MILITARY SERVICES
AND
GENEALOGICAL RECORDS

OF

SOLDIERS

OF

BLAIR COUNTY

PENNSYLVANIA

BY

FLOYD G. HOENSTINE

Southern Historical Press, Inc.
Greenville, South Carolina

This volume was reproduced
from a personal copy located in
the Publishers private library

Please direct all correspondence and book orders to:
SOUTHERN HISTORICAL PRESS, Inc.
1071 Park West Blvd.
Greenville, SC   29611
southernhistoricalpress@gmail.com

Copyright: Floyg G. Hoenstine 1940
ISBN #978-1-63914-331-3
Printed in the United States of America

CONTENTS

	Page
Preface	5
Our Honored Dead of the World War	7
Abbreviations	10
American Decorations	11

PART 1
THE REVOLUTIONARY WAR

Brief History of the War for Independence	17
The Continental Line	19
The Battle of Frankstown	21
Sketches of Veterans of the Revolutionary War	27

PART 2
THE WAR OF 1812

Brief History of the Second War With Great Britain	53
The Pennsylvania Militia	55
The Pennsylvania Volunteers	57
Diary of Captain Allison	67
Sketches of the Veterans of the War of 1812	87

PART 3
THE MEXICAN WAR

Brief History of the Mexican War	97
The Pennsylvania Militia	99
The Pennsylvania Volunteers	101
Sketches of the Veterans of the Mexican War	103

PART 4
THE CIVIL WAR

Brief History of the Civil War	111
The Pennsylvania Militia	113
Constitution and By-laws of the Juniata Rifles	115
The Union Army	119
The "Chicken Raiders"	132
The Grand Army of the Republic	143
Register of Civil War Veterans	153

PART 5
THE SPANISH-AMERICAN WAR

Brief History of the Spanish-American War	285
The Pennsylvania National Guard	287
The Pennsylvania Volunteers	291
The United Spanish War Veterans	293
Register of Spanish-American War Veterans	297

PART 6
THE WORLD WAR

Brief History of the World War	309
The Pennsylvania National Guard	311
The Army of the United States	317
Chronicles of the Hollidaysburg Draft Board	321
The Veterans of Foreign Wars of the United States	335
The American Legion	341
The Disabled American Veterans of the World War	354
Register of Deceased World War Veterans	359

PART 7
INDIVIDUAL RECORDS

Military Services and Genealogical Records	377

THE PREFACE

Local history is the link which connects the past with our present existence. A better understanding and appreciation of national, modern, medieval and ancient history can be had through knowledge of the history which concerns the community in which we live and the history which bears on our immediate relatives or ancestors.

The value of history is ably stated in the words of Patrick Henry, "I know of no way of judging of the future, but by the past."

To determine the direction for our future course it is well to keep fresh in our minds the path we have traveled, using the experiences gained as a guide for the future.

The life of a nation or an individual has changed but little since creation,—life and death—the beginning and the ending,—are but repetition. Only names, places and circumstances change.

In this book an effort has been made to record the historical facts concerning the many soldiers who have lived in Blair County. And a soldier of Blair County is one who was born, lived, died or is buried in this county, regardless of the length of time of residence,—only that such person performed military service during one of the wars or major military campaigns in which the United States was involved.

Back of these records of the soldiers of Blair County, or the history of military units organized in Blair County, and the activities of the posts and camps of the veteran organizations, are untold tales of personal sacrifices, achievements, disappointments and tragic deaths,—the valhalla of men and women who endeavored to serve their God and Country.

The human interest stories of these soldiers cover every phase of our struggle for independence, its preservation, and the building of a great nation out of a vast wilderness.

The gathering of the material which makes up this immense volume originated as a hobby,—a favorite use of spare time and energy—and as time proceeded in its course, interest accordingly increased, until the data at hand became so valuable as to make its preservation a problem.

The registration of veterans graves in Blair County gave impetus to this work, and with the acquisition of a collection of books including local histories, military records, and data from many sources, the idea of a publication of a book was born, and the fulfillment of that ambition is now to be realized.

The amount of material gathered during the past fourteen years would fill several volumes, so in order to limit the publication to this volume and in order that its size would not make the cost of publication prohibitive, only such data as can be classed as vital historical facts are included here and the arrangement is to condense wherever possible.

The most important of all the data recorded herein is the military services of the soldier,—the rank, company and regiment or unit in which he served. The preservation of this information will make possible the acquisition of the complete record as found in the War Department, the pension records, and other official repositories. It will assure the recognition due these soldiers when markers and flags are placed in fond remembrance on each Memorial Day. And it is hoped that it will engender a feeling of respect in the hearts of the people of today, to be carried on to the people of the future, towards perpetuating the memory of the soldiers of Blair County.

Other data of value to the future generations is the year of birth, the year of death, and the name of the cemetery in which many of the soldiers are known to have been buried.

It is anticipated that copies of this publication will be preserved by the historian of the various posts and camps of veterans organizations located in Blair County, and that such historians will enter in the space provided, the subsequent deaths, and that this book will be an incentive for the officers of all veterans organizations to record and preserve the history of their organizations.

Individual owners can aid in this work by making notations in their copies, concerning errors, additions; and records of the military services of members of their families can be here recorded.

The material for this book was collected principly from the following sources: Inscriptions from headstones, Obituaries and military items from newspapers, Genealogical data from local histories, Military and genealogical data from county records, Military services from the Adjutant General's Office, the Bureau of Navigation, and the United States Marine Corps headquarters, at Washington, D. C., Personal narratives from the Pension Department records at Washington, D. C., Records of death and burial from the Veterans Administration, Genealogy and death records from the National Archives at Washington, D. C., Military services and records of military units from the Department of Military Affairs at Harrisburg, Penna., and the Pennsylvania Archives, Military services of Civil War veterans from Bates' "Pennsylvania Volunteers," Military services from Heitman's "Register of Army Officers," Military services from "Pennsylvania Volunteers in the Spanish-American War," and military services and records of military units from Martin's "28th Division In the World War."

The writer is grateful to those three hundred and ten individuals and organizations who by their confidence in the integrity of the sponsor of this enterprise advanced deposits on orders for copies of this book and thereby made possible its completion.

Deep felt thanks is extended to those who supplied data and suggestions, and especially to those two individuals who so ably aided in the proof-reading of the material for this book,—Lemmon C. Stoudnour, of the Hollidaysburg High School Faculty, and Harry A. Jacobs, of Hollidaysburg,—a local historian and former newspaper editor.

The data printed herewith is not intended to be used as official records. It is not claimed that these records are entirely correct, or that they are complete. They are, however, an attempt to preserve the military happenings of Blair County military units and the services of the individual soldiers, who resided in our county at some time in their lives, and it is hoped that the efforts put forth in compiling this book will be followed by other counties, states or future historians.

Persons who have corrections, additional information or who desire any of the data acquired by the author are invited to correspond or visit and inspect the fine collection of Blair County items acquired during the preparation of this book.

FLOYD G. HOENSTINE.

Hollidaysburg, Pa., May, 1940.

OUR HONORED DEAD

THIS BOOK IS RESPECTFULLY DEDICATED TO THOSE WORLD WAR SOLDIERS OF BLAIR COUNTY WHO MADE THE SUPREME SACRIFICE WHILE SERVING THEIR COUNTRY DURING THE PERIOD OF THE WAR, FROM THE 6th OF APRIL, 1917, TO THE 11th OF NOVEMBER, 1918.

Name	*Date of Death*	*Cause of Death*	*Place of Death*
Alexander, John Ralph	Apr. 10, 1918	Drowned at sea	Cape May, N. J.
Allingham, Jess P.	Oct. 8, 1918	Killed in action	France
Anderson, John M.	July 31, 1918	Killed in action	France
Appleman, Clyde E.	Oct. 17, 1918	Died of wounds	France
Auman, Charles L.	Oct. 31, 1918	Died of wounds	Belgium
Aurandt, George Howard	Nov. 6, 1918	**Died of disease**	Camp Cody, N. Mex.
Baker, Thomas	Oct. 18, 1918	Died of wounds	France
Beach, Freeman B.	Oct. 10, 1918	Died of disease	Camp Sherman, Ohio
Beightol, Edward M.	Sept. 28, 1918	Died of wounds	France
Bender, Francis A.	July 30, 1918	Killed in action	France
Bennett, John Henry	Oct. 12, 1918	Killed in action	France
Berkey, Benjamin H.	Sept. 26, 1918	Killed in action	France
Berney, Samuel E.	Oct. 2, 1917	Died of disease	Camp Lee, Virginia
Bickhart, Harry J.	July 19, 1918	Killed in action	France
Black, John Michael	Sept. 7, 1918	Killed in action	France
Bonner, Guy Leslie	Oct. 2, 1918	Died of wounds	France
Borrows, Paul W.	Sept. 26, 1918	Killed in action	France
Brandt, Henry U.	July 30, 1918	Killed in action	France
Briggs, George H.	July 28, 1918	Killed in action	France
Brubaker, Gilbert Earl	Sept. 20, 1918	Died of disease	Camp Jackson, S. Car.
Carson, David F.	July 30, 1918	Killed in action	France
Cashman, William McK.	Sept. 3, 1918	Died of disease	France
Cathers, William S. P.	Aug. 7, 1918	Killed in action	France
Cerullo, Lewis	July 15, 1918	Killed in action	France
Chilcoat, Harry D.	July 29, 1918	Killed in action	France
Claar, Franklin Clyde	July 19, 1918	Killed in action	France
Clarke, John M.	Aug. 11, 1918	Died of wounds	France
Clossin, John Joseph	Oct. 21, 1918	Died of disease	Camp Mills, L. I.
Colabine, John Wesley	July 28, 1918	Died of wounds	France
Cole, Alton C.	July 28, 1918	Died of wounds	France
Corl, Robert A.	Aug. 25, 1918	Died of wounds	France
Crawford, William Morrow	Sept. 30, 1918	Drowned	At sea
Croft, Cloyd Stanley	Oct. 10, 1918	Died of disease	Ft. Ethan Allen, Vt.
Curfman, John Edwin	Oct. 29, 1918	Died of disease	Pittsburgh, Pa.
Denny, Reuben	Oct. 10, 1918	Died of disease	Ft. Benj. Harrison, Ind.
Denocenzo, Angelo	Oct. 17, 1918	Died of disease	Camp Lee, Virginia
Devore, George F.	Sept. 9, 1918	Died of disease	France
Diehl, Francis Richard	July 30, 1918	Killed in action	France
Dodson, Harvey Francis	Oct. 10, 1918	Died of wounds	France
Dossler, Harry G.	Oct. 31, 1918	Died of wounds	France

SOLDIERS OF BLAIR COUNTY

Name	Date of Death	Cause of Death	Place of Death
Earl, Homer W.	July 10, 1918	Died of wounds	France
England, Samuel Arthur	Apr. 7, 1918	Died of disease	Ft. Sam Houston, Texas
Ernest, John Bernard	Feb. 26, 1918	Died of wounds	France
Ewing, Leory Baker	Mar. 2, 1918	Died of disease	Camp Lewis, Wash.
Fagan, William Lawrence	Oct. 5, 1918	Died of disease	Philadelphia, Pa.
Fagley, Ray H.	Oct. 4, 1918	Killed in action	France
Fickes, David Elmer	Sept. 25, 1918	Died of wounds	France
Field, Harry James W.	June 6, 1918	Killed in action	France
Fisher, Richard Gilbert	Sept. 12, 1918	Killed in action	France
Foley, John Francis	July 31, 1918	Died of wounds	France
Fulton, Frank	Nov. 9, 1918	Died of disease	France
Furrer, Jacob Charles	June 14, 1918	Drowned	At sea
Gardner, John Howard	July 28, 1918	Killed in action	France
Gates, John C.	Oct. 21, 1918	Died of disease	At sea
Gearhart, Donald L.	Aug. 1, 1918	Died of wounds	France
Glassco, Simeon H.	Sept. 26, 1918	Killed in action	France
Gleason, Charles H.	Oct. 9, 1918	Died of disease	Camp Sherman, Ohio
Grathwohl, Charles Max.	Oct. 1, 1918	Died of disease	Camp
Gray, Caleb A.	Oct. 6, 1918	Died of wounds	France
Gugluzo, Joseph	June 16, 1918	Killed in action	France
Gullarmod, Norman A.	Nov. 4, 1918	Killed in action	France
Hanley, Michael Clerence	Oct. 8, 1918	Killed in action	France
Herring, Lovey J.	Nov. 18, 1917	Died of disease	Camp Lee, Virginia
Hess, Harry Edison	June 11, 1918	Killed in action	France
Hetherington, Seth C.	Sept. 28, 1918	Killed in action	France
Hewit, Benjamin Hartley	Sept. 29, 1918	Killed in action	France
Hollabaugh, Thomas Lloyd	Oct. 14, 1918	Died of disease	Camp Greenleaf, Ga.
Hommon, Frank Palmer	July 15, 1918	Killed in action	France
Hopkins, Ray Clinton	Sept. 29, 1918	Killed in action	France
Huebner, Leonard William	July 25, 1918	Killed in action	France
Hunter, Roy M.	Oct. 11, 1918	Killed in action	France
Isenberg, Alvin Roy	July 30, 1918	Killed in action	France
Izzo, Frank Xavier	July 20, 1918	Died of wounds	France
Jones, Frank Stanley	Nov. 6, 1918	Died of disease	France
Jones, Russell William	Aug. 13, 1918	Killed in action	Dominican Republic
Kalivay, George John	Nov. 1, 1918	Killed in action	France
Karansta, Achileppa	July 15, 1918	Killed in action	France
Kelley, Cecil A.	July 29, 1917	Died of disease	San Antonio, Texas
Kephart, James Watson	Sept. 6, 1918	Killed in action	France
Killinger, Bert H.	Oct. 14, 1918	Died of wounds	France
Kitto, William	Nov. 2, 1918	Killed in action	France
Klepser, Frank Wilson	Sept. 5, 1917	Died of disease	New York
Kreuz, John	Sept. 28, 1918	Died of wounds	France
Kuhn, Paul Hudson	July 28, 1918	Killed in action	France
Litzinger, Norman J.	July 19, 1918	Killed in action	France
Lodick, Frank	Sept. 12, 1918	Killed in action	France
Lohmer, Michael Albert	Mar. 11, 1918	Died of disease	Norfolk, Virginia
Loucks, Howard M.	May 24, 1918	Died of disease	Ft. Leavenworth, Kan.
Lynn, William E.	July 30, 1918	Killed in action	France
MacArthur, Edwin D.	Feb. 24, 1918	Died of injuries	Camp Sherman, Ohio
Manning, John C.	Oct. 10, 1918	Died of disease	Ft. Adams, R. I.
Marshall, Calvin	Nov. 11, 1918	Died of disease	
Mascia, Leonardo G.	Nov. 5, 1918	Killed in action	France

Name	Date of Death	Cause of Death	Place of Death
Mauk, Paul C.	Sept. 7, 1918	Killed in action	France
McConnell, Charles O.	July 26, 1918	Killed in action	France
McCoy, Raymond B.	Oct. 14, 1918	Killed in action	France
McDowell, Edward B.	Oct. 19, 1918	Died of disease	
McIntosh, Charles Edgar	Sept. 28, 1918	Killed in action	France
McKamey, Robert E.	July 19, 1918	Killed in action	France
McNeal, Orris L.	Sept. 26, 1918	Killed in action	France
Mitchell, Harry Edgar	Nov. 2, 1918	Died of wounds	France
Mock, Arthur C.	July 18, 1918	Killed in action	France
Morse, Harry Elwood	Sept. 27, 1918	Killed in action	France
Murphy, Charles R.	Sept. 25, 1918	Died of disease	France
Murray, Jesse L.	July 22, 1918	Died of wounds	France
Neeley, Calvin G.	Nov. 2, 1918	Died of disease	France
Noel, Herbert W.	Sept. 27, 1918	Killed in action	France
Norman, Charles C.	July 30, 1918	Killed in action	France
Patterson, Francis S.	Sept. 26, 1918	Killed in action	France
Piper, William Fluke	Oct. 2, 1918	Killed in action	France
Reed, Paul Wilson	Oct. 18, 1918	Died of disease	Pittsburgh, Pa.
Rice, Harry Melvin	May 9, 1918	Died of disease	Douglass, Arizona
Rigaldello, Donato	July 30, 1918	Killed in action	France
Ritchey, Francis B.	Oct. 6, 1918	Drowned	At sea
Robinson, Arthur L.	Aug. 13, 1918	Died of wounds	France
Robinson, Joseph F.	Jan. 5, 1918	Died of injuries	Camp
Rockwell, Raymond M.	Nov. 4, 1918	Died of wounds	France
Rowan, Charles R.	Oct. 1, 1918	Died of wounds	France
Ryder, Anthony H.	Sept. 8, 1918	Died of disease	France
Shade, Ralph M.	Oct. 12, 1918	Died of disease	France
Shingler, Charles H.	Nov. 5, 1918	Died of disease	France
Sickler, John J.	July 29, 1918	Killed in action	France
Slagle, David H.	Sept. 6, 1918	Killed in action	France
Smith, William Donald	Oct. 31, 1918	Died of disease	Pittsburgh, Pa.
Smouse, Earl R.	Oct. 24, 1918	Died of disease	Camp Gordon, Ga.
Sollenberger, Robert F.	Aug. 4, 1918	Killed in action	France
Stambaugh, Chester J.	Oct. 8, 1918	Killed in action	France
Stiver, John Warren	July 28, 1918	Killed in action	France
Stoudnour, David B.	Mar. 30, 1918	Died of disease	Camp Custer, Mich.
Sunderland, Grover Earl	July 4, 1918	Killed in action	France
Temple, William S.	Aug. 10, 1918	Killed in action	France
Tipton, D. Merl	Oct. 5, 1918	Killed in action	France
Titler, John J.	Sept. 24, 1918	Killed in action	France
Vadacchino, Gennaro	Oct. 12, 1918	Died of disease	Camp Lee, Virginia
Walker, Ralph G.	Oct. 12, 1918	Died of disease	Camp
Walker, Riley Alden	July 30, 1918	Killed in action	France
Walter, Roy M.	Sept. 30, 1918	Died of disease	Camp
Weible, William E.	July 15, 1918	Killed in action	France
Williams, Howell W.	Oct. 29, 1918	Died of injuries	Bampon Field, Texas
Williams, Maurice B.	Sept. 27, 1918	Killed in action	France
Woomer, Nathan Clark	July 28, 1918	Killed in action	France
Wyandt, Victor Dewy	Apr. 8, 1918	Died of disease	Columbus, Ohio
Wyerman, Albert Raymond	Sept. 10, 1918	Died of disease	France
Yingling, Edgar Dean	Oct. 18, 1918	Died of disease	Camp
Yost, Charles J.	Sept. 16, 1918	Died of disease	France
Zimmerman, Robert L.	Jan. 3, 1918	Died of disease	At sea

ABBREVIATIONS

Adj.—*Adjutant*
Art.—*Artillery*
Atr.—*Artificer*
Bks.—*Blacksmith*
Bn.—*Battalion*
Bug.—*Bugler*
C.A.C.—*Coast Artillery Corps*
Cav.—*Cavalry*
Co.—*Company*
Col.—*Colonel*
Com.—*Commander*
Cpl.—*Corporal*
Cpn.—*Chaplain*
Cpt.—*Captain*
Engr.—*Engineer*
Far.—*Farrier*
Frn.—*Fireman*
Gnr.—*Gunner*
1Lt.—*First Lieutenant*
Inf.—*Infantry*

Lt.—*Lieutenant*
Maj.—*Major*
Mus.—*Musician*
Nrs.—*Nurse*
Q.M.—*Quartermaster*
Q.M.C.—*Quartermaster Corps*
Pa.—*Pennsylvania*
Prov.—*Provisional*
Pvt.—*Private*
Regt.—*Regiment*
Sad.—*Saddler*
2Lt.—*Second Lieutenant*
Sgn.—*Surgeon*
Sgt.—*Sergeant*
Smn.—*Seaman*
U.—*Unassigned*
U.S.—*United States*
Vol.—*Volunteer*
Wgr.—*Wagoner*

AMERICAN DECORATIONS

Awarded to Soldiers of Blair County
Under Authority of the Congress of the United States

CONGRESSIONAL MEDAL OF HONOR

MACLAY, WILLIAM P.—Private, Company A, 43d Infantry, U. S. Volunteers.
Born at Spruce Creek, Pa., resided at Altoona, Pa.
At Hilongas, Leyte, P. I., May 6, 1900.
Charged an occupied bastion, saving the life of an officer in a hand-to-hand combat and destroying the enemy.

ROUSH, J. LEVI—Corporal, Company D, 6th Pennsylvania Reserves.
Born at Bedford County, Pa., resided at Sarah Furnace, Pa.
At Gettysburg, Pa., July 2, 1863.
Was one of six volunteers who charged upon a log house near the Devil's Den, where a squad of the enemy's sharpshooters were sheltered, and compelled their surrender.

DISTINGUISHED SERVICE CROSS

BLACK, JOHN M.—Sergeant, Company G, 110th Infantry, 28th Division.
Born at Royer, Pa., resided at Hollidaysburg, Pa.
Near Villette, on the Vesle River, France, Aug. 29-30, 1918.
Sergeant Black commanded one of four patrols which were sent out to attack and drive out enemy outposts on the railroad embankment a few hundred yards south of the river. As they advanced, the patrols were met by heavy enemy machine-gun and rifle grenade fire which necessitated the withdrawal of three of the patrols. Sergeant Black led his patrol to the railroad, drove out the enemy, and held the position throughout the night and the following day until ordered to retire, although repeatedly attacked by the enemy. During the operations between the Vesle and Aisne Rivers, France, Sept. 7, 1918, Sergeant Black, with utter disregard of his own personal safety, directed the fire of his platoon upon a retreating body of the enemy, and while in this exposed position he was killed in action.
Posthumously awarded. Medal presented to sister, Mrs. Mary Black Andrews, of Hollidaysburg, Pa.

DUEY, ARMA—Private, first class, Company L, 30th Infantry, 3d Division.
Born in Belgium, resided at Houtzdale, Pa.
Near Jaulgonne, France, July 23, 1918.
During the attack made by his company, Private Duey constantly carried messages under heaviest shellfire, insuring and maintaining liaison with all neighboring units.

SOLDIERS OF BLAIR COUNTY

GROVE, GLENN M.—Sergeant, Company D, 11th Machine Gun Battalion, 4th Division.
Born at James Creek, Pa., resided at Tyrone, Pa.
Near Nantillois, France, Sept. 26, 1918.
He, with two officers, using captured German Maxim guns, pushed forward to a heavily shelled area, from which the other troops had withdrawn, and by their accurate and effective fire kept groups of the enemy from occupying advantageous positions. When given permission to withdraw he declined to do so, but maintained fire superiority all afternoon until it became too dark to see. His conspicuous gallantry furnished an inspiration to the other members of the command.

HEWIT, BENJAMIN H.—Captain, 316th Infantry, 79th Division.
Born at Jamestown, N. Dak., resided at Hollidaysburg, Pa.
Near Montfaucon, France, Sept. 28-29, 1918.
He led his men into battle with such fearlessness and valor that he was at all times able to reorganize and continue forward under most difficult circumstances. Although wounded, he remained in command, always being under terrific shell and machine-gun fire, but not until he had received a second wound did he relinquish his command. While being taken from the field he received a third wound.
Posthumously awarded. Medal presented to father, Oliver H. Hewit, of Hollidaysburg, Pa.

INGOLD, WILLIAM J.—Sergeant, Company H, 26th Infantry, 1st Division.
Born at Altoona, Pa., resided at Memphis, Tenn.
Near Cantigny, France, June 3, 1918.
While posting a listening post he encountered a hostile patrol of about 40 men; he attacked the Germans, although armed only with a pistol, and, killing an officer and one soldier, routed the enemy. Carrying the body of the officer, he had just returned to our lines when a raid was attempted by the Germans. Running to the scene of action, he killed two more Germans, aiding materially in routing the raiding party.

LANGHAM, GEORGE W.—Private, Company H, 128th Infantry, 32d Division.
Born at Puzzletown, Pa., resided at Roaring Spring, Pa.
Near Juvigny, north of Soissons, France, Aug. 29-Sept. 2, 1918.
Though he had been severely gassed, he remained on duty with his company while it was in the front line. Later, when it was in support, he voluntarily aided in the work of carrying wounded across an area covered by artillery and machine-gun fire.

LIGHTNER, BLAKE—Second lieutenant, 110th Infantry, 28th Division.
Born at Irvona, Pa., resided at Rosebud, Pa.
At Courmont, France, July 29-31, 1918, and near Montblainville, France, Sept. 27 to Oct. 3, 1918.
Lieutenant Lightner voluntarily established an advance observation post at Courmont. During his work he was knocked down by the concussion of an exploding shell, but remained at his post. Throughout the action in the Argonne he repeatedly exposed himself while leading his men. At Montblainville, although wounded by a shell splinter, he continued in action and succeeded in putting into operation German Machine guns against the enemy, greatly assisting in repulsing their counterattack. He refused to be evacuated until ordered to the rear.

MYERS, JAMES P.—Sergeant, Company C, 16th Infantry, 1st Division.
Born at Philadelphia, Pa., resided at Altoona, Pa.
Near Sommerance, France, Oct. 9, 1918. (Served as James F. Porter.)
During the attack on Hill 272, Sergeant Porter, with four men, exposed himself to heavy machine-gun fire in order to attack an enemy machine gun which was causing heavy casualties among his company. Although all his men were either killed or wounded, he succeeded in capturing the gun. Due to his gallantry, his company was able to continue the advance.

NORTON, FRANK B.—Sergeant, Company M, 328th Infantry, 82d Division.
Born at Philadelphia, Pa., resided at Altoona, Pa.
At Cornay, France, Oct. 9-10, 1918.
After fighting for six hours, he volunteered to accompany 15 other soldiers and an officer on a night patrol of Cornay, which was held by many enemy machine-gun posts. The party worked from 11 o'clock at night till next morning, clearing buildings and dugouts of the enemy, capturing 65 prisoners and two machine guns. With six others Sergeant Norton volunteered and entered a dugout where 23 prisoners were captured. He was wounded while leaving the town, but he refused to go to the aid station until the prisoners had been delivered at brigade headquarters.

OBENOUR, GEORGE G.—Private, first class, Company A, 30th Infantry, 3d Division.
Born at Drab, Pa., and resided at Williamsburg, Pa.
Near Crezancy, France, July 15, 1918.
Three times, under terrific enemy fire, he carried messages to battalion and regimental headquarters. After the company had withdrawn he voluntarily returned to the position his company had held and throughout the night assisted in evacuating the wounded.

OWENS, GILBERT—Sergeant, Company M, 9th Infantry, 2d Division.
Born at Tyrone, Pa., and resided at Tyrone, Pa.
Near Medeah Ferme, France, Oct. 3-5, 1918.
Suffering from three severe scalp wounds, Sergeant Owens remained with his company and for two days performed his duties under intense artillery and machine-gun fire, until sent to the hospital completely exhausted.

ROBERTS, CLAIR C.—Second Lieutenant, 167th Infantry, 42d Division.
Born at Huntingdon, Pa., resided at Altoona, Pa.
Near Landres et St. Georges, France, Oct. 25, 1918.
His platoon suffered heavy casualties and he himself was gassed in the advance on Hill 260. Being the first to reach this hill, he observed that the enemy were forming for a counterattack. Displaying coolness and quick judgment he organized all the available men in the vicinity and launched a vigorous attack upon the enemy, who were routed. The daring and leadership of this officer enabled the support to reach Hill 260 without further fighting.

ROWAN, CHARLES R.—First Lieutenant, 110th Infantry, 28th Division.
Born at Altoona, Pa., resided at Altoona, Pa.
Near Apremont, France, Sept. 29, 1918.
Being familiar with the ground over which an attack was to be made, he volunteered to leave his own company in the reserve and lead another company which was without officers. The enemy attacked before our own operations were begun, and he was wounded by a machine-gun bullet. Exemplifying in the highest degree the spirit of self-sacrifice and devotion to duty he remained with his command for an hour and a half until the hostile attack was repulsed. He has since died from the wounds received in this engagement.
Posthumously awarded. Medal presented to father, R. M. Rowan.

SHRUM, JOHN E.—Private, Company D, 18th Infantry, 1st Division.
Born at Derry, Pa., resides at Hollidaysburg, Pa.
Near Soissons, France, July 19, 1918.
Private Shrum, although wounded, delivered an important message for his platoon commander. In order to accomplish this mission, it was necessary for him to cross an area swept by enemy machine-gun fire.

SMITH, GEORGE L.—Private, Medical Detachment, 125th Infantry, 32d Division.
Born at Blair County, Pa., resided at Hollidaysburg, Pa.
Northeast of Gesnes, France, Oct. 11, 1918.
Private Smith established a collecting point for the wounded in the valley north of Hill 258, during the attack of his battalion. The unit on the right, which was being subjected to an extremely heavy machine-gun fire from the enemy, was unable to advance, thus exposing the right flank of his battalion to a severe machine-gun fire. The terrain afforded no protection to anyone attempting to cross and a runner while attempting to cross this terrain was severely wounded, falling in an exposed position. Private Smith, with splendid heroism and courage, dashed across the exposed area and carried his wounded comrade in to our lines and rendered first aid.

DISTINGUISHED SERVICE MEDAL

FAIR, JOHN S.—Colonel, Quartermaster Corps, U. S. Army.
Born at Dakota, Nebraska, resides at Sylvan Hills, Hollidaysburg, Pa.
He organized and operated the remount service, controlled the purchasing of fuel and forage for the Army, and organized and started into operation the conservation and reclamation division. By his enthusiasm and energy valuable results were obtained.

HARMON, KENNETH B.—Lieutenant Colonel, Ordnance Department, U. S. Army.
Born at San Francisco, Calif, resided at Altoona, Pa.
With exceptionally sound judgment and marked initiative, he displayed a wide comprehension of existing conditions, solving perplexing problems connected with the establishment and operation of the storage system of the Ordnance Department of the American Expeditionary Forces. He opened first a base, then an intermediate depot, and later an advance depot, accomplishing these tasks in spite of numerous obstacles. At all times tireless in energy he worked to insure an adequate supply of Ordnance material for the troops at the front.

McDOWELL, RALPH W.—Lieutenant Commander, Medical Corps, U. S. Navy.
Born at Altoona, Pa., resided in Altoona, Pa.
For services as sanitary inspector and surgeon of the Arrondissement of Tours, France.

PART 1

THE REVOLUTIONARY WAR

A brief history of the Revolutionary War, its causes, important events, battles and ending.

The story of the first military organization to be formed in this section of Pennsylvania, and its history while serving under the Stars and Stripes in the entire thirteen original colonies.

Blair County's most important military event, the Battle of Frankstown,—which was the major engagement with the Indians on the frontier between the forks of the Ohio and the Susquehanna Valley.

Sketches of the military services, the death and burial, and the genealogical history of Veterans of the Revolutionary War who served in Blair County or resided in Blair County.

INDEX TO PART 1

THE REVOLUTIONARY WAR

Brief history of the Revolutionary War 17
Captain Robert Cluggage's Company 19
Battle of Frankstown 21
Sketches of Revolutionary War Veterans 27

A BRIEF HISTORY OF THE REVOLUTIONARY WAR

The principal causes which brought about the war for independence were through matters of trade and the question of the mother country's right to tax the people of the colonies.

England's desire to have the exclusive trade with the colonies resulted in the passage of the Navigation Act of 1761, which eliminated practically all legal trade with other countries. Illegal trading became profitable and enticing, and in order to enforce this law, English War vessels resorted to searching all vessels and seizing those found to be engaged in the illegal trade.

Other efforts were made to control the commerce effecting the colonies and attempts were made to collect taxes from the colonists. All of which became more and more objectionable to the liberty loving people of the new world, so that the right of the English Parliament to tax the colonists became a burning question.

The Stamp Act of 1765 added fuel to the flames and opposition to taxation without representation increased throughout the land and resulted in refusal to pay any taxes to England as a general principle.

This stand led to refusal to use English goods, and following the enactment of laws placing a tax on tea, the people of Boston prohibited the removal of the tea from the ships. On the 16th of December, 1773, a number of persons of Boston, dressed in the garb of Indians, went a step farther and staged a tea party by boarding a vessel in the harbor and emptying the contents of the tea casks into the waters of the harbor.

The English Parliament now adopted strong coercive acts including the Boston Port Bill which prohibited all commerce, and resolved to secure obedience to its laws at all hazards.

To enforce the laws enacted, a fleet with 10,000 troops under command of General Gage were sent to America to put an end to the rebellious course being pursued by the colonists. General Gage learning that military stores were collected at Concord, dispatched a detachment of his troops on the night of the 18th of April, 1775, to seize the stores and to arrest the leaders. At Lexington about seventy minute-men assembled and when failing to disperse and throw down their arms when commanded to do so by Major Pitcairn, they were fired on by the troops and eight Americans remained dead on the field. The British troops continued to Concord and destroyed all they could lay hands on. In the meantime messengers spread the alarm and minute-men assembled from all directions. The returning soldiers were attacked with vigor and spirit from all sides and a running fight became a rout in spite of re-enforcements sent out to support the detachment. Only by a precipitate retreat were they able to reach Boston with any survivors.

Efforts to unite the colonies and pursue a common course of action were inaugurated, and resulted in a meeting of representatives of all colonies except one, as the First Continental Congress, held in Carpenter's Hall at Philadelphia on the 5th of September, 1774. This meeting considered the existing conditions, their relations with Great Britain, and adopted recommendations for the guidance of the colonies in the approaching conflict.

The Second Continental Congress met at Philadelphia on the 10th of May, 1775, and authorized the enlistment of troops, the construction of forts, the raising of finances with which to pursue the struggle for independence, and named George Washington as Commander-in-chief.

During the 1776 session of Congress at Philadelphia, a resolution was presented, declaring, "that the United Colonies are and ought to be free and independent States." Consideration was given this resolution and on the 4th of July, the resolution was unanimously adopted as the Declaration of Independence.

Seven long critical years ensued before the last British army surrendered at Yorktown, and two more years passed before peace was established. This period was marked by many lost battles, trying hours when the cause seemed lost, hardships and suffering such as the American army endured at Valley Forge during the winter of 1777, loss of the large cities and resources, and while the British army with the aid of Hessians captured and destroyed along the seacoast, the interior was harassed by Indians, tories and renegades under pay and promise of reward for scalps and prisoners without any discrimination as to whether men, women or children.

The following list of battles, engagements and events of the Revolutionary War includes those in which soldiers of Blair County participated:

Ticonderoga	New York	May 10, 1775
Bunker Hill	Massachusetts	June 17, 1775
Quebec	Canada	Dec. 31, 1775
Moore's Creek	North Carolina	Feb. 27, 1776
Three Rivers	Canada	June 8, 1776
Charleston	South Carolina	June 28, 1776
Long Island	New York	Aug. 27, 1776
White Plains	New York	Oct. 28, 1776
Fort Washington	New York	Nov. 16, 1776
Trenton	New Jersey	Dec. 26, 1776
Princeton	New Jersey	Jan. 3, 1777
Hubbardton	Vermont	July 5, 1777
Oriskany	New York	Aug. 6, 1777
Bennington	New York	Aug. 16, 1777
Brandywine	Pennsylvania	Sept. 11, 1777
Freeman's Farm	New York	Sept. 19, 1777
Paoli	Pennsylvania	Sept. 20, 1777
Germantown	Pennsylvania	Oct. 4, 1777
Saratoga	New York	Oct. 17, 1777
White Marsh	Pennsylvania	Dec. 5, 1777
Monmouth	New Jersey	June 28, 1778
Wyoming	Pennsylvania	July 1, 1778
Cherry Valley	New York	Nov. 10, 1778
Brier Creek	Georgia	Mar. 3, 1779
Hanging Rock	South Carolina	Aug. 6, 1780
Camden	South Carolina	Aug. 16, 1780
Kings Mountain	North Carolina	Oct. 7, 1780
Cowpens	South Carolina	Jan. 17, 1781
Guilford	North Carolina	Mar. 15, 1781
Hobkirk's Hill	South Carolina	Apr. 25, 1781
Frankstown	Pennsylvania	June 3, 1781
Green Springs	Virginia	July 6, 1781
Eutaw Springs	South Carolina	Sept. 8, 1781
Yorktown	Virginia	Oct. 17, 1781
Sharon	Georgia	May 24, 1782

The English government acknowledged the full and complete independence of the United States under a provisional treaty signed at Paris on the 30th of November, 1782, and the definitive treaty of peace was signed on the 3d of September, 1783, whereby the colonies received proper recognition due a nation and were free to govern themselves.

Of special interest to the people residing on the frontier was the treaty of Fort Stanwix, New York, which was signed in 1783, establishing peace with the Indians and thereby the release of many prisoners who were now able to return to their homes and loved ones.

THE CONTINENTAL LINE
CAPTAIN ROBERT CLUGGAGE'S COMPANY

The first military organization to be formed in this part of Pennsylvania was a company of expert riflemen recruited during May and June, 1775, under command of Captain Robert Cluggage of Shirley Township, Huntingdon County, then Bedford County, whose commission was dated the 25th of June, 1775. Members of this company came from the families who had settled on the frontier and included two of the Holliday boys, three of the McDonalds who resided two miles south of Newry, and others whose homes were located in what is now Blair County.

Captain Cluggage's Company consisted of one captain, three lieutenants, four sergeants, four corporals, one musician and seventy-four privates, and became part of Col. Thompson's Battalion of Riflemen, and later designated as the 2d Regiment of the Army of the United Colonies. Its first encounter with the British occurred at Boston on the 9th of November, 1775, when they drove the British from Lechmere's Point, losing one killed and three wounded, while the British losses were seventeen killed and one wounded. For this victory the battalion received the thanks of General Washington.

Thacher in his "Military Journal of the Revolution" states: "They are remarkably stout and hardy men; many of them exceeding six feet in height. They are dressed in white flocks or rifle shirts and round hats. These men are remarkable for the accuracy of their aim; striking a mark with great certainty at two hundred yards distance. At a review, a company of them, while on a quick advance, fired their balls into objects of seven inches diameter, at the distance of two hundred and fifty yards. They are now stationed in our lines, and their shot have frequently proved fatal to British officers and soldiers who expose themselves to view, even at more than double the distance of common musket shot."

Captain Cluggage resigned on the 6th of October, 1776, in consequence of the appointment of a junior officer to Majority. Lieut. John Holliday was promoted a captain on the 25th of September, 1776; transferred to Captain Ross' Company, and resigned on the first of March, 1778.

Further history of the regiment is found quoted in the "History of Bedford, Somerset and Fulton Counties" and reads as follows: "The Historical Society of Pennsylvania has in its temporary possession a very interesting relic of the revolution. It is the standard of the First Pennsylvania Rifle Battalion, Col. William Thompson, of Carlisle, which was raised upon the reception of the news of the battle of Bunker Hill, and entered the trenches in front of Boston on the 8th of August, 1775. It was in all the skirmishes in front of Boston, and before the British evacuated that city it was ordered to New York to repel their landing there. Colonel Thompson was promoted brigadier on the first of March, 1776, and Lieut. Col. Hand of Lancaster, succeeded him. The term of the battalion expired on the 30th of June, 1776, but officers and men in large numbers re-enlisted for three years or during the war, under Col. Hand, and the battalion became the first regiment of the Continental Line. It was at Long Island, White Plains, Trenton and Princeton, under Hand. On the first of April, 1777, Hand was promoted brigadier, and Lieut. Col. James Chambers, of Chambersburg, became colonel. Under him the regiment fought at Brandywine, Germantown, Monmouth and in every other battle and skirmish of the main army until retired from the service, January 1, 1781.

"Colonel Chambers was succeeded by Col. Daniel Broadhead, and on the 26th of May, 1781, the 1st regiment left York, Pennsylvania, with five others, into which the line was consolidated, under the command of General Wayne, joined Lafayette at Raccoon Ford on the Rappahannock on the 10th of June; fought at Green Springs on the 6th of July; opened the second parallel at Yorktown, which General Steuben, in his division orders of 21st of October, says, "he considered as the most important part of the siege." After the surrender the regiment went southward with Wayne, fought the last battle of the war at Sharon, Georgia, May 24, 1782; entered Savannah in triumph on the 11th of July, and Charleston on the 14th of December, 1782; was in camp on James Island, South Carolina, on the 11th of May, 1783, and only when news of the cessation of hostilities reached that point was it embarked for Philadelphia. In its service it traversed every one of the original thirteen states of the union; for while in front of Boston, October 30, 1775, Captain Parr was ordered with a detachment of this battalion up to Portsmouth, New Hampshire, to defend that point. I noticed this standard on exhibition at the Museum, during the Centennial, but supposed it 'the banner with a strange device' of some revolutionary militia battalion. I identified it the other day at the rooms of the Historical Society from the description contained in a letter from Lieut. Col. Hand to Jasper Yeates, in possession of Gen. Hand's granddaughter, Mrs. S. B. Rogers, of Lancaster. It is dated: "Prospect Hill, 8 March 1776—I am stationed at Cobble Hill with four companies of our regiment. Two companies, Cluggage's and Chambers, were ordered to Dorchester on Monday; Ross' and Lowdens's relieved them yesterday. Every regiment is to have a standard and colors. Our standard is to be a deep green ground, the device a tiger partly enclosed by toils, attempting the pass, defended by a hunter armed with a spear (in white), on crimson field the motto Domari nolo."

The roll of Captain Robert Cluggage's Company, fall of 1776, was as follows:

Captain—Robert Cluggage
First Lieutenant—John Holliday
Second Lieutenant—Robert McKenzie
Third Lieutenant—Benjamin Burd

Sergeants	*Corporals*	*Drummer*
James Holliday	Acquilla White	Timothy Sullivan
Daniel Stoy	William Lee	
Querinus Meriner	Joseph McKenzie	
David Wright	Angus McDonald	

Privates

Anderson, Adam	Gemberland, Daniel	Plumb, Samuel
Bechey, Philip	Gillespy, Reuben	Reynolds, Martin
Bowman, John	Hartister, Richard	Rhoads, Daniel
Broughdon, Thaddeus	Hanning, Conrad	Ritchie, Philip
Brown, Thomas	Jamison, Francis	Shehan, Thomas
Bruner, George	Johnston, Andrew	Shires, Francis
Campbell, John	Judy, Matthias	Simonton, Alexander
Casek, Thomas	Kelley, John	Smith, Emanuel
Cessna, Stephen	King, Peter	Smith, Henry
Clark, Patrick	Knight, James	Stuart, John
Conner, Philip	Laird, William	Taylor, Jonathan
Corrowan, James	Lenning, Charles	Thompson, John
Craig, Joshua	Leonard, Robert	Turmoil, James
Crips, John	Lesley, John	Tweed, Andrew
Crugren, Alexander	McCartney, Henry	VanZandt, James
Cunningham, Thomas	McClain, Daniel	Vanderslice, Daniel
Curran, James	McCune, John	Vaughan, Thomas
Davis, John	McDonald, John	Wallace, Samuel
Dilling, Cornelius	McDonald, Patrick	Walker, Solomon
Donelin, William	McFarlane, Thomas	Warford, James
Dougherty, Matthew	Magee, Thomas	Ward, Thomas
Dowling, Laurence	Mangaw, Daniel	Wilson, Alexander
Franks, Daniel	Miller, Michael	Whitman, George
Freemen, George	Piatt, Robert	Woodward, Samuel
Garrett, Amariah	Pitts, John	

BATTLE OF FRANKSTOWN

During the closing days of the Revolutionary War, an event occurred within the present limits of Blair County which was the major military affair during the war on frontier, in this section of Pennsylvania.

This event was an encounter between the soldiers who were on the frontier and a band of Indians from the Seneca tribe from the State of New York, and took place along an Indian trail leading to the Kittanning Indian trail near the point in Allegheny Township now known as Canan Station.

This historic spot has been marked with a bronze tablet set in a stone, close along the side of the highway, leading from Eldorado to Duncansville, which was placed by the Blair County Historical Society in 1923, the inscription reads as follows: "Forty-five rods east of this spot, along the Kittanning War Path June 3, 1781, a detachment of the Bedford Scouts, under command of Captain Moore and Lieutenant Smith, was ambushed by Indians and Tories. Seventeen of the Scouts were killed and scalped and five wounded."

The only attempt ever made to relate the history of this event is found in "History of the Early Settlement of the Juniata Valley" by U. J. Jones, of Hollidaysburg, who, in 1855, had for his material two letters written by George Ashman, Sublieutenant of Bedford County, who was not present at the time of the event and received his knowledge of the affair during the excitement of the time immediately following its occurrence.

In addition Jones had interviewed local residents who possibly lived on the frontier during the exciting times of the Revolutionary War, or had related to him accounts of the engagement as handed down from generation to generation.

Jones states, in his story of the event, that Lieutenant Ashman's report was pronounced erroneous, by persons who lived in the immediate vicinity during the time of the occurrence. Jones further states that "We sincerely regret that the most strenuous effort on our part to procure a list of this scout proved futile."

As the result of much research work in an effort to procure the names of those who participated in this event it is now possible to give a version of this historic occurrence which agrees in few instances with U. J. Jones or Lieutenant Ashman.

Three muster rolls of the Company of Rangers involved are found in the Pennsylvania Archives. Other references to the men who were engaged are also found in the Archives. Few references or items concerning this event are found in any of the many histories of Pennsylvania or of Blair County, however, from the applications for pensions filed with the Federal Government by those veterans of the Revolutionary War who survived when pension laws were passed in 1818 a great amount of authentic history is procured, giving the individual soldier's part in the military events, as each applicant for a pension was required to give a detailed account of his services, sworn to before the local County Judge and supported by statements of at least two comrades, all in an effort to prove his services, as the Federal Government's record had been destroyed by the British Army when it captured our National Capitol during the War of 1812.

From the mass of information now at hand it is possible to give a different description of the event known until this time as the "Massacre of the Bedford Scouts", and as we proceed with our story we will attempt to establish proof that the title should be the "Battle of Frankstown"; that the organization involved was the Bedford County Rangers under the command of Captain John Boyd, instead of the "Bedford Scouts" in command of Captain Moore and Lieutenant Smith; that the fort which guarded this vicinity was a blockhouse erected near the junction of Blair Creek and the Beaver Dam Branch of the Juniata River instead of Fetter's barn converted into a fort; that the soldiers marched from Bedford, accompanied by a group of volunteers, to the Frankstown Fort upon receiving reports that the Indians had invaded the settlements, instead of a pre-arranged meeting between Captain Boyd's Rangers and a group of local volunteers who would join forces at the fort on the farm of Peter Titus for the purpose of scouring the mountains for signs of Indians.

The description of a military organization or group of soldiers as the "Bedford Scouts" is without definite meaning as no unit of the army was known as a "Scout". Military organizations recruited by a county during the Revolutionary War were known as the "militia" or "rangers", and in this case the unit which participated in the battle was known as Captain John Boyd's Bedford County Rangers, and at the time of the engagement with the Indians, the Rangers were strengthened by the presence of a number of volunteers, residents of the frontier who had had military experience and who accepted the authority of Captain Boyd as their commander.

The authority for the existence of Captain Boyd's Bedford County Rangers was enacted by the General Assembly on the 21st day of February, 1780, and reads, "Resolved that four companies be immediately raised for the Frontier service,.... that the establishment of a company be as follows:—One Captain, One Lieutenant,—One Ensign,—Four Sergeants,—Four Corporals,—One drummer,—One Fifer, and Sixty Privates;.... that, to the officers one hundred dollars levy money for every able bodied recruit who shall pass muster to be paid to the officer enlisting him, and every Commissioned, non commissioned officer and private who shall render faithful service to the State and continue therein during the War, or till honorably discharged shall be entitled to the same gratuity of land, as commissioned, non commissioned officers and privates in the service of the United States, are and shall be entitled to; And that the said land shall be liable to location only in the Counties of Westmoreland, Bedford and Northumberland".

On Friday, February 9, 1781, the Executive Council took the following action: as appears on the Minutes: "The Council taking into consideration the appointing of officers for the four companies of Rangers to be raised in this State for the defense of the Frontier,—on consideration, Resolved, that the following gentlemen be appointed and commissioned accordingly, Viz: John Boyd, Captain; Richard Johnston, Lieutenant; and ————Ensign of the Company to be raised in the county of Bedford".

Captain Boyd being present and in command at the battle with his partly recruited company, reinforced by volunteers, establishes the fact that a duly authorized unit of the armed forces of the United States was engaged rather than a hastily collected group of frontiersmen with no better title than a "Scout".

As to whether the engagement can be described as a massacre, a battle or a skirmish, is a matter of opinion, it being true that the Rangers suffered defeat; however, some resistance was offered as proven by wounds received from the enemy in close combat and that the Indians suffered some casualties. To describe the event as a massacre is to cast an odium upon the character of those brave men who constantly faced danger while guarding the frontier and through whose efforts the lives of many settlers, men, women and children, were saved from destruction by the cruel savages, aided, equipped and supported by the agents of the British Government.

The fact that many survived the engagement, some with wounds, indicates that the Indian's ambush was not entirely successful; that a massacre did not occur and that the dead numbered only those who were killed at the first volley, or possibly a few who were seriously wounded and could not escape. Less than one-half of the number engaged fell victims to the Indian attack, including killed and captured.

The pension application statements of those Revolutionary War veterans refer to this engagement with the Indians as the Battle of Frankstown and in no case is any other title used. These veterans came from many different parts of Pennsylvania and afterwards moved from place to place, eventually, most of them took up residence in western Pennsylvania or Ohio, wherever the lands were located which were granted them for service. Some located in Kentucky, Indiana and even west of the Mississippi, so it was not by agreement that they called the engagement the Battle of Frankstown, but rather for want of any other name.

The entire area within a radius of ten miles of the present village of Frankstown was known as the Frankstown District, and was named for Stephen Franks who conducted a trading post at this point, which was on the Kittanning Trail, close to the Indian village of Assunepachla. Little is known today of Stephen Franks. Possibly he was a French trader who departed from this vicinity prior to 1760, during the period of the French-Indian War, to pursue his trade with the Indians of the Ohio region.

Three forts existed in the Frankstown District during the early days of the Revolution. The barn of Peter Titus located below Hollidaysburg, the home of William Holliday near where Gaysport stands, and the barn of Michael Fetter located near the New Portage Junction. Troops were stationed at these forts at various times and the need for a larger and better constructed fort for use by the troops as quarters and defense against possible attack was greatly needed. From the statements made by a number of veterans to secure pensions it is learned that a blockhouse was constructed during the years 1780, 1781 and 1782, and known as the blockhouse at Frankstown or the Frankstown Fort. It is believed that this blockhouse was located not far from the Fetter barn which would account for the variance in opinion held by many people as to the location of the site of this fort. There being two sites, one marked at Fort Fetter and the other unmarked. The marker for Fort Fetter is located along the William Penn Highway about one mile west of Hollidaysburg and was erected by the Blair County Historical Society in 1922. It contains this inscription, "500 feet northeast of this spot, site of Fort Fetter, built in 1777, first Revolutionary Fort, Frankstown garrison".

Sunday, June 3, 1781, was a day long remembered, especially, by those who happened to be in the Frankstown district of Bedford County, at which time the battle was fought. Some to meet a sudden death, others to receive wounds, suffering and privation as prisoners, while the entire frontier inhabitants were thrown into confusion and the danger of further attacks from the victorious invaders, threatened death to all who could not reach the forts in safety or whose flights eastward could not outdistance the advance of the savages.

Three armed groups converged at the western part of Frankstown Township, Bedford County, and occupied the center of the stage for the event to follow. The first of these armed bodies was the Cumberland County Militia, stationed in the Frankstown Blockhouse. The invading group was a band of Indian warriors bent on laying waste to any improvement made on the frontier and the securing of scalps and prisoners for which they would be handsomely rewarded by the British. The third group consisted of Captain John Boyd's Bedford County Rangers and a number of volunteers, who upon receiving the intelligence that the settlement had been invaded by the savages, hurried to the rescue.

It had been the policy of the Executive Council to guard the frontier by stationing companies of Militia from the more eastern sections of Pennsylvania, in the western forts. These companies of Militia consisted mostly of farmers, or farm boys as the better-to-do were able to pay a substitute as this service was compulsory for a two months period. Two muster rolls of Captain Thomas Askey's Company, 8 "Class, 6" Battalion of Cumberland County Militia commanded by Colonel James Dunlap, are preserved in the Pennsylvania Archives. These rolls indicate that this company was on guard at Frankstown from April 15, 1781 to the 15" of June following. Other references to this event state that Captain James Young's Company, Colonel Albright, was stationed at the Frankstown Fort which can possibly indicate the presence of two companies.

From the accounts of those who were captured we learn that the Indian Warriors, numbering eighty-three, were members of the Seneca tribe from New York State and had traveled from their village near the head waters of the Genesee River. Among those who served as Chiefs of the tribe and who participated in this engagement were Sunfish, Big Snow, Blue Eyes and Colonel Pollard.

Captain John Boyd, after years of service in the Continental Army, had now accepted the Captaincy of the Bedford County Rangers and was at Bedford engaged in guarding the frontier and building up his command for the expected struggle with the Indians, who had annually invaded the settlements during the summer months. His First Lieutenant, Richard M. Johnston, was on recruiting duty in Cumberland County and had succeeded in securing several recruits at Browns Mills, now Armagh Township, Mifflin County.

Word was received at Bedford on Friday June 1, that the Indians had crossed the Allegheny Mountains and had attacked and killed 2 men and carried a woman into captivity. Captain Boyd asked for volunteers to accompany the members of his command and the expedition arrived the next day at the blockhouse on the Frankstown branch of the Juniata River, where they remained until early the next morning. Additional volunteers had been secured on the way from Bedford and according to the account of the battle written by Jones, a number of local residents joined the party at the Fort. It is stated by Jones that no member of the Cumberland County Militia stationed at the fort joined in the party under Captain Boyd and no information being found in the official records to the contrary, it is believed that the militia from Cumberland County were ordered to remain at the fort. As the militia company had only a few days to serve in their tour of duty it seems logical that they would not join an expedition of unknown duration or destination.

Preparations were undertaken to make ready for the party to start the next morning. Ammunition, including lead and powder was supplied each man, and uniforms, rifles, tomahawks and knives were inspected and prepared for use. Rations were issued and much excitement prevailed over the anticipation of engaging the invading savages in combat and driving them from the settlement.

Daybreak Sunday morning found the members of the expedition ready for the march. The command now consisted of a formidable array of men experienced both in army service and in the most effective method of fighting the Indians.

In addition to Captain John Boyd and the regular recruited members of his rangers, the following volunteers are known to have joined the expedition at Bedford or as the party advanced to the fort at Frankstown; Captain Richard Dunlap, Captain Samuel Moore, Captain McDaniel, Lieutenant John Cook, Lieutenant George Smith, Lieutenant Harry Woods, Privates James Henry, Horatio Jones, Patrick McDonald, Adam Wimer, Hugh Means, James Moore and Zadock Casteel.

The above list does not include the names of the local residents mentioned by U. J. Jones as being present and it is quite probable that others arrived during the night and early morning from their homes in the vicinity. The ranks would then be increased by James Somerville, Thomas Coleman, Michael Coleman, two of the Hollidays (Captain John Holliday and probably his brother William) Michael Wallick, Edward Milligan, two brothers named Jones, a man named Gray, one of the Beattys. Making the entire force to number well over forty.

As this armed force marched from the fort in single file along the trail towards the junction of the Kittanning Indian trail little thought was given to the possibility that the Indians would advance close to the fort and prepare an ambuscade, so it was not considered necessary to send out an advance guard or to place flankers.

Captain John Boyd led the way, closely followed by the First Sergeant, Henry Dugan, and the volunteer officers. Captain Boyd's thoughts could not have been of his brother Thomas, who suffered torture and death when captured on a similar expedition while leading fourteen of Morgan's riflemen during Sullivan's expedition into New York state a few years previous, a thought of Thomas Boyd would have warned the Captain of possible danger.

Scouts from the Indian war party watched the movement of the soldiers at the fort and observed the departure of Captain Boyd and his men. Quickly reporting to their chiefs, the plans for an ambuscade were made and the warriors awaited the arrival of their foe. The Indian warriors were noted for two factors in their method of war fare, the first of which was the element of surprise and the other was their bravery and desire for close combat.

As the Rangers and Volunteers reached a point near the mouth of Sugar Run, the Indian Chief gave a loud war-whoop as the signal and a volley of rifle fire poured into the surprised force and several lay dead in the path. The forest rang with the war-whoop of the savages as they sprang forward with the tomahawk poised and the scalping knife ready to complete their work of death, and the scalp cry was heard above the din of the battle. The attack was so sudden and the savages so numerous that the Rangers and Volunteers were thrown into confusion and instead of being able to meet the savages as a unit, each one fought his own battle and tried to gain what protection was possible through retreat and the safety of the fort.

Those in front, consisting mostly of the officers were spared the fire of the savages, as officers were worth more as prisoners than privates, and prisoners were also worth more than scalps when settling with the British Agents.

That resistance was offered the attack of the savages is evident from the fact that Captain Boyd was subdued only after receiving three severe gashes in his head from a tomahawk. Captain Dunlap was killed and Captain McDaniel is reported to have been wounded severely and then to have been tortured and put to death.

One report (Jones) states that Harry Woods shot an Indian, and a quotation found in a pamphlet published at Bedford, Penna., by Miss Annie M. Gilchrist, states that James Henry "had told a companion of a recent dream of being captured by Indians and remarked that he would fight to the end rather than be captured. His friend advised him, in event of capture, to submit and his friends would recue him. Following a battle in which the settlers were defeated, Henry was missing and a posse began a search. His terrible mutilated body was found against a tree and nearby was five dead Indians; the tree and ground showed that there had been a bitter struggle and Henry took five lives before surrendering his own."

The remaining ambushed soldiers fled in all directions and each fought his way to safety. A number were injured, some of whom were overtaken and captured or killed by the pursuing Indians while others concealed themselves or gained the protection of the fort.

The casualties could not be determined at the time of the battle and cannot be definitely counted even to-day, as in the first place, the names of those who marched forth were not recorded in any manner, due to not being regularly enlisted members of any organization, and secondly, it was not known for certain whether those missing had been captured, killed or had gained safety at some distant fort or settlement. It is possible that some who were wounded died in the forest and their bodies never discovered.

From many sources believed to be authentic, we can now publish the names of at least a partial list of the casualties of the battle of Frankstown. Among the dead of Captain Boyd's Rangers are found the names of Sergeant Torrence Grimes and privates: John Conrad, John Downey, Sr., Joseph Martin, Henderson Murphy, Michael Nicholas, John Thomas, William Tucker and Henry Tantinger, while from the volunteer group we have the names of Captain Richard Dunlap, Captain McDaniel and James Henry.

Those captured included Captain John Boyd, Sergeant Henry Dugan, both of the Rangers, and the following volunteers; Captain Samuel Moore, Lieutenant John Cook, Lieutenant George Smith; Privates Patrick McDonald and Horatio Jones.

The wounded Rangers included Sergeant David Beate, Privates Abraham Bodle and Stephen Goble, and the wounded Volunteers were Hugh Means and Adam Wimer.

To the above list of those killed could be added a man named Jones who, as related by U. J. Jones, had stopped to rest and was later found killed and scalped.

The militia who were garrisoning the fort took no part in the battle. However, upon receiving the news of the defeat of the Rangers and Volunteers, they proceeded to prepare the fort to resist an attack, sent messengers to apprise settlers and other forts of the danger and a party was sent from the fort to the aid of the wounded. The next day they went forth to the scene of the battle and buried the dead where they fell.

The members of the Bedford County Rangers who survived returned to Bedford where they were joined a week later by Lieutenant Richard Johnston, who now took over the command of the Company and recruited it to full strength. This Company continued to be known as Captain John Boyd's Bedford County Rangers and remained in active service until the summer of 1783, when it was discharged.

Instead of attacking and plundering the isolated homes of the frontiersmen, many of whom had fled or forted, the Indians were satisfied with their victory, and having taken about a dozen scalps and at least seven prisoners, immediately departed with their prisoners and booty across the mountains to the West Branch of the Susquehanna River, near the mouth of the Sinnemahoning Creek, where they tortured and put to death a captive named Ross who was wounded very badly and unable to walk.

Captain Boyd was forced to witness the death of Ross, and being also wounded and faint from loss of blood, resigned himself to his fate, as his turn was to come next. At the critical moment the life of Captain Boyd was spared by the intervention of an elderly squaw who claimed him as her son, which was following a custom among the Indians where a squaw had lost a son in battle.

Of those who were captured, Captain Boyd, Sergeant Dugan, Lieutenants Cook and Smith, and Private McDonald are known to have returned to their homes during 1783, and to have lived many years, during which time they related their experiences for the benefit of posterity. Horatio Jones was adopted into the Seneca tribe and was not free of the Indians until 1785. He did not return to his home at Bedford but remained in New York State and in later years was appointed Indian Commissioner.

The story of the Battle of Frankstown as gleaned from many official records and related history, through years of research work, is told here but briefly. Further history of each of the participants will be found in this volume under the heading of sketches of Revolutionary War veterans.

SKETCHES OF REVOLUTIONARY WAR VETERANS

ADAMS, JOHN   Ran away from his guardian with whom he was making his home at Conewago and joined the army at Taneytown, Maryland, and was engaged in the Battle of Brandywine.

"Saw a French General there wounded in the leg or thigh, heard him say that it was not dangerous, they should not mind it."

The above quotation is found in the application for a pension filed by John Adams. He did not state who the French General was and probably was not aware that he stood in battle along side General Marquis de Lafayette.

His guardian overtook him after the battle and returned him home. He was then bound to Wendell Kellem of York, Pennsylvania. His master was drafted in 1780, when John Adams served in his place, as a Private in Captain Claar's Company of York County Militia, to guard Hessian prisoners.

He again served as a substitute, this time as a Private in Captain Foreman's Company of York County Militia.

John Adams was born 1764. He married Nancy Beatty at Water Street on the 13th of March, 1790, to which union thirteen children were born. He died at Gaysport on the 2d of August, 1850. Place of burial is unknown.

AITKINS, ROBERT   Served as a Private in Captain John Boyd's Bedford County Rangers during 1781. Received 250 acres donation land as a bounty.

ALLEN, PETER   Enlisted as a Private in Captain James' Company, Colonel Watts, in 1776, and engaged with the enemy at Middletown.

Joined the troops engaged in the defense of the frontier as a Private in the Regiment commanded by Colonel John Piper "and rendezvoused at Lead Mine Fort commanded by General Roberdeau and was actively engaged in every scout." Later served as a Private in Captain William Wilson's Company under Colonel McAlevy and continued in duty along the frontier until the close of the war.

He was born 1754, in Ireland and came to America and settled in Cumberland County in 1775. Resided in Wayne Township, Mifflin County in 1823.

ALLIGAN, WILLIAM   Served as a Corporal in Captain John Boyd's Bedford County Ranging Company during 1781. He received 200 acres donation land.

ARCHER, STEPHEN   Enlisted at Philadelphia in 1776, as a Marine under Captain Robert Mullin on board the U. S. Frigate, the Delaware, commanded by Captain Charles Alexander. Was in the Battles of Trenton and Princeton. Returned to the ship which was captured at the time Philadelphia was taken. Of the one hundred and nine prisoners placed in jail only eighteen or nineteen survived to escape to General Washington's forces at Valley Forge where given bounds and continued in service twenty-one months. He re-enlisted under Captain James Trimble of Augusta County, Virginia, and fought in the Battle of Portsmouth. He then "Came to the back part of Pennsylvania and enlisted in Captain John Boyd's Company of Woods-Rangers". His discharge reads as follows; "I do hereby certify that Stephen Archer has served as a soldier in Captain John Boyd's Company of the Pennsylvania Rangers from the 20th day of May, 1782, to the 30th day of June, 1783, both days included and is hereby honorably discharged agreeable to the orders of Council the 6th June last. Given under my hand at Bedford the 1st of July, 1783. Signed Richard Johnston, Lt."

Stephen Archer resided in Monongahalia County, Virginia, where he died the 12th of May, 1824, at the age of 79.

ARTHUR, JOHN   Enlisted during the year 1776, in Prince Edward County, Virginia, in Captain Baytoff's Company of the 7th Virginia Regiment, later transferred to the 3d Regiment, and served three years, during which time he was in the Battles of Brandywine, Germantown and Monmouth and in sundry skirmishes. He was wounded in the groin by a musket ball, during the Battle of Monmouth.

During the year 1781 he served for a period of seven months as a Private in Captain John Boyd's Bedford County Rangers.

Resided in Greenfield Township, Bedford County, in 1820, aged 55 years and upwards.

ASHMAN, GEORGE   Served as Colonel of the 2d Battalion, Bedford County Militia, the 10th of December, 1777.

Appointed Sub-Lieutenant of Bedford County Militia, the 21st of November, 1780.

"On the 18th of May, 1781. Lieutenant George Ashman and his sub-Lieutenants divided Bedford County into three Battalions. The Townships of Dublin, Shirley, Barree, Hopewell, Frankstown and Huntingdon, then embracing all of the area now constituting Huntingdon and Blair and parts of adjoining counties, composed one Battalion, and the other parts of the County was divided into two. The citizens of the County subject to military duty numbered 1456".

Colonel George Ashman, as sublieutenant, commanded the Bedford County Militia, with headquarters probably at Fort Littleton. His duties no doubt took him through other sections of the frontier, including the Frankstown district.

His letters concerning the Battle fought at Frankstown, the 3d of June, 1781, are as follows:

To Arthur Buchanan at Kishicoquillas (Lewistown) dated the 3d of June, 1781,

"Sir:—By an express this moment from Frankstown, we have the bad news. As a party of volunteers from Bedford was going to Frankstown, a party of Indians fell in with them this morning and killed thirty of them. Only seven made their escape to the garrison at Frankstown. I hope that you'll exert yourself in getting men to go up to the Stone; and pray let the river people know, as they may turn out. I am, in health, George Ashman."

His other letter is addressed to the Executive Council at Philadelphia, dated at Bedford County the 12th of June, 1781,

"Sir:—I have to inform you that on Sunday, the third of this instant, a party of rangers under Captain Boyd, eight in number, with twenty-five volunteers under Captain Moore and Lieutenant Smith, of the militia of this county, had an engagement with a party of Indians (said to be numerous) within three miles of Frankstown, where seventy-five of the Cumberland militia were stationed, commanded by Captain James Young. Some of the party running into the garrison, acquainting Captain Young what had happened, he issued out a party immediately, and brought in seven more, five of whom are wounded, and two made their escape to Bedford—eight killed and scalped—Captain Boyd, Captain Moore and Captain Dunlap missing. Captain Young, expecting from the enemy's numbers that his garrison would be surrounded, sent express to me immediately; but, before I could collect as many volunteers as was sufficient to march to Frankstown with, the enemy had returned over the Allegheny Hill. The waters being high, occasioned by heavy rains, they could not be pursued. This county, at this time, is in a deplorable condition. A number of families are flying away daily ever since the late damage was done. I can assure your Excellency that if immediate assistance is not sent to this county that the whole of the frontier inhabitants will move off in a few days. Colonel Abraham Smith, of Cumberland, has informed me that he has no orders to send us any more militia from Cumberland County to our assistance, which I am surprised to hear. I shall move my family to Maryland in a few days, as I am convinced that not any one settlement is able to make any stand against such numbers of the enemy. If your Excellency should please to order us any assistance, less than three hundred will be of but little relief to this county. Ammunition we have not any; and the Cumberland militia will be discharged in two days. It is dreadful to think what the consequence of leaving such a number of helpless inhabitants may be to the cruelties of a savage enemy.

"Please to send me by the first opportunity three hundred pounds, as I cannot possibly do the business without money. You may depend that nothing shall be wanting in me to serve my country as far as my abilities.

"I have the honor to be, Your Excellency's most obedient, humble servant, George Ashman, Lieut., Bedford County."

ASKEY, THOMAS   Captain Cumberland County Militia 1777-1782.

His company, the 8th Class, 6th Battalion, under Colonel James Dunlap, was "on guard at Frankstown, April 15, 1781, to June 15, following," during which time the Battle of Frankstown was fought, record as above quoted appears in the Pennsylvania Archives, with Ensign Thomas Cessna; Sergeants John Harmony, James Witherow, Andrew Alsworth; Corporals Henry Black, Andrew Bell, Lewis Lee and forty-eight privates.

AURANDT, JOHN DEITRICK   Enlisted in Northumberland County, Buffalo Township, by Lieutenant Jacob Snyder of Captain George Whitzel's Company under Colonel Stewart on the 14th day of January, 1778; transferred to Captain Bankson's Company of the 2d Regiment and discharged on the 14th day of January 1781.

He married the 5th of November, 1782, and his widow, Catharine Reiber Aurandt, survived him. To this union were born the following children: Salome, Catharine, John, David, Jonathan, Hanna and Joshua.

He served as a Minister of the German Reformed Church and died the 24th of April, 1831, at the age of 70 years, 5 months and 16 days. Buried at Shaffersville, Huntingdon County.

BEAMAN, MOSES   Served as a Private in the Bedford County Militia during three tours of two months each, under Captain Patrick Harvey, Edward Rose and John Rush; to guard the frontier from Indian attack, operated from Fort Bedford.

"Went out at time...... to Frankstown and next morning they marched out towards mountains along what was called the "Kittanning Path". Three or four miles from Frankstown they were attacked by Indians, who were lying in ambush, and nearly all killed. Ensign Means was wounded in hand and he thinks only seven or eight besides himself escaped."

Enlisted as a Private in Captain John Boyd's Bedford County Ranging Company and served until the 14th of July, 1783.

Born the 8th of August, 1757, in Cumberland County, resided at Cumberland for twenty years, moved to Stock Township, Morrison County, Ohio, about the year 1826, and died at Brown, Ohio, the 13th of December, 1842.

BEATES, DAVID   Enrolled as a Private in Captain John Boyd's Bedford County Rangers, during the spring of the year 1781. Was wounded during the Battle of Frankstown. Was promoted to first Sergeant and after the capture of Captain Boyd and Sergeant Dugan was in command until Lieutenant Johnston arrived from recruiting duty.

BEATTY, EDWARD   Served in the Bedford County Militia under Lieutenant John VanZant, Captain William Singleton, Colonel Cannon in Matthew Dean's, David Lowery's, Jacob Roller's and Sam Anderson's Forts in the years 1780, 1781, 1782 and 1783.

Was at Fort Pitt and Red Stone, Old Fort and at the treaty held with the Indians at the mouth of the "Maskingham" River.

Born in the year 1756, a son of Robert Beatty and resided on the Juniata River near the Allegheny Mountains. Married Nancy Umstead near Fredericktown, Maryland, and then resided near Huntingdon, Pennsylvania, moved to Lee County, Virginia, in the year 1803, where he died the 27th of December, 1845, survived by his widow and the following children: William, Ann Hagan, Rachael Bales, Robert and Elizabeth.

BEATTY, JOHN Served with the Cumberland County Militia under Ensign John Wilson for a two months tour, in the year 1780.

Enlisted under Lieutenant Johnston as a Private in Captain John Boyd's Bedford County Ranging Company about the 1st of June, 1781, and served for seven months at Bedford to guard the frontier from invasion by the Indians.

Born the 12th of August, 1763, in County of Donegal, Ireland and resided Armagh Township, Mifflin County, in the year 1833.

BEATTY, RICHARD Served in the Bedford County Militia under Captain Singleton.

Son of Robert Beatty who resided on the Juniata River near the Allegheny Mountains at the time of the Revolutionary War.

BEATTY, ROBERT Served in the Bedford County Militia on the frontier under Captain Singleton.

Son of Robert Beatty who resided on the Juniata River near the Allegheny Mountains at the time of the Revolutionary War.

BENNETT, HENRY (HARRY), Born the 24th of October, 1753; settled in what is now Greenfield Township, Blair County, prior to 1790. Died 19th of July, 1837, and buried in the Pressel Cemetery, near Claysburg. Widow Mary, died 13th of February, 1850 aged 82.

A Harry Bennett served in the Bedford County Militia from 1783 to 1790, but unable to locate any record indicating service in the Army during the Revolutionary War period. Grave is being decorated as the grave of a Revolutionary War Veteran.

BLACK, HENRY Commissioned a Captain of Rangers in November 1777. "Their duty was to guard the frontier from Bald Eagle to Bedford......raised his company and was stationed at Frankstown, on the old trading path to Kittanning, he built a Fort at that place". Two other companies of Rangers were raised at the same time, one commanded by Captain Thomas Cluggage, the other by Captain John McDonald, the whole under the command of Major Robert Cluggage.

The authority for the existence of these three companies is found in a Resolution of Congress, dated the 5th of November, 1778 and reads as follows: "Resolved: That the three companies commanded by Captains Cluggage, Black and McDonald, raised for the defense of the frontiers of Pennsylvania be reenlisted and completed to their full complement for the space of one year from the 15th day of December next unless sooner discharged by Congress.

"That every non-commissioned officer and private enlisting in the said companies receive as a bounty a suit of clothes to consist of the articles usually allowed the continental troops, and that it be stipulated with the said non-commissioned officers and privates so enlisting that they shall not be removed from the frontier of the said State on any account whatsoever, except on expeditions against the Indians."

The following is a copy of a letter found in the pension file of Captain Henry Black; dated at Huntingdon the 14th of March, 1779. "Sr. After informing I am in health I would request the favor of you to come over to the Fort as soon as possible as I want to discharge the dues of your company as far as possible-pray inform Captain McDonald to come over with you and Captain Cluggage requests the favor of him to bring over a book that he borrowed.

"I have wrote to William Holliday to send with you time, money. Pray call on him before you come over. My compliments to wife Black. I am your humble servant, Robert Cluggage."

Captain Black was born December 1752, in Chester County, Pennsylvania, and resided in Bedford County during the Revolutionary War. He resided in Adams County, Pennsylvania, the 16th of August, 1832.

BODLE, ABRAHAM   Served as a Corporal with Captain John Boyd's Bedford County Rangers and was wounded in right thigh during the Battle of Frankstown on the 3d of June, 1781.

BOYD, JOHN   Commissioned a Second Lieutenant in the 12th Pennsylvania Regiment, Continental Line, the 16th of October, 1776, promoted First Lieutenant the 20th of May, 1777 and transferred to Third Pennsylvania Regiment. Promoted Captain Lieutenant May, 1780, and retired the Regiment the 1st of January, 1781; commissioned a Captain of Rangers in Bedford County and discharged the 1st of July, 1783.

He was captured by the Indians at the Battle of Frankstown, and the following account of his captivity is found in "Otzinachson or a History of the West Branch Valley of the Susquehanna" by J. F. Meginness: "After the defeat of Captain Boyd's party, he tried to make his escape by running, but was pursued and received three severe gashes in his head with a tomahawk, when he was taken. The Indians immediately struck across the country and came to the West Branch, near the mouth of the Sinnemahoning Creek. They also had another prisoner, named Ross, who was wounded very badly. Being unable to travel further, they determined to massacre him in a very cruel and inhuman manner. He was fastened to a stake, and his body stuck full of pitch pine splinters, when fire was applied, and they danced round him, making the woods resound with their hideous yells. His tortures were terrible, but at length death put an end to his sufferings.

"During this time Captain Boyd, faint from the loss of blood, was tied to a small white oak sapling, and compelled to be a silent spectator of the diabolical scene. His turn was to come next, and he summoned up courage, and quietly resigned himself to his fate. Whilst these incarnate fiends of Pandemonium were making preparations to torture him to death by inches, he sang a very pretty Free Mason song, with a plaintive air, which attracted their attention, and they listened to it very closely, till he was through. At this critical moment an elderly squaw came up and claimed him as her son. The Indians did not interfere. She immediately dressed his wounds and attended to him carefully during their journey to Canada. She accompanied him to Quebec, where he was placed in the hospital and attended by an English surgeon, and rapidly recovered. He was then turned out into the street without money or friends. As he passed along, a large sign, with the letters "Masonic Inn", painted on it, attracted his attention, and observing the landlord standing in the door, gave him the sign of the Order, which was recognized. He was kindly taken in, and cared for till he was exchanged. The wounds on his head occasioned him to keep up a continual winking.

"The old squaw who was the means of preserving his life, belonged to the Oneida tribe. Boyd remembered her as his best friend, and often sent her presents of money. On one occasion he made a journey personally to visit her. Boyd died in Northumberland."

Captain Boyd resided at Northumberland. A brother William Boyd, Second Lieutenant of Captain John Brady's Company 12th Regiment was killed in the Battle of Brandywine the 11th of September, 1777. Another brother, Lieutenant Thomas Boyd, of Morgan's Rifles and fourteen others were captured by the Indians while in advance of Sullivan's Expedition against the Indians of New York State who had committed many depredations against the settlers along the Susquehanna River. All members of Lieutenant Boyd's party were tortured and killed by the Indians, the 14th of Sept. 1779.

Captain John Boyd married a daughter of Colonel John Bull of Northumberland, to which union were born the following children; Sarah, Anima, Mary Elizabeth, John, William and Maria. He served as a Justice of the Peace and was elected a delegate to the Pennsylvania Convention which ratified the Constitution of the United States, the 12th of December, 1787. He died the 13th of February, 1832 at the age of 82 years.

BOYLES, JOHN   Enlisted the 5th of January, 1776, in Captain Persifer Frazier's Company, 4th Battalion, Pennsylvania Militia, and discharged the 26th of November, 1776. Enlisted at Carlisle in Captain William Cross' Company, 4th Pennsylvania Continental

Line; served under Captains Fishbourne, Campbell and Burd, 4th Pennsylvania Regiment under General Sullivan to Schoharie, New York, in 1779. In battles of Brandywine, Germantown, Newton and Appletown. Discharged as a Sergeant in April, 1782.

Born 1751, and resided in Antis Township, Huntingdon County, now Blair County, where he died in 1820. Buried in Logan Valley Cemetery, Bellwood.

BOYLES, WILLIAM Served as a Private and Drummer in the Lancaster County Militia in Captain John Patton's Company, under Colonel James Taylor, from 1777 to 1781.

Buried in Logan Valley Cemetery, Bellwood.

BRICKER, PETER (BRECKER) Went out with the Militia under Colonel Joseph Heister, then enlisted in Berks County during May, 1778, as a Private in Captain Richard Findlay's Company, 6th Pennsylvania Continental Line, and discharged the 19th of March, 1781.

He participated in the Battles of Germantown, Stonypoint, White Plains and Trenton.

Born 1757, and resided in Frankstown Township, Huntingdon County, now Blair County, in 1820.

BROWN, JOHN Served as a Private in Captain John Boyd's Bedford County Rangers for a period of seven months during the year 1781.

BROWN, MICHAEL Served as a Private in Captain John Boyd's Bedford County Rangers for a period of seven months during the year 1781.

BUCHANAN, ARTHUR Colonel of Militia, stationed at Kishacoquillas (Lewistown).

Gathered together a party of militia and marched across the Allegheny Mountains to the waters of the Susquehanna River in pursuit of the Tories, Spring of 1778.

BURTON, JOSHUA Enlisted 1776, and served four years; Private in Captain Thomas Price's Company, Maryland Infantry; taken prisoner at Fort Washington; exchanged and attached to 11th Virginia Regiment; later transferred to Maryland troops under Colonel Smith.

In Battles of Fort Washington, Germantown, Monmouth, and Brandywine where he was wounded in the leg.

"He afterwards enlisted for one year in a company commanded by Captain Boyd of the Pennsylvania Line and served out that year when he was honorably discharged at Bedford, Pennsylvania."

Born 10th of October, 1756, and resided Pickaway County, Ohio, in the year 1831.

CAMPBELL, THOMAS Appointed Captain of Rangers the 7th of April, 1779 and served on the frontier of Bedford County.

CASTEEL, ZADOCK Served for six months as a Private in Captain William Tisue's Company under Colonel Woods and engaged in Battles of Trenton and Princeton.

Enlisted first part of 1781, as a Private in Captain John Boyd's Bedford County Rangers; engaged in Battle of Frankstown and assisted in building a blockhouse at Frankstown.

Born the 17th of January, 1754 in Prince County, Maryland; resided in Bedford County until 1788; married in 1773 in Bedford County; moved to Preston County, Virginia, in 1822; moved to Monroe County, Ohio, where he died the 11th of January, 1844.

CLARK, JAMES Enlisted in 1776, in Chester County Militia, and served enlistments as an Ensign under the following Captains: Anderson, Mordecai, Morgan and Vanderlies. Wounded at the Battle of Brandywine in left leg.

Born 1756, at Lancaster; resided in Franklin Township, Huntingdon County in 1832, and died in Morris Township, Huntingdon County, the 1st of July, 1841.

Buried in the Presbyterian Cemetery at Williamsburg.

CLARKE, JOHN   Served as a Private in Captain Parr's Company, Morgan's Rifle Regiment, from 1777 to 1783. Wounded at Saratoga.

Resided at Martinsburg in 1816, and in Morris Township, Huntingdon County in 1840.

CLUGGAGE, ROBERT   Commissioned Captain, June 1775, and commanded a company recruited in Bedford County which was one of six companies of expert riflemen raised in Pennsylvania under authority of the Continental Congress, on the 14th of June, 1775. The Battalion was known as the 2d regiment until the 1st of January 1776, when it became the 1st regiment of the Continental Line.

Captain Cluggage resigned the 6th of October, 1776, and returned to his home in Black Log Valley, near Orbisonia, now Huntingdon County. He took an active part in the defence of the frontier and served as Major of the Rangers during the years 1778 and 1779. He was active in the development of the lead mines in Sinking Valley and Fort Roberdeau, and succeeded General Daniel Roberdeau.

He served as Justice of the Peace for Bedford County in 1771, and for Shirley Township, Huntingdon County in 1787. He died about 1789, survived by his mother, and the following brothers: James, George, Francis, Thomas and Gavin.

CLUGGAGE, THOMAS   Appointed Captain of Rangers for Bedford County under Major Robert Cluggage and stationed at Fort Roberdeau in Sinking Valley during the years 1778 and 1779.

COLEMAN, MICHAEL   Served as a Private in Bedford County Militia.

Brother of Thomas Coleman; settled in Tuckahoe Valley, Logan Township, Blair County.

COLEMAN, THOMAS   Served as a Private in Bedford County Militia, appointed an Ensign in Rifle Regiment and acted as a volunteer spy and guide for various expeditions.

When applying for a pension in 1833, he made the following statement, "That in the year 1777, he, with a number of his neighbors, who lived in what was then considered the very frontier settlement situate in said County, then known as a part of County of Bedford, collected into a fort called Fetters Fort situate in Frankstown Township in said county, during which year he began to exert himself against the Indians and in the service of the United States; that in the month of November in the same year he discovered the tracks of a parcel of Indians pursuing the path from Kittanning towards Frankstown; that he followed until he found them in the act of making their fires; that he immediately warned the inhabitants of the settlement of their danger who made their escape and that he assisted in collecting men to attack them the following night when five of the Indians were killed and wounded. From that time deponent became a guide to the different companies of men that came to protect the defenseless inhabitants on the frontier. He also turned out and followed the Tories who had meditated the death of the defenseless women and children by joining the Indians and conducting them to the settlement and followed them to the Cherrytree on the Seuwuehanna in the most inclement weather when we encamped and deponent was the first man chosen to proceed to Kittanning to discover, if possible, if the Tories had formed a Junction with the Indians."

On the 1st of August, 1780, he was commissioned by the Supreme Executive Council of Pennsylvania an Ensign and served under Captain John Moore. His commission was for a period of seven months.

He afterwards continued his services as a spy and guide to all that called upon him, during which time he served under Colonel Jack, Captain Black, Colonel Piper, and others, and ranged the frontier to Hannastown and as far as Fort Pitt. "We frequently marched several days without anything to eat. At one time pursued the Indians to near Kittanning. Our jerked beef was out. We then had nothing to eat for four days."

SOLDIERS OF BLAIR COUNTY

Thomas Coleman was born in Cumberland County, in 1748, and resided in Logan Township, Blair County, near Altoona. He died the 2d of February, 1833; and is buried in Grandview Cemetery, Altoona, and was survived by his widow, Pheby, and the following children: John, James, Thomas, Absalom, Michum, William, Sarah married to Frederick Yingling, Catharine married to William Scandred, Margaret married to Thomas Williams, Margaret married to William Bennett and Nancy married to Daniel McCauley.

COLVERT, DANIEL   Served as a Private in Capt. John Boyd's Bedford County Rangers.

CONRAD, JOHN   Served as a Private in Captain John Boyd's Bedford County Rangers. Records indicate that he died during his enlistment, presumably killed at the Battle of Frankstown.

COOK, JOHN   Served as a Private in Captain Herbert's Company, and Colonel Atlee; commissioned Ensign in 12th Pennsylvania Line and according to J. F. Meginnes, he accompanied Captain John Boyd from Northumberland to Bedford and was engaged in the Battle of Frankstown, "They were suddenly surprised by a large body in ambush, and fired upon. A smart engagement took place, but the whites were overcome by superior numbers, and after losing several men, were compelled to fly. Cook received several wounds, and was taken prisoner. Four Indians took him in charge, and started off, he knew not where. On the third night of his captivity they began to amuse themselves by burning his legs with fire brands, and as he was much exhausted from loss of blood from his wounds, was scarcely able to move. After traveling through the wilderness for about twenty days, fed on the entrails of wild animals, they brought him to Niagara. He was brought out one day to run the gauntlet, but being unable to run, as his legs were so badly burned, the Savages at length took mercy on him and let him off. He was then confined in prison until he was finally exchanged and returned."

CORPS, RICHARD   Served as a Private in Captain John Boyd's Bedford County Rangers.

CREVISTON, JACOB   Served as a Private in Captain John Boyd's Bedford County Rangers for which he received in 1802, a grant of 200 acres of land in district No. 10, on the west side of Allegheny River in the County of Westmoreland.

CRISSMAN, JACOB   Reported to have served during the Revolutionary War, but unable to verify services.
Born 1753; died 1856, and buried in Union Cemetery, 11th Avenue and 16th Street, Altoona, but later moved to Fairview Cemetery in 1860; Reserve Section.

CROSSIN, JOHN   Served as a Private in Captain John Boyd's Bedford County Rangers.

CRUSE, JOHN   Enlisted May, 1780, as a Private in Captain Mowerdark's Company, Berks County Militia; re-enlisted in Captain Henry's Company under Major Talbot, in the 6th Regiment of the Continental Line, and discharged in 1781.
Born in Berks County 1761, and died the 28th of April, 1837, at Frankstown.

CURTZ, LUDWIG   Served as a Private in Captain John Boyd's Bedford County Rangers.

DEAN, JOHN   Enlisted at Barrie, as a Private in Captain William Simonton's Bedford County Militia and engaged in scouting parties along the frontier against the Indians.
Born 1762, resided in Huntingdon County in 1833.

DEVINNEY, ANDREW   Served as a Major in Bedford County Militia, from the 18th of March to the 18th of May, 1778.
Resided in Frankstown Township, now Blair County.

THE REVOLUTIONARY WAR

DEWIT, BALTISESSER   Served as a Private in Captain John Boyd's Bedford County Rangers.
Resided in Cumberland County when enlisting, Armagh Township, now Mifflin County.

DICKEY, JOHN   Served several enlistments from Cumberland County, at one time was "sent to a place called Water Street under command of Major Taylor,—at one time sent as a guard with provisions to the lead mines."

"At another time the company was ordered to cross Canoe Mountain, the head of Sinking Valley and the Bald Eagle ridge to the foot of the Allegheny Mountains and range it to Fetters Fort at Frankstown, with Major Taylor—The day before they reached their place of destination the following circumstances occurred—A man and a boy had been out to hunt cows, an Indian shot the man and pursued the boy who having a gun turned towards the Indian; when he saw this he (the Indian) jumped behind a small tree and began to load his gun. Looking round the tree he exposed part of his body which the boy instantly shot at and struck. The Indian dropped his gun and fled, and the boy made his way to the Fort."

John Dickey was born 1752, in Cumberland County and resided at McConnellsburg, 1833.

DODSON, MICHAEL   Enlisted the 20th of July, 1776, at Taneytown, Maryland, for six months, as a Private in Captain Jacob Good's Company.
Enlisted the 20th of April, 1777, at Taneytown, in Captain Lansdale's Company, 4th Maryland, Continental Line, and discharged the 20th of April, 1780. Participated in the Battles of Brandywine, Germantown, White Plains and many skirmishes.
Born the 6th of September, 1751, died the 9th of December, 1830, and buried in the Dodson Cemetery, Greenfield Township, Blair County.

DODSON, THOMAS   Reputed to have served during the Revolutionary War, unable to verify services.
Born the 11th of May, 1741; died the 24th of May, 1831, and buried in the Dodson Cemetery, Greenfield Township, Blair County.

DOWNEY, JOHN, SR.   Served as a Private in Captain Boyd's Bedford County Rangers. Muster rolls indicate that he died while in the services, probably killed at Battle of Frankstown.

DOWNEY, JOHN, JR.   Enlisted at Hagerstown, Maryland, February 1776, in Captain John Nelson's Company, and discharged the 20th of February, 1777. Served under Colonel Butler at Albany, Fort George, Fort Ticonderoga, St. John's Fort and then to Montreal where he joined the 1st Pennsylvania Regiment.

"In 1781, he resided in Bedford County, Pennsylvania and enlisted for and during the War of Revolution under Captain John Boyd in a company of Rangers . . . had a skirmish with Indians and our Captain was taken prisoner. We stayed in a Fort at Frankstown, in the winter in the town of Bedford. Discharged June 4, 1783."

Born the 3d of October, 1755, in Frederick County, Maryland; resided Bedford County during War, moved to Kentucky in 1790, and resided Henry County, Kentucky, in 1833.

DUGAN, HENRY   Enlisted May, 1775, at Old Town, Maryland, as a Private in Captain Michael Cresap's Independent Maryland Company and served one year. Enlisted as a Private in Captain Dean's Company of Rangers in New York City; joined Colonel Malcolm's Regiment and discharged December 1776. Enlisted in 1779 as a Private in Captain William Phillip's Bedford County Militia and served six months.

Enlisted the 30th of March, 1781, as a Sergeant in Captain John Boyd's Bedford County Rangers; captured by the Indians at the Battle of Frankstown, the 3d of June, 1781; returned from captivity to New York the 25th of December, 1782, and discharged the 18th of July, 1783.

Henry Dugan was born in Ireland, the 24th of March, 1736; and came to America in 1760; resided in Cumberland County; moved to the Monongahela district where his wife and three children were killed by the Indians; went to Kentucky in 1774 and was driven off by the Indians; enlisted in Lord Dunmore's Army and fought in the Battle of Kansas River against the Indians.

He resided in Buffalo Valley in 1785, when his home was burned; resided Miami Township, Hamilton County, Ohio, in 1818, with his family consisting of his wife Polly, children Mary, Kitty and William.

DUNLAP, RICHARD (DELAPT) Served as a Captain of the Bedford County Militia, and accompanied Captain John Boyd's Bedford County Rangers from Bedford when they marched to the Frankstown district to drive out the Indians. Killed in Battle of Frankstown, the 3rd of June, 1781. His widow Jane resided at Bedford for many years.

ENSLOW, GEORGE (ENSLEY) Served as a Private in the Bedford County Militia during several tours. Was commissioned a Captain of Bedford County Militia. Served on frontier at the following Forts: Martin's, Frankstown, Wisegarver's, Piper's and Buck's; marched against the Indians and had some skirmishes with them.

Resided in Providence Township, Bedford County, and married Elizabeth Martin on the 2d of December, 1783, whose family resided on the Juniata, in Martin's Fort, which was erected on the land of her father. George Enslow died about 1820.

FEE, JOHN Enlisted January 1778, as a Private in Captain Thomas Cluggage's Company, Bedford County Militia and discharged at Philadelphia in March of same year.

"That soon after, in the course of the same Spring, a large party of Tories to the number of about 90 started off to join the Indians at Kittanning with the intention of bringing them in to murder the inhabitants on the frontier—that as soon as the alarm at this attempt was raised, a party of Militia to the number of about 150 was gathered together by Colonel Buchanan of Lewistown and Colonel McAlevy of Stone Creek and Colonel Jack of Frankstown and marched across the Allegheny Mountains and halted at the waters of the Susquehanna, when they sent out spies, five of whom were shot by the Indians . . . . . returned to Huntingdon, having spent between two and three weeks in said tour and suffered much and endured privation, their provisions having run out on the way" Also, "Turned out at time of massacre of William Eaton; up Raystown Branch when Mrs. Elder was taken prisoner and John Plummer killed who he assisted to bury; with Captain John Shaver to Hair's Valley where they discovered and took several stand of arms secreted by the Tories; up the Little Juniata after the murder of a man named Crum; to the foot of the Allegheny's where it was reported a party of Indians were lurking."

John Fee was born in 1759, and resided east of Huntingdon at the time of the War. His parents were forted for about five years at Carmichael's Fort at the mouth of Aughwick, and Prigmore's Fort at Mill Creek, Married the 16th of June, 1791; died the 26th of August, 1845, survived by his widow Jane.

FINK, MICHAEL Enlisted at York, winter of 1776, as a Private in Captain Albright's Company, 2d Pennsylvania Regiment, and discharged at Trenton, New Jersey, after the meeting or revolt of the Pennsylvania Line in January, 1781. In battles of Long Island, White Plains, Trenton, Princeton, Brandywine, Germantown, Monmouth and Brunswick.

Born 1758; occupation a blacksmith; assessed Frankstown Township 1788; resided Tyrone Township, now Blair County, at time of death in 1836.

FLECK, GEORGE Enlisted in 1776, as a Private in Captain Honey's City Guard; Associators and Militia of Philadelphia, commanded by Lewis Nicola, Town Mayor of the City of Philadelphia; served at the Spring House Tavern and on picket guard at the White Marsh Church in 1778.

Born 1748, in Germany, died the 10th of June 1836; buried in Lutheran Cemetery,

Sinking Valley, Blair County, survived by his widow Catharine, and the following children: Henry, David, Jacob, Elizabeth Crissman, Margaret Fleck, Catharine Crissman and Conrad.

FLECK, PETER Enlisted the 8th of January, 1776, at the Spring House Tavern, 18 miles above Philadelphia as a Private in Captain Thomas Craig's Company, 2d Pennsylvania Regiment, Continental Line; discharged April, 1777, "which discharge he kept until the fall of the year afterwards, when a part of the British Army came to the House in which he resided, and that through fear of them he threw his discharge into the fire and burned it," having participated in the Battles of Brandywine, Three Rivers in Canada and several skirmishes.

Born 1751, in Germany; resided in Huntingdon in 1818; Centre County prior to 1834; Tyrone Township, now Blair County, at the time of his death, the 7th of May, 1837 and buried in the Lutheran Cemetery, Sinking Valley, Blair County.

FRAZIER, BENJAMIN Served as a Private in Captain John Boyd's Bedford County Rangers; received 200 acres donation land located in Westmoreland County; surveyed the 13th of August, 1785.

Resided in Somerset County in 1808.

GALLOWAY, MARSHALL Served as a Corporal in Captain John Boyd's Bedford County Rangers.

GAST, CHRISTIAN Served as a Private in Captain John Sneider's Company of Northumberland County Militia during May-June, 1780.

Born the 11th of August, 1762; resided Rebersburg, Centre County 1789 to 1808, when he moved to Frankstown, Blair County; died the 25th of September, 1843, and buried in the Frankstown Cemetery near Hollidaysburg.

GOBLE, STEPHEN Served a tour of duty as a Private in Captain John Moore's Bedford County Militia, during 1780.

Enlisted in Spring of 1781, served as a Corporal in John Boyd's Bedford County Rangers until the close of the War. "Was in the Battle of Frankstown in his last term of service and was wounded in the right arm by a bullet and Captain Boyd was taken prisoner."

Born March, 1759, in Morris County, New Jersey.

Resided in Bedford County during the Revolutionary War, and in Bartholomew County, Indiana, in 1832.

GRAY, JAMES Enlisted in 1776, at Wilmington, Delaware, as a Private in Captain Joseph Stedman's Company, "Delaware Blues," under Colonel Haslet, and discharged the 26th of March, 1777. In Battles of Long Island and White Plains.

Born 1754, in Ireland; resided in Allegheny Township, Huntingdon County, now Blair County, in 1802, where he died at the residence of his son Thomas, on the 6th of April, 1837.

GRIMES, JAMES Served as a Private in Captain John Boyd's Bedford County Rangers and received 200 acres of donation land.

GRIMES, JOHN Served as a Private in Captain John Boyd's Bedford County Rangers.

GRIMES, TORRENCE Served as a Sergeant in Captain John Boyd's Bedford County Rangers and as records indicate that he died during his period of service it is presumed that he was killed during the Battle of Frankstown, the 3d of June, 1781.

GUTHRIE, GEORGE Enlisted in Cumberland County, as a Private; promoted Lieutenant in Captain Henry Lee's (Light Horse Harry) Legion of Cavalry; served during 1777 and 1778, and engaged in Battle of Brandywine.

Commissioned a Cornet of Cavalry in Count Pulaski's Legion and served during 1779, in the south, at Charleston and Savannah.

Served as a Private in the 2d Battery, Proctor's Artillery, Cumberland County Militia.

Commissioned a Lieutenant 1781, in Colonel Stephen Moylan's Continental Light Dragons and participated in the Capture of Lord Cornwallis at Yorktown, the 19th of October, 1781, and served until the close of the War, in 1783.

Born 1746, at Philadelphia; married 1770, Margaret Campbell (a sister Sarah, married Adam Holliday); resided at Huntingdon 1792; resided at Hollidaysburg 1802; died 1813, and is buried in the Holliday Burial Ground, near Hollidaysburg.

HALL, JAMES Served as a Private in Captain John Boyd's Bedford County Rangers.

HARTZELL, CONRAD Served as a Private in Captain George Shriver's Company, 4th Battalion, under Colonel Philip Boehm, Northampton County Militia, the 14th of May, 1781.

Born 1748, died the 17th of January, 1831, and buried in Antis Cemetery, near Bellwood.

HASLETT, SAMUEL Served as a Private in Captain John Boyd's Bedford County Rangers.

HASSON, JOHN Served as a Private in Captain John Boyd's Bedford County Rangers.

HENRY, JAMES Served as a Private in Captain John Boyd's Bedford County Rangers and was killed during the Battle of Frankstown, the 3d of June, 1781.

His widow Elizabeth, and children, were awarded a pension in 1790, by Orphans Court of Bedford County, payment to be made out of monies arising from Militia fines.

HILEMAN, MICHAEL Served as a Private in Captain Samuel Rodger's Company, 1st Battalion Cumberland County Militia, August 1780.

Born the 30th of September, 1726; died the 6th of September, 1819, and is buried in Frankstown Cemetery near Hollidaysburg.

HOLLIDAY, ADAM Served as a Private in Captain Thomas Paxton's Ranging Company of Bedford County Militia from the 10th of October until the 13th of November, 1776.

Active in the defense of the frontier, assisted in the construction of Forts, and served as Assessor of Frankstown Township for the year 1779.

Came from the north of Ireland about 1750; served during the French and Indian Wars; settled where Hollidaysburg now stands in 1768; married Sarah Campbell the 14th of November, 1776, to which union the following children were born; John and Jane. Died in 1799, and is buried in the Holliday Burial Ground near Hollidaysburg.

HOLLIDAY, JAMES Enlisted in June 1775, as a Sergeant in Captain Robert Cluggage's Company, Thompson's Rifle Battalion, 2d Pennsylvania Regiment; promoted Ensign the 27th of July, 1776, 1st Pennsylvania Regiment, Continental Line; promoted First Lieutenant the 13th of May, 1777, 1st Pennsylvania Regiment, Continental Line. Killed in Action during the Battle of Brandywine on the 11th of September, 1777.

Two hundred acres of donation land was issued the 11th of February, 1800, to his heirs: John Holliday, William Holliday, Ruth, wife of James Sommerville, and Mary, wife of William Galbraith.

Born 1757, a son of William and Mary Holliday.

HOLLIDAY, JOHN Commissioned Second Lieutenant the 25th of June, 1775, in Captain Robert Cluggage's Company, Thompson's Rifle Battalion, 2d Pennsylvania Regiment; promoted First Lieutenant the 1st of January, 1776, 1st Pennsylvania, Regiment, Continental Line; appointed Captain the 25th of September 1776, of Ross' Company, 1st Pennsylvania Regiment, Continental Line; resigned the 1st of March, 1778.

Engaged in battles of Long Island, White Plains, Trenton, Brandywine, Paoli, Germantown, White Marsh, captured at Fort Washington, the 16th of November 1776, also in a skirmish at Mile Square, and wintered at Valley Forge.

"That in the summer of the year 1778, in the early part thereof, his father resided in Bedford County in Frankstown Township, now Huntingdon County aforesaid on the Frontier and a station was kept at his house and that his father moved all his property except some beds into an out house to accommodate the men on duty there. That the Indians attacked the men stationed in the house and burned the out house with nearly all his household property. That in the month of August in the year 1779, this deponent's brothers Adam and Patrick and his sister Jane were killed in Frankstown Township aforesaid by the Indians."

John Holliday was born 1751; died March, 1823, survived by his widow Dorcas, and is buried in the Holliday Burial Ground, near Hollidaysburg.

HOLLIDAY, WILLIAM, SR. Served as Paymaster, Bedford County Militia from the 8th of October, 1776, through 1799. Sublieutenant of Bedford County in 1777.

Born 1730, and came to America from the north of Ireland in 1750; served during the French and Indian Wars; settled where Gaysport now stands in 1768; married Mary McClellan, to which union the following children were born: John, James, William, Ruth, Mary, Adam, Patrick and Jane.

He died in September, 1796, and is buried in the Holliday Burial Ground, near Hollidaysburg.

HOLLIDAY, WILLIAM, JR. Served as a Private in Captain Thomas Paxton's Ranging Company of Bedford County Militia the 10th of October, 1776.

Born 1759; died November 1819, survived by the following children: William, Mary, Jane, Anne and Dorcas.

IRVINE, JOHN, 2D. (IRVIN) (IRWIN) Enlisted January 1776, at Chester County in Captain James Moore's Company, 4th Pennsylvania Regiment, Continental Line, and served one year.

Enlisted winter of 1777, in Captain Thomas Church's Company, under Colonel Francis Johnston, and served three years.

Born 1751; never married; died the 10th of December 1835; and is buried in the Presbyterian Cemetery at Hollidaysburg.

IRWIN, JAMES Served as a Private in Captain Ephriam Allen's Company, 1st Battalion, Chester County Militia.

Born 1738; moved to Frankstown Township, in 1793; died 1820, survived by his widow Molly, and the following children: Robert, James, Jane and Elizabeth.

Buried in Presbyterian Cemetery at Hollidaysburg.

JOHNSTON, RICHARD Commissioned the 9th of February, 1781, as a First Lieutenant in Captain Boyd's Company, Bedford County Rangers; engaged in recruiting of men to complete the strength of the Company and at Browns Mill, Cumberland County, now Armagh Township, Mifflin County. At the time of the Battle of Frankstown, the 3d of June, 1781, assumed command of the Company until the return of Captain Boyd from captivity. The Company continued to guard the frontier with the exception of the time spent at Yorktown, guarding prisoners and on the 23d of February, 1782, was ordered "to march the Company from Yorktown to the County of Bedford to defend the frontier."

Resided in Kishacoquillas Valley, now Mifflin County, in 1783.

JONES, GEORGE   Served as a Private in Captain John Boyd's Bedford County Rangers.

Resided 1828, in Terre Haute, Vigo County, Indiana; married the 28th of July, 1833, in Vigo County and died December, 1834 or March, 1835, in Ohio.

JONES, WILLIAM   Served as a Private in Captain John Boyd's Bedford County Rangers.

JONES, HORATIO   Enlisted during Autumn of 1776 as a musician (fifer) in Captain James Packer's Company under Colonel John Piper, marched to Philadelphia, Trenton and quartered in the College at Princeton; contracted small pox; discharged early summer of 1777; re-enlisted and went with a company to guard the public stores sent from Philadelphia to Pittsburg; guarded Tories imprisoned in Bedford jail; re-enlisted in Captain John Moore's Company of Bedford County Militia, "marched to a blockhouse on the Frankstown Branch of the Juniata River, where the Company was stationed to keep the Indians back from the frontier settlements, that they were frequently engaged in scouting parties."

"In the early summer of 1781 he resided with his father in the Borough of Bedford when word was received that a small party of Indians within a few miles had attacked and killed two men and carried off one woman. Captain John Boyd of the United States Army was at Bedford in a recruiting station, and he asked for volunteers to join the 12 recruits to go after them. The Party consisted of 20 and Jones volunteered to go under Captain Boyd. Next day arrived at the blockhouse on the Frankstown Branch of the Juniata River, where they remained till early next morning when they continued the pursuit and about four miles from said blockhouse met with a party of 83 Indians under the direction of several of their chiefs who immediately commanded a vigorous attack and after killing 8 of the whites and taking seven prisoners and dispersing the residue of the Company immediately removed with this deponent, who with Captain Boyd and five others were prisoners, over the Allegheny Mountains to Canada on the head waters of the Genesee River in New York State. After many perils and severe trials this deponent was adopted into the Indian Nation. Captain Boyd was delivered over to the British and this deponent detained a prisoner until after the Treaty of Fort Stanwix and was not given up by them with the other prisoners in pursuance of that Treaty but remained until the year of 1785 before he got clear of Indians." Sworn statement of the following Indians: "We severally certify that we were of the party of Seneka Indians that took Horatio Jones, now living in the town of Genesee and County Livingston, in the State of New York. He was taken on the waters of the Juniatty in the State of Pennsylvania and fighting under Captain John Boyd in the Revolutionary War. We also certify that he was kept a prisoner among the Indians about four years."

<pre>
                His
      Sunfish   X
                Mark
                His
      Big Snow   X
                 Mark
            His
      Blue X Eyes
         Mark
                  His
      Col. Pollard X
                  Mark
</pre>

Horatio Jones was appointed by George Washington as interpreter of the Six Nations and continued to serve until a few years of his death.

Born 1763, at Great Valley, Chester County, resided at Genesee, Livingston County, New York, where he died the 18th of August, 1836.

KIFER, HENRY   Enlisted at Little York, Pennsylvania in 1776, and served through several important campaigns including the Battle of Trenton.

Died the 11th of February, 1844, at the residence of his son in North Woodbury Township, Bedford County, at the astonishing age of 102 years, and 6 months. Buried in Hickory Bottom Cemetery, Woodbury, in an unmarked grave along fence close to road and of two graves; his is next to church, the other grave being Christian King.

KEELY, JOSEPH   Enlisted in Vincent Township, Chester County, Spring of 1777, in Captain Jacob Hetherling's Company, 4th Battalion, Chester County Militia; captured by the British; escaped after four weeks and returned home; joined Captain George North's Company, under Colonel Caleb North, Continental Line, and served five years and six months.

In Battle of Brandywine, he was wounded by a musket ball in the left arm, the musket ball breaking one of the bones; also, in Battles of Paoli, Germantown and Mud Island Fort; and several skirmishes.

Born 1757; resided Woodbury Township, Huntingdon County, now Blair County; died the 12th of January, 1838, and buried in the Salem Reformed Cemetery, near Williamsburg.

KELLER, JOHN   Served as a Private in the Continental Line.

Born the 24th of February, 1732; died the 1st of March, 1831; buried in Keller Reformed Cemetery, near Williamsburg; survived by his wife Dorothea, and the following children: Elizabeth, Mary, John, Christiana, Margaret, Catharine, Henry, Jacob, Samuel, Susan and Peter.

KELLER, MICHAEL   Veteran of the Revolutionary War. (Services not available)

Died in Canoe Valley, the 1st of April, 1828; aged 96 years, 6 months and 6 days; buried in Keller Reformed Cemetery, near Williamsburg.

KENNEDY, SAMUEL   Served as a Private in Captain John Boyd's Bedford County Rangers.

KING, CHRISTIAN   A veteran of the Revolutionary War. (Services not available) Buried in Hickory Bottom Cemetery, Woodbury, Bedford County.

LANE, JOHN   Enlisted about first day of April, 1779, for nine months in Captain Thomas Cluggage's Company, Bedford County Rangers; stationed at Huntingdon and at Fort Roberdeau, Sinking Valley, to protect the lead mines. Enlisted following Spring in Captain William Phillip's Company, Bedford County Rangers and served six months.

Born the 22d of February, 1756, in Baltimore County, Maryland, and resided Broad Top Township, Bedford County, in 1840.

LEWIS, SAMUEL   Enlisted in 1777, in Captain Fishburn's Company, under Colonel Butler, Continental Line, and served in the 4th and 5th Pennsylvania Regiment until the 17th of September, 1785, having served six years, four months and twenty days for which he received a Badge of Merit for faithful service. In Battles of Brandywine, Germantown and served two years against the Indians of New York State.

Born 1742; resided Greenfield Township, Bedford County, in 1807; Frankstown Township, Huntingdon County in 1821, and living in Huntingdon County in 1835.

LINDSAY, DAVID (LINDSEY)   Enlisted in 1776, as a Private in Captain William Rippey's Company, under Colonel Hartley and served about 15 months. In Battle of Three Rivers in Canada. Following summer enlisted under Colonel Davis in Wagon Department and served six months.

Born 1753, died the 17th of October, 1837, and is buried in the Presbyterian Cemetery at Hollidaysburg.

LIVINGSTON, DANIEL   Enlisted in June, 1779, as a Private in Captain Gilbert McCoy's Company, Pennsylvania Militia, and stationed at Potter's Fort for seven months.

Enlisted, 1781, as a Private in Captain John Boyd's Bedford County Rangers and served for seven months. Joined this Company after Captain Boyd was taken prisoner.

Born 1757, and resided in Potter Township, Centre County in 1833.

LOWER, ADAM (LAUER)   A Veteran of the Revolutionary War (Services not available).

Born 1755, died the 16th of April, 1833; buried in Thompson Cemetery, Williamsburg; headstone inscription reads, "A soldier in Gen. Washington's Army and spent the cold and weary winter at Valley Forge." Survived by his widow Nancy, and the following children: George, Daniel, John and Henry.

MARTIN, JOSEPH   Served as a Private in Captain John Boyd's Bedford County Rangers. Records indicate that he died during this service, presumed to have been killed during the Battle of Frankstown.

McDONALD, ANGUS   Served as a Corporal in Robert Cluggage's Company, First Pennsylvania Rifle Battalion, under Colonel Thompson, during 1775. Served as a Private in the Cumberland County Militia, during 1781 and 1782, under Captains James Bell, Samuel Holliday, Robert Samuels and William Wilson.

Resided in Frankstown Township, Bedford County, 1785.

McDONALD, PATRICK   Enlisted during the Spring of 1775 as a Private in Captain Robert Cluggage's Company, First Pennsylvania Rifle Battalion, under Colonel Thompson; marched to Boston and engaged in the Battles of New York, Long Island, Trenton and Princeton.

While home on a furlough he joined the force under Captain John Boyd and with other volunteers and members of the Bedford County Rangers, they engaged the Indians at Frankstown on the 3d of June, 1781, when he was taken prisoner and carried into Canada where he remained a captive until after peace was restored, when he was released and returned to New York during the Fall of 1783.

Resided in Bedford County in 1775, and in the Township of Colerain, Hamilton County, Ohio, subsequent to the year 1818.

McDOWELL, JAMES   Enlisted the 1st of January, 1776, as a Private in Captain Robert Allison's Company, under Colonel Porter; in Battle of Trenton, and discharged in August.

Served other enlistments under Captains Alexander McCoy, George Bell and William Wilson.

"About the 4th of June 1781, he marched to Bedford, Pennsylvania for a seven months tour under the command of Captain Boyd"; Captain Boyd was captured and Lieutenant Richard Johnston succeeded to the command of the Company; discharged the 3d of January, 1782.

Born February 1755, County of Derry, Ireland, resided in Armagh Township, Cumberland County during the War; resided in Decatur Township, Mifflin County in 1833.

McGUIRE, NICHOLAS   Veteran of the Revolutionary War. (Services not available)

Born 1753; resided in Freedom Township; died the 13th of April, 1813; buried in Nelson Cemetery, near Catfish, Hollidaysburg; inscription on head stone reads: "He served his Country in the Revolutionary War and died esteemed by his neighbors"; his wife Ann Lucas, died the 26th of February, 1846.

McILVAIN, JAMES   Served as a Private in Captain Benjamin Bartholomew's Company, 5th Pennsylvania Regiment, Continental Line, in 1778; also, served as a Private in Captain Samuel Finton's Company, 1st Battalion Cumberland County Militia. The Canal and Portage Register stated he "Died, Dec. 7, 1836, in vicinity of Williamsburg at the residence of his son-in-law, aged 84."

Place of burial is unknown.

McKinney, Felix   Served as a Private in Captain John Boyd's Bedford County Rangers.

McMillan, Thomas   Served in 1776, as a Lieutenant in Captain Martin's Company, Lancaster County Militia; served as a Lieutenant for two months in 1777, as a Lieutenant in Captain Young's Company, under Colonel Boyd, "At Brandywine but took no part in Battle—helped bury the dead"; served two months as a Private in Captain William Lindsay's Company, Lancaster County Militia, guarding prisoners at York.

Born 1756, in Tyrone County, Ireland; arrived in United States in 1760; enlisted from New Holland, Lancaster County; resided in Tyrone Township, Huntingdon County, now Blair County, in 1832; died the 3d of November, 1836, and is buried in Presbyterian Cemetery, Sinking Valley.

McNamara, William   Served as a Private in Captain John Boyd's Bedford County Rangers, but did not participate in the Battle of Frankstown.

McPherran, Andrew   Enlisted March or April, 1776, as a Private in Captain Thomas Church's Company, 5th Pennsylvania Regiment, Continental Line; served for one year and re-enlisted with Captain Church for four years. In Battles of Three Rivers, Couches Bridge, Brandywine, Germantown and several skirmishes.

Born 1755, resided in Huntingdon County; died the 16th of June, 1829, and is buried in the Presbyterian Cemetery in Sinking Valley.

Means, Hugh   Served as an officer in the Continental Army; in Captain John McDonald's Company, Bedford County Militia, for eight months; volunteered for service against the Indians and was wounded in the wrist during the Battle of Frankstown, the 3d of June, 1781; commissioned as Ensign in Captain John Boyd's Bedford County Rangers, and served until the close of the War.

Married the 20th of March, 1783; resided in Catharine Township, Huntingdon County, now Blair County, in 1796; moved to New Wilmington, now Lawrence County, in 1800; died the 12th of February, 1835, survived by his widow Rosanna. Had the following children: Edward, Thomas, Henry, Daniel, Jannie and George.

Means, John   Served as a Lieutenant in Captain Thomas Cluggage's Company, Bedford County Militia, stationed at Fort Roberdeau in Sinking Valley.

Milligan, David   Enlisted in Cumberland County, June 1776, as a Private in Captain Jeremiah Tabott's Company, 6th Pennsylvania Regiment, Continental Line; taken prisoner at Battle of Three Rivers in Canada, and "taken to Quebec—put on board a vessel bound for England. On arriving in the river Thames, he was imprisoned aboard the 74 gunship Cornwall—sailed along the coast of Africa, being absent six months, then placed on board a store ship which sailed for New York. While lying off New York he went out with two others, in a boat to obtain fruit. After landing he prevailed on all the others to desert, which they did and went with him to Philadelphia."

Enlisted the 25th of May, 1781, as a Private in Captain John Boyd's Bedford County Rangers for a term of seven months, re-enlisted for 18 months, quartered at Bedford during the winter; "and the next Spring they marched to Frankstown, where they built a blockhouse, remained stationed there during the summer of 1782. In the succeeding Fall they returned again to Bedford when they again went into winter quarters and continued until the Spring of 1783. They returned to Frankstown and there remained until June."

Born 1749, in County of Down, Ireland; resided in Kishacoquillas Valley, now Mifflin County, in 1781; married Mary Beatty on the 23d of March, 1786; resided in Cadis Township, Harrison County, Ohio, 1833.

Mooney, Arthur   Veteran of the Revolutionary War. (Services not available)
The Hollidaysburg Register of the 13th of November, 1839, contains this item "Arthur Mooney, died Nov. 8, 1839, soldier of the Revolution."

MOORE, DANIEL Enlisted during 1778 for the duration of the War and served as a Corporal in Captain George Calhoun's Company, the Fourth Company of the 10th Pennsylvania Regiment, Continental Line, under Colonel Humpton.

Born in Scotland the 30th of August, 1750; came to Scotch Valley, Bedford County, now Blair County, prior to the Revolutionary War; died the 22d of September, 1827, and buried in the Presbyterian Cemetery at Hollidaysburg.

MOORE, JAMES Served during June, July and August, 1777, as a guard on the frontier as a Sergeant in Captain Patrick McIlhenny's Company, during which time he was stationed "in a house on the waters of the Juniata River situate at a place called Morrisons Cove, also stationed at Bloody Run.

"In April, 1778, he volunteered to go out as a guard on the frontier of Pennsylvania, particularly Bedford County, to guard the country against the Indians. At this time one Captain John Boyd was engaged in those parts in listing soldiers to go against the Indians and deponent volunteered to serve as a guard until said Boyd could make up the Company he wanted and get them organized and ready for marching against the Indians, —he, deponent with a number of other volunteers went out and served as such for four months under the command and direction of Captain Boyd,—a Captain Samuel Moore and Captain McDaniel were also with Boyd but Boyd had the general command. There were no higher officers in said Company than Captain.

"The company to which deponent belonged rendezvoused at the town of Bedford thence they were marched north of Bedford about forty miles to a place called Clearfield. On their march thither they were met about thirty miles from Bedford by a company of Indians before they got to the gap. A sharp conflict ensued with the Indians who greatly exceeding the whites in number, overpowered them and Captains Boyd and Moore were taken prisoner. Captain McDaniel was badly wounded and taken by the Indians a short distance from the battle ground where they killed him. Boyd and Moore were kept by the Indians two years before they got home. Eight men were killed and eight taken prisoners including the Captain. Of those who escaped several were wounded. Boyd never got the company raised that he was first trying to raise when deponent volunteered in their service. After Boyd was taken prisoner some one was appointed to the command. After the engagement the company retreated back seven miles to Frankstown Fort. Deponent and company continued to scour the country constantly until the expiration of his tour which lasted four months. He was at different times marched to Morrisons Cove, Bloody Run, Frankstown Fort and along Juniata River and Snake Spring Valley."

Born in York the 20th of February, 1760, and resided five miles from Bedford when first called into the service. Resided since in Brook County, Virginia, and Brown County, Ohio, in 1837.

MOORE, JOHN Served as a Captain of Bedford County Rangers to guard the frontier and stationed at Frankstown part of the time.

MOORE, JUDE Served as a First Lieutenant in Captain John Moore's Company of Bedford County Rangers, during 1780.

MOORE, SAMUEL Served as a Captain of Bedford County Militia, and joined Captain John Boyd's Company of Bedford County Rangers as a volunteer and engaged in the Battle of Frankstown, the 3d of June, 1781, when he was captured by the Indians.

MOYER, JACOB Enlisted April, 1777, at Reading, Berks County, as a Private in Captain Baker's Company, 4th Pennsylvania Regiment, Continental Line, and served until January 1781. Re-enlisted as a Private in Captain Hartman Sighteiser's Battery of Artillery, under Colonel Carter, and discharged April, 1782.

In Battles of Brandywine, Germantown, Blockhouse and Yorktown.

Born 1758; married Elizabeth Hold, the 1st of August, 1784, at Reading; resided Antis Township, Huntingdon County, now Blair County, and died the 1st of January 1828, leaving issue Elizabeth, Jacob and another daughter married to Anthony Swyers.

MURPHY, HENDERSON   Served as a Private in Captain John Boyd's Bedford County and was killed by the Indians the 3d of June, 1781, at the Battle of Frankstown. Widow and minor children were awarded a pension by Bedford County.

NACHBAR, NICHOLAS (NEIGHBOR)   Served as a Private on the Armed Boat General Washington. Had both eyes shot out at Battle of Brandywine; served as Chaplain Pennsylvania Navy; enlisted the 10th of April, 1777, at Hamburg and discharged the 20th of December, 1781.

Died October 1821 and buried in Logan Valley Cemetery, Bellwood.

NICHOLAS, MICHAEL   Served as a Private in Captain John Boyd's Bedford County Rangers. Records indicate that he died during his enlistment, probably killed at Battle of Frankstown.

PAXTON, JAMES   Served as a Private in Captain Boyd's Bedford County Rangers.

PHILLIPS, ELIJAH   Served as a Private in Captain William Phillip's Rangers, Bedford County Militia, and captured the 16th of July, 1780, in Woodcock Valley, Bedford County, now Huntingdon County, when the Rangers were attacked by a band of Indians. After surrendering, ten of the Rangers were massacred while Elijah Phillips and his father, Captain William Phillips, were taken prisoners. Following the close of the War they were released and returned to their home in Woodbury Township, Bedford County, now Blair County.

Born 1766, he is believed to have died prior to 1796, and to be buried in a small cemetery in field along Clover Creek road on the Elmer Treese farm.

PHILLIPS, WILLIAM   Served as a Captain of Rangers, Bedford County Militia; and was captured the 16th of July, 1780, in Woodcock Valley, Bedford County, now Huntingdon County, when the Rangers were attacked by a band of Indians.

An account of this massacre is found in a letter written the 6th of August, 1780, by Colonel John Piper to President Reed, as follows: "Your favor of the 3d of June, with the blank commissions, has been duly received. Since which we have been anxiously employed in raising our quota of Pennsylvania volunteers, and, at the same time, defending our frontiers; but, in our present shattered situation, a full company cannot be expected from this county, when a number of our militia companies are entirely broken up and the townships laid waste, so that the communication betwixt our upper and lower districts is entirely broken, and our apprehension of immediate danger are not lessened, but greatly aggravated by a most alarming stroke. Captain Phillips, an experienced, good woodsman, had engaged a company of Rangers for the space of two months for the defense of our frontiers, was surprised at his post on Sunday, the 16, day of July, when the Captain with eleven of his Company were all taken and killed. When I received the intelligence, which was the day following, I marched with only ten men directly to the place, where we found the house burned to ashes, with sundry Indian tomahawks that had been lost in the action, but found no person killed at that place. But, upon taking the Indian tracks, within about half a mile we found ten of Captain Phillips' Company with their hands tied and murdered in the most cruel manner. This bold enterprise so alarmed the inhabitants that our whole frontiers were on the point of giving way; but upon application to the Lieutenant of Cumberland County, he hath sent to our assistance one company of the Pennsylvania volunteers, which, with the volunteers raised in our own county, hath so encouraged the inhabitants that they seem determined to stand it a little longer."

The names of those who were massacred are believed to be as follows: Philip Skelly, Joseph Roberts, Hugh Skelly, Philip Sanders, Thomas Sanders, Richard Shirley, M. David, Thomas Gartrell, Daniel Kelly, and one other.

A monument now stands at the spot where the massacre took place and while grading around the site, members of the Saxton American Legion Post, on the 25th of

January, 1933, unearthed the bones of seven of the Rangers. The bones, discovered only eighteen inches under the ground, were re-buried at the spot where they were found.

Captain Phillips with his son Elijah, were taken into captivity by the Indians and not released until the close of the War when they returned to their home which was located about two miles south of Williamsburg, along Clover Creek. William Phillips disposed of his property in 1796, and moved his family to Boone County, Kentucky.

PIPER, JOHN   Appointed Colonel of Bedford County Militia by a resolution of Congress adopted the 18th of July, 1775. He was later appointed Sub-lieutenant of Militia and as such had command of the County Militia and the defense of the frontier. His house located on Yellow Creek, Hopewell Township, Bedford County, was used as a fort. He died the 31st of January, 1816.

PRICE, DORRINGTON   Served as a Sergeant in Captain John Boyd's Bedford County Rangers.

REPLOGLE, RINEHART   Served as a Private in Captain Patrick Hainey's Company, Bedford County Militia.
Buried in a cemetery on the Lee Snyder farm along Potter Creek, Morrisons Cove.

RICKETTS, EDWARD   Enlisted March 1776, in Captain John Little's Company, Bedford County Militia, and served one month; enlisted four months later as a Private in Captain Johnson's Company, later Captain Fisher's Company, Bedford County Militia, and served two months; then assisted in building a fort on his father's place, in Stone Valley; appointed a Lieutenant in Captain John Spencer's, later Captain Arthur Bell's Company, Bedford County Militia, and served until close of War.

"He was kept on the frontier as Commander of spies constantly, and only came home occasionally to get bread and salt and immediately returned,—for four or five years he continued on the back of Tussey Mountain as a guard to the inhabitants. . . . The Indians during moon light nights did much damage by killing people and taking prisoners. They did mischief generally in the morning—they picked moon light nights that they might make their retreat after doing the mischief."

Born the 10th of April, 1758, on the Antietam River below Hagerstown, Maryland; moved to Fairfield County, Ohio, 1800, where he continued to reside in 1832.

ROBERDEAU, DANIEL   At the beginning of the Revolutionary War, he was instrumental in the organization of the Associators and Militia of Pennsylvania. As a Colonel of the 2d Battalion, Associator of the City and Liberties of Philadelphia, he served as Chairman of the Convention of Delegates from the Associated Battalions, held at Lancaster, the 4th of July, 1776, where he was elected the first Brigadier General of the Associators and Militia.

In February, 1777, General Roberdeau became a member of the Continental Congress and having knowledge of the presence of lead in Sinking Valley, Bedford County, now Blair County, he was granted a leave of absence and given authority to mine and smelt this lead which was greatly needed as ammunition for the troops.

General Roberdeau came to Sinking Valley in April, 1778, where he developed several openings into the lead bearing vein and smelted possibly 40,000 pounds of lead. These operations were abandoned during the fall of 1779, as lead when ready for use proved to be rather costly; danger from attack by the Indians and the hardships to the frontier created a shortage of workers, and finally, an ample supply of lead was secured from the French through the efforts of Dr. Benjamin Franklin.

Fort Roberdeau or the Lead Mine Fort, was located near Culp, Tyrone Township, Blair County, and the stockade was constructed of logs laid in a horizontal position. It was used to house and protect the workers of the lead mines, also, as a place of refuge for the settlers from Indian depredations. Troops of the frontier rangers or the Militia were constantly on guard at this Fort.

THE REVOLUTIONARY WAR

General Roberdeau was born 1727, in the West Indies, a son of Isaac and Mary Roberdeau. He became a prominent merchant of Philadelphia, and received many distinctions, including membership in the Assembly of Pennsylvania, a member of the Council of Safety during the Revolutionary War, and a member of the Continental Congress from 1777 to 1779. He resided at Alexandria, Virginia, from 1784 until about 1794, when he moved to Winchester, Virginia, where he died the 5th of January, 1795, and where he is buried.

ROOT, LEMUEL   Enlisted at Amherst, Massachusetts, during the Fall of 1779, as a Private in Captain White's Company; served for a period of three months during which time marched to the Mohawk in New York State. Enlisted again at Amherst on the 6th of July, 1780, as a Private in Captain Hughdang's Company, Colonel Shepard's Regiment, and stationed at West Point until the 8th of January, 1781, when discharged. The Hollidaysburg *Register* of the 13th of October, 1860, reads, "died Oct. 11, 1850, in Antis Township, in Battle of Lexington, April 19, 1775, and was one of the Army confining the British to the City of Boston."

Born the 6th of July, 1760, at city of Tolland, Connecticut, moved to Amherst, Massachusetts, in 1765; resided at Springfield, Massachusetts; moved to Harford County, Maryland, 1793; moved to Frederick County, Maryland, 1802; moved to Antis Township, Huntingdon County, now Blair County, 1809; died the 11th of October, 1850, and buried in the Antis Cemetery, near Bellwood.

ROSEBROUGH, ISAAC   Enlisted October, 1776, as a Private in Captain James Moore's Company, 4th Pennsylvania Battalion, and discharged April, 1778.

Born 1760, resided 1823, in Allegheny Township, Huntingdon County, now Blair County; by occupation he was a blacksmith; died in 1832, survived by his widow Rachael.

SAMPSON, SAMUEL   Enlisted at Bedford in March, 1782, as a Private in Captain John Boyd's Bedford County Rangers; stationed at blockhouse fort at Frankstown during the summer months and at Bedford during the winter; discharged June or July, 1783.

Born 1752; a farmer and school teacher by occupation; resided in Greene County, Pennsylvania; Ohio County, Virginia; moved to Monroe County, Ohio in 1821, and to Athens County, Homer Township, Ohio, in May, 1831.

SANKEY, WILLIAM   Served as a Private in Captain John Boyd's Bedford County Rangers.

SHANNON, GEORGE   Served as a Private in Captain John Boyd's Bedford County Rangers.

SIMONS, HENRY   Served as a Private in Captain John Boyd's Bedford County Rangers.

SIMONTON, WILLIAM   Served as a Captain of Bedford County Militia, a resident of Canoe Valley.

SMITH, GEORGE   Served as a Lieutenant of Bedford County Militia, and on the 3d of June, 1781, while serving as Adjutant of the 1st Battalion of Bedford County Militia, he accompanied the Rangers with other volunteers to the Frankstown district where he was taken prisoner by the Indians, at the Battle of Frankstown and held in captivity until November, 1784.

SOMMERVILLE, JAMES   Served as a Private in Captain William McCall's Bedford County Militia.

Married Ruth Holliday, to which union the following children were born: David, Jane, Mary, William, Rhoda, Martha, Margaret, Ruana, Ruth, James and John.

Buried in Holliday Burial Ground near Hollidaysburg.

SOLDIERS OF BLAIR COUNTY

SPARKS, SOLOMON   Enlisted April, 1782, as a Private in Captain John Boyd's Bedford County Rangers and served for a period of 15 months.

Born in Frederick County, Maryland, 1758, resided at Providence Township, Bedford County in 1833.

STEVENS, GILES (STEPHENS)   Enlisted in Bedford County, the 1st of August, 1778, as a Sergeant in Captain Thomas Cluggage's Company, Bedford County Rangers, under Major Robert Cluggage, and station at Fort Roberdeau; discharged the 29th of March, 1779.

Born 1747, near Baltimore, Maryland; resided in Antis Township, Huntingdon County, now Blair County; married Nancy Tipton and was survived by the following children: Thomas, Shadrack, John William, Vincent, Jabez, Elizabeth, Sarah and Rebecca. Died in the year 1836, and buried in the Charlottesville Cemetery, near Bellwood.

STEVENS, VINCENT   Enlisted at Shirleysburg, Spring of 1779, as a Private in Bedford County Militia and served as a spy and guide: "We erected a Blockhouse at the Three Springs in Springfield Township, now Huntingdon County, families fled there and some erected houses there. . . . Indians killed some men under arms, near Ullery's Mill in Morrisons Cove and some other depredations that gave alarm so applicant had to get out a party . . . had to get out a party to take Capt. McGee into custody (he had taken his company to join the Indians against his own country supposed to be Kittanning town) but on being disappointed owing to some misunderstanding that took place in their first interview, himself and men excaped narrowly and returned, but our party did not succeed and returned without finding him."

Born 1845, in Baltimore, Maryland, moved to Plank Cabin Valley, Bedford County, in 1773, and resided in Dublin Township, Bedford County in 1833.

STONEBRAKER, ADAM   Enlisted August 1776, as a Private in Captain William Hyser's Company, in the German Regiment of Pennsylvania, under Colonel Hunsecker. Engaged in Battles of Trenton, Princeton, and shot through the leg at the Battle of Germantown.

Born 1750; resided in Franklin Township, Huntingdon County, in 1819; died the 1st of November, 1827, at Bald Eagle Furnace.

TANTLINGER, HENRY   Served as a Private in Captain John Boyd's Bedford County Rangers, and was killed at the Battle of Frankstown, the 3d of June, 1781.

THOMAS, JOHN   Served as a Private in Captain John Boyd's Bedford County Rangers. Muster rolls indicate that he died during his period of service and it is presumed that he was killed at the Battle of Frankstown, the 3d of June, 1781.

THOMPSON, JOHN   Served as a Private in Captain John Boyd's Bedford County Rangers.

TIPTON, LUKE   Enlisted August 1778, as a Private in Captain Tarenton's Company, Bedford County Militia, and served two months.

Enlisted in March or April, 1779, as a Private in Captain Thomas Cluggage's Bedford County Rangers and served at Fort Roberdeau in Sinking Valley for one year.

"In March or April, 1779, the Indians and Tories got so bad that my father and family was induced to move into the leadmines fort for safety and there Major Cluggage was recruiting soldiers in and about the fort, offering $60 bounty and $8 per month, and myself and my brother Mishac concluded we had as well enlist as to lay about the fort doing nothing for ourselves or our country and we both took the bounty ($60) for the term of service of 9 months and when the 9 months was expired Captain T. Cluggage discharged all the Company except 8 men and myself and I was one of the eight that was continued in service 3 months longer to guard the magazine, as to our quarters it was in the leadmine fort and as to our provisions we drew from Peter Ryley our commissary and R. Elliott Quartermaster and as to our pay we received $8 per month from a Mr. Thompson who was our paymaster, our daily duty was to parade at the sound of Reveille on the parade ground and then get our breakfast and then prepare for a day or two scout chasing the Indians and Tories, sometimes after them and sometimes they after us."

"As to the probable number there was from 60 to 200 soldiers at our fort at different times."

Also, served as a Private in Captain J. Igo's Company, Bedford County Militia, during the summer of 1780, "to guard the farmers at their homes in order that they could raise a crop."

Born the 14th of May, 1760, in Baltimore County, Maryland; resided in Maryland and Virginia following the War; resided in Homes County, Ohio, in 1832, and in Weakley County, Tennessee, in 1853.

TIPTON, MESHAK Served as a Private in Captain Thomas Cluggage's Bedford County Rangers, at Fort Roberdeau during 1779.

Resided in Antis Township, Huntingdon County, now Blair County, 1787.

TREESE, JOHN Enlisted the 15th of April, 1776, at Kutztown, Berks County, as a Private in Captain Henry Shade's Company, under Colonel Miles, and was discharged the 15th of January 1778. At Battle of Long Island where he lost a finger, and in Battle of White Plains.

Born 1757, died the 4th of March 1826, in Allegheny Township, Huntingdon County, now Blair County, survived by his widow Barbara.

TUCKER, WILLIAM Served as a Private in Captain John Boyd's Bedford County Rangers. Muster rolls indicate that he died during his service and it is presumed that he was killed during the Battle of Frankstown, the 3d of June, 1781.

VAN SCOYOC, TIMOTHY Served with New York troops.

Born on Long Island, New York; came to Huntingdon County, Pennsylvania, in 1793; resided Antis Township, Huntingdon County, now Blair County, in 1840.

VAN ZANT, GEORGE Enlisted in Barree Township, Huntingdon County, December, 1776, as a Private in Captain Samuel Davis' Company, under Colonel John Piper. At Princeton and Bennetts Island.

Enlisted March or April, 1777, as a Private in Captain Henry Black's Company, Bedford County Rangers, and "principally engaged in scouting parties in neighborhood of Frankstown watching Indians and endeavoring to prevent them from committing depredations on the defenseless inhabitants."

Enlisted Spring of 1779, as a Private in Captain Simonton's Company, Bedford County Militia, and served a tour of duty.

Born the 22d of September, 1752, at Philadelphia, and resided in Shirley Township, Huntingdon County, in 1833.

VAN ZANT, JAMES Enlisted July 1775, as a Private in Captain Robert Cluggage's Company, under Colonel Thompson, and marched to Boston. Enlisted Spring of 1778, as a Private in Captain Henry Black's Bedford County Rangers and was stationed at Fort Frankstown. Enlisted Spring of 1779, as a Private in Captain Henry Black's Bedford County Rangers and again stationed at Fort Frankstown.

Born 1756, in Pennsylvania, moved to Kentucky following the War; then to Indiana and resided in Lawrence County, Arkansas, in 1832.

VAN ZANT, JOHN Served as a Lieutenant, Bedford County Rangers, stationed at Dean's, Lowry's, Roller's and Anderson's Forts.

WARD, WILLIAM   Enlisted December 1777, at Kishacoquillas Valley, Pennsylvania, as a Private in Captain Samuel Thompson's Company, under Colonel Lacy, and discharged in March, 1778. Enlisted 1779, as a Private in Captain Doherty's Company, under Major Morrison, and participated in Sullivans' Campaign.

Served as a Sergeant in Captain John Boyd's Bedford County Rangers from April 1781 until the War was over. Joined Company at Bedford following the Battle of Frankstown.

Born April 1750, in Queen County, Ireland; lived at Bedford eleven years; lived at Pittsburgh, Kentucky, Montgomery County, Missouri, and resided in Warren County, Missouri, in 1833.

WHITAKER, JOHN (WHITEACRE)   Served as a Private in Captain John Boyd's Bedford County Rangers.

WILT, THOMAS   Served several tours of duty in the York County Militia under Captains Kurtz, Forrey, Copenhaven, Shields and Foreman; "engaged in several skirmishes with British and Hessians. One of the skirmishes took place near a farm of a Quaker, named Robinson, who had given information of the Company's whereabouts to the enemy who was repulsed."

Born 1757, in Berks County; resided with his father whose farm was on line between York County, Pennsylvania and Frederick County, Maryland; lived in Baltimore two years, returned to father's home, then married and resided in Frederick County, Maryland, for four years; resided at McConnell's Cove, Bedford County, for five years, resided at Greenfield Township, Bedford County, with Jacob Wilt in 1840; died about 1847, survived by his widow Barbara, to whom was born the following children: Jacob, Peter, George, John, David, Daniel, Elizabeth, Margaret, Catharine, Mary and Susanna.

WIMER, ADAM   Enlisted June, 1781, as a Private in Captain John Boyd's Bedford County Rangers and wounded during the Battle of Frankstown, the 3d of June, 1781.

Born the 20th of May, 1763, died the 2d of January, 1845, resided in Lawrence County, Pennsylvania. Had the following children: Jacob, Henry, Abigail, John, David, Nicholas, Adam, Isaac, George, Ann, Eliza and Mary.

WOODS, HENRY   Served several tours of duty during the years 1778 to 1782, inclusive, as a Private in the Bedford County Militia, under Captains Buck, Moore and Lieutenant Johnston. Volunteered to accompany Captain John Boyd's Bedford County Rangers to the Frankstown district when Indians were reported to have crossed the mountains, and engaged in the Battle of Frankstown, the 3d of June, 1781. "This battle was fought on the east side of the Allegheny Mountains, near Burgoon's Gap. The troops after the wounded were taken care of retreated to Bedford. The whole country was driven to their Forts."

Born in Bedford County, about 1757; resided in Bedford County during the Revolutionary War, and resided in Beaver County in 1832.

PART II

THE WAR OF 1812

A brief history of the Second War with Great Britain, giving the causes, important events, battles and ending.

A history of the militia system of Pennsylvania and a record of the military organizations formed in this section prior to and during the War.

Diary and letters written by Captain Robert Allison during the journey of the Huntingdon Light Infantry Company to the Canadian Border.

Sketches of the veterans of the War of 1812 who resided in this section, giving their military services, the death and burial, and genealogical records.

INDEX TO PART II

Brief History of the War of 1812 53

Bedford and Huntingdon County Militia 55

Pennsylvania Volunteer and Drafted Companies 57

    Captain Robert Allison's Company 57

    Captain Moses Canan's Company 58

    Captain Isaac Vandevander's Company 60

    Captain Solomon Sparks' Company 61

    Captain Nicholas Beckwith's Company 61

    Captain William Morris' Company 63

    Captain Edmund Tipton's Company 64

    Captain Samuel Thomas' Company 66

Diary and letters of Captain Robert Allison 67

Sketches of veterans of the War of 1812 87

BRIEF HISTORY OF THE WAR OF 1812

The second war between Great Britain and the United States lasted for over two and a half years, beginning on the 18th of June, 1812.

The principal causes of this war was the interference of Great Britain with American vessels, her efforts to secure the exclusive trade with the United States, and the impressment of seamen from American vessels into her service.

The European war which raged between Napoleon and England for many years affected American trade and commerce, in that, both countries in their efforts to prevent the American vessels from trading with the enemy, seized our ships and impressed our seamen into duty on their vessels. In May, 1806, England declared the entire coast from the Elbe River in Germany, to Brest in France, (over one thousand miles of seacoast) to be in a state of blockade. On the 21st of November, 1806, Napoleon issued the Berlin Decree, which prohibited American vessels from trading with Great Britain.

Other decrees and orders followed and the United States merchants suffered the loss of their trade. In an endeavor to preserve the neutrality of the States, the Tenth Congress passed on the 22d of December, 1807, an embargo act which prohibited American vessels from sailing for foreign ports, all foreign vessels from taking out cargoes, and all coasting vessels were required to furnish bonds to land their cargoes in the United States.

By 1809, the impressment of American seamen into service on British vessels and the violation of our flag so affected the American people that the exclamation "Free trade and sailors rights" was heard on every hand. Several times American men-of-war were fired on and compelled to give up seamen in their crews.

This policy of the foreign governments continued in spite of efforts by the American Government to reach a friendly settlement of their differences, and by 1811, England had captured nine hundred vessels while France had captured one hundred and fifty, all of which were condemned and sold, resulting in the loss of millions of dollars to the merchant and ship owners of America.

Through the influence of British emissaries, the Indians of the Northwest were organized into a confederacy against the Americans, headed by Tecumseh, a Shawnee Chief. The hostilities on the part of the Indians were brought to a temporary stop when troops under General Harrison, Governor of the Indiana Territory, defeated them on the 7th of November, 1811, in the famous battle of Tippecanoe.

Upon the declaration of war with Great Britain on the 18th of June, 1812, the President appointed General Dearborn as command-in-chief, and planned the invasion of Canada from Buffalo and Detroit. General Hull opened the war with an advance from Detroit on the 12th of July, and laid siege to Malden, Canada. He retreated in August, when his line of communication was threatened, and upon being attacked by the British and their Indian allies at Detroit on the 16th of August, he surrendered the entire army of the Northwest with all supplies and possessions to the British without a fight.

The principle battles, engagements and events of the War of 1812, were as follows:

Fort Dearborn	Illinois	Aug. 15, 1812
Queenstown Heights	Canada	Oct. 13, 1812
Fort Niagara	New York	Nov. 21, 1812
Frenchtown	Michigan	Jan. 18, 1813
Ogdensburg	New York	Feb. 22, 1813
York (Toronto)	Canada	Apr. 27, 1813

Fort Meigs	Ohio	May 5, 1813
Fort George	Canada	May 27, 1813
Stony Creek	Canada	June 6, 1813
Lake Erie	Pennsylvania	Sept. 10, 1813
Eccanachaca	Alabama	Dec. 23, 1813
La Cole Mill	Canada	Mar. 30, 1814
Fort Erie	Canada	July 3, 1814
Chippewa	Canada	July 5, 1814
Lundy's Lane	Canada	July 25, 1814
Fort Erie	Canada	Aug. 1, 1814
Washington	District of Columbia	Aug. 24, 1814
Plattsburg	New York	Sept. 6, 1814
Fort McHenry	Maryland	Sept. 13, 1814
Fort Erie	Canada	Sept. 17, 1814
New Orleans	Louisiana	Jan. 8, 1815

Efforts to restore peace were made by the United States Government during 1812 and 1813, but were rejected by Great Britain. The conflict with the armies under Napoleon having ended, veterans of this war were now available for use against the American armies and many were shipped across the ocean. In 1814, the British Government expressed a willingness to negotiate a peace treaty, so in August, the commissioners of the two countries met at Ghent, Belgium, where after a long and weary negotiation, concluded a treaty on the 24th of December, 1814, which was ratified by the United States on the 17th of February, 1815.

During the war, some 1400 American vessels and 20,000 seamen had been captured by British cruisers, while the American warships and privateers captured 2416 British vessels, including fifty-six warships. It was the navy, the arm of the service from which least was expected, that proved by a number of brilliant victories to be the salvation of the American cause, and the heroic conduct of its officers and men established a reputation on the seas that created respect for the United States and its flag.

PENNSYLVANIA MILITIA

The first organization of the citizen soldiery of the Commonwealth of Pennsylvania was initiated by Benjamin Franklin on the 21st of November, 1747, and known as the "Associators." This organization took part in many of the early battles and engagements of the Revolutionary War, and continued in existence until the passage of the fifth section of the Frame of Government of the Constitution of Pennsylvania, in convention at Philadelphia, the 28th of September, 1776.

The fifth section read as follows: "The freemen of this Commonwealth and their sons shall be trained and armed for its defense under such regulations, restrictions, and exceptions as the General Assembly shall by law direct, preserving always to the people the right of choosing their colonels and all commissioned officers under that rank, in such manner and as often as by the said laws shall be directed."

The citizen soldiers of the Commonwealth of Pennsylvania have been known during the history of our country as: Associators, Militia, Volunteers, Uniformed Militia, Organized Militia, Home Guard and National Guard.

The defense system as in effect following the Revolutionary War called for the enrollment of every able bodied male inhabitant within the ages of eighteen and forty-five, into companies, under officers elected by the members of the militia companies.

The regulations required that the enrolled militiamen provide themselves with certain equipment which included a rifle, powder-horn and shot pouch, and that they attend the mustering of their company at the annual or periodical call to be required to pay a fine. The monies secured from the collection of fines were used to pay pensions to the widows and orphans of soldiers of the Revolutionary War.

The Bedford County Militia as organized in May, 1786, for that part of the county now included in Blair County, was known as the Third Battalion and the inhabitants of each township were designated as a company.

Members of the Militia who resided in Tyrone Township were designated as the Fourth Company and were under the command of Captain James Igo, Lieut. William Porter, and Ensign Edward Gray.

The Frankstown Township militiamen were designated as the Fifth Company, and commanded by Captain John Holliday, Lieut. Lazarus Lowry, and Ensign Patrick Cassiday.

The Woodbury Township militiamen were designated as the Sixth Company, and commanded by Captain William Phillips, Lieut. Joseph Sellers, and Ensign William Shirley, Jr.

Upon the formation of Huntingdon County from Bedford County in 1787, the Fourth and Fifth Companies remained the same. The Sixth Company was divided due to the county line running through the township, and the following officers commanded the militiamen who resided in the Huntingdon part of Woodbury Township; Captain William Phillips, Lieut. James Stewart, and Ensign Jacob Server. At this time Tyrone Township had one hundred and forty-four inhabitants liable for military service, Frankstown Township had one hundred and three and Woodbury Township had sixty-nine.

Muster days at this period of the history of our county, when the frontier was being settled, were events to be looked forward to in the life of the inhabitants. The entire community assembled at the designated places and here were settled many of the affairs. Accounts were paid, horses traded, national affairs and local happenings were told, physical contests were decided, and the election of officers was held.

A reorganization of the Pennsylvania Militia went into effect in 1802, and the State was divided into fourteen districts, each district under the command of a Major general. This plan called for many high ranking officers and few effective company commanders with no troops to be depended upon, as their attendance at muster was a matter of choice of being present or having a fine levied.

In 1805 the State had thirteen Major generals enrolled, twenty-eight Brigadier generals and 94,221 troops. This organization was in reality only a paper enrollment.

When trouble threatened with Great Britain, the President issued a call on July 9, 1807, for the Militia of Pennsylvania. The response was rather slow and the trouble blew over before any active service was engaged in.

This system continued until the War of 1812, and with the exception of a few volunteer militia companies existing in the more important towns who drilled regularly and had some equipment, the country was without military protection other than the regular army.

When the second war with Great Britain was thrust upon the people of the United States the country was found to be unprepared for war, either financially or from a military point of view. With the threat of attack and invasion existing along the entire north, east and southern boundaries, the need for a large force of men was apparent.

Huntingdon, Mifflin and Centre Counties constituted the Eleventh Division under the Act of April 9, 1807.

The regulations at this time required that two days of each year be devoted to the training of the Militia. The members being trained by regiments in May and by battalions in October. All male inhabitants subject to military duty were required to be present for muster with their respective companies, or in default be subject to the payment of a fine.

The enrolled members of each company were placed in classes according to their circumstances and ability to promptly respond for a call for military services.

The various companies located in this vicinity constituted the Fifty-eighth regiment which was commanded in 1799 by Lieut.-Colonel John Holliday, and later by Lieut.-Colonel Kellup. This regiment assembled at Hollidaysburg for muster in 1803 and 1812.

A company of volunteers existed in Huntingdon County as early as the first of June, 1792, at which time the officers of a company of Light Infantry at Huntingdon included Captain John Patton, First Lieutenant James Nesbitt, and Second Lieutenant John Armitage.

A return of the officers elected on the 22d of January, 1794, to command a Troop of Horses composed of volunteers of the Brigade included Captain John Galbraith, First Lieutenant Jonathan Henderson, Second Lieutenant Samuel Galbraith, and Cornet Robert McCartney.

On the 5th of October, 1795, the officers of the Light Dragoons were: Captain Jonathan Henderson, and First Lieutenant George Wilson.

The following changes were made in the officers of the Light Infantry Company of Huntingdon on the 11th of July, 1896: Ellis Evans, Lieutenant in place of James Nesbitt, resigned, and John Whitaker, Ensign, instead of John Armitage, resigned.

THE PENNSYLVANIA VOLUNTEERS

Patriotism was not lacking among the members of the existing military organizations at the time of the declaration of war with Great Britain, and the regular army was at once increased by mustering into the service the militia volunteers. However, these volunteer companies were small, in many cases less than forty enrolled members, and upon being called into the Federal Service they were without guns and other arms and equipment so essential to the performance of effective duty during actual warfare.

The present area of Blair County was, at the time of the War of 1812, included in Bedford and Huntingdon Counties. The boundary line between the two counties ran from Elks Gap on the Tussey Mountain beyond Fredericksburg, through McKee's Gap, to the Allegheny Mountain near where the William Penn highway now crosses the mountain to Cresson. So that Greenfield, Juniata, Freedom, parts of Taylor and Huston and North Woodbury Townships as they now exist were in Bedford County, while the northern portion of the present Blair County was in Huntingdon County.

At least four volunteer companies existed in this vicinity at the time of the War of 1812. They tendered their services and were accepted during September of 1812, and served for a period of about two months. These companies were commanded by Captains Robert Allison, Moses Canan, Solomon Sparks and Isaac Vandevander.

The general officers commanding the Militia in this part of the State during the period of the War were as follows:

The appointments of the 3d of August, 1811, included Major James Banks as commander of the 11th Division, consisting of Mifflin, Huntingdon and Centre Counties. On the 4th of July, 1814, the following appointments were made for the 10th Division consisting of Huntingdon, Centre and Clearfield Counties; Major General William Steel, Brigadier Generals Lewis Evans and Arthur Moore, Inspectors of Brigade John Young and Robert Provines. The appointment for the 12th Division comprising Bedford, Somerset and Cambria Counties were: Major General Alexander Ogle, Brigadier Generals John Noble and Robert Philson, Brigade Inspectors Andrew Mann and James Hanna.

CAPTAIN ALLISON'S COMPANY

Captain Robert Allison's Company was organized at Huntingdon and was known as the "Huntingdon Light Infantry." This organization had on the 4th of May, 1812, voted unanimously to tender their services to the President of the United States, in the then impending war with Great Britain, more than a month in advance of the formal declaration of war.

The original plans of operation for the conduct of the war by the northern forces were to attack Canada from two points. Buffalo on the eastern, and Detroit on the western. The attack from Detroit proved disastrous and resulted in the loss of Detroit and the surrender of the western army to the British and their Indian allies. On the Niagara frontier the operations were equally unsuccessful.

The regular forces being unable to cope with the situation and reenforcements being required, it was found necessary to accept the proffered aid of volunteer companies and accordingly, the services of the Huntingdon Light Infantry were accepted and the company left Huntingdon on the 7th of September, 1812, on their march to Niagara.

The only mode of travel existing in the year 1812, between Huntingdon County, Pennsylvania, and Niagara, in the northwestern part of the State of New York, was by horse, wagon or by walking. It is presumed that the officers had mounts available and that a few wagons accompanied the units in order to transport food and supplies, but as to the troops, their method of travel was to march this distance over rough roads through virgin forests, climbing mountains and fording streams as they found them. Captain Allison and his men marched by way of Petersburg and Spruce Creek valley to Bellefonte, and arrived at Buffalo on the 2d of October, the twenty-sixth day after leaving Huntingdon.

No muster roll of this company is obtainable from the authorities at Harrisburg or at Washington. The following list of members has been compiled from the diary and letters of Captain Robert Allison and is believed to be a correct roster as Captain Allison's report to General Hall of the 8th of October, gives the strength of the company as forty-six. The roster published herewith contains forty-seven names. The additional member is believed to have been James Simpson who probably accompanied the company in an unofficial capacity as we find that the captain refers to "Jim" occasionally and in one letter (November 26th) he states that "he has applied for permission to go over."

The complete roster of Captain Robert Allison's Company as published herewith for the first time is as follows:

Captain—Robert Allison
First Lieutenant—Jacob Miller
Ensign—Samuel Swoope
First Sergeant—Henry Miller

Other Members of the Company

Armitage, George	Fee, John	Shultz, Peter
Brown, Robert	Glazier, Charles	Simpson, James
Brown, William	Glazier, John	Snyder, David
Chilcott, Ethan	How, Samuel	Swigarts, Samuel
Cunningham, John	King, Thomas	Thompson, George
Davis, George	Lemon, Samuel	Trappier, Charles
Davis, James	Maize, Wray	Trappier, Joseph
Dean, William	McConnell, John	Vandevander, Abraham
Donalson, William	McFadden, John	Vandevander, Jacob
Dorland, Jacob	Miller, James	Waggoner, John
Eichelberger, Samuel	Nash, John	Westbrook, John
Elliott, Benjamin	Osborn, James	Westbrook, Levi
Engle, Peter	Parks, John	Yocum, Jacob
Fee, George	Ramsey, James	Zimmerman, Jacob
	Saxton, John	

CAPTAIN CANAN'S COMPANY

Captain Moses Canan's Company of Alexandria, known as "The Juniata Volunteers," tendered their services on the 9th of June, 1812, to the Governor of the Commonwealth of Pennsylvania, and were accepted for duty under General Orders of the 25th of August, as issued by Governor Simon Snyder, which read as follows:

"The President of the United States having, through the Secretary of War and General Dearborn, under date respectively of the 13th inst., required a detachment of two thousand Militia, to be marched with the least possible delay from the north-western parts of Pennsylvania to Buffalo, in the State of New York; duty and feeling direct a prompt compliance with a requisition giving scope for action to the patriotism evinced by that portion of our citizen soldiers who have volunteered their services under General Orders on the 12th of May last, in substitution of the draft required of the State.

"To obey this call in defense of rights sacred to freeman—to avenge the injuries of the nation and defend the cause of suffering humanity—the Volunteers of Pennsylvania will not hesitate a moment to meet the avowed enemy of those rights, not only within the bounds of the United States; but will without those limits, with ardor seek, and with determination characteristic of freemen, punish the unprovoked invaders of our rights and property.

"For obvious reasons the Adjutant General has orders to designate for the services of the Volunteers as can, with the least possible delay, be marched to the scene of action; and is charged with the organization of the detachment of two thousand men, conformably to the following plan:—The detachment to constitute a Brigade to consist of four Regiments, and each Regiment to consist of two Battalions, to be arranged by the Adjutant General at the place of rendezvous.

"The general rendezvous will be at Meadville, to which place the Volunteers composing the detachment will march with the requisite expedition, so that they will be there on the 25th of September next......

"Apprised of the generally prevailing desire that those appointed to command may be the choice of the command, the Governor....authorized and directs the officers and privates of the detachment on the day succeeding the 25th of September next, or those who shall have arrived, to elect....one Brigadier General; each Regiment to elect a Colonel Commandant; each Battalion one Major. The Brigadier General to appoint his own Brigade Major; the Field Officers of each Regiment shall appoint their respective regimental staffs."

Captain Moses Canan's Company marched from Alexandria on Friday, the 11th of September, 1812, and upon joining the army at Meadville, his company was mustered into the service of the United States on the 25th of September, 1812, as part of the 1st Pennsylvania Regiment under Colonel Jeremiah Snyder, under command of Brigadier General Adamson Tannehill. This company numbered forty-one officers and men, and continued in the service until the 24th of November, the same year, when the company was discharged and its members returned to their homes.

The company's services were tendered to the State by a letter addressed to the Hon. Nathaniel B. Boileau, Secretary of the Commonwealth, from Captain Canan, dated the 9th of June, 1812, and contained a recommendation from Brigade Inspector William Moore. The letter read as follows; "The Juniata Volunteers, a light infantry company, attached to the One Hundred and Nineteenth Regiment, Pennsylvania Militia, having honored me with their command, I beg leave to inform you that they have, by an agreement filed with the Inspector of this Brigade, tendered their services as part of the quota required by general orders. This company, being but lately formed, are not yet supplied with arms. In order to make their service efficient, I must beg the favor of you to procure from his excellency, the Governor, and forward as early as practicable, forty muskets, bayonets and cartouch boxes, for the safe-keeping of which I will give sufficient security, in such manner as you may direct. Your attention to the above application shall be gratefully remembered by yours, respectfully, M. Canan."

The following names are found on the Muster Roll of Captain Moses Canan's Company and is complete with the exception of the name of one private which cannot be deciphered:

Captain—Moses Canan
Lieutenant—John George Mytinger
Ensign—William Stewart

SOLDIERS OF BLAIR COUNTY

Sergeants	Corporals
John Canan	James Cherry
John Walker	Samuel Fisher
John Ramage	James McGuire
Samuel Ramsey	Jeremiah Cunningham

Privates

Adams, William	Coulter, Samuel	Newman, John
Ake, Jacob	Davis, George	Roberts, Eben
Beans, Alexander	Eckelberger, Jonathan	Scott, James T.
Burley, Cornelius	Harpster, Jacob	Shell, John
Burley, John	Knode, Henry	Simonton, James C.
Caldwell, David	Lenney, John	Simonton, John
Caldwell, Robert	Martin, Samuel	Simonton, Thomas
Canan, Henry	Martin, William	Slonaker, Adam
Carothers, Alexander	Moore, Arthur	White, John
Carothers, Hugh	Mutzebaugh, Joseph	

CAPTAIN VANDEVANDER'S COMPANY

A company of Riflemen from McConnellstown, Huntingdon County, under Captain Isaac Vandevander was accepted by General Orders, dated the 5th of September, 1812, which read as follows: "Names of commanding officers of companies who have patriotically tendered their services, not included in General Orders of the 25th of August, 1812."

This company included one Captain, one Lieutenant, one Ensign and twenty-nine riflemen, and as McConnellstown is directly across the Tussey Moutain from Williamsburg, Blair County, it is believed that several of these volunteers were from what is now Blair County.

Captain Vandevander's Company marched from Alexandria on the 11th of September, 1812, and rendezvoused at Meadville where the Regiment was formed. They then marched to Buffalo and were discharged during the latter part of November.

This Company was attached to the 2d Regiment of Riflemen, commanded by Lieutenant Colonel William Piper, and was mustered into the service of the United States under Brigadier General Adamson Tannehill on the 25th of September, and served until the 25th of November, 1812.

According to information found on the Pay Roll, the monthly pay of a soldier of the War of 1812, was a follows; Captain received forty dollars, Lieutenant thirty dollars, Ensign twenty dollars, Sergeant eight dollars, Corporal seven dollars and thirty-three cents, and a private received six dollars and sixty-six cents.

The following names of members of Captain Vandevander's Company were secured from a copy of a Pay Roll and a Muster Roll:

Captain—Isaac Vandevander
Lieutenant—John Householder, Sr.
Ensign—Jacob Heffner

Sergeants	Corporals	Fifer
William States	Jacob Ridenour	John Lloyd
David Enyeart	Samuel Philabar	
John Baker	John Harnish	*Drummer*
Peter Hughs	Solomon Fink	Richard Hix

THE WAR OF 1812

Privates

Carriher, John	Howry, John	Shaver, John
Dean, Thomas	Householder, John, Jr.	Shaver, Joseph
Graffius, John	Johnston, James	Vaughn, Richard
Helsell, Henry	Norris, William	Wagner, John
Helsell, John	Reed, Charles	Warren, Robert
Herker, Jacob	Ross, Henry	Warren, Samuel
Herker, John		

CAPTAIN SPARKS' COMPANY

Captain Solomon Sparks' Company of Riflemen was recruited at Bedford and marched through the wilderness to Meadville, Pennsylvania, where it was mustered into the service of the United States on the 25th of September, 1812, and became part of the 2d Regiment of Pennsylvania Riflemen, under command of Lieutenant Colonel Piper of Bedford County. The Regiment proceeded to Buffalo where it faced the enemy and was discharged on the 24th of November, 1812.

The following names are found on a Pay Roll of this Company:

Captain—Solomon Sparks
Lieutenant—James Piper
Ensign—David Fletcher

Sergeants	*Corporals*	*Fifer*
Joseph Armstrong	John Mortimore	Solomon Whetstone
John Paxton	James Sparks	
James Wilson	Valentine Steckman	*Drummer*
Philip Steckman	William Wilson	Samuel Lysinger

Privates

Archer, Henry	Hamilton, Robert	Runard, David
Barndollar, Peter	Hinish, John	Runard, Jacob
Carn, Philip	Holler, Solomon	Smith, Henry
Casner, Daniel	Means, Edward	Smith, Samuel
Casner, Jacob	Means, Joseph	Sparks, Abraham
Clinger, Henry	McCarty, William	Sparks, Joseph, Sr.
Cook, William	McCasling, Samuel	Sparks, Joseph, Jr.
Deal, John	Morris, Elijah	Steckman, John
Donaldson, Reason	Morris, Joseph	Stover, Henry
England, James	Phillips, Jacob	Swartz, David
Gardner, James	Pickering, Joshua	Wassing, Henry
Griffith, Abel	Piper, David	Young, Frederick
Griffith, Evan	Richey, Henry	

CAPTAIN BECKWITH'S COMPANY

A volunteer company of Riflemen under the command of Captain Nicholas Beckwith was organized at Bedford, Pennsylvania, and tendered their services to the State on the 11th of September, 1812, which was accepted by the Governor in a letter dated at Harrisburg, the 11th of September, addressed to General John Noble, and read as follows:

"Sir: I have much gratification, on the receipt of your favor of the 7th inst., just handed to me by Mr. David Metzler, and take much pleasure by saying that promptitude with which you have executed general orders of the 5th inst., does you much honor. I accept with great satisfaction the tender of service of the volunteer rifle company which, in the hour of peril and danger, have patriotically stepped forward to serve their country in substitution of the remainder of the draft required of the Fifty-fifth regiment, part of the detachment ordered to rendezvous at Pittsburgh, on the 2d of October next. In compliance with the Company's conditions; first, commissions are forwarded; on the second, can only say the State owns not a single tent. These camp kettles and other camp equipments will be furnished at Pittsburgh, by the United States Deputy Superintendent of Military Stores, or may be furnished at Carlisle, as has been done in case of volunteers marched from Franklin county, if Mr. Metzler will make the application founded on my requisition to the deputy there. The third condition, must be referred to those patriotic feelings inherent in the bosom of every true American. Very respectfully, sir, your obedient servant, Simon Snyder".

Captain Beckwith's Company was mustered into the service of the United States on the 2d of October, 1812, and mustered out on the 2d of April, 1813, during which period it was part of the 5th Battalion, Pennsylvania Militia, commanded by Major D. Nelson, of the United States, under the command of Brigadier General Richard Crooke, and in the army commanded by General W. H. Harrison.

The following names of members of this company are found on a Pay Roll:

Captain—Nicholas Beckwith
Lieutenant—David Metzler
Ensign—Thomas Alexander

Sergeants	*Corporals*	*Musician*
V. Michael Mulwits	Alexander Wilson	M. Henry Suck
Robert Gibson	Daniel Metzler	
T. John Smith	Thomas Brown	
David Dryden	Adam Bowers	

Privates

Airley, Samuel	Glass, John	Noble, Robert
Bender, Henry	Humbert, John	Rinedollar, Christopher
Bender, John	Isor, Henry	Rinedollar, George
Brown, David	Isor, John	Sirley, Samuel
Duffield, William	Irwin, Jerret	Smith, Joseph
Fortney, Daniel	Lynn, John	Snider, Michael
Forsythe, David	Martin, Samuel	Stephens, William
Full, John	McClain, Robert	Whitstone, David
Gaff, William	McCorcle, Joseph	Wilson, Hance

THE WAR DURING 1813

The campaign of 1812 having proven disastrous, new plans for carrying on the war with Great Britain were adopted for the year 1813, and which required that greater efforts be made to drive the British from the soil of the United States, and in retaliation for the invasion of the border states that the army of the United States proceed to invade Canada at several points.

Finding it impossible to secure sufficient volunteers, it was decided to inaugurate a draft. Therefore, Governor Snyder, by General Orders dated the 12th of May, 1813, directed that fourteen hundred men be drafted from Pennsylvania in the manner pre-

THE WAR OF 1812

scribed by law, and that they be formed into two Divisions, four Brigades, and twenty-two Regiments. The quota of the Eleventh Division, comprising Huntingdon, Mifflin and Centre Counties, consisted of two Brigades, one of 255 men and the other of 431 men.

The work of putting the draft into effect progressed and two companies were so raised in Huntingdon County. Captain William Morris commanded the company raised in the eastern part of the county and Captain Edmund Tipton commanded the draftees from the western part of the county, which included all men so enrolled from the area now included in Blair County that was formerly Huntingdon County.

CAPTAIN MORRIS' COMPANY

Captain William Morris' Company of Infantry consisting of drafted militiamen marched to the Canadian border during June of 1813, and were discharged in November, of the same year.

The names of the members of this Company were as follows:

Captain—William Morris
1st Lieutenant—Daniel Weaver
2d Lieutenant—William Isgrig
3d Lieutenant—Cornelius Crum
Ensign—John McIlroy
Ensign—William Love

Sergeants	*Corporals*	*Drummer*
Alexander Cresswell	Samuel Hollinshead	William Hannen
Henry Newingham	John McNamara	
John Stratton	John B. Riddle	*Fifer*
Joseph Mutzebaugh	John Mack	George Wilson
William Wilson	Benjamin Scott	
John Brotherland	John Galbraith	
Joseph Eckley	Jacob Bowersock	
	John Camberling	
	Robert Logan	
	James Stewart	

Privates

Baugher, Henry	Forsley, Thomas	McGiffin, Samuel
Bingham, Hugh	Fridgill, William	McKeehen, David
Bingham, John	Galbraith, William	McKeehen, Samuel
Black, Robert	Gettes, Robert	Moorehead, Samuel
Bollinger, Jacob	Glen, James	Nelson, William
Booth, Thomas	Gooshorn, Samuel	Ralston, Thomas
Burns, Isaac	Grady, George	Rickets, Hezekiah
Camberling, Henry	Griffin, John	Rudy, Daniel
Campbell, Hugh	Gutrie, William	Scott, John
Clabaugh, Henry	Hewett, Henry	Shade, George
Clark, Samuel	Hockenberry, Adam	Shaw, James
Clemens, Robert	Hollis, William	Shorthill, Thomas
Cornelius, Jacob	Hyte, James	Shoup, George
Cutshall, Jacob	Irwin, Samuel	Smice, John
David, William	Johnson, Anthony	Stewart, John
Dean, George	Johnson, Hugh	Stewart, William
Dearmet, William	Johnston, Thomas	Strong, Daniel

SOLDIERS OF BLAIR COUNTY

Dougherty, Edward
Dunn, John
Duncan, Daniel
Ellsworth, Samuel
Ewing, David
Fagin, Asoph
Fitzsimmons, Henry
Fleming, John
Flenner, Jonathan

Kelly, William
Kent, Nicholas
King, Patrick
Larrimore, Thomas
Lennox, John
Lightner, Matthias
Long, Henry
Long, John
McCammon, John

Swartz, Michael
Taylor, William Wilson
Thompson, Matthew
Thompson, Rees
Walls, Jacob
Weston, Joseph
Wharton, Samuel
Williamson, Hugh

CAPTAIN TIPTON'S COMPANY

Captain Edmund Tipton's Company of Pennsylvania Infantry was organized during May, 1813, and marched to Erie where it became part of the Fourteenth Regiment, commanded by Colonel C. Rees Hill, of the Second Brigade, Eleventh Division.

It appears from the rolls of this company that a shortage of arms and weapons existed, as it is recorded that eight members of the company carried "private" rifles, while only ten were charged with public rifles and eleven had public muskets.

Captain Tipton's Company, upon arriving at Erie, was engaged for sometime in guarding the property and operations in connection with the building of vessels for Commodore Perry's fleet, during which time they were cannonaded by the British fleet on Lake Erie. At least part of the company was with the expedition to Sandusky, where it engaged and captured part of the British forces at Fort Stevens. The company reassembled at Erie and guarded the prisoners and shipping on Barr's Island, that had been captured by Commodore Perry in his famous victory on Lake Erie, the 10th of October, 1813.

Among the crew selected to man the vessels and guns during the battle of Lake Erie were a number of men from the central part of Pennsylvania. It is noted on the rolls of Captain Tipton's Company that at least four members of this company enrolled for service with the fleet. James Wilson, and Samuel Smithy joined the Marine Service, while Daniel Mutzebaugh and Samuel Patton joined for duty on board the fleet.

Captain Tipton's Company was discharged at Erie on the 26th of October, 1813, and returned home a few days later.

The names of the members of this company as gathered from various sources are as follows:

Captain—Edmund Tipton
First Lieutenant—John McCabe
Second Lieutenant—Isaac Vantrees
Third Lieutenant—John Cox
Fourth Lieutenant—Christian Denlinger
Ensign—Patrick Madden

Sergeants	Corporals	Drummer
John Calderwood	Abraham Law	Elisha Ross
Peter Hewit	James Mathers	
Jesse Moore	James Parks	
Benjamin McCune	Thomas Rees	
Jacob Shafer	Zadock Westover	

Privates

Aurandt, John
Bailey, George
Bailey, William
Bauher, Henry
Boyd, Alexander
Brotherton, John
Brown, Joseph
Buell, Joseph
Brumbarger, Joseph
Burgart, Samuel
Burns, Daniel
Cramer, Daniel
Dailey, Henry
Dellinger, George
Dixon, Samuel
Doyle, Dennis
Dunn, Alexander
Elliott, John
Ellis, William
Emy, John
Fox, Jacob
Fulton, Henry
Gallagher, James
Ganoe, James
Ganoe, Samuel
Gardner, William
Gaut, William
Gearhart, John
Gibson, Gideon
Gibson, Jesse
Guthrie, William
Harpst, John
Harrigher, John
Hewit, Joseph
Hollingshead, Samuel
Hollis, William
Hopkins, James
Hunter, John
Hunter, Samuel
Hyle, John
Jamison, John
Johnson, Anthony
Johnston, David
Jones, James
Keighley, Jacob
Kelly, Davis
Kemberling, Ludgick
Kephart, Henry
Kerr, Joseph

Lanzer, Abraham
Laughlin, Hugh
Lenox, John
Locketts, Zacharia
Long, Henry
Lukehart, Conrad
Lukehart, George
Maurer, Jacob
Miller, Henry
Miller, John M.
Mooney, George
Moore, Abraham
Moore, Ephraim
Mong, Henry
Mutzebaugh, Daniel
McClelland, James
McClelland, Joseph
McClelland, Nathaniel
McLin, John W.
McMillen, John
McNamara, John
McWilliams, William
McWilliams, James
Newell, Joseph
Parker, Ira
Patton, Samuel
Raub, Henry
Rees, Thomas, Jr.
Sackett, Ezria
Shank, John
Sharp, Thomas
Shoener, Solomon
Shoop, George
Smith, John
Smithy, Samuel
Smithy, Stofel
Smock, Abraham
Stewart, Isaac
Thompson, William
Tippery, Abraham
Vanpool, Henry
Walls, Jonathon
Welsh, William
Wilhelm, Jacob
Willerman, Jacob
Williamson, James
Wilson, Abraham
Wilson, James

CAPTAIN THOMAS' COMPANY

A number of residents of Bedford County served in a Company of Artillery of the Pennsylvania Militia, under Captain Samuel Thomas, under command of Colonel Rees Hill.

This company was mustered into the service on the 5th of May, 1813, and was discharged at Erie on the 5th of November, 1813.

The names of the Bedford County soldiers who served in this company are as follows:

Captain—Samuel Thomas
Third Lieutenant—Andrew Sheets
Sergeant—George W. Smith

Privates

Beavers, Andrew
Becker, Henry
Booth, Robert
Bridenhall, Henry
Brown, John
Casteer, Thomas
Chamberlain, John
Craig, Benjamin
Crosson, Thomas
Donalston, Levi
Easter, George
Fenstermaker, Jacob
Fight, John
Fleegle, Jacob
Frederical, William, Jr.
Frederical, William, Sr.
French, Arthur
Giles, Martin
Graham, John
Hamler, Nicholas
Jones, Henry
Kizer, John
McAtee, Samuel
Moyer, John
Pittman, William
Rice, George
Richey, John
Shreaves, Edward
Sliger, George
Stechman, John
Stillwell, James
Wallick, Philip
Weyer, Jacob
Whimset, John Z.
Woolford, Jacob

DIARY AND LETTERS

Written by

CAPTAIN ROBERT ALLISON

of the

HUNTINGDON LIGHT INFANTRY, DURING HIS MARCH TO THE CANADIAN BORDER IN THE WAR OF 1812

NOTE

The following is a graphic account of the happenings and events which occurred during the march of the members of the Huntingdon Light Infantry to the Canadian Border in the War of 1812.

This account is compiled in chronological order from a diary kept during the march and from the letters written by Captain Robert Allison to his wife, Polly, (Mary Elliott). The letters are in an excellent state of preservation, while the diary is somewhat used and parts of several pages are missing.

It was necessary in order to present a comprehensive account of the experiences of the members of this company, to supply missing words and to insert additional data. Other liberties were taken in the spelling, punctuation, and construction of sentences.

This account of the march of a military unit from central Pennsylvania to the Canadian border is a remarkable historical record of that day, and is presented as not being an exception to that experienced by the companies recruited in this section of the state, but rather is typical of the trials and privations endured by the soldiers of the war of 1812, who enlisted from this part of Pennsylvania and served on the Canadian Border.

SATURDAY, AUGUST 22, 1812

Huntingdon, Pennsylvania. Received from Captain Joseph Wheaton, Assistant Deputy Quartermaster, commissions from the President for myself and two subaltern officers bearing date of the 14th of the present month and orders from the Secretary of War at Washington, to march my Company to headquarters at Niagara,—also received bill of exchange on W. Eutis to be negotiated at Chambersburg Bank in the sum of $632.40, for which purpose I set out for that place and received the money—having spent five entire days in transacting the business. Captain Wheaton stated to me that I was considered as holding a......command and would be entitled to double rations.

MONDAY, AUGUST 31

The Company members and officers are to appear before Dr.......who is to examine the men and report whether any of them have bodily infirmity and unable to perform the duties required of them.

TUESDAY, SEPTEMBER 1

The Doctor reported Henry Swoope as unfit—he is therefore discharged.

67

WEDNESDAY, SEPTEMBER 2

Advanced for flour, bags, whiskey and fish $31.50; paid to J. McCahan for hams and bacon $20.75; M. Grafeus for camp kettle $7.00; J. McCahan for bacon $4.62; and A. M. Connell for sugar and chocolate $13.00.

SUNDAY, SEPTEMBER 6

Reported to the Brigade Inspector and received for use of the Company twelve pounds powder,......dozen of ball and twelve dozen......, the property of the State.
Copy of a letter sent to T. H. Cushing, Exq., Adjutant General.
Sir: Agreeable to the instructions from the Secretary of War. I have the honor to inform you that tomorrow at 2 o'clock my Company will march from this place for the headquarters at Niagara. Enclosed I send you a muster roll or what is intended to take the place of one, having never been in service or ever seen a roll, must be an apology for lack of form and military style. There is some variations between the enclosed roll and that furnished to Captain Wheaton owing to some men having joined the Company and others being totally unable from bodily infirmities to march. Other changes will no doubt yet take place.

Twenty-four days is the time for which the allotment of expenses was made by.... and myself for marching to Niagara, allowing for bad weather, and computing the distance at 250 miles by the road I must go, but on further inquiry the distance is greater and my men are all young and inexperienced in the toils of war. I must therefore use great caution and make short marches at the out-set. Every exertion in my power consistent with the abilities of the men shall be made to be at headquarters within the estimated time. I found it would be altogether impractical to transport my Company without the aid of a baggage wagon. I have employed one at the expense of the Company in hopes with economy to be able to save some out of the estimate. Is it improper for me to ask you to intercede and write to the person who employs wagons at headquarters concerning our situation, in order that it might be got into public service on our arrival there. I have the honor to be.

MONDAY, SEPTEMBER 7

At 2 o'clock P. M. we left Huntingdon and arrived at Petersburg, six miles, at 5 o'clock. Spent a night without much sleep owing in part to anxiety of mind and more to the noise of the soldiers and intemperance and noisy conduct of private citizens. We were handsomely and hospitably entertained by Mr. M......who refused taking any compensation.

TUESDAY, SEPTEMBER 8

We left Petersburg at half past five o'clock and arrived at Mr. Marshall's (on Spruce Creek) at half past 9 o'clock, distance nine miles. We were refreshed and well entertained for which Mr. Marshall refused to receive any compensation. At half past 12 o'clock we resumed our march and arrived at Grays (Graysville) at 4 o'clock, distance seven miles, in all sixteen miles, and paid his bill and expense amounting to $9.00.

WEDNESDAY, SEPTEMBER 9

We marched from John Gray's at half past five o'clock and arrived at Frederick Dale's at 9 o'clock, distance six miles. There we breakfasted and a number of neighboring citizens refused to let the soldiers pay any bill and advanced the amount to the landlord,-- a well disposed liberal man. We then moved to James Johnston's at Centreville where we arrived at half past three o'clock, distance eight miles, making the entire day's march fourteen miles. The men were considerably fatigued, several of them unable to walk. We were badly entertained, four soldiers obliged to go to bed supperless and the landlord anxious to receive tavern fees for each man's victuals. With difficulty he accepted ......per man for the midlings and he charged one dollar for a bottle of cherry bounce. The officers and men generally dissatisfied. Expenses $9.17.

THURSDAY, SEPTEMBER 10

We marched from Johnston's to Bellefonte where we found an elegant breakfast prepared at the house of Evan Miles and given at the expense of the citizens. We remained there until 5 o'clock P. M. to get washing done for Company.

Thursday afternoon—My dear Polly: We have got this far on our journey without any particular trouble or misfortune. Some of the men have complained of fatigue but none of them have any serious reason for it. I appear to be the hardiest fellow among them all and have no doubt but the march will be of great service and make me stronger than I have ever been. The people generally on the road have been very kind and attentive to us. Our men are getting some washing done today and this evening we contemplate marching about three miles further. John will give you all the particulars of our march and I will write again by next mail. I pray you to be contented and if possible make yourself happy. It will add much to my satisfaction to know that you do not fret on account of my absence. It would surprise you to see what fine spirits I appear to be in. Give my kind love to the children and tell Catherine I kissed her when she was sleeping before I left home. That God may bless you and them, shall be my constant prayer till I return. Write to me and direct your letter "Lindley Town, State of New York" put it into the post office on Friday next. Your truly affectionate husband.

We marched down the Nittany valley to George N....s and remained there during the night, an obliging man. Paid expenses for the Company amounting to $4.00. The whole day's march was eleven miles.

FRIDAY, SEPTEMBER 11

We marched to Isaac McKinney's who had prepared an excellent breakfast and the whole Company partook of it with great cheerfulness, and each Sergeant and Corporal had his canteen filled with whiskey for his men all gratuitously bestowed. We then moved on to Alexander Robinson's. Making the march of the day fourteen miles, taking into view that we went half a mile out of the road to Mr. McKinney's. Paid expenses at Alexander Robinson's $9.20.

SATURDAY, SEPTEMBER 12

We marched from Alexander Robinson's to Sebastian Shade's for breakfast, distance five miles, and were well entertained by a liberal man. Paid expenses $7.20. We then proceeded to the ferry on the Susquehanna opposite Dunnsburg, paid ferriage of the soldiers at three cents per man, $1.44. We then arrived at John White's in Dunnsburg, distance six miles. We were well entertained. Paid expenses $8.20.

SUNDAY, SEPTEMBER 13

We marched this morning from Dunnsburg to Stephen Duncan's, distance nine miles. Had breakfast and were liberally entertained without expense. Moved on to Jersey Shore, distance three miles. Here the citizens had provided a handsome entertainment for us at their expense.

MONDAY, SEPTEMBER 14

We left Jersey Shore and marched to Bennett's, distance six miles, for breakfast. A number of citizens paid the soldiers' bill. We then moved on to Williamsport, distance ten miles.

TUESDAY, SEPTEMBER 15

We remained at Williamsport to get washing and baking done. A detachment of Regular Troops under command of Colonel Parker arrived, which determined me to remain one day longer in order they might go ahead. Paid expenses of cleaning fish, an axe, and baking bread.

WEDNESDAY, SEPTEMBER 16

Paid Henry Pickle expenses of the soldiers.

THURSDAY, SEPTEMBER 17

Marched to John Hays for breakfast, distance six miles. Paid expenses $7.20. Moved to Reynolds, distance eight miles, making this day's march fourteen miles. Commenced a slight rain at 12 o'clock and appearance of bad weather. Mr. Reynolds was a very liberal man, charging us 12 cents a man. Total expense paid $6.62½.

My Dear Polly: My company remained at Williamsport until this morning in order to give Colonel Parker's detachment an opportunity of being one day before us on the march. They march as soldiers and always pitch their tents. We march yet as gentlemen soldiers and are gladly received by the inhabitants. We had a quantity of herring cleaned and dried, and bread baked at Williamsport, in order to carry us through the wilderness which we are to attack tomorrow morning, but from all the information I can collect we will be able to quarter in a house and barn each night by making long marches. We have fared remarkably well and are in good quarters for this night. We marched fourteen miles and arrived here at 2 o'clock. Something is being prepared to eat and I could not delay the pleasure of writing to you this letter, which must be left to be taken up by the post boy and deposited in the next office. I am perfectly in health and walking agrees with me. All the men are in good health and spirits as usual.

Mr. Rose died yesterday morning at his residence near Williamsport. I have made and will make arrangements with the different post-masters to forward any letters directed to me, provided I should have passed the offices to which I directed them to be forwarded. Tell my friend McCahan that I am as yet too much engaged to write to him, but will when I arrive at headquarters. The next letter you write direct it to me at "Williamsburg, York". I do not know whether any of the soldiers intends writing or not—but you may inform their friends and families that they are well and able to eat hearty and laugh merrily.

I have promised to write to a great many people when I get to Niagara but fear I will neglect my promises. You, my Dear, cannot be forgotten. We have 218 miles march before us on starting this morning. God bless and protect you and our dear children and all my good Huntingdon friends, is my constant prayer. It is not necessary to say that I shall expect a letter from you every week.

FRIDAY, SEPTEMBER 18

We left Reynolds and marched up Trout Run at the head of which, about six miles, we breakfasted on cold bacon, herring, etc., previously prepared. We then moved on to Hew's one of the worst roads ever traveled either by man or beast. The total distance said to be fourteen and one-half miles, to the place called the Blockhouse. Paid expenses for Company $9.60.

SATURDAY, SEPTEMBER 19

Left Hew's and after marching about five miles, had breakfast at a small Inn, on the same fare as Friday, then proceeded to Bloss', previously called Peter's Camp, through almost an entire wilderness, especially bad roads of stones and swamps. Arrived at

Bloss' at half-past two o'clock. The men were much fatigued and the horses of the baggage wagon much wearied.

This day at the breakfasting place George Thompson strayed into the woods and became lost. Soldiers were dispatched in pursuit of him and returned without him, he having found the road in pursuing the Company. Crossed the Tioga River at Bloss'. Paid Aaron Bloss Expenses $9.60.

I commence, my dear Polly, this letter today in order to give you an account of our march and shall continue to add to it until it can be forwarded by mail. On yesterday morning our prospects were gloomy, every appearance of rain and a wilderness to pass through, but the day became fine. We left Reynolds, the place from where I last wrote, in Lycoming County in which we still are, and moved on through an uninhabited country for six miles which distance we waded a small stream of water three times, then sat down on logs and partook of a most sumptuous breakfast composed of bread, cold herring and cold bacon prepared the night before. Last night we lodged rather uncomfortably at a small house after making the entire day's march of fifteen miles over the highest hills, part of the Allegheny Mountains, and the worst roads I ever saw. This morning we marched about five miles and at a small inn, ate our breakfast in the same style as yesterday, there being no house from where we set out until this place. This is the part of the road called the wilderness and a dreary one it is. We have not heard the chirping of a bird for two days, our day's march has been twelve miles, and we appear all fatigued. There is but one apartment and the soldiers are sleeping on their chairs around me while I write. At our breakfasting place George Thompson, without my knowledge took his gun and went into the woods in search of game. When the roll was called he did not answer and I became alarmed least he should not again find us. I had the drum beat and guns fired, all without effect and I was obliged to dispatch two soldiers in search of him and since our arrival here they have come in with him. He had strayed so far from our little encampment as to have lost himself. The poor fellow was in great trouble and I inflicted no punishment on him, although it is contrary to orders that any soldier should leave the place of rendezvous more than one hundred yards without leave.

Jim behaves himself remarkably well and attends to his duty. He is tired soldiering and says if myself and him had stayed at home, we would not have had so much trouble.

SUNDAY, SEPTEMBER 20

Left Bloss' a little after light and marched to John C. Youngman's for breakfast, distance five and one-half miles. Rained part of the time. We then proceeded to D. Willard's, making the day's march altogether nineteen and one-half miles. Crossed the Tioga three times. Paid expenses of $20.00.

Dear Polly: We have arrived here after a march of nineteen miles principally along the bank of Tioga River. The drum aroused us at the dawn of day and we immediately started. It rained on us for about half an hour and then became pleasant. We have comfortable quarters for the night, the evening has become cold and I have a fire put on in my room from where I now write, but cannot look around me without calling to my recollection how great my happiness would be were it possible to be transported in an instant to my own fire side and surrounded by you and my poor little girls, but these reflections unman me and I must endeavor to dissipate them, it will be only an attempt. It is said we now have good roads and a pleasant country to pass through.

MONDAY, SEPTEMBER 21

Remained here for breakfast and then proceeded on our way. Crossed the line into New York at Linley Town, passed the Conaneague and halted at the house of James Ford, a genteel liberal man who well entertained us. Total amount of expense $6.50. Distance this day ten miles.

Dear Polly: For the first time since we started I agreed to take breakfast before our march and have arrived at Linley Town in the State of New York, about 170 miles from Huntingdon. To this place I requested you to write and the post is to arrive this evening. My anxiety is great but I fear from the arrangements of the post office at Williamsport that I shall have to wait one week longer. We have been marching among the Yankees for three days, they have behaved very politely, but evince a great disposition to make money off us. Yesterday evening being Sunday, a number collected and this morning a Colonel, a Major, a Captain, a Doctor and God knows how many other officers waited on me and escorted my Company for a mile carrying two stand of colors in front of us, and swearing we were the handsomest set of men as soldiers, they ever saw. Indeed the compliments we have received ever since our setting out have been such that under any other circumstances than mine at home would make me proud of my present situation, but my mind is too much engrossed about my family and affairs at home for compliments to make any impression on me. The regular troops who have passed before us have been guilty of such outrageous conduct that we are considered as gentlemen. They are one day's march before us and I am determined they shall remain so unless they stop a few days and then I will proceed ahead of them. We are now at a genteel house on the bank of the River Cowanesque, commonly called Conanesky, about twelve miles on this side of Painted Post, where I expect to reach tomorrow, perhaps further. Myself, officers and soldiers are all well and stand the march much better than they expected. My feet have not yet got sore and I have been obliged to administer salve for sole feet and laudenum for the lax, brought on by eating fresh provisions, to only one or two men. I never was in better health in my life.

The soldiers have got a fiddle in the adjoining room and are dancing briskly. It annoys me a good deal, but I am willing to submit to it, as their spirits are revived in consequence of the music. The Post will leave this place tomorrow and I must close my letter. I have given you all the news I can think of. Tell the families of the soldiers, they are well, and I will endeavor to take them home so.

No doubt you will show my letter to Mrs. H. and all our other friends. If it gives them as much pleasure to read, as me to write, under an idea that you and them will be gratified, it will be some little consolation. God bless you, my dear children and all my friends is the wish nearest the heart of your ever affectionate husband. Write to my mother where I am.

TUESDAY, SEPTEMBER 22

We moved from Ford's, crossed the Tioga twice, paid James Cook for transporting the Company over one crossing of the Tioga, one dollar, crossed the Canisteo River, halted a few minutes at Irwin's near the Canisteo and then moved on across the Cohocton River over a bridge to Irwin's at the Painted Post, distance twelve miles. A rain commenced at half-past 8 o'clock and wet the soldiers considerably. Paid expenses $9.60.

WEDNESDAY, SEPTEMBER 23

Left Painted Post and marched to Campbell's for breakfast. Purchased bread and milk for men $2.00, then proceeded to Bath, total day's march eighteen and one-half miles. Halted at the house of Captain Bull.

THURSDAY, SEPTEMBER 24

Remained at Bath to have washing done, bread baked, etc. Paid for bacon $2.20, paid Samuel Nixon for bread $5.00, paid Howell Bull, expenses $37.50.

Dear Polly: I have not received no letter from you but one since I left home nor can I expect any till my arrival at Niagara, and have directed the different postmasters where I requested you to write to forward them after me, which will be done. My last letter to you was from Linley Town to which place I gave you an account of our journey.

The next morning we marched off and ate our breakfast on the bank of the Tioga River at which place rain commenced and continued on us during our march that day. We got twelve miles, crossed the Cohocton River to the Painted Post, and yesterday arrived at this place where we are remaining today for the purpose of resting, washing, etc. Nothing of moment has occurred to any of us. We still continue to be improving in health and all have good appetites. Tomorrow morning we shall again resume our march and suppose it will be nearly two days before we reach headquarters. The distance being about 120 miles. I feel astonished at myself to think that I can walk eighteen and nineteen miles a day without being fatigued or my feet getting sore. Snyder frequently complains of his ankles but after riding a short distance in the baggage wagon, is restored.

We have generally been well lodged on our march, the men always having a house or barn to sleep in, and I have as yet had a good bed. You will not receive this letter until Friday two weeks, and perhaps at some time receive another which may be written when I get some further on. You must not be uneasy if a week should slip by without you receiving a letter, for although I will not neglect writing, the arrangements of the mails are so that there is no certainty. I hope Elizabeth and Catherine behave well and are a comfort to you, but I must not think too much about you and them, or I will not be considered a soldier, which I wish I never had been.

That God may grant you fortitude to bear our separation without too much unhappiness is my most sincere prayer. Give my love as usual to all friends and kiss the children for me.

FRIDAY, SEPTEMBER 25

We marched from Bath along the turnpike road to Hornell, distance twenty miles. Paid expenses of Company $6.80.

SATURDAY, SEPTEMBER 26

Moved on to Mr. Hurlbrut's for breakfast and paid for milk $.50, distance five miles, then marched on to Dansville, twelve miles, making this day's march seventeen miles. Paid expenses at Dansville $12.00.

SUNDAY, SEPTEMBER 27

Left Dansville and marched to Mr. Kennedy's where we breakfasted, distance five miles. Marched on to Bigtree. (Genesco) Paid for bread $.75.

MONDAY, SEPTEMBER 28

Left Genesee and marched to Lege's for breakfast. Paid for bread on the road $.25. Paid for milk at Bigtree $.25. Arrived at Calidonia, making this day's march eighteen miles.

My Dear Polly: This day three weeks I left Huntingdon and all I hold most dear to me this side the grave and am now two hundred and seventy-three miles distant from them and about ninety-five miles yet to go. For two days we have had good roads, fine weather and a pleasant country. The men still continue well and cheerful. No particular accident has befallen any of us.

The officers breakfast and sup at public houses. I provide provisions and the soldiers cook for themselves much to their satisfaction. This evening while sitting at supper my friend Mich. T. Simpson rode up to the door on his way to headquarters in the capacity of an officer, but what it is I have not yet asked him. I presume in the Commissary department.

We have now got on the State road from Albany to Niagara, having crossed the Genesee River. Three volunteer rifle companies passed on before this morning and one overtook us. There are one thousand troops about twenty-five miles behind and five thousand others are on their march from Albany. The whole country is alive with soldiers and everything has a warlike appearance. Honor calls me to the scene of action, effection and inclination call me home where all my happiness rests. A great variety of incidents and little anecdotes along the road tend much to amuse and keep me from reflecting too much. At Niagara I shall expect to receive several letters from you and some of my Huntingdon friends. I wrote to McCahan as well as you from Bath and this is the sixth time I have written you since my leaving home, but am fearful you will not receive all the letters. I cannot see any little children along the road without thinking about my dear girls at home. I feel the great necessity of my presence at Huntingdon, both on account of my family and that of Mr. Henderson. Tell John he must write to me and when I arrive at Niagara I shall give him an account of our situation. May God protect you, our little girls and all friends is the ardent prayer of your affectionate husband.

TUESDAY, SEPTEMBER 29

Left Calidonia and marched to . . . . for breakfast. Marched on to Batavia, making the whole day's march eighteen miles.

Dear Polly: I wrote you yesterday from Calidonia but lest the letter should miscarry, have thought it advisable to write from this place. The distance being eighteen miles from Calidonia, we have had a most delightful day and the people here are very genteel and polite.

I yesterday passed through a small Indian village where there were a great many Indian warriors who are preparing to espouse the American cause and will in a few days follow us. I purchased from one of the Squaws a musk mellon.

Tell Catherine I saw a great many little Indian girls like her. I just hear the sound of drums approaching at the head of two regular troops from the eastward. Farewell and believe me most affectionately yours.

WEDNESDAY, SEPTEMBER 30

Left Batavia and marched to McCracken's for breakfast. Paid for milk $1.25. Moved on and at Bruce's paid for two quarts of whiskey $.75. Marched to Vandevander's (damp dirty uncomfortable house) making the whole day's march eighteen miles.

THURSDAY, OCTOBER 1

Left Vandevander's and moved to Harris for breakfast. Then marched to Landis, the whole day's march being fourteen miles.

FRIDAY, OCTOBER 2

Moved towards Buffalo, distance eight miles, having on the road called on General Smythe, who had no orders for me, but to go to Buffalo and ordered my stay there until he would receive a communication from General Van Rensselaer. Arrived at Buffalo.

SATURDAY, OCTOBER 3

Remained at Buffalo to wash, etc. Having on yesterday called on General Hall who recommended my remaining at Buffalo until he would write and receive an answer from General Van Rensselaer with regard to my destination.

My Dear Polly: On yesterday afternoon we got to this place which was not one of the points contemplated to pass by when I left home. It is about twenty miles around to come this way to get to Niagara, but the roads were so bad the other course and all the other troops pursuing this route, I thought proper to follow. I am remaining here today for orders and expect on Monday to resume our march and probably be stationed at Lewiston about thirty miles from this place and eight from Niagara.

I have not yet been able to learn what number of troops are at the different points, but regiments and companies are hourly coming on and in a very few weeks something final will be done. The strong presumption at present is that we will be ordered into Canada which I can now see from my window across the point of Lake Erie. There are a great number of friendly Indians in this town and neighborhood and one of their great men informed me last night that in about four weeks there would be a body of eight hundred assembled at this place to assist in making the attack.

There are two regiments of regular troops stationed about three miles behind me and a great many others two miles further down the river, but I will not distress you by writing an account of the military transactions. The scene is new to me and I am heartily tired of it. What the result of our operations will be is very uncertain but all the officers appear to be in good spirits and confident of success. I have not yet received any of your letters but expect they are at Niagara, to which place you will continue to direct them.

The distance to this place from Huntingdon is three hundred and thirty-one miles; and I did not ride one foot of the road. My feet were sometimes a little sore but I now feel no inconvenience from them and am not even tired. The soldiers continue well and appear contented. The compliments paid our Company has a good effect to keep them cheerful. This letter will be put into the Post office to go by the way of Albany as being the most expeditious way of reaching you. This is a very rainy, stormy day and Lake Erie has a grand and terrible appearance. The surrounding country is pleasant and fine but there is no comfort for me separated from you and my dear children. Farewell my dear wife, take care not to spoil our little girls and endeavor to be contented. Give my love to the children and all friends.

SUNDAY, OCTOBER 4

Remained in Buffalo awaiting for orders and drew a provision return for forty-eight rations of bread for use of my Company.

MONDAY, OCTOBER 5

Remained at the same place and drew a provision order for my Company consisting of forty-eight men and one woman, for ninety-eight complete rations, at 2 o'clock, P. M. for Company exclusive of officers.

TUESDAY, OCTOBER 6

Remained at same place.

WEDNESDAY, OCTOBER 7

Drew a provision order for ninety-eight complete rations for the Company exclusive of officers, commencing on the 7th of October. This evening I received a verbal communication from General Hall that he had orders from General Van Rensselaer to remain at Buffalo until further orders and that all the Pennsylvania Troops were to do so.

THURSDAY, OCTOBER 8

Reported to General Hall as follows: Buffalo, 8th of October, 1812, Sir: In obedience to orders from the Honorable William Eustis, Secretary of War, bearing date the 16th of August, last, I have the honor to report to you that I am arrived at this place (after a march of 331 miles) with a Company of Volunteer Infantry from Pennsylvania consisting of one Captain, two Subalterns, four Sergeants, four Corporals, two musicians and thirty-three privates, all of whom are now subject to your orders. I am respectfully yours.

FRIDAY, OCTOBER 9

Drew a provision order for ninety-eight rations for my Company, exclusive of officers and servants.

SATURDAY, OCTOBER 10

My beloved Wife: At this place we are ordered to remain until further orders. We have very comfortable quarters both for officers and men and all continue well. I have written to John Henderson an account of the particulars of the war which he will communicate to you. I have not yet been able to get your letters from Niagara, but will send for them tomorrow by the mail. It is not safe going down the river or I would have sent before this time, but have no wish to unnecessarily expose myself. You may assure the families of all soldiers that they are well. I can form no idea yet of what will take place or whether anything this winter. In future direct your letters to this place. As usual give my love to the children and believe me to be most affectionately your tender husband.

SUNDAY, OCTOBER 11

Drew a provision order for ninety-eight rations.

My Dear Polly: I wrote you a short letter yesterday which left this day and must go round by the way of Albany to Huntingdon as the most expeditious route. Not being able to make any correct calculation how soon a letter will reach you from this place, I write by almost every mail leaving here. I am in hopes that my Company will be stationed here until the whole army is ordered to cross the river into Canada which is much talked of. This morning about twenty-three hundred regular troops march to a place called Lewiston, where the other part of the army is stationed. By some it is suggested that the object is to have a sufficient force collected in order to cross at that point. The volunteer corps to which Canan and Vandevander's Companies are attached have not yet arrived nor any news of them. Major Cuyler, aide to General Hall, who was killed by a cannon ball was yesterday buried with the honors of war. My Company was selected by the General to perform the ceremony and firing at the grave. We all cleaned ourselves up, made a brilliant appearance and acquitted ourselves with honor much to the satisfaction of the General who was pleased to compliment us for our correct military conduct. We are much in favor and not yet put to any very hard duty, except that in General Orders we are directed to exercise six hours every day. At the home where I lodge there are two British officers who were taken prisoners on Friday in a Brig which was taken by the Americans. There are also here a number of American officers who were surrenderd by General Hull at Detroit, among whom is Captain Hickman and his lady who is the Daughter of General Hull. Their situation is very unpleasant owing to the conduct of Hull being frequently the subject of conversation and much censured.

We have had no alarm today from the British. This morning a few cannons were fired across the river at our fort two miles from Buffalo but no injury done. This is the most unpleasant country at this season of the year I ever saw, there being continual storms and rains. I am getting so fat that my clothes will scarcely button on me and I eat hearty three times a day, and have not yet become either lazy or dissipated, or forget that I have a family and comfortable home, where I should rather be than gaining all the laurels which military ambition could possible desire. I hope the children and you are well, frequently do I awake dreaming that Catherine is prattling to me. I fear paying the postage of so many letters will break you up and I must not write so often. Tomorrow I expect to get all the letters which you wrote and directed to Niagara and other places. It will be a great treat to me. With my love to all friends. I am your loving husband.

MONDAY, OCTOBER 12

(No entry in diary)

TUESDAY, OCTOBER 13

Drew a provision order for one hundred rations, having recruited one other female.

SATURDAY, OCTOBER 17

My Dear Polly: David Snyder has been discharged and now goes home. It would give me great pleasure if we were all in the same situation, but I cannot form any opinion yet, whether we will remain all winter or not, but my fears are that we will be obliged to stay. There has been one hard battle fought by the Americans in attempting to take possession of Canada, in which a great many valuable lives were lost, and at the place where we were to have been and no doubt would be, provided we had tents, so that you see all things are for the best. I am sorry to say that I have not yet been able to obtain either clothing or money for my men and they are getting uneasy. I hope soon to get warm clothing for them. For three days past all has been peace and quietness, until last night when we were alarmed and out immediately under arms, but it turned out to be in consequence of some drunken Indians in the neighborhood firing their guns. There are a number of Indians who drew their rations and say they are ready and willing to fight for us. Owing to the confusion in the neighborhood of the post office where your letters were directed I have got none of them yet, but hope in a few days to receive them all. Heaven protect you and my children. Your ever affectionate husband.

P. S. Mr. Simpson, Miller, Swope and myself have got boarding at a small house in a retired part of the town with a poor family. The man of the house drinks hard, the woman is neat and clean, and has one little girl, the size of Catherine. We have a room to sit and sleep in and eat in the kitchen. Jim still behaves well but is heartily tired of campaigning. I have written so often that I have nothing to say.

MONDAY, OCTOBER 19

To the Secretary of War. Sir: In obedience to your orders dated 16th of August, last, delivered by Captain Wheaton on the 22d of the same month, I marched with my Company of Volunteers from Huntingdon, Pennsylvania, on the 7th of September, and arrived at this place (after a march of 331 miles without tents) on the 2d of the present month, where I was halted by orders from the Commander-in-chief. We are yet without tents or any prospect of getting them, my men have no winter underdress, being directed to leave home with linen pantaloons and waistcoats, their shoes are worn out and many of them have no stockings and are entirely without the means of procuring any kind of comfortable clothing suitable for the approaching season, which this climate particularly requires. After diligent inquiry I cannot find any person authorized or who has the means of advancing to my men the amount of clothing, agreeable to the act of Congress, or even to pay the men their wages as soldiers. I am willing to submit to many inconveniences, but the clamors of my men and seeing them shivering with cold for want of clothing morning and evenings, when on guard are very distressing. My company is not the only one in this situation, there are two others from Pennsylvania, out of which five of their men have deserted and unless some pecuniary relief is shortly afforded, I fear it will be impossible to keep our men together.

Having received my orders direct from you and there being no person here to whom I can apply must be my apology for this communication which I hope will not be overlooked but immediately attended to for the good of the service. I have the honor, etc.

My Dear Wife: No doubt before you receive this the news of the Battle of Queenstown will have reached you, and in my last letter I stated the reason why my

Company were so fortunate as not to be there, viz, what we all consider a misfortune, the want of tents. A true account of the engagement cannot yet be given. I have spent a great part of the day in company with General Van Rensselaer who commanded the expedition and he has but an imperfect knowledge of the number killed. The total amount of killed and wounded and taken prisoners will be about one thousand. The officers and privates taken (except the regulars) will be permitted to return on their parole not take up arms during the war. A flag of truce came over the river today. I was ordered by the General to receive the officers. They had nothing particular to communicate, only to inquire for some friends. An armistice has taken place and hostilities are not to commence until thirty hours notice is given. My opinion at present is that there will be no further attempt to invade Canada this winter and I hope that a peace will shortly take place, for which I do most sincerely hope. This evening I received two Huntingdon papers which were going on to Niagara, directed to me. They were a great treat. The letters are gone on, they could not be opened, but will return on the day after tomorrow. Write every post, direct to Buffalo. I heard yesterday by a gentlemen direct from Meadville that the two thousand volunteers were in a State of confusion, desertions daily taking place and doubtful whether they will come on or not. If they do not come on they will be disgraced. My love to all my friends, Your affectionate husband.

SATURDAY, OCTOBER 24

My Dear Polly: On Tuesday last I started from this place for Niagara to see the country, and more for the purpose of receiving letters from you which I expected certainly, but may you well guess my disappointment and mortification to find on examination that there were twelve or fifteen for the different soldiers and both the other officers but none for me. I am certain they must have miscarried and yet cannot well reconsile this opinion on reflection that the others were forwarded from the different offices to which they were directed.

I spent an hour in viewing the falls of Niagara, which are certainly one of the wonders of nature, but I was a little out of temper in consequence of my disappointment and did not enjoy the scene so much as I otherwise would have done. Neither McCahan or J. Henderson have any reason to expect any more letters from me. It is impossible for me to make up any decided opinion as to what will be the operations of the army during the winter, but present appearance indicate an intention to retire into quarters.

Major General Van Rensselaer who was Commander-in-chief of all the forces is still at this place but has given the command of the army to General Smythe of the regulars, and is going home. Major General Hall has gone home not to return, and I am sorry to say that things relative to the war appear to be in much confusion. It is impossible to get a correct account of the late unfortunate battle, particularly the number killed, but from the best idea I can form there must have been about two hundred killed and nearly the same number wounded, many of whom are daily dying. The day after the battle an armistice took place which still continues and uncertain how long it will be, but hostilities are not to commence on either side without thirty hours previous notice. I saw the ground on which the battle was fought, the river is not more than one hundred yards wide at the place the Americans crossed and the British soldiers, their forts and batteries were in full view. Colonel Wynders Regiment of regulars are stationed at Niagara Fort, the others encamped about three miles from this place.

The whole force now on the lines who can be compelled to go into Canada does not exceed two thousand, and I presume the General, who is said to be a cautious man, will not attempt it with so small a number. The Meadville volunteers have not yet arrived and doubts are entertained that they will not come over. Out of one of the Pennsylvania Volunteer companies now here, nine have deserted and three from the other. None of my men have yet disgraced themselves by such conduct. They are comfortably situated in the courthouse but I cannot tell how long they will remain there.

Give my compliments to our friends and love and kisses to each of the children, and believe me most affectionately your tender husband.

WEDNESDAY, OCTOBER 28

My Dear Polly: When I wrote you last, I had not received your letters nor one from McCahan, both of which arrived on the evening of the day I wrote and much pleased was I to hear from home. We are going on as usual, all well, but the greatest number of the Company's beginning to grow uneasy and anxious to get home. We have not yet went into tents, but were very near it yesterday, being ordered out of the courthouse to give room for the sick. However, I made out to provide a house into which the men go this day. I have purchased warm clothing for them, under an expectation that the paymaster will shortly be on and remunerate me. The regular troops who are encamped about two miles from this town are becoming sickly, owing to their being obliged to sleep on the damp ground, about three hundred out of one thousand are laid on their backs and many of the poor fellows who were wounded in the late battle have died. This day at 1 o'clock I am to go out to the encampment with my Company to see a soldier shot for desertion.

All is peace and quietness here at present, the armistice is not yet at an end. When it ceases, no doubt some little trouble will commence, but there will be no danger unless we are ordered to cross over into Canada. The Pennsylvania troops have not yet arrived. I am anxious to hear from home and no doubt in a few days will receive letters. I seldom suffer myself to think of my business which is suffering much, of you, the children and my friends, it is impossible for me to forbear thinking too much for my own happiness. I hope Mary is come home and that you are all well. Heaven protect you. Your affectionate husband.

SATURDAY, OCTOBER 31

I called on General Smythe and received his direction to appoint the Officer of the Day and give the countersign till further orders.

My Dear Polly: The same day on which I wrote you last, your letter of the 9th of October, together with McCahan's paper were both received and there is little doubt but all your letters will safely arrive. I have not been able yet to receive any money for the men, either their pay or in lieu of clothing, they are becoming very fretful and unless I can get some from the government shortly I fear they will become more so. I have laid out nearly all my own money to buy clothing for them and unless I get some shortly, will be obliged to get it sent from home. Captain Collin's Company who are in my situation have determined to the number of forty-two to stack their arms and go home. They are all republicans and the officers have had more trouble with them, than I have yet had. Tell Mr. Henderson that so soon as I have any news to give, I will write. At present all is peace on the lines, both parties making preparations, the Americans for the invasion, the British for defense. I was all day yesterday engaged on the Court Martial, trying soldiers for desertion, and am today to be on another. The soldier who I stated in my last letter was to be shot, was executed in the presence of the whole army in and near this place. He met his fate with great resolution, and I think had hopes of pardon till the last moment. I can form no opinion as to the course the war will take or whether it will soon be at an end, but hope for the best. I am growing very fat and of late had so little hard duty to perform that I am getting lazy, but not dissipated.

I am glad Mary has got home. She will be company for you, though Tho. Blair will add to your comfort. Tell all the children, I hope they will be good and obedient to you. Does ever Elizabeth talk of me? Remember me affectionately to Mr. H. and all other relatives and friends. I am your affectionate husband.

TUESDAY, NOVEMBER 3

George Armitage, James Simpson, Abraham Vandevander, L. Westbrook and J.

Westbrook deserted,—to pursue them to Cattaraugus. I proceeded towards Conewago, overtook them, and the three first returned.

My Dear Polly: The occurrence which causes the date of my letter from this place is a very unpleasant one for me. The volunteers have not yet had one cent of pay and have became very impatient and much dissatisfied with their situation. On Tuesday night five of my Company deserted. Yesterday at twelve o'clock I procured a horse and pursued them to this place, being thirty miles distant from Buffalo, up Lake Erie. This morning I started at 3 o'clock with a man to carry a lantern to guide me through a wilderness of nine miles and arrived at a house at day light, where I found my men, very much to their confusion and astonishment. After a good deal of persuasion, they agreed to return to their duty and began to retrace their steps. I remained with them for sometime and then rode on before. Three of them have came on and two I fear much have determined to go off. I have first dispatched a messenger to raise the militia to go in search of them. They were all making their way home.

Yesterday morning before I left Buffalo, every member of Captain Phillips' Company and several of Captain Collin's (both from Fayette County) stacked their arms and refused to do duty until they were paid their wages and money in lieu of clothing. They were all reported to the General, and I have just received information that they were put under guard and marched out to the encampment where the regulars are,—poor fellows, I feel much for their present situation. It is a hard one and I know not what the consequences will be.

They are almost naked and barefooted, and without money, or any to be had for them,—yet all these hardships will not justify mutiny or desertion. My men are much better off, as I purchased pantaloons for all of them that wanted, but the novelty of a soldier's life is over and they want to go home. It is shameful that we have not yet received our money from the government. I have repeatedly applied to General Smythe, who is now our commander, but without redress. He is willing to do all in his power for our accommodation, but has not the means. The Pennsylvania troops from Meadville have not yet arrived. What can occasion their delay, we are at a loss to know. An express was sent after them last Monday, who has not yet returned. On their arrival, it will be ascertained whether the campaign closes for this fall or not. I hope it may and the war too.

Since I wrote you last, one other of your letters arrived. They will all come on. McCahan's paper containing a statement of the election is to hand.

I shall remain here tonight and tomorrow return to Buffalo. The ride under any other circumstances than being so far from you, my children and friends, would be pleasant. The whole distance being along the beach of Lake Erie, but my mind is too much engrossed about the situation of my business and family, to enjoy with great pleasure some of the magnificent scenes of nature exhibited in this quarter of the world. I am becoming quite accustomed to the appearance and society of Indians, seeing them daily and frequently meeting with them at their camps in the woods. I feel much for your situation next week during the Court, so many inquiries will be made respecting my business. George Thompson has not been very well but is getting better. Ensign Swoope says if he was once more at home he would give security not to leave the Borough for two years. Neither officers or men enjoy the greatest possible contentment of mind, but all appear to be growing fat, which is not strong evidence of too much anxiety.

As usual, present my love kindly to all our friends and give each of the children a kiss from me. I am your truly affectionate husband,

TUESDAY, NOVEMBER 10

My Dear Polly: I wrote you a few days since from Cattaraugus when I was in pursuit of deserters from my Company. Levi Westbrook and John Westbrook have not yet been taken and I fear much will reach home before they are apprehended. Their conduct was so dishonorable and unprincipalled that I hope the citizens of Huntingdon will have them immediately apprehended and confined in prison in order that a detachment of men may be sent to bring them back. The other three who were persuaded off by them are in excellent spirits and glad they returned. No punishment has been or will be inflicted on them. We are generally well. George Thompson is still a little better.

All is yet doubt and uncertainty as to our movements this fall. The regular troops have been ordered to build huts, which looks like retiring into winter quarters. I am in great hopes the campaign is at an end and that peace will be made. The war is badly carried on. No money yet for the volunteers. The Company who stacked arms were kept under guard for three days and nights exposed to the weather without tents and then discharged with each a suit of clothes. Their Captain had his sword taken from him and is yet under arrest.

So far as I can learn there is a very general wish, particularly among all the volunteers, that the war would cease.

The armistice still continues, consequently all is peace and quietness. My Company is attached to a battalion of volunteers from Albany and New York. We have no hard duty to perform and are doing but little good.

In future write to me at this place and direct your letters to come by the western mail. They will arrive several days sooner. John Henderson, John Miller and J. McCahan have not performed their promises to write. I think you must receive at least three letters from me weekly by the different mails as I write that often. The mail will close in a few minutes and I have not time to write any more.

May happiness attend you, my darling children and all friends is the wish of your affectionate husband.

THURSDAY, NOVEMBER 12

Received from Captain James Thomas, Divisional Quartermaster, $1737.60 in lieu of clothing for the men of my Company.

SATURDAY, NOVEMBER 14

My Dear Polly: Yesterday we had a slight fall of snow, this morning is cold and everything has a gloomy appearance. The poor soldiers who are obliged to lay in tents have a very uncomfortable time. My men are in a house, and with great exertion I have been able to procure pay for their clothing, which has elevated their spirits a little and they are better satisfied. A few days since the General issued an order for the soldiers to build huts which was considered as putting an end to the campaign for the season, but it was afterwards countermanded and every arrangement is making for crossing over into Canada in a few days. The Meadville troops will be here this day or tomorrow and then something conclusive will be done. I am still in expectation that the General will retract his orders for crossing. The weather is becoming so cold and unpleasant, I have got my flannel made up and a cloth waistcoat made. I shall make myself as warm as possible as the nature of the circumstances will admit of. George Thompson has not yet entirely recovered, his complaint appears to be of the rheumatic kind and has settled principally in his left arm, otherwise he is well enough. I am sorry you were so much tortured with the reports of part of my Company being cut off, as we have never had even a skirmish. Waggoner was standing sentinel a few nights since, it being dark, something approached, he hailed and for want of an answer fired his musket, immediately on report of which a dog yelped loudly and ran off. Should we go over the river you cannot expect to hear from me so often, but I will write before we start. A company of volunteers from Baltimore have came on and are united to the regiment I am attached to. Our whole regiment consists of about four hundred volunteers under command of Colonel McClure, an Irish democrat from New York. He is a clever man and very friendly with me. This day the mail arrives by which I expect to receive letters from home. That God may protect you, my children and all our friends is the unceasing prayer of your affectionate husband.

FRIDAY, NOVEMBER 20

My Dear Polly: The Meadville troops arrived here the day before yesterday, all in good health and spirits, but I believe will not generally cross the water, indeed from what I can learn I don't believe that more than one fourth of them will, but perhaps when they see others crossing it will encourage them. Everything preparatory to our entering Canada in a few days is progressing. The weather at present is extremely unfavorable, very cold and repeated snow storms. The soldiers who are in tents complain much and not without reason. The volunteers are generally tired of soldiering and if once more at home would remain there. From the present movements, it is generally understood and believed that a descent will be made, even without the aid of the Pennsylvanians. It is considered imprudent but I fear will be persevered in. If a landing is effected, we shall have a pretty severe winter. The armistice which has continued since the battle of Queenstown is taken off, and this night at nine o'clock hostilities on either side may commence.

As you might hear more unfavorable reports of our situation and circumstances, than are in reality founded in facts, I have thought advisable to give you the above statement of what appears to be intended. Captain Canan looks well, he says his men will cross, but after conversing with them I find the general cry of all the Pennsylvanians is they will be the fewest number. That if there was a sufficient force to go over they would not remain behind. Knowing that we are compelled to cross, myself and Company are relieved from suspence.

Perhaps this may be the last letter you will receive from me while we remain here, as it is probably the orders for embarkation of the troops will be given immediately before it is done. After orders are received, if possible, I will write.

My health is very good, my spirits more depressed than those of a soldier should be. I cannot help it. The men are well except George Thompson, whose rheumatism in his arm has become so bad that I will endeavor to have him discharged and sent home. I pray that you will endeavor to be contented and not distress yourself too much on my account. Give my love most affectionately to the children and also my friends, and believe me most truly your loving husband.

SUNDAY, NOVEMBER 22

George Thompson discharge from service by Colonel McClure.

My Dear Polly: The bearer George Thompson has been dismissed from service in consequence of a complaint in his arm. I am sorry he was no longer able to do duty as he has always conducted himself with great propriety and as a good soldier.

I wrote you by the mail which left this place yesterday and write generally three times each week as many of the letters miscarry. Your letter bearing date the 31st of October arrived by the mail last night, none from J. Henderson have yet come to hand and only three from McCahan.

On the arrival of every mail I am at the postoffice. In a letter written you from Cattaraugus I requested you to forward your letters by the western mail. Continue to do so, they will come more certain and more expeditious. If the two Westbrooks have got to Huntingdon I hope they are safely lodged in prison and will there remain until sent for. Their conduct is of that kind which cannot, nor will it, be overlooked. They have added baseness to cowardice. There will be no humanity in the citizens refusing to confine them.

I hope the recruiting officer has attended to my request in having them confined. In the course of this day it will be determined how many of the Pennsylvania troops will volunteer to cross the line. The number at present is extremely doubtful. Several of Captain Canan's Company, and amongst others, Arthur Moore, have said that if his company will not go over, they will join mine.

The whole country is bustle and confusion. In this town and within three miles around, there are not less than five thousand soldiers, but not more than two thousand regulars and volunteers who are compelled to cross the water. I think in less than five days we will, without fail, embark the troops. A severe cannonading has been heard the greater part of this day, supposed to be at Lewiston, but the cause of it is not yet known.

It is now late on Sunday evening, part of this letter was written in the morning, since when I have been to the encampment of the Pennsylvania troops. They have not yet determined how many will go over. Volunteers are hourly arriving from this State under the General's invitation to assist in the conquest. As I have no time to write any other person than you, it will be necessary to communicate the intelligence herein contained. I am so much engaged procuring good arms and blankets for my men that I scarcely know what I am doing, much less writing. For want of an . . . I have a bayonet fixed on the end of a pole. Miller and Swoope will take a musket and bayonet. If anything particular occurs during the night, I shall inform you. It would give me much pleasure, and no doubt my friends, if I had leisure to write all the passing occurrences of the times.

No two men appear to be of the same opinion except that the better opinion at present is the idea of crossing is imprudent with our present forces and provisions. If we remain here for ten days, they will be scarce, and should we cross over, they will be difficult to be had. A lady has engaged to have me a boiled tongue and some cakes to put in my knapsack.

Monday—Last night there was an alarm and we were under arms for an hour, but there was no danger. I am just returning from a ride along the river and am so cold that I can scarcely write.

As usual, remember me to all friends, and kiss the children for me. Your affectionate husband.

MONDAY, NOVEMBER 23

Drew from Captain James Thomas, Divisional Quartermaster, Forty-five cartridge boxes and bayonet belts for use of my Company.

WEDNESDAY, NOVEMBER 25

My Dear Polly: I commence this letter, my dear wife, with feeling which by me cannot be described. Your ever reading it depends entirely on my fate. Should I fall in Canada, then you must read this to me, distressing and melancholy, last assurance of my unbounded and unalterable affection for you. For my own fate, I am somewhat careless, for your situation my dear little children and my friends to whom I might be of some assistance, I feel the keenest regret. My pen trembles in my hand, and the tears trickle from my eyes on the paper while I write, at the idea of the pain and distress which you will feel at reading this. Perhaps it would have been better had I desisted, but my feelings would not permit me. I deemed it proper to make a will, which is herein enclosed. I can write no more. Kiss each of the children for me. Tell them that their father's lips are cold, and that his prayer was for you and them. Farewell alast—a long farewell. I hope to meet you in heaven. Your affectionate husband.

THURSDAY, NOVEMBER 26

My Dear Polly: The determination of the General is publicly made known, that we are in a very short time, even tomorrow morning, to make the conquest of Canada. This morning I was ordered to parade my men with their knapsacks and everything in a state of preparation for crossing. I have mine ready packed with two good boiled tongues and a half a loaf of bread, one shirt and cravat, one pair of stockings, and a pair of blankets. We moved on some distance when we were ordered to return. The regulars having attempted an embarkation of the troops, which for some reasons not yet publicly known, failed. Great trouble has been given by the men of the Pennsylvania troops to their officers about crossing. Captain Canan informed me yesterday that out of the battalion to which he belongs, commanded by Major John Scott consisting of 285 men, nineteen had volunteered to go over, twelve of whom were from his Company. It is generally believed that the whole brigade will not turn out more than two or three hundred men. The Commanding General has ordered four hundred of those who refused going over to be marched about thirty miles down the Niagara River to build a fort. The remainder will be stationed at some other place. This is done by way of degradation for their refusal to go over. I am in great hopes they will yet do better. The question is to be again agitated this day. Out of Captain Ox's Green Castle Company, two including Lieutenant Wilson have agreed to volunteer.

Captain Clackner and all his men from Pennsylvania have absolutely refused. None of Vandevander's men will cross. Kinote, who deserted, has returned to Canan. I hope the two Westbrooks are secured. Tell all my friends that unless they have them taken, they want spirit and a due regard to order. A very unpleasant occurrence took place in our regiment a few days since. All the companies, mine accepted, took umbrage at a Landlord whom they pleased to call a Tory. The Baltimore Company, well versed in the management of mobs, proposed pulling down his house and began by breaking the windows which they effected and were proceeding when my company was called upon to protect it. We drove them from the house, charged bayonets, and protected it for about two hours, and could have done so. The mob appeared to disperse when General Porter and my Colonel came and directed me to remove my men. Scarcely was this done when they returned doubly enraged, entered the house with axes and destroyed the floors, the roof, the sides, and threw the furniture out of the windows, and attempted to set fire to it. A company of regular artillery armed with loaded pistols and sabres were ordered to enter and clear the house dead or alive. They immediately entered and began cutting with their swords when the rioters got out of the windows in a great hurry. None of them were killed, but several wounded. One had his hand cut off with the stroke of a sabre. One of the artillery men had his nose cut off by one of his own company. Patrols were kept up during the night but no injury done. Vengeance has been sworn against many of the inhabitants who are called federalists—denominated tories —by the Baltimorians. My men are in high spirits and in great estimation for their manly conduct in the affair of the riot. They are now warmly clothed and by great exertions, I loaned each of them an additional blanket this morning. Every favor which a soldier could expect has been granted them, and by great exertions on my part, they have been rendered comfortable. This they all acknowledge which is some little satisfaction, but is far from being any compensation for the deprivations I suffer on account of being from home. Jim was at first delighted at being left on this side of the water, as he was never considered very courageous. Today, he has applied for permission to go over. I have got a place for him to stay here for a while. When we make a stand, if necessary, I can send for him. Doctor Dean is appointed Surgeon of our regiment with which I am well pleased. It was on the solicitation of W. Simpson and myself. I have neither more paper or time to write you further at present. With my love to all friends, and kisses to the children, I am your loving husband.

SUNDAY, NOVEMBER 29

My Dear Polly: In my last letter I stated that the time was fixed when the descent was to be made on Canada, and in pursuance of the order, each officer and soldier was provided with two days' provisions in his knapsack. The night before last about two hundred regulars and sailors passed over and stormed several batteries, spiked a number of British Cannon, threw others into the river. They set fire to a house, took about forty prisoners with the loss of about fifty men killed and wounded. Yesterday morning at the dawn of day, the whole army marched to the place of embarkation. One whole regiment embarked and rowed about half over the river when the grape shot from the British field artillery poured so heavily on them that they were obliged to put back and return. The whole of the regular troops not amounting to 1000 then embarked on board the boats and went some distance up the river in order to strike across. The American forces were paraded in detachments on this shore. The British regulars, Militia, Lighthorse and Indians were all drawn up in line of battle in different places on the opposite shore where it was probable we would endeavor to effect a landing. Their cannon playing at our boats all the time and endeavoring to rake them. Our cannon firing at their soldiers and batteries, the balls were whistling about in every direction and appeared to be totally disregarded. The scene was extremely grand and yet something awful in it. During its continuance, three bold sailors crossed over, set fire to three houses, killed almost in face of the British army, stole two turkeys and returned safe. Our boats attempted a second time to enter the stream when the cannon began to fire at them. It was then growing towards evening, a Council of War was called by the General, immediately after the breaking up of which, orders were issued that all troops should return their different encampments. They all appeared in high spirits and anxious to get over. Victory, to them, appeared in vain. They returned with great indignation and much dissatisfied at the General. I was in expectation that this would put an end to the expedition, for the present season and such was the prevailing opinion, but since I commenced writing, an order has been shown me that we are to cross tomorrow morning at 9 o'clock, and preparations are again making for that purpose. I had been unwell for a few days and for two days had not went out of the house, owing to a bad cold. Yesterday, I marched with my company to the place of embarkation which is about three miles distance with a determination to cross with them. Owing to the fatigue of walking and standing all day on the damp ground, I am not quite so well today, and unless I get better, I will not be able to go over with them in the morning. Indeed it was imprudent for me to go yesterday, but knowing that the tongue of calumny would be directed against me by illiberal minds, I determined to risk it at all events, and when it was thought I could not go the men appeared so disheartened that I appeared compelled to move with the rest. I have pains in my limbs and a considerable headache with a slight cough. I have taken an emetic and got bled. In a very few days, I shall, with care, be perfectly well. Owing to the severe fatigue of yesterday, Mr. Swoope is unwell with a pain in his back and his going is extremely doubtful. In short he cannot go, because being out one night without shelter, which must inevitably be the case, would knock us both up. It is a most unfortunate and mortifying circumstance at the present momentuous crisis. I shall not close this letter till tomorrow and then give you further details. Your letter of the seventh of November received this morning. I have never yet received any from J. Henderson and only two from McCahan. I wrote you always by the same mail that I wrote any other person, and never less than two and frequently four letters each week. I have not received one third of the letters you have written and never but three newspapers. So gross is the negligence somewhere. In the future, write only by the western mail. I wrote John H. three very lengthy letters giving a precise and particular account of our situation and prospects.

MONDAY, NOVEMBER 30

This morning our regiment was under arms in order to proceed to the place of embarkation. I went part of the way with them, not being able, nor intending to cross over, when our march was countermanded and we ordered to remain at our encampment till further orders. There is to be a general Council of War held this day at which all the Colonels will be present. Something will then finally be determined on. Every person is dissatisfied at the present trifling mode of managing the affairs of the invasion. Had the business been properly conducted on Saturday morning early, I have no doubt but we could have subdued part of Canada without even a life being lost, more than had been in taking the batteries, etc. I feel considerably better today and only a little weak. Knowing that you would hear more alarming accounts of our situation, than were true, I have thought it best to give a candid narrative of what has really taken place. In my next, I hope to relieve you from all anxiety, and that we will be either in quiet possession of Canada or the expedition given up for the season. Two hundred of the Pennsylvania Troops have deserted since their arrival here. Many of them are sick. Provisions are scarce. Butter is three cents per pound, and there is no bread to be had at meal time in any of the public houses. Potatoes are substituted. I have never been obliged to eat but one meal without bread. We are still in comfortable quarters. The desolation of the war in this country is truly distressing. Give my love affectionately to the children and all friends, and believe me, Your affectionate husband.

SUNDAY, DECEMBER 27

To the Secretary of War—Sir: I have returned from the Niagara frontier on furlough, and finding the situation of my private concerns such that it is totally impossible for me to remain longer in the Army, I therefore resign my commission as Captain of Infantry Volunteers in the service of the United States. Should it be necessary for me to repair to Washington to settle my account of transportation, I shall on receiving notice, proceed there during the month of February. Since my departure from my company they have all (except one who was unable, some who had been previously discharged, and two who who had ran off) went off and scattered over the country. With a full determination not to return into service, I have the honor to be Robert Allison.

SKETCHES OF VETERANS OF THE WAR OF 1812

ADAIR, JOHN   Served as a Private in Captain John Robinson's Company, Pennsylvania Militia, from the 5th of September, 1814, until the 5th of December, 1814. Entered service again in 1835 and died while serving in Florida against the Seminole Indians. His widow, Mary, resided in Blair County, and died the 15th of January, 1875.

ALBERT, WILLIAM   The *Hollidaysburg Register* of the 10th of February, 1869, contains the following item "William Albert, a soldier of 1812, was recently frozen to death in Greenfield Township." No record of military services available.

ALEXANDER, JAMES   Served as a Trumpeter in Captain Joseph Markle's Light Dragoons, Lieutenant Colonel James N. Ball's Squadron, Pennsylvania Volunteers, North Western Army, for twelve months ending the 29th of March, 1813.
Served as a Private in Captain Matthew Rodger's Company, Colonel C. Rees Hill, Pennsylvania Militia, from the 5th of May, 1813, to the 5th of November 1813.
Born 1791; married Margaret Holliday; died 1852, and buried in the Presbyterian Cemetery at Hollidaysburg.

ARFORD, FREDERICK   Served as a Private in Captain Thomas Huston's Company, under Lieutenant Colonel John Lutz; Pennsylvania Militia; rendezvoused at York, Pennsylvania.
Buried in Grandview Cemetery at Tyrone.

BARR, WILLIAM   Believed to have served during the War of 1812. Services are not available. However, a William Barr served as a Private in Captain Hummel's Company, during 1814, also, a William Barr served as a Private in Captain James Murvin's Company, under Colonel Andrew Jenkins, during the early part of 1814.
Born 1791; died on the 18th of May, 1848, and buried in the Presbyterian Cemetery at Hollidaysburg.

BEAMER, MATHIAS   Believed to be a veteran of the War of 1812. Record of military services unavailable.
Buried in Logan Valley Cemetery at Bellwood.

BECKWITH, CLEMENT   Served as a Private in Captain John Adams' Company, Delaware Militia, during March and April, 1813.
Died at Port Matilda, Pennsylvania, on the 25th of December, 1868. His widow Mary, resided in Altoona in 1879.

BELL, ISAAC   Served as a Private in Captain Morrow's Company, in Captain S. W. Kearney's Company, and in Captain Joseph Henderson's Company, under Colonel Hugh

Bailey; in 22d United States Infantry, and in 2d United States Infantry; enlisting on the 17th of February, 1814, and discharged on the 28th of February, 1819.

Participated in several battles and received a wound in the right eye during the battle of Lundy's Lane. "Marched back to Fort Erie where on the 15th of August, 1819, the British followed and stormed Fort Erie,—and while the British were in possession of the out works, General Gaines and the United States Troops in the Fort blew up the outer magazine and the enemy with it."

Born on the 13th of July, 1799; resided at Cove Forge, Woodbury Township, in 1871; died on the 27th of September, 1874, survived by his widow Mary Ann; buried in the Presbyterian Cemetery at Williamsburg.

BENDER, HENRY   Served as a Private in Captain Nicholas Beckwith's Company from Bedford; Pennsylvania Militia.

Buried at Waterside, South Woodbury Township, Morrison's Cove, Bedford County; survived by widow Susan.

BENTON, JOHN   Served as a Private in Captain Jacob Marshall's Company, under Lieutenant Colonel Jeremiah Shappel, Pennsylvania Militia, from the 1st of September, 1814, until the 4th of December, 1814, at two dollars a month.

Born in Berks County, the 4th of August, 1786; married Eve Conser in 1825; died at East Freedom, Blair County the 29th of November, 1868; and buried in Lutheran Cemetery at Newry. Widow resided at Tyrone in 1879.

BERRY, JOHN, SR.   The *Hollidaysburg Register* of the 22d of August, 1866, records the death as, "He was a soldier of the War of 1812; born in 1793; died at Duncansville on the 17th of August, 1866, survived by several children and numerous grand children." Military services not available and place of burial unknown.

BRIDENTHAL, HENRY   Served as a Private in Captain Samuel Thomas' Artillery Company, under Colonel Rees Hill, Pennsylvania Militia, from the 5th of May, 1813, until the 5th of November, 1813.

Born 1784; died 1868, and buried in the Fairview Cemetery at Martinsburg.

BROWN, JACOB   Served as a Private in Captain George Ritter's Company, Pennsylvania Militia.

Died in Perry County, the 4th of September, 1854; widow Elizabeth, resided in Altoona in 1871.

CANAN, MOSES   Recruited and commanded a Company of the Pennsylvania Militia Volunteers from Alexandria; promoted a Major.

Born 1783, in Huntingdon County; resided in Ebensburg, 1831; married Mary Henderson; died at Johnstown in 1863.

CARROTHERS, ALEXANDER   Served as a Private in Captain Moses Canan's Company, Pennsylvania Militia Volunteers.

Buried in Presbyterian Cemetery at Williamsburg.

CARROTHERS, HUGH   Served as a Private in Captain Moses Canan's Company, Pennsylvania Militia Volunteers.
Buried in Presbyterian Cemetery at Williamsburg.

CHAMBERLAIN, JOHN   Served as a Private in Captain Samuel Thomas' Artillery Company, Pennsylvania Militia, and Lieutenant Sheets Company, Kentucky Militia; enlisted on the 12th of April, 1813, and discharged on the 16th of October, 1814.
Born on the 24th of August, 1787; married Elizabeth A. Ashman on the 17th of December, 1816; died at Pattonville, Morrison Cove, the 14th of March, 1873; and buried in an old cemetery near Loysburg.

COOPER, JOHN   Served as a Private in Matthew Rodger's Company, Pennsylvania Militia; enlisted at Petersburg on the 10th of April, 1813, and discharged on the 5th of November, 1813.
Born 1784; married Jane Milliken in October, 1811; died at Hollidaysburg on the 11th of November, 1872. Place of burial unknown.

CREAMER, DANIEL   Served as a Private in Captain Edmund Tipton's Company, Pennsylvania Militia.
Born 1794; died on the 30th of June, 1863 and buried in the Lutheran Cemetery at Hollidaysburg.

CUNNINGHAM, JEREMIAH   Served as a Private in Captain Jonathan Jones' Company, Pennsylvania Militia, from the 1st of September, 1814, until the 4th of December, 1814.
Born on the 15th of March, 1796; married Eliza Hutchinson on the 13th of January, 1825; died at Gaysport, on the 26th of October, 1847, and buried in the Presbyterian Cemetery at Hollidaysburg.

DAILEY, HENRY   Served as a Private in Captain Edmund Tipton's Company, Pennsylvania Militia, from the 13th of April, 1813, until the 5th of November, 1813. "He went to Erie and did Garrison duty till July, 1813, and was cannonaded by the British. Then went to General Harrison's Army at Sandusky in July, 1813,—here they had a slight encounter but captured the enemy and then they went back to Erie and were discharged after staying at Barr's Point guarding the prisoners and shipping taken by Commodore Perry."
Born the 13th of January, 1783; resided on Clover Creek near Fredericksburg, Blair County; married Catherine Dilling at Rebecca Furnace in October, 1815; died on the 14th of October, 1872, while attending a convention of the Society of the War of 1812, in Ohio, and probably buried in Ohio.

DAVIS, GEORGE   Served as a Private in Captain Moses Canan's Company of Alexandria, Pennsylvania, from September, 1812 until 24th of November, 1812.
Born in Huntingdon County; resided at Yellow Springs or Franklin Forge, Blair County; daughter Jane married Henry K. Hammond.

DONALDSON, WILLIAM   Served as a Private in Captain Robert Allison's Company, Pennsylvania Volunteer Militia, from September, 1812, until the 24th of November, 1812.
Born 1790; died at Hollidaysburg on the 11th of August, 1860, and buried in the Presbyterian Cemetery at Hollidaysburg.

FULTON, HENRY   Served as a Private in Captain Edmund Tipton's Company, Pennsylvania Militia, from May, 1813, until the 26th of October, 1813.

Widow Sarah, resided at Tyrone in 1870.

FURRY, DANIEL   *Hollidaysburg Register* of the 30th of March, 1864, states that he "was a soldier of the War of 1812, and was buried with the honors of war. The funeral was attended by Van Tries Cornet Band, a squad of the 84th Regiment at home on furlough, a detachment of the Provost Guard and a large concourse of friends and citizens."

Born 1793; died on the 25th of March, 1864. Buried in Lutheran Cemetery at Hollidaysburg.

GATES, JACOB   Served as a Private in Captain Burd's, Captain Hall's and Captain Pierce's Companies, enlisting at Carlisle on the 8th of May, 1812, and discharged on the 30th of June, 1817. "Was at Battle of Fort George, Stoney Creek and Beaver Dams, at latter place taken prisoner. Was taken to jail at Little York, thence to Kingston, thence to Montreal, then to Quebec and to Halifax, in Nova Scotia, and was imprisoned on Melvin Island, remained until last of February and was sent to Boston" and rejoined regiment. In Battle of Chippewa, Lundy's Lane, and Bridgewater, where he was wounded by a musket ball in the hip.

Born on the 17th of March, 1795; married Mary Bowers on the 22nd of July, 1819, had six sons serve during the Civil War; died at Duncansville on the 5th of February, 1878, and buried in the Carson Valley Cemetery, near Duncansville.

GLANDING, JAMES ARCHIBALD   Served as a Private in the Maryland Militia, from the 10th of September, 1814, until March, 1815. Received a gun shot wound in the right leg during the Battle of North Point, Maryland.

Born on the 17th of June, 1776; died on the 1st day of September, 1864, and buried in the Fairview Cemetery at Altoona.

GRUBER, NICHOLAS   Served as a Private in Captain Adam Hawk's Company of Pennsylvania Militia from the 17th of February, 1814, until the 20th of December, 1814.

Born on the 18th of May, 1795; married Susannah Daniel at Bartonsville, Monroe County, in 1818; resided at Martinsburg, Blair County; died on the 15th of November, 1873, and buried in the Spring Hope Cemetery at Martinsburg.

HARPST, JOHN   Served as a Private in Captain Edmund Tipton's Company of Pennsylvania Militia from the 13th of April, 1813, until the 25th of October, 1813. "Mustered in at Hollidaysburg,—thence to Erie, where the regiment remained four months in guarding the building of vessels at that point, thence to Cleveland, to Fort Stevens."

Born, 1792, married Julia Ann Cox at Warrior's Mark, on the 1st of June, 1815; resided in Logan Township, Blair County, 1872; died on the 8th of October, 1880. Place of burial is unknown.

HART, EZRA   Served as a Private in Captain Shankin's Company of Maryland Militia.

Born in Frederick County, Maryland, on the 10th of January, 1790; died on the 25th of December, 1853; buried in Carson Valley Cemetery, near Duncansville; survived by widow, Mary, who resided in Altoona in 1880.

HOPKINS, JAMES   Served as a Private in Captain Edmund Tipton's Company of Pennsylvania Militia during 1813.

Born on the 6th of September, 1792, and died in Blair County in 1828. Place of burial unknown.

HORRELL, IRWIN   Military services not available, but supposed to have served as a Captain.

Born on the 8th of February, 1786; died on the 23rd of October, 1859, and buried in the Luthern Cemetery at Hollidaysburg.

HULL, ANDREW   Military services not available.

Born on the 25th of September, 1781; died on the 4th of May, 1856, and buried in the Antis Cemetery, near Bellwood.

HYLE, JOHN   Served as a Private in Captain Edmund Tipton's Company, Pennsylvania Militia, from May, 1813, until the 5th of October, 1813.

Born, 1797, died on the 15th of August, 1847; survived by his widow Catharine and nine children. Place of burial unknown.

KANE, BENJAMIN   Military services not available.

Born on the 2nd of August, 1772; died on the 6th of June, 1857, and buried in the Fairview Cemetery at Martinsburg.

LEMON, SAMUEL   Served as a Private in Captain Robert Allison's Company of the Pennsylvania Volunteer Militia from the 25th of August, 1812 until the 24th of November, 1812.

Born at Manor Hill, Huntingdon County, in 1793; married Jane Moore; died on the 25th of February, 1867, and buried in the Presbyterian Cemetery at Hollidaysburg.

LINGENFELTER, MICHAEL   Served as a Private in Captain Frederick Hoff's Company of Pennsylvania Militia from the 2nd of October, 1812, until the 16th of April, 1813.

Born on the 15th day of August, 1781, died on the 2nd of March, 1849, and buried in the Union Cemetery at Claysburg.

LOVE, ROBERT   Military services not available.

Born on the 12th of July, 1782; died during the fall of 1866; buried in Grandview Cemetery at Tyrone.

LYSINGER, SAMUEL   Served as a Drummer in Captain Solomon Sparks' Company of Pennsylvania Militia from the 25th of September, 1812, until the 24th of November, 1812.

Survived by widow Margaret, who resided in Woodbury Township, in 1868.

MAIZE, WRAY   Served as a Private in Captain Robert Allison's Company of Pennsylvania Militia from the 25th of August, 1812, until the 24th of November, 1812.

Born in 1779; died on the 27th of July, 1862; buried in the Methodist Cemetery at Williamsburg; survived by widow Anna C., who resided at Williamsburg, in 1868.

MATHERS, JAMES   Served as a Private in Captain Edmund Tipton's Company of Pennsylvania Militia from May, 1813, until the 26th of October, 1813.

Survived by widow Elizabeth, who resided at Frankstown in 1868.

MAURER, JACOB   Served as a Private in Captain Edmund Tipton's Company of Pennsylvania Militia from May, 1813, until the 26th of October, 1813.

Born, 1789; died on the 6th of December, 1868; buried in the Maurer's Cemetery, near Altoona; survived by widow Barbara, who resided in Logan Township, Blair County, in 1870.

MAUS, JOHN S.   Served as a Private in Captain John Snyder's Company of Pennsylvania Militia from the 24th of September, 1814, until the 31st of December, 1814.

Born 1795; died on the 13th of September, 1840; buried in the Presbyterian Cemetery at Hollidaysburg; survived by widow Rachael, who resided in Hollidaysburg, in 1878.

MERRITTS, GEORGE, SR.   Served as a Private in Captain Joseph Henderson's Company, 22nd United States Infantry, from the 27th of February, 1814, until the 4th of October, 1814.

Born in Bucks County in 1793; resided at Springfield Furnace, Blair County, in 1822; died in 1869, and buried in Indiana County, Pennsylvania.

MILLER, HENRY   Served as a Private in Captain Edmund Tipton's Company of Pennsylvania Militia from the 13th of April, 1813, until the 24th of June, 1813; wounded in left arm in battle.

Born on the 14th of February, 1788; died on the 24th of December, 1824; buried in Walters Cemetery, near Duncansville; survived by widow Elizabeth, who resided at Duncansville, in 1868.

MOORE, JESSE   Served as a Sergeant in Captain Edmund Tipton's Company of Pennsylvania Militia from the 12th of April, 1813, until the 24th of October, 1813.

Born on the 30th of May, 1790; died on the 3d of March, 1875; buried in the Presbyterian Cemetery at Hollidaysburg.

NEWBERRY, JAMES   Served as a Private in the Cumberland Blues under Captain Handel.

Born at Chadd's Ford, Cumberland County, on the 22nd of January, 1796; resided at Gaysport, Blair County; served during the Mexican and the Civil Wars; died on the 9th of September, 1885, and buried in the National Cemetery at Hampton, Virginia.

POWELL, MATHIAS   Served in the United States Navy, on the old war ship, *Constitution*, and participated in twenty-one engagements between 1809 and 1814; served as a Private in Captain Heitzelberger's Company of the Pennsylvania Militia from the 1st of September, 1814, until the 4th of December, 1814, and was in Fort Henry when the British General Ross was slain.

Born March, 1781; died on the 26th day of April, 1877; buried in the Presbyterian Cemetery at Williamsburg; survived by his widow Mary, who resided in Williamsburg in 1879.

RAMEY, FREDERICK Military services not available. It is related that he served on board Commodore Perry's fleet during the Battle of Lake Erie, on the 10th of September, 1813.

Born in Alsace-Loraine, on the 14th of December, 1785; died on the 4th of July, 1865, buried in the Lutheran Cemetery in Sinking Valley.

ROBLY, MATTHEW Served as a Private in Captain Wool's Company of Militia.

Born in Connecticut on the 25th of February, 1784; died on the 26th of November, 1870; buried in Oak Ridge Cemetery at Altoona; survived by his widow, Martha A. Brown, whom he married at Spruce Creek on the 18th of May, 1837, and who resided in Altoona in 1880.

SIMONTON, JAMES C. Served as a Private in Captain Moses Canan's Company of Pennsylvania Volunteer Militia from the 25th of August, 1812, until the 24th of November, 1812.

Born on the 2nd of October, 1776; died on the 14th of October, 1857. Place of burial is unknown.

SWOPE, HENRY Commissioned Second Lieutenant in Captain Robert Allison's Company of Pennsylvania Militia, on the 14th of August, 1812; discharged from Company before it left for Canadian Border.

Born on the 18th of November, 1791; died on the 9th of October, 1829, and buried in the Fairview Cemetery at Martinsburg.

SWOPE, SAMUEL Served as an Ensign in Captain Robert Allison's Company of Pennsylvania Militia from the 7th of September, 1812, until the 24th of November, 1812.

Born in 1798; died in 1874, and buried in the Spring Hope Cemetery at Martinsburg.

TRIMBLE, JAMES Served as a Surgeon in the 2d United States Artillery from the 6th of July, 1812, until the 1st of September, 1816.

Born in Pennsylvania, on the 18th of April, 1790; resided at Williamsburg in 1831; died on the 22d of June, 1838; and buried in the Presbyterian Cemetery at Williamsburg.

WALKER, JOHN Served as a Sergeant in Captain Moses Canan's Company of Pennsylvania Militia from the 25th of September, 1812, until the 24th of November, 1812.

Born in 1793; first wife was Susan Blair; second wife Prudence Paine; died on the 15th of December, 1863, and buried in the Presbyterian Cemetery at Hollidaysburg.

WEIR, JACOB Served as a Private in Captain Samuel Thomas' Company of Pennsylvania Militia from the 5th of May, 1813, until the 5th of November, 1813.

Born 1791; died on the 8th of October, 1878; buried in the St. Patrick's Cemetery at Newry; survived by his widow Margaret, who resided in Eldorado, in 1879.

WELSH, WILLIAM Served as a Private in Captain Edmund Tipton's Company of Pennsylvania Militia from May, 1813 until the 26th of June, 1813.

Born on the 27th of January, 1777; died on the 21st of February, 1844, and buried in the Logan Valley Cemetery at Bellwood.

WESTLEY, DANIEL Served as a Private in Captain John May's Company of Pennsylvania Militia from the 28th of August, 1814, until the 5th of March, 1815.

Born 1795; enlisted Robinson Township, near York; died at Davidsburg, Antis Township, Blair County, on the 1st of January, 1870. Place of burial is unknown.

WILLIAMSON, JAMES Served as a Private in Captain Edmund Tipton's Company of Pennsylvania Militia from May, 1813, until the 24th of November, 1813.

Born on the 20th of January, 1785; died on the 10th of April, 1863; and buried in the Carson Valley Cemetery near Duncansville.

PART III

THE MEXICAN WAR

A brief history of the Mexican War, giving the causes, the Texans' struggle for independence, important events, battles, and the ending.

A history of the military organizations formed in this section prior to and during the Mexican War.

Sketches of the veterans of the Mexican War, giving their military services, death and burial records, and genealogical data.

INDEX TO PART III
THE MEXICAN WAR

Brief history of the Mexican War	97
Pennsylvania Militia prior to the Mexican War	99
Union Cavalry	99
Washington Grays	100
Williamsburg Blues	100
Warriors Mark Fencibles	100
Pennsylvania Volunteers in the Mexican War	101
Second Pennsylvania Volunteer Infantry	101
Sketches of Mexican War Veterans	103

A BRIEF HISTORY OF THE MEXICAN WAR

The war with Mexico was brought about by the disregard of the Mexican Government for the lives and property of the Americans, the settlement of Texas by the Americans, their declaration of independence from Mexico, and lastly, by the annexation of Texas by the United States as a State of the union.

By the Treaty of 1819 with Spain, and the purchase of Louisiana, the United States relinquished whatever claim it had to Texas, then a part of Mexico. However, in 1821, Mexico revolted and established her independence, which placed Texas under Mexican authorities, who, being jealous of the rapid settlement of Texas, inaugurated measures to impede the progress of that part of Mexico laying north of the Rio Grande River, to the extent of reducing the State of Texas to the status of a province, and prohibiting the immigration of all persons from the United States.

Efforts to purchase Texas from the Mexican Government were made in the year 1827, and again in 1829, by the United States, but without success. Disrespect had been shown the American flag on a number of occasions, depredations had been committed upon American commerce, and the property of American citizens had been confiscated over a period of time, without redress, and all efforts to reach a settlement only resulted in evasions and delays on the part of the Mexican Government.

In 1835 the Texans proclaimed their independence from the rule of Mexico, and when the Mexican army attempted to subjugate the revolutionists, they were met by the Texan army and defeated. In March, 1836, the strongly reinforced Mexican army captured a detachment of four hundred Texans under Colonel Fannin near Goliad. This entire force was marched out under guards and shot down by their captors. Only a few of the captives managed to escape, one of them being John Holliday, a grandson of Adam, after whom the town of Hollidaysburg is named.

After days of privation, living on roots and uncooked food, hiding by day and traveling by night, John Holliday finally joined his companions of the Texan army and related the fate of his comrades at Goliad, and his experiences in surviving the Mexican cavalry who hunted the escaping Texans like rabbits, and sabred them down where found.

John Holliday returned to his home at Hollidaysburg to recuperate. Here he was honored in every possible way, and on his return was handed a sum of money to carry to the Texans to aid them in their war for independence. Upon his return he was commissioned a Captain in the Texan army and sent on the ill-fated Sante Fe expedition which resulted in the capture of the entire force, and his imprisonment near Mexico City. Being released about two years later and while returning to the States aboard a steamer, he died of typhoid fever and was buried in the Gulf of Mexico.

The siege and annihilation of the Texan forces under Colonel Travis in the Alamo at San Antonio followed. The determination of the Texans to be free of Mexican authority, and the revenge of the death of their countrymen who died in the Alamo and at Goliad, brought them complete victory over the Mexicans, when on the 21st of April, 1836, the Texan army under General Sam Houston utterly routed the Mexican army at San Jacinto, and captured Santa Ann, President of Mexico and Commander-in-chief of the Mexican army.

The people of Texas then desired to join the United States, but the danger of war with Mexico and other political questions delayed the annexation until the 4th of July, 1845. Upon this action being taken, the Mexican Minister at Washington demanded his passports, and the American Minister left Mexico.

The President of the United States sent an army of 1500 men under the command of General Zachary Taylor to Corpus Christi, on the west bank of the Nueces River, to protect the Texans from invasion during the negotiations, so that at the time of the annexation of Texas as a State, the United States army was in a position to oppose the Mexican army, and actual hostilities soon started, when on the 24th of April, 1846, a detachment of American Dragoons were attacked by a large body of Mexican troops, resulting in the killing of a dozen or more of the American soldiers, and the capture of the remainder.

Following the formal declaration of war on the 11th of May, 1846, the plans of operation included: first, an army of the west to march under General Kearney against New Mexico, and thence westward to co-operate with the fleet, which was to be reinforced, against California; second, an army of the centre under General Wool to invade Mexico from the north. These plans were augmented by a change of operations which involved the use of the fleet to transport an army under General Winfield Scott to Vera Cruz, and from there to invade the country to its capital, Mexico City, and to force the Mexican Government to accept terms of peace.

The principal events and engagements during the Mexican War were as follows:

Palo Alto	Texas	May 8, 1846
Resaca de la Palma	Texas	May 9, 1846
Matamoras	Mexico	May 18, 1846
Monterey	Mexico	Sept. 21, 1846
Buena Vista	Mexico	Feb. 22, 1847
Vera Cruz	Mexico	Mar. 9, 1847
Cerro Gordo	Mexico	Apr. 17, 1847
Churubusco	Mexico	Aug. 18, 1847
Contreras	Mexico	Aug. 18, 1847
Molino Del Ray	Mexico	Sept. 8, 1847
Chapultepec	Mexico	Sept. 12, 1847
Mexico City	Mexico	Sept. 14, 1847

A treaty was concluded at Guadalupe-Hildaga, Mexico, on the 2nd of February, 1848, and ratified by the Congress of the United States on the 16th of March, 1848, which acknowledged the Rio Grande to be the boundary between Texas and Mexico, and an immense area including New Mexico, Upper California, Nevada, Arizona, and a part of Colorado, was ceded to the United States for the sum of $15,000,000 and the settlement in part of the American claims against Mexico.

PENNSYLVANIA MILITIA

During the period following the War of 1812, interest in military affairs and the national defense received very little attention as was the case following all wars in which the United States has been involved. This was due to the Nation's desire to heal the wounds and re-adjust itself to the changes brought about by the war, also, being victorious, no other Nation desired to become involved and receive a taste of warfare as meted to the British at New Orleans. Interest, therefore, lagged in the formation of military units and it was not until many years after the war that the first company was organized in this section.

As military units were formed throughout the State and interest increased in such matters, these companies were organized into battalions, battalions into regiments and divisions were designated. The Militia muster days of the Revolutionary War and the War of 1812 gave way to the Military encampments, which lasted for several days' duration, when the companies assembled at some designated place, held competitive and combined drills, parades and social affairs, which all added interest and zest to the life of the soldiers. At these encampments the annual election of officers was held, and were often marked with spirited campaigning of a political nature. The first military encampment to be held at Hollidaysburg, for training was on the 13th. of May, 1839, and included the enrolled militia of the 151st Regiment, 2nd Brigade, 10th Division.

Another early encampment was held by the 4th Battalion of Huntingdon County, composed of the Union Cavalry of Antis Township, Washington Grays of Hollidaysburg and the Williamsburg Blues, assembled at Williamsburg for drill on the 12th of May, 1841.

The 4th Battalion of Huntingdon held an encampment on the 19th of October, 1841, at the Race Track, Northfield, Hollidaysburg which was attended by the following companies:

Cambria Guards	Captain W. A. Smith
Williamsburg Blues	Captain McKiernan
Bedford Artillery	Captain Reamer
Independent Grays (Bedford)	Captain Arnod
Union Cavalry	Captain Bell
Washington Grays	Major Williams

A grand military encampment was held October, 1843, on the Jackson farm in Gaysport, (Camp Warren) which was attended by seventeen companies and as many bands, and proved to be a great military and social success.

UNION CAVALRY

The first military company known to have been organized entirely within the area which now constitutes Blair County was the Union Cavalry. Men for this company came from Pleasant Valley, Sinking Valley and Tuckahoe Valley, with headquarters probably at Bells Mills, now Bellwood.

This Company met at the home of David Robison in Pleasant Valley on the 2nd. of June, 1838, for the purpose of organizing a company of cavalry, and the officers known to have served were Captain Martin Bell, Captain Benjamin F. Bell, First Lieutenant William S. Hamilton and Second Lieutenant James W. Riddle.

WASHINGTON GRAYS

The first military company ever formed in Hollidaysburg, was organized Oct. 5, 1839. Its original officers being William Williams, Captain; J. A. Landis, First Lieutenant; and George R. McFarlane, Second Lieutenant. This company passed out of existence at the time of the Mexican War, when, not being accepted for service as a unit, many of its members enlisted in the American Highlanders, (Company M, 2nd Pennsylvania Infantry) of Ebensburg. This Company drilled every Saturday at the Warehouse of the Western Transportation Company during 1839, and in later years at the Hollidaysburg Depot. Its commanding officers for the various years were Captains James King and William Williams.

WILLIAMSBURG BLUES

A company of "light" infantry was organized at Williamsburg prior to 1841, and designated as the 60th Company, 29th Regiment, 2nd Brigade, 10th Division, but known locally as the Williamsburg Blues. The officers for this company during the various years, were Captains McKiernan and Thomas K. Fluke; First Lieutenant James M. Kinkead and Second Lieutenants Joseph Rees and Alexander R. McKamey.

This company tendered its services to the President as is evidenced by the following resolution which appeared in the newspapers of that day.

"Armory, Williamsburg Blues, May 22, 1846. 'Whereas, the President of the United States has been authorized to accept the services of fifty thousand volunteers, to ensure effective operation against the Mexican aggressors, and believing that duty calls loudly upon every American to respond to the call of his country when our rights are invaded or our flag insulted; therefore, Resolved, that we hereby tender our services to President Polk, in the event of the War requiring our aid, to repair to the scene of conflict, and battle for the glorious cause of American liberty.'"

"Resolved, that Lieutenant J. M. Kinkead transmit a copy of the above preamble and resolutions to President Polk. 'Resolved, That the foregoing preamble and resolutions be published in all papers of the County.'" Thomas K. Fluke, Captain.

WARRIOR'S MARK FENCIBLES

A company of Pennsylvania Militia was organized at Warrior's Mark sometime prior to the war with Mexico and was known as Company Number 57, the Warrior's Mark Fencibles, consisting of eighty-five members.

A number of the residents of that section of Blair County now included in Snyder Township and Tyrone Borough were members of this company.

The officers of the Warrior's Mark Fencibles at the time of offering their services to the Governor of Pennsylvania for duty during the Mexican War were as follows: Captain James Bell; First Lieutenant James Thompson; Second Lieutenant James A. Gano.

THE PENNSYLVANIA VOLUNTEERS

War was declared against Mexico, on the 13th of May, 1846, by an Act of Congress which stated that "by the act of the Republic of Mexico a state of war exists between that government and the United States."

The President of the United States made a requisition on the Governor of Pennsylvania for six regiments and the Governor's call for volunteers brought responses from over ninety volunteer companies, numbering eight thousand three hundred and seventy-four men. Among the companies located in this section of Pennsylvania, known to have volunteered, were the Washington Grays of Hollidaysburg, the Williamsburg Blues and the Warrior's Mark Fencibles. None of these companies were accepted, however, a number of the enrolled members were accepted for duty in other companies, principally in companies included in the Second Pennsylvania Infantry.

SECOND PENNSYLVANIA INFANTRY

Practically all soldiers who enlisted from Blair County for service in the Mexican War served in the 2nd Pennsylvania Regiment of Infantry, commanded by Colonel William B. Roberts, and Lieutenant Colonel John W. Geary, later governor of Pennsylvania.

Colonel Geary had previously commanded the American Highlanders from Ebensburg, and his company having been under strength, he suggested to William Williams of Hollidaysburg that he recruit a group of men in Blair County and accepted a lieutenancy in the Company. The American Highlanders were designated Company B, Second Pennsylvania Infantry and went out with seventy-six officers and men under the command of Captain John Humphrey; First Lieutenant Samuel W. Black; and Second Lieutenants Elisha Lucketts and William Williams.

A similar arrangement, to recruit a group of men at Williamsburg to bring Company M up to strength was effected and Alexander R. McKamey of Williamsburg received a Commission as Lieutenant and was later promoted to Captain.

Captain Samuel M. Taylor's Company from Bedford which became Company L, of the second regiment, also, had several members from Blair County, so that in all, the number of Blair County men enrolled in the various companies of the regiment were almost sufficient to make up one company.

The various companies whose services were accepted for duty in the War with Mexico proceeded to Pittsburgh during the last of December 1846, where the regiment was organized, the companies were re-designated as units of the Second Pennsylvania Infantry, and the battalion and regimental officers elected.

The regiment then embarked on steamboats and went down the Ohio and Mississippi Rivers to New Orleans where they encamped at Plaine Chalmette. The troops from many states assembled here, to embark on ships for Vera Cruz. Companies B, D, and G, embarked on board the *Gen. Veizie* and being driven out of its course by a storm, came to the coast of Cuba after twenty-five days. Smallpox broke out on board and the transport was placed in quarantine at Lobos Island for a month. By the time these three companies joined the main army under General Scott the army had captured Vera Cruz, fought a battle at Cerro Gordo and Jalapa and were on their way to Mexico City.

The Second Pennsylvania Regiment being re-united, it joined in the attack on the Castle of Chapultepec, the West Point of Mexico, which was well defended and only captured by assault during which many ladders were used to scale the walls. The final victory came with the capture of the City of Mexico, in which this regiment participated, and upon the surrender of the City the Second Pennsylvania Infantry was the first to enter the city.

Going into camp at San Angel, nine miles from the City of Mexico, the regiment recuperated and took count of the losses suffered during the army's successful march to the Capital of Mexico. In Company B, alone, of the 76 officers and men who went out with the company, only thirty-five remained fit for duty on the 7th of February, 1848, while 24 had been killed or died of wounds and 13 had been discharged for injuries, wounds and other causes.

The route of march from Vera Cruz to the City of Mexico was marked with mounds and small crosses, indicating the burial places of members of the Second Pennsylvania Regiment. Similar mounds indicated the graves of members of other units, and among those who "slept" in soldiers' graves were Texas Rangers, Yankees from New England States, Volunteers from Tennessee, cowboys of the Plains, adventurers, soldiers of fortune, and gentlemen "unafraid," but "Americans all", who had avenged the "Alamo" and moved the western boundary of the United States from the plains of the Mississippi Valley to the coast of the Pacific Ocean.

At Colonia San Rafael, near Mexico City, is the oldest National Cemetery owned and maintained by the United States government. In this Cemetery repose the remains of those whose bodies were not returned to the States, numbering 1363. A stone shaft with the following inscribed words stands sentinel: "To the memory of the American Soldiers who perished in this Valley in 1847, whose bones, collected by their Country's order, are buried here."

SKETCHES OF MEXICAN WAR VETERANS

BARBOUR, SAMUEL S. G.   Enrolled at Hollidaysburg as a Private in Company B, 2nd Pennsylvania Infantry on the 21st of December, 1846, and discharged at Pueblo, Mexico, on the 5th of November, 1847.

BEEGLE, JOHN M.   Military services not available, possibly served as a Captain. Born on the 24th of June, 1805; died on the 28th of July, 1863, and buried in the Lutheran Cemetery at Newry.

CAMPBELL, JOHN   Enrolled at Newry as a Private in Company B, 2nd Pennsylvania Infantry on the 21st of December, 1846, and discharged on the 14th of July, 1848.
Born in Ireland on the 8th of August, 1826, died on the 14th of May, 1903, and was buried in the St. Patrick's Cemetery at Newry.   Survived by his widow, Sarah Ann Hoover.

CAMPBELL, SYLVESTER H.   Enrolled at Williamsburg as a Private in Company M, 2nd Pennsylvania Infantry on the 5th of May, 1847, and discharged on the 21st of July, 1848.

CANNON, JOSEPH N.   Served as a Private in Company B, 2nd United States Infantry from the 4th of July, 1845, until December, 1848.
Born on the 4th of July, 1829; died on the 25th of April, 1907, and buried in the Logan Valley Cemetery at Bellwood.   Also served during the Civil War.

CASWELL, WILLIAM R.   Served in the United States Navy as a 1cl Boy from the 21st of August, 1846, until the 17th of November, 1847.
Born in 1827; died on the 9th of August, 1891, and buried in the St. Paul's Lutheran Cemetery near Williamsburg.

CLARK, THOMAS   Enrolled at Hollidaysburg as a Private in Company C, 2nd Pennsylvania Infantry on the 6th of December, 1847, and discharged on the 20th of July, 1848.

CLARKE, JOHN MORRIS   Served as a Private in Company I, 2nd United States Dragoons.
Born in Delaware County, Pennsylvania, on the 6th of February, 1829; died on the 15th of June, 1890, and buried in the Fairview Cemetery at Altoona.   Also served during the Civil War.

CONDO, JOHN   Served as a Private in Company A, 1st Pennsylvania Infantry from the 26th of November, 1846, until the 24th of March, 1847.
Born on the 17th of September, 1816; died on the 22nd of July, 1882, and buried in the Fairview Cemetery at Altoona.

CONFER, JACOB M.   Enrolled at Hollidaysburg as a Private in Company B, 2nd Pennsylvania Infantry, on the 21st of December, 1847, and discharged on the 14th of July, 1848.

CRAWFORD, DAVID   Commissioned a First Lieutenant in the 9th Company, 1st Oregon Territory Infantry, on the 14th of May, 1848, and served against the Cayuse Indians.
Born at Newry on the 19th of November, 1820; joined an emigrant train in 1844 and crossed the plains to Oregon; died on the 21st of August, 1903, and buried in the Presbyterian Cemetery in Sinking Valley.

SOLDIERS OF BLAIR COUNTY

CROZIER, RICHARD J. Served as a Private in Company D, 2nd Pennsylvania Infantry from the 4th of January, 1847, until the 14th of July, 1848.

Born in Ireland, in 1825; died on the 15th of May, 1900, and buried in the Fairview Cemetery at Altoona. Also served in the Civil War.

CULP, SAMUEL Served as a Private in Company D, 5th United States Infantry from May, 1847, until September, 1848.

Born on the 1st of March, 1824; died on the 3rd of February, 1899, and buried in the Lutheran Cemetery in Sinking Valley. Also served during the Civil War.

DITCH, DAVID Enrolled at Williamsburg as a Private in Company M, 2nd Pennsylvania Infantry, on the 5th of May, 1847, and discharged on the 21st of July, 1848.

DRIPPS, ANDREW W. Served as a Private in Company B, 2nd Pennsylvania Infantry from the 4th of January, 1847, until the 14th of July, 1848.

Born 1825, and resided at Hollidaysburg in 1850.

DUNLAP, MATTHEW Enrolled at Williamsburg as a Private in Company M, 2nd Pennsylvania Infantry, on the 5th of May, 1847, and discharged on the 21st of July, 1848.

EDWARDS, JONATHAN Enrolled at Williamsburg as a Private in Company M, 2nd Pennsylvania Infantry, on the 5th of May, 1847, and discharged on the 21st of July, 1848.

FEATHER, JOHN Enrolled at Bedford as a Corporal in Company L, 2nd Pennsylvania Infantry, on the 6th of May, 1846, and discharged on the 14th of July, 1848.

Born on the 10th of April, 1827; died on the 6th of May, 1892, and buried in the Lutheran Cemetery at Claysburg.

FILEY, GEORGE Enrolled at Williamsburg as a Sergeant in Company M, 2nd Pennsylvania Infantry, on the 5th of May, 1847.

Died on board the steamship *Col. Yell*, at Louisville, on the 1st of June, 1847.

FOCKLER, ELI Enrolled at Williamsburg as a Private in Company M, 2nd Pennsylvania Infantry, on the 5th of May, 1847, and discharged on the 21st of July, 1848.

GARDNER, JOSEPH W. Enrolled at Williamsburg as a Private in Company M, 2nd Pennsylvania Infantry, on the 5th of May, 1847, was wounded on the 10th of September, 1847 at Chapultepec, Mexico, and discharged on the 20th of July, 1848.

Born on the 16th of June, 1825; died on the 12th of December, 1898, and buried in the Oak Ridge Cemetery at Altoona. Also served during the Civil War.

GIFFORD, JAMES Military services not available. Obituary states that he served in the Mexican and Civil Wars.

Born on the 26th of July, 1816; died on the 4th of November, 1895, and buried in the Presbyterian Cemetery in Sinking Valley.

HANNAH, DAVID W. Enrolled at Williamsburg as a Musician, Company M, 2nd Pennsylvania Infantry, on the 5th of May, 1847, and discharged on the 21st of July, 1848.

HASSETT, JOHN Enrolled at Newry as a Private in Company B, 2nd Pennsylvania Infantry, on the 21st of December, 1846, and discharged on the 20th of March, 1847.

HELSEL, HENRY S. Enrolled at Bedford as a Private in Company L, 2nd Pennsylvania Infantry, on the 6th of May, 1846, and discharged on the 14th of July, 1848.

Born on the 14th of August, 1826; died on the 19th of December, 1914, and buried in the Mt. Moriah Cemetery at Blue Knob.

HENRY, HARRISON Served as a Corporal in Company B, 2nd Pennsylvania Infantry, from the 21st of December, 1846; died of disease in Mexico City on the 22nd of October, 1847; age 24, and buried in the Presbyterian Cemetery at Hollidaysburg.

HENRY, JOHN Enrolled at Hollidaysburg as a Private in Company H, 2nd Pennsylvania Infantry, on the 17th of November, 1847, and discharged on the 12th of July, 1848.

HERD, JAMES H. Enrolled at Hollidaysburg as a Private in Company B, 2nd Pennsylvania Infantry, on the 21st of December, 1846, and discharged on the 25th of July, 1847.

HIGGINS, JACOB C. Enrolled at Williamsburg as a Private in Company M, 2nd Pennsylvania Infantry, on the 5th of May, 1847, and discharged on the 21st of July, 1848.
Born at Williamsburg on the 7th of March, 1826; died on the 1st of June, 1893, and buried in the Grandview Cemetery at Johnstown. Also served during the Civil War.

HOFIUS, DAVID H. Enrolled at Bedford as a Second Lieutenant of Company I, 2nd Pennsylvania Infantry, on the 6th of May, 1846, and discharged on the 1st of November, 1847.
Born on the 4th of August, 1818; died on the 25th of July, 1859, and buried in the Presbyterian Cemetery at Hollidaysburg.

HOLLAND, THOMAS W. Served as a Sergeant in Company B, 2nd Pennsylvania Infantry, from the 21st of December, 1846, until the 14th of July, 1848.
Born in 1821; died on the 14th of June, 1902, and buried in the St. Patrick's Cemetery at Newry. Also served during the Civil War.

HOUCK, JAMES Enrolled at Williamsburg as a Private in Company M, 2nd Pennsylvania infantry, on the 5th of May, 1847, and died in a hospital at Mexico City on the 17th of January, 1848, aged 20.

HUFF, GEORGE Military services not available.
Born on the 24th of August, 1812; died on the 19th of January, 1858, and buried in the Fairview Cemetery at Altoona.

KELLY, JAMES Military services not available.
Died on the 10th of April, 1865, and buried in the Greenwood Cemetery near Altoona.

KENSINGER, GEORGE Enrolled at Williamsburg as a Private in Company M, 2nd Pennsylvania Infantry, on the 5th of May, 1847, and discharged on the 21st of July, 1848.
Born in 1803; died on the 22nd of September, 1886, and buried in the Schmucker's Cemetery near Williamsburg. Also served during the Civil War.

KIDD, JOSEPH L. Enrolled at Williamsburg as a Sergeant in Company M, 2nd Pennsylvania Infantry, on the 5th of May, 1847, and discharged on the 21st of July, 1848.
Born on the 7th of October, 1823, died on the 8th of May, 1903, and buried in the Presbyterian Cemetery at Williamsburg. Also served during the Civil War.

KOUNSMAN, WILLIAM S. Military service not available.
Born on the 23rd of April, 1811; died on the 24th of October, 1876, and buried in the Carson Valley Cemetery near Duncansville.

LIEBIG, FREDERICK R. Served as a Private in the United States Marines from the 3rd of July, 1846, until the 28th of September, 1848.
Born on the 19th of May, 1826; died on the 13th of October, 1914, and buried in the Oak Ridge Cemetery at Altoona. Also served during the Civil War.

LEWIS, THOMAS Enrolled at Hollidaysburg as a Private in Company B, 2nd Pennsylvania Infantry, on the 21st of December, 1846, and died in the hospital at Pueblo, Mexico.

McCLANAHAN, JAMES C. Enrolled at Hollidaysburg as a Private in Company M, 2nd Pennsylvania Infantry, on the 5th of May, 1847, and was killed in battle on the 14th of September, 1847.

McCLOSKEY, CORNELIUS K. Served as a Private in Company B, 2nd Pennsylvania Infantry, from the 21st of December, 1846, until the 6th of December, 1848.

Born in 1817; died on the 24th of October, 1889, and buried in the St. Patrick's Cemetery at Tunnel Hill.

McDERMOT, BARNABAS Enrolled at Ebensburg as a Sergeant in Company D, 2nd Pennsylvania Infantry, on the 4th of December, 1846, and discharged on the 14th of July, 1848.

Born in 1822; died on the 16th of August, 1890, and buried in the St. John's Cemetery in Altoona. Also served during the Civil War.

McDERMOT, FRANCIS C. Enrolled at Ebensburg as a Private in Company D, 2nd Pennsylvania Infantry, on the 4th of December, 1846, and discharged on the 14th of July, 1848.

Born 1828, resided in Altoona in 1885.

McELHATAN, FRANKLIN Enrolled at Hollidaysburg as a Private in Compnay B, 2nd Pennsylvania Infantry, on the 21st of December, 1846, and discharged on the 28th of February, 1848.

McKAMEY, ALEXANDER R. Served as a Captain of Company M, 2nd Pennsylvania Infantry, from the 5th of May, 1847, until the 21st of July, 1848.

Born 1816; died in 1854, and buried in the Presbyterian Cemetery at Williamsburg.

McKEAGE, JOHN (Military record not available)

Born on the 15th of April, 1827; died on the 12th of February, 1874, and buried in the Presbyterian Cemetery at Hollidaysburg. Also served during the Civil War.

McKIERNAN, JOHN S. Enrolled at Williamsburg as a Private in Company M, 2nd Pennsylvania Infantry, on the 5th of May, 1847, and served until the 1st of August, 1847.

McLAUGHLIN, JOHN Enrolled at Hollidaysburg as a Private in Company B, 2nd Pennsylvania Infantry, on the 10th of December, 1846, and served until the 18th of February, 1848.

McNAMARA, JOHN Enrolled at Newry as a Private in Company B, 2nd Pennsylvania Infantry, on the 21st of December, 1846, and served until the 25th of April, 1847.

Born 1820; died in hospital at San Angel, Mexico, on the 25th of April, 1847, and buried in the Presbyterian Cemetery at Hollidaysburg.

McPHERSON, ALEXANDER Military services not available.

Born in 1813; died on the 6th of November, 1892, and buried in the Greenlawn Cemetery at Roaring Spring. Also served during the Civil War.

McCHESNEY, JAMES Enrolled at Hollidaysburg as a Private in Company B, 2nd Pennsylvania Infantry, on the 21st of December, 1846, and served until the 14th of July, 1848.

MASON, SAMUEL D. Served as a Corporal in Company H, 4th United States Artillery, from 1847 until the 25th of August, 1850.

Born on the 27th of March, 1825; died on the 25th of April, 1889, and buried in the St. John's Cemetery at Altoona.

MAUK, PAUL S. Enrolled at Bedford as a Private in Company L, 2nd Pennsylvania Infantry, on the 6th of May, 1846, and served until the 14th of July, 1848.

Born on the 16th of March, 1829; died on the 27th of July, 1896, and buried in the Union Cemetery at Claysburg.

MONTGOMERY, JOHN Enrolled at Williamsburg as a Private in Company M, 2nd Pennsylvania Infantry, on the 5th of May, 1847, and served until the 21st of July, 1848.

THE MEXICAN WAR

MURRAY, WILLIAM GRAY   Served as a Sergeant in Company G, 2nd Pennsylvania Infantry from the 26th of December, 1846, until the 9th of April, 1847, when commissioned a Second Lieutenant and assigned to the 11th United States Infantry. Resigned on the 14th of August, 1848.

Born in Ireland, on the 25th of July, 1825; died on the 23rd of March, 1862, and buried in the St. Mary's Cemetery at Hollidaysburg. Killed in action during the Civil War.

MYERS, AUGUSTUS   Enrolled at Hollidaysburg as a Private in Company A, 2nd Pennsylvania Infantry, on the 17th of November, 1847, and served until the 21st of July, 1848.

NEALY, JAMES   Enrolled at Hollidaysburg as a Private in Company B, 2nd Pennsylvania Infantry, on the 21st of December, 1846, and served until the 14th of July, 1848.

NEWBERRY, JAMES   Served as a Private, Company B, 2nd Pennsylvania Infantry, sick and left at Fort Independence, Missouri. Resided at Gaysport.

Born at Chad's Ford, Cumberland County, on the 22nd of January, 1796; died on the 9th of September, 1885, and buried in the National Cemetery at Hampton, Virginia. Also served in the War of 1812 and the Civil War.

O'ROURKE, MICH   Enrolled at Hollidaysburg as a Private in Company B, 2nd Pennsylvania Infantry, on the 11th of November, 1847, and served until the 14th of July, 1848.

OVER, DAVID   Served as a Private in Company L, 2nd Pennsylvania Infantry, from the 6th of May, 1847, until the 14th of July, 1848.

Born at Bedford on the 5th of April, 1825; died on the 21st of December, 1900, and buried in the Presbyterian Cemetery at Hollidaysburg.

PEFFER, HENRY   Enrolled at Hollidaysburg as a Private in Company M, 2nd Regiment of Pennsylvania Infantry, on the 13th of December, 1846, and discharged on the 21st of July, 1848.

REED, PETER S.   Enrolled at Danville on the 26th of December, 1846, as a Private and elected a Second Lieutenant of Company C, 2nd Pennsylvania Infantry, on the 6th of January, 1847. Discharged on the 20th of July, 1848.

Born at Danville in 1824; was one of the original settlers of Altoona; died on the 11th of June, 1882, and buried in Golden City, Colorado. Also served during the Civil War.

REILLY, JOHN   Enrolled at Hollidaysburg on the 21st of December, 1846, as a Fifer in Company B, 2nd Pennsylvania Infantry.

RHODES, ABRAM J.   Enlisted on the 21st of December, 1846, as a Private in Company B, 2nd Pennsylvania Infantry, and discharged on the 14th of July, 1848.

Born on the 1st of January, 1824; died on the 1st of December, 1919, and buried in the Presbyterian Cemetery at Hollidaysburg. The last surviving Mexican War Veteran residing in Blair County.

ROACH, THOMAS   Enrolled at Williamsburg on the 5th of May, 1846, as a Private in Company M, 2nd Pennsylvania Infantry, and was discharged on the 21st of July, 1848.

SHRIVER, FREDERICK   Enrolled at Hollidaysburg on the 21st of December, 1846, as a Private in Company B, 2nd Pennsylvania Infantry, and discharged on the 14th of July, 1848.

STONE, WASHINGTON J.   Enrolled at Hollidaysburg on the 21st of December, 1846, as a Private in Company B, 2nd Pennsylvania Infantry, and discharged on the 11th of May, 1847.

Born on the 27th of July, 1826; died on the 4th of June, 1862, and buried in the Lutheran Cemetery at Hollidaysburg. Also served during the Civil War.

TAYLOR, JAMES R. Served as a Private in Company M, 2nd Pennsylvania Infantry, from the 5th of May, 1847, until the 21st of July, 1848.

Born on the 15th of September, 1830; died on the 23rd of July, 1892, and buried in the Oak Ridge Cemetery at Altoona. Also served during the Civil War.

WHITE, LORENZO E. Enrolled at Williamsburg on the 5th of May, 1847, as a Corporal in Company M, 2nd Pennsylvania Infantry, and discharged on the 5th of May, 1848.

Born on the 10th of May, 1821; died on the 8th of January, 1904, and buried in the Oak Ridge Cemetery at Altoona.

WILLIAMS, WILLIAM Commissioned a Second Lieutenant on the 21st of December, 1846, of Company B, 2nd Pennsylvania Infantry; promoted a First Lieutenant on the 1st of February, 1848, and discharged on the 14th of July, 1848.

Born at Greensburg, Pennsylvania, on the 7th of June, 1827; died on the 30th of January, 1906, and buried in the Presbyterian Cemetery at Hollidaysburg. Also served during the Civil War.

WILSON, JOHN S. Enrolled at Hollidaysburg on the 18th of December, 1847, as a Private in Company B, 2nd Pennsylvania Infantry, and discharged on the 14th of July, 1848.

WILSON, WILLIAM H. Enrolled at Williamsburg on the 5th of May, 1847 as a Private in Company M, 2nd Pennsylvania Infantry.

Born in 1827; died on the 19th of February, 1891, and buried in the Presbyterian Cemetery at Williamsburg.

WISEGARVER, GEORGE W. Served as a Sergeant in Company F, 5th United States Infantry.

Born on the 17th of April, 1825; died on the 1st of June, 1852, and buried in the Sarah Furnace Cemetery near Claysburg.

ZENTRY, GEORGE W. Enrolled at Hollidaysburg on the 21st of December, 1846, as a Private in Company B, 2nd Pennsylvania Infantry, and discharged on the 17th of August, 1847.

PART IV

THE CIVIL WAR

Sketches of the Military Organizations of Blair County during the period from the close of the Mexican War to the close of the Civil War.

A history of the Posts of the Grand Army of the Republic and other veterans' organizations of Blair County.

Register of all Civil War Veterans, giving the rank, organization, year of birth and death, and place of burial.

SPECIAL ABBREVIATIONS USED IN THIS SECTION

Bn	*Battalion*	Nrs	*Nurse*
Bgd	*Brigade*	Prov	*Provisional*
Bug	*Bugler*	Q.M.	*Quartermaster*
Cpn	*Chaplain*	Res	*Reserve*
Cpl	*Corporal*	2Lt	*Second Lieutenant*
Cpt	*Captain*	Sig	*Signal*
Frn	*Fireman*	Smn	*Seaman*
Gnr	*Gunner*	Sgn	*Surgeon*
Ind	*Independent*	U	*Unassigned*
1Lt	*First Lieutenant*	U.S.C.T.	*United States Colored Troops*
Mil	*Militia*	V.R.C.	*Veterans' Reserve Corps*
Mus	*Musician*		

(m)....also served Mexican **War**

(s)......also served Spanish-American **War**

INDEX TO PART IV
THE CIVIL WAR

Brief history of the Civil War	111
Military organizations prior to the Civil War	113
Constitution and By-laws of the Juniata Rifles	115
Military organizations during the Civil War	119
Third Pennsylvania Infantry	120
Fourteenth Pennsylvania Infantry	120
Sixty-second Pennsylvania Infantry	121
Thirty-first Pennsylvania Infantry	122
First Pennsylvania Cavalry	122
Eighty-fourth Pennsylvania Infantry	123
Fifty-fifth Pennsylvania Infantry	124
Fifty-third Pennsylvania Infantry	124
Seventy-sixth Pennsylvania Infantry	125
Ninth Pennsylvania Cavalry	126
One hundred and Tenth Pennsylvania Infantry	126
Twelfth Pennsylvania Cavalry	127
Second Pennsylvania Cavalry	128
One hundred and Twenty-fifth Pennsylvania Infantry	128
One hundred and Thirty-seventh Pennsylvania Infantry	129
Pennsylvania Militia of 1862	130
Pennsylvania Militia of 1863	131
"The Chicken Raiders"	132
Bell's Independent Cavalry, Pennsylvania Militia	134
Forty-sixth Pennsylvania Militia	134
Independent Battalion, Pennsylvania Militia	135
Twenty-second Pennsylvania Cavalry	135
Thirteenth Pennsylvania Cavalry	136
Nineteenth Pennsylvania Cavalry	136
One hundred and Eighty-fourth Pennsylvania Infantry	137
One hundred and Ninety-first Pennsylvania Infantry	138
Pennsylvania Militia of 1864	138
Ninety-first Pennsylvania Infantry	138
Two hundred and Eighth Pennsylvania Infantry	139
Two hundred and Fifth Pennsylvania Infantry	139
First Pennsylvania Artillery	140
Fifty-seventh Pennsylvania Infantry	140
One hundred and Ninety-second Pennsylvania Infantry	141
One hundred and Fourth Pennsylvania Infantry	141
Seventy-seventh Pennsylvania Infantry	141
One hundred and Third Pennsylvania Infantry	142
Veterans' Organizations	143
Col. William G. Murray Post No. 39, G.A.R.	144
Lt. S. C. Potts Post No. 62, G.A.R.	145
Lieut. H. N. Lower Post No. 82, G.A.R.	146
Col. D. M. Jones Post No. 172, G.A.R.	147
Sanford F. Beyer Post No. 426, G.A.R.	148
Jas. H. Gibboney Post No. 466, G.A.R.	149
Fred C. Ward Post No. 468, G.A.R.	150
Lt. Robert M. Johnston Post No. 474, G.A.R.	151
Peter Shuman Post No. 574, G.A.R.	152
Register of Civil War Veterans	153

A BRIEF HISTORY OF THE CIVIL WAR

In April, 1865, more than a million of men were in the military service of the United States. A still larger number had been previously enrolled and discharged.

To these must be added a roll of names which, at that time, numbered over three hundred and fifty thousand,—THE GRAND ARMY OF THE DEAD.

The Union Army suffered the following casualities:

Killed in battle	67,058
Died of wounds and other injuries	43,032
Died of disease	224,586
Died from causes not classified	24,852
Total	359,528

The Army had taken part in more than two thousand engagements, many of them of minor importance as to numbers engaged or results attained, while others were mighty battles which strained all the resources and tested the fullest powers of endurance of great opposing armies.

The Navy, with 122,000 men employed, had borne an equally important part, following, watching, and capturing privateers of the enemy in foreign seas, patrolling the long line of coast from Cape Charles to the Rio Grande, blockading ports, capturing forts, and giving, often at critical times, assistance and protection to the Army in many of its engagements.

The Secretary of War, Edwin M. Stanton, suggested that the armies of Major General George G. Meade and Major General William T. Sherman should be formally reviewed in the city of Washington before their final discharge from the service of the United States.

The Army of the Potomac, the Army of the Tennessee, and the Army of Georgia therefore marched to the vicinity of Washington to be reviewed on the 23rd and 24th of May, 1865, for which the necessary orders were issued by Lieutenant General Ulysses S. Grant. The Army of the Ohio remained in North Carolina under command of Major General John M. Schofield.

The public and private buildings of the National Capital were profusely decorated; triumphal arches and reviewing-stands were erected at different points, and vast crowds of people gathered from all sections to honor the returning veterans.

The teachers and pupils of the public schools of Washington were assembled on the terrace and balconies of the capital and waved banners and sang patriotic songs as the soldiers passed. Upon a strip of canvas along the front of the capital was inscribed the legend: "The ONLY NATIONAL DEBT WE CAN NEVER PAY IS THE DEBT WE OWE THE VICTORIOUS UNION SOLDIERS."

Representatives of various States had erected stands, which were filled by their sons and daughters, who, while heartily joining in the honors accorded to all troops, enthusiastically applauded those who more directly represented their own particular States.

The principal reviewing-stand was erected near the Executive Mansion, and was occupied by President Andrew Johnson and his Cabinet, by diplomats and envoys of foreign nations, and by governors of States. Among the latter were some especially beloved by the soldiers and honored by the nation for their invaluable and patriotic services as "war governors,"—notably John A. Andrews, of Massachusetts, and Andrew G. Curtin, of Pennsylvania.

On the first day Lieutenant General Grant occupied a position near the President, with distinguished naval officers and General Sherman, Brigadier General Oliver A. Howard, Brigadier General John A. Logan, and others, whose troops were to parade on the next day. It was while on this stand that General Logan was informed that he had been assigned to the command of the Army of the Tennessee. General Howard having been appointed Commissioner of the Freedman's Bureau.

Many of the officers and large numbers of the soldiers were garlanded with flowers as they passed along the line of march.

"Sherman's bummers" helped to relieve whatever of monotony there was in the continual tramp, tramp, tramp of the armies. A number were mounted on mules or on sorry-looking horses borrowed from some quartermaster's camp of condemned animals, and carrying chickens, pigs and vegetables; others on foot swung along in the free-and-easy gait learned on their march to the sea.

It was estimated that nearly 150,000 men participated in these ceremonies—the Army of the Potomac, 80,000; the Army of the Tennessee, 36,000; and the Army of Georgia, 33,000.

Never before had such a pageant been witnessed at the capital of any nation—the passage of an army of citizen soldiers who, having by their valor saved the nation, were now present only that those necessary details might be completed which would enable them to take places in the ranks of peaceful citizens.

With worn uniforms and tattered ensigns telling eloquently of service in the field, these men were now only anxious to return to their homes and loved ones. Though joyfully returning, and, as representatives of all who had honorably served in the armies and navies of the Union, thus receiving the plaudits of the people whom they had so ably served, there were sad thoughts not inharmonious with the occasion.

As they passed the reviewing-stand where representative men were assembled in their honor, the marching soldiers missed above all others that rugged, homely face which now would have been lit with a halo of glory. The great patient heart, that for four years had borne such a fearful strain, was now stilled. In all the land no one was nearer the soldier's heart than Abraham Lincoln.

Other forms were missing from the group—leaders of corps and of armies of whom Major General John F. Reynolds, of Pennsylvania, Major General James B. McPherson, of Ohio, and Major General John Sedgwick, of Connecticut, were types.

But the thoughts of the soldiers were not then so much with the absent leaders as with the more familiar forms of comrades, dear to their hearts, but now numbered with the dead. Perchance they had been playmates in school-boy days and bosom friends in maturer years.

Together they had responded to the call of an imperiled country, together had faced the dangers of the service. In camp and bivouac they had slept under the same blankets and shared the contents of their haversacks and canteens.

These, their comrades, had not lived to hear the joyful shouts of victory, and were not to receive the embraces of their loved ones. They had died that the Nation might live, and their graves were mute reminders that there was no longer a question as to whether one flag or two should kiss the northern breezes as they swept towards the gulf.

The fond affection cherished for the honored dead but stimulated the ties of sympathy and love for comrades living and sharing the thrilling memories of the years of national strife and warfare now happily over.

They were soon to part, each in his own way to fight the battle of life, to form new ties, new friendships, but never could they forget the sacred bond of comradeship welded in the fire of battle, that in after years, should be their stimulus to take upon themselves the work confided to the people by President Lincoln "to bind up the Nation's wounds," "to care for him who shall have borne the battle, and for his widow and his orphan."

PENNSYLVANIA MILITIA

It appears that all military units functioning prior to the Mexican War passed out of existence with the war and as far as known none were revived under the same name or same group of officers. No drastic changes occurred in the laws pertaining to the Pennsylvania Militia. The Adjutant General issued orders and regulations according to the laws governing the volunteer and uniformed Militia. Companies were organized at various towns and communities according to need and the local interest.

Interest increased in military affairs with the question of secession becoming acute and the possibility of a civil conflict, so that, by 1859, Blair County had eleven military units with regimental and brigade officers to command them. Lieutenant Colonel Jacob Higgins, of Williamsburg, commanded the local regiment, designated as the 1st Regiment, 4th Brigade, 16th Division, Pennsylvania Volunteer Militia, and his appointments to the regimental staff for the year beginning August, 1858, were as follows: Surgeon R. W. Christy with the rank of Major, Assistant Surgeon John Fay with the rank of Captain, Judge Advocate D. H. Hofius with rank of Major, Adjutant J. C. Osterloh with rank of First Lieutenant, Quartermaster C. R. Hostetter with the rank of First Lieutenant, Staff Sergeant-major Lorenzo E. White, and Drum Major Frederick E. Shindel.

The Brigade and Regimental officers elected in June, 1859, by the various units, with each member having a vote, were as follows: Brigadier General B. F. Bell, Brigade Inspector J. C. Osterloh, Colonel Jacob Higgins, Lieutenant Colonel William Williams, and Major A. J. Crissman.

A short sketch of the various military units existing in Blair County prior to the Civil War, arranged in order as to their date of organization, with the number of enrolled members, follows:

HOLLIDAYSBURG GUARDS

The first military unit to be formed in Blair County following the Mexican War was at Hollidaysburg. A company known as the Hollidaysburg Guards was in existence prior to November, 1850, as the newspapers of the 6th of November, 1850, in recording the obsequies in honor of General Zachary Taylor held at Hollidaysburg, states that the visiting militia companies, all from Cambria County, "were handsomely escorted into town by the Hollidaysburg Guards, under command of Captain Drips."

The Hollidaysburg Guards remained in existence but a few years. Their officers were Captain George Bingham, Captain Andrew W. Drips, and Lieutenants William Stone and Washington J. Stone.

BLACK PLUMED RIFLES

Another company to be organized at Hollidaysburg within a few years after the Mexican War, was the Black Plumed Rifles. The officers were Captain Robert McNamara, and Lieutenants James W. Storm and John Campbell. This company disbanded after a few years.

ALTOONA GUARDS

A company of infantrymen formed, probably, about 1855, in Altoona, with a membership of twenty-nine under Captain H. W. Snyder, Lieutenant Joseph W. Gardner, Lieut. G. W. Gwin, became Company B, 3rd Penna. Infantry during the Civil War.

LOGAN RIFLE RANGERS

A company of riflemen, numbering thirty-nine, was organized in Altoona under Captain Jacob S. Szink, Lieutenants Christ R. Hostetter and Frederick Shillinger, and became Company E, 3rd Pennsylvania Infantry.

ALLEGHENY CAVALRY

A troop of Cavalry, numbering twenty-eight, was commanded by Captain David Stiteler, Lieutenants Thomas Hamilton, P. Harpster and David Gardner. Disbanded when not accepted for service in the Civil War.

SCOTT RIFLES

A company of riflemen, numbering twelve, was organized at Duncansville, and later named the Blair County Rifles under Captain Thomas W. Holland, Lieutenants J. C. McCloskey, William McGraw, Samuel A. Andrews, became Company H, 14th Pennsylvania Infantry during the Civil War.

WASHINGTON ARTILLERY

A Martinsburg Company, numbering thirty men, was commanded by Captain A. S. Morrow, Lieutenant I. A. Oellig, and disbanded prior to the Civil War.

HOLLIDAYSBURG FENCIBLES

A company of infantrymen, numbering thirty-eight, existed at Hollidaysburg and commanded by Captains David H. Hofius, Francis P. Minier, John R. McFarlane, Lieutenants John C. Osterloh, Thomas McFarlane, Ensign Anthony Vowinkle, became Company A, 3rd Pennsylvania Infantry during the Civil War.

TYRONE ARTILLERY

A battery of artillery, numbering forty-nine, commanded by Captain James M. Bell, Lieutenants J. G. Ebling, Francis M. Bell, Ensign John L. Burley, became Company D, 3rd Pennsylvania Infantry during the Civil War.

WAYNE GUARDS

A company of infantrymen, numbering twenty-two, of Williamsburg, under Captain William L. Neff, Lieutenants B. Shipley, William R. Ayers, became Company C, 3rd Pennsylvania Infantry during the Civil War.

JUNIATA RIFLES

A company of riflemen, numbering fifty-eight, of Hollidaysburg, was organized on the 22nd of October, 1858, under Captain Alexander M. Lloyd, Lieutenants Robert L. Horrell, E. H. Gardner, George Cunningham, Ensign H. T. Conrad, became Company H, 3rd Pennsylvania Infantry.

EMMETT GUARDS

A company of infantrymen, numbering forty-seven, of Hollidaysburg, under Captain William Williams, Jr., Lieutenants Patrick T. Keyes, M. McNally, Ensign P. T. Walsh, was disbanded when not accepted for duty in the Civil War.

TYRONE CAVALRY

A troop of cavalry, numbering twenty-eight, commanded by Captain James Crowther, Lieutenants R. C. Galbraith, J. H. Burley, Cornet J. H. Cramer, became Company D, 14th Pennsylvania Infantry during the Civil War.

KEYSTONE FENCIBLES

A company of infantrymen was organized at Altoona during the summer of 1859, under Captain William R. Leonard; disbanded.

MARTINSBURG INFANTRY

A company of infantrymen was organized a short time prior to the Civil War, commanded by Captain Alexander Bobb, Lieutenants Josiah C. Sanders, John H. Typher, became Company I, 14th Pennsylvania Infantry during the Civil War.

The Adjutant General's report for 1860, indicated that eleven companies of Militia existed in Blair County, viz: two companies of cavalry, two artillery, four infantry, and three riflemen. This report also stated that these eleven units had the following arms and equipment; two brass six-pounder field pieces, 193 muskets, 193 bayonets, 193 cartridge boxes, 110 bayonet scabbards with belts and plates, 125 rifles, 110 powder horns, 35 pouches, 100 pistols, 50 horses, 50 cavalry swords, and 50 sword belts.

CONSTITUTION AND BY-LAWS

OF THE

Juniata Rifles of Hollidaysburg

"Whereas: We are desirous of forming ourselves into an organized Volunteer Company for the purpose of improvement in Military drill and tactics and believing that all our efforts to that end will be ineffectual and nugatory unless the members thereof are governed and controlled by suitable rules and regulations. We the undersigned members of said Company who hereby subscribe and pledge ourselves severally to keep and maintain inviolate the following Constitution and By-Laws for our organization and government. Hereby holding ourselves subject and liable for any infringement of said Constitution and By-Laws to the fines and forfeitures therein imposed.

Article 1. This Company shall be called and known by the name of the "Juniata Rifles."

Article 2. The officers of this Company shall consist of Commissioned Officers: One Captain, 1 First Lieutenant, 1 Second Lieutenant, Non-commissioned officers: First, Second, Third and Fourth Sergeants. One Quartermaster Sergeant, and First, Second, Third and Fourth Corporals. And all of the above officers shall be elected by the Company and any candidate having a majority of the votes poled shall be declared duly elected.

Article 3. Every member of the Company shall uniform and equip himself according to the orders and regulations of the Adjutant General of Pennsylvania, and shall in all things submit to and be governed by the requirements of the Act of Assembly for the government of Volunteers and Uniformed Militia.

Article 4. This Company shall have stated parades in each year including the 22 day of February, 4 day of July, (unless these days shall happen on Sunday) and the day in May required by Law. Three other stated parades to be held at such times as shall be fixed by the Commissioned officers provided that nothing herein contained shall prevent the Captain with concurrence of the Company from holding special meetings of the Company for ordinary business, parades, drills and target firing, whenever in his opinion it shall be necessary and useful for the Company.

Article 5. A majority of the members present at any Company meeting or parade shall have power and be competent to pass any By-Law for the regulation of the Company and shall constitute a quorum to transact any business relating to the same excepting cases otherwise provided for in this Constitution.

Article 6. The officers for the transaction of the business of the Company shall be a President, Secretary, and Treasurer. The Captain by virtue of his office to be President, First Sergeant to be Secretary, and the Treasurer to be elected from members of the Company.

Article 7. The duty of the President shall be to preside at all the meetings of the Company and decide on all questions of order. The duty of the Secretary shall be to keep the minutes and proceedings of each meeting of the Company in a book to be provided for that purpose. And the duty of the Treasurer shall be to keep an exact and regular account of all the receipts and expenditures of the Company and make a report thereof at each stated parade of the Company.

Article 8. Of the time when and the place where of each stated parade the First Sergeant shall give at least six days' notice by written or printed handbills posted in conspicuous places or sent to each member of the Company.

Article 9. One Commissioned officer, one non-commissioned officer, and one Private to be appointed by the Commanding Officer of the Company shall be and will constitute a Court of Appeals to decide on cases of absentees from any parade or meeting of the Company. When so constituted and appointed there shall be held four Courts of Appeals for the Company each year, the time when and the place where the same shall be held to be fixed by the Commanding Officer who shall cause at least ten days' notice to be given of the time and place of each Appeal.

Article 10. All Court-Martials for the trial of any non-commissioned Officer or Private for a mis-conduct on parade shall consist of One Commissioned Officer, one non-commissioned officer and one Private. None of whom shall be excused to be appointed by the Commanding Officer, provided that should charges be brought against the Commanding Officer then the next highest Officer in rank shall appoint said Court-Martial.

Article 11. All fines and forfeitures imposed upon any member or officer of this Company by Court-Martial or otherwise by virtue of the Constitution and By-Laws thereof shall be levied and collected by the Captain or Commanding Officer, of the Company or by his warrant attested by the Secretary or First Sergeant directed to any Constable of Blair County in the manner provided for the collection of fines by the Militia Laws of Pennsylvania.

Article 12. All the necessary expenses of the Company shall be paid by the Treasurer out of the funds raised by fines, penalties, dues and apportionments directed by law to be paid to Uniform Militia, provided that in no case shall the Treasurer pay out or expend any of the funds or defray any of the expenses of the Company unless by written order of the Commanding Officer attested by the Secretary or First Sergeant.

Article 13. The Commanding Officer of the Company shall yearly appoint a standing committee of three persons to inspect the uniforms, arms and accoutrement of each member and report to the Court of Appeals any and every member who shall appear on parade not having his uniform and equipment in good order.

Article 14. The above and foregoing Constitution shall not be altered or amended unless by the vote of two-thirds of the members of the Company.

BY-LAWS

Section 1. Any member of the Company appearing on parade not being fully and legally equipped subject to the inspection of the Standing Committee shall be fined one dollar.

Section 2. Any member of the Company appearing on drill or parade without his arms being in good order subject to the inspection of the Standing Committee shall be fined one dollar.

Section 3. Any non-commissioned officer or private not attending on any day of stated parade without a good excuse to be decided by the Court of Appeals shall be fined two dollars.

Section 4. Should the Captain of the Company absent himself from any stated parade without a good excuse he shall incur the penalty of five dollars, and any other Commissioned Officer not being present on any stated parade day shall incur a penalty of three dollars to be decided in manner provided in Section 3.

Section 5. Any officer or private absenting himself from a special meeting of the Company shall pay a fine of twenty-five cents each and every member of the Company, officers and privates, shall pay into the funds of the Company the sum of twenty-five cents a month.

Section 6. No member of the Company shall be expelled from the Company unless by the votes of two-thirds of the members present at any stated meeting and in all cases the vote to be taken by ballot except in cases otherwise provided for in Constitution and By-Laws.

Section 7. The resignation of a member shall not be received or accepted until he pays to the Treasurer of the Company Five Dollars or delivers to the Treasurer his uniform and produces a certificate from the Treasurer that all arrearages are paid.

Section 8. No substitute for a member absent from parade shall be accepted unless by consent of Captain.

Section 9. Any member or members directly or indirectly attempting to make this Company a political one or to subserve political ends shall be publicly expelled.

Section 10. Any member or officer of this Company appearing on parade in a state of intoxication or becoming so while on parade, shall for the first offense be fined one dollar, for the second offense two dollars and for the third offense the Orderly Sergeant shall strike his name off the Constitution and he shall be publicly expelled.

Section 11. Any member or officer guilty of unsoldierly conduct on any day of parade shall for the first offense be fined fifty cents, for the second offense one dollar and for the third offense shall be expelled.

Section 12. Any resolution passed and voted upon by a majority of the members of this Company shall be equally binding with these By-Laws.

Section 13. Any member appearing on parade without having his boots or shoes properly blacked or in good order shall be fined fifty cents.

Section 14. At the time of our signing this Constitution and By-Laws we bind ourselves respectively to pay into the hands of the Treasurer the sum of three dollars each. Which sum shall be forfeited in case we do not provide ourselves with the necessary uniform.

WAR RESOLUTION

ADOPTED BY THE

Juniata Rifles of Hollidaysburg

At a meeting held by the members of the Juniata Rifles, the 8th day of January, 1861, attended by General William Williams, Jr., and Captain A. M. Lloyd, the following resolution was unanimously adopted with nine cheers. Three for our Country, Three cheers for General Williams and Three for Captain Lloyd;

RESOLVED, First,—Andrew Jackson the Second Washington of America, great alike in the field and cabinet, him whose iron nerve grappled with the secessionists nullification of that day, and who if living would never have allowed treason to assume its present dimensions,

RESOLVED, Second,—That "The Union in the language of him who made this day immortal" "must and shall be preserved" "and that we pledge unreservedly our lives our fortunes and our sacred honor" "in its maintenance,"

RESOLVED, Third,—That the gallant Kentuckian, Major Robert Anderson, by his strategic movement from Moultrie to Fort Sumter has shown himself to be an apt scholar of the Hero of Chippewa and Lundy Lane and that the movement merits the hearty approbation of the Government and people of the United States—and that we are ready when government demands it of us, to reinforce him with men who know but one Flag,—The Flag of our Union,

RESOLVED, That the thanks and congratulations of the people of this Union are due to General Scott, Senators Crittenden and Johnston, Gen. Wool and others who have thrown their whole weight against the traitorous monster Secession.

RESOLVED, Fourth—That as the Flag of our Union has been trampled under foot in the Forts of Moultrie and Pinkney in Charles Harbor, we call upon the Government to grant the gallant Anderson force sufficient to place it in its former position where "Long may it wave, o'er the land of the Free and Home of the Brave,"

RESOLVED, Fifth—That if the report be true Gov. Curtin has bestowed the greatest boon in his power on the Volunteer system by appointing our favorite Gen. James S. Nagley, (one of the brave of Pueblos Seige) to preside over our destinies during the momentous time now in our history—And that we advise our Senator and Legislators to aid him in every way possible, that our profession may not as it has heretofore been a "laughing stock" in our Halls of Legislation, that whatsoever may be the opinion of the Three Solons (who as we are informed visited our State Capitol lately for the purpose of disparaging the proposed appropriation for arming the State) that we must have arms or disband, that we consider ourselves aggrieved that not one stand of arms has been brought into our Brigade (the 4th) under the "Fuss and Feather" rule of our late distinguished Adjutant General C. C. Wilson,

RESOLVED, That we this day authorize our Commander to tender our services in defense of the Flag of our Union to the Commander in Chief.

THE UNION ARMY

President Lincoln's proclamation declaring war on seceded southern states was issued on the 15th of April, 1861, and his call for seventy-five thousand volunteer soldiers to suppress the rebellion followed immediately. His appeal was responded to from all parts of the northern states. The Honorable S. S. Blair of Hollidaysburg, wired Governor Andrew G. Curtin of Pennsylvania, on the 16th of April, that "Two companies of forty-five men each will leave tomorrow evening. Blair County will send eight companies within a week." The *Altoona Tribune* of the 19th of April, contained the following item, "On yesterday morning the Juniata rifles of Hollidaysburg, Capt. A. M. Lloyd, passed through this place on their way to Harrisburg. This evening the Hollidaysburg Fencibles, and the Wayne Guards from Williamsburg passed through this place, enroute to Harrisburg." Other companies hastened to assemblying points and then to Washington, to defend the capital, and the Pennsylvania troops were the first to arrive for this purpose.

The call for seventy-five thousand troops for a period of three months was followed by calls for larger forces for nine months, then for one year, then for three years and finally as the war was prolonged, the enlistments were for the duration of the war. Regardless of the number of men called, or the length of term, Blair County responded with her quota of volunteers, and when three hundred thousand were called in August, 1862, Blair County's quota of two companies, or two hundred men, was exceeded by four or five hundred men. At this time Blair County had furnished between 1500 and 2000 men for the war, a proportion almost equal to one-half or her voting population. At the time of the first draft in September, 1862, Deputy Marshal A. M. Lloyd reported that Blair County had 1771 soldiers in the federal service, not including those who had enlisted in the regular army, navy, marine, teamsters, and blacksmiths.

A Provost Marshal's office was maintained at Hollidaysburg, where recruits were received, sworn, their bounty paid, and mustered into the service; also drafts were conducted from this office. During August, 1864, the Hollidaysburg Borough paid a bounty amounting to two hundred dollars; the Federal government gave one hundred dollars. Other boroughs and the townships paid bounties, and sometimes the bounties totaled over four hundred dollars.

As an inducement to secure volunteers, many townships, as well as the County, paid bounties ranging from twenty-five to two hundred dollars. As the war continued, it became necessary to put into effect several drafts, and a number of Blair County men were thus called into the service or were able to engage substitutes. The draft ages were from 21 to 45, and as almost eighty per cent of the enlistments were young men under twenty-one, the number of draftees were, therefore, very low in proportion to the total of 4,776,376 enlistments. The total number of soldiers to serve in the Union Army was 2,400,000, this being 10 out of every 100 inhabitants.

The following is a record of the principal companies and regiments in which Blair County soldiers served enlistments, as secured through extensive examination of muster rolls and much research work. Some of these companies have never been mentioned in previous histories of Blair County, as being recruited in this county, so it is with pride that we now include such companies in this history.

Soldiers of Blair County served in all major engagements of the Civil War and in many skirmishes. The individual story of the soldier is almost the history of the war as they fought on land and sea, performed picket duty during the long hours of the night, took part in raids into the enemy's lines, marched with Sherman to the sea, suffered starvation and disease in southern prison camps at Andersonville, Libby and at Salisbury, proudly passed in review before Abraham Lincoln, witnessed the surrender of General Lee, captured and guarded Jefferson Davis, and finally, were pallbearers at the funeral of Abraham Lincoln.

The following sketches of Pennsylvania organizations which include companies or groups recruited in Blair County, are arranged in order of the date of being mustered into the service.

THIRD PENNSYLVANIA INFANTRY

The Third Pennsylvania Infantry of which six of its ten companies, numbering 415 men, were Blair County soldiers, was mustered into the service of the United States at Camp Curtin, Harrisburg, on the 20th of April, 1861, five days after the President's call for volunteers. This regiment left Camp Curtin on the evening of the 20th for Baltimore, but was halted at Cockeyville, Maryland, by reason of the destruction of the railroad bridge. The regiment returned to Camp Scott at York where it remained until the 27th of May, when it proceeded to Chambersburg, and on the 7th of June arrived at Hagerstown. On the 1st of July the command proceeded to Williamsport, crossed the Potomac River the following day, and arrived at Martinsburg. The regiment was ordered back to Williamsport to guard the main depot, where it remained until the 26th of July, when it returned to Harrisburg without having been engaged with the enemy, and was mustered out of the service on the 29th of July, its term of enlistment for three months having expired.

Field and Staff officers of the regiment included Colonel Francis P. Minier of Hollidaysburg, Lieutenant Colonel Oliver M. Irvine of Duncansville, and Assistant Surgeon William C. Roller of Williamsburg.

Company A, formerly the Hollidaysburg Fencibles, was commanded by Captain John R. McFarlane, First Lieutenant John McKeage, Second Lieutenant Thomas McFarlane, all of Hollidaysburg. Fifty-nine of its seventy-eight members were recruited at Hollidaysburg.

Company B, formerly the Altoona Guards, was commanded by Captain Henry Wayne, First Lieutenant Joseph W. Gardner, Second Lieutenant John M. Clark, all of Altoona. Fifty-seven of its eighty-two members were recruited at Altoona.

Company C, formerly the Wayne Guards of Williamsburg, was commanded by Captain William L. Neff, First Lieutenant Jacob C. Yingling, Second Lieutenant Robert Johnson, all of Williamsburg. Seventy-four of its seventy-eight members were recruited at Williamsburg.

Company D, formerly the Tyrone Artillery, was commanded by Captain James Bell, First Lieutenant William B. Darlington, Second Lieutenant Francis M. Bell, all of Tyrone. Fifty-eight of its seventy-seven members were recruited at Tyrone.

Company E, formerly the Logan Rifle Rangers of Altoona, was commanded by Captain Jacob Szink, First Lieutenant Richard J. Crozier, Second Lieutenant Frederick Shillinger, all of Altoona. Fifty of its seventy-seven members were recruited at Altoona.

Company H, formerly the Juniata Rifles of Hollidaysburg, was officered by Captain Alexander M. Lloyd of Hollidaysburg, First Lieutenant Christian N. Snyder of Altoona, Second Lieutenant Stephen C. Potts of Hollidaysburg. Thirty-four of its seventy-nine members were from Hollidaysburg, twenty-one from Altoona, fifteen from Frankstown, and the remainder from other points in the County.

FOURTEENTH PENNSYLVANIA INFANTRY

The Fourteenth regiment of Pennsylvania Infantry was mustered into the service of the United States at Camp Curtin, Harrisburg, on the 30th of April, 1861, and encamped at Lancaster, Chambersburg and at Hagerstown for training. The regiment crossed the Potomac River on the 2nd of July and arrived at Martinsburg, West Virginia, on the 14th. It was ordered to Carlisle, Pennsylvania, without being engaged in action, and was mustered out of the service on the 7th of August, its term of enlistment for three months having expired.

Company D, formerly the Tyrone Cavalry, was commanded by Captain James Crowther of Tyrone, First Lieutenant John S. McKiernan of Smith's Mills, Clearfield County, Second Lieutenant William Stoke of Tyrone. Twenty-five of its eighty-five members were enrolled at Tyrone, and fifty-nine at Smith's Mills.

Company H, formerly the Scott Rifles of Duncansville, was commanded by Captain Thomas Holland of Duncansville, First Lieutenant William McGraw of East Freedom, Second Lieutenant Samuel A. Andrews of Hollidaysburg. Twenty-two of its seventy-seven members were enrolled from Duncansville, thirty-two from East Freedom, eleven from Newry, five from Hollidaysburg, and four from Claysburg.

Company I, formerly the Martinsburg Infantry, was commanded by Captain Alexander Bobb, First Lieutenant J. C. Saunders, Second Lieutenant John H. Typher, all from Martinsburg and vicinity. This company of ninety men was recruited in Morrison's Cove.

SIXTY-SECOND PENNSYLVANIA INFANTRY

Company M of the Sixty-second regiment of Pennsylvania Infantry, known as the Blair County Sharp Shooters, was the first company from Blair County to be enlisted for a term of three years. This company was mustered into the service of the United States on the 9th of August, 1861. Sixty-eight of its 118 members were enrolled at Hollidaysburg, nine at Altoona and the remainder from other counties, all under the command of Captain Richard J. Crozier of Altoona, Captain John H. Murray of Hollidaysburg, First Lieutenant Stephen C. Potts of Hollidaysburg, First Lieutenant Robert N. Martin of Hollidaysburg and Second Lieutenant Patrick Morris, of Hollidaysburg.

The regiment assembled at Pittsburgh, then proceeded to Harrisburg, to Baltimore and Washington, D. C., where it received full war equipment. On the 11th of September, it crossed the Potomac River and went into camp near Fort Corcoran where the men were drilled and trained for active field duty. On the 5th of April, 1862, the regiment took its place in the line of battle at Yorktown, Virginia, where it was engaged in action for the first time.

A flag presented by the young ladies of Hollidaysburg to members of this company was carried throughout the war as a guidon, and is now on display in the new Hollidaysburg High School building where it is being preserved.

Other engagements and battles in which the regiment participated as lettered on the flag were:

Hanover Court House	Virginia	May 26, 1862
Seven Days' Battle	Virginia	June 27, 1862
Gaines Mills	Virginia	June 27, 1862
Antietam	Maryland	Sept. 16, 1862
Blackford's Ford	Virginia	Sept. 30, 1862
Fredericksburg	Virginia	Dec. 13, 1862
Chancellorsville	Virginia	May 1, 1863
Gettysburg	Pennsylvania	July 2, 1863
Manassas Gap	Virginia	Nov. 5, 1863
Rappahannock Station	Virginia	Nov. 11, 1863
Mine Run	Virginia	Dec. 3, 1863
Wilderness	Virginia	May 5, 1864
Laurel Hill	Virginia	May 9, 1864
Spottsylvania Court House	Virginia	May 12, 1864
Jerico Ford	Virginia	May 25, 1864
Totopotomoy	Virginia	May 30, 1864
Bethesda Church	Virginia	June 2, 1864
Petersburg	Virginia	June 18, 1864

The Regiment with the exception of Companies L and M, returned to Pittsburgh, Pennsylvania, on the 4th of July, 1864, where it was mustered out of the service. Company M, still having some time to serve was transferred to the Ninety-first Pennsylvania Infantry and was finally discharged on the 15th of August, 1864. Thirty-two of its members re-enlisted in Company K, of the Ninety-first, for the duration of the war.

THIRTY-FIRST PENNSYLVANIA INFANTRY

A company containing fifty men was recruited at Altoona and vicinity, and mustered into the service on the 27th of August, 1861, under the command of Captain John M. Clarke, First Lieutenant Robert J. Clark, both of Altoona, Pa.

This Company was attached to the First District of Columbia Volunteers, and was assigned to the Thirty-first Regiment of Pennsylvania Infantry, on the 2nd of April, 1862. Upon reporting for duty with the Thirty-first Regiment, this Company was designated as Company F, and ordered to take charge of the extra line of caissons for the artillery battalion of the Reserves, and continued on detached service until the 8th of March, 1863, when it joined the regiment at Union Mills, Virginia.

The Thirty-first Regiment of Pennsylvania Infantry was also known as the Second Pennsylvania Reserve Regiment. The Pennsylvania Reserve Volunteer Corps consisted of thirteen Regiments of Infantry, one Regiment of Cavalry and one Regiment of Artillery, organized and equipped by the Commonwealth of Pennsylvania for duty either at home or when needed by the Federal Government. Upon being accepted for Federal service the Second Regiment of the Pennsylvania Reserve became the Thirty-first Pennsylvania Infantry.

The engagements and battles in which the Regiment participated during the period that the Blair County members were with the Regiment, were as follows:

Gettysburg	Pennsylvania	July 2, 1863
Bristoe Station	Virginia	Jan. 24, 1864
Wilderness	Virginia	May 4, 1864
Spottsylvania Court House	Virginia	May 8, 1864
North Anna	Virginia	May 23, 1864
Shady Grove Church	Virginia	May 30, 1864

The Thirty-first returned to Pennsylvania during the first part of June, 1864, and was mustered out of the service. The term of enlistment of Company F, not having expired, the Blair County members, forty-four in number, were transferred to Company A, One Hundred and Ninety-first Pennsylvania Infantry, in which organization they served until the 27th of August, 1864.

FIRST PENNSYLVANIA CAVALRY

A troop of Cavalry, later designated Troop G, of the First Regiment of Pennsylvania Cavalry, numbering one hundred members, was recruited in Blair County by Captain Jacob Higgins, First Lieutenant David Gardner, and Second Lieutenants Henry C. Beamer and George J. Geiser, all of Blair County.

The Regiment rendezvoused at Camp Curtin, Harrisburg, where it was mustered into the service on the 28th of August, 1861, being the Fifteenth Regiment of the Pennsylvania Reserve Corps. It joined the division of reserve regiments at its camp at Tenallytown, Maryland; then moved to Camp Pierpont, Virginia, on the 10th of October.

Captain Jacob Higgins became Lieutenant Colonel of the Regiment upon the organization of the Regimental Staff, which position he resigned on the 7th of January, 1862. During the history of Company G, it had three additional Captains, namely: David Gardner, Henry C. Beamer and Francis T. Confer.

The members of this company saw considerable service and were engaged in many battles and skirmishes, the most important of which were:

Falmouth	Virginia	May 13, 1862
Strasburg	Virginia	June 1, 1862
Cross Keys	Virginia	June 8, 1862
Cedar Mountain	Virginia	Aug. 7, 1862
Thoroughfare Gap	Virginia	Aug. 28, 1862
Second Bull Run	Virginia	Aug. 29, 1862
Fredericksburg	Virginia	Dec. 13, 1862
Brandy Station	Virginia	June 9, 1863
Gettysburg	Pennsylvania	July 2, 1863
Shepardstown	Virginia	July 16, 1863
Haws Shop	Virginia	May 25, 1864
Trevellian Station	Virginia	June 11, 1864
Reams Station	Virginia	July 12, 1864
Malvern Hill	Virginia	July 28, 1864

The First Pennsylvania Cavalry was relieved from active duty on the 30th of August, 1864, its term of service having expired, however, a number of men of this Company, including Blair County members, re-enlisted in the Second Provisional Cavalry for the duration of the war.

EIGHTY-FOURTH PENNSYLVANIA INFANTRY

Two companies and parts of three others, were Blair County's contribution to the personnel of the Eighty-fourth Regiment of Pennsylvania Infantry, which was recruited under authority issued to William G. Murray, of Hollidaysburg, Pennsylvania.

Recruiting was well under way by the 20th of September, 1861, and the companies rendezvoused at Camp Crossman, near Huntingdon, Pennsylvania, and subsequently at Camp Curtin, Harrisburg. William G. Murray was elected Colonel and Thomas C. Craig, of Hollidaysburg, was later promoted to Lieutenant Colonel.

The Regiment arrived at Hancock, Maryland, on the 2nd of January, 1862, where it was armed with Belgian muskets, and two days later deployed in line of battle, receiving its baptism of fire from Stonewall Jackson's advancing forces near Berkeley Springs, West Virginia.

This Regiment suffered heavy losses, including the death of Colonel Murray at Kernstown, near Winchester, Virginia, on the 23rd of March, 1862.

The most important battles and engagements in which this Regiment participated were as follows.

Winchester	Virginia	Mar. 22, 1862
Kernstown	Virginia	Mar. 23, 1862
Cedar Mountain	Virginia	Aug. 9, 1862
Second Bull Run	Virginia	Aug. 30, 1862
Fredericksburg	Virginia	Dec. 30, 1862
Chancellorsville	Virginia	May 2, 1863
Wilderness Campaign	Virginia	May 5, 1864
Petersburg	Virginia	June 14, 1864

In October, 1864, the men whose three year enlistment had expired were mustered out of the service and those who re-enlisted, their number supplemented by recruits, were organized into a battalion of four companies, which remained on duty until the 13th of January, 1865, when the battalion was consolidated with the Fifty-seventh Regiment of Pennsylvania Infantry.

Those men who re-enlisted were allowed a veteran's furlough of thirty-five days, during which time they returned to their homes, arriving on the 26th of February, 1864, and returning on the 30th of March, 1864.

The Blair County Companies and their officers were as follows:
Company A, under the command of Captain Robert L. Horrell of Hollidaysburg.
Part of Company C, under Captain Abram J. Crissman of Martinsburg.
Company E, under the command of Captain Patrick Gallagher of Hollidaysburg.
Part of Company H, under First Lieutenant James C. Mitchell of Hollidaysburg.
Part of Company I, under Captain John R. Ross of Duncansville.

FIFTY-FIFTH PENNSYLVANIA INFANTRY

Company I, of the Fifty-fifth Regiment of Pennsylvania Infantry was recruited in Morrison's Cove by Captain David W. Madara, of Bloomfield Furnace. Sixty-three of its members were enrolled from the Cove, many of whom were from the Blair County section. The names of the officers who were enrolled from Blair County were: Captain Benjamin Rough of East Freedom, First Lieutenant Andrew Rough from East Freedom, First Lieutenant Solomon W. Fry and Second Lieutenant William C. Williams, both from Blair County.

This Company was mustered into the service on the 20th of September, 1861, and rendezvoused at Camp Curtin, Harrisburg. It numbered thirty-eight officers and 757 men. The Regiment proceeded to Fortress Monroe, Virginia, on the 22nd of November, and embarked on the 8th of December for Port Royal, South Carolina, arriving there on the 12th.

Parts of the Regiment were engaged with the enemy on Edison Island, on the 29th of March, and at Pocotaligo Bridge, on the 21st of December, 1862.

The majority of the men re-enlisted for a second three year term, on the first of January, 1864, and were given a veteran's furlough. Upon their return and the acquisition of recruits, the Regiment embarked for Virginia, on the 12th of April, 1864.

Other engagements in which the Regiment participated in were:

Petersburg	Virginia	June 15, 1864
Chapin's Farm	Virginia	Sept. 29, 1864
Hatcher's Run	Virginia	Mar. 31, 1865
Fort Baldwin	Virginia	Apr. 2, 1865
Appomattox Court House	Virginia	Apr. 9, 1865

The Fifty-fifth Regiment was mustered out of the service at Petersburg, Virginia, on the 30th of August, 1865, having served the longest period of any Blair County Company.

FIFTY-THIRD PENNSYLVANIA INFANTRY

Twenty-six members of Company C, of the Fifty-third Regiment of Pennsylvania Infantry were recruited in Blair County and mustered into the service on the 17th of October, 1861. The remainder of Company C, was recruited from Huntingdon County, all under the command of Captain John H. Wintrode, of Huntingdon County, Captain Henry J. Smith of Blair County, Captain Andrew J. Merrett of Williamsburg, First Lieutenant Robert McNamara of Hollidaysburg, First Lieutenant Samuel M. Royer of Springfield Furnace, First Lieutenant Dewalt S. Fouse of Blair County.

The Regiment moved to Washington, D. C., on the 7th of November; crossed the Potomac River on the 27th, and went into camp near Alexandria, Virginia.

The major battles and engagements in which this unit participated were:

Seven Pines	Virginia	June 1, 1862
Gaines Mills	Virginia	June 27, 1862

Antietam	Maryland	Sept. 17, 1862
Fredericksburg	Virginia	Dec. 12, 1862
Chancellorsville	Virginia	Apr. 28, 1863
Gettysburg	Pennsylvania	July 2, 1863
Po River	Virginia	May 9, 1864
Spottsylvania Court House	Virginia	May 11, 1864
Cold Harbor	Virginia	June 2, 1864
Petersburg	Virginia	June 12, 1864
Ream's Station	Virginia	Aug. 12, 1864
Boydton's Plank Road	Virginia	Mar. 31, 1865
Five Forks	Virginia	Apr. 1, 1865

The Fifty-third Regiment returned to Harrisburg, Pennsylvania, on the 27th of December, 1863, and those members who enlisted for a second three year term were granted a veteran's furlough. Returning to the front the regiment took part in many battles and engagements and was present at the surrender of the southern army. It then participated in the grand review of the armies at Washington on the 23rd of May, and was mustered out on the 30th of June, 1865.

SEVENTY-SIXTH PENNSYLVANIA INFANTRY

Two companies of the Seventy-sixth Regiment of Pennsylvania Infantry were recruited in Blair County and mustered into the service of the United States, on the 17th of October, 1861. Oliver M. Irvine and John W. Hicks of Blair County served as Lieutenant Colonels. The Regiment, known as the Keystone Zouaves, left Harrisburg on the 19th of November, for Fortress Monroe, Virginia, where it embarked for Hilton Head, South Carolina, arriving on the 8th of December.

Company C, was recruited principally at Hollidaysburg, Duncansville, Frankstown and Martha Furnace, and had enrolled a total of one hundred and nine men, all from Blair County. Its officers were: Captain John W. Hicks, Captain Alfred Hicks, Captain John McNevin of Hollidaysburg, First Lieutenant George S. Hoover of Newry, First Lieutenant Joseph Harlin of Newry, Second Lieutenant Joseph D. Keech of Frankstown, Second Lieutenant Philemon N. Hicks of Duncansville, and Second Lieutenant Benjamin White of Frankstown.

Company F, was recruited principally at Altoona, and contained one hundred and twelve men, under the command of Captain Henry Wayne, Captain Joseph R. Findley, Captain Thomas L. McGlathery, First Lieutenant George H. Gwin, Second Lieutenant John Hubert, all of Altoona, and Second Lieutenant Joseph W. Cannon of Bellwood.

The regiment was engaged in the following battles and engagements:

Charleston	South Carolina	June 16, 1862
Pocotaligo	South Carolina	Oct. 22, 1862
Fort Wagner	South Carolina	July 10, 1863
Drury's Bluff	Virginia	May 16, 1864
Cold Harbor	Virginia	June 1, 1864
Petersburg	Virginia	July 26, 1864
Deep Bottom	Virginia	Aug. 14, 1864
Bermuda Hundred	Virginia	Aug. 25, 1864
Chapin's Farm	Virginia	Sept. 28, 1864
Darbytown Road	Virginia	Oct. 27, 1864
Fort Fisher	Virginia	Dec. 23, 1864
Fort Fisher	Virginia	Jan. 15, 1865

The Seventy-sixth Regiment was mustered out at Raleigh, North Carolina, on the 18th of July, 1865, and reached Harrisburg, on the 23rd, where it was paid and finally disbanded.

NINTH PENNSYLVANIA CAVALRY

Company M, of the Ninth Regiment of Pennsylvania Cavalry, was recruited in Blair and Huntingdon Counties, and mustered into the service on the 24th of October, 1861. It contained fifty-four soldiers of Blair County, twenty-one having enlisted at Tyrone and thirty-three at Hollidaysburg, and was commanded by the following officers: Captain George W. Patterson of Spruce Creek, Captain James Bell of Tyrone and Captain Thomas S. McCahan of Spruce Creek.

The Ninth Cavalry left Harrisburg on the 20th of November, by rail for Pittsburgh, where it boarded a steamboat for Louisville, Kentucky. It trained at Jeffersonville, Indiana, opposite to Louisville, and proceeded on the 10th of January, 1862, to the front where it guarded the Louisville and Nashville Railroad until the 5th of March, when it was ordered to Tennessee.

The Regiment saw much service and many hard campaigns in the saddle. The principal battles and engagements in which it fought were as follows:

Lebanon	Kentucky	May 4, 1862
Spring Creek	Tennessee	May 14, 1862
Moore's Hill	Tennessee	June 6, 1862
Franklin	Tennessee	Mar. 4, 1863
Chickamaugua	Georgia	Aug. 16, 1863
Readyville	Tennessee	Sept. 6, 1864
Lovejoy's Station	Georgia	Nov. 16, 1864
Bear Creek	Georgia	Nov. 20, 1864
Aiken	South Carolina	Feb. 11, 1865
Averysboro	North Carolina	Mar. 16, 1865
Morrisville	North Carolina	Apr. 13, 1865

The Ninth Cavalry, after participating in Sherman's march to the sea, had the distinction of receiving the flag of truce which terminated in the surrender of General Joseph E. Johnston. It also provided the escort for General Sherman when he proceeded to the Bunett House at Durban, North Carolina, to meet General Johnston, and again upon the occasion of agreeing to the terms of surrender.

The Ninth Cavalry was mustered out of the service at Lexington, North Carolina, on the 18th of July, 1865, and returned to Harrisburg.

ONE HUNDRED AND TENTH PENNSYLVANIA INFANTRY

Two companies and part of a third of the One Hundred and Tenth Regiment of Pennsylvania Infantry were recruited from Blair County and mustered into the service about the 24th of October, 1861, and served under the following Field and Staff officers: Colonel James Crowthers of Tyrone, Lieutenant Colonel David M. Jones of Tyrone, Lieutenant Colonel Franklin B. Stewart of Altoona, Major Isaac T. Hamilton of Allegheny Township, Adjutant Matthias H. Jolly of Tyrone, Adjutant William H. Shelow of Tyrone, and Surgeon David S. Hays of Hollidaysburg.

The regiment rendezvoused at a camp near Huntingdon, and was transferred to Camp Curtin, Harrisburg, about the first of December. The regiment left Camp Curtin on the 2nd of January, 1862, and proceeded to Hancock, Maryland, where arms were issued on the 5th and the regiment formed to resist an expected attack from Stonewall Jackson's forces, which did not materialize, when the regiment marched to Cumberland where it was engaged in guarding the Baltimore and Ohio Railroad until the 8th of March, when it moved to Martinsburg, West Virginia, and then to Winchester, Virginia.

The battles and engagements in which this regiment participated were:

Kernstown	Virginia	Mar. 23, 1862
Port Republic	Virginia	June 8, 1862

THE CIVIL WAR

Cedar Mountain	Virginia	Aug. 9, 1862
Thoroughfare Gap	Virginia	Aug. 28, 1862
Second Bull Run	Virginia	Aug. 29, 1862
Fredericksburg	Virginia	Dec. 13, 1862
Chancellorsville	Virginia	May 2, 1863
Gettysburg	Pennsylvania	July 1, 1863
Kelly's Ford	Virginia	Nov. 7, 1863
Wilderness	Virginia	May 6, 1864
Spottsylvania Court House	Virginia	May 12, 1864
Chickahominy	Virginia	June 3, 1864
Petersburg	Virginia	June 15, 1864
Fort Steadman	Virginia	Mar. 25, 1865
Amelia Springs	Virginia	Apr. 6, 1865

The One hundred and Tenth Pennsylvania Infantry was granted a veterans' furlough in January, 1864, at which time the men re-enlisted for a second three year term. Upon rejoining the regiment they brought with them many recruits to replace casualties and those discharged. The regiment was at Clover Hill, near Richmond, when General Lee surrendered and it immediately took up its homeward march and participated in the grand review of the armies at Washington on the 28th of June, and returned to Harrisburg.

Company A was recruited at Altoona and Tyrone and was commanded by the following officers from Blair County: Captain David M. Jones of Tyrone, Captain Fleming Holliday of Bellwood, First Lieutenant Hiram H. Hopkins of Altoona, First Lieutenant William H. Shelow of Tyrone.

Company C was recruited in Blair and Bedford Counties and served under the following officers from Blair County: Captain Ezra D. Brisbin of Tyrone, Captain Isaac T. Hamilton of Allegheny Township, Captain James C. Hamilton of Tyrone, First Lieutenant George W. Burley of Altoona, First Lieutenant Charles Copelin of Altoona, and Second Lieutenant William Roberts of Martinsburg.

Company H was recruited throughout Blair County and the officers who served in this company were: Captain Franklin B. Stewart of Altoona, Captain Hiram H. Hopkins of Altoona, Captain Francis Cassiday of Newry, First Lieutenant Matthias H. Jolly of Tyrone, and First Lieutenant John W. Nanning of Tyrone.

TWELFTH PENNSYLVANIA CAVALRY

During the history of the Twelfth Regiment of the Pennsylvania Cavalry, over four hundred men were recruited at Hollidaysburg and Martinsburg, where recruiting stations were maintained. The first members from Blair County were mustered into the service at Camp McReynoldsville at Philadelphia, during January, 1862. The troops that had the largest number of members from Blair County, according to the muster rolls, were Troop D with Thirty-four, Troop F with thirty-three, Troop G with one hundred and one, Troop H with thirty-two, Troop L with thirty-five and Troop M with seventy-five.

The officers who were enrolled from Blair County were: First Lieutenant Erastus W. Kellogg of Troop D, from Martinsburg, First Lieutenant John W. Miller of Troop F, from Martinsburg, Second Lieutenant Henry E. Gutelius of Troop F, from Martinsburg, First Lieutenant John H. Black of Troop G, from Duncansville, and First Lieutenant Daniel W. Overlander of Troop H, from Martinsburg.

The Regiment proceeded to Washington, during April, 1862, where it received arms and remained in camp until the 20th of June, when it was ordered to the front. During the early part of 1864, the members re-enlisted for a second term of three years and the regiment was ordered home on a veterans' furlough, and through the efforts of its members many recruits were obtained.

SOLDIERS OF BLAIR COUNTY

The battles and engagements in which the regiment participated were:

Bristoe Station	Virginia	Aug. 26, 1862
Antietam	Maryland	Sept. 17, 1862
Front Royal Road	Virginia	June 14, 1863
Cunningham's Cross Roads	Pennsylvania	July 5, 1863
Kernstown	Virginia	July 23, 1864
Harmony	Virginia	Mar. 22, 1865

The regiment was mustered out of the service on the 20th of July, 1865, and returned in a body to Philadelphia.

SECOND PENNSYLVANIA CAVALRY

Fifteen members of Troop F, of the Second Regiment of Pennsylvania Cavalry were recruited in Blair County by Lieutenant Charles S. W. Jones of Tyrone, and mustered into the service of the United States on the first of March, 1862.

The Regiment rendezvoused at Camp Patterson, Philadelphia, and arrived at Washington on the 25th of March. It crossed the Potomac River into Virginia on the 27th of June, and joined the army at Madison Court House on the 5th of August.

The battles and engagements in which the regiment participated were:

Culpepper Court House	Virginia	Aug. 27, 1862
Chantilly	Virginia	Sept. 1, 1862
Occoquan River	Virginia	Dec. 28, 1862
Gettysburg	Pennsylvania	July 1, 1863
Haws Shop	Virginia	May 28, 1864
Malvern Hill	Virginia	Aug. 14, 1864
Charles City Cross Road	Virginia	Aug. 16, 1864
Five Forks	Virginia	Mar. 30, 1865

The Second Pennsylvania Cavalry was present at the surrender of the Confederate Army at Appomattox Court House on the 9th of April, 1865; participated in the grand review of the armies at Washington on the 23rd of May, and also, on the 7th of June. The Regiment was consolidated with the Twentieth Pennsylvania Cavalry, forming the First Pennsylvania Provisional Cavalry, and mustered out of the service at Cloud's Mill, Virginia, on the 13th of July, 1865.

ONE HUNDRED AND TWENTY-FIFTH PENNSYLVANIA INFANTRY

Six of the ten companies of the One Hundred and Twenty-fifth Regiment of Pennsylvania Infantry were recruited in Blair County and the remaining four companies were recruited in Huntingdon County, all under the authority given to Jacob Higgins of Williamsburg, to organize a regiment.

The term of service was for nine months and the regiment was mustered into the service of the United States at Camp Curtin, Harrisburg, on the 16th of August, 1862, when the following named officers from Blair County were included in the regimental staff; Colonel Jacob Higgins, Lieutenant Colonel Jacob Szink of Altoona, Adjutant Robert M. Johnston of Williamsburg, Quartermaster William C. Bayley of Hollidaysburg, Assistant Surgeon John Fay of Williamsburg, Assistant Surgeon Lafayette F. Butler of East Freedom, Assistant Surgeon Francis B. Davidson of Williamsburg, and Chaplain John D. Stewart of Tyrone.

The Regiment left Camp Curtin on the 16th of August, 1862, for Washington, from where it was ordered into Virginia on the 18th, and stationed at Hunter's Chapel, and subsequently at Fort Bernard, Virginia.

Company A, numbering one hundred and four members, was recruited at Tyrone and commanded by the following officers; Captain Francis M. Bell, First Lieutenant

Jesse S. Stewart, First Lieutenant Wilbur F. Stewart, and Second Lieutenant David G. Ganoe, all from Tyrone.

Company B, numbering ninety members, was recruited at Williamsburg, and commanded by the following named officers: Captain Ulysses I. Huyett, First Lieutenant Joseph R. Higgins, and Second Lieutenant Garian Shellenberger, all from Williamsburg.

Company D, numbering ninety-five members, was recruited at Altoona, and commanded by the following named officers: Captain Jacob Szink, Captain Christ R. Hostetter, Captain Alexander W. Marshall, First Lieutenant Thomas E. Campbell, Second Lieutenant Peter S. Treese, and Second Lieutenant George H. Hawksworth, all from Altoona.

Company E, numbering eighty-six members, was recruited in East Freedom and vicinity, under the following named officers: Captain William McGraw, First Lieutenant Samuel A. Kephart, Second Lieutenant John G. Cain, Second Lieutenant John H. Robertson, all from East Freedom and vicinity.

Company G, numbering ninety-six members, was recruited at Hollidaysburg, and commanded by the following named officers: Captain John McKeage, First Lieutenant Samuel A. Andrews, and Second Lieutenant Thomas McCamant, all from Hollidaysburg.

Company K, numbering ninety members, was recruited at Altoona, and commanded by the following named officers: Captain Joseph W. Gardner, First Lieutenant Edward R. Dunegan, and Second Lieutenant Daniel J. Travis, all from Altoona.

The principle battles in which this Regiment participated were:

Antietam	Maryland	Sept. 17, 1862
Chancellorsville	Virginia	May 1, 1863

The term of nine months' service having expired on the 16th of May, 1863, the One Hundred and Twenty-fifth Regiment returned to Harrisburg, where it was mustered out of the service on the 18th of May. The Blair County members of this Regiment returned to Altoona on the 26th of May, and were welcomed home with a public reception.

ONE HUNDRED AND THIRTY-SEVENTH PENNSYLVANIA INFANTRY

Company I, of the One Hundred and Thirty-seventh Regiment of Pennsylvania Infantry was recruited at Hollidaysburg and mustered into the service of the United States at Camp Curtin, Harrisburg, on the 20th of August, 1862.

This Company, numbering eighty-eight members, known as the Hammond Guards of Hollidaysburg, was enrolled for a term of nine months and served under command of the following officers: Captain Thomas McFarlane, Captain William F. Johnson, First Lieutenant Joseph G. Isenberg, all of Hollidaysburg, and Second Lieutenant John L. May of Martinsburg.

The various companies which made up this Regiment rendezvoused at Harrisburg, where a regimental organization was effected and Colonel Henry M. Bossert of Clinton County was elected to command. The Regiment was then ordered to Washington, where it encamped and was drilled by officers from the neighboring forts. On the 31st of August it was attached to General Hancock's Brigade, then marching through Washington, after the defeat at Bull Run, and about to enter on the Maryland campaign. At Crampton's Gap, in the South Mountain, the corps came up with the enemy's and the regiment was there for the first time under fire.

Following the battle of Antietam, the Regiment was assigned to guard duty along the Potomac River and at the time of Stuart's cavalry raid into Pennsylvania it was sent in pursuit. The men were aroused at midnight and put upon the march, and no halt was called until they were far into Pennsylvania. The pursuit was fruitless, and the command went into camp a few miles from Hagerstown, near the State line.

Other battles, engagements and campaigns in which this Regiment participated were:

Antietam	Maryland	Sept. 17, 1862
Franklin Crossing	Virginia	Apr. 29, 1863
Chancellorsville	Virginia	May 2, 1863

The term of enlistment having expired on the 20th of August, 1863, the Regiment was ordered to Washington, where it was mustered out of the service on the 1st of June, 1863.

The *Hollidaysburg Register* of the 10th of June, 1863, printed the following item: "On Tuesday evening last, the "Hammond Guards," of this place, Company I, 137th Regiment Pennsylvania Volunteers came home. When they arrived, Van Tries' Cornet Band, a large delegation of the soldiers of the 125th, and a crowd of People were waiting for them. The cars stopped at the west end of Gaysport, and the "Guards" were escorted into town amidst the welcome of the whole population. Captain Reamey, with his usual good taste and liberality, had the American House handsomely decorated, and at Squire Bowers' on Wayne Street, and other places, the display was tasteful. After marching to the Town Hall, the soldiers were dismissed. They then proceeded to the American House, where they partook of an elegant supper, provided by Essington Hammond, Esq. Mr. Hammond greatly assisted by pecuniary and other means, in the organization of the Company, and it was after him that it was named."

No history of Blair County mentions Company I, of the One Hundred and Thirty-seventh Regiment, as being recruited in this county, or that the members of this Company were from Hollidaysburg, and Samuel P. Bates in his official history of the Pennsylvania Volunteers of the Civil War gives the place of enrollment for this Company as Bradford. An examination of the muster roll discloses the place of enrollment as Hollidaysburg and a glance at the names of the members of this company proves without question the fact that they were from Hollidaysburg as practically all of them had been substantial citizens of this community and well known to many persons. The last member of this company to survive, was Augustus R. Deal, who died at Hollidaysburg, in 1929.

MILITIA OF 1862

Following the second battle of Bull Run on the 29th and 30th of August, 1862, the victorious southern army, taking advantage of its success, continued crossing the Potomac River in its march to the north. The close proximity of the southern border of Pennsylvania to the Potomac made possible an invasion of Pennsylvania through one day's march.

The Governor of Pennsylvania, accordingly, issued a proclamation on the 4th of September calling on the people to arm and prepare to defend their homes by the formation of companies and regiments, for the purpose of drill and instruction, and that after 3 P. M., of each day, all business houses be closed.

On the 10th, the enemy having invaded Maryland, the Governor issued a General Order, calling on all able bodied men to enroll immediately for the defense of the State, and to hold themselves in readiness to march upon an hour's notice; to select officers, to provide themselves with such arms as could be obtained, with sixty rounds of ammunition to the man, tendering arms to such as had none, and promising that they should be held for service, for such time only as the pressing exigency for the State defense should continue. The following day the Governor called for fifty thousand men to take the field.

The troops called under the State authority, known as the Pennsylvania Militia, responded promptly and many were stationed along the Pennsylvania border as well as at various points in the State of Maryland, when the Army of the Potomac met the invading forces at Antietam, Maryland, on the evening of the 16th, and the day of the 17th of September, 1862, and defeated them, hurling them back across the Potomac River into Virginia.

The Blair County units which responded to the Governor's Call were; Company A of the Twenty-third Regiment of Pennsylvania Militia, numbering ninety-one men, was recruited at Hollidaysburg; mustered into the service on the 21st of September, 1862; mustered out of the service on the 27th of September, and commanded by the following officers; Captain John R. McFarlane, First Lieutenant George B. Bowers, Second Lieutenant Anthony Vowinkle, all of Hollidaysburg.

The following companies were organized at Altoona and not being mustered into the service were known as Home Guards:

McClellan Guards,—under Captain A. C. Devlin, First Lieutenant J. T. Prengergast, Second Lieutenant William A. Boyden.

Altoona Riflemen,—under Captain George Hartzell, First Lieutenant Washington Foust, Second Lieutenant Jacob Hesser.

The Mountaineers,—under Captain Charles B. Street, First Lieutenant William A. Ware, Second Lieutenant Thomas H. Savery.

Altoona Fencibles,—under Captain William Boyden, First Lieutenant Charles Bushman, Second Lieutenant George W. Sparks.

Thos. A. Scott Corp,—under Captain Samuel Barber, First Lieutenant William Hough, Second Lieutenant William E. Albright.

Corcoran Guards,—under Captain Charles E. Collins, First Lieutenant John J. Redder, Second Lieutenant Thomas Drumgold.

Mountain Rangers,—under Captain Alexander Heverly, First Lieutenant Andrew Kipple, Second Lieutenant David Robinson.

MILITIA OF 1863

The rebel army's victory at Fredericksburg, on the 13th of December, 1862, and their more signal success at Chancellorsville in May, 1863, encouraged their leaders to again attempt an invasion of the north. Plans were accordingly laid over a long period of time and veiled in secrecy. Discontent was spread among certain elements in the north through the efforts of the "Copperheads", and the rebels' spy system kept them well informed of conditions throughout the northern States. Foreign supplies, guns and munitions of war had been received and the hopes of the southern confederacy were bright, while the north was disheartened and tired of the prolonged war. Recruiting was at a standstill, as evidenced by the fact that not a single company had been raised in Blair County since the previous summer and many soldiers had returned from the service on account of the termination of their enlistments.

Well informed circles, especially the newspapers of the north, did not believe that the southern army would attempt an invasion, in fact they calmed any alarm of danger, and on the 15th of June, with the rebels in possession of Chambersburg, Pennsylvania, the country had not as yet awakened to the immediate threat of an invasion of the State in force.

As a precautionary measure, the War Department, on the 9th of June, 1863, created two new military departments, one in the Monongahela District, and the other extending from the Laurel Hill range, eastward to the Delaware River, and to be known as the Susquehanna Department. This later department was placed under command of Major-General Darius N. Couch, and on assuming command, orders were issued calling for the people of the State to volunteer as members of the various units which would constitute the Army Corps of the Susquehanna. The Governor's proclamation of the 12th of June, in support of General Couch's orders, stated that, "Information has been obtained by the War Department, that a large rebel force, composed of cavalry, artillery, and mounted infantry, has been prepared for the purpose of making a raid into Pennsylvania."

The situation becoming more serious, the President, on the 15th, called for one hundred thousand men, to serve for a period of six months, unless sooner discharged, fifty thousand to be from the State of Pennsylvania. Governor Curtin's proclamation followed, urging all men capable of bearing arms to enroll themselves in military organizations, and to urge all others to give aid and assistance in the emergency. At that time the care and gathering of the crops was uppermost in the minds of many, while others were busily engaged in carrying on their daily work, tasks made harder by the absence of many men who were then in the service, so that but few realized the pending danger, until the rebel army had crossed the Pennsylvania border and his ultimate destination became a matter of grave concern.

To the people of south-central Pennsylvania every cloud of dust on the distant highway became a possible enemy patrol. Alarms sprang up everywhere and organizations of volunteers marched towards the south to guard the passes in the mountains, to protect the railroad bridges, and the towns. The rebel army continued its march without serious opposition, and it was not until the first of July, when General Meade, with his army of the Potomac, hastening northward by forced marches along parallel roads to that which the enemy were following, came in contact with General Lee's invading army at Gettysburg, Pennsylvania, and during the days, July 2nd, 3rd and 4th, fought one of the world's greatest battles.

"THE CHICKEN RAIDERS"

Blair County being a community of military importance, by reason of having large railroad shops at Altoona, a main railroad system traversing the county, and being a highly developed farming center, was therefore, a possible destination for the southern army. The *Hollidaysburg Register and Blair County Weekly News*, of the 1st of July, 1863, states that, "The rebels had for weeks been threatening an invasion of the State, but not until two weeks ago did we fully realize the truth of their threats, and their purpose to carry them out."

On Monday evening, the 14th of June, the residents of Blair County began to organize a force to resist the advancing enemy, when several units of an emergency force was formed.

This force consisted of men of the community, many of them too old or young for regular military duty, and many of them had families and other responsibilities, which exempted them from military services. However, when their homes and firesides were threatened by an invasion from the rebel army, they laid aside all duties of civil life and took up arms in defense of their homes. They were not enrolled, mustered or sworn into the service of the State or the Federal Government, neither were they examined for physical fitness, but went forth as the minute-men of Revolutionary War days to prepare defenses with which to obstruct the advance of the enemy, and if necessary to offer their bodies to the enemy's bullets, and their lives in defense of their country.

For want of a military title, this army of emergency troops, were called Pennsylvania Emergency Militia, or Minute-men, but in later years they were referred to locally as the "Chicken Raiders". This latter title was acquired probably by reason of an inadequately organized commissary department, and when sufficient rations were not forth coming, it became necessary for the soldiers to, individually and in groups, visit the farms in the neighborhood of their camps, in order to secure food. Some provisions and possessions of the farmers were requisitioned and paid for eventually, but no doubt much was obtained by these emergency soldiers without formalities, and chickens being plentiful, easy to prepare, and pleasing to the taste, constituted the principal item on the menu during the week that the "Chicken Raiders" marched to the vicinity of Everett, and returned to their homes in Blair County and elsewhere.

Colonel Jacob Higgins was named to command the emergency forces (Chicken Raiders) in this vicinity, and he in turn named the following as members of his staff: Captain John H. Keatley of Hollidaysburg as Assistant Adjutant General, Captain D. K. Reamey of Hollidaysburg and Lieutenant Charles S. Derland of Hollidaysburg as Aides-de-camp, Captain A. A. Cohill as Assistant Engineer, Captain S. S. Blair as Assistant Quartermaster, and Captain Samuel Calvin as Provost Marshal.

Colonel Higgins had, by the end of the week, the following forces under his command; one regiment of infantry from Johnstown under Colonel W. A. McCartney, one battalion of infantry under Colonel Jacob Szink, one battalion of infantry under Colonel William McGraw, and one battalion of cavalry under Major Henry C. Beamer.

On Tuesday, the 23rd of June, Colonel Higgins, with a part of his forces, advanced as far as McKee's Gap, where he took possession of that point and under the direction of Captain R. H. Lamborn, began to fortify the pass by constructing trenches along the mountain side, and by building obstructions to be placed in the road. Colonel McAllister, with a detachment of one hundred men took possession of Loy's Gap, near Pattonville, and began to obstruct it in a similar manner.

On the 24th, part of the forces at McKee's Gap moved to Loy's Gap, and the following day the main body of the troops marched in the direction of St. Clairsville, Bedford County, from where they intended to take possession of all the gaps and passes fronting the valley and lying upon the eastern slope of the Allegheny Mountains. They arrived at a pass south of St. Clairsville about three o'clock, and commenced to construct a series of fortifications, work on which was continued during the night and part of the following day.

During the 26th of June orders were received from General Milroy, then at Bedford, for Colonel Higgins to march his forces immediately toward Bloody Run. The troops moved at once by way of Bedford and arrived at their destination in due course of time. Colonel Higgins and his staff, being mounted, proceeded by way of Morrison's Cove and arrived at Bloody Run in advance of the main body.

The following letter, published in *War of the Rebellion*, addressed to Major General Couch, from N. L. Yarnall, Lieutenant Colonel, Commanding, and dated at Altoona, the 28th of June, 1863, deals with the matter of local defense; "I have been out examining the country. I find three or four gaps from fifteen to twenty miles out, that should be guarded, in order to protect this place. I can guard them with twelve hundred or fifteen hundred men and four or six pieces of artillery. I leave here with five companies at 12 o'clock today for McKee's Gap, and if I had a mustering officer at this place I could raise the remaining number sufficient to guard the gaps. Can you send me four or six pieces, or can I get them from Pittsburgh? We have the men for them. It is necessary that I should have them."

The *Hollidaysburg Register* of the 1st of July, 1863, contains the following item, "The six hundred of our citizens of Hollidaysburg who were serving as "Minute men" in defense of our country, have returned to their homes, because the authorities did not wish their services longer, unless they would consent to be mustered into the United States service for six months. They were willing to remain while the emergency might last but could not have been sworn in for six months, as when they shouldered the musket they left business and other considerations at an hour's notice. Many of them will return to the service in companies which are being formed under the call for ninety days."

The rebel forces did not cross the county line into Blair County. However, they did invade Bedford County on the south, and some action took place below Bloody Run. Blair County did not escape the rumors of war and like many towns and villages of the southern part of Pennsylvania, it had its war scare. This occurred on the 2nd of July, 1863, while the battle of Gettysburg was raging in all its fury.

The effect of the war scare at Hollidaysburg, as recorded by the *Hollidaysburg Register* of the 18th of July, was as follows: "Early on Thursday morning last, our citizens were aroused from their slumber by the ringing of the Court House bell. All kinds of reports were in circulation on the streets, such as that the rebel advance guard had entered Martinsburg, on the night before, and ordered the women and children to be taken out, as they intended to fire the town, and many other rumors equally alarming. Great excitement was the consequence,—frightened citizens were on the streets adding to the rumors which were in circulation, until it was thought that the rebels were certainly "coming".

"Preparations were made for their arrival,—valuables were secreted, the county records and other valuable documents belonging to the county were hastily packed by the officials, horses and cattle were sent to the mountains, terrified clothing dealers removed their stock to places of safety, recruiting officers suddenly appeared in citizen's dress, and consternation reigned supreme. The report which had been received by messenger from McKee's Gap, was that the rebel pickets were eight miles on the other side of Martinsburg. Mounted scouts from town were sent out in different directions, who returned in the evening, and reported that the excitement had been caused by little or nothing, and that the rebels had not been nearer to us than usual, as far as they could learn, and that the Broad Top Railroad was still in operation, notwithstanding the reliable (?) information which we had received that eight hundred rebels had visited Marklesburg and other places along the line of the railroad."

Some consolation may have been felt by the more timid persons of this vicinity, when on the following day a squad of rebel prisoners who had been captured below Bloody Run, were taken through Hollidaysburg. It is not recorded that any person sought vengeance on these prisoners for the confusion and the unnecessary excitement of the previous day, and it is more likely that food and refreshments were provided for the captured foe.

BELL'S INDEPENDENT CAVALRY, PENNSYLVANIA MILITIA

Several companies of the Pennsylvania Militia were recruited in Blair County from the emergency troops who went forth to fortify and guard the mountain passes, and were mustered into the Federal service under the Governor's call for fifty thousand volunteers, to serve for the period of three months.

The first of these companies to be mustered into the service was Bell's Independent Cavalry Troop of the Pennsylvania Militia, numbering one hundred and two men, ninety-three of whom were from Altoona, was mustered on the 30th of June, 1863, under the command of Captain James M. Bell of Tyrone, First Lieutenant Marshall McCormick of Altoona, and Second Lieutenant John B. Cunningham of Altoona. This Company was mustered out of the service on the 10th of August, 1863.

FORTY-SIXTH PENNSYLVANIA MILITIA

Two companies and parts of two other companies were recruited in Blair County and made part of the Forty-sixth Regiment of Pennsylvania Militia, and mustered into the service at a camp at Huntingdon on the 1st of July, 1863. Among the staff officers of this Regiment were: Major Francis M. Bell of Tyrone, Surgeon Jacob M. Gemmill of Altoona, Quartermaster Matthew T. Gill of Altoona, and Quartermaster Sergeant Hugh Pitcairn of Altoona.

The Regiment was ordered to Philadelphia where it rendered important service, at a most critical time, in restoring order and supporting the laws and recognized authority. It was mustered out of the service at Harrisburg on the 18th of August, 1863.

Company C, numbering eighty-five members, was recruited at Altoona, under the command of Captain Henry B. Huff, First Lieutenant Joseph H. Bryan, and Second Lieutenant George W. Russell, all of Altoona.

Company D, numbering eighty men, was recruited at Altoona, under the command of Captain Thomas E. Campbell, First Lieutenant Wilbur B. Blake, and Second Lieutenant Benjamin R. Rumberger, all of Altoona.

Thirty-four of the seventy members of Company E, were recruited at Tyrone, and served under the following Officers: Captain Charles Merryman, and First Lieutenant Levi Clabaugh, both of Tyrone.

Thirty-six of the sixty-seven members of Company K, were recruited at Tyrone, and served under Captain Joseph W. Gardner of Altoona.

INDEPENDENT BATTALION, PENNSYLVANIA MILITIA

Two companies and part of a third were recruited in Blair County, as part of the Independent Battalion of the Pennsylvania Militia, and mustered into the service at Camp

Juniata, Huntingdon, on the 3rd of July, 1863. Blair County men who served as staff officers were; Lieutenant Colonel John McKeage of Hollidaysburg, Major Richard J. Crozier of Altoona, Quartermaster John H. Keatley of Hollidaysburg, and Surgeon John Fay of Williamsburg.

The Blair County companies were stationed for some time at Camp Crozier, near Hopewell, Bedford County. This camp was located on the rising ground in the rear of the village. The Battalion was mustered out of the service on the 8th of August, 1863. The Hollidaysburg companies, arrived home on the 9th of August, and were dismissed at the railroad depot, and returned to their homes without display.

Company A, numbering ninety-nine members, of which eighty-four were recruited at Hollidaysburg, was commanded by Captain Oliver M. Irvine of Duncansville, First Lieutenant David Stiteler of Hollidaysburg, and Second Lieutenant James Rodgers of Hollidaysburg.

Company B, numbering seventy-eight members of which sixty-six were recruited at Hollidaysburg, was commanded by Captain John Swires, First Lieutenant Augustus Batton, and Second Lieutenant John Miller, all of Hollidaysburg.

Company F, numbering seventy-nine members was recruited in Blair and Cambria Counties. Thirty-five members were recruited at Altoona, six at Hollidaysburg and one at Bell's Mills, under the command of the following officers: Captain Daniel J. Travis, and Second Lieutenant William Strong, both of Altoona.

The two Hollidaysburg companies were known at the time of performing their service as Companies E and F, of the Fifty-fourth Pennsylvania Militia, but they are described by Samuel P. Bates, in his official history of the Pennsylvania Volunteers of the Civil War, as Companies A and B, Independent Battalion, Pennsylvania Militia.

TWENTY-SECOND PENNSYLVANIA CAVALRY

During the latter part of June, 1863, upon the occasion of the rebel advance into Pennsylvania, a battalion of Cavalry, four troops, was organized to serve under the call of the President for volunteers to serve for a six months' term. Two troops of the battalion were recruited in Blair County and mustered into the service during the early part of July, under the command of the following Blair County officers who were members of the battalion headquarters: Major B. Mortimer Morrow of Hollidaysburg, Adjutant C. Sanford Derland of Hollidaysburg, and Quartermaster Abram J. Crissman of Martinsburg.

The battalion was employed in guarding the fords of the Susquehanna, above and below Harrisburg, and in picketing the roads leading into the Cumberland Valley. After the defeat of the rebel army at Gettysburg, it was pushed up the valley in pursuit, and until the close of its term of service, was engaged with the cavalry in holding the Shenandoah Valley.

Troop C, composed of fifty men recruited at Tyrone and thirty-three recruited in Bedford County, was commanded by Captain Matthias H. Jolly, and Second Lieutenant Albert A. Abbott, both of Tyrone.

Troop D, composed of forty-six men recruited in Blair County and thirty-seven recruited in Huntingdon County, was commanded by Captain William L. Neff of Williamsburg, First Lieutenant William Gayton of Blair County, and Second Lieutenant J. Brown Wingate of Hollidaysburg.

At the end of its term of enlistment of six months, the battalion was reorganized and its members re-enlisted for a term of three years. The Ringgold Battalion was united with the re-organized units on the 22nd of February, 1864, and the regimental staff included the fol.owing Blair County officers: Colonel Jacob Higgins of Williamsburg, Adjutant Joseph G. Isenberg of Hollidaysburg, and Quartermaster William C. Bayley of Hollidaysburg.

SOLDIERS OF BLAIR COUNTY

The period up until the third of July, 1864, was used in organizing, equipping and training the members of the command, when the regiment was ordered to the front and received its baptism of fire.

The battles and engagements in which the regiment participated were:

Leetown	Virginia	July 3, 1864
Maryland Heights	Maryland	July 6, 1864
Snicker's Ferry	Virginia	July 17, 1864
Newmarket	Virginia	July 25, 1864
Kernstown	Virginia	Aug. 21, 1864
Charlestown	West Virginia	Aug. 25, 1864
Moorefield	West Virginia	Aug. 26, 1864
Martinsburg	West Virginia	Aug. 31, 1864
Opequon	Virginia	Sept. 18, 1864
Cedar Creek	Virginia	Oct. 19, 1864

The regiment was consolidated with the Eighteenth during June, 1865, forming the Third Provisional Cavalry, and was mustered out of the service on the 31st of October, 1865.

Troop H contained forty-four men from Hollidaysburg and one from Tyrone, under command of the following officers from Blair County: Captain Matthias H. Jolly of Tyrone, First Lieutenant Alfred A. Abbott of Tyrone, and Second Lieutenant David G. Ganoe of Hollidaysburg.

Troop I contained twenty-seven men from Blair County, under command of Captain C. Sanford Derland of Hollidaysburg, Second Lieutenant William H. Adams, and Second Lieutenant Robert A. Laird, both of Tyrone.

Troop K contained forty-nine men from Hollidaysburg; however, none of the officers were from Blair County.

Troop M contained twenty-three men from Hollidaysburg, under command of First Lieutenant J. Brown Wingate of Hollidaysburg. Twenty-six other soldiers of Blair County were scattered throughout the regiment, making a total of one hundred and seventy from Blair County.

THIRTEENTH PENNSYLVANIA CAVALRY

One hundred and three members of Troop D of the Thirteenth Regiment of Pennsylvania Cavalry were recruited in Blair County, and commanded by the following officers from Blair County: Captain James M. Bell of Tyrone, and Second Lieutenant George W. Cruse of Frankstown. Forty-nine of the Blair County members were enrolled at Altoona, seventeen at Frankstown, sixteen at Hollidaysburg and the remainder from scattered points throughout the County. The Blair County members were mustered into the service during September, 1863, and joined the Regiment at Catlett's Station, Virginia.

The battles and engagements in which the Regiment participated during the period that the Blair County members were part of it, were:

Sulphur Springs	Virginia	Oct. 12, 1863
Wilderness	Virginia	May 5, 1864
Beaver Dam Station	Virginia	May 26, 1864
Haws Shop	Virginia	May 28, 1864
St. Mary's Church	Virginia	June 24, 1864
Wyatt's Farm	Virginia	Sept. 29, 1864
Gravelly Run	Virginia	Feb. 5, 1865
Raleigh	North Carolina	Mar. 19, 1865

THE CIVIL WAR

Many of the members of the Thirteenth Cavalry were captured by the rebel army and confined in prison at Andersonville, Georgia, where at least sixty-seven members of the Regiment died of starvation and disease.

The Regiment was mustered out of the service at Raleigh, North Carolina, on the 14th of July, 1865, and returned to Camp Cadwallader, Philadelphia, where it was finally discharged.

NINETEENTH PENNSYLVANIA CAVALRY

Thirty-seven men from Blair County served in the Nineteenth Regiment of Pennsylvania Cavalry; twenty-six of these were assigned to Troop L, and were later transferred to Troop A. They were mustered into the service on the 9th of September, 1863, and served under the following officers who were from Blair County: Captain D. Ross Miller of Altoona, First Lieutenant Wilbur B. Blake of Altoona.

The Regiment left Camp Stanton, Philadelphia, on the 5th of November, and arrived at Columbus, Kentucky, on the 3rd of December,

The major battles and engagements in which this Regiment participated were as follows:

Egypt	Tennessee	Feb. 19, 1864
Cypress Swamp	Tennessee	Apr. 6, 1864
Big Blue River	Arkansas	Oct. 20, 1864
Nashville	Tennessee	Dec. 15, 1864
Franklin	Tennessee	Dec. 17, 1864
Sugar Creek	Tennessee	Dec. 26, 1864
Clinton	Louisiana	July 25, 1865

This Regiment was consolidated into four companies, and were detailed for provost duty at important points in Louisiana, where they remained until the 14th of May, 1866, when they were mustered out of the service.

ONE HUNDRED AND EIGHTY-FOURTH PENNSYLVANIA INFANTRY

A number of men, including practically all of the officers and non-commissioned officers, of Companies D and E, of the One hundred and Eighty-fourth Regiment of Pennsylvania Infantry, were recruited from Blair County, and rendezvoused at Camp Curtin, Harrisburg, where they were mustered into the service on the 13th of May, 1864.

Company D was commanded by Captain Henry B. Huff of Hollidaysburg, First Lieutenant James C. Dysart of Altoona, and Second Lieutenant Joseph H. Bryan of Altoona.

Company E was commanded by Captain John McKeage of Hollidaysburg, First Lieutenant Hugh T. Harpham of Altoona, and Second Lieutenant Daniel W. Reynolds of Altoona.

The Regiment left Camp Curtin on the 14th of May, and on the 1st of June it led in two desperate assaults upon the enemy's fortification at Cold Harbor, Virginia.

The battles and engagements in which this Regiment participated were as follows:

Cold Harbor	Virginia	June 1, 1864
Petersburg	Virginia	June 22, 1864
Deep Bottom	Virginia	Aug. 16, 1864
Weldon Railroad	Virginia	Aug. 25, 1864
Hatcher's Run	Virginia	Oct. 27, 1864
Appomattox Court House	Virginia	Apr. 9, 1865

The Regiment marched back to the vicinity of Washington, and participated in the grand review of the armies on the 23rd of May, 1865, and was mustered out of the service on the 14th of July, 1865.

ONE HUNDRED AND NINETY-FIRST PENNSYLVANIA INFANTRY

Forty-four former members of the Thirty-first Pennsylvania Infantry, who were from Blair County, were transferred to Company A of the One Hundred and Ninety-first Regiment of Pennsylvania Infantry, on the 6th of June, 1864. These men had been enrolled at Altoona under Captain John M. Clark on the 27th of August, 1861. No officers from Blair County were transferred or served with the Regiment.

The battles and engagements in which the Regiment participated during the period that the Blair County men were part of it were:

Cold Harbor	Virginia	May 30, 1864
Charles City Cross Roads	Virginia	June 13, 1864
Petersburg	Virginia	June 18, 1864
Weldon Railroad	Virginia	Aug. 19, 1864
Gravelly Run	Virginia	Mar. 30, 1865

Of the forty-four Blair County members of Company A, twenty-one were captured at Weldon Station, Virginia, on the 19th of August, 1864, and of this number ten died in rebel prisons.

The regiment returned to the neighborhood of Washington and was mustered out of the service on the 28th of June, 1865.

MILITIA OF 1864

During the year 1864 a number of units were recruited throughout Pennsylvania for short periods of service to perform some specific duty, such as guarding certain strategic points or to strengthen the border guard when threatened by enemy cavalry raids.

Twenty-one men were recruited in Blair County as part of Company G of an Independent Battalion of Pennsylvania Militia, of which Major Jacob Szink of Altoona served on the Staff.

Company G was mustered into the service on the 16th of July, 1864, under the command of Captain Jacob Szink, and First Lieutenant Josiah D. Hicks of Altoona, and was mustered out of the service on the 10th of November, 1864.

NINETY-FIRST PENNSYLVANIA INFANTRY

Thirty-two former members of Company M of the Sixty-second Pennsylvania Infantry, who were from Blair County, were transferred to Company K of the Ninety-first Regiment of Pennsylvania Infantry, on the 20th of July, 1864. These men were enrolled at Hollidaysburg on the 9th of August, 1861, under Captain Richard Crozier of Altoona. No officers from Blair County were transferred or served in the Ninety-first Regiment.

THE CIVIL WAR

The battles and engagements in which the Regiment participated during the period that the Blair County men were part of it, were:

Petersburg	Virginia	July 30, 1864
Weldon Railroad	Virginia	Aug. 19, 1864
Peebles Farm	Virginia	Sept. 30, 1864
David House	Virginia	Oct. 8, 1864
Hatcher's Run	Virginia	Oct. 28, 1864
Five Forks	Virginia	Mar. 30, 1865
Appomattox Court House	Virginia	Apr. 9, 1865

The Regiment participated in the formal surrender of the rebel army at Appomattox Court House, when on the following day the command was drawn up while the enemy stacked their arms, the ceremony lasting the entire day.

The Regiment participated in the grand review of the armies at Washington on the 23rd of May, and was mustered out of the service on the 10th of July, 1865.

TWO HUNDRED AND EIGHTH PENNSYLVANIA INFANTRY

One company of the Two Hundred and Eighth Regiment of Pennsylvania Infantry was recruited in Blair County, principally at Williamsburg and vicinity, and mustered into the service of the United States on the 26th of August, 1864, at Camp Curtin, Harrisburg. Major Alexander Bobb of Martinsburg served as a Staff officer.

Company B was under command of Captain James S. Shollar and First Lieutenant Calvin C. Hewitt, both of Williamsburg.

The regiment left for the front on the 13th of September, 1864, and joined the army at Bermuda Hundred, Virginia.

The battles and engagements in which the regiment participated were:

Fort Steadman	Virginia	Mar. 25, 1865
Fort Sedgwick	Virginia	Apr. 2, 1865

Bates, *History of Pennsylvania Volunteers* states that, "After the retaking of the main line, (at Fort Steadman) the picket line was re-established, and Captain Shollar of Company B, was detailed as brigade officer in charge. The enemy's dead were delivered under flag of truce, many of whom were found to have been shot in the head, and a large proportion were lying in front of the position occupied by the Two hundred and Eighth. "When you were about to make your final charge," said a rebel officer to Captain Shollar, "A council of war was being held by our Generals; but it was the shortest council of war you ever saw; for when they beheld such magnificent lines advancing, they adjourned, by each taking to his heels without ceremony."

The Regiment encamped near Alexandria, Virginia, until mustered out of the service on the first of June, 1865.

TWO HUNDRED AND FIFTH PENNSYLVANIA INFANTRY

Blair County furnished well over three hundred men for duty in the Two hundred and Fifth Regiment of Pennsylvania Infantry, which was mustered into the service at Camp Curtin, Harrisburg, on the 27th of August, 1864, with B. Mortimer Morrow of Hollidaysburg serving as Major.

Company A, numbering one hundred and nine members, was recruited at various points throughout Blair County; commanded by the following officers from Blair

County: Captain George C. Gwinner, First Lieutenant Levi W. Port of Martinsburg, and Second Lieutenant Morris Davis of Altoona.

Company C, numbering one hundred and two members, was principally recruited at Spring Mills, now Roaring Spring, and commanded by Captain Louis D. Spiece, First Lieutenant Henry N. Lower, and Second Lieutenant David M. Butler, all of Roaring Spring.

Forty members of Company D were recruited at Hollidaysburg, but not commanded by any Blair County officers.

Seventy-two of the one hundred and eighteen members of Company I were recruited in Blair County. Of this number, sixty-three were recruited at Hollidaysburg, under command of Captain John A. McCahan of Hollidaysburg, First Lieutenant Henry Hawk of Altoona, and Second Lieutenant Henry Elway of Altoona.

The Regiment left Harrisburg on the 5th of September, 1864, and joined the army at the front at City Point, Virginia.

The battles and engagements in which the Regiment participated were:

Fort Steadman	Virginia	Mar. 25, 1865
Fort Sedgwick	Virginia	Apr. 2, 1865

The Regiment encamped near Alexandria, Virginia, until mustered out of the service on the 2nd of June, 1865.

FIRST PENNSYLVANIA ARTILLERY

At least one hundred and twelve men, were enrolled in Blair County for duty with the First Pennsylvania Artillery, during August and September, 1864. One hundred and nine of this number were recruited at Hollidaysburg, and assigned to the various batteries of the Regiment. The largest number, fifty-six, served in Battery D. None of the officers of the Regiment were from Blair County.

The only engagement in which Battery D participated during the period that the Blair County members were with it, was:

Cedar Creek	Virginia	Oct. 18, 1864

Battery D was posted on Maryland Heights during the spring of 1865, and was ordered to Harrisburg, where it was mustered out of the service on the 29th and 30th of June, 1865.

FIFTY-SEVENTH PENNSYLVANIA INFANTRY

At least one hundred and seventy Blair County members of the Eighty-fourth Pennsylvania Infantry were transferred on the 13th of January, 1865, to the Fifty-seventh Regiment of Pennsylvania Infantry. These members had enlisted during September, 1861, and had seen considerable service in battle and field under Colonel William G. Murray and his successors.

The Blair County men were principally assigned to Company G and I, thirty-six being assigned to the former and ninety-six to the latter. The only Blair County officers known to have served in the Regiment were: Captain John R. Ross of Duncansville and First Lieutenant James S. Mitchell of Hollidaysburg.

The battles and engagements in which the Regiment participated, during the period that the Blair County members were part of it, were:

Hatcher's Run	Virginia	Feb. 5, 1865
Fort Steadman	Virginia	Mar. 25, 1865
Sailor's Creek	Virginia	Apr. 6, 1865

THE CIVIL WAR 141

The Regiment marched to Richmond during May, 1865, then to camp at Alexandria, Virginia, where it was mustered out of the service on the 22nd of June.

Upon disbanding, the following address was issued by the line officers to the men: "Parting as a band of brothers, let us cling to the memory of those tattered banners, under which we have fought together, and which without dishonor, we have just now restored to the authorities who placed them in our hands. Till we grow gray headed and pass away let us sustain the reputation of this noble old Regiment. Fortune threw together two organizations, the Eighty-fourth and the Fifty-seventh, to make the present command. Both regiments have been in service since the beginning of the strife, and the records of both will command respect in all coming time. Very many of those who were enrolled with us have fallen, and their graves are scattered here and there throughout the South. We shall not forget these, and the people of this nation must and will honor their memory. Comrades, Farewell!"

ONE HUNDRED AND NINETY-SECOND PENNSYLVANIA INFANTRY

Company D, numbering one hundred members, of the One hundred and Ninety-second Regiment of Pennsylvania Infantry, was recruited at Hollidaysburg, and mustered into the service of the United States, on the 6th of February, 1865; and served under command of the following officers from Blair County: Captain Samuel A. Andrews, First Lieutenant James Rodgers, and Second Lieutenant John Swires, all of Hollidaysburg.

This company was assigned to the Regiment as replacement and reported for duty at Harper's Ferry, West Virginia, where a regimental re-organization was effected about the middle of March, when the spring campaign opened, and the Regiment moved to Staunton and Lexington, Virginia. Few of the enemy were met as the fighting here was substantially at an end.

The Regiment continued in the service, without being engaged with the enemy, and was mustered out on the 24th of August, 1865.

ONE HUNDRED AND FOURTH PENNSYLVANIA INFANTRY

Company E, numbering ninety-six members, of the One Hundred and Fourth Regiment of Pennsylvania Infantry, was recruited at Altoona, and mustered into the service on the 25th of February, 1865, at Harrisburg, under the following officers: Captain Robert Johnson of Altoona, First Lieutenant John H. Keatley of Hollidaysburg, and Second Lieutenant William Rodamer of Altoona.

The company joined the Regiment as replacements, at Bermuda Hundred, Virginia, on the first of March, and on the 12th, fifteen days after being mustered, the men were doing picket duty within one hundred yards of rebel works, on the point of land between the Appomattox and the James River.

The Blair County Company participated in the following battle:

    Petersburg   Virginia   Apr. 3, 1865

The Regiment was mustered out of the service at Portsmouth, Virginia, on the 25th of August, 1865.

SEVENTY-SEVENTH PENNSYLVANIA INFANTRY

Company F, numbering one hundred and five members, of the Seventy-seventh Regiment of Pennsylvania Infantry, was principally recruited at Hollidaysburg, and mustered into the service about the 27th of February, 1865, under command of Captain Daniel Shock of Claysburg.

The company joined the regiment as replacements at Strawberry Plains, East Tennessee, and served in this vicinity until the close of the war, without being engaged with the enemy. The Regiment was then ordered to Texas where it served until the 6th of December, 1865, when it was mustered out of the service.

ONE HUNDRED AND THIRD PENNSYLVANIA INFANTRY

Company H, numbering eighty-seven members, of the One hundred and Third Regiment of Pennsylvania Infantry, was recruited in Blair County, and mustered into the service during March and April, 1865, under the command of Captain Joseph W. Daugherty of Altoona.

The company joined the Regiment as replacements in April, 1865, and served with the army in Virginia, without being engaged with the enemy. It was mustered out of the service at Newbern, North Carolina, on the 25th of June, 1865.

VETERANS' ORGANIZATIONS

A number of attempts were made following the close of the Civil War by various groups to unite the returning Union soldiers into Veterans' organizations. Some of these attempts were successful and brought forth national organizations, of which, the Grand Army of the Republic was the largest and most popular.

Possibly the earliest effort made in Blair County to organize the returned soldiers is recorded by the following item which appeared in the *Hollidaysburg Register* of 1866: "The Soldiers' Union No. 1, of Pennsylvania, meets in the Town Hall, 2nd Floor, every Monday evening at 7 o'clock, J. R. McFarlane, President; H. H. Snyder, Secretary."

The Grand Army of the Republic was first suggested and planned by Doctor B. F. Stephenson of Springfield, Illinois, and the first unit was instituted at Springfield during the early part of 1866. Other units were formed, and on the 12th of July, 1866, representative soldiers from all parts of the State met at Springfield to perfect a permanent and national organization. It is highly significant that this great organization of union soldiers should have its incipience in the town of Springfield, Illinois, where the great Commoner and friend of the soldier, Abraham Lincoln, received his early law training and where he resided at the time of his election to the Presidency of the United States.

Based on those cardinal principles of Loyalty, Charity and Fraternity:— the Grand Army of the Republic grew rapidly and at the height of its influence, about 1890, it was considered of great value to the welfare of the soldiers and their dependents, and was held in high esteem by the community and was influential in determining the national policies of the United States.

Nine G.A.R. Posts were formed in Blair County between the years 1867 and 1888, and continued in existence until insufficient numbers attended the meetings due to infirmities of old age and lack of members. In addition to the nine G.A.R. Posts of Blair County, one other, the James D. Noble Post No. 451, of Woodbury, formed about 1883, by its close proximity to Blair County, contained members from Blair County.

A group of soldiers of Tyrone formed themselves into an organization known as the Major C. S. W. Jones Garrison No. 58, Army and Navy Union, in honor of Major Charles Sullivan Worrell Jones who was born at Graysville, Huntingdon County, on the 29th of October, 1842, a son of Samuel and Elizabeth Jones. He enlisted in Company F, 2nd Pennsylvania Cavalry, on the 1st of March, 1862, as a Private, and after serving successively as Corporal, Sergeant, Lieutenant and Captain, was discharged on the 13th of July, 1865. He organized the Sheridan Troop of Tyrone in 1871, and served as its Captain until his death on the 6th of May, 1905, including service during the Spanish-American War, as a Major of Pennsylvania Cavalry.

Encampment Number 17, Union Veteran League, of Altoona was chartered on the 20th of August, 1887. A bronze plaque containing the names and organizations of its members, as of July, 1911, was placed on the 14th Street side of the Second National Bank building, Altoona, and later removed to the American Legion building, 1123 13th Avenue, Altoona. The inscription on this plaque reads as follows: "Union Veteran League composed of officers, soldiers, sailors and marines, of the Union Army, Navy and Marine Corps, during the War of the Rebellion who volunteered prior to the first of July, 1863, for a term of three years, and were honorably discharged for any cause after a service of at least two continuous years, or were at any time discharged by reason of wounds received in line of duty. No drafted person or substitute, nor any one who at any time bore arms against the United States, shall be eligible to Membership."

The following history of the G.A.R. Posts of Blair County is not complete due to many important historical facts being unavailable at this time.

COL. WILLIAM G. MURRAY POST NO. 39

The first Blair County unit of the Grand Army of the Republic was formed at Hollidaysburg during April, 1867, and mustered by H. H. Snyder on the 4th of March, 1867. This Post was titled Col. William G. Murray Post No. 39, and continued active until the 15th of October, 1869. A re-organization meeting was held in Stehley's Hall, corner Mulberry and Wayne Streets, on the 17th of July, 1877, when the following named members "whose names appeared on the descriptive book were duly mustered by Captain A. J. Hamilton, Deputy District Adjutant General," of Philadelphia; William C. Roller, Isaac F. Beamer, James Tearney, Henry L. Bunker, James R. Williamson, Charles H. Young, John R. McFarlane, George W. Cruse, Jonothan Derno, Ephraim Gerst, Henry A. Miller, James P. Stewart, Johnson C. Akers, John Wighaman, John B. McKee and Thomas Tierney.

The officers elected at this meeting to serve for the year 1867, were as follows: Commander, Isaac F. Beamer; Senior Vice-Commander, James Tearney, Junior Vice-Commander, Jonathan Derno; Surgeon, William C. Roller; Chaplain, Henry L. Bunker, Quartermaster, John Wighaman; Officer of the Day, Johnson C. Akers; Officer of the Guard Ephraim Gerst.

Post No. 39 was named in honor of the memory of William Gray Murray, who was born in Ireland on the 25th of July, 1825, and who resided in Harrisburg, where he enlisted for service during the Mexican War on the 26th of December, 1846. He served as a Sergeant in Company G, (Cameron Guards) 2nd Pennsylvania Infantry and was later commissioned a Second Lieutenant and assigned to the 11th United States Infantry. He was discharged on the 14th of August, 1848, after performing arduous service in Mexico under General Scott.

Shortly after the close of the Mexican War, William Gray Murray moved to Hollidaysburg, where, during the fall of 1861, he recruited men to make up the 84th Regiment of Pennsylvania Infantry, and upon the organization of the Regiment he was chosen its Colonel, and commissioned by Governor Curtin of Pennsylvania under date of the 28th of December, 1861. Colonel Murray continued in command of the 84th until the 23rd of March, 1862, when he was instantly killed while engaged in battle at Kerntown, near Winchester, Virginia. His horse having been shot from under him, he lead his men on foot against the enemy when he received a bullet in the forehead. He was the first Pennsylvania Colonel to be killed in the war and the sad event created deep feeling throughout the entire country. His remains were returned to Hollidaysburg, where many citizens and soldiers paid their respects and burial was held in the St. Mary's Cemetery in Hollidaysburg.

Colonel Murray's name is handed down to the present generation by reason of the respect and esteem in which he was held by his comrades. Even though the last member of Post 39 has passed to the great beyond, history will forever record the death and sacrifice of this soldier and the achievements of the G.A.R. Post named in his honor. The surviving members of the Hollidaysburg Post of the G.A.R., namely: Harrison T. Stiffler, Levi Leedom and John A. Smith, held the final meeting of the Post at the home of Levi Leedom at Hollidaysburg on the 2nd of June, 1931, at which time it was decided to disband and to surrender the charter to the Department Headquarters. The last commander to serve this Post was D. M. Lotz of Duncansville, and the last Adjutant was Levi Leedom of Hollidaysburg.

The three surviving members who attended the last meeting of the Post have answered the last summons and passed to the great beyond. The last survivor was Harrison T. Stiffler of Canoe Creek, who died on the 28th of December, 1932.

The monument at the Court House, corner of Union and Allegheny Streets, was erected by the Commissioners of the County of Blair, as the citizens' tribute to the memory of the soldiers and sailors of the Civil War, and was unveiled on the 11th of June, 1896. The designer and erector was the Badger Brothers, of West Quincy, Massachusetts, and the cost was ten thousand dollars.

LT. S. C. POTTS POST NO. 62

The Lt. S. C. Potts Post No. 62, Department of Pennsylvania, Grand Army of the Republic, was instituted at Altoona on the 20th of July, 1877, with the following fourteen veterans of the Civil War as charter members: George H. Gwin, Jacob D. Fries, George F. Dern, Isaiah W. Toomey, Josiah W. Fries, John B. Brady, Harrison O'Burn, Franklin B. Stewart, Charles Copeland, Jacob D. Hirst, Albert Boyer, Caleb H. Closson, David W. Eakins and Theodore Burchfield.

The *Altoona Tribune* of the 16th of January, 1879, contained the following item, "The Officers of Lieut. Stephen C. Potts Post No. 62, Grand Army of the Republic, were mustered on Thursday evening, the 9th inst., by mustering officer Theodore Burchfield, assisted by Comrade J. N. Reber of Post 8, of Philadelphia. The following are the officers for the present term: Post Commander, William Few; Senior Vice-Commander, Malden Valentine; Junior Vice-Commander, Henry Hawk; Adjutant, Isaiah W. Toomey; Quartermaster, Edward McLean; Surgeon, William D. Hall; Chaplain, Henry B. Kendig; Officer of the Day, John R. Garden; Officer of the Guard, David W. Eakins; Sergeant Major, Theodore Stroh; Quartermaster Sergeant, Reuben M. Lewis; Inside Sentinel, Harry Miller; Outside Sentinel, Henry E. Fettinger. Meetings to be held semi-monthly at the Odd Fellows' Hall, over the Altoona Bank."

Post No. 62 was named in honor of the memory of Stephen Collins Potts, who was born at Butler, Pennsylvania, on the 24th of July, 1841. He was commissioned at the age of 19, a Second Lieutenant of Company H, 3rd Pennsylvania Infantry, (Juniata Rifles of Hollidaysburg) and served from the 20th of April, 1861, until the 29th of July, 1861. On the 9th of August, 1861, he was commissioned a First Lieutenant in Company M, 62nd Pennsylvania Infantry, and was wounded during the battle of Fredericksburg on the 13th of December, 1862, dying the following day. The *Altoona Tribune* of the 23rd of December, 1862, contained the following item, "The body of Lt. S. C. Potts was taken to Hollidaysburg on a special train, on Sunday, accompanied by the Good Will Fire Company, of which he was a member, and the Mountaineers."

Memorial Day and Grand Army Day were observed with special attention each year by the soldiers of this vicinity. The *Altoona Tribune* of the 20th of May, 1875, reports the proceedings of a meeting on Decoration Day observance, as follows: "The meeting at the Council Chamber on Thursday evening last completed the arrangements for the proper observance of Decoration Day. A Committee of arrangements was elected consisting of Robert Johnson, Chairman; Captain H. B. Huff, Colonel F. B. Stewart, Captain R. J. Crozier, Lt. J. G. Shollenberger, Captain F. P. Confer, Major John R. Garden, Captain E. M. Warren, R. Morgan, Alex. Blakely, W. H. Harkness and W. P. Spielman. The object of this committee is to effect an organization of a Soldiers' Memorial Association to exist in perpetum. Sub-committees were appointed for music, contribution of flowers and invitations. Captain E. M. Warren was chosen Chief Marshal, and Captain R. Johnson and R. Morgan, assistants."

It is with pride that it can be recorded here that the wishes of the committee of 1875 has been complied with and that the Memorial Day Committee of Altoona continues to function. The observance of Grand Army Day was an annual event held at Lakemont Park during the first part of September, when many veterans and their friends assembled to greet the living and to honor the dead.

The final meeting of Post 62 was held in the G.A.R. Hall, 911 Chestnut Avenue, on the 8th of September, 1934, and the charter surrendered. A Memorial Scroll was presented to the Post, recording the date organized, date disbanded, and the names of the following surviving members: Isaac P. Patch, Patrick Laughlin, John G. Wolf, John W. Swartz, John B. Harnden, William Lee Woodcock, John W. McAlarney, Thompson Davis and Richard F. Fowler. The only survivor of this group today is John W. McAlarney of Loop Station, Penna.

LIEUT. H. N. LOWER POST NO. 82

A Post of the Grand Army of the Republic was organized by the Union soldiers of Roaring Spring and vicinity, during the summer of 1867, and mustered on the 24th of September, the same year, as the General John Sedgwick Post. This Post was named in honor of the memory of Major General John Sedgwick, a native of the state of Connecticut, who commanded troops during the Civil War and was killed in action on the 9th of May, 1864, at the battle of Spottsylvania, Virginia.

The General John Sedgwick Post was disbanded on the 30th of September, 1881, and re-organized on the 17th of November, 1881, as the Lieut. H. N. Lower Post No. 82, and its rolls contained the names of fifty members during the year 1882.

The names of the charter members were as follows: William Hite, John W. Young, William F. Kyle, Charles Wilson, James W. Hayes, George W. Lingenfelter, Martin Lingenfelter, David B. Carpenter, George W. Hoover, John W. Daugherty, David R. P. Gilliland, Benjamin F. Shoemaker, George Hainsey, Daniel Lear, George Neff, William L. Snyder and John A. J. Williams.

The officers elected to serve during the year 1882 were as follows: Commander, William Hite; Senior Vice-Commander, John W. Young; Junior Vice-Commander, David B. Carpenter; Quartermaster, Charles Wilson; Chaplain, John A. J. Williams; Officer of the Day, Benjamin F. Shoemaker; Officer of the Guard, George W. Hoover; Sergeant Major, John W. Daugherty; Quartermaster Sergeant, James W. Hayes.

Post No. 82 was named in honor of the memory of Henry N. Lower who was born in 1841, on the Lower homestead, Taylor Township, near Roaring Spring. He served first as a Private in Company I, 137th Pennsylvania Infantry, enlisting on the 20th of August, 1862 and discharged on the 1st of June, 1863, and later commissioned a First Lieutenant in Company C, 205th Pennsylvania Infantry. Eighty-four members of Company C, were recruited during August, 1864, by Lieut. Henry N. Lower, Captain Louis D. Spiece and Lieut. David M. Butler, at Roaring Spring. However, at that time the town was known as Spang's Mills, and on the muster rolls for Company C, 205th, it was designated as Spring Mills. The 205th Regiment of Pennsylvania Infantry participated in the battle of Petersburg where Lieutenant Lower was killed on the 2nd of April, 1865, in the charge on Fort Sedgwick, in the capture of Battery 30. His body was not returned to Blair County, but was buried in the battlefield cemetery at Petersburg.

The Lieut. H. N. Lower Post met every Friday evening in the Odd Fellows' Hall, and remained active until the year 1927, when it disbanded and its records were surrendered to the Department Headquarters of the Grand Army of the Republic, whose headquarters were maintained during recent years in room 340, City Hall, Philadelphia. Upon inquiry we are informed that the descriptive book had been deposited in the State Library Building at Harrisburg. The descriptive books of the various G.A.R. Posts contained a complete record of members including their military organization, dates of enlistment and discharge, when mustered as a member of the Post, date of muster out or death, and often showed the place of burial. These books are a valuable record of the Post and should be preserved.

The Commander for the year 1889 was John W. Blake, who entered the Army at the age of fifteen, and who died on the 5th of March, 1936, being, probably the last survivor of those who held membership in the Lieut. H. N. Lower Post. John W. Blake served as a First Lieutenant in Company F, 3rd Pennsylvania Artillery and while stationed at Fortress Monroe he had the distinction of shaking hands with President Abraham Lincoln, an honor and privilege that he prided and related with pleasure throughout his life, as a resident of Morrison's Cove.

COL. D. M. JONES POST NO. 172

A Post of the Grand Army of the Republic was organized at Tyrone during the summer of 1868 and mustered in on the 9th of November, 1868.

This Post disbanded on the 15th of October, 1869, and was re-organized and mustered in on the 8th of May, 1880, as the Col. D. M. Jones Post No. 172, with a membership of nearly four hundred at the height of its career, which was about 1890.

The names of the first officers elected to serve this Post after its re-organization were as follows: Commander, Graham M. Closson; Senior Vice-Commander, James C. Bell; Junior Vice-Commander, Thomas S. McCahan; Adjutant, Josiah D. Hicks; Quartermaster, Cicero M. Ewing; Officer of the Day, Charles S. W. Jones; Officer of the Guard, Lewis J. Givler; Sergeant Major, Henry B. Piper; Sergeant Major, Stephen V. Haslett; Quartermaster Sergeant, William T. Henderson.

This Post held its meetings during the early days of its existence on the 2nd and 4th Saturdays of each month, in the Harris Hall and later in the Study building, and of late years in the Municipal building.

Post No. 172 was named in honor of the memory of David Mattern Jones who was born in Huntingdon County on the 24th of April, 1838, a son of Samuel and Elizabeth Jones. He first enlisted for service during the Civil War as a Corporal on the 20th of April, 1861, and served in Comapny D, 3rd Regiment of Pennsylvania Infantry for three months, being discharged with the Company on the 29th of July, 1861. During the fall of 1861, he recruited a company at Tyrone and vicinity, for a three year term of service and was commissioned Captain on the 24th of October, 1861. This company was designated Company A, 110th Pennsylvania Infantry and participated in many important battles during the War. Captain Jones was promoted to Major on the 16th of June, 1862, in recognition of meritorious service during several engagements. He was wounded in the wrist during the battle of Bull Run and taken prisoner at the battle of Chancellorsville but was exchanged in a couple of weeks and rejoined his command. While serving as commander of a battalion of the 110th Regiment during the battle of Gettysburg, he had his left leg shot off which incapacitated him for further military service. Before being discharged, he was, on the 21st of December, 1862, promoted to the rank of Lieutenant Colonel of the Regiment and finally left the service on the 9th of October, 1863. Colonel Jones died on the 16th of July, 1877, at Denver, Colorado, where he had gone in the hope of regaining his health. His body was returned to Blair County and the burial took place in the Grandview Cemetery at Tyrone.

During the year 1886, Carey H. Russell served as Post Commander, and the officers for the year 1897 were as follows: Commander, Charles S. W. Jones; Senior Vice-Commander, P. H. Meadville; Junior Vice-Commander, J. P. Bateman; Adjutant, Martin Burley; Trustees, C. S. W. Jones, J. A. Loudon and H. F. Copelin.

The Col. D. M. Jones Post of the Grand Army of the Republic disbanded during the year 1930 and its records were surrendered to the Department Headquarters at Philadelphia. An historical record book was kept of the members of this Post which is still in existence. This record gave the military record and a sketch of the services of the members during the War.

The last surviving member of the Tyrone Post of the G.A.R. was John W. Bookhamer, a Past Commander, who died on the 8th of February, 1936, a resident of Tyrone.

The only surviving veteran of the Civil War residing in Tyrone at this time is Henry H. Bryan who is now 98 years old. He served as a Private in Company H, 3rd Pennsylvania Infantry, (Juniata Rifles of Hollidaysburg) and later as the Quartermaster Sergeant of Company H, 22nd Regiment of Pennsylvania Cavalry.

SANFORD F. BEYER POST NO. 426

A Post of the Grand Army of the Republic was organized at Bellwood by the veterans of the Civil War who resided in that vicinity, during the early spring of 1884 and was mustered on the 18th of April, 1884. The names of the charter members and other important historical facts appears to be lost or destroyed as such information is unavailable at this time.

The Bellwood Post of the G.A.R. was named in honor of the memory of Sanford Frederick Beyer who was born at Beyer's Mills, near Tipton, Blair County, about 1841, a son of Aaron and Lydia Ramey Beyer. Sanford F. Beyer enlisted as a Private in Company A, 110th Regiment of Pennsylvania Infantry on the 24th of October, 1861, and served through many battles and engagements with his company. He was taken prisoner and after months of confinement in a tobacco warehouse at Richmond, Virginia, he was exchanged and came home to recuperate. Afterwards, rejoining his regiment and while engaged in the Petersburg Campaign, he was killed by a minnie ball during the battle at Hatcher's Run on the 25th of March, 1865. His body was returned to his home and buried in the Mt. Zion Cemetery, near Bellwood.

An older sister, Catharine Blake Beyer who was born at Charlottesville, Blair County, on the 1st of January, 1840, served as a Nurse with the Army of the Potomac during the year 1863, being stationed at the General Hospital, Harper's Ferry, Virginia.

The first Commander to serve Post No. 426 of Bellwood was Solomon F. Forgeus, and the first Adjutant was Arthur F. Alward. Solomon F. Forgeus continued to serve as commander until 1888 when he became Adjutant which office he held for many years, being one of the most active members of this Post until moving elsewhere.

This Post enrolled fifty-eight members by the first of the year 1885, and was active in community affairs as well as contributing to the welfare of the disabled veterans and their dependents.

According to the minutes of this Post, ten French rifled muskets were purchased from the War Department on the 9th of December, 1884, and on the 28th of September, 1885, the Post contributed the sum of $10.20 to the General Grant Memorial Fund.

The names of other members of this Post who served as Commanders are: William A. McDermitt, Graham M. Meadville, Adolphus H. Smith, H. C. Roth, Elijah Estep and George M. Miles.

The Sanford F. Beyer Post disbanded in 1924 and its charter was surrendered to Department Headquarters. Each Post of the G. A. R. received a charter signed by the Department Commander and the Assistant Adjutant General. These charters recorded the names of the members who participated in the organization of the Post, known as the charter members, and in the top center appeared a cluster of Union Flags with the American Eagle in front. Beneath appeared in writing the names of the charter members. Between the tiers of names appeared the Grand Army insignia and the wording appearing on the charter was as follows: "Grand Army of the Republic: To all unto whom these Presents come, Greetings: Know Ye, That reposing full trust and confidence in the fidelity and faithfulness of these members, . . . I do hereby in conformity with the rules and regulations of the Grand Army of the Republic, and by virtue of the power and authority in me vested, constitute them and their associates and successors, a post of the Grand Army of the Republic to be known as ...... Post, No. ...., of Blair County, Department of Pennsylvania.

"And I authorize and empower them to perform all acts necessary to conduct said organization in accordance with the rules and regulations of the G. A. R.

"Dated at the headquarters of the Department of Pennsylvania of the Grand Army of the Republic at Philadelphia on the .... day of ...., in the year of our Lord one thousand eight hundred and .... and of our independence the one hundred and .....

JAS. H. GIBBONEY POST NO. 465

The Duncansville Post of the Grand Army of the Republic, Department of Pennsylvania, was organized by veterans of the Civil War who resided in that vicinity about 1884.

Neither the names of the charter members, the names of the officers, or other important historical facts concerning this Post are available at the present time and may have been destroyed.

This Post was named in honor of the memory of James H. Gibboney, who was born at Duncansville, in 1839. He enlisted first as a Private in Company H, 14th Regiment of Pennsylvania Infantry, (Blair County Rifles of Duncansville) on the 24th of April, 1861, for a three month term, and was discharged on the 3rd of August, 1861. On the 13th of August, 1862, he re-enlisted as a Corporal in Company G, 125th Regiment of Pennsylvania Infantry, and was killed in action during the battle of Antietam, Maryland, on the 17th of September, 1862, exactly one month after the arrival of the regiment at Washington, D. C., from Camp Curtin, Harrisburg, Pennsylvania.

One of the members of the 125th Regiment of Pennsylvania Infantry, a survivor of the Battle of Antietam, wrote the following description of the day's events in his diary: "Wednesday, September 17, 1862. The Regiment was ordered forward by the flank, was then thrown into column of companies and marched one-fourth mile where we formed line of battle, passing through a strip of woods driving the enemy before us into an open field, very heavy musketry all the time, when half-way between this wood, and the road leading from Hagerstown to Sharpsburg we were ordered to lay down in an open field, remaining in this position about one hour we received orders to go forward double quick, halting on the edge of a strip of woods on the right of the stone church on the road leading from Hagerstown to Sharpsburg. We then sent forward our skirmish line, some ten or fifteen minutes elapsed before we received orders to fire, having the enemy in sight and picking our man, made every shot effective, and from the account of a rebel Colonel given us while over the lines under a flag of truce to get our wounded and dead. He stated that we had killed more than eight hundred of their men, they could hardly be made to believe it was only a single regiment. We were sent in alone as a bait to draw them (the enemy) out of the woods. We were ordered to fall back several times before our men could be made to leave the ground so intent were they in firing into the enemy's ranks. We were almost surrounded and suffered greatly from an enfilading fire, whole companies would seem to fall at a single volley. After we got back across the open field out of range of the batteries, and were resting when several officers rode up to our regiment and stated that we had won great laurels for the bravery we had shown in the engagement. Having had nothing to eat all day, 'Hard Tack' was issued to us just before dark, we then laid down on the ground until morning."

The only soldier of Company G, to be killed during the day's action was James H. Gibboney of Duncansville. However, of the fifteen wounded, several died as a result of their wounds. The body of James H. Gibboney was returned to his home and burial took place in the Presbyterian Cemetery at Hollidaysburg.

The name of the commander of the G. A. R. Post of Duncansville for the year 1886 was William H. McKee.

This Post held its meetings at one time in the building over the store recently conducted by J. Lee Wilt.

The only surviving Civil War veteran of this vicinity is James C. Megahan, who resides at 510 West 14th Street, aged 92, who is also one of the three surviving veterans residing in Blair County.

FRED C. WARD POST NO. 468

A second Altoona Post of the Grand Army of the Republic was instituted on the 7th of January, 1885, at which time the following members were present: William T. Miller, Martin H. Mackey, David Counsman, Thomas Moore, John Currie, Josiah D. Hicks, Abraham Rhodes, Joseph R. Brashears, Joseph W. Gardner, Thomas C. Nicholson and John A. Hindman. This Post maintained its Post home at 800 Eighth Avenue until recent years when it joined other organizations in the maintenance of the G. A. R. rooms at 911 Chestnut Avenue.

Post No. 468 was named in honor of the memory of Frederick Calloway Ward, who was born on the 12th of November, 1842, and who enlisted on the 14th of August, 1862, as a Private in Company K, 125 Pennsylvania Infantry. He was wounded severely in the hip during the battle of Antietam, Maryland, on the 17th of September, 1862, and died from his wounds on the 19th. His body was not returned home but was buried in the National Cemetery at Antietam.

The members of Post 468 joined with the citizens, and members of other organizations in honoring the soldier dead who are buried in the cemeteries located in Altoona and vicinity by placing metal markers, flags and flowers on each grave prior to Memorial Day of each year. Among the graves to be cared for are those in the Circle in the Fairview Cemetery, where burial of Union soldiers was first made in 1862.

The monument within the circle of soldiers' graves was dedicated on the 4th of July, 1867, with appropriate ceremonies, being presented by the citizens of Altoona to the memory of those who made the supreme sacrifice during the Civil War. A Soldiers' Monument Association was organized at Altoona during 1866, and chartered in the Blair County Courts. A sum of money in excess of $4000 was raised by a "Ladies' Fair" which was held in the Masonic Temple, Altoona, from January 8th to the 12th, 1867, during which time various articles were "presented and voted for at the prices per vote, as annexed." The monument, composed of a granite base and an Italian marble column, standing twenty-six feet high, was erected by John Baird of Philadelphia, at a cost of four thousand dollars.

The names of the soldiers of Altoona and vicinity, as inscribed on the monument are as follows: Capt. Henry Wayne, Capt. T. L. McGlathery, Capt. P. T. Keys, Lt. Geo. W. Burley, Lt. P. Morris, Lt. S. C. Potts, Lt. R. J. Clarke, J. Kelly, C. R. Everson, Jr., J. S. McLaughlin, B. J. Burley, D. Foust, L. M. Beals, J. G. Bowers, J. McLaughlin, J. Bush, J. Markley, G. Williams, B. F. Tipton, F. Hench, G. G. Kress, F. G. Ward, J. T. Moore, W. H. Wilgis, M. A. Riggle, S. B. Stewart, W. J. Reid, W. Moore, C. B. Bates, H. Burkholder, S. F. Stevens, A. Fry, J. Fry, L. Valentine, J. D. Hagerty, D. W. Oswalt, S. L. Hoar, F. Wentzell, D. Ragan, T. T. McClain, H. Kentner, Jas. Maxwell, W. Battenberg, W. H. Buck, T. G. Arble, J. Meloy, J. Maurer, W. Walker, D. B. Webber, D. M. Burkholder, W. Haggerty, J. R. Morrow, J. Aurandt, G. R. Daugherty, J. E. Davis, L. Davis, L. Mabus, A. C. Gwin, H. Bartlebaugh, J. B. Brown, L. Fleck, W. Fry, W. Boyles, H. C. Buel, D. Kounsman, J. A. Boyles, D. Coho, I. K. Morgan, J. M. Knox, J. Hurley, W. Weirbaugh, J. A. Brown, J. S. Hamilton, J. G. Morrow, E. Evers, R. P. Engles, J. Allison, J. B. Kinsel, J. L. Kinsel.

The final meeting of Post 468 was held in the G. A. R. hall on the 15th of August, 1934, at which time action was taken to disband, and the charter was accordingly surrendered to Department Headquarters on the 16th. A Memorial Scroll was presented to the Post, recording the date of organization, date disbanded, and the names of the following surviving members: Henry V. Carls, John F. Kelly, Stewart C. Wilson, James Yount, David R. Demaree, Millard F. Singiser, and Adam C. Hammaker. Of this group, the last to answer the final summons was Henry V. Carls, who died on the 23rd of August, 1938. The last Post Commander was Stewart C. Wilson, who had served in this capacity for the past twelve years.

The last surviving Civil War veterans of Altoona were John B. Harnden and Robert L. Rohm.

LT. ROBT. M. JOHNSTON POST NO. 474

The Williamsburg Post of the Grand Army of the Republic, Department of Pennsylvania, was instituted about 1885.

This Post was named in honor of the memory of Robert M. Johnston, who was born on the 17th of October, 1842. He enlisted first as a Private in Company C, 3rd Pennsylvania Infantry and served for three months, from the 20th of April, 1861, until the 29th of July. Upon the organization of the 125th Regiment of Pennsylvania Infantry, during the summer of 1862, he was commissioned a First Lieutenant, to date from the 16th of August, and appointed as Regimental Adjutant. While acting Major during the Battle of Antietam on the 17th of September, 1862, he was mortally wounded, dying two days later. The body of Lieutenant Johnston was returned to his home and buried in the Presbyterian Cemetery at Williamsburg.

The members of the Williamsburg Post of the G. A. R. were always active in the welfare of their comrades, and the observance of Memorial Day. This Post included the veterans of previous wars in its list of graves to be decorated and by similar action elsewhere, Decoration Day acquired a broader meaning and became known as Memorial Day, and dedicated to the soldiers of all wars.

General James A. Logan, Commander-in-chief of the Grand Army of the Republic, issued orders to the members of his organization requesting them to decorate the graves of their fallen comrades. General Orders No. 11, reads as follows:

"The 30th of May, 1868, is designated for the purpose of strewing with flowers or otherwise decorating the graves of comrades who died in defense of their country during the late rebellion and whose bodies now lie in almost every city, village and hamlet churchyard in the land. In this observance no form of ceremony is prescribed, but Posts and comrades will in their own way arrange such fitting services and testimonials of respect as circumstances may permit. We are organized, comrades, as our regulations tell us for the purpose among other things, 'of observing and strengthening these kind and fraternal feelings which have bound together the soldiers, sailors and marines who united to suppress the late rebellion.' What can aid more to assure this result than cherishing tenderly the memory of our heroic dead who made their breasts a barricade between our country and its foes? Their soldiers' lives were the reveille of freedom to a race in chains, and their death the tattoo of rebellious tyranny in arms. We should guard their graves with sacred vigilance. All that the consecrated wealth and taste of the Nation can add to their adornment and security is but a fitting tribute to the memory of her slain defenders. Let no wanton foot tread rudely on such hallowed ground. Let pleasant paths invite the coming and going of reverent visitors and fond mourners. Let no vandalism or avarice or neglect, no ravages of time testify to the present or the coming generations that we have forgotten as a people the cost of a free and undivided Republic. If other eyes grow dull and other hands slack, and other hearts grow cold in the solemn trust, ours shall keep it well as long as the light and warmth of life remain in us. Let us, then, at the time appointed gather around their sacred remains and garland the passionless wounds above them with the choicest of flowers of spring time; let us raise above them the dear old flag they saved from dishonor; let us in this solemn presence, renew our pledges to aid and assist those whom they left among us a sacred charge upon a Nation's gratitude —the soldier's and sailor's widow and orphan. It is the purpose of the Commander-in-chief to inaugurate this observance with the hope that it will be kept from year to year, while a survivor of the war remains to honor the memory of his departed comrades."

The Lt. Robt. M. Johnston Post No. 474, of Williamsburg, surrendered its charter on the 20th of October, 1918, and the Post disbanded. The last surviving Civil War veteran was William H. Lower, who died in 1934.

PETER SHOEMAN POST NO. 574

The last Post of the Grand Army of the Republic to be formed in Blair County was organized at Martinsburg on the 1st of May, 1888; the charter being dated at Philadelphia on the 18th of May, which was also the date of muster. The names of the charter members are as follows: John M. Bateman, David S. Bloom, Christian H. Bowers, James S. Brantner, William M. Chaplin, George Emigh, Jr., Daniel W. Fix, Jacob S. Keagy, Jacob C. Kochendarfer, Levi W. Port, William Roberts, David Shoeman, James Snyder, William L. Spanogle, Jacob M. Smith and George T. Vallance. The first Commander of this Post was Levi W. Port, and the meetings were held in the Odd Fellows' Building, but as the membership dwindled during the more recent years, the meetings were held in the office of John H. Nicodemus.

Post No. 574 was named in honor of the memory of Peter Shoeman, a young soldier of North Woodbury Township, whose military record we are unable to obtain. All efforts to secure the rank and organization, or the date and place of his death, have been futile. To Miss Ella M. Snowberger, of North Woodbury Township, we are indebted to for the only printed reference to this soldier. In her writings for the *Morrison's Cove Herald*, entitled "Recollections of By-gone Days in the Cove," she relates, from interviews with Cove resident, that Peter Shoeman was, "Detailed to carry water from a spring which was exposed to the fire of the enemy, he had been shot down. They found the body three days later. He had tried to staunch a gaping wound in his chest with a wad of grass and leaves which he thrust into the hole."

It is reported in the columns of the *Morrison's Cove Herald* of the 10th of January, 1889, that "William Young, Martinsburg cigar maker, presented the Peter Shoeman Post of the G.A.R. with a gavel made from a piece of wood taken from Culp's Hill on the Gettysburg battlefield. A bullet shot from a gun in the battle was sticking from the end of the gavel. The gift was greatly appreciated by the Grand Army men and it was decided to use the gavel at their meetings.

The Martinsburg Post of the Grand Army of the Republic disbanded about 1916, and the charter is being preserved by Miss Ella Nicodemus, daughter of John H. Nicodemus, one of the last surviving Civil War veterans of Martinsburg.

A worthy project has been undertaken by Doctor C. N. Johnson, of Martinsburg, towards beautifying the entrance to the park, and at the same time, to erect a memorial to the soldiers of Morrison's Cove. The Park, now incorporated is managed by a Board of Directors elected by the people of the Cove, and there has been erected a monument built of stones secured from the Gettysburg battlefield, on which a granite tablet has been placed containing the following inscription: "Morrison's Cove Memorial Park, dedicated July 4, 1934, in memory of the soldiers and sailors of Morrison's Cove."

Eight pillars supporting anchor chains secured from the Philadelphia Naval Yard, containing 109 links, surround the monument. Each link represents a soldier of the Cove who died in the service. Two anchors, located back of the monument, support a large link which represents the unknown soldiers of the Cove. The anchors were secured from the Philadelphia Naval Yard, while the link was forged from pig iron secured from the Valley Forge Park Commission. The expenses in connection with the link were contributed by 1041 pupils of the Morrison's Cove schools. A large sandstone secured from the site of Fort Necessity is placed in front of the anchor and will be used to support a bronze tablet. The twenty-four stone pillars support anchor chains, secured from the Norfolk Naval Yards, containing 1249 links representing the soldiers who returned from the wars. One hundred pound cannon balls, from the Watervliet Arsenal, rest on top of the pillars. Links painted black represent deceased soldiers and white ones, the living. The flag pole was the main mast of the U. S. Destroyer *Fanning*, and the 4.7 field piece was secured from the Aberdeen Arsenal.

REGISTER OF CIVIL WAR VETERANS

Name	Rank Organization	Born	Died	Cemetery	Location
Abbott, Alfred A.	Sgt. A, 125 Pa. Inf.				
	2 Lt. C, 22. Pa Cav.				
	1 Lt. H, 22 Pa. Cav.	1837			
Abbott, Amos	Pvt. C, 110 Pa. Inf.				
	Pvt. C, 53 Pa. Inf.				
Abbott, Charles A.	Pvt. I, 123 Pa. Inf.		1912	Grandview	Altoona
Abott, Jackson S. R.	Atr. D. 1 Pa. Art.	1835	1905	Carson Valley	Duncansville
Abbott, Peter M.	Pvt. M, 62 Pa. Inf.				
	Pvt. K, 91 Pa. Inf.				
Abt, Joseph	Pvt. I, 84 Pa. Inf.				
Ackers, Abner	Pvt. I, 192 Ohio Inf.		1895	Reformed	Loysburg
Ackison, David	Pvt. F, 11 Pa. Inf.		1862		
Acre, Henry H.	Pvt. D. 13 Pa. Cav.	1841			
Acre, William	Pvt. D. 13 Pa. Cav.	1839			
Adams, Alexander	Pvt. H, 22 Pa. Cav.	1844			
Adams, George S.	Pvt. Marine Corps	1845	1919	Fairview	Altoona
Adams, James W.	Pvt. F. 21 Pa. Cav.	1846	1916	Carson Valley	Duncansville
Adams, Nathan	Mus. D, 46 Pa. Mil.	1815	1878	Fairview	Altoona
Adams, Robert H.	Pvt. H, 57 Pa. Inf.	1848			
Adams, William A.	Pvt. E, 104 Pa. Inf.	1831	1901	St. Augustine	Cambria Co.
Adams, William H.	2 Lt. I, 22 Pa. Cav.	1837			
Affierbach, George	Pvt. C, 110 Pa. Inf.				
Africa, Henry	Pvt. B, 192 Pa. Inf.	1851	1907	Grandview	Tyrone
Africa, Samuel	Mus. A, 110 Pa. Inf.				
Ager, James	Pvt. K, 28 Pa. Inf.	1837	1906	Grazierville	Tyrone
Agnew, Daniel C.	Pvt. I, 22 Pa. Cav.	1846			
Agnew, Samuel Kyle	Far. I, 22 Pa. Cav.	1816	1870	Fairview	Altoona
Agnew, William	Pvt. H, 55 Pa. Inf.	1835	1926	Bedford	Penna.
Ague, George B.	Pvt. B, 19 Ohio Inf.	1848	1922	Logan Valley	Bellwood
Aikens, Alexander	Pvt. G, 55 Pa. Inf.	1831	1922	Greencastle	Penna.
Aikens, John	Pvt. I, 102 Pa. Inf.	1828	1865	St. Marys	Hollidaysburg
Aiken, Matthew	Sgt. G, 12 Pa. Cav.	1840			
Aiken, Stephen D.	Pvt. D, 125 Pa. Inf.	1841	1913	Fairview	Altoona
Aikens, William	Sgt. F, 76 Pa. Inf.	1839	1916	Oak Ridge	Altoona
Aimaker, John	Pvt. C, 110 Pa. Inf.				
Ainsworth, James W.	Pvt. A, 3 Pa. Inf.				
	Pvt. C, 110 Pa. Inf.	1828	1875	Rebecca Furnace	Martinsburg
Ainsworth, Samuel H.	Pvt. C, 110 Pa. Inf.				
Ake, Joseph H.	Sgn. 111 Pa. Inf.	1827	1887	Presbyterian	Williamsburg
Ake, Joseph W.	Pvt. A, 125 Pa. Inf.				
Ake, Joseph W.	Pvt. G, 12 Pa. Cav.	1843	1917	Rose Hill	Altoona
Ake, Joseph W.	Pvt. U, 205 Pa. Inf.	1843			
Ake, Samuel V. B.	Pvt. E, 84 Pa. Inf.				
Akers, Henry H.	Pvt. D, 13 Pa. Cav.	1841	1903	Carson Valley	Duncansville
Akers, John R.	Pvt. A, 133 Pa. Inf.	1845	1862	Sharpsburg	Maryland
Akers, John T.	Pvt. D, 101 Pa. Inf.	1846	1917	Presbyterian	Hollidaysburg
Akers, Johnson C.	Cpl. I, 14 Pa. Inf.				
	1 Lt. E, 1 Pa. Cav.	1839	1923	Lutheran	Hollidaysburg
Akers, William C.	Pvt. A, 84 Pa. Inf.	1845	1864	Wilderness	Virginia
Akers, Wilson Lee	Pvt. K, 125 Pa. Inf.				
	Cpl. C, 186 Pa. Inf.	1841	1918	Oak Ridge	Altoona
Akin, Matthew	Pvt. E, 3 Pa. Inf.	1840			
Albaugh, Henry A.	Pvt. A, 3 Pa. Inf.				
	Pvt. D, 84 Pa. Inf.				
	Pvt. M, 22 Pa. Cav.	1839	1864	Lutheran	Hollidaysburg
Albert, Francis	Pvt. A, 3 Pa. Inf.				
	Pvt. A, 84 Pa. Inf.	1840	1864	St. Marys	Hollidaysburg
Albert, John A.	Pvt. C, 84 Pa. Inf.				

SOLDIERS OF BLAIR COUNTY

Name	Rank Organization	Born	Died	Cemetery	Location
Albert, Thaddeus	Mus. F, 84 Pa. Inf.	1835	1881	St. Johns	Altoona
Albright, George B.		1827			
Albright, John	Pvt. A, 23 Pa. Mil.	1833			
Albright, Josiah C.	1 Lt. K, 158 Pa. Inf.	1826	1908	Oak Ridge	Altoona
Alcutt, David	Pvt. H, 33 Pa. Inf.	1834			
Alexander, Alfred	Pvt. A, 84 Pa. Inf.				
Alexander, George	Pvt. F, Ind. Bn. Pa. Mil.	1834			
Alexander, Hugh H.	Pvt. C, 159 O. N. G.	1845			
Alexander, James		1831	1862	Presbyterian	Hollidaysburg
Alexander, John A.	Ldn. U. S. Navy	1844	1935	Union	Hollidaysburg
Alexander, John S.	Pvt. B, 208 Pa. Inf.	1834	1905	Fairview	Altoona
Alexander, R. H.	Pvt. 97 Ohio Inf.				
Alexander, William H.	Pvt. B, 208 Pa. Inf.	1843	1888	Fairview	Altoona
Alleman, Jacob	Pvt. Ind. Cav. Pa. Mil.	1827			
Allen, George		1843	1916	Springfield	Ohio
Allen, Henry C.	Pvt. G, 148 Pa. Inf.	1846	1910	Fairview	Altoona
Allen, James J.	Pvt. C, 199 Pa. Inf.	1849	1881	Grandview	Tyrone
Allen, John T.	Cpl. F, 77 Pa. Inf.	1845			
Allen, John Westley	Sgn. 148 Pa. Inf.	1838	1895	Carlisle	Penna.
Allen, Samuel	Pvt. C, 76 Pa. Inf.	1842			
Allen, William	Pvt. C, 110 Pa. Inf.				
Allender, James D.	Pvt. C, 3 Pa. Inf.				
	Sgt. B, 125 Pa. Inf.				
	Sgt. E, 104 Pa. Inf.	1839	1902	Presbyterian	Williamsburg
Alley, Henry	Pvt. E, 104 Pa. Inf.	1832	1882	Methodist	Williamsburg
Alley, James H.	Pvt. F, Ind. Bn. Pa. Mil.	1845			
Alley, William	Pvt. E, 45 Pa. Inf.	1841	1915	Logan Valley	Bellwood
Allison, Jacob M.	Sgt. G, Pa. Mil.				
Allison, James	Pvt. I, 55 Pa. Inf.		1864	Charleston	S. Carolina
Allison, James M.	Pvt. C, 46 Pa. Mil.	1827			
Allison, Nathanuel	Pvt. K, 55 Pa. Inf.	1847	1912	Albrights	Roaring Spring
Alloway, John W.	Cpl. B, 1 Pa. Art.	1843	1921	Chicago	Ill.
Almaker, John	Pvt. C, 110 Pa. Inf.				
Alward, Arthur F.	Pvt. C, 187 Pa. Inf.	1845	1909	Logan Valley	Bellwood
Alward, John	Pvt. E, 12 U. S. Inf.				
	Pvt. B, 13 U. S. Inf.	1843	1891	Logan Valley	Bellwood
Ambrose, William	2 Lt. F, 31 Pa. Inf.				
	Sgt. A, 191 Pa. Inf.	1831			
Amheiser, Daniel	Pvt. B, 125 Pa. Inf.				
	Pvt. E, 104 Pa. Inf.				
Amheiser, George W.	Pvt. B, 3 Pa. Inf.				
	Cpl. D, 22 Pa. Cav.				
	Pvt. E, 104 Pa. Inf.	1841	1906	Fairview	Altoona
Ammerman, John T.	Pvt. G, 51 Pa. Inf.	1839	1910	Fairview	Altoona
Ammerman, Joseph	Cpl. G, 51 Pa. Inf.	1830	1920	Grandview	Tyrone
Ammerman, Joseph	Pvt. C, 49 Pa. Inf.		1883	Unionville	Penna.
Anderson, Alexander	Pvt. D, 120 Ohio Inf.		1900	Lewistown	Penna.
Anderson, David	Pvt. A, 110 Pa. Inf.				
Anderson, Henry	Bks. K, 22 Pa. Cav.	1843			
Anderson, James G.	Pvt. H. 4 Pa. Inf.				
	Pvt. E, 20 Pa. Cav.				
	Pvt. C, 1 Prov. Cav.	1836		Grandview	Tyrone
Anderson, Henry N.	Pvt. E, 3 Pa. Inf.				
	Sgt. C, 46 Pa. Mil.	1840			
Anderson, Johnson	Pvt. H, 110 Pa. Inf.				
Anderson, Sample	Pvt. H, 110 Pa. Inf.	1820		Grandview	Tyrone
Anderson, Samuel T.	Pvt. E, 3 Pa. Inf.	1832	1878	Fairview	Altoona
Anderson, William	Pvt. I, 205 Pa. Inf.				
Anderson, William	Pvt. A, 205 Pa. Inf.				
Andrews, Artemus	Pvt. E, 46 Pa. Mil.	1845			
Andrews, Charles	Pvt. C, 110 Pa. Inf.		1862	Port Republic	Virginia

THE CIVIL WAR

Name	Rank Organization	Born	Died	Cemetery	Location
Andrews, Charles	Sgt. C, 110 Pa. Inf.	1839	1879	Grandview	Tyrone
Andrews, David	Pvt. G, 125 Pa. Inf.				
Andrews, Jacob W.	Cpl. H. 14 Pa. Inf.				
	Pvt. K, 13 Pa. Cav.	1831	1925	Lutheran	Hollidaysburg
Andrews, James M.	Sgt. M, 12 Pa. Cav.	1839	1876	Carson Valley	Duncansville
Andrews, John C.	Pvt. C, 76 Pa. Inf.	1837			
Andrews, Samuel A.	2 Lt. H, 14 Pa. Inf.				
	1 Lt. G, 125 Pa. Inf.				
	Cpt. D, 192 Pa. Inf.	1833			
Andrews, William	Pvt. E, 46 Pa. Mil.	1803			
Andrews, William A.	Pvt. C, 110 Pa. Inf.		1864	Wilderness	Virginia
Anthony, Raymond S.	Pvt. M, 62 Pa. Inf.				
	Pvt. K, 91 Pa. Inf.				
Apple, Jacob	Pvt. M, 62 Pa. Inf.				
	Pvt. K, 91 Pa. Inf.		1864		
Applebaugh, Charles E.	Pvt. B, 110 Pa. Inf.				
	Pvt. D, 6 U. S. Cav.				
	Sgt. 76 Pa. Inf.	1837	1929	Oak Ridge	Altoona
Applegate, William R.	Pvt. 7 Bn. D. C. Mil.	1844	1878	Fairview	Altoona
Arble, Jacob C.	Pvt. Ind. Cav. Pa. Mil.				
	Cpl. D, 13 Pa. Cav.	1834	1917	Fairview	Altoona
Arble, James	Pvt. B, 3 Pa. Inf.	1842			
Arble, James B.	Pvt. A, 84 Pa. Inf.				
Arble, John H.	Pvt. K, 125 Pa. Inf.	1842	1929	Rose Hill	Altoona
Arble, John M. C.	Pvt. D, 46 Pa. Mil.	1847	1909	Fairview	Altoona
Arble, Thomas G.	Pvt. K, 125 Pa. Inf.				
	Pvt. Ind. Cav. Pa. Mil.				
	Pvt. B, 13 Pa. Cav.	1844	1864	Andersonville	Georgia
Arble, William	Pvt. D, 13 Pa. Cav.	1841			
Arbogast, Henry C.	Cpl. G, 49 Pa. Inf.	1842	1912	Rose Hill	Altoona
Arford, John H.	Pvt. K, 78 Pa. Inf.			Grandview	Tyrone
Armstrong, D. B.	Sgt. F, 37 Pa. Inf.				
Armstrong, Isaac W.	Sgt. D, 46 Pa. Mil.	1833			
Arnet, Frederick	Pvt. E, 1 Pa. Art.	1847			
Ash, Henry M.	Cpl. E, 46 Pa. Mil.	1840			
Ashburn, George M.	Pvt. E, 2 Pa. Art.	1846	1932	Rose Hill	Altoona
Askey, William	Pvt. F, 200 Pa. Inf.	1846	1895	Philipsburg	Penna.
Athey, Wesley B.	Pvt. B, Ind. Bn. Pa. Mil.				
	Cpl. M, 22 Pa. Cav.	1845			
Attick, David P.	Pvt. Ind. Cav. Pa. Mil.	1839			
Attig, George S.	Cpl. A, 54 Pa. Inf.	1841	1911	Fairview	Altoona
Attig, James H.	Pvt. E, 3 Pa. Inf.				
	Sgt. D, 125 Pa. Inf.				
	Sgt. Ind. Cav. Pa. Mil.	1840			
Attig, John D.	Pvt. B, 46 Pa. Inf.	1833	1912	Calvary	Altoona
Attig, Peter	Pvt. G, 133 Pa. Inf.				
Attleberger, George	Pvt. H, 1 Pa. Art.	1825			
Atwell, John	Pvt. C, 110 Pa. Inf.				
Aucker, Abraham		1832			
Auker, Ephraim N.	Pvt. C, 103 Pa. Inf.	1845	1900	Oak Ridge	Altoona
Aults, Ambrose M.	Sgt. D, 131 Pa. Inf.				
	Cpt. G, 205 Pa. Inf.	1844	1875	Grandview	Tyrone
Ault, C. E.	Pvt. H, 13 Md. Inf.				
Aunkst, Martin L.	Cpl. C, 76 Pa. Inf.	1831	1915	Rose Hill	Altoona
Aurandt, Alfred	Pvt. E, 84 Pa. Inf.				
	Sgt. I, 57 Pa. Inf.	1842			
Aurandt, Jacob M.	Pvt. M, 9 Pa. Cav.	1842			
Aurandt, John	Pvt. D, 184 Pa. Inf.		1864	Andersonville	Georgia
Aurandt, Joseph F.	Pvt. B, 125 Pa. Inf.		1863	Chancellorsville	Virginia
Aurandt, William	Cpl. C, 208 Pa. Inf.	1827	1891	Bald Eagle	Tyrone
Austin, Ashnel	Pvt. E, 84 Pa. Inf.				
Ayers, Charles	Cpl. I, 55 Pa. Inf.	1818			

SOLDIERS OF BLAIR COUNTY

Name	Rank Organization	Born	Died	Cemetery	Location
Ayers, Jacob	Pvt. H, 22 Pa. Cav.	1840			
Ayers, Jacob	Pvt. A, 125 Pa. Inf.	1819	1898	Bald Eagle	Tyrone
Ayers, James M.	Pvt. F, 76 Pa. Inf.	1840	1920	Pittsburgh	Penna.
Ayers, John	Pvt. A, 84 Pa. Inf.	1821		Sarah Furnace	Claysburg
Ayers, John J.	Pvt. F, 76 Pa. Inf.	1833			
Ayers, Robert H.	Pvt. B, 192 Pa. Inf.	1844	1907	Rose Hill	Altoona
Ayers, William	Pvt. F, Ind. Bn. Pa. Mil.	1828			
Ayers, William R.	Pvt. C, 76 Pa. Inf.	1827			
Babcock, Allen K.	Cpt. A, 54 Pa. Inf.	1837	1922	Presbyterian	Hollidaysburg
Babcock, William R.	Pvt. K, 136 Pa. Inf.	1843			
Bacon, Daniel	Cpl. E, 84 Pa. Inf.	1823	1864	Deep Bottom	Virginia
Bacon, John D.	Pvt. C, 6 U. S. Cav.	1853	1931		Washngtn, D.C.
Baer, Harrison D.	Pvt. E, 3 Pa. Inf.	1836			
Bailey, Edward C.	Pvt. D, 192 Pa. Inf.				
Bailey, Francis J.	Pvt. A, 84 Pa. Inf.				
	Pvt. G, 57 Pa. Inf.	1843			
Bailey, John	Pvt. I, 55 Pa. Inf.	1835	1864	St. Marys	Hollidaysburg
Bailey, John	Pvt. C, 110 Pa. Inf.		1864		
Bailey, John R.	Pvt. D, 4 U. S. Art.		1864	Point Lookout	Maryland
Bailey, Joseph	Pvt. G, 77 Pa. Inf.	1845	1921	Geeseytown	Hollidaysburg
Bailey, Valentine	Pvt. A, 1 Pa. Art.	1842			
Bailey, William	Pvt. G, 12 Pa. Cav.	1846	1864		
Bailey, William T.	Pvt. E, 110 Pa. Inf.				
	Pvt. H, 22 Pa. Cav.	1846	1919	Charlottesville	Bellwood
Bair, John	Pvt. C, 84 Pa. Inf.	1845	1873	Fairview	Altoona
Baird, Albert	Pvt. I, 137 Pa. Inf.				
Baird, David	Pvt. H, 125 Pa. Inf.	1804	1867	Lutheran	Hollidaysburg
Baird, George L.	Pvt. H, 208 Pa. Inf.	1845	1902	Dry Hill	Woodbury
Baird, Jacob W.	Pvt. I, 205 Pa. Inf.	1847	1889	Fairview	Altoona
Baith, George	Pvt. D, 88 Pa. Inf.		1908	Cornelus	Huntingdon Co.
Baith, Peter	Pvt. H, 22 Pa. Cav.	1841			
Baker, Abraham	Pvt. K, 78 Pa. Inf.	1828	1911	Huntingdon	Penna.
Baker, Adolphus R.	Pvt. I, 137 Pa. Inf.				
Baker, Andrew C.	Pvt. B, 13 Pa. Cav.	1842	1918	Greenlawn	Roaring Spring
Baker, Andrew J.	Pvt. K, 22 Pa. Cav.	1846			
Baker, Andrew J.	Pvt. H, 133 Pa. Inf.				
Baker, Benedict B.	Pvt. G, 12 Pa. Cav.				
Baker, Calvin B.	Pvt. A, 19 Pa. Cav.	1848			
Baker, David N.	Pvt. C, 13 Pa. Cav.	1843	1864	Hickory Bottom	Martinsburg
Baker, Francis	Pvt. C, 184 Pa. Inf.	1846	1911	Oak Ridge	Altoona
Baker, Franklin S.	Pvt. E, 125 Pa. Inf.	1844	1862	Holsingers	Bakers Summit
Baker, Gemmel	Mus. E, 84 Pa. Inf.				
	Mus. I, 57 Pa. Inf.				
Baker, Granville	Pvt. I, 137 Pa. Inf.				
Baker, Henry	Pvt. C, 19 Pa. Cav.	1837	1880	Logan Valley	Bellwood
Baker, Henry N.	Pvt. H, 110 Pa. Inf.				
Baker, Isaac F.	Pvt. A, 125 Pa. Inf.				
Baker, Jacob S.	Pvt. D, 99 Pa. Inf.	1843	1902	Brumbaugh	Martinsburg
Baker, John	Pvt. A, 205 Pa. Inf.	1843			
Baker, John	Pvt. M, 62 Pa. Inf.				
	Pvt. K, 91 Pa. Inf.	1841			
Baker, John	Pvt. D, 125 Pa. Inf.				
	Pvt. Ind. Cav. Pa. Mil.	1816	1885	Fairview	Altoona
Baker, John C.	Sgt. I, 55 Pa. Inf.	1840	1921	Albrights	Roaring Spring
Baker, John D.	Pvt. E, 84 Pa. Inf.				
Baker, Luther S.	Pvt. A, 126 Pa. Inf.	1844	1877	Fairview	Altoona
Baker, Samuel	Pvt. K, 49 Pa. Inf.				
	Sgt. L, 19 Pa. Cav.	1837			
Baker, Samuel G.	Pvt. C, 3 Pa. Inf.				
	Sgt. B, 125 Ra. Inf.	1829	1863	Stafford C. H.	Virginia
Baker, Thomas J.	Pvt. H, 110 Pa. Inf.	1841	1909	Lutheran	Newry
Baker, William	Pvt. I, 55 Pa. Inf.	1831	1914	Holsingers	Bakers Summit

THE CIVIL WAR 157

Name	Rank Organization	Born	Died	Cemetery	Location
Baker, William W.	Pvt. D, 192 Pa. Inf.	1847			
Baldridge, Howard M.	Pvt. A, 23 Pa. Mil.				
	Pvt. A, Inf. Bn. Pa. Mil.	1842	1895	Presbyterian	Hollidaysburg
Baldwin, Samuel	Pvt. D, 13 Pa. Cav.	1839			
Bales, Adam	Pvt. C, 84 Pa. Inf.				
Ball, Peter	Pvt. K, 184 Pa. Inf.	1847	1928	St. Thomas	Ashville
Balling, Thomas	Pvt. A, 147 N. Y. Inf.	1843	1922	Bald Eagle	Tyrone
Baltzell, Charles D.	Sgt. K, 196 Ohio Inf.		1906	Rose Hill	Altoona
Bankert, Robert F.	Pvt. G, 14 Pa. Inf.				
	Sgt. E, 105 Pa. Inf.	1842	1929	Fairview	Altoona
Banks, Cecil R.	Pvt. A, 23 Pa. Mil.				
	Pvt. A, Ind. Bn. Pa. Mil.				
	Pvt. 22 Pa. Cav.	1844			
Banks, John	Pvt. C, 110 Pa. Inf.				
Baptish, John H.	Pvt. D, U. S. C. T	1833	1910	Union	Hollidaysburg
Barclay, David T.	Pvt. D, 79 Pa. Inf.	1843	1906	Reform	Loysburg
Bare, Francis	Pvt. A, 205 Pa. Inf.	1846	1921	Greenwood	Altoona
Bare, Walter	Pvt. F, 76 Pa. Inf.	1821	1902	Greenwood	Altoona
Barger, James C.	Pvt. E, 13 Pa. Cav.	1844	1915	Fairview	Altoona
Barger, Robert B.	Cpt. H, 56 Pa. Inf.	1841	1917	Newton	Kansas
Barkdoll, Peter	Pvt. C, 13 Md. Inf.	1848	1920	Fairview	Altoona
Barker, Marcus L.	Pvt. F, 102 Pa. Inf.	1843	1930	Carson Valley	Duncansville
Barker, Samuel	Pvt. B, 3 Pa. Inf.	1837			
Barker, William F.	Pvt. B, 125 Pa. Inf.		1880	Chambersburg	Penna.
Barkla, Isaac	Pvt. D, 46 Pa. Mil.	1825			
Barkla, William	Pvt. D, 46 Pa. Mil.	1836			
Barkley, J. T.	Pvt. H, 208 Pa. Inf.			Dry Hill	Woodbury
Barkman, Christopher M.	Pvt. I, Pa. Cav.	1845			
Barlett, John	Pvt. I, 149 Pa. Inf.	1842	1924	Rose Hill	Altoona
Barley, Peter	Cpl. I, 14 Pa. Inf.	1835			
Barnacle, John E.	Cpt. F, 31 Pa. Inf.				
Barnes, Edward E.	Cpl. A, 110 Pa. Inf.		1864	Petersburg	Virginia
Barnes, George W.	Pvt. F, 18 Pa. Cav.	1841	1917	Grandview	Tyrone
Barnes, Hayes	Pvt. A, 110 Pa. Inf.		1864	City Point	Virginia
Barns, John A.	Pvt. A, 110 Pa. Inf.			Deep Bottom	Virginia
Barnes, John A.	Pvt. D, 3 Pa. Inf.	1840			
Barnes, Solomon B.	Sgt. 2 Pa. Art.				
	Cpt. H, 16 Pa. Cav.	1830	1898	Chambersburg	Penna.
Barnes, William	Pvt. H, 22 Pa. Cav.	1845			
Barnet, David	Pvt. A, 184 Pa. Inf.		1906	Lutheran	Claysburg
Barnett, Joseph	Pvt. C, 2 Md. Inf.	1834	1906	Carson Valley	Duncansville
Barnett, Samuel	Pvt. I, 149 Pa. Inf.	1838	1920	Albrights	Roaring Spring
Barnhart, George R.	Pvt. K, 211 Pa. Inf.	1848	1914	Oak Ridge	Altoona
Barnhart, John	Pvt. K, 7 U. S. Cav.				
	Far. L, 1 U. S. Cav.	1838	1902	Oak Ridge	Altoona
Barnhart, John A.	Pvt. E, 5 Pa. Art.	1824	1885	Oak Ridge	Altoona
Barr, Albert D.	Pvt. A, 23 Pa. Mil.	1845			
Barr, Allen S.	Pvt. A, Ind. Bn. Pa. Mil.				
	Pvt. U, 205 Pa. Inf.	1829			
Barr, David	Cpl. H, 3 Pa. Inf.				
	Cpl. A, 84 Pa. Inf.				
Barr, Franklin R.	Pvt. H, 41 Pa. Inf.				
	Sgt. H, 103 Pa. Inf.	1846	1920	Fairview	Martinsburg
Barr, Henry	Cpl. A, 3 Pa. Inf.	1833			
Barr, Henry	Pvt. C, 205 Pa. Inf.	1842	1913	Fairview	Martinsburg
Barr, James	Pvt. H, 3 Pa. Inf.				
	Cpt. A, 84 Pa. Inf.	1840	1884	Presbyterian	Hollidaysburg
Barr, John	Sgt. A, 3 Pa. Inf.	1816	1890	Presbyterian	Hollidaysburg
Barr, Joseph	Pvt. B, 192 Pa. Inf	1822	1900	Presbyterian	Hollidaysburg
Barr, Reuben	Pvt. I, 14 Pa. Inf.				
	Cpl. I, 137 Pa. Inf.				
	Sgt. C, 205 Pa. Inf.	1836			

Name	Rank Organization	Born	Died	Cemetery	Location
Barr, Samuel C.	Pvt. A, 3 Pa. Inf.				
	Sgt. A, 84 Pa. Inf.	1836			
Barr, Silas J.	Pvt. E, 84 Pa. Inf.	1845	1864	St. Patricks	Newry
Barr, Simon B.	Sgt. H, 3 Pa. Inf.				
	Sgt. A, 84 Pa. Inf.	1840	1912	Presbyterian	Hollidaysburg
Barr, Theodore	Pvt. G, 125 Pa. Inf.				
	Cpl. D, 192 Pa. Inf.	1836	1876	Lutheran	Hollidaysburg
Barr, Thomas M.	Pvt. H, 3 Pa. Inf.				
	Cpl. G, 125 Pa. Inf.	1843		Fockler	Saxton
Barr, William	Pvt. A, 23 Pa. Inf.	1846			
Barr, William N.	Sgt. H, 103 Pa. Inf.	1822	1877	Fairview	Altoona
Barr, William W.	Pvt. C, 22 Pa. Cav.	1844			
Barrett, Conrad	Pvt. B, 149 Pa. Inf.		1922	Kerrmoor	Clearfield Co.
Barrett, Miles	Pvt. L, 3 Pa. Art.	1826	1892	Logan Valley	Bellwood
Barron, David H.	Cpn. A, 23 Pa. Mil.	1828			
Barry, David R. P.	2Lt. D, 9 Pa. Cav.	1840			
Bart, Peter	Pvt. A, 55 Pa. Inf.				
Bartlebaugh, David	Pvt. B, 3 Pa. Inf.				
	Pvt. G, 125 Pa. Inf.	1840	1897	Greenwood	Altoona
Bartlebaugh, Henry	Pvt. F, 76 Pa. Inf.	1837	1864	Hampton	Virginia
Bartlebaugh, James	Cpl. I, 57 Pa. Inf.	1838	1869	Methodist	Williamsburg
Bartlebaugh, John	Cpl. I, 55 Pa. Inf.	1831			
Bartlebaugh, M.	Pvt. I, 14 Pa. Inf.	1838			
Bartlebaugh, Philip	Pvt. H, 14 Pa. Inf.				
	Pvt. H, 12 Pa. Cav.	1839	1897	Holsingers	Bakers Summit
Bartlebaugh, Silas	Pvt. I, 14 Pa. Inf.	1839			
Bartlebaugh, Silas M.	Sgt. I, 55 Pa. Inf.	1843	1870	Lutheran	Newry
Bartley, Ignatius	Pvt. D, 192 Pa. Inf.	1828	1896	St. Marys	Altoona
Bartley, Jesse B.	Pvt. I, 49 Pa. Inf.		1833	Coin	Iowa
Bartley, John M.	Pvt. C, 46 Pa. Mil.	1840	1915	Oak Ridge	Altoona
Bartley, William B.	Cpl. E, 3 Pa. Inf.	1832	1895	Fairview	Altoona
Barto, Benjamin H.	Pvt. A, 110 Pa. Inf.				
Barto, George W.	Sgt. I, 74 Pa. Inf.	1840	1918	Fairview	Altoona
Barto, John	Pvt. I, 34 Pa. Inf.				
	Pvt. C, 191 Pa. Inf.	1841	1893	Oak Ridge	Altoona
Bartow, Thomas C.	Pvt. E, 3 Pa. Inf.				
	Pvt. F, 125 Pa. Inf.				
	Pvt. M, 20 Pa. Cav.				
	Pvt. F, 188 Pa. Inf.	1845			
Baseler, Levi	Pvt. F, Ind. Bn. Pa. Mil	1845			
Bateman, John M.	Cpl. G, 12 Pa. Cav.	1832	1904	Spring Hope	Martinsburg
Bateman, Joseph Porter	Pvt. E, 45 Pa. Inf.	1838	1926	Grandview	Altoona
Bateman, Thomas H.		1835			
Bates, C. B.					
Bathurst, Andrew G.	Pvt. D, 49 Pa. Inf.				
Bathurst, Henry A.	Pvt. A, 46 Pa. Inf.		1906	Graysville	Huntingdon Co.
Baton, Augustus	Sgt. H, 3 Pa. Inf.				
	Sgt. G, 125 Pa. Inf.				
	1Lt. B, Ind. Bn. Pa. Mil.				
	Sgt. D, 192 Pa. Inf.	1830	1873	Presbyterian	Hollidaysburg
Bauer, Alexander	Pvt. D, Durell's Art.				
Baughman, Abraham	Pvt. F, 99 Pa. Inf.	1838	1926	Brumbaugh	Martinsburg
Baughman, David	Pvt. M, 62 Pa. Inf.				
	Cpl. K, 91 Pa. Inf.			Grazierville	Tyrone
Baughman, John H.	Pvt. I, 22 Pa. Cav.				
Baughman, Lorenzo	Pvt. H, 103 Pa. Inf.	1841	1925	Baughmans	Tyrone
Baum, Henry	Pvt. A, 23 Pa. Mil.	1812			
Bayles, William T.	Pvt. H, 110 Pa. Inf.				
Bayley, William C.	Cpt. Q.M.C.				
	1Lt. 22 Pa. Cav.	1824	1889	Presbyterian	Hollidaysburg
Baymer, Frederick	Pvt. C, 46 Pa. Mil.	1842			
Bayme, William J.	Pvt. M, 9 Pa. Cav.	1838			

THE CIVIL WAR 159

Name	Rank Organization	Born	Died	Cemetery	Location
Beach, Bartholomew	Cpl. E, 13 Pa. Cav.	1833	1906	Carson Valley	Duncansville
Beals, Abraham	Cpl. C, 76 Pa. Inf.	1840			
Beals, George W.	Pvt. K, 46 Pa. Mil.	1837		Fairview	Altoona
Beals, Jacob R.	Pvt. E, 3 Pa. Inf.	1847	1873	Fairview	Altoona
Beal, John S.	Pvt. K, 125 Pa. Inf.				
Beals, John T.	Pvt. H, 3 Pa. Inf.				
	Pvt. M, 62 Pa. Inf.	1846	1874	Fairview	Altoona
Beals, Lemuel M.	Pvt. C, 46 Pa. Mil.				
	Pvt. D, 13 Pa. Cav.	1846	1864	Fairview	Altoona
Beal, William H.	Pvt. K, 125 Pa. Inf.				
Beal, William H.	Sgt. C, 46 Pa. Mil.	1839			
Beams, John	Pvt. E, 3 Pa. Inf.	1839			
Beams, Stephen F.	Pvt. A, 26 U.S.C.T.	1835	1904		
Beam, Theodore M.	Pvt. C, 102 Pa. Inf.	1832	1920	Fairview	Altoona
Beamenderfer, C. W.	Pvt. A, 84 Pa. Inf.				
Beemer, Alfred	Pvt. E, 46 Pa. Mil.	1833			
Beamer, Albert Scott	Pvt. G, 125 Pa. Inf.	1845	1869	Lutheran	Newry
Beamer, David	Pvt. U, 205 Pa. Inf.	1831			
Beamer, David B.	Pvt. K, 210 Pa. Inf.	1832	1916	Logan Valley	Bellwood
Beamer, Henry C.	Cpt. G, 1 Pa. Cav.				
Beamer, Isaac F.	Sgt. F, 49 Pa. Inf.	1841	1879	Presbyterian	Hollidaysburg
Beamer, John	Pvt. A, 110 Pa. Inf.				
Beamer, Samuel	Pvt. E, 184 Pa. Inf.		1864	Andersonville	Georgia
Beamer, Thomas D.	Sgt. H, 110 Pa. Inf.	1834	1907		Tyrone
Beamer, Thomas W.	Pvt. A, 125 Pa. Inf.		1863	Stafford C. H.	Virginia
Bears, Reuben	Pvt. E, 84 Pa. Inf.				
Bear, Samuel	Pvt. D, 13 Pa. Cav.	1839			
Beard, Alexander	Pvt. I, 137 Pa. Inf.				
	Cpl. A, 205 Pa. Inf.	1830	1904	Frankstown	Hollidaysburg
Beard, George W.	Pvt. C, 110 Pa. Inf.				
Beard, Hezekiah	Cpl. H, 3 Md. Cav.	1845	1923	Rose Hill	Altoona
Beard, Joseph C.	Pvt. D, 13 Pa. Cav.	1845			
Beard, William H.	Pvt. I, 137 Pa. Inf.				
Bearstler, Edward	Pvt. B, 128 Pa. Inf.	1842	1917	Rose Hill	Altoona
Beatle, Samuel	Pvt. D, 13 Pa. Cav.	1844			
Beatty, Franklin	Cpl. K, 125 Pa. Inf.				
Beatty, Franklin M.	Pvt. E, 3 Pa. Inf.	1840			
Beatty, Jacob	Pvt. K, 125 Pa. Inf.				
	Sgt. F, Ind. Bn. Pa. Mil.	1841			
Beatty, Joseph Walter K.	Pvt. A, 125 Pa. Inf.				
	Pvt. Marine Corps	1835	1903	Fairview	Altoona
Beatty, Oscar	Pvt. F, 31 Pa. Inf.				
Beatty, Oscar	Pvt. D, 3 Pa. Inf.	1838			
Beatty, William	Pvt. H, 36 Pa. Inf.	1844	1893	Fairview	Altoona
Beaver, John	1Lt. I, 158 Pa. Inf.	1841	1898	Fairview	Altoona
Bechtel, John	Pvt. C, 84 Pa. Inf.	1821			
Bechtel, Martin Luther	Sgt. A, 14 U. S. Inf.	1836	1916	Fairview	Martinsburg
Beck, Felix	Sgt. G, 12 Pa. Cav.	1838		St. Michaels	Loretto
Beck, Frederick	Pvt. C, 46 Pa. Mil.	1835			
Beck, Henry L.	Pvt. I, 22 Pa. Cav.	1833			
Beck, Isaiah	Sgt. G, 22 Pa. Cav.	1843			
Beck, John	Pvt. F, 97 Pa. Inf.	1849			
Beck, Reuben	Pvt. F, 77 Pa. Inf.	1830			
Beckhart, Jacob	Cpt. H, 110 Pa. Inf.				
Beckweth, Thomas	Pvt. D, 14 Pa. Inf.	1834			
Beegle, Henry W.	Pvt. H, 110 Pa. Inf.		1863	Gettysburg	Pa.
Beegle, John A.	Pvt. E, 125 Pa. Inf.				
	Cpl. C, 110 Pa. Inf.	1840	1916	Lutheran	St. Clairsville
Beegle, Solomon	Pvt. G, 207 Pa. Inf.	1841	1910	Carson Valley	Duncansville
Beeler, James H.	Pvt. I, 22 Pa. Cav.	1845	1907	Fairview	Altoona
Beeman, Henry S.	Cpl. M, 9 Pa. Cav.	1838	1865	Annapolis	Maryland
Beers, George S.	Cpl. S, 125 Pa. Inf.				

Name	Rank	Organization	Born	Died	Cemetery	Location
Beichler, William E.	Pvt.	U. Inf.	1846	1920	Rose Hill	Altoona
Beichtel, Lewis G.	Pvt. E,	4 Pa. Cav.	1841	1865	Union	Claysburg
Beighel, David E.	Sgt. M,	9 Pa. Cav.	1842	1895	Fairview	Altoona
Beigle, Daniel	Pvt. D,	192 Pa. Inf.		1886	St. Patricks	Newry
Beigle, Jacob	Pvt. H,	110 Pa. Inf.		1863	Falmouth	Virginia
Beigle, Jacob	Pvt. E,	46 Pa. Mil.	1844			
Beikstein, George	Bug. M,	9 Pa. Cav.				
Beissert, Herman	Pvt. C,	84 Pa. Inf.	1819			
Bell, Benjamin J.	Pvt. G,	2 Pa. Art.	1833	1928	Grandview	Tyrone
Bell, Elias Cline	Pvt. K,	123 Pa. Inf.	1842	1898	Presbyterian	Hollidaysburg
Bell, Francis Marion	2Lt. D,	3 Pa. Inf.				
	Cpt. A,	125 Pa. Inf.				
	Maj.	46 Pa. Mil.	1826	1901	Grandview	Tyrone
Bell, G. Thomas	Cpl. A,	205 Pa. Inf.	1845	1906	Oak Ridge	Altoona
Bell, George	Pvt. M,	62 Pa. Inf.				
Bell, Irwin W.	Mus. D,	14 Pa. Inf.				
Bell, James C.	Pvt. D,	3 Pa. Inf.				
	Sgt. C,	110 Pa. Inf.	1835	1924	Homestead	Pa.
Bell, James H.	Pvt. A,	23 Pa. Mil.	1819			
Bell, James M.	Cpt. D,	3 Pa. Inf.				
	Cpt. M,	9 Pa. Cav.				
	Cpt. Ind. Cav. Pa. Mil.					
	Cpt. D,	13 Pa. Cav.	1819	1874	Grandview	Tyrone
Bell, James W.	Pvt. H,	Ind. Pa. Art.				
Bell, John J.	Pvt. G,	N. Y. Inf.	1825	1907	Fairview	Altoona
Bell, John Thomas	Pvt. D,	102 Pa. Inf.	1849	1912	Oak Ridge	Altoona
Bell, Joseph H.	Pvt. F,	Ind. Bn. Pa. Mil.	1836			
Bell, Joseph H.	Pvt. K,	125 Pa. Inf.				
Bell, Lemon	Pvt. H,	110 Pa. Inf.				
Bell, Richard M.	Cpl. F,	76 Pa. Inf.	1840	1864	Logan Valley	Bellwood
Bell, Thomas G.	Pvt. Ind. Cav. Pa. Mil.				Logan Valley	Bellwood
Bell, William H.	Mus. E,	40 Pa. Inf.	1840	1925	Patton	Pa.
Bell, William H.	Pvt. C,	3 Pa. Inf.	1841			
Bendell, Edmund	2Lt. G,	Ind. Bn.				
Benden, James	Pvt. K,	125 Pa. Inf.	1809	1892	St. Patricks	Gallitzin
Benden, Simen	Pvt. K,	125 Pa. Inf.				
Benden, Theodore	Pvt. C,	19 U. S. Inf.	1842	1907	St. Patricks	Gallitzin
Bender, Peter	Pvt. D,	6 N. Y. Cav.	1850			
Bender, Sabastian	Pvt. Ind. Cav. Pa. Mil.		1844	1924	St. Johns	Altoona
Benedick, Myron A.						
Benner, David H.	Pvt. D,	110 Pa. Inf.	1844	1922	Fairview	Altoona
Benner, Peter	Pvt. I,	57 Pa. Inf.	1819			
Benner, Thomas M.	Pvt. C,	125 Pa. Inf.	1835	1902	Reform	Sinking Valley
Bennett, Alexander	Pvt. A,	125 Pa. Inf.				
Bennett, Arthur S.	Pvt. E,	49 Pa. Inf.	1818	1897	Carson Valley	Duncansville
Bennett, Joseph	Pvt. M,	16 Pa. Cav.	1823	1890	Carson Valley	Duncansville
Bennett, Robert	Pvt. C,	33 Pa. Mil.	1843	1912	St. Johns	Altoona
Benscoter, Crawford L.	Pvt. F,	143 Pa. Inf.	1845			
Benson, Aaron P.	Pvt. Ind. Cav. Pa. Mil.					
	Pvt. B,	13 Pa. Cav.	1846			
Benson, Fleetwood W.	Pvt. F,	104 Pa. Inf.	1827	1882	Fairview	Martinsburg
Benton, David H.	Pvt. A,	84 Pa. Inf.	1837	1918	Birmingham	Pa.
Benton, Emanuel E.	Pvt. E,	125 Pa. Inf.	1825	1907	Greenfield	Bedford Co.
Benton, Franklin	Pvt. C,	205 Pa. Inf.	1846			
Benton, George R.	Pvt. F,	Ind. Bn. Pa. Mil.				
	Cpl. F,	76 Pa. Inf.	1846	1897	St. Patricks	Newry
Benton, Jesse L.	Pvt. E,	125 Pa. Inf.				
	Pvt. A,	13 Pa. Cav.	1839	1914	Grandview	Tyrone
Benton, John	Pvt. E,	125 Pa. Inf.	1822	1887	St. Patricks	Newry
Benton, John	Pvt. C,	205 Pa. Inf.	1844	1910	St. Patricks	Newry
Benton, Miles	Pvt. E,	84 Pa. Inf.	1842	1917	Willow Grove	Petersburg
Berkey, Hiram J.	Pvt. K,	5 Pa. Art.	1834	1916	Holsopple	Somerset Co.

THE CIVIL WAR

Name	Rank Organization	Born	Died	Cemetery	Location
Birkhimer, Charles	Pvt. K, 13 Pa. Cav.	1840	1922	Greenlawn	Roaring Spring
Berkheimer, Daniel B.	Pvt. M, 22 Pa. Cav.	1845	1915	Salemville	Bedford Co.
Barkheimer, Jacob	Pvt. A, 205 Pa. Inf.	1822	1910	Fairview	Altoona
Barkhimer, John	Pvt. K, 55 Pa. Inf.	1844	1921	Mt. Hope	Blue Knob
Barkhammer, Levi	Pvt. H, Ind. Bn. Pa. Mil.				
	Pvt. A, 184 Pa. Inf.			Bechtel Farm	Bedford Co.
Burkheimer, Martin	Pvt. K, 125 Pa. Inf.				
	Pvt. A, 205 Pa. Inf.	1843			
Birkhimer, Samuel	Pvt. I, 137 Pa. Inf.				
	Pvt. I, 55 Pa. Inf.			Reform	St. Clairsville
Berkheimer, William	Pvt. E, 3 Pa. Cav.	1840	1900	Oak Ridge	Altoona
Berkheimer, William	Pvt. H, 11 N. J. Inf.	1837	1926	Presbyterian	Hollidaysburg
Berkstresser, Daniel S.	Cpl. F, 77 Pa. Inf.	1820			
Berkstresser, John	Pvt. C, 84 Pa. Inf.	1817			
Berkstresser, John Y.	Pvt. I, 137 Pa. Inf.		1916	Saxton	Pa.
Berlin, David	Sgt. G, 3 Pa. Cav.				
Berlin, John Milton	Cpl. D, 3 Pa. Inf.	1838	1861	Grandview	Tyrone
Berlin, Samuel L.	Sgt. C, 22 Pa. Cav.	1843			
Bernard, Robert	Boy, U. S. Navy	1830	1879	Fairview	Altoona
Berry, George	Pvt. A, 23 Pa. Mil.				
	Pvt. A, Ind. Bn. Pa. Mil.				
	Pvt. H, 13 Pa. Cav.	1845			
Berry, Jeremiah	Pvt. D, 205 Pa. Inf.	1820			
Berry, John	Pvt. C, 84 Pa. Inf.	1843			
Berry, William H. H.	Cpl. A, 125 Pa. Inf.				
Bertram, George A.	Cpl. D, 125 Pa. Inf.				
Bertram, George J.	Pvt. F, 133 Pa. Inf.	1838	1891	St. Patricks	Gallitzin
Bertram, Peter A.	Pvt. B, 208 Pa. Inf.				
Bertren, Peter	Pvt. M, 62 Pa. Inf.		1863	Chancellorsville	Virginia
Bettorf, John G.	Cpl. D, 184 Pa. Inf.	1830			
Betz, Joel H.	Pvt. H, 25 Pa. Inf.				
	Pvt. G, 48 Pa. Inf.	1839	1925	Fairview	Altoona
Bewley, Stephen	Cpl. G, 192 Pa. Inf.	1842	1892	Greenwood	Altoona
Beyer, Catharine Blake	Nrs. U. S. Army	1840			
Beyer, Ezra Crum	Pvt. E, 46 Pa. Mil.				
	Pvt. A, 125 Pa. Inf.	1844	1864	Mt. Zion	Bellwood
Beyer, James S.	Pvt. I, 149 Pa. Inf.	1837	1899	Grandview	Tyrone
Beyer, Sanford F.	Pvt. A, 110 Pa. Inf.		1865	Mt. Zion	Bellwood
Beyer, Solomon	Sgt. H, 110 Pa. Inf.				
Bickel, David J.	Pvt. D, 36 Ohio Inf.	1846	1928	Fairview	Altoona
Bickel, Henry	Pvt. A, 84 Pa. Inf.				
	Pvt. G, 57 Pa. Inf.	1843	1911	Carson Valley	Duncansville
Biddle, Charles	Pvt. M, 62 Pa. Inf.	1824	1861	Minors Hill	Virginia
Biddle, George C.	Pvt. C, 205 Pa. Inf.	1843	1865	Arlington	Virginia
Biddle, Jacob S.	Pvt. I, 194 Pa. Inf.				
	Pvt. M, 22 Pa. Cav.			Loysburg	Bedford Co.
Bierman, Frederick	Pvt. K, 125 Pa. Inf.				
	Pvt. K, Ind. Bn. Pa. Mil.				
Biesicker, George A.	Cpl. K, 87 Pa. Inf.	1834	1922	Carson Valley	Duncansville
Bigham, Alphonsus J.	Bug. M, 12 Pa. Cav.	1845	1929	St. Johns	Altoona
Bilestine, George W.	Pvt. A, 110 Pa. Inf.				
Biller, Joseph I.	Smn. U. S. Navy		1919	Loretto	Pa.
Bing, William H.	Pvt. E, Ind. Bn. Pa. Mil.				
	Pvt. B, 210 Pa. Inf.	1846	1913	Grandview	Tyrone
Bish, Joseph H.	Pvt. A, 46 Pa. Inf.			Presbyterian	Hollidaysburg
Bishop, David P.					
Bitel, Philip	Pvt. D, 192 Pa. Inf.				
Bitner, Jonathan W.	Pvt. B, 1Bn. Pa. Mil.				
	Sgt. I, 211 Pa. Inf.	1829	1902	Greenwood	Altoona
Bitner, William S.	Pvt. Ind. Cav. Pa. Mil.	1833			
Bittle, Charles	Pvt. C, 3 Pa. Inf.	1825			
Bittle, Charles F.	Bug. 22 Pa. Cav.	1845			

SOLDIERS OF BLAIR COUNTY

Name	Rank Organization	Born	Died	Cemetery	Location
Black, Amos R.	Pvt. D, 46 Pa. Inf.	1847			
Black, Archibald A.	Cpl. G, 149 Pa. Inf.	1843	1907	Oak Ridge	Altoona
Black, Daniel	Pvt. E, 84 Pa. Inf.		1862	Point Lookout	Maryland
Black, David M.	Pvt. G, 125 Pa. Inf.				
	Pvt. G, 12 Pa. Cav.	1834	1902	Asbury	Altoona
Black, George W.	Pvt. K, 22 Pa. Cav.	1832			
Black, George W.	Pvt. H, 3 Pa. Inf.	1840			
Black, George Washington	Pvt. E, 45 Pa. Inf.	1843	1913	Royer Mt.	Williamsburg
Black, Jacob Martin	Pvt. G, 46 Pa. Inf.	1845	1923	Oak Ridge	Altoona
Black, James Augusta	Pvt. H, 103 Pa. Inf.	1843	1928	Oak Ridge	Altoona
Black, John H.	Cpl. H, 14 Pa. Inf.				
	1Lt. G, 12 Pa. Cav.	1834	1922	Carson Valley	Duncansville
Black, Samuel P.	Pvt. F, 31 Pa. Inf.		1863	Arlington	Virginia
Black, Steele S.	Pvt. B, 1 Pa. Art.	1846			
Black, William	Mus. C, 191 Pa. Inf.			Fairview	Altoona
Black, William A.	Sgt. F, 19 Pa. Cav.	1840	1914	Water Street	Pa.
Blackburn, George	Pvt. C, 200 Pa. Inf.	1843	1912	Fairview	Altoona
Blackburn, Harmon	Pvt. F, 77 Pa. Inf.				
	Pvt. G, 194 Pa. Inf.	1845	1918	Sarah Furnace	Claysburg
Blackburn, Joseph H.	Sgt. A, 23 Pa. Mil.	1828			
Blackburn, Moses	Pvt. M, 22 Pa. Cav.	1826	1899	Lutheran	Newry
Blackstone, Dill	Pvt. H, 3 Pa. Inf.				
	Cpl. M, 62 Pa. Inf.	1841	1889	Rose Hill	Altoona
Blackstone, Joseph S.	Pvt. A, 5 U. S. Art.	1842	1912	Dayton	Ohio
Blackwood, William J.	Pvt. G, 12 Pa. Cav.	1825			
Blair, Samuel Steel	Pvt. E, 13 Pa. Cav.				
	Pvt. A, Ind. Bn. Pa. Mil.	1821	1890	Presbyterian	Hollidaysburg
Blair, William Henry	Sgt. I, 58 Pa. Inf.		1920	Lock Haven	Pa.
Blair, William J.	Cpl. M, 62 Pa. Inf.	1830			
Blair, William J.	Pvt. H, 3 Pa. Inf.	1833			
Blake, Burdine	Pvt. F, 46 Pa. Inf.	1850	1915	Fairview	Martinsburg
Blake, Christopher	Pvt. A, 110 Pa. Inf.				
Blake, James	Pvt. 84 Pa. Inf.				
	Pvt. H, 57 Pa. Inf.				
	Pvt. B, 208 Pa. Inf.	1819	1896	Fairview	Martinsburg
Blake, John W.	Pvt. F, 152 Pa. Inf.				
	1Lt. F, 3 Pa. Art.	1848	1936	Rose Hill	Altoona
Blake, Samuel	Pvt. C, 110 Pa. Inf.	1835		Fockler	Saxton
Blake, Samuel	Pvt. D, 125 Pa. Inf.				
	Pvt. Ind. Cav. Pa. Mil.	1844			
Blake, Simon	Pvt. C, 110 Pa. Inf.				
Blake, Thomas	Pvt. C, 110 Pa. Inf.				
Blake, Wilbur B.	Pvt. D, 125 Pa. Inf.				
	1Lt. D, 46 Pa. Cav.				
	1Lt. C, 19 Pa. Cav.	1843	1898	Fairview	Altoona
Blake, William B.	Pvt. B, 125 Pa. Inf.				
	2Lt. B, 208 Pa. Inf.			Hopewell	Bedford Co.
Blakely, Alexander R.	Pvt. A, 74 Pa. Inf.	1841	1878	Fairview	Altoona
Blakely, Robert	Pvt. H, 7 Pa. Cav.				
Blakely, William	Pvt. I, 82 Pa. Inf.			Collinsville	Altoona
Bleiler, George	Pvt. Ind. Cav. Pa. Mil.				
	Pvt. H, 9 Pa. Cav.	1838	1925	Fairview	Altoona
Bloom, David S.	Pvt. I, 137 Pa. Inf.	1834	1894	Fairview	Martinsburg
Bloom, Thomas	Pvt. H, 202 Pa. Inf.	1848	1925	Fairview	Altoona
Bloomfield, Henry	Ldn. U. S. Navy	1836	1904	Oak Ridge	Altoona
Bloomfield, James	Ldn. U. S. Navy	1844			
Bloomfield, William	Pvt. A, 1 N. Y. Cav.	1831	1883	Oak Ridge	Altoona
Blumer, John H.					
Blummer, John R.	Pvt. K, Pa. Inf.	1843			
Blyler, James M.	Pvt. F, 29 Ind. Inf.	1847		Presbyterian	Hollidaysburg
Boartman, A. H.	Pvt. K, 125 Pa. Inf.		1862	Mt. Kalma	Pa.

THE CIVIL WAR

Name	Rank Organization	Born	Died	Cemetery	Location
Bobb, Alexander	Cpt. I, 14 Pa. Inf.				
	Cpt. C, 133 Pa. Inf.				
	Maj. 208 Pa. Inf.	1823	1910	Fairview	Martinsburg
Bock, Peter	Sgt. A, 23 Pa. Mil.	1824			
Bodley, Mark	Pvt. A, 13 Ohio Inf.	1839	1886	Presbyterian	Arch Spring
Boell, Harry	Pvt. H, 3 Pa. Inf.	1834			
Boell, William	Pvt. H, 3 Pa. Inf.	1838			
Bogart, Jesse W.	Pvt. A, 13 Ind. Inf.	1849	1921	Greenlawn	Roaring Spring
Boggs, Alexander	Pvt. A, 3 Pa. Inf.				
	Cpl. G, 125 Pa. Inf.				
	Smn. U. S. Navy	1837			
Boggs, George W.	Atr. E, Knaps. Pa. Art.	1835	1863	Presbyterian	Hollidaysburg
Bohn, Valentine H.	Pvt. I, 79 Pa. Inf.		1865	Arlington	Virginia
Bolan, Lewis D.	Pvt. B, 49 Pa. Inf.	1844			
Bolch, George	Pvt. D, 13 Pa. Cav.	1838			
Bollinger, David	Pvt. E, 21 Pa. Cav.	1837	1915	Fairview	Altoona
Bollinger, George	Bks. D, 13 Pa. Cav.	1829			
Bollinger, Henry L.	Pvt. G, 125 Pa. Inf.				
Bollinger, Jacob B.	Pvt. B, 22 Pa. Cav.	1845			
Bollinger, James	Pvt. C, 53 Pa. Inf.	1835			
Bollinger, John W.	Pvt. C, Ind. Bn. Pa. Mil.	1845	1913	Fairview	Altoona
Bollinger, Michael A.	Pvt. A, 23 Pa. Mil.	1843			
Bollman, George F.	Pvt. G, Ind. Bn. Pa. Mil.				
	Pvt. M, 22 Pa. Cav.			Reform	Hopewell
Bond, George M.	Cpl. F, 12 Pa. Cav.				
Bonebreak, Daniel W.	Sgn. C, Med. Dept.	1841	1894	Fairview	Martinsburg
Bonghama, John					
Boner, H.	Mus. I, 14 Pa. Inf.	1842			
Bonner, Henry W.	Pvt. A, 84 Pa. Inf.				
	Pvt. G, 57 Pa. Inf.	1843			
Bookhamer, John W.	Pvt. F, 77 Pa. Inf.	1842	1936	Grandview	Tyrone
Bookhammer, Thomas R.	Pvt. D, 22 Pa. Cav.				
	Pvt. F, 77 Pa. Inf.	1842	1930	Greenlawn	Roaring Spring
Bookhammer, William G.	Pvt. B, 208 Pa. Inf.			Hopewell	Bedford Co.
Books, Jonas	Pvt. I, 13 Pa. Cav.	1844	1877	Greenlawn	Roaring Spring
Boone, J. Albert	Pvt. F, Ind. Bn. Pa. Mil.	1842			
Boone, Frank	Mus. F, Ind. Bn. Pa. Mil.	1847			
Boose, Isaac	Pvt. C, 84 Pa. Inf.	1842			
Booth, John W.	Sgt. A, 201 Pa. Inf.	1833	1888	Presbyterian	Hollidaysburg
Booth, Nathaniel	Pvt. B, 2 W. Va. Cav.	1843			
Border, Andrew	Cpl. C, 110 Pa. Inf.				
Border, John	Pvt. C, 110 Pa. Inf.				
	Pvt. B, 22 Pa. Cav.			Bethel	Bedford Co.
Border, John S.	Pvt. C, 110 Pa. Inf.	1840	1915	Potters Creek	Pa.
Boring, Henry J.	Pvt. H, 14 Pa. Inf.	1838			
Boring, Thomas	Pvt. M, 22 Pa. Cav.	1833	1911	Huntingdon	Pa.
Bosler, Henry	Pvt. I, 14 Pa. Inf.	1838			
Bossert, Jacob R.	Cpl. H, 110 Pa. Inf.				
Bossinger, Daniel W.	Pvt. C, 46 Pa. Mil.	1839			
Bossinger, Henry C.	Pvt. C, 46 Pa. Mil.	1838			
Boswell, William	Pvt. F, 77 Pa. Inf.	1836			
Bottonberg, William	Pvt. Ind. Cav. Pa. Mil.				
	Pvt. D, 13 Pa. Cav.	1830	1864	Annapolis	Maryland
Bottorf, David	Pvt. E, 125 Pa. Inf.				
Boughamer, Henry J.	Cpl. A, 125 Pa. Inf.				
	Cpl. C, 208 Pa. Inf.			Charlottesville	Bellwood
Boughamer, John	Pvt. E, 93 Pa. Inf.	1820	1892	Asbury	Altoona
Boughamer, John	Pvt. G, 130 Pa. Inf.				
	Pvt. A, 20 Pa. Cav.	1843			
Bougher, John	Sgt. F, 62 Pa. Inf.	1830		Derry	Pa.
Bowen, Francis	Pvt. D, 125 Pa. Inf.		1862	Antietam	Maryland

SOLDIERS OF BLAIR COUNTY

Name	Rank Organization	Born	Died	Cemetery	Location
Bowers, Abraham	Pvt. B, 3 Pa. Inf.	1839			
Bowers, Adam	Cpl. A, 205 Pa. Inf.				
Bowers, Adam	Pvt. 187 Pa. Inf.	1820	1864	Cypress Hill	Long Island
Bowers, Christian H.	Pvt. I, 56 Pa. Inf.	1840	1903	Spring Hope	Martinsburg
Bowers, Cornelius D.	Pvt. A, 3 Pa. Inf.				
	Pvt. D, 84 Pa. Inf.	1838	1905	Presbyterian	Hollidaysburg
Bowers, George B.	1Lt. A, 23 Pa. Mil.	1813	1886	Presbyterian	Hollidaysburg
Bowers, Henry C.	Pvt. K, 57 Pa. Inf.		1867	Fairview	Altoona
Bowers, John C.	Pvt. C, 46 Pa. Mil.				
	Cpl. D, 184 Pa. Inf.	1845	1864	Fairview	Altoona
Bowers, Michael D.	Pvt. A, 205 Pa. Inf.	1843	1926	Logan Valley	Bellwood
Bower, Moses					
Bowers, William D.	Pvt. A, 23 Pa. Mil.	1843			
Bowles, Crawford B.	Pvt. H, 92 Ill. Inf.	1838	1918	Fairview	Altoona
Bowles, James B.	Pvt. A, 125 Pa. Inf.	1838	1915	Fairview	Altoona
Bowman, Daniel H.	Pvt. C, 110 Pa. Inf.	1839	1864	Potters Creek	Bedford Co.
Bowman, George	Pvt. C, 110 Pa. Inf.	1837	1862	Potters Creek	Bedford Co.
Bowman, Jacob H.	Pvt. K, 22 Pa. Cav.	1846			
Bowman, Micheal	Pvt. F, 31 Pa. Inf.				
	Pvt. A, 191 Pa. Inf.	1841	1865	Salisbury	N. Car.
Bowman, Peter	Pvt. F, 31 Pa. Inf.				
	Pvt. A, 191 Pa. Inf.	1837			
Bowman, Thomas	Pvt. C, 110 Pa. Inf.				
Bowser, Daniel L.	Pvt. K, 55 Pa. Inf.	1833	1902	Greenfield	Bedford Co.
Bowser, David	Pvt. K, 55 Pa. Inf.	1842	1911	Mt. Hope	Claysburg
Bowser, George W.	Pvt. F, 76 Pa. Inf.	1839			
Bowser, Jacob	Pvt. C, 205 Pa. Inf.	1839	1864	City Point	Virginia
Bowser, John B.	Pvt. D, 192 Pa. Inf.	1849	1904	Presbyterian	Hollidaysburg
Bowser, John J.	Pvt. G, 12 Pa. Cav.	1844	1868		
Bowser, Joseph M.	Pvt. C, 205 Pa. Inf.	1843			
Bowser, Moses	Pvt. F, 49 Pa. Inf.		1897	Mt. Hope	Claysburg
Bowser, Valentine		1821	1891	Mt. Hope	Claysburg
Boyden, John Augustus	Mus. D, 125 Pa. Inf.				
	Mus. G, Pa. Mil.	1846	1920	Oak Ridge	Altoona
Boyer, Abraham A.	Pvt. I, 49 Pa. Inf.				
	Cpl. C, 3 Pa. Art.	1839	1908	Oak Ridge	Altoona
Boyer, Adam	Pvt. F, 77 Pa. Inf.	1844			
Boyer, Albert	Pvt. D, 125 Pa. Inf.				
	Sgt. D, 46 Pa. Mil.	1844	1922	Fairview	Altoona
Boyer, George	Pvt. E, 104 Pa. Inf.				
Boyer, Lewis	Pvt. C, 50 Pa. Inf.	1826	1886	Logan Valley	Bellwood
Boyer, William	Pvt, F, 77 Pa. Inf.	1842			
Boyer, William H.	Pvt. A, 110 Pa. Inf.	1840	1910	Logan Valley	Bellwood
Boylan, P. M.	Pvt. D, 127 Pa. Inf.	1836	1912	St. Patricks	Gallitzin
Boyle, Alfred H.	Smn. U. S. Navy				
Boyles, Andrew A.	Pvt. A, 205 Pa. Inf.	1836	1921	Hutchison	Altoona
Boyles, David K.	Pvt. C, 2 Pa. Art.	1836	1894	Logan Valley	Bellwood
Boyle, George	Pvt. B, 3 Pa. Inf.				
	Sgt. F, 76 Pa. Inf.	1845	1894	Antis	Bellwood
Boyles, Henry	Pvt. A, 205 Pa. Inf.				
Boyles, Jacob	Pvt. F, 76 Pa. Inf.	1844			
Boyles, James B.	Pvt. A, 125 Pa. Inf.				
Boyles, John	Pvt. D, 55 Pa. Inf.				
	Pvt. B, 208 Pa. Inf.	1849			
Boyles, John A.	Pvt. B, 3 Pa. Inf.				
	Sgt. F, 76 Pa. Inf.	1838	1863	Charleston	S. Car.
Boyles, John C.	Pvt. G, 12 Pa. Cav.	1818	1884	Fairview	Altoona
Boyles, Martin W.	Pvt. B, 3 Pa. Inf.				
	Cpl. D, 46 Pa. Mil.				
	Pvt. C, 19 Pa. Cav.	1838	1906	Rose Hill	Altoona
Boyles, William	Pvt. B, 3 Pa. Inf.				
	Pvt. F, 76 Pa. Inf.	1842	1862	Pocataligo	S. Car.

THE CIVIL WAR

Name	Rank Organization	Born	Died	Cemetery	Location
Boyles, William T.	Pvt. E, 3 Pa. Inf.				
	Pvt. H, 110 Pa. Inf.	1809	1886	Logan Valley	Bellwood
Bracken, Foster	Pvt. D, 13 Pa. Cav.	1843			
Bradley, Benjamin F.	Pvt. H, 21 Pa. Cav.	1845	1929	Oak Ridge	Altoona
Bradley, Francis P.	Pvt. I, 55 Pa. Inf.	1840	1882	St. Patricks	Newry
Bradley, Hugh	1Lt. F, 3 Pa. Inf.	1833	1909	St. Marys	Hollidaysburg
Bradley, James	Pvt, B, Ind. Bn. Pa. Mil.	1840			
Bradley, John	Pvt. U, 84 Pa. Inf.				
	Pvt. I, 57 Pa. Inf.	1838			
Bradley, John C.	Pvt. E, 104 Pa. Inf.				
Bradley, William J.	Pvt. H, 3 Pa. Inf.				
	Cpl. K, 125 Pa. Inf.				
	A. E. U. S. Navy	1849	1925	Calvary	Altoona
Brady, James F.	Pvt. F, 2 N. J. Inf.	1833			
Brady, John B.	Pvt. D, 46 Pa. Mil.				
	Bks. C, 19 Pa. Cav.	1834	1908	Fairview	Altoona
Brady, Patrick	Pvt. D, 14 Pa. Inf.	1840			
Brady, Patrick	Cpl. M, 62 Pa. Inf.	1839			
Brandt, Daniel W.	Pvt. A, 126 Pa. Inf.				
	Pvt. D, 11 Pa. Cav.	1843	1930	Oak Ridge	Altoona
Brandt, Jacob S.	Pvt. 84 Pa. Inf.	1844	1913	Calvary	Altoona
Brant, William	Pvt. K, 125 Pa. Inf.				
Brannen, John	Pvt. B, 202 Pa. Inf.	1835	1894	Oak Ridge	Altoona
Brannan, Michael	Pvt. M, 62 Pa. Inf.				
	Pvt. F, Ind. Bn. Pa. Mil.	1820	1890	St. Johns	Altoona
Brannan, Patrick	Pvt. M, 62 Pa. Inf.	1832	1862	Gaines Mill	Virginia
Brannon, William	Pvt. M, 62 Pa. Inf.	1843			
Brannen, William	Pvt. H, 110 Pa. Inf.	1835	1918	Frankstown	Hollidaysburg
Brantner, James Scott	Pvt. B, 125 Pa. Inf.				
	Pvt. B, 208 Pa. Inf.		1902	Schmuckers	Williamsburg
Brantner, John H.	Pvt. B, 125 Pa. Inf.	1840	1899	Methodist	Williamsburg
Brantner, Stewart F.	Pvt. F, 1 Pa. Art.		1894	Schmuckers	Williamsburg
Brashears, Joseph R.	Pvt. H, 1 Md. Inf.				
	Sgt. F, 11 Md. Inf.				
	Sgt. U, 2 Md. Inf.	1843	1915	Oak Ridge	Altoona
Bratton, John D.	Pvt. B, 110 Pa. Inf.	1846	1920	Grandview	Tyrone
Bratton, Edmund E.	Pvt. C, 46 Pa. Mil.	1844			
Bratton, Harvey A.	Pvt. A, 205 Pa. Inf.				
Bratton, Henry H.	Pvt. H, 110 Pa. Inf.	1820	1893	Grandview	Tyrone
Brawley, John	Pvt. C, 93 Pa. Inf.	1831			
Brawn, Joseph F.	Pvt. A, 4 N. H. Inf.		1882	Fairview	Altoona
Brechbiel, Abraham	Pvt. K, 133 Pa. Inf.				
	Cpl. D, 13 Pa. Cav.	1844	1907	Fairview	Altoona
Breckbill, Jacob W.	Cpl. A, 148 Pa. Inf.	1838	1926	Oak Ridge	Altoona
Breakbill, Jeremiah	Pvt. C, 13 Pa. Cav.				
Breichbeil, Thomas D.	Pvt. C, 101 Pa. Inf.	1843	1928	Greenwood	Altoona
Breeze, Samuel	Pvt. H, 14 Pa. Inf.				
	Pvt. C, 76 Pa. Inf.	1820			
Brehman, John Andrew	Mus. C, 4 Pa. Mil.	1840	1911	Fairview	Altoona
Brenick, John	Pvt. B, 3 Pa. Inf.	1838			
Brenneman, David	Sgt. I, 14 Pa. Inf.	1836			
Brenneman, Francis	Pvt. E, 104 Pa. Inf.				
Brenneman, Isaac N.	Cpl. C, 3 Pa. Inf.	1836			
Brenneman, Michael	Pvt. C, 3 Pa. Inf.	1841			
Brenner, Amos	Pvt. I, 14 Pa. Inf.	1832			
Brenner, Joseph	Pvt. D, 192 Pa. Inf.	1827	1920	Presbyterian	Hollidaysburg
Brenner, Mitchell C.					
Breon, Jacob	Cpt. F, 148 Pa. Inf.	1829	1901	Fairview	Altoona
Bressler, Lindley H.	Pvt. A, 125 Pa. Inf.		1862	Alexandria	Virginia
Bressler, Mahlon H.	Pvt. D, 3 Pa. Inf.				
	Pvt. F, 31 Pa. Inf.				
	Cpl. A, 191 Pa. Inf.	1840	1911	Oak Ridge	Altoona

SOLDIERS OF BLAIR COUNTY

Name	Rank Organization	Born	Died	Cemetery	Location
Bressler, Samuel	Pvt. K, 3 Pa. Art.	1834	1909	Grandview	Tyrone
Breth, Samuel J.	Pvt. G, 11 Pa. Cav.	1839	1903	Fairview	Altoona
Brewer, Thomas H.	Pvt. D, 14 Pa. Inf.				
	Cpl. A, 61 Pa. Inf.	1833	1904	Oak Ridge	Altoona
Bridaham, John G.	Pvt. E, 13 Pa. Cav.				
Bridenthal, David S.	Pvt. F, 99 Pa. Inf.	1822	1897	Hickory Bottom	Woodbury
Briggle, John M.	Pvt. C, 99 Pa. Inf.	1843	1914	Greenfield	Bedford Co.
Briggs, Alolphus E.	Pvt. H, 110 Pa. Inf.				
Briggs, Daniel C.	Pvt. M, 9 Pa. Cav.	1844	1864	Louisville	Kentucky
Brindle, Emanuel	Pvt. M, 62 Pa. Inf.	1837			
Brindle, George W.	Pvt. E, 125 Pa. Inf.				
Brindle, John	Pvt. M, 102 Pa. Inf.		1905	Franklinville	Hunt'gdon Co.
Briner, James	Pvt. E, 84 Pa. Inf.		1864	Alexandria	Virginia
Briney, Henry	Pvt. H, 205 Pa. Inf.	1843	1912	Alto Reste	Hollidaysburg
Briney, John	Pvt. A, 205 Pa. Inf.				
Bringhurst, Thomas F.	Cpt. F, 31 Pa. Inf.				
Brininger, Simon	Pvt. I, 55 Pa. Inf.	1820			
Brinner, William B.	Pvt. I, 57 Pa. Inf.	1844			
Brisbin, Ezra Dougherty	Cpt. C, 110 Pa. Inf.		1895	Grandview	Tyrone
Brissell, John	Pvt. G, 12 Pa. Cav.	1844			
Brogan, Charles F.	Cpl. A, 110 Pa. Inf.				
Brogan, Samuel	Pvt. D, 205 Pa. Inf.	1829			
Brookbank, David E.	Pvt. C, 19 Pa. Inf.	1840	1888	St. Johns	Altoona
Brooks, Isaac	Pvt. U, 1 Pa. Art.	1835			
Brooks, James E.	Pvt. E, 26 Pa. Mil.				
	Pvt. B, 13 Pa. Cav.	1846	1903	Greenwood	Altoona
Brooks, John	Pvt. A, 84 Pa. Inf.				
Brooks, John	Pvt. K, 46 Pa. Mil.	1846			
Brooks, Jonas W.	Pvt. C, 110 Pa. Inf.				
Brooks, Thomas	Pvt. C, 63 Pa. Inf.				
	Sgt. A, 17 Pa. Cav.	1842	1922		
Brooks, William W.	Pvt. D, 13 Pa. Cav.	1845			
Brotherlin, John	Maj. Paymaster	1812	1879	Presbyterian	Hollidaysburg
Brown, Absalom C.	Mus. B, 56 Pa. Inf.	1840	1909	Fairview	Altoona
Brown, Amos G.	Pvt. C, 76 Pa. Inf.	1846			
Brown, Andrew W.	Pvt. C, 21 U. S. C. T.			Union	Hollidaysburg
Brown, George C.	Pvt. K, 46 Pa. Mil.	1844			
Brown, George D.	Pvt. A, 184 Pa. Inf.	1844	1927	Potter Creek	Bedford Co.
Brown, George W.	Pvt. I, 149 Pa. Inf.	1832	1898	Oak Ridge	Altoona
Brown, Henry P.	Pvt. B, 54 Mass. Inf.	1843	1895	Union	Hollidaysburg
Brown, Isaac E.	Sgt. D. 125 Pa. Inf.				
	Pvt. Ind. Cav. Pa. Mil.	1834			
Brown, Jacob	Pvt. I, 14 Pa. Inf.	1836			
Brown, Jacob C.	Cpl. G, 12 Pa. Cav.	1843	1906	Rose Hill	Altoona
Brown, Jacob D.	Cpl. D, 101 Pa. Inf.			Potter Creek	Bedford Co.
Brown, James	Pvt. F, 76 Pa. Inf.	1839			
Brown, James B.	Pvt. B, 3 Pa. Inf.				
	Pvt. F, 76 Pa. Inf.	1836	1864	Cold Harbor	Virginia
Brown, James E.	Cpl. H, 203 Pa. Inf.		1883	Oregan Hill	Penna.
Brown, John	Pvt. E, 22 U. S. C. T.				
Brown, John	Pvt. 13 Md. Inf.				
Brown, John A.	Pvt. D, 125 Pa. Inf.		1862	Antietam	Maryland
Brown, John T.	Pvt. G, 12 Pa. Cav.	1839			
Brown, Joseph T.	Pvt. B, 3 Pa. Inf.				
	Pvt. F, 76 Pa. Inf.	1839	1911	Greenwood	Altoona
Brown, Josiah R.	Pvt. A, 190 Pa. Inf.		1864	Salisbury	N. Car.
Brown, Michael A.	Pvt. B, 148 Pa. Inf.	1835	1879	Fairview	Altoona
Brown, Nathan	Pvt. F, 76 Pa. Inf.	1832	1902	Greenwood	Altoona
Brown, Philip S.	Pvt. A, 184 Pa. Inf.	1840	1903	Greenlawn	Roaring Spring
Brown, Robert	Pvt. F, 45 U. S. C. T.	1829	1893	Union	Hollidaysburg
Brown, Samuel D.	Pvt. D, 101 Pa. Inf.	1842	1897	Potter Creek	Bedford Co.

Name	Rank Organization	Born	Died	Cemetery	Location
Brown, William	Sgt. B, Ind. Bn. Pa. Mil.	1842			
Brown, William	Pvt. I, 51 Pa. Inf.		1904	Unionville	Penna.
Brown, William	Pvt. A, 51 Pa. Inf.	1824	1910	Fairview	Martinsburg
Brown, William A.	Pvt. D, 22 U.S.C.T.	1831	1916	Union	Hollidaysburg
Brown, William E.	Pvt. F, 31 Pa. Inf.	1838	1877	Fairview	Altoona
Brown, William H.	Pvt. A, 1 Pa. Cav.	1840	1937	Fairview	Altoona
Brubaker, Emanuel	Pvt. H, 14 Pa. Inf.				
	Pvt. E, 84 Pa. Inf.	1839	1862	Winchester	Virginia
Brubaker, George	Pvt. D, 125 Pa. Inf.				
	Pvt. D, 46 Pa. Mil.				
	Pvt. I, 7 Pa. Cav.	1846	1878	Fairview	Altoona
Brubaker, Jacob	Pvt. H, 110 Pa. Inf.				
Brubaker, Samuel H.	Cpl. B, 208 Pa. Inf.				
Brubaker, Samuel	Pvt. F, 203 Pa. Inf.	1840	1928	Carson Valley	Duncansville
Brumbaugh, David	Pvt. A, 23 Pa. Mil.	1843			
Brumbaugh, David D.	Pvt. K, 50 Pa. Inf.	1837	1883	Spring Hope	Martinsburg
Brumbaugh, F. M.	Pvt. C, 110 Pa. Inf.				
Brumbaugh, George	Pvt. E, 84 Pa. Inf.	1827	1887	St. Pauls	Williamsburg
Brumbaugh, Henry C.	Pvt. H, 103 Pa. Inf.	1831	1880	Fairview	Altoona
Brumbaugh, Isaac C.	Pvt. H, 103 Pa. Inf.	1844	1872	St. Pauls	Williamsburg
Brumbaugh, Jacob	Pvt. D, 125 Pa. Inf.				
	Cpl. A, 205 Pa. Inf.	1831	1916	Rose Hill	Altoona
Brumbaugh, Jacob C.	Pvt. B, 125 Pa. Inf.	1838	1908	Presbyterian	Williamsburg
Brumbaugh, John	Pvt. D, 9 Pa. Cav.				
	Pvt. F, 133 Pa. Inf.	1833	1908	Rose Hill	Altoona
Brumbaugh, Joseph	Pvt. E, 104 Pa. Inf.				
Brumbaugh, Joseph	Pvt. A, 77 Pa. Inf.	1840	1913	Grandview	Tyrone
Brumbaugh, Samuel	Pvt. A, 205 Pa. Inf.				
Brumbaugh, William A.	Mus. D, 125 Pa. Inf.				
Brumbaugh, William	Pvt. G, 133 Pa. Inf.				
	Pvt. F, 13 Pa. Cav.	1839	1923	Fairview	Altoona
Brunell, Theodore	Pvt. B, 125 Pa. Inf.				
	Mus. B, 208 Pa. Inf.	1836	1894	Oak Ridge	Altoona
Brunell, William	Pvt. B, 125 Pa. Inf.				
Brunker, Richard P.	Mus. M, 62 Pa. Inf.	1844	1922	Bloomington	Illinois
Bryan, Charles	Pvt. M, 9 Pa. Cav.	1844			
Bryan, Edmund	Sgt. Ord. Dept.		1873	Washington	D. C.
Bryan, George W.	Pvt. C, 205 Pa. Inf.	1845			
Bryan, Henry H.	Pvt. H, 3 Pa. Inf.				
	Sgt. H, 22 Pa. Cav.	1842			
Bryan, James M.	Pvt. A, 13 Pa. Cav.	1847	1927	Logan Valley	Bellwood
Bryan, John	Sgt. E, 125 Pa. Inf.				
Bryan, Joseph H.	1Lt. C, 46 Pa. Mil.				
	2Lt. D, 184 Pa. Inf.	1841			
Bryant, James	Pvt. B, 62 Pa. Inf.	1835	1901	Oak Ridge	Altoona
Bryny, Michael	Pvt. B, 208 Pa. Inf.	1822	1900	Methodist	Williamsburg
Buchanan, James W.	Sgt. K, 78 Pa. Inf.	1840	1898	Hutchisons	Altoona
Buchanan, Robert J.	Pvt. H, 125 Pa. Inf.	1844	1886	Hutchisons	Altoona
Buchanan, William	Pvt. D, 22 Pa. Cav.				
	Pvt. K, 22 Pa. Cav.	1842	1931	Cassville	Huntingdon Co.
Buck, Christian M.	Pvt. I, 22 Pa. Cav.	1846	1921	Grandview	Tyrone
Buck, George W.	2Lt. A, 110 Pa. Inf.	1840	1915	Oak Ridge	Altoona
Buck, Ira	Pvt. E, 45 Pa. Inf.	1845	1872	Carson Valley	Duncansville
Buck, Miles	Mus. K, 50 Pa. Inf.	1848	1909	Graziersville	Tyrone
Buck, Samuel David	Pvt. C, 46 Pa. Inf.	1844			
Buck, Travanian	Pvt. F, 76 Pa. Inf.	1843	1920	Carson Valley	Duncansville
Buck, William	Pvt. E, 125 Pa. Inf.	1832	1905	Carson Valley	Duncansville
Buck, William Harrison	Cpl. E, 45 Pa. Inf.		1864	Wilderness	Virginia
Buckius, George	Pvt. M, 192 Pa. Inf.				
	Pvt. A, 201 Pa. Inf.	1847			
Buel, Henry G.	Pvt. F, 76 Pa. Inf.	1843	1863	Ft. Wagner	S. Car.

SOLDIERS OF BLAIR COUNTY

Name	Rank Organization	Born	Died	Cemetery	Location
Buffington, Charles L.	2Lt. E, 1 Pa. Cav. Adj. 200 Pa. Inf.	1837	1914	Grandview	Tyrone
Bulger, Andrew	Pvt. C, 110 Pa. Inf.	1842	1863	Kifer	Woodbury
Bulger, Daniel B.	Pvt. H, 208 Pa. Inf.	1817	1890	Kifer	Woodbury
Bulger, David	Pvt. H, 208 Pa. Inf.	1833	1905	Woodbury	Bedford Co.
Bulger, Levi M.	Cpl. C, 110 Pa. Inf.				
Bulick, Thomas M.	1Lt. C, 45 Pa. Inf.				
Bullard, Owen	Pvt. C, 84 Pa. Inf.	1831	1862	Handcock	Maryland
Bullers, William H.	Pvt. A, 84 Pa. Inf.				
Bumgardner, Alfred	Cpl. D, 125 Pa. Inf.				
Bumgardner, Israel	Pvt. E, 104 Pa. Inf.				
Bumgardner, Lewis	Pvt. K, 22 Pa. Cav.	1827			
Bumgardner, Zachariah	Pvt. C, 76 Pa. Inf.	1838	1864	Chester Field	Virginia
Bunker, Henry L.	Pvt. A, 84 Pa. Inf.	1845	1896	Lutheran	Hollidaysburg
Bunker, Isaiah W.	Pvt. D, 84, Pa. Inf.	1815	1884	Lutheran	Hollidaysburg
Bunker, N. R.	Cpt. D, 58 Pa. Inf.				
Bunnels, John R.	Pvt. A, 110 Pa. Inf.				
Buoy, Austin	Sgt. F, 107 Pa. Inf.	1840	1885	Dayton	Ohio
Buoy, James A.	Sgt. U. S. Inf.		1865	Phila.	Penna.
Burchfield, Theodore(s)	Pvt. F, 126 Pa. Inf. Cpl. K, 196 Pa. Inf.	1842	1923	Fairview	Altoona
Burge, Adam	Pvt. E, 125 Pa. Inf.		1862	Washington	D. C.
Burge, Jacob	Pvt. D, 53 Pa. Inf.	1826	1905	Lutheran	Hollidaysburg
Burger, David	Pvt. H, 112 Ill. Inf.	1830	1909	Spring Hope	Martinsburg
Burger, Joseph S.	Pvt. F, 77 Pa. Inf.	1833	1922	Salemville	Penna.
Burger, Reuben	Pvt. M, 62 Pa. Inf. Cpl. K, 91 Pa. Inf.				
Burget, Elias S.	Pvt. E, 84 Pa. Inf. Pvt. G, 57 Pa. Inf.	1835	1899	Nicodemus	Henrietta
Burk, Francis Patrick	Pvt. H, 14 Pa. Inf.	1837	1927	St. Marys	Hollidaysburg
Burke, James M.	Pvt. M, 62, Pa. Inf.	1826	1886	Oak Grove	Tyrone
Burke, John	Cpl. M, 9 Pa. Cav.	1837			
Burk, John	Pvt. A, 110 Pa. Inf.				
Burk, Samuel	Pvt. A, 84 Pa. Inf.				
Burket, Abram	2Lt. G, 11 Pa. Cav.	1842	1923	Reform	Claysburg
Burket, Adam	Pvt. D, 13 Pa. Cav.	1847	1865	Burkets	Henrietta
Burket, Beightal	Pvt. I, 22 Pa. Cav.	1846	1865	New Creek	Virginia
Burket, David	Pvt. E, 138 Pa. Inf.			Mt. Zion	Bedford Co.
Burket, David	Pvt. F, 77 Pa. Inf.	1846	1928	Saxton	Penna.
Burket, Ephriam	Cpt. D, 110 Pa. Inf.	1830	1901	Lutheran	Sinking Valley
Burket, Ephraim J.	Pvt. B, 3 Pa. Inf. Sgt. A, 205 Pa. Inf.	1835	1915	Fairview	Altoona
Burket, Gabriel	Pvt. K, 55 Pa. Inf.			Mt. Zion	Bedford Co.
Burket, George M.	Pvt. I, 14 Pa. Inf. Pvt. D, 13 Pa. Cav.	1842			
Burket, Henry	Pvt. C, 205 Pa. Inf.	1848			
Burkett, Henry	Pvt. E, 76 Pa. Inf.		1898	New Baltimore	Penna.
Burket, Jacob	Pvt. D, 55 Pa. Inf.	1843	1912	Imlertown	Penna.
Burket, Jacob D.	Pvt. I, 171 Pa. Inf.	1839	1912	Reform	Claysburg
Burket, John B.	Pvt, A, 205 Pa. Inf.	1849			
Burket, John W.	Pvt. F, 77 Pa. Inf.	1837	1931	Brumbaugh	Martinsburg
Burket, Samuel C.	Pvt. E, 2 Bn. Pa. Inf.	1844	1919	Greenwood	Altoona
Burkey, Aaron	Pvt. H, 14 Pa. Inf. Pvt. M, 12 Pa. Inf.	1837	1913	Carson Valley	Duncansville
Burkheart, George W.	Pvt. E, 177 Pa. Inf.	1842	1881	Carson Valley	Duncansville
Burkhart, James H.	Pvt. Ind. Cav. Pa. Mil.	1841			
Burkhart, John	Pvt. C, 19 Pa. Cav.	1842			
Burkhart, William	Pvt. F, 76 Pa. Inf.	1813	1890	Carson Valley	Duncansville
Burkhart, William D.	Pvt. F, 76 Pa. Inf.	1844	1921	Rose Hill	Altoona
Burkhire, William	Pvt. M, 62 Pa. Inf.				
Burkholder, David M.	Pvt. D, 184 Pa. Inf.	1844	1864	Antis	Bellwood
Burkholder, Henry	Pvt. F, 76 Pa. Inf.	1822	1862	Hilton Head	S. Car.

THE CIVIL WAR 169

Name	Rank Organization	Born	Died	Cemetery	Location
Burley, Benjamin F.	Pvt. D, 46 Pa. Mil.	1818	1897	Fairview	Altoona
Burley, Caleb R.	Sgt. D, 3 Pa. Inf.	1821	1892	Grandview	Tyrone
Burley, David	Pvt. H, 110 Pa. Inf.	1823	1881	Fairview	Altoona
Burley, Emanuel J.	Pvt. D, 125 Pa. Inf.	1828	1862	Fairview	Altoona
Burley, Francis M.	Pvt. D, 3 Pa. Inf.				
	Sgt. A, 110 Pa. Inf.	1834	1863	Gettysburg	Penna.
Burley, George W.	Sgt. D, 3 Pa. Inf.				
	1Lt. C, 110 Pa. Inf.	1833	1862	Fairview	Altoona
Burley, John L.	Sgt. D, 3 Pa. Inf.	1832	1902	Fairview	Altoona
Burley, John Wesley	Pvt. D, 46 Pa. Mil.	1842	1912	Fairview	Altoona
Burley, Levi R.	Pvt. D, 125 Pa. Inf.				
	Cpl. Ind. Bn. Cav. Pa. Mil.	1845	1903	Fairview	Altoona
Burley, Martin	Cpl. D, 14 Pa. Inf.				
	Cpl. F, 2 Pa. Cav.	1835	1904	Grandview	Tyrone
Burley, William H. H.	Pvt. A, 110 Pa. Inf.	1831	1900	St. Johns	Altoona
Burley, William	Sgt. D, 125 Pa. Inf.	1835	1893	Fairview	Altoona
Burne, Joseph	Pvt. A, 23 Pa. Mil.	1825			
Burnett, Charles	Smn. U. S. Navy	1834	1888	Oak Ridge	Altoona
Burns, Albert	Pvt. C, 99 Pa. Inf.	1847	1926	Orbisonia	Huntingdon Co.
Burns, Alexander	Pvt. H, 131 Pa. Inf.				
	Pvt. A, 205 Pa. Inf.	1828	1913	Logan Valley	Bellwood
Burns, Francis P.	Pvt. E, 104 Pa. Inf.	1847	1877	St. Johns	Altoona
Burns, Isaac	Pvt. E, 49 Pa. Inf.	1835	1902	Charlottsville	Bellwood
Burns, James	Pvt. F, 32 U. S. C. T.	1823			
Burns, John	Pvt. F, 31 Pa. Inf.				
	Pvt. A, 191 Pa. Inf.	1835	1921	St. Patricks	Gallitzin
Burns, Joseph G. W.	Pvt. F, Ind. Bn. Pa. Mil.				
	Pvt. A, 87 Pa. Inf.	1825	1893	Carson Valley	Duncansville
Burns, Lafayette W.	Pvt. H, 208 Pa. Inf.	1832	1906	Kifer	Woodbury
Burns, Michael	Cpl. C, 205 Pa. Inf.	1843	1899	St. Johns	Altoona
Burns, Patrick	Pvt. A, 84 Pa. Inf.				
Burns, Patrick A.	Pvt. F, 133 Pa. Inf.	1844	1892	St. Patricks	Gallitzin
Burns, Patrick A.	Pvt. F, 133 Pa. Inf.	1849	1901	St. Patricks	Gallitzin
Burns, Sylvester W.	Pvt. K, 22 Pa. Cav.	1845	1890	St. Johns	Altoona
Burns, Thomas	Pvt. G, 125 Pa. Inf.	1802		St. Marys	Hollidaysburg
Burns, William	Pvt. I, 1 Pa. Art.	1845	1908	Oak Ridge	Altoona
Burns, William Jackson	2Lt. M, 16 Pa. Cav.	1838	1918	Huntingdon	Penna.
Burns, William H.	Pvt. I, 22 Pa. Cav.	1839	1902	St. Johns	Altoona
Burns, William M.	Pvt. A, 110 Pa. Inf.				
Burris, James	Pvt. F, 32 U. S. C. T.	1823	1902	Oak Ridge	Altoona
Burtnett, David A.	Cpl. D, 125 Pa. Inf.				
	Sgt. Ind. Cav. Pa. Mil.	1836	1890	Oak Ridge	Altoona
Burtnett, John R.	Pvt. B, 54 Pa. Mil.				
	Pvt. L, 11 Pa. Cav.	1846			
Burtnett, John	Pvt. E, 125 Pa. Inf.	1824	1893	Allegheny Fur.	Altoona
Bush, George C.	Sgt. G, 41 Pa. Inf.				
	Sgt. F, 190 Pa. Inf.		1865		
Bush, Jacob D.	Pvt. B, 149 Pa. Inf.	1828	1880	Fairview	Altoona
Bush, John	Pvt. B, 99 Pa. Inf.	1843	1902	Reform	Claysburg
Bush, John Henry	Pvt. E, 3 Pa. Inf.				
	Pvt. A, 46 Pa. Inf.	1838		Lutheran	Hollidaysburg
Bush, Joseph	Cpl. F, 2 Pa. Cav.	1804	1863	Fairview	Altoona
Bushman, Thomas	Sgt. K, 101 Pa. Inf.	1840	1918	Oak Ridge	Altoona
Buskin, George W.	Pvt. C, 205 Pa. Inf.	1845			
Buterbaugh, Samuel	Pvt. G, 125 Pa. Inf.				
	Cpl. B, 208 Pa. Inf.				
Butler, Andrew			1863	Beauford	S. Car.
Butler, Charles	Cpl. E, 125 Pa. Inf.				
Butler, David M.	Pvt. E, 125 Pa. Inf.				
	1Lt. C, 205 Pa. Inf.	1838	1898	Greenlawn	Roaring Spring
Butler, James J.	Pvt. E, 181 Pa. Inf.		1883	Ryde	Penna.
Butler, John B.	Pvt. C, 205 Pa. Inf.	1845	1930	Greenlawn	Roaring Spring

SOLDIERS OF BLAIR COUNTY

Name	Rank Organization	Born	Died	Cemetery	Location
Butler, Lafayette F.	Sgn. 125 Pa. Inf.				
	Sgn. 42 Pa. Inf.				
Butler, Solomon	Sgn. 190 Pa. Inf.	1824	1873	Lutheran	Newry
Butler, William	Pvt. D. 192 Pa. Inf.	1823	1896	Lutheran	Hollidaysburg
Butt, Jeremiah P.	Pvt. H, 211 Pa. Inf.	1841	1928	Calvary	Altoona
Butts, George M.	Cpl. F, 77 Pa. Inf.				
Butts, Henry A.	Pvt. F, 77 Pa. Inf.				
Butts, James B.	Mus. C, 133 Pa. Inf.				
	Mus. A, 184 Pa. Inf.	1839	1907	Reform	Loysburg
Butts, William G.	Cpl. B, 125 Pa. Inf.	1837	1903	Presbyterian	Hollidaysburg
Byers, Abraham	Pvt. F, 57 Pa. Inf.				
Byers, Benjamin F.	Pvt. D, 184 Pa. Inf.	1837	1923	Rose Hill	Altoona
Byers, Henry W.	Pvt. F, Ind. Bn. Pa. Mil.	1845			
Byers, Walter P.	Pvt. H, 3 Pa. Inf.				
	Pvt. M, 62 Pa. Inf.	1842			
Byrns, Patrick	Pvt. B, Ind. Bn. Pa. Mil.	1835			
Byrne, Patrick E.	Pvt. G, 12 Pa. Cav.	1843			
Cain, Frederick	Pvt. D, 13 Pa. Cav.	1845			
Cain, Jeromiah	Pvt. D, 149 Pa. Inf.	1830	1918	Union	
Cain, John	Cpl. E, 104 Pa. Inf.				
Cain, John G.	Adj. 125 Pa. Inf.				
Cain, John J.	Pvt. E, 77 Pa. Inf.	1847	1906	St. Johns	Altoona
Cain, Thomas	Pvt. M, 9 Pa. Cav.		1883	Antis	Bellwood
Calderwood, Andrew P.	Sgn. U. S. Army	1824	1887	Grandview	Tyrone
Calderwood, Millard F.	Pvt. G, 97 Pa. Inf.				
	149 Pa. Inf.	1848	1935	Fairview	Altoona
Calderwood, Thomas	Pvt. B, 13 Pa. Cav.	1843	1916	Grandview	Tyrone
Caldwell, Hiram	Pvt. C, Ind. Bn. Pa. Mil.				
Caldwell, James			1864	Wilderness	Virginia
Caldwell, John M.	Pvt. A, Ind. Bn. Pa. Mil.	1844			
Caldwell, Nelson	Pvt. G, 203 Pa. Inf.		1904	Clinton Co.	Penna.
Caldwell, Sylvester K.	Pvt. K, 13 Pa. Cav.	1845	1906	Frankstown	Hollidaysburg
Caldwell, Thomas	Pvt. A, 110 Pa. Inf.				
Caldwell, William	Pvt. B, Ind. Bn. Pa. Mil.	1846			
Callagan, Michael	Pvt. C, 76 Pa. Inf.	1831			
Callaghan, Andrew	Pvt. K, 125 Pa. Inf.				
Calvert, John S.	Sgt. B, 3 Pa. Inf.	1836	1888	Fairview	Altoona
Calvert, William H.	Pvt. A, Ind. Bn. Pa. Mil.				
	Pvt. C, 77 Pa. Inf.	1838	1914	Fairview	Altoona
Calvin, Joseph A.	Pvt. E, 136 Pa. Inf.	1843-1919		Presbyterian	Hollidaysburg
Calvin, Matthew R.	Pvt. A, Ind. Bn. Pa. Mil.	1845			
Calvin, Samuel	Pvt. A, 23 Pa. Mil.	1811	1890	Lutheran	Hollidaysburg
Camerer, Daniel	Pvt. C, 84 Pa. Inf.			Spring Hope	Martinsburg
Camerer, Henry	Pvt. I, 14 Pa. Inf.	1838		Fairview	Martinsburg
Camerer, John	Pvt. C, 84 Pa. Inf.				
	Pvt. H, 57 Pa. Inf.	1839		Lutheran	Hollidaysburg
Camerer, Samuel	Pvt. I, 14 Pa. Inf.	1821	1876	Spring Hope	Martinsburg
Cameron, John C.	Pvt. H, 41 Pa. Inf.	1842	1926	Logan Valley	Bellwood
Cameron, Simon Rufus	Pvt. B, 12 Pa. Cav.	1845	1884	Presbyterian	Sinking Valley
Cameron, William S.	Pvt. G, 125 Pa. Inf.				
Campbell, David H.	Pvt. C, 49 Pa. Inf.				
	Pvt. G, Pa. Mil.			Spring Hope	Martinsburg
Campbell, Harvey B.	Cpl. I, 135 Pa. Inf.	1834	1890	Methodist	Williamsburg
Campbell, James	Pvt. M, 9 Pa. Cav.	1837			
Campbell, James	Pvt. F, 2 Pa. Cav.	1820	1864	Grandview	Tyrone
Campbell, John	Pvt. M. 62 Pa. Inf.	1842	1861	Logan Valley	Bellwood
Campbell, John	Pvt. C, 13 Pa. Cav.	1826	1894	Frankstown	Hollidaysburg
Campbell, John L.	Pvt. C, 84 Pa. Inf.	1822			
Campbell, Lawrence	Pvt. I, 14 Pa. Inf.				
	Pvt. M, 62 Pa. Inf.	1831			
Campbell, Robert	Pvt. F, 75 Pa. Inf.	1836	1892	St. Patricks	Gallitzin
Campbell, Robert M.	Pvt. A, 110 Pa. Inf.				

THE CIVIL WAR   171

Name	Rank Organization	Born	Died	Cemetery	Location
Campbell, Thomas E.	1Lt. D, 125 Pa. Inf.				
	Cpt. D, 46 Pa. Mil.	1839			
Campbell, Thomas J.	Mus. I, 14 Pa. Inf.	1840		Fairview	Martinsburg
Campbell, William	Pvt. D, 14 Pa. Cav.	1842	1864	Andersonville	Georgia
Campbell, William	Sgn. 202 Pa. Inf.	1831	1883	Fairview	Altoona
Campbell, William D.	Pvt. A, 7 Pa. Cav.	1826	1908	Carson Valley	Duncansville
Campbell, William H. H.	Pvt. B, 6 Pa. Cav.	1838	1865	Logan Valley	Bellwood
Canan, David H.	Pvt. C, 22 Pa. Cav.				
	Pvt. H, 184 Pa. Inf.	1845	1895	Grandview	Tyrone
Canan, Henry	Pvt. C, 125 Pa. Inf.	1824	1907	Greenwood	Altoona
Canan, William H.	Pvt. G, 125 Pa. Inf.	1840	1872	Fairview	Altoona
Cannon, Joseph W. (M)	Cpl. B, 3 Pa. Inf.				
	2Lt. F, 76 Pa. Inf.				
	Sgt. E, 7 Ohio Cav.	1829	1907	Logan Valley	Bellwood
Capstick, James C.	Pvt. E, 8 Pa. Inf.	1840	1904	Fairview	Altoona
Caraher, Alfred	Cpl. C, 208 Pa. Inf.	1829	1900	Bald Eagle	Tyrone
Carbaugh, Jonathan	Pvt. A, 110 Pa. Inf.			Elkhurst	Tyrone
Carey, James C.	Pvt. C, 3 Pa. Inf.				
	Cpl. B, 125 Pa. Inf.	1838	1913	St. Patricks	Newry
Carls, Henry	Pvt. B, 125 Pa. Inf.				
	Pvt. B, 208 Pa. Inf.	1845	1938	Fairview	Altoona
Carl, James	Pvt. K, 205 Pa. Inf.	1838			
Carls, John	Pvt. E, 104 Pa. Inf.				
Carl, John W.	Pvt. 46 Pa. Mil.	1831	1896	Grandview	Tyrone
Carl Lemuel	Pvt. I, 205 Pa. Inf.	1838			
Carmon, Howard C.	Pvt. D, 1 Pa. Art.	1845			
Carnell, David	Pvt. E, 125 Pa. Inf.				
	Pvt. I, 55 Pa. Inf.	1842	1898	Greenlawn	Roaring Spring
Carner, Charles B.	Pvt. D, 192 Pa. Inf.	1828	1906	Lutheran	Hollidaysburg
Carnes, John	Pvt. H, 13 Md. Inf.	1827	1878	Fairview	Altoona
Carnes, William	Pvt. D, 13 Md. Inf.	1845		Warriors Mark	Penna.
Carney, Allison H.	Pvt. U, 22 Pa. Cav.	1841			
Carney, Martin	Pvt. I, 137 Pa. Inf.	1822	1883	Presbyterian	Hollidaysburg
Carpenter, David B.	Pvt. C, 110 Pa. Inf.				
	Pvt. L, 6 U. S. Cav.	1846	1928	Greenlawn	Roaring Spring
Carpenter, John W.	Pvt. H, 41 Pa. Inf.	1842	1926	Stockton	California
Carpenter, Samuel S.	Pvt. B, 13 Pa. Cav.	1848	1902	Reform	Loysburg
Carr, William	Pvt. D, 14 Pa. Inf.	1833			
Carrell, Joseph	Cpl. G, 125 Pa. Inf.	1839	1892	Presbyterian	Hollidaysburg
Carroll, Thomas	Pvt. C, 84 Pa. Inf.	1831			
Carson, Daniel	Pvt. C, 133 Pa. Inf.	1838	1900	Salemville	Bedford Co.
Carson, Jacob Z.	Pvt. I, 171 Pa. Inf.	1841	1909	Albrights	Roaring Spring
Carson, Samuel M.	Pvt. C, 62 Pa. Inf.	1845	1912	Huntingdon	Penna.
Carson, Thomas F.	Pvt. A, 46 Pa. Mil.			Grandview	Tyrone
Carter, Floyd	Pvt. E, 32 Pa. Inf.			Union	Hollidaysburg
Carter, Jacob L.	Pvt. C, 148 Pa. Inf.	1843	1900	Fairview	Altoona
Carter, Samuel B.	Pvt. B, 57 Pa. Inf.				
Carter, Samuel M.	Smn. U. S. Navy	1838	1921	Allegheny Fur.	Altoona
Carter, William B.	Pvt. F, 31 Pa. Inf.				
	Pvt. A, 191 Pa. Inf.	1842		Logan Valley	Bellwood
Cartwright, Austin	Pvt. G, Ind. Bn. Pa. Mil.	1847			
Cartwright, Franklin J.	Pvt. G, 205 Pa. Inf.	1846		Hopewell	Bedford Co.
Cartwright, William	Pvt. E, 49 Pa. Inf.	1832	1912	Frankstown	Hollidaysburg
Case, Reuben	Pvt. A, 84 Pa. Inf.			Lutheran	Hollidaysburg
Case, Thomas	Pvt. D, 13 Pa. Cav.	1836			
Case, Willis B.	Pvt. 109, 2Bn. Vt. Corps		1910	West Newton	Penna.
Casey, James					
Casey, John	Pvt. 55 Pa. Inf.			St. Patricks	Gallitzin
Casey, Patrick	Pvt. 192 Pa. Inf.	1842	1891	St. Patricks	Gallitzin
Cashling, Michael	Pvt. D, 46 Pa. Mil.	1824	1909	Fairview	Altoona
Caskey, Abednego	Pvt. D, 192 Pa. Inf.				
Casner, Charles					

SOLDIERS OF BLAIR COUNTY

Name	Rank Organization	Born	Died	Cemetery	Location
Casner, John	Sgt. H, 12 Pa. Cav.	1838	1929	Presbyterian	Hollidaysburg
Casner, John W.	Pvt. C, 110 Pa. Inf.				
Cassell, Andrew	Pvt. E, 20 Pa. Cav.			Grandview	Tyrone
Cassell, George	Pvt. U, 84 Pa. Inf.				
	Pvt. I, 57 Pa. Inf.	1834			
Casselberry, John F.	Pvt. D, 131 Pa. Inf.	1846	1918	Cleveland	Ohio
Cassidy, Christopher	Pvt. I, 84 Pa. Inf.				
Cassaday David F.	Cpl. F, 31 Pa. Inf.				
	Cpl. A, 191 Pa. Inf.	1839	1869	Fairview	Altoona
Cassiday, Francis	Cpt. H, 110 Pa. Inf.	1821	1904	Lutheran	Newry
Cassiday, George E.	Pvt. H, 110 Pa. Inf.				
Cassidy, George W.	Pvt. F, 31 Pa. Inf.				
	Pvt. A. 191 Pa. Inf.	1840			
Cassady, James L.	Pvt. C, 208 Pa. Inf.		1878	Warriors Mark	Penna.
Cassiday, Michael	Pvt. M, 62 Pa. Inf.	1841			
Cassidy, Michael	Pvt. G, 12 Pa. Cav.	1809	1872	Fairview	Altoona
Cassiday, Peter V.	Pvt. F, 1 Pa. Art.	1843			
Cassidy, Samuel Ambrose	Pvt. A, 2 Pa. Art.	1825	1918	St. Johns	Altoona
Cassidy, Solomon	Cpl. B, 46 Ohio Inf.	1837	1909	Rose Hill	Altoona
Cassidy, Solomon	Pvt. B., 3 Pa. Inf.				
	Pvt. K, 84 Pa. Inf.				
	Pvt. K, 57 Pa. Inf.	1841	1914	Oak Ridge	Altoona
Cassidy, William E.	Pvt. M, 3 Pa. Art.		1925		
Cassady, William M.	Pvt. K, 110 Pa. Inf.				
	Pvt. I, 6 U. S. Cav.	1840	1906	Bald Eagle	Tyrone
Caswell, George A.	Pvt. H, 13 Md. Inf.	1818	1908	Fairview	Altoona
Caughling, William T.	Pvt. B, 49 Pa. Inf.				
Cavender, Charles	Pvt. C, 46 Pa. Mil.	1821			
Cessna, George W.	Pvt. E, 76 Pa. Inf.	1842	1898	Fairview	Altoona
Chamberlain, Daniel	Pvt. I, 34 Pa. Inf.	1842	1918	Warriors Mark	Penna.
Chamberlain, Eli Gabriel	Pvt. G, Ind. Bn. Pa. Mil.				
	Pvt. K, 208 Pa. Inf.	1845	1865	Rodman	Roaring Spring
Chamberlain, Ferando C.	Pvt. C, 194 Pa. Inf.		1930	Clearville	Bedford Co.
Chamberlin, Jacob	Cpl. H, 22 Pa. Cav.	1832			
Chamberlain, Jacob	Pvt. F, 77 Pa. Inf.	1844		St. Pauls	Williamsburg
Chamberlain, James	Pvt. C, 110 Pa. Inf.				
Chamberlain, William P.	Pvt. C, 76 Pa. Inf.	1835			
Chambers, James W.	Pvt. I, Bn. Ind. Art.	1846	1916	Grandview	Altoona
Chambers, William A.	Pvt. I, 22 Pa. Cav.	1845			
Champeno, George		1839			
Champeno, William	Cpl. C, 76 Pa. Inf.	1843	1889	Fairview	Altoona
Chandler, Harrison J.	Pvt. F, 10 Pa. Inf.				
	2Lt. K, 76 Pa. Inf.	1840	1928	Rochester	Pa.
Chaplin, Samuel	Pvt. D, 205 Pa. Inf.	1816			
Chaplin, William M.	Pvt. I, 25 U. S. C. T.	1847	1914	Fairview	Martinsburg
Chappell, C. W.	Sgt. B, 111 Pa. Inf.			Mt. Zion	Bedford Co.
Charles, Henry	Pvt. D, 192 Pa. Inf.				
Charles, Samuel W.	Pvt. A, 3 Pa. Inf.	1836			
Charles, Thomas J.	Pvt. G, 125 Pa. Inf.				
	Pvt. M, 22 Pa. Cav.	1840	1925	Oak Ridge	Altoona
Charters, William C.	Pvt. F, 31 Pa. Inf.				
	Pvt. A, 191 Pa. Inf.	1835			
Chase, John H.					
Chase, William S.	Cpl. A, 6 Pa. Cav.	1831	1898	Oak Ridge	Altoona
Cherry, Alfred	Pvt. F, 31 Pa. Inf.		1864	Fredericksburg	Virginia
Cherry, Calvin F.	Pvt. Ind. Bn. Pa. Mil.	1844			
Cherry, Edward	Pvt. A, 110 Pa. Inf.	1843	1861	Antis	Bellwood
Cherry, George	Pvt. G, 12 Pa. Cav.	1844	1888	Antis	Bellwood
Cherry, John E.	Pvt. E, 104 Pa. Inf.	1839	1929	Charlottesville	Bellwood
Cherry, Thomas A.	Pvt. H, 103 Pa. Inf.	1832	1901	Antis	Bellwood
Chesley, Edwin	Pvt. B, 40 Pa. Inf.				
	Cpl. A, 206 Pa. Inf.	1838	1882	Homer City	Pa.

Name	Name Organization	Born	Died	Cemetery	Location
Chesney, Simon	Pvt. G, 13 Pa. Cav.		1910	Mooresville	Hunt'gdon Co.
Chestnutwood, Augustine	Pvt. D, 13 Pa. Cav.				
Chilcoat, Benjamin	Pvt. M, 9 Pa. Cav.	1835	1865	Florence	S. Car.
Chilcoat, Hilany	Pvt. C, 110 Pa. Inf.				
Chilcoat, Isaac	Pvt. C, 110 Pa. Inf.				
Chilcoat, William Lee	Pvt. K, 9 Pa. Cav.	1845	1917	Grandview	Altoona
Christ, Robert	Pvt. F, Ind. Bn. Pa. Mil.	1843			
Christian, John G.	Pvt. H, 14 Pa. Inf.				
	Cpl. G, 125 Pa. Inf.	1839	1864	Carson Valley	Duncansville
Christy, Henry C.	Sgn. 55 Pa. Inf.				
	Sgn. 58 Pa. Inf.				
Christy, Josiah M.	Pvt. K, 28 Pa. Inf.	1827	1882	St. Patricks	Gallitzin
Christy, Livingston L.	Pvt. G, 125 Pa. Inf.	1841			
	Sgt. Ind. Bn. Pa. Mil.				
Claar, Daniel	Pvt. H, 99 Pa. Inf.	1833	1892	German Baptist	Claysburg
Claar, Henry I.	Pvt. K, 55 Pa. Inf.			Upper Claar	Bedford Co.
Claar, Jacob C.	Pvt. E, 138 Pa. Inf.			Upper Claar	Bedford Co.
Claar, Lewis	Pvt. H, 99 Pa. Inf.			Upper Claar	Bedford Co.
Claar, Samuel	Pvt. F, 1 Pa. Art.	1842	1914	Upper Claar	Bedford Co.
Claar, Thomas	Pvt. H, 99 Pa. Inf.		1900	Upper Claar	Bedford Co.
Clabaugh, Andrew	Bug. Ind. Cav. Pa. Mil.	1835			
Clabaugh, Benjamin	Pvt. D, 46 Pa. Mil.	1837			
Claubaugh, James		1834	1916	Hopewell	Bedford Co.
Clabaugh, John E.	Pvt. I, 205 Pa. Inf.	1844	1924	Rose Hill	Altoona
Clabaugh, Levi L.	1Lt. E, 46 Pa. Mil.	1830	1898	Fairview	Altoona
Clabaugh, S.	Pvt. G, 11 Pa. Cav.				
Clan, Samuel					
Clapper, Adolphus	Pvt. I, 137 Pa. Inf.	1833	1898	Canoe Creek	Williamsburg
Clapper, Daniel	Pvt. B, 208 Pa. Inf.	1848	1874	St. Johns	Williamsburg
Clapper, Jacob	Pvt. E, 104 Pa. Inf.	1850	1868	Carson Valley	Duncansville
Clapper, Jacob M.	Pvt. I, 137 Pa. Inf.	1833	1911	Frankstown	Hollidaysburg
Clapper, James	Sgt. D, 13 Pa. Cav.	1841			
Clapper, James	Pvt. I, 137 Pa. Inf.				
Clapper, William	Pvt. C, 19 Pa. Cav.	1846			
Clark, David	Pvt. D, 3 Pa. Inf.				
	Pvt. D, 49 Pa. Inf.				
	Pvt. H, 143 Pa. Inf.	1832	1902	Fairview	Altoona
Clark, Jacob F.	Pvt. U, 22 Pa. Cav.	1840			
Clark, James	Pvt. D, 192 Pa. Inf.	1828	1883	St. Marys	Hollidaysburg
Clark, James N.	Pvt. K, 46 Pa. Mil.	1846			
Clark, Jamison	Pvt. H, 22 Pa. Cav.	1846	1864	Charleston	W. Va.
Clark, John	Pvt. C, 84 Pa. Inf.	1838			
Clark, John	Pvt. M, 62 Pa. Inf.				
	Pvt. K, 91 Pa. Inf.	1841	1897	Sarah Furnace	Claysburg
Clark, John	Pvt. H, 3 Pa. Inf.	1821			
Clark, John A.	Pvt. E, 3 Pa. Inf.				
	Pvt. D, 84 Pa. Inf.	1836	1907	Rose Hill	Altoona
Clark, Lewis L.	Pvt. I, 34 Pa. Inf.	1831	1861		Sinking Valley
Clark, Lewis M.	Pvt. F, 140 Pa. Inf.	1843	1913	Greenlawn	Hollidaysburg
Clark, Pinkney J.	Pvt. D, 46 Pa. Inf.	1827	1890	Fairview	Altoona
Clark, Robert	Pvt. B, 3 Pa. Inf.	1841			
Clark, Robert	Pvt. G, 125 Pa. Inf.				
Clark, Thaddeus B.	Pvt. A, 84 Pa. Inf.				
	Pvt. G, 57 Pa. Inf.	1845	1873	Lutheran	Hollidaysburg
Clark, William E.	Pvt. H, 22 Pa. Cav.	1843	1864		
Clarks, John Morris (M)	2Lt. B, 3 Pa. Inf.				
	Maj. F, 31 Pa. Inf.	1829	1890	Fairview	Altoona
Clark, Robert J.	1Lt. F, 31 Pa. Inf.		1864		
Clarks, Samuel	Pvt. A, 23 Pa. Mil.	1822			
Clauss, George F.	Pvt. A, 3 Pa. Inf.				
	Sgt. A, 23 Pa. Mil.	1820	1904	Lutheran	Newry
Claycomb, Frederick	Pvt. K, 55 Pa. Inf.			Mt. Zion	Bedford Co.

SOLDIERS OF BLAIR COUNTY

Name	Organization	Born	Died	Cemetery	Location
Claycomb, John	Pvt. K, 55 Pa. Inf.	1819	1873	Fairview	Altoona
Claycomb, Nathaniel	Pvt. C, 1 Pa. Art.	1841			
Claycomb, Samuel	Pvt. G, 11 Pa. Cav.	1834	1905	Rose Hill	Altoona
Clemens, Peter	Pvt. B, 96 Pa. Inf.	1841	1923	Mifflin	Pa.
Clevenger, Harrison	Pvt. B, 3 Md. Inf.	1847	1903	Everett	Pa.
Clevenger, Jonathan J.	Pvt. E, 84 Pa. Inf.				
	Pvt. I, 57 Pa. Inf.	1831			
Clifford, Carson W.	Pvt. F, 135 Pa. Inf.				
	Cpl. A, 186 Pa. Inf.	1845	1918	Indiana	Pa.
Clinefelter, Robert W.	Cpl. Tanners Pa. Inf.			Leisburg	Pa.
Clites, Solomon	Pvt. F, 77 Pa. Inf.	1847			
Clodious, Charles	Pvt. A, 125 Pa. Inf.				
Clopper, Daniel	Pvt. B, 208 Pa. Inf.				
Closs, Peter	Pvt. A, 23 Pa. Mil.	1824			
Closson, Caleb Horace	Pvt. G, 119 Pa. Inf.	1845	1911	Fairview	Altoona
Closson, David	Pvt. B, Ind. Bn. Pa. Mil.				
	Pvt. E, 49 Pa. Inf.	1843	1915	Carson Valley	Duncansville
Closson, Graham McC.	Pvt. A, 110 Pa. Inf.		1917	Freeport	Illinois
Closson, Josiah S.	Pvt. G, 125 Pa. Inf.	1842	1901	Fairview	Altoona
Clossin, Martin	Pvt. F, 77 Pa. Inf.	1826	1865	Victoria	Texas
Closson, Thomas S.	Pvt. E, 46 Pa. Mil.				
	Cpl. A, 110 Pa. Inf.	1847	1910	Logan Valley	Bellwood
Clouner, Isaac	Pvt. G, 21 Pa. Cav.	1836	1910	Fairview	Altoona
Cluck, Britten E.	Cpl. K, 125 Pa. Inf.				
Cluck, Jacob	Pvt. K, 125 Pa. Inf.				
Coats, Thomas C.	Pvt. A, 84 Pa. Inf.				
Coble, Benjamin F.	Pvt. C, 53 Pa. Inf.	1836	1914	Brumbaugh	Hunt'gdon Co.
Coble, John	Pvt. C, 110 Pa. Inf.				
Cobler, Francis C.	Pvt. G, Ind. Bn. Pa. Mil.				
	Pvt. K, 55 Pa. Inf.	1847			
Cochran, Jeremiah	Pvt. B, Ind. Bn. Pa. Mil.				
	Cpl. I, 205 Pa. Inf.	1832	1911	Carson Valley	Duncansville
Cochran, John	Pvt. A, 3 Pa. Inf.	1842			
Cochran, Peter	Pvt. B, Ind. Bn. Pa. Mil.				
	Pvt. H, 110 Pa. Inf.	1847	1915	Carson Valley	Duncansville
Cochran, Robert	Pvt. D, 125 Pa. Inf.				
Cochran, William	Pvt. A, 56 Pa. Inf.			Carson Valley	Duncansville
Cogan, George	Pvt. F, 148 Pa. Inf.				
	Pvt. G, 53 Pa. Inf.	1839	1910	Frankstown	Hollidaysburg
Cogley, George W.	Pvt. E, 1 Pa. Art.	1840			
Coho, David	Pvt. B, 3 Pa. Inf.	1834	1861	Fairview	Altoona
Coho, John	Pvt. A, 3 Pa. Inf.				
	Sgt. K, 125 Pa. Inf.				
	Sgt. Ind. Cav. Pa. Mil.				
	Sgt. E, 184 Ohio Inf.	1838	1927	Fairview	Altoona
Colabine, William D.	Pvt. I, 205 Pa. Inf.	1841			
Colbert, James	Pvt. E, 84 Pa. Inf.				
	Cpl. I, 57 Pa. Inf.	1828			
Colbert, Jonathan	Pvt. D, 13 Pa. Cav.	1832	1865	Salisbury	N. Car.
Colbert, Robert	Pvt. D, 13 Pa. Cav.	1829	1897	Methodist	Williamsburg
Colclesser, Henry	Ldn. U. S. Navy	1843	1902	Carson Valley	Duncansville
Colclesser, John	Pvt. C, 46 Pa. Mil.				
	Cpl. D, 13 Pa. Cav.	1837	1912	Carson Valley	Duncansville
Cole, James	Pvt. G, 46 Pa. Mil.				
	Pvt. A, 19 Pa. Cav.	1846	1899	Fairview	Altoona
Cole, Samuel S.	Pvt. G, 127 Pa. Inf.		1895	Logan Valley	Bellwood
Coleman, Thomas L.	Mus. B, 3 Pa. Inf.				
	Sgt. F, 31 Pa. Inf.	1843	1920	Fairview	Altoona
	Sgt. A, 191 Pa. Inf.	1841			
Colledge, David	Pvt. M, 9 Pa. Cav.				
College, David	Pvt. C, 110 Pa. Inf.				
College, James	Pvt. C, 110 Pa. Inf.		1862	Hopewell Twp.	Bedford Co.

THE CIVIL WAR

Name	Rank Organization	Born	Died	Cemetery	Location
College, John W.	Pvt. C, 110 Pa. Inf.		1862	Hopewell Twp.	Bedford Co.
Collier, Elias B.	Pvt. K, 125 Pa. Inf.				
Collier, George	Cpl. D, 184 Pa. Inf.		1891	Antis	Bellwood
Collier, Nathaniel	Pvt. M, 21 Pa. Cav.	1836	1928	Logan Valley	Bellwood
Collins, George	Cpl. D, 158 Pa. Inf.				
Collins, John B.	Pvt. Ind. Cav. Pa. Mil.	1828	1886	Presbyterian	Hollidaysburg
Collins, Michael	Pvt. C, 84 Pa. Inf.	1821			
Colvin, Joseph A.	Pvt. E, 136 Pa. Inf.	1843			
Comb, Henry	Pvt. F, 77 Pa. Inf.	1831			
Commerford, James	Cpl. K, 125 Pa. Inf.				
Conagan, Cyrus	Pvt. B, 208 Pa. Inf.				
Condon, J. Frank	Pvt. A, 133 Pa. Inf.	1844	1901	Fairview	Altoona
Condon, J. H.	Sgt. I, 192 Pa. Inf.	1834			
Condon, Patrick	Pvt. B, 11 Pa. Inf.	1839			
Conden, Thomas	Cpl. M, 62 Pa. Inf.				
Condron, Angus B.	Pvt. A, 23 Pa. Mil.				
	Pvt. A, Ind. Bn. Pa. Mil.	1847	1924	Presbyterian	Hollidaysburg
Condron, Jacob	Pvt. B, 192 Pa. Inf.	1846	1928	Presbyterian	Williamsburg
Condron, James	Pvt. A, 23 Pa. Mil.	1813			
Condron, William	Pvt. D, 192 Pa. Inf.				
Confer, Francis P.	Pvt. K, 3 Pa. Inf.				
	Cpl. G, 1 Pa. Cav.	1837	1917	St. Johns	Altoona
Confer, George	Pvt. D, 13 Pa. Cav.	1847			
Confer, James S.	Pvt. A, Ind. Bn. Pa. Mil.				
	Pvt. D, 13 Pa. Cav.	1845			
Conley, John	Pvt. M, 9 Pa. Cav.	1844			
Conlon, James	Pvt. H, 13 Pa. Cav.		1896	Salem Reform	Williamsburg
Conlon, James	Pvt. B, 23 Pa. Inf.	1829			
Connell, Jerome M.					
Connelly, Patrick	Pvt. D, 14 Pa. Inf.	1830			
Connelly, Thomas	Cpl. M, 62 Pa. Inf.	1842			
Connelly, Thomas T.	Pvt. D, 14 Pa. Inf.				
	Sgt. I, 22 Pa. Cav.	1827			
Conner, Isaac	Cpl. H, 22 Pa. Cav.	1832			
Conners, John	Pvt. F, 76 Pa. Inf.	1841			
Conner, Lewis	Sgt. H, 22 Pa. Cav.	1844			
Connor, Samuel	Pvt. F, Ind. Bn. Pa. Mil.	1836			
Conrad, Augustine	Pvt. G, 12 Pa. Cav.	1839			
Conrad, Cornelius A.	Pvt. I, 55 Pa. Inf.	1847	1923	St. Patricks	Gallitzin
Conrad, David E.	Pvt. I, 137 Pa. Inf.	1828	1902	Lutheran	Hollidaysburg
Conrad, Edward	Pvt. F, 77 Pa. Inf.	1847			
Conrad, Henry	Pvt. F, 76 Pa. Inf.	1827			
Conrad, Henry A.	Pvt. C, 205 Pa. Inf.	1820	1901	Lutheran	Newry
Conrad, Henry A.	Sgt. F, 1 Pa. Art.	1833			
Conrad, Henry F.	Sgn. 111 Pa. Inf.				
	Sgn. 174 Pa. Inf.			St. Patricks	Newry
Conrad, Isaac	Pvt. I, 14 Pa. Inf.	1837			
Conrad, Jacob	Pvt. H, 205 Pa. Inf.	1846			
Conrad, Joseph	Pvt. A, 199 Pa. Inf.		1865	Point of Rocks	Virginia
Conrad, Robert A.	Pvt. E, 84 Pa. Inf.	1840	1898	St. Patricks	Newry
Conrad, Samuel	2Lt. I, 206 Pa. Inf.			Grandview	Tyrone
Conrad, Samuel T.	Pvt. B, 46 Pa. Mil.	1843	1876	Grandview	Tyrone
Correy, James W.	Pvt. D, 125 Pa. Inf.		1863	Harpers Ferry	Virginia
Conrey, Joseph R.	Pvt. I, 137 Pa. Inf.	1836	1910	Frankstown	Hollidaysburg
Conroy, Nicholas	Pvt. C, 49 Pa. Inf.	1836			
Conroy, William	Pvt. G, 35 Pa. Inf.	1835	1912	St. Marys	Altoona
Conway, John A.	Pvt. K, 125 Pa. Inf.				
Cook, Charles	Pvt. I, 14 Pa. Inf.	1828			
Cook, Cyrus G.	Pvt. G, 138 Pa. Inf.	1842	1911	Grandview	Tyrone
Cook, Henry H.	Pvt. K, 125 Pa. Inf.				
	Cpl. C, 46 Pa. Mil.				
Cook, John F.					

SOLDIERS OF BLAIR COUNTY

Name	Rank Organization	Born	Died	Cemetery	Location
Cook, John W.	Sad. Hqs. 22 Pa. Cav.	1834	1892	St. Marys	Hollidaysburg
Cook, Reuben Wiser	Sgt. E, 138 Pa. Inf.	1843	1923	Everett	Pa.
Coons, David A.	Pvt. G, 12 Pa. Cav.	1843	1921	St. Patricks	Gallitzin
Cooper, Benjamin F.	Pvt. H, 3 Pa. Inf.				
	Pvt. F, 5 U.S. Art.				
	Sgt. D, 58 Pa. Inf.	1843	1907	Presbyterian	Hollidaysburg
Cooper, Charles	Pvt. U, 22 Pa. Cav.	1842			
Cooper, George	Cpl. E, 22 U. S. C. T.		1864	Newark	New Jersey
Cooper, James M.	Pvt. C, 3 Pa. Inf.				
	Pvt. B, 125 Pa. Inf.	1840	1902	Presbyterian	Williamsburg
Cooper, James M.	Pvt. A, 23 Pa. Mil.	1816			
Cooper, Thaddeus			1864	Wilderness	Virginia
Cooper, Theodore N.	Pvt. B, 125 Pa. Inf.		1863	Fairfax	Virginia
Copeland, Charles	Cpt. C, 110 Pa. Inf.	1835	1904	Fairview	Altoona
Copelin, David	1Lt. A, 110 Pa. Inf.				
Copelin, Hugh F.	Cpl. I, 6 U. S. Cav.	1842	1907	Grandview	Tyrone
Copelin, Isaiah	Pvt. D, 46 Pa. Mil.				
	Pvt. C, 110 Pa. Inf.	1829			
Copenhaven, Jacob	Pvt. B, 1 Pa. Art.	1846			
Copenhaven, John	Pvt. B, 1 Pa. Art.	1844			
Copp, Randall B.	Pvt. K, 46 Pa. Mil.	1841			
Corbin, Abraham B.	Pvt. H, 23 Pa. Cav.	1840			
Corbett, David M.	Pvt. D, 13 Pa. Cav.	1845			
Corbin, David P.	Cpl. I, 137 Pa. Inf.				
Corbin, George W.	Pvt. B, 149 Pa. Inf.	1839	1880	Three Springs	Hunt'gdon Co.
Corbin, Joseph	Pvt. D, 12 U. S. Inf.	1842	1919	Greenlawn	Hollidaysburg
Corbin, Matthew W.	Pvt. B, 147 Pa. Inf.	1832	1912	Rose Hill	Altoona
Corbin, Wescott	Pvt. G, 100 Pa. Inf.	1847	1899	Lutheran	Hollidaysburg
Core, Joseph C.	Sgt. A, 110 Pa. Inf.				
Corl, Anthony	Pvt. A, 84 Pa. Inf.				
Corle, Francis	Pvt. G, 91 Pa. Inf.			Mt. Zion	Bedford Co.
Corle, Franklin	Pvt. E, 138 Pa. Inf.			Mt. Zion	Bedford Co.
Corle, Fred K.	Pvt. F, 99 Pa. Inf.			Mt. Zion	Bedford Co.
Corl, Jonathan	Pvt. G, 91 Pa. Inf.		1864	Petersburg	Virginia
Corle, Michael	Pvt. D, 91 Pa. Inf.			Mt. Zion	Bedford Co.
Corle, William	Pvt. D, 138 Pa. Inf.			Mt. Zion	Bedford Co.
Cornelius, Benjamin F.	Pvt. F, 23 Ind. Inf.		1897	Philadelphia	Pa.
Cornelius, Conrad	Pvt. A, 55 Pa. Inf.	1845	1923		Gallitzin
Cornelius, David	Pvt. F, 31 Pa. Inf.				
Cornelius, Isaac	Pvt. F, 31 Pa. Inf.				
	Pvt. A, 191 Pa. Inf.				
Cornelius, James	Pvt. D, 1 Pa. Art.	1825	1893	Grandview	Tyrone
Cornelius, Joseph H.	Pvt. K, 202 Pa. Inf.	1825			
Cornelius, Thomas C.	Pvt. M, 62 Pa. Inf.	1842			
Cornell, William H.	Pvt. K, 208 Pa. Inf.	1839	1913	Fairview	Altoona
Cornmesser, Augustus	Pvt. E, 46 Pa. Mil.				
	Pvt. 87 Pa. Inf.	1826	1879	Logan Valley	Bellwood
Cornmesser, Charles P.	Pvt. C, 84 Pa. Inf.	1844	1862	Logan Valley	Bellwood
Costley, Samuel	Pvt. Ind. Cav. Pa. Mil.	1836			
Cotterell, John	1Lt. H, 110 Pa. Inf.				
Coughlin, James	Pvt. M, 9 Pa. Cav.				
Coughlin, William P.	Pvt. B, 49 Pa. Inf.				
Coulter, John S.	Pvt. F, 46 Pa. Mil.				
	Pvt. F, 102 Pa. Inf.	1839	1917	Eastlawn	Tyrone
Counsman, David	Pvt. C, 46 Pa. Mil.	1842			
Counsman, David	Sgt. E, 3 Pa. Inf.	1841	1925	Fairview	Altoona
Courter, John C.	Pvt. F, 77 Pa. Inf.	1829			
Cover, William	Sgt. D, 5 Pa. Art.	1840	1909	Oak Ridge	Altoona
Cowen, David	Pvt. I, 55 Pa. Inf.	1837	1864	Fortress Monroe	Virginia
Cowen, George H.	Pvt. I, 137 Pa. Inf.				
	Sgt. C, 205 Pa. Inf.	1837	1865	Greenlawn	Roaring Spring
Cowen, Jacob	Pvt. 50 Ill. Inf.		1873		Colorado

THE CIVIL WAR

Name	Rank Organization	Born	Died	Cemetery	Location
Cowan, Robert	Pvt. H, 110 Pa. Inf.				
Cowen, Stewart	Pvt. M, 13 Pa. Cav.	1832	1897	Grandview	Tyrone
Cowen, Thomas	Pvt. H, 110 Pa. Inf.		1864	Wilderness	Virginia
Cowen, William L.	Pvt. C, 205 Pa. Inf.	1846			
Cox, Francis R.	Cpl. I, 22 Pa. Cav.	1846	1912		
Cox, Henry	Pvt. A, 205 Pa. Inf.	1827	1888	Fairview	Altoona
Cox, John	Pvt. C, 76 Pa. Inf.	1842	1863	Ft. Wagner	S. Car.
Cox, Levi A.	Pvt. M, 62 Pa. Inf.				
Cox, Marshall	Pvt. E, 45 Pa. Inf.	1847	1893	Grandview	Tyrone
Cox, Robert	Cpl. A, 46 Pa. Mil.	1826	1907	Fairview	Altoona
Cox, William F.	2Lt. H, 84 Pa. Inf.	1840	1912	Oak Ridge	Altoona
Coy, John	Pvt. A, 125 Pa. Inf.				
Coykendall, Philo	Pvt. E, 1 Pa. Inf.			Costello	Pa.
Cozzens, Anderson	Pvt. D, 1 Pa. Art.	1830			
Cozzens, Hiram	Pvt. D, 1 Pa. Art.	1826			
Craig, George W.	Pvt. A, Ind. Bn. Pa. Mil.				
	Pvt. M, 22 Pa. Cav.	1847	1920	St. Johns	Altoona
Craig, George W.	Pvt. I, 55 Pa. Inf.	1828	1862	Cypress Hill	Long Island
Craig, James H.	Pvt. H, 3 Pa. Inf.				
	Pvt. E, 14 U. S. Inf.	1832	1910	St. Marys	Hollidaysburg
Craig, John	Pvt. C, 3 Pa. Inf.	1828	1898	Lutheran	Williamsburg
Craig, John	Pvt. E, 84 Pa. Inf.				
Craig, John J.	Pvt. Signal Corps	1845	1919	Oak Ridge	Altoona
Craig, Thomas H.	Col. 84 Pa. Inf.	1837	1915	San Francisco	Cal.
Crain, Andrew P.	Pvt. A, 125 Pa. Inf.	1835	1914	Oak Ridge	Altoona
Cramer, Amos Alexander	Cpl. H, 110 Pa. Inf.		1863	Grandview	Tyrone
Cramer, David	Pvt. A, 23 Pa. Mil.	1835			
Cramer, David J.	Pvt. D, 192 Pa. Inf.				
Cramer, Henry	Pvt. U, 205 Pa. Inf.	1818			
Cramer, Jacob	Pvt. C, 110 Pa. Inf.				
Cramer, Jacob	Pvt. E, 84 Pa. Inf.				
	Pvt. I, 57 Pa. Inf.	1832	1865	Annapolis	Maryland
Cramer, James C.	Cpl. H, 110 Pa. Inf.	1834	1916	Grandview	Tyrone
Cramer, James H.	Pvt. A, 23 Pa. Mil.	1829			
Cramer, John	Pvt. Palmers Pa. Inf.	1816	1896	St. Johns	Altoona
Cramer, John B.	Cpl. I, 22 Pa. Cav.	1843	1914	Greenlawn	Roaring Spring
Cramer, Joseph	Cpl. G, 12 Pa. Cav.	1845			
Cramer, Levi	Pvt. H, 208 Pa. Inf.	1819	1887	Woodbury	Bedford Co.
Cramer, Matthew	Pvt. I, 205 Pa. Inf.	1847	1930	Oak Ridge	Altoona
Cramer, Samuel	Pvt. C, 77 Pa. Inf.	1843	1904	Oak Ridge	Altoona
Cramer, Silas	Cpl. G, 12 Pa. Cav.				
Cramer, William	Pvt. C, 97 Pa. Inf.	1846	1906	Greenlawn	Roaring Spring
Crampton, Benjamin	Pvt. K, 30 U. S. C. T.				
	Ldn. U. S. Navy	1839	1907	Grandview	Tyrone
Crawford, George	Mus. D, 205 Pa. Inf.	1847			
Crawford, John	Pvt. K, 131 Pa. Inf.	1839	1908	St. Patricks	Gallitzin
Crawford, John H.	Pvt. A, 23 Pa. Mil.	1833			
Crawford, Joseph H.	Pvt. B, 49 Pa. Inf.	1840	1905	Salem Reform	Williamsburg
Crawford, William	Pvt. C, 76 Pa. Inf.	1843	1862	Pocataligo	S. Car.
Crayton, John A.	Pvt. H, 110 Pa. Inf.				
Cretin, Joshua	Pvt. K, 125 Pa. Inf.		1862	Antietam	Maryland
Criswell, John T.	Pvt. D, 151 Pa. Inf.	1835	1926	Mifflin	Pa.
Creswell, Thomas	Pvt. E, 38 Wis. Inf.	1836			
Cresswell, Thomas	Pvt. B, 46 Pa. Mil.				
Criley, Benjamin F.	Cpl. K, 175 Pa. Inf.			Waybrook	Pa.
Crissman, Abraham J.	Cpt. C, 84 Pa. Inf.				
	Q. M. 22 Pa. Cav.	1828		Comptonville	Cal.
Crissman, Austin	Pvt. A, 125 Pa. Inf.	1841	1862	Lutheran	Sinking Valley
Crissman, Frederick	Pvt. F, 76 Pa. Inf.	1822	1870	Asbury	Altoona
Crissman, Harrison H.	Sgt. 31 Pa. Inf.				
	Sgt. A, 191 Pa. Inf.	1840	1890	Fairview	Altoona
Crist, Francis T.	Pvt. G, 91 Pa. Inf.			Mt. Zion	Bedford Co.

SOLDIERS OF BLAIR COUNTY

Name	Rank Organization	Born	Died	Cemetery	Location
Crist, Isaac	Pvt. I, 54 Pa. Inf.			Mt. Zion	Bedford Co.
Crist, John C.	Pvt. C, 12 Pa. Cav.	1833	1902	Reform	Claysburg
Criste, Samuel A.	Lt. F, 28 Pa. Inf.	1840	1882	St. Patricks	Gallitzin
Crocker, Henry H.	Pvt. A, 125 Pa. Inf.				
Croft, Alexander	Sgt. C, 110 Pa. Inf.	1825	1862	Potter Creek	Bedford Co.
Croft, George	Pvt. B, 22 Pa. Cav.			Potter Creek	Bedford Co.
Croft, Jeremiah	Pvt. I, 55 Pa. Inf.			Holsingers	Bakers Summit
Croft, Levi G.	Pvt. C, 11 Ohio Inf.	1847	1937	Dry Hill	Woodbury
Croft, Penrose	Pvt. K, 200 Pa. Inf.	1839			
Croft, Phillip P.	Pvt. C, 110 Pa. Inf.		1862	Potters Creek	Bedford Co.
Cronan, Dennis	Pvt. D, 192 Pa. Inf.	1831	1891	St. Patricks	Gallitzin
Crownauer, Frank	Pvt. D, 192 Pa. Inf.	1831	1895	St. Patricks	Gallitzin
Crone, William	Pvt. A, 125 Pa. Inf.	1829	1902	Fairview	Altoona
Cronemiller, John	Pvt. D, 1 Pa. Art.		1865	Salisbury	N. Car.
Cronister, Dorsey	Pvt. I, 22 Pa. Cav.	1847	1918	Huntingdon	Pa.
Cronister, Jacob	Pvt. I, 34 Pa. Inf.	1838	1920	Cross Roads	Martinsburg
Crook, Peter	Pvt. K, 125 Pa. Inf.	1837	1872	St. Johns	Altoona
Crosby, William E.	Pvt. A, 110 Pa. Inf.				
Crosta, Charles	Mus. A, 205 Pa. Inf.				
Crouse, Levi	Pvt. A, 84 Pa. Inf.				
Crouse, Peter R.	Pvt. C, 46 Pa. Mil.	1826			
Crowell, Dan A.	Cpl. I, 137 Pa. Inf.				
Crowell, John	Pvt. H, 22 Pa. Cav.	1844			
Crowell, John	Pvt. A, 125 Pa. Inf.		1926	Birmingham	Pa.
Crowl, Francis	Pvt. A, 110 Pa. Inf.				
Crownover, William H.	Pvt. K, 22 Pa. Cav.	1845			
Crowther, James	Cpt. D, 14 Pa. Inf. Col. 110 Pa. Inf.	1818	1863	Fredericksburg	Virginia
Crothers, William	Pvt. C, 84 Pa. Inf.				Tyrone
Crowther, William E.	Cpl. F, 2 Pa. Cav.	1845	1864	Grandview	Tyrone
Croyle, James A.	Pvt. K, 133 Pa. Inf. Pvt. D, 55 Pa. Inf.	1844	1916	Kifer	Woodbury
Crozier, Richard J. (M)	1Lt. E, 3 Pa. Inf. Cpt. M, 62 Pa. Inf. Maj. Ind. Bn. Pa. Mil.	1825	1900	Fairview	Altoona
Crum, Abraham	Pvt. A, 205 Pa. Inf.		1865	Arlington	Virginia
Crum, Allison H.	Sgt. K, 22 Pa. Cav.	1841			
Crum, Moses	Pvt. I, 205 Pa. Inf.	1826	1900	Carson Valley	Duncansville
Crum, Oliver	Pvt. G, 149 Pa. Inf.	1834	1864	Andersonville	Georgia
Crum, Simon	Pvt. I, 55 Pa. Inf.		1865	St. Marys	Hollidaysburg
Crum, William	Pvt. A, 3 Pa. Inf.	1840			
Cruse, George W.	Pvt. H, 3 Pa. Inf. Sgt. C, 76 Pa. Inf.	1835	1918	Oak Ridge	Altoona
Cruse, George W.	Pvt. E, 3 Pa. Inf. 2Lt. D. 13 Pa. Cav.	1829	1889	St. Patricks	Gallitzin
Cruse, John Madison	Pvt, A, 84 Pa. Inf. Pvt. M, 22 Pa. Cav.	1843		Dayton	Ohio
Cruse, Joseph R.	Pvt. A, 23 Pa. Mil.	1829			
Cruse, Lewis	Cpl. A, 84 Pa. Inf.	1835	1907	Presbyterian	Hollidaysburg
Cruse, Michael	Pvt. C, 84 Pa. Inf.	1831			
Cruse, William H.	Pvt. D, 13 Pa. Cav.	1831		St. Marys	Hollidaysburg
Cullen, Charles	Pvt. C, 54 Pa. Inf.	1842			
Culley, Robert	Pvt. E, 93 Pa. Inf.	1839	1912	Lock Haven	Pa.
Cullison, John	Pvt. M, 22 Pa. Cav.	1833	1922	Greenlawn	Roaring Spring
Culp, Samuel (M)	Sgt. A, Ind. Bn. Pa. Mil. Sgt. A, 205 Pa. Inf.	1824	1899	Lutheran	Sinking Valley
Cummins, Timothy	Pvt. D, 7 Pa. Cav.				
Cumpson, Benjamin	Pvt. E, 99 Pa. Inf.	1847	1915	Keagy	Woodbury
Cunningham, David T.	Pvt. A, 125 Pa. Inf.				
Cunningham, Hamilton	Far. A, 20 Pa. Cav.	1842	1903	Logan Valley	Bellwood
Cunningham, J. W.	Pvt. G, 12 Pa. Cav.	1833			
Cunningham, James D.					

THE CIVIL WAR 179

Name	Rank Organization	Born	Died	Cemetery	Location
Cunningham, James M.	Pvt. B, Ind. Bn. Pa. Mil.	1843			
Cunningham, Jeremiah J.	Pvt. A, 23 Pa. Mil.				
	Pvt. A, Ind. Bn. Pa. Mil.	1846			
Cunningham, John B.	Pvt. K, 12 Pa. Cav.				
	2Lt. Ind. Cav. Pa. Mil.	1831	1903	Fairview	Altoona
Cunningham, Owen M.	Pvt. K, 101 Pa. Inf.	1841	1897	Fairview	Altoona
Cunningham, William H.	Pvt. H, 206 Pa. Inf.		1901	Boliver	Pa.
Cupp, John H.	Pvt. E, 103 Pa. Inf.	1834	1908	Grandview	Tyrone
Cupp, Joseph	Pvt. D, 3 Pa. Inf.				
	Pvt. H, 143 Pa. Inf.	1835	1909	Birmingham	Pa.
Cupp, Perry	Cpl. E, 45 Pa. Inf.	1841	1927	Warriors Mark	Pa.
Curfman, Joseph C.	Pvt. F, 31 Pa. Inf.				
	Pvt. A, 191 Pa. Inf.				
Curran, James C.	Mus. M, 62 Pa. Inf.	1813	1891	St. Marys	Hollidaysburg
Curran, James	Pvt. C, 76 Pa. Inf.	1841			
Curran, Michael	Pvt. Ind. Cav. Pa. Mil.	1838			
Currie, John	Pvt. C, 46 Pa. Inf.	1838	1913	Fairview	Altoona
Currie, William	Pvt. B, 72 Pa. Inf.	1832	1910	Fairview	Altoona
Curry, Abraham	Pvt. M, 22 Pa. Cav.	1838	1932	Presbyterian	Hollidaysburg
Curry, Charles W.	Pvt. H, 3 Pa. Inf.				
	Sgt. C, 84 Pa. Inf.	1824	1902	Calvary	Altoona
Curry, Constantine	Pvt. C, 84 Pa. Inf.				
	Pvt. B, Ind. Bn. Pa. Mil.				
	Pvt. D, 13 Pa. Cav.	1845	1914	Calvary	Altoona
Curry, George W.	Pvt. F, 12 Pa. Cav.	1848	1922	Presbyterian	Hollidaysburg
Curry, George W.	Pvt. B, 149 Pa. Inf.	1886			
Curry, James W.	Pvt. 3 Va. Inf.				
	Cpn. 138 Pa. Inf.	1831	1892	Fairview	Altoona
Curry, John	Pvt. H, 3 Pa. Inf.				
	Cpl. C, 76 Pa. Inf.	1843	1864	Hampton	Virginia
Curry, Peter	Pvt. G, 205 Pa. Inf.	1835			
Curry, Robert	Pvt. G, 50 Wis. Inf.	1833	1888	Carson Valley	Duncansville
Curry, Samuel	Pvt. I, 84 Pa. Inf.	1823	1902	Calvary	Altoona
Curtis, George A.	Pvt. G, 18 Pa. Cav.	1848			
Curtis, George R.	Pvt. G, 125 Pa. Inf.				
	Cpl. D, 192 Pa. Inf.	1840	1925	Presbyterian	Hollidaysburg
Curtis, William	Sgt. A, 84 Pa. Inf.				
	Sgt. I, 57 Pa. Inf.	1832			
Cutler, William T.	Pvt. A, 130 Pa. Inf.				
	Pvt. Signal Corps	1838	1892	Fairview	Altoona
Cutshall, Richard	Pvt. E, 104 Pa. Inf.				
Daily, James W.	Pvt. G, 12 Pa. Cav.	1842			
Dallas, John	Pvt. H, 14 Pa. Inf.	1841			
Daltry, Thomas	Cpl. H, 137 Pa. Inf.	1831			
Daniels, Charles	Pvt. I, 205 Pa. Inf.	1827			
Daniels, Edward	Pvt. I, 14 Pa. Inf.	1826			
Daniels, James	Pvt. F, Ind. Bn. Pa. Mil.	1839			
Daniels, John	Pvt. F, 76 Pa. Inf.				
Dannals, Charles R.	Pvt. G, 125 Pa. Inf.			Presbyterian	Hollidaysburg
Dannals, William S.	Pvt. A, 84 Pa. Inf.	1843	1925	Presbyterian	Hollidaysburg
Danner, George I.					
Dannley, William	Pvt. B, 202 Pa. Inf.	1849			
Dare, Richard A.	Mus. I, 34 Pa. Inf.	1848	1911	Calvary	Altoona
Darlington, William B.	1Lt. D, 3 Pa. Inf.				
	Adj. 76 Pa. Inf.				
	Maj. 18 Pa. Cav.	1829			
Darr, Joseph A.	Pvt. D, 46 Pa. Mil.	1847	1886	St. Johns	Altoona
Dasher, Alexander	Sad. D, 13 Pa. Cav.	1841			
Dasher, James	Pvt. E, 125 Pa. Inf.				
Dasher, John A.	Pvt. D, 125 Pa. Inf.	1829	1903	Fairview	Altoona
Dasher, John W.	Pvt. C, 76 Pa. Inf.	1842			
Dasher, Levi	Pvt. C, 76 Pa. Inf.	1843	1863	Hilton Head	S. Car.

SOLDIERS OF BLAIR COUNTY

Name	Rank Organization	Born	Died	Cemetery	Location
Dasher, Samuel	Pvt. C, 76 Pa. Inf.	1842		Rodman	Roaring Spring
Dasher, Samuel D.	Pvt. G, 125 Pa. Inf.				
	Sgt. D, 192 Pa. Inf.				
Daughenbaugh, David	Pvt. I, 22 Pa. Cav.	1839			
Daughenbaugh, Ephriam G.	Pvt. B, 208 Pa. Inf.	1837	1905	Oak Ridge	Altoona
Daughenbaugh, W.	Pvt. A, 205 Pa. Inf.				
Daugherty, Aaron	Sgt. G, 12 Pa. Cav.	1840			
Daugherty, Charles W.	Pvt. G, 205 Pa. Inf.	1843	1915	Fairview	Altoona
Daugherty, Edward T.	Pvt. H, 201 Pa. Inf.	1841	1875	Baltimore	Maryland
Daugherty, G. R.					
Dougherty, George A.	Cpl. B, Ind. Bn. Pa. Mil.	1845			
Dougherty, George A.	Pvt. A, 84 Pa. Inf.				
	Pvt. M, 22 Pa. Cav.	1844			
Daugherty, George R.	Pvt. C, 46 Pa. Mil.	1829			
Dougherty, George W.	Pvt. A, 13 Pa. Cav.	1836	1888	Fairview	Altoona
Dougherty, George W.	Pvt. C, 77 Pa. Inf.	1844	1916	Baltimore	Maryland
Dougherty, James	Pvt. C, 110 Pa. Inf.				
Daugherty, Jeremiah C.	Pvt. F, 49 Pa. Inf.		1877	Asbury	Altoona
Dougherty, John	Pvt. B, 3 Pa. Inf.	1842			
Dougherty, John H.	Sgt. G, 12 Pa. Cav.	1843	1915	Fairview	Altoona
Daugherty, John H.	Pvt. G, 12 Pa. Cav.	1814	1872	Fairview	Altoona
Daugherty, John M.	Cpl. D, 125 Pa. Inf.				
Daugherty, John W.	Pvt. H, 110 Pa. Inf.	1833	1924	Greenlawn	Roaring Spring
Dougherty, Joseph W.	Pvt. A, 3 Pa. Inf.				
	Cpt. A, 84 Pa. Inf.				
	Cpt. H, 103 Pa. Inf.	1838	1893	Oak Ridge	Altoona
Dougherty, Michael	Pvt. H, 14 Pa. Inf.	1838			
Daugherty, Thomas	Pvt. B, Ind. Bn. Pa. Mil.	1845			
Dougherty, Thomas H.	Pvt. B, 110 Pa. Inf.	1836	1910	Fairview	Altoona
Daugherty, Victor V.	Pvt. B, 125 Pa. Inf.				
Dougherty, William	Pvt. A, 3 Pa. Inf.	1840			
Davenport, John	Pvt. G, 16 Pa. Cav.	1838	1903	Gospel	Gallitzin
Davidson, Francis B.	Sgn. 125 Pa. Inf.				
Davidson, George C.	Cpl. A, 125 Pa. Inf.				
	Sgt. L, 2 Pa. Art.	1845	1916	Grandview	Tyrone
Davidson, John A.	Pvt. D, 3 Pa. Inf.				
	Pvt. H, 103 Pa. Inf.	1831	1916	Grandview	Tyrone
Davidson, John W.	Pvt. H, 110 Pa. Inf.				
	H. S. 110 Pa. Inf.				
Davison, Rees J.	Pvt. D, 3 Pa. Inf.	1833			
Davidson, Robert G.	Pvt. A, 7 Pa. Cav.	1847	1907	Grandview	Tyrone
Davis, Abel	Pvt. D, 125 Pa. Inf.				
Davis, Amos C.	Pvt. A, 3 Pa. Inf.				
	C. M., U. S. Navy	1839	1912	Greenwood	Altoona
Davis, Benjamin S.	Pvt. A, 205 Pa. Inf.	1832	1893	Fairview	Altoona
Davis, David	Pvt. I, 8 Wis. Inf.				
Davis, Edward J.	Pvt. C, 1 Pa. Inf.		1893	McVeytown	Pa.
Davis, George W.	Pvt. H, 14 Pa. Inf.				
	Cpl. C, 76 Pa. Inf.	1841	1912	Oak Ridge	Altoona
Davis, Guyon Irvin	1Lt. A, 11 Ill. Inf.	1827	1901	Presbyterian	Hollidaysburg
Davis, Hezekiah	Pvt. D, 192 Pa. Inf.				
Davis, J. Gemmill	Pvt. F, 195 Pa. Inf.				
	Pvt. F, 79 Pa. Inf.	1849	1930	Fairview	Altoona
Davis, James C.	Pvt. E, 104 Pa. Inf.				
Davis, James D.	Pvt. B, Ind. Bn. Pa. Mil.	1819			
Davis, James D.	Cpl. C, 76 Pa. Inf.	1841		Carson Valley	Duncansville
Davis, James E.	Pvt. F, 77 Pa. Inf.	1823			
Davis, James S.	Pvt. A, 205 Pa. Inf.	1838	1895	Fairview	Altoona
Davis, Jeremiah	Pvt. C, 46 Pa. Mil.	1843			
Davis, John	Q. M, U. S. Navy				
	Pvt. B, 5 U. S. Cav.	1845	1927	Carson Valley	Duncansville
Davis, John	Pvt. D, 46 Pa. Mil.	1833			

Name	Rank Organization	Born	Died	Cemetery	Location
Davis, John	Pvt. G, 125 Pa. Inf.				
Davis, John A.	Pvt. M, 62 Pa. Inf.				
Davis, John E.	Pvt. D, 125 Pa. Inf.		1862	Antietam	Maryland
Davis, John H.					
Davis, John N.	Pvt. C, 110 Pa. Inf.		1881	Everett	Pa.
Davis, John P.	Pvt. F, 31 Pa. Inf.				
	Pvt. A, 191 Pa. Inf.	1835			
Davis, John W.	Cpl. A, 23 Pa. Inf.	1839	1886	Asbury	Altoona
Davis, John W.	Pvt. A, Ind. Bn. Pa. Mil.	1845			
Davis, Joseph		1843	1934	Harrisburg	Pa.
Davis, Joshua V.	Pvt. H, 14 Pa. Inf.				
	Pvt. C, 76 Pa. Inf.	1843	1938	West Hartford	Conn.
Davis, Kessler	Pvt. K, 46 Pa. Mil.				
	Pvt. C, 19 Pa. Cav.	1847	1907	Fairview	Altoona
Davis, Leonard	Pvt. D, 125 Pa. Inf.	1863			
Davis, Lewis	Pvt. K, 9 Pa. Cav.	1840	1914	Fairview	Martinsburg
Davis, Martin	Pvt. C, 110 Pa. Inf.				
Davis, Morris	Cpl. D, 125 Pa. Inf.				
	2Lt. A, 205 Pa. Inf.	1842	1914	Fairview	Altoona
Davis, Nathan H.	Cpl. A, 84 Pa. Inf.			Pleasantville	Bedford Co.
Davis, Peter	Pvt. H, 110 Pa. Inf.		1864	Deep Bottom	Virginia
Davis, Porter R.	Pvt. C, 110 Pa. Inf.			Everett	Pa.
Davis, Robert	Pvt. M, 62 Pa. Inf.	1826	1862	Gaines Mills	Virginia
Davis, Robert	Pvt. D, 13 Pa. Cav.	1835	1881	Fairview	Altoona
Davis, Thomas P.	Pvt. I, 55 Pa. Inf.	1847	1864	Carson Valley	Duncansville
Davis, Thomas W.	Pvt. A, 205 Pa. Inf.	1847	1916	Fairview	Altoona
Davis, Thompson	Pvt. G, 12 Pa. Cav.	1845	1937	Alto Reste	Hollidaysburg
Davis, William	Pvt. B, 3 Pa. Inf.	1831			
Davis, William A.	Pvt. A, 205 Pa. Inf.	1830	1903	Fairview	Altoona
Davis, William A.	Pvt. A, 84 Pa. Inf.			Friends	Bedford Co.
Davis, William H.	Cpl. C, 209 Pa. Inf.				
	Pvt. F, 133 Pa. Inf.	1842	1919	Lloyds	Cambria Co.
Davis, William K.	Pvt. K, 177 Pa. Inf.		1904	Reedsville	N. Car.
Dawson, Theobold M.	Sgt. H, 57 Pa. Inf.	1845			
Deal, Augustus R.	Pvt. I, 137 Pa. Inf.				
	Sgt. B, 192 Pa. Inf.	1839	1929	Presbyterian	Hollidaysburg
Dean, Adin B.	Pvt. K, 46 Pa. Mil.	1840			
Dean, George W.	Pvt. D, 184 Pa. Inf.	1838	1888	Grandview	Tyrone
Dean, John	Cpl. A, 23 Pa. Mil.				
	Pvt. A, Ind. Bn. Pa. Mil.	1832			
Dean, William	Pvt. D, 188 Pa. Inf.	1834	1901	Lutheran	Hollidaysburg
Dearmitt, Alex	Sgn. 16 Pa. Cav.	1828	1864	Lutheran	Hollidaysburg
Dearmit, Franklin	Pvt. E, 25 Pa. Inf.	1844	1891	Fairview	Altoona
Dearmitt, George W.	Pvt. A, 110 Pa. Inf.	1840	1914	Rose Hill	Altoona
DeBeck, Benjamin	Pvt. D, 192 Pa. Inf.				
Deck, James S.	Pvt. U. S. Signal Corps		1889		Nebraska
Deck, Frederick	Pvt. B, 208 Pa. Inf.				
Decker, David	Pvt. K, 22 Pa. Cav.	1844			
Decker, Henry P.	Sgt. K, 22 Pa. Cav.	1841			
Decker, Isaac J.	Pvt. B, 208 Pa. Inf.	1830	1902	Methodist	Williamsburg
Decker, Martin	Pvt. I, 211 Pa. Inf.				
Decker, William S.	Pvt. F, 31 Pa. Inf.				
	Sgt. A, 191 Pa. Inf.				
Deeter, Daniel	Pvt. F, 143 Pa. Inf.	1840	1919	Royer	Williamsburg
Defibaugh, Adam C.	Pvt. C, 76 Pa. Inf.	1817		Rodman	Roaring Spring
Defibaugh, Harland W.	Pvt. G, 78 Pa. Inf.	1841	1916	Fairview	Altoona
Defibaugh, Thomas	Pvt. C, 76 Pa. Inf.	1842			
Deford, Asbury O.	Cpl. I, 137 Pa. Inf.	1840	1910	Fairview	Martinsburg
DeHaven, Wesley	Pvt. B, 125 Pa. Inf.				
	Pvt. D, 192 Pa. Inf.	1833	1894	Fairview	Altoona
Deitrick, George A.	Pvt. A, 115 Pa. Inf.	1841			
Deitrich, John L.	Sgt. B, 126 Pa. Inf.		1864	Oak Ridge	Altoona

SOLDIERS OF BLAIR COUNTY

Name	Rank Organization	Born	Died	Cemetery	Location
Delaney, Daniel	Pvt. F, 31 Pa. Inf.				
	Pvt. A, Pa. Inf.		1864	Salisbury	N. Car.
Delaney, George J.					
Delaney, George W.	Pvt. H, 57 Pa. Inf.				
Delaney, James C.	Pvt. H, 57 Pa. Inf.				
Delaney, John	Pvt. F, 76 Pa. Inf.	1840	1862	Hilton Head	S. Car.
Delahunt, Joseph	Pvt. A, 3 Pa. Inf.	1839			
Delehunt, Joseph	Cpt. A, 84 Pa. Inf.	1837	1913	St. Patricks	Gallitzin
Dell, Ephriam	Pvt. D, 192 Pa. Inf.				
Dell, Henry H.	Pvt. C, 3 Pa. Inf.	1838			
Dell, Isaac	Pvt. D, 192 Pa. Inf.				
Dell, James	Pvt. H, 12 Pa. Cav.	1844	1924	St. Patricks	Newry
Dell, John	Pvt. G, 11 Pa. Cav.	1837	1907	Fairview	Altoona
Dell, John S.	Pvt. A, 125 Pa. Inf.	1840	1914	Rose Hill	Altoona
Dell, Moses	Pvt. F, 1 Pa. Art.	1840	1928	Holsingers	Bakers Summit
Dell, Peter	Pvt. E, 125 Pa. Inf.	1842	1929	Carson Valley	Duncansville
Dell, Samuel	Pvt. F, 76 Pa. Inf.	1849	1927	Oak Ridge	Altoona
Delo, Jeremiah	Pvt. Ind. Cav. Pa. Mil.	1830			
Delozier, Robert	Cpl. D, 184 Pa. Inf.	1845	1894	St. Johns	Altoona
Dem, George F.					
Demarre, David R.	Pvt. E, Ind. Bn. Mil.		1935	Newport	Pa.
Dengate, Christopher	Pvt. K, 78 Pa. Inf.	1846	1937	Logan Valley	Bellwood
Dennhoefer, Simon	Pvt. E, 15 N. Y. Art.				
	Sgt. A, 2 U. S. Cav.	1835	1873	Oak Ridge	Altoona
Denning, Samuel A.	Pvt. A, 127 Pa. Inf.				
	Sgt. Ind. Cav. Mil.	1841	1895	Chillicothe	Ohio
Denning, William J.	Pvt. H, 15 Pa. Cav.	1843	1918	Fairview	Altoona
Denny, Daniel	Pvt. 3 Pa. Inf.				
	Pvt. 110 Pa. Inf.				
	Pvt. B, 192 Pa. Inf.			Elkhurst	Tyrone
Denny, John	Pvt. D, 3 Pa. Inf.				
	Pvt. B, 48 Pa. Inf.	1820		Grandview	Tyrone
Denny, Joseph	Pvt. D, 3 Pa. Inf.				
	Pvt. A, 110 Pa. Inf.	1844	1910	Grandview	Tyrone
Denny, Peter	Pvt. D, 14 Pa. Inf.				
	Pvt. A, 2 Pa. Cav.	1841	1889	Grandview	Tyrone
Derland, C. Sanford	Cpt. I, 22 Pa. Cav.				
Dern, George F.	Pvt. L, 3 N. Y. Cav.	1833		Fairview	Altoona
Dernell, Jonathan K.	Pvt. M, 62 Pa. Inf.				
	Pvt. K, 91 Pa. Inf.				
Derno, Jonathan	Sgt. A, 3 Pa. Inf.				
	Cpt. A, 84 Pa. Inf.	1831	1908	Lutheran	Hollidaysburg
Derrick, John B.	Pvt. U, 84 Pa. Inf.				
	Pvt. K, 57 Pa. Inf.	1847			
Derrick, Levi H.	Pvt. K, 84 Pa. Inf.				
	Pvt. K, 57 Pa. Inf.	1844			
Detrick, George F.	Pvt. A, 126 Pa. Inf.				
	Pvt. B, 61 Pa. Inf.	1845	1926	New Florence	Pa.
Detrich, John L. P.	Pvt. B, 126 Pa. Inf.				
	Pvt. U. S. Signal Corps	1835	1894	Oak Ridge	Altoona
Detrich, John M.	Pvt. D, 99 Pa. Inf.	1848	1880	Greenlawn	Roaring Spring
Deturk, Benjamin H.	Sgt. C, 1 N. Y. Engrs.	1837	1913	Rose Hill	Altoona
Detwiler, Andrew	Pvt. A, 84 Pa. Inf.				
	Pvt. I, 57 Pa. Inf.	1842	1913	St. Johns	Williamsburg
Detwiler, George W.	Pvt. B, 3 Pa. Inf.				
	Sgt. H, 12 Pa. Cav.	1844	1912	Fairview	Altoona
Detwiler, Jacob M.	Pvt. E, 143 Pa. Inf.	1845	1923	Holsingers	Bakers Summit
Detwiler, James Oliver	Pvt. C, 46 Pa. Mil.	1844	1936	Danville	Ill.
Detwiler, John M.	Pvt. D, 13 Pa. Cav.	1838	1909	Greenlawn	Roaring Spring
Detwiler, John W.	Sgt. F, 76 Pa. Inf.	1847	1919	Beaver Valley	Clearfield Co.
Detweiler, Joseph	Pvt. K, 55 Pa. Inf.	1808	1883	Fairview	Altoona

THE CIVIL WAR

Name	Rank Organization	Born	Died	Cemetery	Location
Detwiler, Joseph	Pvt. B, 84 Pa. Inf.				
	Pvt. I, 57 Pa. Inf.	1839	1903	Keller Reform	Williamsburg
Detwiler, Moses H.	Cpl. E, 104 Pa. Inf.				
Devine, Henry S.	Cpl. M, 62 Pa. Inf.	1841			
Devine, Michael B.	Sgt. 28 Pa. Inf.	1839	1863	St. Marys	Hollidaysburg
Devore, Daniel	Pvt. E, 84 Pa. Inf.				
DeVore, Samuel Baker	Pvt. K, 84 Pa. Inf.				
	Pvt. K, 57 Pa. Inf.	1842	1920	Oak Ridge	Altoona
Dibert, Michael H.	Pvt. H, 14 Pa. Inf.	1841			
Dick, Daniel P.	Pvt. C, 205 Pa. Inf.	1837	1917	Albrights	Roaring Spring
Dick, Michael P.	Pvt. C, 205 Pa. Inf.	1840	1909	Albrights	Roaring Spring
Dickell, Isaac S.	Cpl. E, 195 Pa. Inf.	1845			
Dickey, Samuel	Pvt. E, 79 Pa. Inf.	1847	1918	Presbyterian	Hollidaysburg
Dickson, Andrew I.					
Dickson, David	Pvt. A, 125 Pa. Inf.				
Dickson, James	Pvt. A, 110 Pa. Inf.				
Dickson, Matthew	Pvt. A, 205 Pa. Inf.			De Moines	Iowa
Dickson, Samuel F.	Pvt. A, 205 Pa. Inf.	1832	1906	Grandview	Tyrone
Dickson, William D.	H. S. U. S. Navy				
	Sgt. K, 209 Pa. Inf.	1842	1891	Fairview	Altoona
Diehenbacher, James	Pvt. A, 23 Pa. Mil.	1837			
Diehl, Daniel	Cpl. E, 125 Pa. Inf.				
Diehl, George	Sgt. F, 77 Pa. Inf.	1838			
Diehl, George	Pvt. I, 137 Pa. Inf.				
Diehl, George C.	Pvt. F, 77 Pa. Inf.	1845	1929	Portage	Pa.
Diehl, Henry	Pvt. A, 125 Pa. Inf.				
Diehl, James S.	Pvt. K, 55 Pa. Inf.	1847	1908	Lutheran	Newry
Diehl, Samuel	Pvt. F, 77 Pa. Inf.	1841			
Diggins, Jesse	Pvt. A, 77 Pa. Inf.	1839			
Dill, Mathew T.	Q. M., 46 Pa. Mil.				
Dilling, Jacob L.	Pvt. B, 20 Pa. Cav.	1847	1922	Brumbaugh	Martinsburg
Dillman, Simon P.	Pvt. H, 14 Pa. Inf.	1831			
Dillon, Charles	Pvt. D, 13 Pa. Cav.	1822			
Dillen, Charles	Pvt. K, 125 Pa. Inf.				
Dillon, John A.	Cpl. M, 9 Pa. Cav.				
Dilser, Lawrence	Pvt. I, 14 Pa. Inf.	1823			
Ditch, David	Pvt. Ind. Cav. Pa. Mil.	1841			
Ditch, Henry	Pvt. F, 76 Pa. Inf.	1839			
Ditch, John	Pvt. B, 208 Pa. Inf.				
Ditterline, Smith F.	Pvt. P, 192 Pa. Inf.	1843	1907	Old Point Comfort	Virginia
Dively, Gabriel	Pvt. E, 125 Pa. Inf.				
	Pvt. H, 12 Pa. Cav.			Reform	St. Clairsville
Dively, George C.	Pvt. F, 77 Pa. Inf.				
Dively, George M.	Pvt. F, 77 Pa. Inf.	1831	1908	Greenfield	Bedford Co.
Dively, James	Pvt. H, 12 Pa. Cav.	1845	1897	Reform	Claysburg
Dively, John	Pvt. C, 110 Pa. Inf.		1864	Andersonville	Georgia
Dively, Martin	Pvt. F, 77 Pa. Inf.	1841	1894	Claar	Bedford Co.
Dively, Morgan	Pvt. F, 77 Pa. Inf.	1839	1906	Claar	Bedford Co.
Dively, Paul	Pvt. D, 11 Pa. Cav.	1841	1895	Union	Claysburg
Dively, William M.	Pvt. G, 11 Pa. Cav.	1843	1897	Fairview	Altoona
Diven, Daniel N.	Pvt. F, 76 Pa. Inf.	1838			
Divine, John N.	Pvt. E, 3 Pa. Inf.	1839			
Divinney, James J.	Pvt. H, 72 Pa. Inf.				
	Pvt. A, 183 Pa. Inf.	1847	1886	St. Johns	Altoona
Dixon, John	Pvt. 54, Mass. C. T.				
Dixon, George W.	Pvt. C, 49 Pa. Inf.	1835	1909	Grandview	Tyrone
Dixon, James	Pvt. H, 110 Pa. Inf.				
Dixon, John C.	Pvt. A, 205 Pa. Inf.				
Dixon, Miles	Pvt. E, 46 Pa. Mil.				
	Cpl. A, 110 Pa. Inf.	1847	1926	Cross Roads	Hunt'gdon Co.
Dixon, Milton	Pvt. I, 7 Pa. Cav.	1845	1920	Charlottsville	Bellwood
Dixon, Robert C.	Pvt. A, 23 Pa. Mil.	1829			

SOLDIERS OF BLAIR COUNTY

Name	Rank Organization	Born	Died	Cemetery	Location
Doak, John H.	Pvt. A, 122 Pa. Inf.				
	Pvt. E, 188 Pa. Inf.	1837	1914	Lancaster	Pa.
Dobbins, Alexander	Cpt. E, 84 Pa. Inf.	1831	1879	St. Josephs	Williamsburg
Dodson, Samuel B.	Pvt. C, 19 Pa. Cav.	1842	1872	Union	Claysburg
Dodson, William	Pvt. E, 13 Pa. Cav.			Union	Claysburg
Doll, William E.	Pvt. G, 8 Ind. Inf.	1837	1873	Fairview	Altoona
Domer, William	Pvt. Andersons Pa. Cav.	1827	1891	Antis	Bellwood
Donahay, David A.	Pvt. H, 14 Pa. Inf.	1830			
Donahay, George B.	Cpt. D, 36 Pa. Inf.	1829			
Donahoe, Patrick	Pvt. K, 125 Pa. Inf.				
	Pvt. F, Ind. Bn. Pa. Mil.	1840			
Donald, John	Pvt. D, 13 Pa. Cav.	1839			
Donnelly, David R.	Pvt. B, 125 Pa. Inf.	1841	1907	Fairview	Altoona
Donnelly, John	Pvt. B, 110 Pa. Inf.	1830	1906	Keller Reform	Williamsburg
Donoly, Joseph	Pvt. D, 110 Pa. Inf.		1885		
Donnely, Walter B.	Pvt. K, 13 Pa. Cav.			Soldiers Home	Sandusky, Ohio
Donoughe, John	Pvt. D, 5 Pa. Inf.		1900	Ashville	Pa.
Donoughe, Robert E.	Pvt. F, 28 Pa. Inf.	1842	1905	St. Patricks	Gallitzin
Dorsey, William C.	Pvt. H, 3 Pa. Inf.	1840			
Doughman, Frederick	Pvt. B, 148 Pa. Inf.	1827	1901	Grazierville	Tyrone
Douglass, George W.	Pvt. G, 130 Pa. Inf.		1872	Logan Valley	Bellwood
Douglass, William K.	Pvt. G, 12 Pa. Cav.	1844			
Dow, Frank				Calvary	Altoona
Dowling, John H.	Pvt. A, 1 Del. Inf.				
	Cpt. B, 4 Del. Inf.	1835	1917	St. Johns	Altoona
Downing, George W.	Pvt. F, 175 Pa. Inf.				
Downing, James	Pvt. E, 84 Pa. Inf.	1834	1916	Keller Reform	Williamsburg
Downs, Daniel	Cpl. C, 76 Pa. Inf.	1838	1904	Greenwood	Altoona
Downs, Elias	Sgt. K, 46 Pa. Mil.	1841			
Downs, James	Cpl. D, 47 Pa. Inf.	1837	1921	Brookville	Pa.
Downs, Joseph	Sgt. K, 46 Pa. Mil.	1845			
Downs, Thomas	Pvt. E, 84 Pa. Inf.		1863	Chancellorsville	Virginia
Doyle, Michael	Pvt. D, 192 Pa. Inf.				
Drass, Jacob G.	Pvt. D, 192 Pa. Inf.	1840	1900	St. Johns	Altoona
Drips, Andrew W. (M)	Capt. Iowa Inf.	1862			
Drips, Henry W. L.	Mus. H, 41 Pa. Inf.				
	Pvt. E, 190 Pa. Inf.	1848	1934	Derry	Pa.
Drips, Samuel W.	Pvt. H, 41 Pa. Inf.				
	Pvt. E, 190 Pa. Inf.				
Driver, Henry	Pvt. Ind. Cav. Pa. Mil.	1809	1881	Oak Ridge	Altoona
Driver, William H.	Pvt. D, 46 Pa. Mil.	1845			
Duck, Henry B.	Cpl. A, 125 Pa. Inf.				
	Pvt. E, 104 Pa. Inf.	1827	1900	Royer	Williamsburg
Duclas, John	Cpl. G, 21 N. Y. Cav.				
Dudley, Charles B.	Pvt. A, 114 N. Y. Inf.	1842	1909	Bryn Mawr	Pa.
Duffy, Francis	Pvt. F, 3 Pa. Inf.	1834			
Duffy, John	Pvt. B, 9 U. S. Inf.	1843	1872	St. Johns	Altoona
Dugan, James	Pvt. B, 9 Pa. Inf.	1845	1915	Pressel	Claysburg
Dumm, Thomas P.	Pvt. A, 40 Pa. Inf.				
	Pvt. D, 9 Pa. Cav.	1839			
Dumm, Valentine	Pvt. A, 11 Pa. Cav.	1841			
Dunahay, David	Pvt. H, 12 Pa. Cav.	1829	1892	Dodsons	East Freedom
Duncan, David	Pvt. H, 110 Pa. Inf.				
Duncan, Joseph M.		1822	1880	Presbyterian	Arch Spring
Duncan, William S.	Pvt. Miss. Marines				
	Pvt. E, 1 Mo. Art.	1830	1908	Presbyterian	Sinking Valley
Dunegan, Edward R.	1Lt. K, 125 Pa. Inf.	1906			
Dunlap, Benjamin	Pvt. E, 45 Pa. Inf.		1893	Presbyterian	Hollidaysburg
Dunlap, Caleb E.	Pvt. I, 22 Pa. Cav.	1845			
Dunlap, Essington	Pvt. E, 125 Pa. Inf.				
Dunlap, Franklin	Pvt. M, 62 Pa. Inf.				
	Pvt. D, 192 Pa. Inf.	1824			

THE CIVIL WAR

Name	Rank Organization	Born	Died	Cemetery	Location
Dunlap, John	Pvt. C, 49 Pa. Inf.				
	Pvt. G, 13 Pa. Cav.	1838	1922	Oak Ridge	Altoona
Dunlap, John	Pvt. I, 14 Pa. Inf.				
	Pvt. E, 125 Pa. Inf.	1839		Elkhurst	Tyrone
Dunlap, Martin	Pvt. I, 22 Pa. Cav.	1846		Grandview	Tyrone
Dunlap, S. Bigler	Pvt. B, 100 Pa. Inf.	1840	1916	Rose Hill	Altoona
Dunlap, William	Pvt. A, 46 Pa. Mil.			Grandview	Tyrone
Dunmire, Elijah C.	Pvt. C, 125 Pa. Inf.	1834	1862	Georgetown	D. C.
Dunmire, George B.	Pvt. A, 125 Pa. Inf.				
Dunn, James Bradley	Pvt. G, 125 Pa. Inf.	1844	1932	Spring Hope	Martinsburg
Dunn, John	Mus. A, 6 U. S. Cav.	1845	1864	Andersonville	Ga.
Dunn, John	Pvt. E, 84 Pa. Inf.	1812	1869	St. Marys	Hollidaysburg
Dunn, Joseph M.	Pvt. A, 3 Pa. Inf.				
	Pvt. A, 23 Pa. Mil.	1839	1906	Calvary	Altoona
Dunn, Patrick	Smn. U. S. Navy	1824	1888	St. Johns	Altoona
Dunn, Patrick	Pvt. E, 125 Pa. Inf.				
Dunn, Robert	Pvt. B, Ind. Bn. Pa. Mil.	1845			
Dunn, Roman B.	Pvt. A, 84 Pa. Inf.				
	Pvt. G, 57 Pa. Inf.	1844			
Durbin, Stephen A.	Pvt. A, 55 Pa. Inf.	1834	1898	St. Patricks	Gallitzin
Dutrow, George B.	Pvt. F, 13 Md. Inf.	1826	1918	Fairview	Altoona
Dwyer, William J.	Smn. U. S. Navy	1837	1899	St. Johns	Altoona
Dysart, Edward	Pvt. A, Ind. Bn. Pa. Mil.	1844			
Dysart, James	Pvt. A, 23 Pa. Inf.	1842			
Dysart, James C.	Cpt. F, 46 Pa. Mil.				
	1Lt. D, 184 Pa. Inf.	1834	1902	Oak Ridge	Altoona
Dysart, Sarah Elizabeth	Nrs. Medical Corps	1837	1909	Dysart	Bellwood
Eakins, David W.	Pvt. A, 125 Pa. Inf.	1845	1925	Oak Ridge	Altoona
Eakens, Stephen	Pvt. A, 110 Pa. Inf.				
Eaken, William R.	Pvt. I, 22 Pa. Cav.	1847	1923	Graziersville	Tyrone
Earhart, George Wm.	Pvt. K, 46 Pa. Mil.	1838		Fairview	Altoona
Earhart, Peter	Pvt. F, 133 Pa. Inf.	1840	1915	St. Patricks	Gallitzin
Earhart, William	Pvt. A, 7 Md. Inf.	1841	1880	Fairview	Altoona
Earlenbaugh, Andrew S.	Pvt. E, 125 Pa. Inf.				
Earlenbaugh, Andrew S.	Cpl. C, 205 Pa. Inf.	1843			
Earlenbaugh, George	Pvt. K, 76 Pa. Inf.	1843	1864	East Sharpsburg	Roaring Spring
Early, John H.	Pvt. K, 22 Pa. Cav.	1844			
Eastop, William	Pvt. D, 5 Pa. Inf.	1820	1898	St. Johns	Williamsburg
	Cpl. C, 53 Pa. Inf.				
Eastman, Henry K.	Pvt. I, 31 Maine Inf.	1846	1922	Rose Hill	Altoona
Eastman, Smith J.	Pvt. A, 1 Pa. Art.	1844			
Eaton, Bird C.	Pvt. A, 23 Pa. Mil.				
	Pvt. B, 192 Pa. Inf.	1829	1900	Presbyterian	Hollidaysburg
Eaton, Hannibal V.	Pvt. M, 62 Pa. Inf.	1843	1862	Presbyterian	Hollidaysburg
Eaton, Harry K.	Smn. U. S. Navy	1828	1868	Presbyterian	Hollidaysburg
Eberle, Alexander	Pvt. D, 46 Pa. Mil.	1827	1900	Fairview	Altoona
Eberly, Henry	Pvt. G, 12 Pa. Cav.	1846			
Eberman, Edwin S.	Pvt. A, 3 Pa. Inf.				
	Pvt. A, 23 Pa. Mil.	1816	1896	Fairview	Martinsburg
Eby, George S.	Pvt. Ind. Cav.Pa. Mil.	1817			
Eby, Jacob Q.	Cpl. A, 1 Pa. Cav.	1842	1909	Oak Ridge	Altoona
Eby, John W.	Sgt. D, 22 Pa. Cav.				
	Pvt. Ind. Cav. Pa. Mil.	1837			
Eckard, Henry H.	Pvt. D, 13 Pa. Cav.	1841			
Eckard, Jacob	Pvt. B, Ind. Bn. Pa. Mil.				
	Pvt. I, 55 Pa. Inf.	1846	1906	Fairview	Altoona
Eckard, William	Pvt. D, 13 Pa. Cav.	1839	1909	Greenlawn	Hollidaysburg
Eckard, Winfield S.	Pvt. D, 22 Pa. Cav.				
	Pvt. B, 208 Pa. Inf.	1846			
Eckenrode, Joseph A.	Pvt. A, 109 Pa. Inf.	1844	1888	St. Patricks	Gallitzin
Eckle, Joseph	Cpl. A, 3 Pa. Inf.	1830			
Eckley, Charles	Sgt. A, 110 Pa. Inf.		1864	City Point	Virginia

SOLDIERS OF BLAIR COUNTY

Name	Rank Organization	Born	Died	Cemetery	Location
Eckley, Henry L.	Pvt. A, 110 Pa. Inf.				
Eckley, Joseph	Pvt. B, 3 Pa. Inf.				
	Cpl. H, 110 Pa. Inf.	1831	1890	Birmingham	Pa.
Eckroth, Daniel	Pvt. G, 104 Pa. Inf.	1846	1927	Grandview	Tyrone
Eddleblute, James L.	Pvt. D, 13 Pa. Cav.	1844			
Edelman, Samuel S.	Pvt. E, 84 Pa. Inf.				
	Pvt. I, 57 Pa. Inf.	1845	1910	Rose Hill	Altoona
Edminson, Alexander S.	Pvt. D, 149 Pa. Inf.	1836	1921	Cambria Mills	Pa.
Edmiston, Franklin B.	Pvt. D, 53 Pa. Inf.				
	Pvt. A, 4 U. S. Art.	1845	1900	Fairview	Altoona
Edmiston, Isaac	Pvt. F, 77 Pa. Inf.	1838	1922	Grazierville	Tyrone
Edmiston, Lewis	Pvt. B, 208 Pa. Inf.		1901	Grandview	Tyrone
Edmiston, Lisle	Pvt. H, 110 Pa. Inf.	1827	1913	Osceola Mills	Pa.
Edmondson, Owen	Pvt. E, 61 Pa. Inf.	1839	1908	Lutheran	Newry
Edmondson, Samuel	Pvt. G, Ind. Bn. Pa. Mil.	1845			
Edmiston, Samuel B.	Pvt. K, 125 Pa. Inf.				
	Cpl. C, 46 Pa. Mil.				
	Cpl. B, 13 Pa. Cav.	1834			
Edmiston, William	Pvt. A, 205 Pa. Inf.	1829	1898	Fairview	Altoona
Edwards, Amon G.	Cpl. A, 125 Pa. Inf.		1861	Chambersburg	Pa.
Edwards, David H.	Pvt. C, 19 U. S. Inf.	1843	1915	Oak Ridge	Altoona
Edwards, John	Pvt. H, 199 Pa. Inf.		1910	Enid	Fulton Co.
Edwards, Jonathan B.	Cpl. C, 133 Pa. Inf.	1835	1910	Methodist	Williamsburg
Edwards, William	2Lt. F, 31 Pa. Inf.				
Egan, Michael	Cpl. G, 11 Pa. Cav.		1891	Wilmore	Pa.
Ehman, George	Sgt. D, 3 Pa. Inf.				
	Pvt. C, 125 Pa. Inf.				
	Pvt. C, 1 Pa. Art.	1842	1915	Grandview	Tyrone
Ehman, John H.	Pvt. A, 22 Pa. Cav.	1837	1889	Grandview	Tyrone
Ehrenfelt, Jacob M.	Pvt. D, 184 Pa. Inf.		1864	Andersonville	Georgia
Ehrenfelt, Jacob M.	Pvt. K, 125 Pa. Inf.				
	Sgt. D, 184 Pa. Inf.				
Ehrenfelt, John	Pvt. Ind. Cav. Pa. Mil.				
	Pvt. K, 46 Pa. Mil.	1845			
Ehringer, John	Pvt. C, 91 Pa. Inf.	1839	1916	Dayton	Ohio
Eichelberger, David	Pvt. M, 22 Pa. Cav.	1824	1888	Union	Claysburg
Eichelberger, John	Pvt. M, 22 Pa. Cav.	1848	1916	Lutheran	Claysburg
Echelberger, Michael					
Eichenlaub, Joseph	Pvt. K, 143 Pa. Inf.	1842	1916	Coupon	Cambria Co.
Eichenlaub, Valentine	Cpl. A, 2 Pa. Cav.				
	Cpl. A, 1 Pa. Cav.	1846			
Eicher, Samuel	Pvt. H, 99 Pa. Inf.	1832	1900	Greenfield	Claysburg
Eicholtz, Alfred	Pvt. B, 125 Pa. Inf.				
Eicholtz, Charles	Cpl. E, 92 Ill. Cav.	1835	1922	Frankstown	Hollidaysburg
Eicholtz, Henry S.	Pvt. C, 3 Pa. Inf.	1837	1861	Lutheran	Williamsburg
Einstein, Max A.	Col. 27 Pa. Inf.				
Elder, Charles	Pvt. K, 22 U. S. C. T.			Union	Hollidaysburg
Elder, Henry R.	Pvt. K, 125 Pa. Inf.				
	Sgt. D, 184 Pa. Inf.				
Elder, Reuben	Pvt. M, 62 Pa. Inf.		1864		
Elder, Samuel T.	Pvt. B, Ind. Bn. Pa. Mil.	1842			
Elder, William L.	Pvt. A, 3 Pa. Inf.	1841	1868	Lutheran	Hollidaysburg
Ellenberger, James Ross	Cpl. C, 148 Pa. Inf.	1841	1915	Carson Valley	Duncansville
Ellenberger, John	Pvt. D, 98 Pa. Inf.	1833	1900	Lutheran	Sinking Valley
Ellenberger, William	Pvt. 149 Pa. Inf.	1822	1908	Ross Church	Hunt'gdon Co.
Eller, Henry	Mus. A, 188 Pa. Inf.			Claar	Bedford Co.
Ellet, James	Pvt. 54 Mass. C.T.				
Ellet, Samuel	Pvt. 54 Mass. C.T.				
Elway, Henry	Pvt. D, 46 Pa. Mil.				
	2Lt. I, 205 Pa. Inf.	1827	1913	Fairview	Altoona
Elway, John S.	Pvt. D, 46 Pa. Mil.				
	Sgt. I, 205 Pa. Inf.	1841			

THE CIVIL WAR

Name	Rank Organization	Born	Died	Cemetery	Location
Ely, Hiram F.	Pvt. A, 147 Pa. Inf.	1832			
Emeigh, Charles	Pvt. H, 14 Pa. Inf.	1840			
Emigh, Christopher	Pvt. C, 205 Pa. Inf.	1844	1896	Metzlers	Martinsburg
Emeigh, Christopher	Cpl. H, 12 Pa. Cav.	1829	1913	Reform	Claysburg
Emigh, George J.	Pvt. C, 205 Pa. Inf.	1843	1925	Fairview	Martinsburg
Emigh, George C.	Cpl. C, 205 Pa. Inf.	1823	1895	Metzlers	Martinsburg
Emigh, Jacob	Pvt. H, 22 Pa. Cav.	1844			
Emigh, Reuben	Pvt. I, 136 Pa. Inf.	1822	1888	Bald Eagle	Tyrone
Emigh, Thomas	Pvt. B, 192 Pa. Inf.	1828	1872	Greenlawn	Roaring Spring
Enfield, David	Pvt. G, 12 Pa. Cav.	1844			
Emfield, George	Pvt. F, 76 Pa. Inf.	1841	1915	Antis	Bellwood
Emsfield, Thomas S.	Pvt. H, 110 Pa. Inf.				
Emswiler, Michael K.	Pvt. B, 191 Pa. Inf.	1843	1902	Fairview	Altoona
Enders, Joseph	Pvt. A, 84 Pa. Inf.				
	Cpl. I, 57 Pa. Inf.	1830			
Enders, Michael	Pvt. E, 84 Pa. Inf.				
	Pvt. G, 57 Pa. Inf.				
England, Isaac	Pvt. K, 82 Pa. Inf.	1845	1919	Rose Hill	Altoona
England, Johnson					
Engle, Bernard	Pvt. G, 12 Pa. Cav.	1842	1866	Presbyterian	Hollidaysburg
Engle, Henry	Pvt. H, 14 Pa. Inf.	1821			
Engle, John	Pvt. I, 40 Pa. Inf.		1861	Pierpont	Virginia
Engle, Joseph E.	Far. G, 12 Pa. Cav.	1819	1889	Fairview	Altoona
Engles, Robert P.	Pvt. K, 125 Pa. Inf.		1863	Washington	D. C.
Enyeart, Thomas L.	Cpl. B, 208 Pa. Inf.	1845	1923	Pittsburgh	Pa.
Eppleman, Emmanuel G.	Pvt. G, 138 Pa. Inf.	1840	1919	Bendersville	Pa.
Eppley, Lewis H.	Pvt. D, 1 Pa. Art.				
	Pvt. H, 200 Pa. Inf.				
Erb, James M.	Pvt. C, 46 Pa. Mil.	1845			
Erbe, William	Pvt. C, 3 Pa. Inf.	1842			
Ermine, John H.	Sgt. H, 110 Pa. Inf.	1846	1921	Charlottsville	Bellwood
Erok, Daniel	Pvt. F, 147 Pa. Inf.				
Eshelman, Joseph	Pvt. D, 46 Pa. Mil.	1825	1901	Carson Valley	Duncansville
Espy, Calvin M.	Cpl. A, 110 Ohio Inf.	1836	1919	Rose Hill	Altoona
Estep, David	Pvt. E, 84 Pa. Inf.		1864	Salisbury	N. Car.
Estep, Elijah	Pvt. C, 3 Pa. Inf.				
	Pvt. E, 84 Pa. Inf.				
	Cpl. I, 57 Pa. Inf.	1840	1914	Logan Valley	Bellwood
Estep, Elijah H.	Cpl. B, 125 Pa. Inf.				
	Pvt. C, 19 Pa. Cav.	1842	1899	Fairview	Altoona
Estep, Henry C.	Pvt. E, 84 Pa. Inf.				
	Pvt. I, 57 Pa. Inf.	1844			
Estep, James	Pvt. C, 22 Pa. Cav.	1841	1863	Chambersburg	Pa.
Estep, John J.	Pvt. E, 104 Pa. Inf.	1826	1897	Logan Valley	Bellwood
Esterline, John	Pvt. B, 3 Pa. Inf.	1839			
Esterline, John M.	Pvt. A, 125 Pa. Inf.				
Estright, George W.	Pvt. L, 12 Pa. Cav.	1843	1865	Collinsville	Altoona
Estright, Henry	Pvt. B, 208 Pa. Inf.				
Estright, William	Pvt. G, 11 Pa. Cav.	1843	1929	Oak Ridge	Altoona
Etchison, Perry O.	Sgt. K, 22 Pa. Cav.	1825			
Etzler, Daniel	Pvt. F, 78 Pa. Inf.	1831			
Evans, Albert	Pvt. D, 125 Pa. Inf.				
Evans, Asabel Y.	Pvt. K, 22 Pa. Cav.	1845	1928	Huntingdon Co.	Pa.
Evans, Caleb C.	Pvt. A, 22 Pa. Cav.	1844	1913	Petersburg	Pa.
Evans, Charles	Lt. K, 76 Pa. Inf.	1823			
Evans, David E.	Pvt. D, 192 Pa. Inf.				
Evans, Frank	Pvt. A, 84 Pa. Inf.				
Evans, George	Pvt. I, 55 Pa. Inf.	1834			
Evans, Henry	Pvt. D, 22 Pa. Cav.	1844			
Evans, Henry	Pvt. D, 12 Pa. Cav.		1915	Oak Ridge	Altoona
Evans, John J.	Pvt. I, 84 Pa. Inf.			Stone Church	Bedford Co.
Evans, Llewllyn	Pvt. H, 110 Pa. Inf.				

SOLDIERS OF BLAIR COUNTY

Name	Rank Organization	Born	Died	Cemetery	Location
Evans, Oswald D.	Pvt. C, 110 Pa. Inf.	1839	1864	Lutheran	Hollidaysburg
Evans, Samuel O.	Sgt. G, 12 Pa. Cav.	1842			
Evans, Thomas	Cpl. A, 110 Pa. Inf.				
Evans, William	Pvt. K, 133 Pa. Inf.				
	Sgt. E, 21 Pa. Cav.	1834	1888	Lutheran	Hollidaysburg
Everhart, Alfred	Pvt. K, 57 Pa. Inf.	1839			
Everhart, David L.	Pvt. C, 110 Pa. Inf.				
Eberhart, Jacob M.	Pvt. E, 84 Pa. Inf.				
Everhart, Joel	Pvt. F, 49 Pa. Inf.				
Everhart, Joseph David	Pvt. I, 57 Pa. Inf.	1837	1916	United Brethren	Canoe Creek
Eberhart, Peter	Pvt. D, 46 Pa. Mil.	1819	1907	Fairview	Altoona
Everhart, William	Pvt. B, 208 Pa. Inf.				
Ebbert, James T.	2Lt. D, 3 Pa. Cav.	1836	1888	Oak Ridge	Altoona
Everly, William	Pvt. F, 22 Pa. Cav.	1845			
Evers, Edward	Pvt. E, 8 Pa. Cav.	1826	1861	Fairview	Altoona
Eversch, Charles	Cpl. D, 46 Pa. Mil.	1845			
Everson, George R. J.	Pvt. B, 37 Pa. Inf.	1839	1862	Fairview	Altoona
Ewing, Alexander B.	Pvt. I, 205 Pa. Inf.	1847	1890	Franklinville	Hunt'gdon Co.
Ewing, Cicero M.	Pvt. E, 11 Pa. Inf.				
	Pvt. E, 211 Pa. Inf.	1840	1930	Grandview	Tyrone
Ewing, Levi M.	Pvt. B, 125 Pa. Inf.		1862	Hagerstown	Maryland
Ewing, Samuel	Pvt. K, 49 Pa. Inf.	1844	1912	Newton Hamilton	Pa.
Exline, William	Pvt. F, 3 Pa. Inf.				
	Pvt. G, 11 Pa. Cav.	1839	1895	Oak Ridge	Altoona
Eyre, Henry C.	Pvt. C, 46 Pa. Mil.				
	Sgt. Pa. Mil.	1844			
Fackler, Samuel	Pvt. C, 110 Pa. Inf.				
Fagans, James	Pvt. E, 125 Pa. Inf.				
	Pvt. I, 55 Pa. Inf.				
Fagan, Patrick	Pvt. C, 14 Pa. Cav.	1842	1904	St. Johns	Altoona
Fagley, Miller	Pvt. I, 22 Pa. Cav.	1848	1915	Grazierville	Tyrone
Fair, James	Pvt. A, 23 Pa. Mil.				
	Pvt. D, 13 Pa. Cav.	1830		Springfield	Ill.
Fair, Henry	Pvt. C, 53 Pa. Inf.	1834	1908	Oil City	Pa.
Fair, Lemuel L.	Pvt. D, 206 Pa. Inf.	1843	1932	Oak Ridge	Altoona
Fairbanks, Ira	Pvt. C, 205 Pa. Inf.	1846			
Falkender, John L.	Pvt. D, 3 Pa. Inf.	1830			
Falkender, William D.	Pvt. H, 208 Pa. Inf.	1836	1909	Waterside	Bedford Co.
Faloon, Joseph	Pvt. H, 12 Pa. Inf.			Indiana	Pa.
Farley, John C.	Pvt. B, 1 D. C. Inf.	1842	1927	Rose Hill	Altoona
Farrell, James	Pvt. K, 125 Pa. Inf.				
Farrell, Michael	Pvt. A, 84 Pa. Inf.		1864	Washington	D. C.
Fausnaught, Isaac S.	Pvt. G, 12 Pa. Cav.	1836			
Fawks, Jerome	Pvt. B, 125 Pa. Inf.	1847	1905	Frankstown	Hollidaysburg
Faxon, Edward L.	Pvt. A, 23 Pa. Mil.	1821			
Fay, Andrew J.	Pvt. E, 3 Pa. Inf.	1842			
Fay, David	Cpl. C, 3 Pa. Inf.				
	Sgt. Q. M. 125 Pa. Inf.	1837	1893	Presbyterian	Williamsburg
Fey, John					
Fay, John	Sgn. 125 Pa. Inf.				
	Sgn. Ind. Bn. Pa. Mil.	1830	1907	Fairview	Altoona
Fay, Robert R.	Cpl. B, 125 Pa. Inf.				
	Sgt. B, 208 Pa. Inf.	1844	1906	Presbyterian	Williamsburg
Feather, David	Pvt. A, 81 Pa. Inf.		1897	Claar	Bedford Co.
Feathers, Henry	Pvt. H, 99 Pa. Inf.			Union Township	Bedford Co.
Feather, Henry C.	Pvt. C, 205 Pa. Inf.	1826	1899	Reform	Claysburg
Feather, John	Pvt. C, 205 Pa. Inf.	1833	1908	Claar	Bedford Co.
Feather, Josiah	Pvt. A, 84 Pa. Inf.				
Feathers, Josiah	Pvt. G, 91 Pa. Inf.			Claar	Bedford Co.
Feather, Michael	Cpl. I, 171 Pa. Inf.			Union Township	Bedford Co.
Feather, Michael	Pvt. H, 14 Pa. Inf.				
	Sgt. H, 110 Pa. Inf.	1841	1918	Carson Valley	Duncansville

THE CIVIL WAR

Name	Rank Organization	Born	Died	Cemetery	Location
Feather, Simon M.	Pvt. E, 138 Pa. Inf.			Union Township	Bedford Co.
Feather, Samuel	Pvt. C, 205 Pa. Inf.	1830	1876	Lutheran	Newry
Feathers, William	Pvt. K, 55 Pa. Inf.	1840	1933	Claar	Bedford Co.
Feay, Andrew	Cpl. B, Ind. Bn. Pa. Mil.	1842			
Fechter, Ignatius J.	Pvt. E, 3 Pa. Inf.				
	Pvt. A, 84 Pa. Inf.				
	Pvt. G, 57 Pa. Inf.	1844			
Fechtner, Clemens	Pvt. I, 14 Pa. Inf.	1838			
Feenan, Michael	Pvt. A, 110 Pa. Inf.				
Feeny, Christopher D.	Pvt. A, 205 Pa. Inf.				
	Pvt. K, 125 Pa. Inf.	1836	1864	St. Johns	Altoona
Feeney, Francis	Pvt. K, 125 Pa. Inf.	1837	1901	St. Johns	Altoona
Feeney, Patrick	Pvt. C, 208, Pa. Inf.	1824	1881	St. Johns	Altoona
Feichter, Martin	Pvt. I, 17 Pa. Cav.	1847	1921	St. Patricks	Newry
Felgar, John	Cpl. C, 84 Pa. Inf.				
Fell, Thomas C.	Sgt. H, 5 Pa. Cav.	1835			
Fellenbaum, James	Pvt. C, 46 Pa. Mil.	1847			
Feltenbarger, Jacob	Pvt. I, 205 Pa. Inf.	1834			
Feltwell, Joshua	Pvt. 149 Pa. Inf.	1828	1907	Fairview	Altoona
Fanno, Melvin H.	1Lt. L, 12 Pa. Cav.	1839			
Fentiman, William H.	Pvt. B, 2 Pa. Inf.				
	Pvt. D, 126 Pa. Inf.	1836			
Fenton, Charles M.	Pvt. H, 3 Pa. Inf.	1839			
Ferguson, Daniel	Pvt. Ind. Cav. Pa. Mil.	1837			
Ferguson, John	Pvt. C, 110 Pa. Inf.		1862	Reform Church	Hopewell Twp.
Ferguson, William	Pvt. B, 3 Pa. Inf.	1822			
Ferree, Isaac	Pvt. A, 55 Pa. Inf.		1865	Petersburg	Virginia
Ferry, Joseph	Pvt. A, 3 Pa. Inf.				
	Pvt. A, 84 Pa. Inf.	1839	1906	St. Johns	Altoona
Fessenden, William	Pvt. K, 46 Pa. Mil.	1844			
Fetterhoof, Daniel	Pvt. M, 9 Pa. Cav.	1836			
Fetterolf, Henry	Cpl. H, 49 Pa. Inf.	1841			
Fettinger, Charles L.	Pvt. C, 46 Pa. Mil.				
	Pvt. A, 20 Pa. Cav.	1848	1897	Fairview	Altoona
Fettinger, Henry E.	Pvt. A, 95 Pa. Inf.	1844	1903	Fairview	Altoona
Fettinger, W. D.		1846	1877	Fairview	Altoona
Fetters, George	Pvt. B, 202 Pa. Inf.	1846	1932	Birmingham	Pa.
Fetters, Lewis A.	Pvt. K, 46 Pa. Mil.				
	Pvt. G, 12 Pa. Cav.	1847			
Fetters, William	Cpl. A, 110 Pa. Inf.	1843	1920	Grandview	Tyrone
Few, William	Pvt. E, 26 Pa. Mil.	1847	1907	Fairview	Altoona
Fick, Henry C.	Pvt. H, 184 Pa. Inf.	1832	1910	Fairview	Altoona
Fickes, Henry	Pvt. F, 49 Pa. Inf.	1827	1908	Oak Ridge	Altoona
Fickes, Silas S.	Sgt. H, 95 Pa. Inf.	1847	1929	Fairview	Altoona
Fields, Charles B.	Pvt. G, 55 Pa. Inf.	1849	1905	Fairview	Altoona
Fields, John R.	Pvt. K, 16 Pa. Cav.	1848	1929	Alto Reste	Hollidaysburg
Fields, John	Pvt. F, 205 Pa. Inf.	1849	1918	Grandview	Tyrone
Fields, William H.	Pvt. A, 22 Pa. Cav.	1836	1911	Rose Hill	Altoona
Fiester, David	Pvt. A, 110 Pa. Inf.				
Figart, Andrew M.	Pvt. F, 31 Pa. Inf.				
	Pvt. A, 191 Pa. Inf.	1840			
Figart, Francis G.	Pvt. K, 46 Pa. Mil.	1846			
Filer, George	Pvt. A, 3 Pa. Inf.	1840		Fairview	Altoona
Finch, Miles	Pvt. F, 77 Pa. Inf.	1842	1865	Green Lake	Texas
Findley, John W.	Pvt. F, 74 Pa. Inf.	1844	1916	Rose Hill	Altoona
Findley, Joseph R.	Cpt. F, 76 Pa. Inf.	1838	1903	Fairview	Altoona
Findley, William	Pvt. D, 110 Pa. Inf.			Walls	Williamsburg
Fink, Abraham	Pvt. C, 148 Pa. Inf.	1835	1911	Replogle	Woodbury
Fink, Benjamin C.	Pvt. A, 110 Pa. Inf.	1834	1905	Mt. Pleasant	Centre Co.
Fink, David A.	Pvt. A, 205 Pa. Inf.	1847	1933	Antis	Bellwood
Fink, Frederick	Pvt. B, 3 Pa. Inf.	1841			
Fink, Isaac	Pvt. A, 110 Pa. Inf.				

SOLDIERS OF BLAIR COUNTY

Name	Rank Organization	Born	Died	Cemetery	Location
Fink, Jacob	Pvt. I, 14 Pa. Inf.	1817			
Fink, John H.	Pvt. A, 205 Pa. Inf.	1839	1914	Oak Ridge	Altoona
Fink, John W.	Pvt. D, 14 Pa. Inf.	1837			
Fink, Reuben	Pvt. D, 14 Pa. Inf.	1839			
Fink, Reuben	Pvt. A, 110 Pa. Inf.				
Fink, William	Pvt. A, 110 Pa. Inf.				
Fink, William H.	Pvt. D, 206 Pa. Inf.	1844	1907	Logan Valley	Bellwood
Findley, Stephen	Pvt. F, 76 Pa. Inf.	1841	1863	Ft. Wagner	S. Car.
Findley, William J.	Pvt. A, 19 Pa. Inf.				
	Sgt. E, 106 Pa. Inf.	1844			
Finn, John	Pvt. C, 91 Pa. Inf.	1825	1900	St. Marys	Hollidaysburg
Finnegan, Daniel	Pvt. I, 55 Pa. Inf.	1818	1864	City Point	Virginia
Finney, Andrew W.	Pvt. D, 125 Pa. Inf.	1862			
Finney, Francis	Pvt. K, 125 Pa. Inf.				
Finney, Francis	Pvt. E, 3 Pa. Inf.	1840			
Finney, Orren P.	Pvt. M, 62 Pa. Inf.	1841	1934	Fairview	Altoona
Firth, Jacob	Pvt. I, 14 Pa. Inf.	1835			
Fishel, George W.	Pvt. C, 110 Pa. Inf.				
Fisher, Benjamin F.	Pvt. D, 46 Pa. Mil.	1839			
Fisher, Daniel J.	Pvt. F, 77 Pa. Inf.	1829			
Fisher, Henry S.	Pvt. C, 133 Pa. Inf.			Woodbury Twp.	Bedford Co.
Fisher, Harry L.	Pvt. Ind. Cav. Pa. Mil.				
	Sgt. F, 22 Pa. Cav.	1838			
Fisher, John A.	Pvt. A, 46 Pa. Mil.	1803			
Fisher, Joseph	Pvt. C, 3 Pa. Inf.		1870	Friends Grove	Pa.
Fisher, Joseph	Pvt. A, 77 Pa. Inf.	1841			
Fisher, Joseph E.	Pvt. D, 192 Pa. Inf.				
Fisher, Levi	Lt. M, 12 Pa. Cav.	1840	1909	Oak Ridge	Altoona
Fisher, Michael	Pvt. E, 104 Pa. Inf.	1827	1904	St. Marys	Altoona
Fissel, Henry	2Lt. G, 149 Pa. Inf.	1833	1893	Lutheran	Newry
Fitch, John A.	Pvt. G, 18 Pa. Inf.				
	Pvt. D, 8 Pa. Cav.	1833	1923	Grandview	Altoona
Fitzgerald, William	Pvt. C, 10 N. J. Inf.		1917	Osceola Mills	Pa.
Fitzharris, Michael	Pvt. C, 110 Pa. Inf.				
	Pvt. A, 84 Pa. Inf.				
	Sgt. G, 57 Pa. Inf.	1844	1916	St. Patricks	Gallitzin
Fitzpatrick, James M.	Gun. U. S. Navy	1846	1911	Oak Ridge	Altoona
Fitzsimmons, James	Pvt. M, 62 Pa. Inf.				
	Sgt. K, 91 Pa. Inf.		1865	Petersburg	Virginia
Fix, Daniel W.	Pvt. G, 97 Pa. Inf.	1841	1911	Spring Hope	Martinsburg
Flanagan, Augustus	Sgt. A, 55 Pa. Inf.	1844	1924	Tecumseh	Nebraska
Flanagan, George A.	Pvt. E, 84 Pa. Inf.				
	Pvt. I, 57 Pa. Inf.	1827	1864	Salisbury	N. Car.
Flanigan, John	Cpl. E, 3 Pa. Inf.	1841	1903	St. Johns	Altoona
Fleck, Abraham M.	Pvt. H, 22 Pa. Cav.	1845			
Fleck, Conrad	Pvt. G, 12 Pa. Cav.	1825	1908	Lutheran	Sinking Valley
Fleck, Edward	Pvt. D, 192 Pa. Inf.				
Fleck, Jacob Martin	Pvt. A, 205 Pa. Inf.	1830	1914	Fairview	Altoona
Fleck, John	Pvt. H, 14 Pa. Inf.				
	Pvt. F, 5 U. S. Art.	1838		Lutheran	Hollidaysburg
Fleck, John A.	Cpl. H, 148 Pa. Inf.				
	Sgt. G, 53 Pa. Inf.		1898	Lutheran	Sinking Valley
Fleck, Luther E.	Pvt. F, 76 Pa. Inf.	1840	1864	Hampton	Virginia
Fleck, Thomas	Pvt. K, 48 Pa. Inf.	1824	1903	Charlottsville	Bellwood
Fleck, William	Pvt. F, 77 Pa. Inf.	1821	1865	Galveston	Texas
Fleck, William E.	Pvt. I, 137 Pa. Inf.				
	Pvt. M, 13 Pa. Cav.	1846	1914	Fairview	Altoona
Fleigle, William W.	Pvt. B, 208 Pa. Inf.			Helixville	Bedford Co.
Fleming, John J.	Sgt. D, 148 Pa. Inf.	1839	1908	Johnstown	Pa.
Fleming, Stephen C.	Pvt. E, 84 Pa. Inf.			St. Marys	Hollidaysburg
Flemmings, James W.	Pvt. C, 11 Pa. Cav.		1901	Fetterhoofs Cl.	Franklin Co.
Flenner, Samuel T.	Pvt. F, 1 Pa. Art.	1846			

THE CIVIL WAR

Name	Rank Organization	Born	Died	Cemetery	Location
Flenner, William H.	Sgt. D, 5 Pa. Inf.				
	Sgt. H, 125 Pa. Inf.	1839	1912	Grandview	Tyrone
Flelninken, H. B.	Cpl. M, 62 Pa. Inf.				
Fletcher, David	Pvt. K, 211 Pa. Inf.	1837	1918	Replogle	Woodbury
Fletcher, G. E.	Pvt. D, 58 N. Y. Inf.				
Flick, William	Pvt. K, 131 Pa. Inf.		1894	Lincoln	Nebraska
Flock, Francis					
Flood, Albert B.	Sgt. C, 3 Pa. Inf.				
	Sgt. F, 125 Pa. Inf.	1839	1906	Methodist	Williamsburg
Flood, Theodore L.	2Lt. C, 125 Pa. Inf.	1842		Meadville	Pa.
Flood, Thomas Barlow	Pvt. B, 46 Pa. Mil.				
	Pvt. B, 1 Pa. Art.	1844		Methodist	Williamsburg
Flough, Casper	Cpl. A, 55 Pa. Inf.		1889	St. Patricks	Newry
Flough, Francis	Pvt. E, 104 Pa. Inf.	1825	1901	St. Patricks	Newry
Fluke, James J.	Pvt. A, 55 Pa. Inf.				
	Pvt. D, 1 U. S. Art.	1843	1904	St. Johns	Altoona
Fluck, John R.	Pvt. H, 208 Pa. Inf.	1840	1924	Tatesville	Pa.
Fluke, Oliver	Pvt. C, 110 Pa. Inf.				
	Sgt. C, 22 Pa. Cav.				
	Sgt. C, 205 Pa. Inf.	1844		Reform Church	Hopewell Twp.
Fluke, Samuel B.	Fife Maj. 205 Pa. Inf.	1840	1935	Loysburg	Bedford Co.
Fluke, William	Pvt. C, 3 Pa. Inf.	1841	1924	St. Johns	Altoona
Flynn, Samuel	Pvt. H, 14 Pa. Inf.				
	Cpl. C, 76 Pa. Inf.	1840	1864	Chesterfield Hs.	Virginia
Flynn, William	Pvt. I, 54 Pa. Inf.				
Fogle, Joseph	Pvt. I, 82 Pa. Inf.	1838	1885	Fairview	Altoona
Fogle, Peter	Sgt. F, 76 Pa. Inf.	1840	1920	Fairview	Altoona
Folk, Henry A.	Pvt. D, 45 Pa. Inf.	1842	1914	Fairview	Altoona
Folk, Jonathan	Pvt. C, Ind. Bn. Pa. Inf.	1847	1897	Fairview	Altoona
Fonner, John	Pvt. E, 49 Pa. Inf.	1829	1884	Antis	Bellwood
Fonner, Joseph B.	Pvt. R, 19 Pa. Cav.	1847	1914	Frankstown	Hollidaysburg
Fonner, Joseph F.	Pvt. B, 46 Pa. Mil.				
Fonse, Reuben I.	Pvt. C, 53 Pa. Inf.				
Foose, Michael H.	Pvt. G, 16 Pa. Cav.	1847	1923	Oak Ridge	Altoona
Ford, Patrick J.	Pvt. E, 84 Pa. Inf.	1825	1884	Presbyterian	Williamsburg
Fore, Yost	Pvt. I, 14 Pa. Inf.	1832	1903	St. Marys	Hollidaysburg
Foreman, Henry B.	Pvt. D, 53 Pa. Inf.	1835	1903	Fairview	Altoona
Foreman, John C.	Pvt. A, 110 Pa. Inf.	1844	1883	Longs	Tyrone
Foreman, Joseph C.	Pvt. A, 110 Pa. Inf.	1840			
Foreman, Michael K.	Pvt. F, 77 Pa. Inf.	1830	1865	Louisville	Kentucky
Forgeus, Solomon F.	Pvt. C, 134 Pa. Inf.				
	Pvt. C, 3 Pa. Art.				
	1Lt. G, 9 U. S. C. T.	1844			
Formhalts, Charles	Pvt. D, 192 Pa. Inf.	1825	1901	Lutheran	Hollidaysburg
Forney, John W.	Pvt. D, 13 Pa. Cav.	1843			
Fornwalt, George F.	Pvt. J, 206 Pa. Inf.		1907	Taylorsville	Pa.
Fornwalt, William M.	Cpl. C, 53 Pa. Inf.	1841	1928	Royer	Williamsburg
Forshey, Henry	Cpl. K, 3 Pa. Art.			Grandview	Tyrone
Forsht, David	Pvt. C, 205 Pa. Inf.	1846			
Fortna, Matthias	Pvt. A, 3 Pa. Inf.	1833		Bald Eagle	Tyrone
Foster, Isaiah	Pvt. I, 22 Pa. Cav.	1826			
Foster, Jacob	Pvt. G, 1 Md. Cav.	1836	1911	Rose Hill	Altoona
Fouse, Adam G.	Cpl. E, 104 Pa. Inf.	1842	1917	Salem Reform	Williamsburg
Fouse, Benjamin	Pvt. K, 78 Pa. Inf.		1865	Marklesburg	Pa.
Fouse, Dewalt S.	1Lt. C, 53 Pa. Inf.	1841			
Fouse, Henry G.	Pvt. B, 208 Pa. Inf.	1845	1919	Salem Reform	Williamsburg
Fource, John D.	Cpl. E, 181 Pa. Inf.	1824	1891	Grandview	Tyrone
Fouse, John G.	Pvt. E, 104 Pa. Inf.				
Fouse, William D.	Pvt. B, 125 Pa. Inf.				
	Sgt. D, 22 Pa. Cav.				
	Pvt. B, 208 Pa. Inf.	1846	1916	Rose Hill	Altoona
Foust, Daniel	Pvt. I, 205 Pa. Inf.	1846			

Name	Rank Organization	Born	Died	Cemetery	Location
Foust, Daniel	Pvt. D, 205 Pa. Inf.	1846	1865	Fairview	Altoona
Foust, George W.	Cpl. E, 3 Pa. Inf.				
	Sgt. Ind. Cav. Pa. Mil.	1834	1900	Fairview	Altoona
Foust, Henry	Pvt. A, 110 Pa. Inf.				
Foust, William W.	Pvt. D, 149 Pa. Inf.	1847	1908	Rose Hill	Altoona
Fowler, Augustus	Pvt. A, 195 Pa. Inf.		1904	Carson Valley	Duncansville
Fowler, James	Pvt. C, 97 Pa. Inf.			St. Johns	Altoona
Fowler, James M.	Pvt. K, 21 N. J. Inf.		1862	Winchester	Virginia
Fowler, John E.	Pvt. C, 46 Pa. Mil.	1837	1899	Fairview	Altoona
Fowler, Richard F.	Pvt. A, 23 Pa. Mil.				
	Pvt. A, Ind. Bn. Pa. Mil.				
	Pvt. M, 22 Pa. Cav.	1846	1938	Fairview	Altoona
Fox, John H.	Pvt. A, 3 Pa. Inf.				
	Pvt. A, 23 Pa. Mil.				
	Pvt. A, Ind. Bn. Pa. Mil.	1842			
Fox, Michael		1839	1916	Marshalltown	Iowa
Fox, Reuben J.	Pvt. A, Ind. Bn. Pa. Mil.				
	Pvt. B, 13 Pa. Cav.	1844	1931	Greenlawn	Hollidaysburg
Fox, Watson R.	Pvt. D, 22 Pa. Cav.				
	Pvt. B, 208 Pa. Inf.	1845	1865	Petersburg	Virginia
Foy, Andrew J.	Pvt. A, 49 Pa. Inf.	1832	1898	Logan Valley	Bellwood
Fraily, John T.	Pvt. I, 3 Md. Inf.	1830	1917	Grandview	Tyrone
Fraley, Jacob	Pvt. D, 46 Pa. Mil.	1842	1913	Fairview	Altoona
Fraley, Samuel	Pvt. C, 46 Pa. Mil.	1847			
Francis, Albert	Pvt. E, 76 Pa. Inf.	1847			
Franey, Michael	Pvt. F, 5 W. Va. Cav.	1820	1894	St. Patricks	Gallitzin
Frank, Adam	Pvt. A, 84 Pa. Inf.				
	Pvt. F, 84 Pa. Inf.	1830	1869	St. Marys	Hollidaysburg
Frank, Christian	Pvt. H, 3 Pa. Inf.	1828	1892	St. Marys	Hollidaysburg
Frank, John	Pvt. D, 107 Pa. Inf.	1839	1903	Presbyterian	Hollidaysburg
Franks, Joseph	Pvt. H, 184 Pa. Inf.	1848			
Frank, Joseph S.	Bks. E, 20 Pa. Cav.	1846	1917	Fairview	Altoona
Franks, William	Pvt. H, 184 Pa. Inf.	1845	1918	Rose Hill	Altoona
Franklin, Thomas J.	Pvt. I, 133 Pa. Inf.				
	Pvt. U. A. Signal Corps	1843	1912	Rose Hill	Altoona
Frantz, Abraham	Sgt. C, 22 Pa. Cav.	1841	1911	Bald Eagle	Tyrone
Frantz, Daniel	Pvt. D, 1 Pa. Art.	1845			
Fraser, John Royer	Pvt. A, 1 Conn. Inf.				
	Sgt. B, 8 Conn. Inf.	1841	1916	Fairview	Altoona
Fredergill, Thomas	Pvt. C, 76 Pa. Inf.	1818			
Frederick, Benjamin F.	Pvt. C, 3 Pa. Inf.	1834			
Frederick, Benjamin F.	Pvt. M, 62 Pa. Inf.				
	Pvt. K, 91 Pa. Inf.	1836	1885	Asbury	Altoona
Frederick, John	Sad. G, 12 Pa. Cav.	1840	1900	Antis	Bellwood
Frederick, Michael	Pvt. F, 16 Vet. Res. Cps.	1815	1887	Burket	Henrietta
Frederick, William	Pvt. H, 208 Pa. Inf.	1831	1896	Dry Hill	Woodbury
Frederick, William H.	Pvt. F, 1 Pa. Art.	1836	1917	Lutheran	Hollidaysburg
Freeman, James E.	Pvt. M, 62 Pa. Inf.				
	Pvt. K, 91 Pa. Inf.				
Freet, George L.	Cpl. E, 126 Pa. Inf.	1839	1907	Fairview	Altoona
Freitag, Herman	Pvt. E, 148 Pa. Inf.	1838	1907		
French, Alexander	Pvt. E, 88 Pa. Inf.	1845	1912	Frankstown	Hollidaysburg
Fresh, John	Pvt. Ind. Cav. Pa. Mil.	1827	1899	St. Johns	Altoona
Frey, William B.	Pvt. E, 200 Pa. Inf.	1835	1901	Lutheran	Hollidaysburg
Fribley, Charles W.	Cpt. F, 84 Pa. Inf.				
	Col. 8, U. S. C. T.		1864	Olustee	Florida
Friday, Hiram	Pvt. E, 148 Pa. Inf.				
	Pvt. E, 53 Pa. Inf.	1838	1907	Baughmans	Tyrone
Friday, John H.	Pvt. C, 125 Pa. Inf.				
	Pvt. I, 91 Pa. Inf.			Baughmans	Tyrone
Friel, Hugh	Pvt. E, 84 Pa. Inf.				
Friend, Israel	Pvt. E, 104 Pa. Inf.	1845	1880	Salemville	Bedford Co.

THE CIVIL WAR 193

Name	Rank Organization	Born	Died	Cemetery	Location
Fries, J. W.	2Lt. H, 11 Pa. Inf.	1840	1916	Tacoma	Washington
Fries, Jacob D.	Cpl. E, 28 Pa. Inf.	1842	1937	Oak Ridge	Altoona
Frueauff, John F.	Maj. 153 Pa. Inf.				
Fry, Abraham	Pvt. I, 46 Pa. Mil.				
	Pvt. C, 53 Pa. Inf.		1864	Arlington	Virginia
Fry, Adam	Pvt. F, 76 Pa. Inf.	1841	1862	Pocatigo	S. Car.
Fry, Daniel	Pvt. K, 187 Pa. Inf.	1836	1916	Fairview	Altoona
Fry, Edward D.	Pvt. A, 55 Pa. Inf.	1846			
Fry, George	Pvt. A, 165 Pa. Inf.		1915	Franklin Co.	Pa.
Fry, George		1821	1870	Sniveleys	Williamsburg
Fry, John	Pvt. A, 55 Pa. Inf.	1844	1938	Blairsville	Pa.
Fry, John	Pvt. G, 12 Pa. Cav.	1844	1865	Asbury	Altoona
Fry, John	Pvt. D, 21 Pa. Cav.	1841	1912	Logan Valley	Bellwood
Fry, John	Pvt. H, 110 Pa. Inf.				
Fry, John C.	Pvt. E, 84 Pa. Inf.				
	Pvt. H, 57 Pa. Inf.				
Fry, Levi	Pvt. F, 76 Pa. Inf.	1843	1863	Ft. Wagner	S. Car.
Fry, Michael	Pvt. A, 84 Pa. Inf.			Upper Claar	Bedford Co.
Fry, Robert	Cpl. D, 125 Pa. Inf.				
Fry, Robert J.	Pa. Res.		1883		
Fry, Solomon W.	Pvt. H, 14 Pa. Inf.	1832			
Fry, Solomon W.	1Lt. I, 55 Pa. Inf.	1829			
Fullmer, John	Pvt. F, 46 Pa. Inf.	1841	1901	Fairview	Altoona
Fulton, David S.	Cpl. B, 209 Pa. Inf.	1849			
Fulton, Samuel A.	Pvt. G, 125 Pa. Inf.				
Fultz, Elisha	Pvt. G, 12 Pa. Cav.	1812			
Fultz, William M.	Pvt. G, 12 Pa. Cav.	1846			
Funk, Alexander	Pvt. I, 84 Pa. Inf.				
Funk, Alexander	Pvt. C, 19 Pa. Cav.				
Funk, Amos H.	Pvt. B, Ind. Bn. Pa. Mil.	1845			
Funk, David	Pvt. B, 3 Pa. Inf.	1837			
Funk, David	Pvt. I, 14 Pa. Inf.	1837			
Funk, David P.	Pvt. G, 12 Pa. Cav.	1837	1922	Rose Hill	Altoona
Funk, David P.	Pvt. G, 12 Pa. Cav.	1841			
Funk, George	Pvt. A, 125 Pa. Inf.		1862	Antietam	Maryland
Funk, Harrison	Pvt. H, 110 Pa. Inf.				
Funk, James	Pvt. A, 23 Pa. Mil.	1823			
Funk, James P.	Pvt. G, 12 Pa. Cav.	1846	1929	Asbury	Altoona
Funk, Thomas	Pvt. D, 13 Pa. Cav.	1842	1864	Arlington	Virginia
Funk, William	Pvt. D, 3 Pa. Inf.	1843			
Funk, William	Sgt. A, 125 Pa. Inf.				
Funk, William	2Lt. E, 46 Pa. Mil.	1842			
Furnalman, Adam	Pvt. D, 13 Pa. Cav.	1834	1915	Presbyterian	Birmingham
Gable, Adam G.	Cpl. M, 20 Pa. Cav.	1840	1880	St. Marys	Altoona
Gable, Theodore	Pvt. A, 101 Pa. Inf.	1846	1907	Carson Valley	Duncansville
Gable, William M.	Cpl. K, 22 Pa. Cav.	1838	1864	Charleston	W. Va.
Gaff, Samuel	Bks. A, 21 Pa. Cav.				
	Pvt. 126 Pa. Inf.	1840	1931	Chambersburg	Pa.
Gailey, Joseph	Pvt. C, 110 Pa. Inf.	1829			
Gailly, William	Pvt. F, Ind. Bn. Pa. Mil.	1844			
Gaines, George	Pvt. F, 76 Pa. Inf.	1841	1864	Hampton	Virginia
Galbraith, William	Pvt. D, 45 Pa. Inf.	1820	1883	Fairview	Altoona
Gallagher, Charles	Pvt. I, 55 Pa. Inf.	1836			
Gallagher, James	Pvt. I, 57 Pa. Inf.	1842			
Gallagher, John	Pvt. E, 125 Pa. Inf.	1841			
Gallagher, Patrick F.	Cpt. E, 84 Pa. Inf.		1862	Presbyterian	Hollidaysburg
Gallagher, William	Pvt. E, 84 Pa. Inf.				
Gallaher, Wilson	Pvt. E, 104 Pa. Inf.				
Galloway, Henry S.	Cpl. M, 62 Pa. Inf.	1840	1864	Presbyterian	Hollidaysburg
Galloway, John	Pvt. E, 84 Pa. Inf.	1840			
Galloway, Joseph D.	Pvt. A, 84 Pa. Inf.				
	Sgt. B, 13 Pa. Inf.	1845	1888	St. Johns	Altoona

SOLDIERS OF BLAIR COUNTY

Name	Rank Organization	Born	Died	Cemetery	Location
Gamble, Andrew G.	Pvt. F, 194 Pa. Inf.	1843	1904	Fairview	Altoona
Ganoe, Andrew L.	Sgt. A, 110 Pa. Inf.	1835			
Ganoe, Benjamin	Pvt. A, 205 Pa. Inf.				
Ganoe, David G.	2Lt. A, 125 Pa. Inf.				
	2Lt. H, 22 Pa. Cav.	1835	1883	Bald Eagle	Tyrone
Ganoe, Jeremiah	Sgt. D, 3 Pa. Inf.	1839			
Ganoe, Martin L.	Pvt. F, 2 Pa. Cav.	1844	1917	Chambersburg	Penna.
Ganoe, Thomas	Pvt. A, 110 Pa. Inf.				
Ganoe, William V.	Mus. I, 205 Pa. Inf.	1845			
Gans, Cloyd	Sgt. G, 25 U.S.C.T.	1832	1916	Oak Ridge	Altoona
Garber, Charles	Pvt. M, 62 Pa. Inf.				
Garber, George C.	Pvt. H, 3 Pa. Inf.	1830			
Garber, Jacob	Pvt. M, 62 Pa. Inf.				
Garber, John B.	Pvt. E, 50 Pa. Inf.	1826	1889	Greenlawn	Roaring Spring
Garber, John J.	Cpl. C, 205 Pa. Inf.	1838	1927	St. Patricks	Newry
Garber, Michael C.	Col. Q.M.C.		1881	Madison	Wisconsin
Garbrick, George	Pvt. D, 198 Pa. Inf.	1828	1911	Logan Valley	Bellwood
Garden, Edward D.	Mus. M, 62 Pa. Inf.				
	Pvt. K, 91 Pa. Inf.				
Garden, John R.	Pvt. H, 3 Pa. Inf.				
	Sgt. M, 62 Pa. Inf.				
	Sgt. K, 91 Pa. Inf.				
	2Lt. H, 215 Pa. Inf.	1842	1919	Oak Ridge	Altoona
Garden, Robert B.	Pvt. E, 3 Pa. Inf.				
	Cpl. Ind. Cav. Pa. Mil.	1839			
Gardner, Adam	Pvt. D, 55, Pa. Inf.			Mt. Zion	Bedford Co.
Gardner, Andrew	Pvt. K, 78 Pa. Inf.	1828	1911	Grandview	Tyrone
Gardner, David	Col. 1 Pa. Cav.				
Gardner, David	Pvt. K, 110 Pa. Inf.			Baughmans	Tyrone
Gardner, Harry	Pvt. F, 32 Mass. Inf.	1835	1887	Lutheran	Hollidaysburg
Gardner, James	Sgt. E, 125 Pa. Inf.				
Gardner, John F.	Cpl. G, 12 Pa. Cav.	1841	1905	Fairview	Altoona
Gardner, John T.	Cpt. E, 2 Kan. Cav.	1823	1888	Lutheran	Newry
Gardner, Joseph W. (M)	1Lt. B, 3 Pa. Inf.				
	Cpt. K, 125 Pa. Inf.				
	Cpt. K, 46 Pa. Mil.	1825	1898	Oak Ridge	Altoona
Gardner, Peter	Pvt. I, 205 Pa. Inf.	1839			
Gardner, Robert	Pvt. E, 125 Pa. Inf.				
Gardner, Thaddius S.	Sgn. 62 Pa. Inf.				
	Sgn. 17 Pa. Cav.	1839	1893	Presbyterian	Hollidaysburg
Gardner, W. J.	Pvt. K, 20 Pa. Cav.				
Gardner, William	Pvt. K, 46 Pa. Mil.	1846			
Garland, David	Pvt. I, 91 Pa. Inf.	1828	1909	Bald Eagle	Tyrone
Garland, David W.	Pvt. C, 125 Pa. Inf.	1844	1917	Carson Valley	Duncansville
Garland, Joseph	Pvt. B, 81 Pa. Inf.	1838			
Garland, Moses K.	Pvt. C, 3 Pa. Inf.				
	Cpl. G, 125 Pa. Inf.				
	Pvt. C, 76 Pa. Inf.	1844	1865	Carson Valley	Duncansville
Garlick, Adam	Pvt. K, 12 Pa. Inf.		1916	Saxton	Penna.
Garman, Adam	Pvt. K, 187 Pa. Inf.				
Garman, Philip F.	Pvt. A, 125 Pa. Inf.				
	Cpl. K, 187 Pa. Inf.	1841	1919	Logan Valley	Bellwood
Garner, George	Pvt. A, 84 Pa. Inf.				
	Pvt. I, 57 Pa. Inf.	1818	1865		
Garner, Jacob H.	Pvt. D, 205 Pa. Inf.	1843			
Garner, Joseph E.	Pvt. B, 125 Pa. Inf.				
Garner, Matthew	Pvt. D, 205 Pa. Inf.	1831			
Garner, Peter	Pvt. C, 22 Pa. Cav.	1840			
Garret, Alexander A.	Pvt. C, 3 Pa. Inf.	1840			
Garrett, Albert T.	Pvt. C, 110 Pa. Inf.				
Garret, John C.	Pvt. C, 110 Pa. Inf.				
Garet, Peter	Pvt. A, Ind. Bn. Pa. Mil.	1845			

THE CIVIL WAR 195

Name	Rank Organization	Born	Died	Cemetery	Location
Garrett, William L.	Pvt. A, 3 Pa. Inf.	1835	1907	Rose Hill	Altoona
Garrettson, Benjamin H.	Pvt. C, 205 Pa. Inf.	1841	1865	E. St. Clair Twp.	Bedford Co.
Garretson, Frederick	Pvt. C, 205 Pa. Inf.	1836			
Garretson, Thomas	Pvt. A, 84 Pa. Inf.				
Garrigan, Thomas	Pvt. F, Ind. Bn. Pa. Mil.	1833			
Gates, Charles McC.	Sgt. C, 76 Pa. Inf.	1844	1911	Rose Hill	Altoona
Gates, Flemmery N.	Pvt. E, 84 Pa. Inf.	1841			
Gates, Frederick	Pvt. G, 12 Pa. Cav.	1836			
Gates, George W.	Pvt. D, 42 Pa. Inf.				
	Cpl. D, 190 Pa. Inf.	1842	1922	Greenwood	Altoona
Gates, George W.	Pvt. C, 76 Pa. Inf.	1829			
Gates, Henry A.	Pvt. K, 125 Pa. Inf.				
Gates, Jeremiah	Pvt. E, 84 Pa. Inf.	1839	1862	Winchester	Virginia
Gates, John	Pvt. H, 3 Pa. Inf.	1838			
Gates, Joseph	Pvt. H, 3 Pa. Inf.	1824			
Gates, Joseph	Sgt. 110 Pa. Inf.				
	Sgt. H, 208 Pa. Inf.	1838	1896	Carson Valley	Duncansville
Gates, Joseph	Pvt. H, 18 Pa. Cav.	1841			
Gates, Joseph	Cpl. D, 1 Pa. Cav.	1843	1926	Brumbaughs	Martinsburg
Gates, Martin V. B.	Pvt. H, 14 Pa. Inf.				
	Sgt. C, 76 Pa. Inf.	1839		Hopewell	Penna.
Gates, Martin	Pvt. C, 110 Pa. Inf.			Hopewell Twp.	Bedford Co.
Gates, Phillip	Pvt. H, 110 Pa. Inf.	1820	1887	Stormestown	Penna.
Gates, Samuel	Pvt. C, 110 Pa. Inf.	1843	1862	Hopewell Twp.	Bedford Co.
Gates, Theophilus R.	Cpl. K, 55 Pa. Inf.	1831	1927	Logan Valley	Bellwood
Gates, William	Pvt. B, 88 Pa. Inf.	1829	1912	Grandview	Tyrone
Gates, William	Pvt. C, 110 Pa. Inf.			Hopewell Twp.	Bedford Co.
Gates, William B.	Pvt. B, Ind. Bn. Pa. Mil.	1846			
Gates, William B.	Pvt. I, 55 Pa. Inf.	1846	1907	McKeesport	Penna.
Gates, William E.	Pvt. B, 192 Pa. Inf.	1832	1900	Greenlawn	Roaring Spring
Gates, William H.	Pvt. C, 110 Pa. Inf.				
	Pvt. K, 208 Pa. Inf.	1838	1915	Loysburg	Penna.
Gates, William H.	Pvt. E, 84 Pa. Inf.			Broad Top Twp.	Bedford Co.
Gayton William	1Lt. D, 22 Pa. Cav.	1828			
Gearhart, Frederick W.	Pvt. D, 125 Pa. Inf.	1841	1907	Fairview	Altoona
Gearhart, Jacob	Pvt. L, 102 Pa. Inf.	1833	1900	Fairview	Altoona
Geesey, Christ	Cpl. A, 84 Pa. Inf.	1833	1872	Frankstown	Hollidaysburg
Geesey, Henry	Pvt. I, 137 Pa. Inf.	1845	1919	Rose Hill	Altoona
Geesey, John	Pvt. Ind. Cav. Pa. Mil.	1830			
Geesey, John	Pvt. E, 13 Pa. Inf.				
Gehrelt, Benjamin F.	Pvt. C, 126 Pa. Inf.	1844	1884	Fairview	Altoona
Gehrett, Adam	Pvt. F, 31 Pa. Inf.		1864	Alexandria	Virginia
Gehrett, James W.	Pvt. I, 1 Pa. Art.				
Gehrett, John J.	Pvt. K, 22 Pa. Cav.	1846			
Gehrett, Samuel W.	Sgt. 22 Pa. Cav.	1845			
Geiser, George J.	Pvt. C, 3 Pa. Inf.				
	2Lt. G, 1 Pa. Cav.	1841			
Geiser, James	Pvt. C, 3 Pa. Inf.				
	Cpl. B, 125 Pa. Inf.				
	Cpt. G, 3 Pa. Art.				
	Col. D, 188 Pa. Inf.	1839	1922	Oak Ridge	Altoona
Geiser, Tighlman	Pvt. F, 1 Pa. Art.				
	Pvt. B, 125 Pa. Inf.				
	Pvt. I, 22 Pa. Cav.	1841			
Geisinger, David	Pvt. D, 205 Pa. Inf.	1846			
Geisinger, Miles G.	Pvt. A, 22 Pa. Cav.	1845	1927	Fairview	Altoona
Geisler, Louis H.	Pvt. E, 125 Pa. Inf.				
	Sgt. F, 77 Pa. Inf.	1825		E. St. Clair Twp.	Bedford Co.
Geisler, Lydwik					
Geist, Andrew W.	Cpl. H, 188 Pa. Inf.	1846	1918	Rose Hill	Altoona
Geist, George	Pvt. D, 192 Pa. Inf.				
Geitly, Jacob	Pvt. I, 14 Pa. Inf.	1837			

SOLDIERS OF BLAIR COUNTY

Name	Rank Organization	Born	Died	Cemetery	Location
Gemmill, Jacob M.	Sgn. 46 Pa. Mil.				
Gensimore, George	Sgt. I, 34 Pa. Inf.	1842			
George, Barnabus	Pvt. A, 107 Pa. Inf.		1903	St. Patricks	Newry
George, James P.	Pvt. M, 16 Pa. Cav.		1897	McVeytown	Penna.
George, William F.	Pvt. K, 3 Pa. Art.	1837	1907	Logan Valley	Bellwood
Gern, Charles L.	Pvt. A, 84 Pa. Inf.	1819	1879	Oak Ridge	Altoona
Gerst, Ephriam	Sgt. B, 125 Pa. Inf.	1835	1910	Presbyterian	Hollidaysburg
Gettleman, Jacob	Pvt. E, 104 Pa. Inf.	1838	1915	Royer	Williamsburg
Gettys, James	Pvt. F, 27 Pa. Mil.			Fairview	Altoona
Getz, Henry	Pvt. E, 104 Pa. Inf.			Grandview	Tyrone
Gibboney, Benjamin F.	Pvt. G, 125 Pa. Inf.				
Gibboney, George W.	Pvt. F, 76 Pa. Inf.	1843			
Gibboney, James H.	Pvt. H, 14 Pa. Inf.				
	Cpl. G, 125 Pa. Inf.	1839	1862	Presbyterian	Hollidaysburg
Gibboney, John Calvin	Pvt. C, 76 Pa. Inf.	1844	1920	Carson Valley	Duncansville
Gibboney, Luther M.	Pvt. H, 14 Pa. Inf.	1842	1861	Carson Valley	Duncansville
Gibson, David	Pvt. A, 3 Pa. Inf.	1835			
Gibson, George G.	Pvt. H, 208 Pa. Inf.	1831	1901	Grandview	Tyrone
Gibson, William	Pvt. A, 205 Pa. Inf.				
Gibson, William D.	Pvt. D, 13 Pa. Cav.	1842			
Gifford, James	Sgt. I, 1 Pa. Art.	1816	1895	Presbyterian	Sinking Valley
Gilbert, Samuel W.	Pvt. G, 5 Pa. Inf.				
	2Lt. C, 93 Pa. Inf.				
Gildea, David A.	Sgt. H, 14 Pa. Inf.	1838	1906	St. Patricks	Newry
Gill, Richard	Pvt. D, 46 Pa. Mil.	1829	1877	Fairview	Altoona
Gill, William	Pvt. A, 205 Pa. Inf.				
Gill, William H.	Pvt. F, 2 Pa. Cav.	1844			
Gillam, James S.	Sgt. I, 149 Pa. Inf.	1841	1923	Eastlawn	Tyrone
Gilland, David A.	Sgt. I, 137 Pa. Inf.	1841	1906	Oak Ridge	Altoona
Gillaspie, John Wilson	Pvt. A, 3 Prov. N. Y. Cav.	1829	1920	Grandview	Altoona
Gille, Charles	Pvt. K, 5 Md. Inf.	1835	1908	Salemville	Bedford Co.
Gillen, James	Pvt. F, 76 Pa. Inf.	1842			
Gillen, James P.	Frn. U. S. Navy	1830	1913	St. Johns	Altoona
Gillen, William	Pvt. D, 14 Pa. Inf.	1831			
Gillhousen, Albert E.	Pvt. D, 3 Pa. Inf.				
	Pvt. F, 76 Pa. Inf.				
	Pvt. K, 7 Pa. Cav.	1841	1868	Logan Valley	Bellwood
Gillet, Anthony	Pvt. 14, 2Bn. V.R.C.			Spring Hope	Martinsburg
Gilliland, David R. P.	Pvt. C, 77 Pa. Inf.	1838	1917	Greenlawn	Roaring Spring
Gilliland, James	Pvt. C, 77 Pa. Inf.		1864	Jefferson	Indiana
Gilliland, Matthew	Pvt. B, 46 Pa. Mil.				
Gillmen, John F.	Pvt. C, 77 Pa. Inf.	1841	1908	Grandview	Tyrone
Gilmore, James Frank	Pvt. A, 199 Pa. Inf.	1846	1931	Logan Valley	Bellwood
Gilmore, John	Pvt. A, 84 Pa. Inf.		1862	Winchester	Virginia
Gilroy, Patrick	Pvt. A, 84 Pa. Inf.				
Gilroy, William	Ldn. U. S. Navy	1835	1873	St. Johns	Altoona
Gilsinger, David	Pvt. I, 205 Pa. Inf.	1846			
Gilson, Jackson	Pvt. C, 110 Pa. Inf.				
Gingerick, Augustus	Pvt. E, 1 Pa. Art.	1844			
Ginerich, Rudolph	Cpl. F, 2 Pa. Cav.	1843	1916	Grandview	Tyrone
Ginner, Martin	Pvt. E, 104 Pa. Inf.				
Ginter, Augustus	Pvt. H, 12 Pa. Cav.	1840	1873	Oak Grove	Tyrone
Ginter, Daniel	Pvt. C, 194 Pa. Inf.	1846	1919	Bald Eagle	Tyrone
Ginter, David	Pvt. H, 22 Pa. Cav.	1833	1876	Bald Eagle	Tyrone
Ginter, David M.	Sgt. G, 12 Pa. Cav.	1840			
Ginter, David M.	Pvt. E, 3 Pa. Inf.	1843			
Ginter, George W.	Pvt. E, 84 Pa. Inf.		1880	Smiths	Martinsburg
Ginter, James	Pvt. A, 205 Pa. Inf.				
Ginter, John	Pvt. E, 125 Pa. Inf.				
Ginter, John C.	Pvt. C, 205 Pa. Inf.	1844	1864	Greenlawn	Roaring Spring
Ginter, John E.	Pvt. B, 208 Pa. Inf.	1834	1888	Oak Ridge	Altoona

Name	Rank Organization	Born	Died	Cemetery	Location
Ginter, Jonathan	Mus. D, 3 Pa. Inf.				
	Cpl. M, 62 Pa. Inf.	1838	1906	Grandview	Tyrone
Girod, Abram	Mus. 45 Pa. Inf.	1842			
Gissner, Jacob	Pvt. K, 142 Pa. Inf.	1836			
Givin, James S.	Sgt. E, 49 Pa. Inf.	1842	1904	Grandview	Tyrone
Given, Joseph D.	Pvt. A, 97 Pa. Inf.	1842	1902	Oak Ridge	Altoona
Given, William	Pvt. A, 97 Pa. Inf.	1840			
Givler, Lewis J.	Pvt. I, 126 Pa. Inf.		1883	Grandview	Tyrone
Glasgow, George W.	Pvt. D, 14 Pa. Inf.				
	Pvt. D, 192 Pa. Inf.	1831	1884	Logan Valley	Bellwood
Glasgow, James E.	Pvt. H, 1 Pa. Art.	1821	1900	Fairview	Altoona
Glasgow, Joseph F.	Pvt. H, 84 Pa. Inf.	1828	1888	Fairview	Altoona
Glasgow, Taylor W.	Pvt. H, 110 Pa. Inf.	1833	1863	Logan Valley	Bellwood
Glasgow, Thomas	Pvt. A, 110 Pa. Inf.				
Glass, Augustine	Pvt. F, 28 Pa. Inf.		1877	Loretta	Penna.
Glass, George W.	Pvt. I, 137 Pa. Inf.	1839	1904	Frankstown	Hollidaysburg
Glass, James R.	Pvt. D, 125 Pa. Inf.				
Glass, John	Pvt. E, 84 Pa. Inf.		1864	Carlisle	Penna.
Glass, John J.	Pvt. I, 55 Pa. Inf.	1840	1914	St. Patricks	Newry
Glaub, Jacob	Pvt. K, 79 Pa. Inf.		1877	St. Johns	Altoona
Glenn, William B.	Pvt. A, 46 Pa. Mil.				
Glenn, William F.	Pvt. E, 3 Pa. Inf.	1840			
Glunt, Abraham	Pvt. I, 84 Pa. Inf.	1796	1862	Fairview	Altoona
Glunt, Henry	Pvt. G, 12 Pa. Cav.	1838	1906	Fairview	Altoona
Glunt, Jacob	Pvt. C, 76 Pa. Inf.	1824	1864	Petersburg	Virginia
Glunt, Joseph	Pvt. F, 49 Pa. Inf.	1836	1917	Fairview	Altoona
Glunt, William C.	Pvt. F, 31 Pa. Inf.				
	Pvt. A, 191 Pa. Inf.	1842	1926	Carson Valley	Duncansville
Gochnaur, David	Pvt. G, 3 Pa. Inf.				
	Pvt. F, 54 Pa. Inf.	1900			
Gochnour, John A.	Pvt. K, 14 Pa. Inf.				
	Pvt. A, 139 Ohio Inf.				
	Cpl. B, 133 Pa. Inf.	1842	1912	Fairview	Altoona
Godderman, A. B.	Pvt. F, 28 Pa. Inf.				
Godfrey, Patrick	Pvt. 5, U. S. Cav.		1884	St. Patricks	Gallitzin
Gonsman, Frederick G.	Pvt. C, 205 Pa. Inf.	1845	1910	St. Patricks	Newry
Gonter, Samuel	Pvt. A, 13 Md. Inf.		1898	Congregational	Washington, D. C.
Good, Jacob	Pvt. Ind. Cav. Pa. Mil.	1822			
Good, John	Pvt. C, 76 Pa. Inf.	1841	1864	Petersburg	Virginia
Good, Samuel	Pvt. A, 205 Pa. Inf.				
Gooderham, Abraham B.	Pvt. F, 28 Pa. Inf.	1840	1909	Rose Hill	Altoona
Gooderham, P. J.	Pvt. A, 110 Pa. Inf.		1862	Mt. Kalma	Harrisburg
Goodfellow, John W.	Cpl. E, 2 Mass. Cav.	1837	1913	St. Marys	Hollidaysburg
Goodman, Benjamin F.	Pvt. K, 22 Pa. Cav.	1842			
Goodman, David L.	Pvt. I, 46 Pa. Mil.	1839	1890	Hutchinsons	Altoona
Goodman, George	Pvt. E, 148 Pa. Inf.				
	Pvt. E, 53 Pa. Inf.	1830	1910	Grandview	Tyrone
Goodman, George W.	Pvt. K, 79 Pa. Inf.	1837	1916	Oak Ridge	Altoona
Gordon, George C.	Pvt. B, 158 Pa. Inf.			Mt. Zion	Bedford Co.
Gordon, Harry	Pvt. F, 77 Pa. Inf.	1835			
Gordon, Joseph	Pvt. C, 12 Pa. Cav.	1838	1909		Roaring Spring
Gorecht, John M.	Pvt. B, 122 Pa. Inf.		1893	Lancaster	Penna
Gorley, William R.	Pvt. A, 84 Pa. Inf.				
	Cpl. G, 57 Pa. Inf.	1843			
Gorman, Samuel	Pvt. M, 21 Pa. Cav.	1843	1910	Fairview	Altoona
Gorman, Thomas	Pvt. E, 84 Pa. Inf.	1821	1901	Royer Mt.	Williamsburg
Gormand, Frederick	Pvt. D, 19 Pa. Cav.	1844			
Gorsuch, Elijah	Pvt. I, 57 Pa. Inf.	1844	1916	Royer Mt.	Williamsburg
Goshorn, Solomon B.	Pvt. A, 110 Pa. Inf.		1864		
Gosnell, David M.	Pvt. B, 2 Pa. Art.	1845	1930	Presbyterian	Williamsburg
Goss, Adam	Cpl. A, 110 Pa. Inf.	1841	1912	Grandview	Tyrone

Name	Rank Organization	Born	Died	Cemetery	Location
Goss, Elias	Pvt. C, 22 Pa. Cav.				
	Pvt. C, 110 Pa. Inf.	1844	1890	Logan Valley	Bellwood
Goss, Fredrick	Pvt. A, 110 Pa. Inf.	1839	1862	Mt. Zion	Tyrone
Goss, Harrison	Pvt. A, 110 Pa. Inf.				
Goss, Joseph Ritner	Pvt. D, 3 Pa. Inf.				
	Lt. A, 110 Pa. Inf.	1836	1907	Rose Hill	Altoona
Goss, Lloyd	Pvt. E, 45 Pa. Inf.	1842	1927	Logan Valley	Bellwood
Gottshall, Samuel	Pvt. D, 19 Pa. Cav.	1841	1902	Greenwood	Altoona
Gottschall, William H.	Pvt. G, 39 Pa. Mil.	1844	1913	Rose Hill	Altoona
Gowen, Edward					
Grabill, Emanuel	Pvt. F, 77 Pa. Inf.	1845	1865	Galveston	Texas
Grace, Israel	Pvt. L, 102 Pa. Inf.		1889	Marysville	Bedford Co.
Gracey, Daniel	Pvt. K, 21 Pa. Cav.		1922		Indiana
Gracey, George E.	Pvt. H, 107 Pa. Inf.	1845	1911	Fairview	Altoona
Grady, James Stephens	Pvt. E, 104 Pa. Inf.	1837	1912	Grandview	Tyrone
Graering, Levi	Pvt. F, 169 Pa. Inf.				
	Cpl. F, 211 Pa. Inf.	1834	1914	Presbyterian	Williamsburg
Graff, James B.	Sgt. A, 23 Pa. Mil.				
	Pvt. A, Ind. Bn. Pa. Mil.	1842			
Graffius, Christian	Pvt. M, 13 Pa. Cav.	1845	1898	Carson Valley	Duncansville
Graffius, Jonathan	Pvt. D, 13 Pa. Cav.	1841	1864		
Graffius, Josiah	Pvt. D, 13 Pa. Cav.	1842	1865	Salisbury	N. Car.
Graft, William P.	Pvt. A, 3 Pa. Inf.	1835			
Graham, James M.	Pvt. F, 46 Pa. Mil.				
	Cpl. F, 194 Pa. Inf.	1845	1927	East Lawn	Tyrone
Graham, John	Sgt. G, 149 Pa. Inf.		1910	Duncannon	Penna.
Grant, James W.					
Grass, Cephas	Pvt. G, Ind. Bn. Pa. Mil.				
	Pvt. C, 205 Pa. Inf.	1847	1920	Fairview	Martinsburg
Graw, William	Sgt. K, 125 Pa. Inf.				
Gray, George W.	Pvt. I, 55 Pa. Inf.	1829	1900		
Gray, George W.	Pvt. G, 125 Pa. Inf.				
Gray, George W.	Pvt. E, 93 Pa. Inf.				
Gray, John H.	Cpl. I, 55 Pa. Inf.	1838	1906	Warriors Mark	Penna.
Grey, Mercer D.	Pvt. G, I Pa. Cav.	1840	1921	Frankstown	Hollidaysburg
Gray, Milton	Pvt. F, 76 Pa. Inf.	1833			
Gray, Silas	Pvt. F, 76 Pa. Inf.				
	Pvt. C, 46 Pa. Mil.	1841			
Gray, William Y.	Pvt. B, 49 Pa. Inf.	1843	1865	Fairview	Altoona
Grazier, Abnednego	Pvt. B, 192 Pa. Inf.	1831	1895	Grandview	Tyrone
Grazier, John Wesley	Cpl. A, 125 Pa. Inf.	1836	1907	Grazierville	Tyrone
Grazier, Israel	Pvt. B, 13 Pa. Cav.	1834	1906	Asbury	Bellwood
Green, Albert	Pvt. I, 137 Pa. Inf.				
Greene, Alfred	Pvt. Ind. Cav. Pa. Mil.	1838			
Green, Alfred	Pvt. B, 54 Mass. Inf.	1838	1921	Union	Hollidaysburg
Green, Andrew	Pvt. C, 46 Pa. Mil.	1835	1909	Fairview	Altoona
Green, Benjamin F.	Pvt. F, 31 Pa. Inf.				
	Pvt. A, 191 Pa. Inf.	1843	1894	Oak Ridge	Altoona
Green, David M.	Pvt. Ind. Cav. Pa. Mil.	1830	1873	Fairview	Altoona
Greene, Edward S.	Pvt. C, 76 Pa. Inf.	1837			
Greene, Franklin P.	Pvt. B, 46 Pa. Mil.				
	Pvt. D, 205 Pa. Inf.	1835			
Green, James M.	Pvt. 69 N. Y. Inf.	1839	1905	St. Johns	Altoona
Green, John W.	Pvt. G, 12 Pa. Cav.	1842	1932	Logan Valley	Bellwood
Green, Lemuel M.	Pvt. D, 192 Pa. Inf.				
Green, Martin	Pvt. F, 31 Pa. Inf.				
	Pvt. A, 191 Pa. Inf.		1864	Salisbury	N. Car.
Green, Peter	Pvt. K, 201 Pa. Inf.	1833	1906	Oak Ridge	Altoona
Green, Samuel	Pvt. D, 125 Pa. Inf.	1829	1920	Fairview	Altoona
Green, Thomas	Pvt. H, 3 Pa. Inf.				
	Cpl. M, 62 Pa. Inf.	1839			
Green, William	Pvt. A, 125 Pa. Inf.	1845	1905	Fairview	Altoona

THE CIVIL WAR

Name	Rank Organization	Born	Died	Cemetery	Location
Green, William R. T.	Pvt. E, 195 Pa. Inf.		1900	Woodbury Twp.	Bedford Co.
Greenawalt, William	Pvt. F, 77 Pa. Inf.	1844	1897	Shellys	Williamsburg
Greenland, Thomas J.	Cpl. C, 110 Pa. Inf.		1864		
Greenwood, Charles M.	Pvt. F, Ind. Bn. Pa. Mil.	1842			
Greer, Adam J.	Pvt. B, 3 Pa. Inf.				
	Cpl. F, 126 Pa. Inf.	1826	1890	Fairview	Altoona
Gregory, Lewis L.	Pvt. K, 3 Ill. Cav.	1835	1911	Grandview	Tyrone
Gregg, David McMurtrie	Cpt. 6 U. S. Cav.				
	Col. 8 U. S. Cav.				
	Brigadier General	1833	1916	Reading	Penna.
Gregg, James	Pvt. E, 104 Pa. Inf.				
Gregg, John	Pvt. C, 53 Pa. Inf.	1836	1862	Hampton	Virginia
Greiger, William	Pvt. D, 13 Pa. Cav.	1824			
Greist, Leander	Sgt. E, 46 Pa. Mil.	1833			
Grenand, Alfred	Pvt. 54 Mass. Inf.				
Grier, George W.	A. E. U. S. Navy	1842			
Griffin, John	Pvt. C, 3 Pa. Inf.	1839			
Griffin, Russell H.	Pvt. H, 3 Pa. Inf.				
	Cpl. C, 46 Pa. Mil.				
	Sgt. D, 13 Pa. Cav.	1840	1898	Fairview	Altoona
Griffin, Theodore A.	Pvt. C, 46 Pa. Mil.				
	Pvt. D, 13 Pa. Cav.	1837	1866	Fairview	Altoona
Griffith, Abel	Pvt. H, 191 Pa. Inf.			Waterside	Bedford Co.
Griffith, Napoleon B.	Pvt. E, 3 Pa. Inf.				
	Pvt. H, 12 Pa. Cav.	1840	1866	Fairview	Altoona
Grimes, Henry	Pvt. C, 84 Pa. Inf.	1841			
Grimes, Henry	Pvt. A, 84 Pa. Inf.				
Grimes, Jacob	Pvt. C, 84 Pa. Inf.			Liberty Twp.	Bedford Co.
Grimes, Jacob R.	Cpl. C, 205 Pa. Inf.	1841			
Grimes, John C.	Cpl. I, 14 Pa. Inf.				
	Pvt. C, 84 Pa. Inf.	1812	1892	Hickory Bottom	Woodbury
Grogan, Daniel	Pvt. B, 192 Pa. Art.			St. Patricks	Gallitzin
Groom, Amos	Pvt. H, 22 Pa. Cav.	1841			
Groomer, Anthony	Pvt. F, 77 Pa. Inf.	1828		Hopewell	Bedford Co.
Grooms, David	Pvt. H, 14 Pa. Inf.	1826		Carson Valley	Duncansville
Gross, Charles	Pvt. B, 2 Md. Cav.	1838	1891	Grandview	Tyrone
Gross, George D.	Sgt. B, 11 Pa. Cav.	1840	1927	Greenlawn	Roaring Spring
Grossman, Frederick	Pvt. F, 76 Pa. Inf.				
	Pvt. C, 143 Pa. Inf.	1848	1864	Wilderness	Virginia
Grove, Amos	Pvt. I, 14 Pa. Inf.	1830			
Grove, Benjamin H.	Pvt. I, 149 Pa. Inf.		1925	Crafton	Penna.
Grove, Harry	Sgt. D, 46 Pa. Mil.	1838			
Grove, John W.	Pvt. E, 126 Pa. Inf.	1845	1911	Fairview	Altoona
Grove, Joseph	Pvt. D, 1 Pa. Art.	1832			
Grove, Samuel D.	Bug. K, 22 Pa. Cav.	1846			
Grove, William	Pvt. D, 192 Pa. Inf.	1841	1914	Carson Valley	Duncansville
Growden, Joseph	Pvt. C, 45 Pa. Inf.	1834	1901		Bedford Co.
Gruber, George S.	Pvt. C, 176 Pa. Inf.	1831	1911	Fairview	Martinsburg
Guestwhite, Peter	Pvt. F, 56 Pa. Inf.	1809	1898	Fairview	Altoona
Gummo, Edward R.	Pvt. F, 12 Pa. Cav.	1844	1920	Fairview	Altoona
Gummo, John W.	Pvt. F, 12 Pa. Cav.	1843	1912	Rose Hill	Altoona
Gunkle, Joseph	Pvt. E, 3 Pa. Inf.	1840			
Gunnet, Thomas	Pvt. F, 77 Pa. Inf.	1834	1913	Royer Mt.	Williamsburg
Gunter, Abraham S.	Pvt. E, 20 Pa. Cav.	1838	1908	Grandview	Tyrone
Gushman, William	Pvt. E, 104 Pa. Inf.				
Gutshall, George	Pvt. G, 202 Pa. Inf.	1840	1899	Fairview	Altoona
Guyer, Thomas S.	2Lt. I, 34 Pa. Inf.				
Guyer, William	1Lt. K, 9 Pa. Cav.	1833	1891	Fairview	Altoona
Gwin, Alexander C.	Pvt. B, 3 Pa. Inf.				
	Sgt. F, 76 Pa. Inf.	1836	1863	Morris Island	S. Car.
Gwin, George H.	Pvt. B, 3 Pa. Inf.				
	1Lt. F, 76 Pa. Inf.	1832	1914	Fairview	Altoona

Name	Rank Organization	Born	Died	Cemetery	Location
Gwin, James A.	Sgt. F, 76 Pa. Inf.	1838	1911	Asbury	Bellwood
Gwin, Maxwell	Pvt. K, 76 Pa. Inf.	1834	1901	Maurers	Altoona
Gwinn, William M.	2Lt. C, 84 Pa. Inf.				
Gwin, William W.	Pvt. G, 12 Pa. Cav.	1844	1891	Lutheran	Newry
Gwinner, George C.	Cpt. A, 205 Pa. Inf.				
Hackenberg, James W.	Sgt. D, 131 Pa. Inf.		1862	Frederick	Maryland
Hackett, Robert S.	Pvt. K, 46 Pa. Mil.	1821			
Haddell, William	Pvt. K, 1 Md. Inf.	1843			
Haderman, Matthew J.	Cpl. C, 205 Pa. Inf.	1846			
Hads, Henry J.	1Lt. G, 11 Pa. Cav.	1844			
Hadsdan, William	Pvt. 45, 2 Bn. Vet. Res.	1832	1918	Huntingdon	Huntingdon Co.
Haffley, David S.		1827	1892	Deihl	Henrietta
Hagen, Henry J.	Smn. U. S. Navy	1828	1919	Calvary	Altoona
Hagans, John	Pvt. D, 125 Pa. Inf.				
Hagans, John	Pvt. D, 205, Pa. Inf.	1831			
Hagerty, David	Pvt. B, 1 Pa. Art.	1841			
Haggerty, Jacob C.	Cpl. L, 3 Pa. Art.	1839	1915	Fairview	Altoona
Hagerty, Joseph	Pvt. A, 107 Pa. Inf.	1812	1868	Grandview	Tyrone
Hagerty, Joseph D.	Pvt. F, 76 Pa. Inf.	1846	1864	Petersburg	Virginia
Hagerty, Luther Calvin	Pvt. D, 110 Pa. Inf.	1850	1899	Antis	Bellwood
Haggerty W.					
Haines, Charles M.	Sgt. A, 22 Pa. Cav.	1842	1907	Oak Ridge	Altoona
Haines, David W.	Pvt. G, 208 Pa. Inf.	1837	1914	Newport	Penna.
Haines, Edward R.	Pvt. B, 77 Pa. Inf.	1847			
Hains, Franklin M.	Cpl. F, 1 Pa. Art.	1839	1919	Fairview	Altoona
Hanes, Rudolph	Pvt. A, 45 Pa. Inf.	1835	1899	Presbyterian	Hollidaysburg
Hains, William R.	Pvt. M, 9 Pa. Cav.	1843	1910	Fairview	Altoona
Hainley, Christian F.	Pvt. C, 76 Pa. Inf.	1843	1900	Greenlawn	Roaring Spring
Hanley, David S.	Pvt. E, 125 Pa. Inf.				
	Sgt. B, 192 Pa. Inf.	1827	1880	Sharpsburg	Roaring Spring
Hainley, John D.	Pvt. B, 208 Pa. Inf.				
Hanley, John S.	Pvt. C, 205 Pa. Inf.	1843			
Hanley, Samuel H.	Pvt. L, 19 Pa. Cav.	1838	1909	Greenlawn	Roaring Spring
Hainzey, Adam	Cpl. C, 76 Pa. Inf.	1840			
Hainsey, Frederick	Sgt. I, 55 Pa. Inf.	1841	1920	Geeseytown	Hollidaysburg
Hainsey, George	Pvt. H, 14 Pa. Inf.	1840			
Hainsey, George	Pvt. C, 76 Pa. Inf.	1838	1903	Greenlawn	Roaring Spring
Hainsey, Henry					
Hainsey, John	Pvt. C, 76 Pa. Inf.	1837	1915	Greenlawn	Roaring Spring
Hainsey, Valentine	Pvt. I, 55 Pa. Inf.				
	Pvt. A, 188 Pa. Inf.		1864	Sarah Furnace	Claysburg
Halderman, Baltzer	Pvt. D, 20 Pa. Cav.	1838	1905	Rose Hill	Altoona
Hale, Henry	Pvt. C, 76 Pa. Inf.	1827	1908	Rose Hill	Altoona
Hale, Henry	Pvt. E, 125 Pa. Inf.				
Hale, Samuel	Pvt. E, 84 Pa. Inf.				
	Pvt. I, 57 Pa. Inf.	1843	1887	Methodist	Williamsburg
Hale, William H.	Pvt. I, 55 Pa. Inf.	1837	1913	Albright	Roaring Spring
Halfpenny, John I.	Pvt. K, 7 Pa. Cav.	1845	1862	National	Nashville, Ten.
Halk, Henry	Pvt. C, 17 Pa. Cav.	1843	1922	Riverview	Huntingdon
Hall, Adolphus	Pvt. B, 3 Pa. Inf.				
	Pvt. F, 31 Pa. Inf.	1811			
Hall, Edward Samuel	Pvt. K, 125 Pa. Inf.				
	Sgt. G, Pa. Mil.	1843	1900	Fairview	Altoona
Hall, George M.	Pvt. H, 14 Pa. Inf.				
	Pvt. C, 76 Pa. Inf.				
	Pvt. Ind. Bn. Pa. Mil.				
	Pvt. A, 205 Pa. Inf.	1838	1914	Oak Ridge	Altoona
Hall, George W.	Pvt. G, 12 Pa. Cav.	1842	1910	Calvary	Altoona
Hall, James	Pvt. H, 37 Pa. Inf.	1841	1914	Fairview	Altoona
Hall, John	Pvt. G, Ind. Bn. Pa. Mil.	1845			
Hall, John	Pvt. G, 125 Pa. Inf.				
Hall, John	Pvt. D, 13 Pa. Cav.	1843			

Name	Rank Organization	Born	Died	Cemetery	Location
Hall, William D.	Pvt. K, 17 Pa. Inf.				
	2Lt. I, 1 N.Y. Cav.	1845	1897	Oak Ridge	Altoona
Hall, William E.	Sgn. 54 Pa. Inf.				
Haller, David	Pvt. A, 101 Pa. Inf.	1835	1915	Fairview	Altoona
Halliwell, John J.	Pvt. B, 202 Pa. Inf.	1843	1901	Fairview	Altoona
Halloran, Michael M.	Pvt. H, 3 Pa. Inf.				
	Pvt. M, 62 Pa. Inf.	1846	1908	St. Johns	Altoona
Halloran, Stephen	Mus. E, 84 Pa. Inf.		1895	Point Pleasant	Virginia
Hallowell, Robert A.	Pvt. I, 49 Pa. Inf.	1840	1891	Logan Valley	Bellwood
Halpan, James	Pvt. A, 84 Pa. Inf.				
Halpin, Patrick	Pvt. A, 23 Pa. Mil.	1828			
Halsep, George J.	Pvt. F, 31 Pa. Inf.		1864	Andersonville	Georgia
Ham, Robert	Pvt. H, 3 Pa. Inf.				
	Pvt. C, 76 Pa. Inf.				
Hamer, Alexander		1827	1868	Hanibal	Mo.
Hamer, John	Pvt. D, 1 Pa. Art.	1844			
Hamilton, Asbury W.	Pvt. I, 29 Pa. Inf.	1847	1904	Fairview	Altoona
Hamilton, Baxter	Pvt. G, 205 Pa. Inf.	1845	1925	Greenlawn	Roaring Spring
Hamilton, Charles H.	Pvt. G, 12 Pa. Cav.	1845			
Hamilton, David	Pvt. H, 103 Pa. Inf.	1824	1897	Royer Mt.	Williamsburg
Hamilton, Essington, K.	Pvt. C, 205 Pa. Inf.	1845	1903	Fairview	Altoona
Hamilton, George	Pvt. B, 3 Pa. Inf.	1843			
Hamilton, George H.	Pvt. F, 201 Pa. Inf.	1840			
Hamilton, Hugh	Pvt. D, 1 Pa. Art.				
Hamilton, Isaac T.	Maj. 110 Pa. Inf.				
Hamilton, J. C.	Pvt. A, 12 Pa. Cav.	1837			
Hamilton, James	Cpt. C, 110 Pa. Inf.	1845			
Hamilton, John	Pvt. M, 62 Pa. Inf.				
	Pvt. K, 91 Pa. Inf.		1864	Petersburg	Virginia
Hamilton, John C.	Pvt. C, 110 Pa. Inf.				
Hamilton, Joseph Smith	Pvt. H, 110 Pa. Inf.	1844	1863	Fairview	Altoona
Hamilton, Mahlon B.	Cpl. H, 14 Pa. Inf.	1830			
	Pvt. I, 55 Pa. Inf.				
Hamilton, Milton H.	Pvt. A, 87 Pa. Inf.	1845	1889	Fairview	Altoona
Hamilton, William H.	Pvt. K, 187 Pa. Inf.			Logan Valley	Bellwood
Hamilton, William L.	Pvt. A, 38 Pa. Mil.	1831	1900	Rose Hill	Altoona
Hamlin, James S.	Pvt. E, 201 Pa. Inf.		1891	Fairview	Altoona
Hamm, David K.	Pvt. C, 205 Pa. Inf.			Hopewell	Bedford Co.
Hamm, John K.	Pvt. C, 205 Pa. Inf.		1902	Carson Valley	Duncansville
Hammaker, Adam Curtis	Cpl. B, 12 Md. Inf.	1845	1935	Rose Hill	Altoona
Hammaker, Peter	Pvt. B, 12 Md. Inf.	1847	1919	Rose Hill	Altoona
Hamel, Alfred Henry	Pvt. F, 77 Pa. Inf.	1848	1934	Rose Hill	Altoona
Hammel, Peter S.	Pvt. E, 54 Pa. Inf.	1841	1861	Sarah Furnace	Claysburg
Hammers, Martin	Pvt. E, 54 Pa. Inf.	1829	1891	Oak Ridge	Altoona
Hammill, Samuel Royer					
	Col. Q. M. Corps	1840	1881	Royer Mt.	Williamsburg
Hammond, Edward	Pvt. H, 14 Pa. Inf.	1833			
Hammond, Edwin	Sgt. D, 125 Pa. Inf.				
Hammond, Essington	Sgt. A, 23 Pa. Mil.	1828			
Hammond, Greenbury	Pvt. H, 14 Pa. Inf.	1841			
Hamor, James J.	Pvt. H, 14 Pa. Inf.				
	Pvt. G, 125 Pa. Inf.	1838	1894	Riverview	Huntingdon
Hampson, Solomon C.	Pvt. M, 9 Pa. Cav.	1843	1864	Louisville	Kentucky
Hancuff, Thomas W.	Pvt. E, 84 Pa. Inf.	1827	1862	Yellow Spring	Williamsburg
Hand, James	Pvt. I, 55 Pa. Inf.				
	Pvt. M, 1 U.S. Art.	1825	1908	Calvary	Altoona
Haney, Patrick	Pvt. D, 125 Pa. Inf.				
Haney, Patrick	Pvt. D, 125 Pa. Inf.				
Hanlon, John	Pvt. A, 55 Pa. Inf.	1825	1894	St. Johns	Altoona
Hanna, John	Pvt. C, 53 Pa. Inf.	1843	1861	Military	Washington, D. C.

SOLDIERS OF BLAIR COUNTY

Name	Rank Organization	Born	Died	Cemetery	Location
Hanna, Matthew	Pvt. M, 62 Pa. Inf.				
	Pvt. K, 91 Pa. Inf.				
Hannah, Robert F.	Pvt. I, 205 Pa. Inf.	1846	1926	Burkets	Warriors Mark
Happersett, John C. G.	Maj. U. S. Army		1893		
Harbaugh, Alley	Pvt. I, 205 Pa. Inf.	1846			
Harbaugh, Jason	Pvt. A, 84 Pa. Inf.			Pleasantville	Bedford Co.
Harbaugh, John	Pvt. C, 205 Pa. Inf.	1845			
Harbaugh, William H.	Pvt. A, 84 Pa. Inf.			Pleasantville	Bedford Co.
Harber, George	Cpl. I, 117 Ill. Inf.	1844	1902	St. Augustine	Cambria Co.
Harbison, Andrew K.	Sgt. C, 46 Pa. Mil.	1830			
Harding, James	Cpl. H, 110 Pa. Inf.				
Hardman, William H.	Pvt. D, 65 N. Y. Vol.	1842	1916	Rose Hill	Altoona
Hardwick, William	Pvt. G, 12 Ind. Art.				
Hardy, Daniel	Pvt. D, 131 Pa. Inf.	1837	1906	Grandview	Tyrone
Hardy, Samuel E.	Pvt. C, 45 Pa. Inf.	1843	1908	Grandview	Tyrone
Hardy, William H.	Pvt. D, 192 Pa. Inf.	1830	1912	Oak Ridge	Altoona
Hare, Adam L.	Pvt. D, 1 Pa. Inf.				
	Pvt. A, 1 U. S. Cav.				
	Pvt. E, 3 U. S. Art.				
	Pvt. D, 1 Mich. Inf.	1847	1911	Presbyterian	Hollidaysburg
Hare, Henry	Pvt. K, 210 Pa. Inf.	1848	1922	Holsingers	Bakers Summit
Hare, John F.	Pvt. I, 137 Pa. Inf.				
Hare, Samuel L.	Cpl. E, 84 Pa. Inf.				
	Cpl. I, 57 Pa. Inf.	1841	1916	Rose Hill	Altoona
Hare, William	Pvt. G, 57 Pa. Inf.	1837			
Harker, Andrew	Pvt. D, 205 Pa. Inf.	1831	1888	Royer Mt.	Williamsburg
Harkins, Albert	Pvt. D, 22 Pa. Cav.	1842			
Harkins, Patrick P.	Pvt. E, 84 Pa. Inf.				
Harklerode, A. H.	Pvt. E, 125 Pa. Inf.				
Harklerode, David	Pvt. E, 125 Pa. Inf.			Everett	Penna.
Harklerode, Henry	Atr. D, 1 Pa. Art.	1831			
Harkness, Albert	Pvt. Ind. Cav. Pa. Mil.	1842			
	Pvt. D, 22 Pa. Cav.				
Harkness, Charles S.	Pvt. A, 36 Pa. Inf.	1842	1891	Oak Ridge	Altoona
Harkness, William H.	Pvt. A, 36 Pa. Inf.	1821	1884	Oak Ridge	Altoona
Harlin, Joseph	1Lt. C, 76 Pa. Inf.	1831	1913	Lutheran	Newry
Harmon, Newton	Pvt. I, 190 Pa. Inf.				
Harn, David K.	Pvt. C, 205 Pa. Inf.	1832			
Harn, John K.	Pvt. C, 205 Pa. Inf.	1834			
Harnden, John B.	Pvt. D, 49 Pa. Inf.				
	Pvt. K, 1 Pa. Cav.	1841	1938	Rose Hill	Altoona
Harnish, John			1863	Chancellorsville	Virginia
Harnish, John	Pvt. C, 3 Pa. Inf.	1828			
Harnish, John W.	Pvt. L, 13 Pa. Cav.	1843	1929	Presbyterian	Hollidaysburg
Harnish, Samuel C.	Pvt. M, 92 Pa. Inf.	1824	1899	Keller Reform	Williamsburg
Harold, Jacob	Pvt. F, 77 Pa. Inf.	1834			
Harper, Samuel G.	Pvt. H, 110 Pa. Inf.	1846	1864	Grandview	Tyrone
Harpham, Hugh T.	1Lt. E, 184 Pa. Inf.	1826	1899	Oak Ridge	Altoona
Harpster, Enoch H.	Pvt. I, 3 Pa. Art.	1835	1905	Lutheran	Newry
Harpster, George W.	Pvt. I, 22 Pa. Cav.	1844			
Harpster, William	Pvt. M, 9 Pa. Cav.	1840	1865	Florence	S. Car.
Harrington, John	Smn. U. S. Navy	1843	1902	Antis	Bellwood
Harris, Daniel	Pvt. F, 53 Pa. Inf.	1837	1892	Soldiers Home	Erie
Harris, George H.	Pvt. A, 23 Pa. Mil.	1838			
Harris, John	Pvt. M, 9 Pa. Cav.	1843			
Harris, Robert	Pvt. B, 22 Pa. Cav.	1839			
Harris, Samuel O.	Pvt. E, 3 Pa. Art.		1875	Keagy	Woodbury
Harrison, Andrew S.	Pvt. F, 19 Pa. Cav.	1843	1911	Rose Hill	Altoona
Harrison, John T.	Pvt. 3 Wis. Inf.	1840			
Harshbarger, William	Pvt. I, 205 Pa. Inf.	1839			
Hart, Ellis	Sgt. I, 84 Pa. Inf.	1820	1904	Carson Valley	Duncansville
Hart, Israel	Pvt. G, 205 Pa. Inf.			Grandview	Huntingdon

THE CIVIL WAR

Name	Rank Organization	Born	Died	Cemetery	Location
Hart, Jonathan	Pvt. A, 125 Pa. Inf.			Bellwood	Penna.
Hart, Joseph	Pvt. D, 192 Pa. Inf.	1826	1900	St. Marys	Hollidaysburg
Hart, Peter S.	Pvt. I, 84 Pa. Inf.				
	Pvt. K, 57 Pa. Inf.	1842	1921	Oak Ridge	Altoona
Hart, Thomas	Pvt. C, 110 Pa. Inf.				
Hartle, John B.	Pvt. B, 99 Pa. Inf.			Mt. Zion	Bedford Co.
Hartman, George L.	Cpl. C, 110 Pa. Inf.		1863	Chancellorsville	Virginia
Hartman, John P. C.	Pvt. C, 110 Pa. Inf.	1840	1900	Greenlawn	Roaring Spring
Hartman, Samuel	Pvt. B, 55 Pa. Inf.	1834	1903	St. Patricks	Gallitzin
Hartsock, John S.	Pvt. C, 46 Pa. Mil.	1843			
Hartsock, Joseph F.	Pvt. K, 8 Mich. Inf.	1833	1899	Oak Ridge	Altoona
Hartz, Frank	Pvt. G, U. S. Inf.	1845	1896	Methodist	Williamsburg
Hartzell, David R.	Pvt. Ind. Cav. Pa. Mil.				
	Sgt. 22 Pa. Cav.	1828			
Hartzell, Solomon	Pvt. A, 205 Pa. Inf.	1829	1894	Fairview	Altoona
Harvey, David P.	Sgt. B, 110 Pa. Inf.				
	Cpl. F, 19 Pa. Cav.		1892	Shirleysburg	Huntingdon
Harvey, Robert B.	Pvt. B, 110 Pa. Inf.				
	Pvt. F, 19 Pa. Cav.	1844			
Harvey, Thomas	Pvt. D, 58 Pa. Inf.	1829	1888	Oak Ridge	Altoona
Harvey, William	Pvt. I, 41 Pa. Inf.	1813	1908	Fairview	Altoona
Harwood, Richard	Pvt. C, 110 Pa. Inf.				
Haryman, Adam	Cpt. G, 12 Pa. Cav.				
Haslet, G. M.	Pvt. E, 76 Pa. Inf.			Mt. Sinai	Blue Knob
Haslett, James	Pvt. G, 14 Pa. Mil.			Fairview	Altoona
Haslett, James	Pvt. H, 110 Pa. Inf.	1820	1893	Leechburg	Penna.
Haslett, John	Pvt. A, 61 Pa. Inf.	1820	1903	Carson Valley	Duncansville
Haslett, Stephen V.	Mus. A, 125 Pa. Inf.				
	Mus. E, 46 Pa. Mil.	1847	1881	Grandview	Tyrone
Hastings, Joseph	Pvt. D, 1 Pa. Art.	1846			
Hastings, William	Pvt. I, 22 Pa. Cav.	1845			
Hasty, William	Cpl. A, Ind. Bn. Pa. Mil.	1831			
Hatfield, William	Pvt. D, 22 Pa. Cav.	1845			
Haughawout, B. S.	Pvt. F, 149 Pa. Inf.	1845			
Haun, Augustus	Pvt. D, 1 Pa. Art.				
Haupt, L. Allison	Pvt. H, 2 Pa. Inf.				
	Sgt. E, Ind. Bn. Pa. Mil.	1839	1920	Grandview	Tyrone
Havens, John	Pvt. D, 205 Pa. Inf.	1846	1919	Grandview	Tyrone
Hawk, Henry	Cpl. I, 137 Pa. Inf.				
	1Lt. I, 205 Pa. Inf.	1834	1928	Fairview	Altoona
Hawk, Norval F.	Pvt. I, 11 Pa. Inf.	1840	1900	Greenwood	Altoona
Hawksworth, Francis A.	Pvt. D, 46 Pa. Mil.	1845			
Hawksworth, George H.	2Lt. D, 125 Pa. Inf.				
Hawksworth, George W.	Pvt. H, 3 Pa. Inf.				
	Sgt. F, 76 Pa. Inf.				
	Sgt. U. S. Signal Corps	1840	1916	Fairview	Altoona
Hawksworth, Thomas A.	Cpl. C, 46 Pa. Mil.	1832			
Hawn, Albert	Pvt. D, 205 Pa. Inf.	1841			
Hawn, Samuel	Pvt. D, 205 Pa. Inf.	1844			
Hay, J. Y.				Asbury	Altoona
Hayden, Patrick	Pvt. H, 110 Pa. Inf.		1863		
Hays, Alexander Y.	Pvt. C, 110 Pa. Inf.				
Hays, David Sterret	Sgn. 110 Pa. Inf.	1833	1898	Presbyterian	Hollidaysburg
Hayes, James W.	Pvt. C, 205 Pa. Inf.	1833	1915	Greenlawn	Roaring Spring
Hays, Samuel	Sgt. 14 U. S. Inf.				
Hayes, Samuel B.	Pvt. B, 110 Pa. Inf.				
	Pvt. G, 51 Pa. Inf.	1841	1896	Grandview	Tyrone
Hazzard, George W.	Pvt. D, 49 Pa. Inf.				
Heard, Thomas W.	Pvt. A, 125 Pa. Inf.				
Hearn, Servedas	Pvt. C, 125 Pa. Inf.			Schmuckers	Williamsburg
Hearn, James A.	Pvt. C, 205 Pa. Inf.	1841			
Heatter, George					

SOLDIERS OF BLAIR COUNTY

Name	Rank Organization	Born	Died	Cemetery	Location
Heater, John	Pvt. A, 28 Pa. Inf.			Replogles	Woodbury
Heck, George W.	Pvt. E, 101 Pa. Inf.	1849	1930	Mifflintown	Penna.
Heckman, Sylvester	Pvt. I, 22 Pa. Cav.		1892	Oak Ridge	Altoona
Hedden, Joseph	Pvt. G, 60 N. Y. Inf.	1837	1912	Oak Ridge	Altoona
Hedding, Samuel E.	Pvt. H, 3 Md. Inf.	1846	1914	Rose Hill	Altoona
Heffner, Daniel	Pvt. D, 1 Pa. Art.	1844			
Heffner, George	Pvt. D, 1 Pa. Art.	1845			
Heffner, Jacob	Pvt. C, 53 Pa. Inf.	1830	1864	City Point	Virginia
Heidler, George D.	Cpl. C, 22 Pa. Cav.	1845			
Helfrick, Aaron Sipe	Pvt. D, 74 Pa. Inf.	1846	1934	Rose Hill	Altoona
Heller, Augustus E.	Sgt. C, 49 Pa. Inf.	1824	1914	Fairview	Altoona
Heller, Edward	Pvt. H, 22 Pa. Cav.	1844			
Heller, Edward W.	Pvt. B, 125 Pa. Inf.	1841	1882	Fairview	Altoona
Heller, John A.	Pvt. C, 53 Pa. Inf.				
	Pvt. A, 4 Pa. Art.	1842	1902	Greenwood	Altoona
Helwig, John	Pvt. M, 22 Pa. Cav.				
Hellwig, John L.	Sgt. G, 125 Pa. Inf.				
Hellwig, John J.	Pvt. A, 3 Pa. Inf.	1839			
Helm, Edward	Pvt. C, 110 Pa. Inf.				
Helsel, Edward	Pvt. C, 76 Pa. Inf.	1843		Hopewell	Bedford Co.
Helsel, George L.	Pvt. C, 53 Pa. Inf.	1822	1894	Lutheran	Newry
Helsel, Henry S. (m)	Pvt. G, 3 Pa. Inf.				
	Pvt. E, 76 Pa. Inf.	1826	1914	Mt. Moriah	Blue Knob
Helsel, John F.	Pvt. A, 54 Pa. Inf.	1844	1919	St. Patricks	Newry
Helsel, Joseph	Pvt. G, 12 Pa. Cav.	1841	1921	Mt. Moriah	Blue Knob
Helsel, William	Cpl. A, 54 Pa. Inf.	1836	1912	Logan Valley	Bellwood
Heltzel, George L.	Pvt. C, 53 Pa. Inf.	1842			
Heltzel, Jonathon D.	Pvt. C, 110 Pa. Inf.		1864	Wilderness	Virginia
Hemler, Joseph H.	Pvt. A, 84 Pa. Inf.				
Hemminger, Abraham O.	Pvt. H, 3 Prov. Cav.			Mt. Olivet	Bedford Co.
Hempfield, George	Pvt. B, 3 Pa. Inf.				
	Pvt. F, 76 Pa. Inf.	1842			
Hempfield, J. Dysart	Pvt. A, 23 Pa. Mil.				
	Pvt. B, Ind. Bn. Pa. Mil.				
	Pvt. H, 110 Pa. Inf.	1846	1939	Presbyterian	Hollidaysburg
Hemphill, Thomas W.	Pvt. E, 104 Pa. Inf.				
Hench, Frederick	Pvt. F, 76 Pa. Inf.	1843	1862	Hilton Head	So. Carolina
Hench, Henry H.	Pvt. H, 110 Pa. Inf.	1847	1903	Greenwood	Altoona
Henschey, David C.	Pvt. A, Ind. Bn. Pa. Mil.	1845			
Henshey, John B.	Pvt. H, 3 Pa. Inf.				
	Pvt. M, 62 Pa. Inf.				
	Sgt. C, 46 Pa. Mil.	1841	1871	Alto Reste	Hollidaysburg
Henchey, John F.	Pvt. A, 110 Pa. Inf.	1842			
Henchey, John T.	Pvt. E, 46 Pa. Mil.	1843			
Henshey, Samuel A.	Pvt. A, 125 Pa. Inf.		1862	Harpers Ferry	West Virginia
Henshey, Thomas C.	Cpl. D, 3 Pa. Inf.	1835	1908	Fairview	Altoona
Henshey, Thomas J.	Pvt. H, 3 Pa. Inf.				
	Cpl. M, 62 Pa. Inf.	1841	1864		
Hendershot, John W.	Cpl. A, 125 Pa. Inf.				
	Cpl. H, 22 Pa. Cav.	1840	1892	Bald Eagle	Tyrone
Hendershot, Isaac	Pvt. F, 28 Pa. Inf.				
Hendershot, Andrew	Cpl. K, 22 Pa. Cav.	1830			
Henderson, John A.	Pvt. H, 110 Pa. Inf.				
Henderson, John W. D.	Pvt. 49 Pa. Inf.	1840	1912	Malvern	Chester Co.
Henderson, Joseph	Pvt. F, 84 Pa. Inf.	1835	1911	Presbyterian	Williamsburg
Henderson, Samuel T.	Pvt. H, 110 Pa. Inf.	1821	1880	Grandview	Tyrone
Henderson, William	Pvt. H, 14 Pa. Inf.	1824			
Henderson, William	Pvt. C, 76 Pa. Inf.	1844			
Henderson, Wm. Thomas	Pvt. B, 192 Pa. Inf.	1843	1931	Grandview	Tyrone
Hengst, Daniel	Pvt. G, 11 Pa. Cav.	1837	1903	Presbyterian	Hollidaysburg
Henry, Daniel B.	Cpl. I, 55 Pa. Inf.	1841			
Henry, John	Sgt. B, 22 Pa. Cav.			Hetrick	Woodbury

THE CIVIL WAR 205

Name	Rank Organization	Born	Died	Cemetery	Location
Henry, John	Pvt. D, 1 Pa. Art.	1846			
Henry, Russell R.	Pvt. I, 137 Pa. Inf.				
Henry, Samuel	1Lt. H, 21 Pa. Cav.	1843			
Hensel, Charles H.	Pvt. D, 165 Pa. Inf.	1841	1899	Fairview	Altoona
Herman, Moses	Pvt. A, 125 Pa. Inf.				
Herr, Henry	Pvt. B, 110 Pa. Inf.				Houtzdale
Herr, Samuel	Sgt. M, 62 Pa. Inf.	1835	1902	Fairview	Altoona
Herrick, George	Sgt. K, 110 Pa. Inf.	1820	1863	National	Gettysburg
Herrington, James T.	Pvt. H, 149 Pa. Inf.	1838	1922		Osceola Mills
Hershell, Anthony	Pvt. B, 208 Pa. Inf.	1837	1892	Royer Mountain	Williamsburg
Hershell, Lemuel	Pvt. B, 208 Pa. Inf.		1865	Petersburg	Virginia
Hershey, John B.	Sgt. C, 46 Pa. Mil.				
Hershey, John R.	Pvt. A, 1 Pa. Res. Cav.	1840	1925	Riverview	Huntingdon
Hertzler, Abraham	Pvt. C, 84 Pa. Inf.	1843			
Hesley, Abraham	Pvt. M, 9 Pa. Cav.	1844	1912	Warriors Mark	Penna.
Hess, David L.	Pvt. C, 2 Pa. Inf.	1833	1901	Oak Ridge	Altoona
Hess, Frederick C.	Cpl. G, 57 Pa. Inf.	1843			
Hess, James M.	Pvt. D, 46 Pa. Mil.	1848			
Hess, Samuel		1837			
Hesser, Frederick	Cpl. Ind. Cav. Pa. Mil.	1832			
Hetrick, George G.	Pvt. M, 19 Pa. Cav.		1903	Methodist	Marklesburg
Hetrick, Michael	Pvt. B, 208 Pa. Inf.	1834	1898	Salem Reform	Williamsburg
Houston, Joseph	Pvt. C, 12 Pa. Cav.	1838	1909	Greenlawn	Roaring Spring
Houston, William H.	Pvt. B, 192 Pa. Inf.	1844	1926	Greenlawn	Roaring Spring
Heverly, Chas. W.	Pvt. A, 110 Pa. Inf.			Grandview	Tyrone
Heverly, Henry	Pvt. I, 57 Pa. Inf.	1833			
Heverly, Jacob F.	Pvt. F, 2 Pa. Cav.	1835	1905	Grandview	Tyrone
Heverly, Samuel J.	Pvt. A, 110 Pa. Inf.	1840	1862	Grandview	Tyrone
Heverly, William	Pvt. E, 125 Pa. Inf.		1891	Grandview	Tyrone
Heverly, William	Pvt. C, 22 Pa. Cav.	1844			
Hewit, Benjamin L.	Pvt. A, 23 Pa. Mil.				
	Pvt. A, Ind. Bn. Pa. Mil.				
	Mjr. Paymaster	1833	1894	Presbyterian	Hollidaysburg
Hewitt, Calvin C.	Pvt. C, 3 Pa. Inf.				
	Mus. B, 125 Pa. Inf.				
	1Lt. B, 208 Pa. Inf.	1845	1873	Presbyterian	Williamsburg
Hewit, Henry H.	Pvt. G, 125 Pa. Inf.				
	Cpl. A, Ind. Bn. Pa. Mil.				
	Cpl. C, 76 Pa. Inf.	1844			
Hewitt, Robert		1828			
Hewitt, Thomas R.	Pvt. M, 62 Pa. Inf.	1845	1863	Presbyterian	Hollidaysburg
Hewit, William G.	Pvt. G, 125 Pa. Inf.	1842	1921	Presbyterian	Hollidaysburg
Heyser, Jacob	Pvt. Ind. Cav. Pa. Mil.	1824			
Hickey, Michael	Pvt. F, Ind. Bn. Pa. Mil.	1842			
Hickman, John P.	Frn. U. S. Navy	1836	1904	Calvary	Altoona
Hickman, Sylvester	Pvt. I, 22 Pa. Cav.	1834	1892	Calvary	Altoona
Hicks, Alexander C.	Pvt. C, 3 Pa. Inf.	1842			
Hicks, Alfred	Cpt. C, 76 Pa. Inf.	1838	1916	Pittsburgh	Penna.
Hicks, Daniel	Sgt. E, 46 Pa. Mil.				
Hicks, Daniel	Sgt. C, 19 Pa. Cav.	1846			
Hicks, Daniel A.	Pvt. A, 125 Pa. Inf.	1845	1911	Logan Valley	Bellwood
Hicks, Daniel B.	Mus. H, 14 Pa. Inf.	1835	1915	Carson Valley	Duncansville
Hick, David	Pvt. U, 205 Pa. Inf.	1831			
Hicks, George W.	Pvt. D, 177 Pa. Inf.	1843			
Hicks, Jackson	Pvt. C, 110 Pa. Inf.				
Hicks, James	Pvt. I, 1 Pa. Art.	1843			
Hicks, John	Pvt. B, 2 Pa. Inf.	1823	1894	Presbyterian	Williamsburg
Hicks, John	Sgt. L, I Md. Cav.	1839	1925	Carson Valley	Duncansville
Hicks, John Calvin	Pvt. D, 41 Pa. Inf.				
	Pvt. E, 190 Pa. Inf.	1837	1907	Rose Hill	Altoona
Hicks, John G.	Pvt. K, 22 Pa. Cav.	1845			
Hicks, John J.	Pvt. K, 3 Pa. Inf.	1844	1923	Orbisonia	Penna.

Name	Rank Organization	Born	Died	Cemetery	Location
Hicks, John K.	Pvt. D, 1 Pa. Art.		1865		
Hicks, John W.	1Lt. I, 3 Pa. Inf.				
	Col. 76 Pa. Inf.	1836	1867	Carson Valley	Duncansville
Hicks, Jonathan	Pvt. K, 78 Pa. Inf.	1849	1920	Fairview	Altoona
Hicks, Josiah D.	Pvt. K, 125 Pa. Inf.				
	Sgt. C, 46 Pa. Mil.				
	1Lt. G, Pa. Mil.	1844	1923	Fairview	Altoona
Hicks, Owen	Pvt. C, 7 Ohio Inf.				
	Sgt. B, 5 Ohio Inf.				
Hicks, Philemon N.	Pvt. G, 125 Pa. Inf.				
	1Lt. 76 Pa. Inf.	1844	1907	Glenlock	Kansas
Hicks, Philemon N.	Pvt. C, 76 Pa. Inf.	1825	1901	Fairview	Martinsburg
Hicks, Thomas J.	Pvt. D, 205 Pa. Inf.	1847	1923	Presbyterian	Williamsburg
Hicks, William	Pvt. H, 3 Pa. Inf.	1829			
Hicks, William	Pvt. B, 192 Pa. Inf.	1848	1919	Grandview	Tyrone
Higgins, Jacob C. (M)	Cpt. Q. M. Corps				
	Col. 1 Pa. Cav.				
	Col. 125 Pa. Inf.				
	Col. Pa. Mil.				
	Col. 22 Pa. Cav.	1826	1893	Grandview	Johnstown
Higgins, Joseph R.	1Lt. B, 125 Pa. Inf.	1817	1882	Lutheran	Williamsburg
High, William	Pvt. F, 5 Pa. Cav.	1829	1891	Collinsville	Altoona
Higo, Peter	Cpl. F, 205 Pa. Inf.			Alto Reste	Hollidaysburg
Hikes, George W.	Pvt. D, 1 Pa. Art.		1932	Calvary	Altoona
Hileman, Aaron G.	Pvt. I, 137 Pa. Inf.	1840	1862	Frankstown	Hollidaysburg
Hileman, Adolphus P.	Pvt. A, 13 Pa. Cav.	1830	1874	Fairview	Altoona
Hileman, Albert	Pvt. I, 137 Pa. Inf.	1838	1892	Presbyterian	Hollidaysburg
Hileman, James	Pvt. K, 202 Pa. Inf.	1832	1897	Oak Ridge	Altoona
Hileman, John	Cpl. C, 46 Pa. Mil.	1844	1904	Fairview	Altoona
Hileman, Joseph	Pvt. 137 Pa. Inf.	1834	1877	Frankstown	Hollidaysburg
Hileman, Joseph B.	Pvt. Ind. Cav. Pa. Mil.	1823			
Hileman, William	Pvt. H, 3 Pa. Inf.	1840			
Hileman, William C.	Cpl. C, 84 Pa. Inf.	1840	1862	Presbyterian	Hollidaysburg
Hileman, William K.	Pvt. A, 84 Pa. Inf.	1840	1915	Frankstown	Hollidaysburg
Hilings, Samuel Reed	Pvt. F, 1 Pa. Art.	1840	1914	Presbyterian	Williamsburg
Hill, Alexander M.	Pvt. D, 4 Pa. Cav.	1842	1927	Homer City	Penna.
Hill, Edward	Cpl. C, 22 Pa. Cav.	1841			
Hill, Frederick	Pvt. D, Pa. Cav.	1819	1865		
Hill, George W.	Pvt. D, 13 Pa. Cav.	1842			
Hill, Isaac	Pvt. F, 135 Pa. Inf.		1863	Fairview	Altoona
Hill, Isaac	Sgt. E, 46 Pa. Mil.				
	Sgt. B, 22 Pa. Cav.	1840	1892	Bald Eagle	Tyrone
Hill, James	Sgt. K, 13 Pa. Inf.	1847	1918	Curwensville	Penna.
Hill, John L.	Pvt. D, 14 Pa. Inf.	1816			
Hill, John L.	Sgt. A, 110 Pa. Inf.				
Hill, Oscar	Pvt. I, 205 Pa. Inf.	1834			
Hill, Thomas	Cpl. A, 133 Pa. Inf.				
	Pvt. D, 4 Pa. Cav.	1839	1902	Greenwood	Altoona
Hill, William	Pvt. U, 22 Pa. Cav.	1845			
Hillard, John	Pvt. D, 105 Pa. Inf.		1862		
Hiltner, John A.	Pvt. H, 133 Pa. Inf.	1841	1926	Grandview	Tyrone
Himes, Adam	Pvt. E, 76 Pa. Inf.	1826	1920	St. Marys	Hollidaysburg
Himes, George	Pvt. A, 2 D. C. Inf.				
	Pvt. G, 186 Pa. Inf.			New Enterprise	Penna.
Himes, John	Pvt. I, 14 Pa. Inf.	1841			
Himmelsbaugh, Charles	Pvt. B, 22 Pa. Cav.	1846			
Himstead, Augustus	Pvt. M, 12 Pa. Cav.	1828	1888	Fairview	Altoona
Hindman, John A.	Pvt. H, 122 Pa. Inf.	1844			
Hinds, Joseph S.	Pvt. C, 3 Pa. Inf.	1836			
Hinebaugh, William	Pvt. K, Pa. Inf.		1892	Marklesburg	Penna.
Hiney, Samuel	Pvt. D, 46 Pa. Mil.		1903	Westport	Penna.
Hinkle, David	Pvt. E, 84 Pa. Inf.	1812	1871	Snivelys	Williamsburg

THE CIVIL WAR

Name	Rank Organization	Born	Died	Cemetery	Location
Hinton, Samuel	Pvt. D, 13 Pa. Cav.	1845	1864	North Anna River	Virginia
Hippensteel, William A.	Pvt. I, 55 Pa. Inf.	1829	1898	Frankstown	Hollidaysburg
Hippo, William R.	Pvt. B, 49 Pa. Inf.	1831	1906	Fairview	Altoona
Hirst, Jacob D.	Pvt. M, 62 Pa. Inf.	1842	1904	Fairview	Altoona
Hirst, William	Pvt. K, 22 Pa. Cav.	1845	1910	Marklesburg	Penna.
Hitchcock, Robert S.	Cpn. 2 Md. Inf.	1818	1891	Lexington	Conn.
Hite, Daniel	Pvt. C, 200 Pa. Inf.	1842	1889	Greenlawn	Roaring Spring
Hite, George	Pvt. A, 87 Pa. Inf.	1824	1904	Lutheran	Newry
Hite, John	Pvt. I, 205 Pa. Inf.	1830	1865	Meade Station	Virginia
Hite, John H.	Pvt. B, Ind. Bn. Pa. Mil.	1845			
Hite, Josiah M.	Pvt. C, 19 Pa. Cav.	1828	1906	Greenlawn	Roaring Spring
Hixenbaugh, Thomas C.	Pvt. I, 22 Pa. Cav.	1841			
Hoar, Albert	Pvt. D, 192 Pa. Inf.				
Hoar, Samuel L.	Pvt. Ind. Cav. Pa. Mil.				
	Pvt. K, 46 Pa. Mil.	1846			
Hoar, Samuel L.	Cpl. C, 19 Pa. Cav.		1865	Monroe	Louisiana
Hoar, William S.	Pvt. D, 125 Pa. Inf.				
Hobart, Bartholomew	Pvt. K, 125 Pa. Inf.				
Hobart, John W.	Pvt. E, 104 Pa. Inf.				
Hobbs, Alexander	Pvt. C, 2 Md. Inf.				
	Pvt. H, 11 Md. Inf.	1843	1901	Oak Ridge	Altoona
Hockenberry, John	Pvt. I, 55 Pa. Inf.	1842			
Hockinberry, Uriah	Pvt. D, 46 Pa. Mil.	1819			
Hockenberry, Samuel	Pvt. I, 55 Pa. Inf.	1838	1864	Hampton	Virginia
Hockter, William I.	Pvt. G, 11 Pa. Inf.				
Hodge, Patrick F.	Pvt. H, 14 Pa. Inf.	1839			
	Cpt. A, 55 Pa. Inf.				
Hoe, John T.	Pvt. Ind. Bn. Pa. Mil.	1845			
Hoefler, Frederick	Pvt. K, 125 Pa. Inf.				
	Pvt. D, 46 Pa. Mil.	1831			
Hoefler, George	Pvt. D, 46 Pa. Mil.	1847			
Hoell, Andrew	Pvt. B, 9 Pa. Cav.		1873	Johnstown	Penna.
Hoffer, Alexander	Pvt. F, 31 Pa. Inf.		1863		
Hoffman, Anthony	Pvt. A, 3 Pa. Inf.				
Hoffman, Daniel	Pvt. A, 84 Pa. Inf.				
	Pvt. G, 57 Pa. Inf.				
Hoffman, Enos	Pvt. B, 53 Pa. Inf.	1840			
Hoffman, Frederick		1823	1905	Oak Grove	Tyrone
Hoffman, George	Pvt. K, 84 Pa. Inf.			St. Marys	Hollidaysburg
Hoffman, Henry A.	Cpl. C, 125 Pa. Inf.				
	2Lt. B, 192 Pa. Inf.	1843	1918	Lancaster	Penna.
Hoffman, John A.	Pvt. F, 195 Pa. Inf.				
	Pvt. F, 45 Pa. Inf.			Baughmans	Tyrone
Hoffman, Thomas	Pvt. I, 137 Pa. Inf.				
	Pvt. M, 9 Pa. Cav.	1829	1867	Lutheran	Hollidaysburg
Hoffner, Jonathan N.	Pvt. G, 148 Pa. Inf.	1843	1921	Croffs Mills	Huntingdon
Hofius, Henry M. L.	Pvt. D, 186 Pa. Inf.	1841	1896	Carson Valley	Duncansville
Hogan, Henry O.	Pvt. F, 28 Pa. Inf.	1835	1922	Calvary	Altoona
Hogentogler, John S.	Pvt. B, Ind. Bn. Pa. Mil.	1844			
Hogle, Gilbert B.	Pvt. C, 76 Pa. Inf.	1843	1912	Lewistown	Penna.
Hogmire, John I.	Pvt. D, 110 Pa. Inf.				
	Sgt. A, 19 Pa. Cav.	1842	1913	Presbyterian	Williamsburg
Hogue, Samuel	Pvt. Signal Corps	1849	1919	Oak Ridge	Altoona
Hohloch, Frederick	Pvt. F, 84 Pa. Inf.	1834	1890	Lutheran	Hollidaysburg
Hoke, Adam	Pvt. Ind. Cav. Pa. Mil.				
	Pvt. F, Ind. Bn. Pa. Mil.	1845			
Hoke, David	Pvt. A, 2 Pa. Inf.	1827			
Holcomb, Guy	Sgt. G, 57 Pa. Inf.	1841			
Holder, John	Pvt. M, 62 Pa. Inf.				
Holes, Samuel	Sgt. H, 110 Pa. Inf.				
Holland, Patrick F.	1Lt. H, 110 Pa. Inf.				
Holland, Richard C.	Pvt. C, 105 Pa. Inf.	1848			

SOLDIERS OF BLAIR COUNTY

Name	Rank Organization	Born	Died	Cemetery	Location
Holland, Thomas W. (M)	Cpt. H, 14 Pa. Inf.	1821	1902	St. Patricks	Newry
Hollen, John A.	Pvt. I, 205 Pa. Inf.	1849	1906	Greenwood	Altoona
Hollen, Joseph G.	Pvt. I, 205 Pa. Inf.	1831			
Hollen, Joseph R.	Pvt. R, 187 Pa. Inf.	1843	1922	Glasgow	Penna.
Hollin, Thomas	Pvt. H, 205 Pa. Inf.	1836			
Hollen, William	Pvt. H, 110 Pa. Inf.				
Hollen, William C.	Pvt. I, 205 Pa. Inf.	1840			
Hollen, William R.	Pvt. G, 12 Pa. Cav.	1839	1869	Fairview	Altoona
Holler, James M.	Pvt. G, 125 Pa. Inf.				
	Pvt. E, 13 Pa. Cav.	1837	1894	Fairview	Altoona
Holliday, Fleming	Cpt. A, 110 Pa. Inf.	1827	1902	Logan Valley	Bellwood
Holliday, William V.	Sgt. H, 110 Pa. Inf.	1836	1902	Fairview	Altoona
Hollinger, Stephen	Pvt. A, 43 U.S.C.T.	1842	1866	Eastern Light	Altoona
Hollingshead, John L.	Pvt. F, 31 Pa. Inf.				
	Pvt. A, 191 Pa. Inf.	1831	1910	Eastlawn	Tyrone
Hollingshead, William F.	Pvt. D, 39 Pa. Inf.				
	Pvt. B, 192 Pa. Inf.	1833	1913	Hutchinsons	Altoona
Hollingshead, Wilson	Pvt. D, 1 Pa. Art.	1836	1912	Fairview	Altoona
Hollingsworth, John	Pvt. F, 31 Pa. Inf.				
	Pvt. A, 191 Pa. Inf.				Tyrone
Hollis, William K.	Pvt. G, 12 Pa. Cav.	1842			
Hollock, Fred	Pvt. F, 84 Pa. Inf.	1833			
Holsinger, Josiah	Pvt. C, 110 Pa. Inf.				
Holzinger, Albert H.	Pvt. E, 195 Pa. Inf.	1842	1927	Wrightsville	Penna.
Homan, Thomas	Pvt. D, 125 Pa. Inf.		1863	Fairfax	Virginia
Homan, William H.	Pvt. A, 110 Pa. Inf.				
	Pvt. D, 6 U. S. Cav.	1841	1923	Lutheran	Williamsburg
Honley, Levi	Pvt. M, 9 Pa. Cav.	1833			
Hook, Andrew	Pvt. H, 110 Pa. Inf.		1863	Chancellorsville	Virginia
Hook, Maddock	Pvt. C, 76 Pa. Inf.	1828			
Hook, Samuel	Pvt. A, 125 Pa. Inf.				
	Sgt. K, 187 Pa. Inf.	1844	1915	Fairview	Altoona
Hook, William	Cpl. B, 3 Pa. Inf.				
	Pvt. E, 6 Pa. Cav.	1838	1899	Fairview	Altoona
Hoopengarner, George	Cpl. E, 125 Pa. Inf.				
Hooper, Henry John	Pvt. K, 7 Ill. Inf.	1831	1886	Collinsville	Altoona
Hoover, Allen E.	Pvt. M, 9 Pa. Inf.	1841			
Hoover, Andrew J.	Pvt. D, 149 Pa. Inf.	1837	1911	St. Augustine	Cambria Co.
Hoover, Daniel	Sgt. D, 14 Pa. Inf.	1841			
Hoover, Daniel G.	Cpl. E, 104 Pa. Inf.	1836	1910	Fairview	Martinsburg
Hoover, George	Pvt. I, 14 Pa. Inf.	1822			
Hoover, George F.	Cpl. C, 76 Pa. Inf.	1844	1916	Calvary	Altoona
Hoover, George S.	Pvt. C, 76 Pa. Inf.	1845	1874	St. Patricks	Newry
Hoover, George S.	Sgt. H, 14 Pa. Inf.				
	1Lt. C, 76 Pa. Inf.	1817	1862	Hilton Head	S. Car.
Hoover, George W.	Pvt. B, 76 Pa. Inf.	1822	1899	Greenlawn	Roaring Spring
Hoover, George W.	Pvt. H, 3 Pa. Prov. Cav.	1832	1900	Friends	Warriors Mark
Hoover, George W.	Pvt. E, 125 Pa. Inf.				
Hoover, Henry	Pvt. F, 77 Pa. Inf.	1827	1865	Victoria	Texas
Hoover, Jacob W.	Pvt. C, 55 Pa. Inf.		1891	Carson Valley	Duncansville
Hoover, John	Pvt. F, 31 Pa. Inf.				
Hoover, John I.	Pvt. C, 19 Pa. Cav.	1843	1930	Union	Claysburg
Hoover, Levi G.	Pvt. E, 104 Pa. Inf.	1832	1910	Carson Valley	Duncansville
Hoover, Phillip	Sgt. H, 22 Pa. Cav.	1843			
Hoover, Samuel	Pvt. D, 14 Pa. Inf.				
	Cpl. C, 208 Pa. Inf.	1838	1906	Grandview	Tyrone
Hoover, Samuel	Pvt. A, 23 Pa. Mil.				
	Pvt. A, Ind. Bn. Pa. Mil.	1821			
Hoover, Samuel	Pvt. A, 110 Pa. Inf.				
Hoover, Thomas L.	Pvt. C, 76 Pa. Inf.	1840			
Hopkins, Hiram H.	Cpt. H, 110 Pa. Inf.			Uniondale	Pittsburgh
Hopkins, James A.	Pvt. H, 22 Pa. Cav.	1846			

THE CIVIL WAR 209

Name	Rank Organization	Born	Died	Cemetery	Location
Hopkins, James	Pvt. G, Ind. Bn. Pa. Mil.	1847	1915	Logan Valley	Bellwood
Hopkins, Turner B.	Pvt. A, 23 Pa. Mil.	1822	1871	Presbyterian	Hollidaysburg
Hopkins, William M.	Pvt. F, 31 Pa. Inf.				
	Pvt. F, 190 Pa. Inf.	1843	1903	Oak Ridge	Altoona
Horn, Ira C.	Cpl. A, 110 Pa. Inf.				
Horn, Levi A.	Pvt. K, 25 Pa. Inf.				
	Pvt. M, 62 Pa. Inf.	1848			
Horne, Thaddeus	Pvt. F, 45 Pa. Inf.	1842	1898	St. Johns	Altoona
Horner, Jeremiah	Pvt. F, 21 Pa. Inf.	1840	1914	Conemaugh	Penna.
Horning, Martin	Pvt. B, 13 Pa. Cav.				
	Pvt. A, 50 Pa. Inf.	1844	1913	St. Marys	Hollidaysburg
Horning, Matthew	Pvt. A, Ind. Bn. Pa. Mil.	1844			
Horning, Peter	Pvt. A, Ind. Bn. Pa. Mil.	1842			
Horrell, Albert	Pvt. I, 137 Pa. Inf.				
Horrell, Robert L.	Cpt. A, 84 Pa. Inf.	1822	1887	Presbyterian	Hollidaysburg
Horton, Jacob L.	Pvt. C, 205 Pa. Inf.	1843	1901	Greenlawn	Roaring Spring
Horton, John A.	Pvt. A, 61 Pa. Inf.	1848	1917	Royer Mt.	Williamsburg
Hossinger, William H.	Pvt. E, 104 Pa. Inf.				
Hostetter, Christ	Cpl. D, 125 Pa. Inf.				
Hostler, Jacob Frank	Pvt. A, 205 Pa. Inf.	1845	1928	Fairview	Altoona
Hotchkin, Gordon Beriah	Sgn. 1 Pa. Cav.	1830	1915	Greenwood	Altoona
Houck, Aaron	Pvt. U, 84 Pa. Inf.				
	Cpl. I, 57 Pa. Inf.	1843			
Houck, Dorsey B.	Pvt. C, 3 Pa. Inf.				
	Sgt. E, 84 Pa. Inf.	1826			
Houck, Francis A.	Pvt. C, 46 Pa. Mil.	1842			
Houck, George A.	Pvt. B, 125 Pa. Mil.				
	Pvt. I, 22 Pa. Cav.	1844	1881	Fairview	Altoona
Houck, James H.	Pvt. C, 3 Pa. Inf.				
	Sgt. B, 125 Pa. Inf.				
	Sgt. B, 208 Pa. Inf.	1838	1918	Oak Ridge	Altoona
Houck, John S.	Pvt. C, 46 Pa. Mil.	1830			
Houck, Marshall	Pvt. F, 31 Pa. Inf.				
	Pvt. A, 191 Pa. Inf.	1840			
Houch, Thomas L.	Cpl. B, 208 Pa. Inf.	1828	1904	Fairview	Altoona
Houck, William A.	Pvt. I, 125 Pa. Inf.				
	Cpl. I, 46 Pa. Mil.				
	Pvt. E, 84 Pa. Inf.				
	Pvt. I, 57 Pa. Inf.	1841	1932	Oak Ridge	Altoona
Houp, Joseph	Sgt. B, 46 Pa. Mil.				
	Pvt. D, 205 Pa. Inf.	1829	1898	Grandview	Tyrone
Householder, Jacob	Pvt. C, 110 Pa. Inf.				
Householder, M. C.	Pvt. C, 110 Pa. Inf.				
Housel, Seth I.	Sgt. G, 4 Pa. Inf.				
	Sgt. H, 51 Pa. Inf.				
	Pvt. 8 U. S. Inf.	1839	1914	Grandview	Tyrone
Houseman, Andrew J.	Pvt. B, 3 Pa. Inf.				
	Pvt. F, 76 Pa. Inf.				
	Pvt. U. S. Signal Corps	1838	1893	Fairview	Altoona
Houseman, Daniel	Sgt. D, 13 Pa. Cav.	1832	1921	Oak Ridge	Altoona
Houseman, James	Pvt. A, 125 Pa. Inf.				
Houseman, William E.	Sad. C, 22 Pa. Cav.	1841			
Houser, Christian	Pvt. A, 23 Pa. Mil.	1824	1897	Logan Valley	Bellwood
Houser, Michael W.	Cpt. C, 57 Pa. Inf.	1822	1883		Altoona
Houser, Reuben	Mus. E, 20 Pa. Cav.	1848	1888	Bald Eagle	Tyrone
Houser, William Miller	Cpl. C, 9 Pa. Cav.	1834	1878	Fairview	Altoona
Housley, William	Pvt. C, 46 Pa. Mil.	1842	1891	Fairview	Altoona
Howard, George	Pvt. I, 105 Pa. Inf.	1818	1904	Maurers	Altoona
Howard, Harrison J.	Pvt. D, 13 Pa. Cav.				
	Pvt. 45 N. Y. Inf.	1842			
Howard, John	Pvt. I, 125 Pa. Inf.	1844	1904	Fairview	Altoona

Name	Rank Organization	Born	Died	Cemetery	Location
Howard, John	Pvt. M, 19 Pa. Cav.				
	Cpl. A, 19 Pa. Cav.	1844	1904	Fairview	Altoona
Howard, William T.	Cpl. F, 1 Md. Cav.	1844	1913	Oak Ridge	Altoona
Howden, Andrew T.	2Lt. M, 62 Pa. Inf.				
Howe, James M.	Pvt. H, 3 Pa. Inf.	1840			
Howe, James M.	Pvt. A, 14 Pa. Cav.	1839	1869	St. Johns	Altoona
Howe, Robert C.	Pvt. C, 76 Pa. Inf.	1844	1913	Oak Ridge	Altoona
Howe, Thomas	Pvt. G, 3 Pa. Inf.				
Howell, John C.	Pvt. D, 125 Pa. Inf.	1824	1913	St. Patricks	Gallitzin
Howell, Thomas A.	Pvt. B, 192 Pa. Inf.		1895	St. Patricks	Gallitzin
Howell, William	Pvt. A, 55 Pa. Inf.	1843	1906	St. Patricks	Gallitzin
Howsel, Seth I.	Pvt. A, 8 U. S. Inf.	1839	1914	Lewisburg	Penna.
Hubert, John	Pvt. E, 3 Pa. Inf.				
	2Lt. F, 76 Pa. Inf.	1842			
Hubert, Nicholas	Cpl. F, 31 Pa. Inf.				
Hudson, Edward	Pvt. A, 205 Pa. Inf.				
Huey, Samuel	Pvt. K, 55 Ohio Inf.	1824	1904	St. Patricks	Gallitzin
Huff, Charles	Pvt. A, 125 Pa. Inf.				
Huff, George F.	Pvt. C, 46 Pa. Mil.	1843			
Huff, Henry B.	Pvt. H, 3 Pa. Inf.				
	Sgt. K, 125 Pa. Inf.				
	Cpt. C, 46 Pa. Mil.				
	Cpt. D, 184 Pa. Inf.	1840	1907	Fairview	Altoona
Huff, Reuben C.	Pvt. D, 5 Mass. Cav.	1841	1906	Union	Hollidaysburg
Hughes, David H.	Cpl. B, Ind. Bn. Pa. Mil.	1844			
Hughes, Jacob G.	Pvt. B, 11 Pa. Cav.	1844	1935	Charlottesville	Bellwood
Hughes, James H.	Cpl. F, 76 Pa. Inf.	1839	1864	Chesterfield Hts.	Virginia
Hughes, John	Pvt. H, 14 Pa. Inf.	1840			
Hughes, John A.	Pvt. D, 12 Md. Inf.				
Hughes, John D.	Cpl. E, 46 Pa. Mil.	1825	1885	Fairview	Altoona
Hughes, John W.	Pvt. D, 4 Pa. Cav.	1840	1903	Johnstown	Penna.
Hughes, Joseph	Pvt. H, 3 Pa. Inf.	1839			
Hughes, Joseph H.	Cpl. F, 76 Pa. Inf.		1864	Chesterfield Hts.	Virginia
Hughes, Joseph M.	Pvt. B, 143 Pa. Inf.	1835	1905	Grandview	Tyrone
Hughes, Patrick F.	Sgt. A, 55 Pa. Inf.	1840	1904	St. Johns	Altoona
Hughes, Samuel	Pvt. D, 192 Pa. Inf.	1837	1896	Peoria	Illinois
Hughes, Stephen	Pvt. G, 3 Pa. Inf.	1828	1909	Presbyterian	Hollidaysburg
Hugo, Henry	Pvt. A, 110 Pa. Inf.				
Hulings, Samuel C.	Pvt. C, 19 Pa. Cav.	1841	1897	Mount Union	Penna.
Humes, James G.	Pvt. B, 30 Pa. Inf.	1839	1864	Fairview	Altoona
Hummel, Hiram H.	Cpl. D, 192 Pa. Inf.				
Humphrey, George M.	Pvt. F, 16 Vir. Inf.		1910	Williamsport	Penna.
Hunsbarger, David	Pvt. H, 110 Pa. Inf.				
Hunt, George E.	Pvt. A, 132 Pa. Inf.	1838	1911	Rose Hill	Altoona
Hunter, Benjamin F.	Pvt. M, 62 Pa. Inf.	1840	1862	Gaines Mills	Virginia
Hunter, David G.	Pvt. E, 61 Pa. Inf.	1817	1874	Logan Valley	Bellwood
Hunter, James H.	Pvt. A, 125 Pa. Inf.		1862	Charlottesville	Bellwood
Hunter, John Anderson	Pvt. A, 110 Pa. Inf.			Logan Valley	Bellwood
Hunter, Matthew S.	Pvt. A, 3 Pa. Inf.	1834	1912	Presbyterian	Hollidaysburg
Hunter, Ralph	Pvt. E, 27 Pa. Mil.	1823	1886	Oak Ridge	Altoona
Hunter, Robert L.	Pvt. H, 125 Pa. Inf.				
Hunter, Thomas	Pvt. A, 125 Pa. Inf.	1834		Charlottesville	Bellwood
Hunter, William	Pvt. E, 46 Pa. Mil.				
	Pvt. C, 208 Pa. Inf.	1830	1900	Bald Eagle	Tyrone
Hunter, William	Pvt. F, Ind. Bn. Pa. Mil.	1846			
Hunter, William W.	Pvt. B, 22 Pa. Cav.	1847	1867	Logan Valley	Bellwood
Huntington, William	Pvt. A, 205 Pa. Inf.				
Huntsbarger, S.	Pvt. H, 110 Pa. Inf.				
Huntsman, Thomas L.	Pvt. I, 149 Pa. Inf.	1831	1907	Logan Valley	Bellwood
Hurd, John	2Lt. M, 12 Pa. Cav.	1843	1901	Fairview	Altoona
Hurd, Thomas W.	Pvt. A, 125 Pa. Inf.	1824	1914	Lutheran	Hollidaysburg
Hurdman, David	Pvt. A, 110 Pa. Inf.				

Name	Rank Organization	Born	Died	Cemetery	Location
Hurley, Allen E.	Pvt. G, 21 Pa. Inf.	1842	1899	Carson Valley	Duncansville
Hurley, G. Washington	Pvt. I, 22 Pa. Cav.	1816	1886	Carson Valley	Duncansville
Hurley, Granville	Cpl. G, 8 U.S.C.T.	1836	1922	Eastern Light	Altoona
Hurley, John	Pvt. F, 76 Pa. Inf.	1841	1861	Hampton	Virginia
Hurley, Warner	Pvt. U, 84 Pa. Inf.				
	Pvt. I, 57 Pa. Inf.	1845			
Hurley, William	Pvt. E, 84 Pa. Inf.				
	Pvt. I, 57 Pa. Inf.	1830	1911	Greenlawn	Roaring Spring
Huston, James	Pvt. B, 148 Pa. Inf.	1835	1915	Grandview	Tyrone
Hutchison, John J.	Ldn. U. S. Navy	1842	1865	Guilford	Altoona
Huyett, Miles C.	Pvt. B, 125 Pa. Inf.				
	Sgt. B, 208 Pa. Inf.				
Huyett, Samuel L.	Cpt. D, 110 Pa. Inf.				
	Cpt. G, 46 Pa. Mil.				
	Cpt. A, 19 Pa. Cav.	1838		Philadelphia	Penna.
Huyett, Ulysses S.	Pvt. C, 3 Pa. Inf.				
	Cpt. B, 125 Pa. Inf.	1841			
Huyo, Charles F.	Cpl. M, 62 Pa. Inf.				
Hyskell, William D.	Pvt. H, 2 Pa. Art.	1846	1929	Beulah	Ramey
Ickes, Adam	Pvt. H, 14 Pa. Inf.				
	Pvt. A, 12 U. S. Inf.	1841	1909	Mt. Hope	Claysburg
Ickes, Alexander	Pvt. B, 91 Pa. Inf.			Mt. Zion	Bedford Co.
Ickes, Henry	Pvt. F, 99 Pa. Inf.			Mt. Zion	Bedford Co.
Ickes, Joseph H.	Pvt. A, 84 Pa. Inf.	1838		Imler	Bedford Co.
Ickes, William H.	Pvt. G, Ind. Bn. Pa. Mil.	1840			
Ickes, William M.	Pvt. I, 91 Pa. Inf.	1847	1926	Albrights	Roaring Spring
Iddings, Ellis	Pvt. K, 91 Pa. Inf.	1847			
Igou, Caleb	Pvt. E, 104 Pa. Inf.	1828	1887	Antis Twp.	Bellwood
Igo, James Malvern	Pvt. F, 49 Pa. Inf.		1864	Sandy Hook	Maryland
Imler, George	Pvt. E, 138 Pa. Inf.				Bedford Co.
Imler, John	2Lt. K, 55 Pa. Inf.	1831	1872	Mt. Hope	Claysburg
Imler, Jonas C.	Pvt. C, 205 Pa. Inf.	1844	1938		Bedford Co.
Imler, Martin	Pvt. C, 91 Pa. Inf.	1831	1867	Greenfield	Kimmell Twp.
Ingram, William D.	Pvt. F, 2 Pa. Cav.	1844			
Inlow, Francis	Pvt. K, 125 Pa. Inf.				
Irons, George	Pvt. K, 22 U.S.C.T.	1832	1909	Union	Hollidaysburg
Irvin, Adie Franklin	Cpl. F, 76 Pa. Inf.	1839	1909	Logan Valley	Bellwood
Irvine, Alfred C.	Pvt. G, 125 Pa. Inf.		1907	Washington	D. C.
Irvin, Andrew	Pvt. E, 45 Pa. Inf.	1845	1906	Maple Grove	Bellville
Irwin, Daniel	Pvt. G, 34 Pa. Inf.		1864	Spottsylvania	Virginia
Irvin, Daniel P.	Sgt. C, 3 Pa. Inf.				
	Cpl. B, 125 Pa. Inf.				
	Pvt. F, 22 Pa. Cav.	1837	1885	Presbyterian	Williamsburg
Irvin, George M.	Pvt. D, 125 Pa. Inf.				
Irwin, George M.	Pvt. D, 188 Pa. Inf.			Logan Valley	Bellwood
Irvin, Henry	Sgt. E, 45 Pa. Inf.	1835	1915	Oak Ridge	Altoona
Irvine, Henry Lloyd	Sgt. G, 125 Pa. Inf.				
	Sgt. Ind. Bn. Pa. Mil.	1842	1904		Cumberland Co.
Irwin, Jacob Tippery	Pvt. F, 76 Pa. Inf.	1837	1889	Logan Valley	Bellwood
Irwin, James	Pvt. C, 110 Pa. Inf.				
Irwin, James A.	Pvt. H, 110 Pa. Inf.	1846	1931	Alto Reste	Hollidaysburg
Irvine, James McC.	Pvt. M, 12 Pa. Cav.	1844	1919	Lutheran	Newry
Irwin, Jerret	Pvt. C, 110 Pa. Inf.				
Irwin, John E.	Pvt. C, 76 Pa. Inf.	1824	1866	Logan Valley	Bellwood
Irwin, Joseph	Pvt. A, 23 Pa. Mil.				
	Pvt. A, Ind. Bn. Pa. Mil.	1819	1883	Presbyterian	Hollidaysburg
Irwin, Lewis	Sgt. D, 22 Pa. Cav.	1842			
Irvine, Oliver Mayberry	Maj. 3 Pa. Inf.				
	Maj. 76 Pa. Inf.				
	Cpt. A, Ind. Bn. Pa. Mil.				
	Maj. 84 Pa. Inf.	1833	1899	Carson Valley	Duncansville
Irvin, Samuel	Pvt. G, 34 Pa. Inf.	1833	1908	Grandview	Tyrone

Name	Rank Organization	Born	Died	Cemetery	Location
Irvin, William	1Lt. M, 9 Pa. Cav.	1841	1913	St. Johns	Altoona
Irwin, William C.	Pvt. E, 46 Pa. Mil.	1847	1903	Grandview	Tyrone
Irwin, William K.	Sgt. M, 12 Pa. Cav.	1843	1895	St. Johns	Altoona
Isenberg, Abraham	Pvt. D, 122 Pa. Inf.	1838	1903	Frankstown	Hollidaysburg
Isenberg, Daniel	Sgt. M, 9 Pa. Cav.	1837	1902	Oak Ridge	Altoona
Isenberg, Ephraim	Pvt. D, 1 Pa. Art.	1843			
Isenberg, Franklin B.	Cpl. M, 9 Pa. Cav.	1844			
Isenberg, James	Pvt. K, 22 Pa. Cav.	1845			
Isenberg, John	Pvt. A, 125 Pa. Inf.	1841	1897	Greenwood	Altoona
Isenberg, Joseph G.	1Lt. I, 137 Pa. Inf.				
	Adj. 22 Pa. Cav.	1837			
Isenberg, Peter S.	Pvt. D, 1 Pa. Art.	1845	1932	Logan Valley	Bellwood
Isenberg, Samuel N.	Pvt. D, 1 Pa. Cav.	1842			
Isenberg, Thomas J.	Pvt. K, 22 Pa. Cav.	1844			
Isenberg, William H.	Pvt. D, 1 Pa. Art.	1839			
Isett, Aaron B.	Pvt. H, 14 Pa. Inf.				
	Pvt. G, 125 Pa. Inf.	1837	1914	Myersdale	Penna.
Isett, Jacob H.	Pvt. A, 110 Pa. Inf.				
Isett, Jacob H.	Sgt. K, 15 Pa. Cav.	1828	1897	Presbyterian	Sinking Valley
Isett, Henry J.	Pvt. Palmers Inf.	1840	1917	Presbyterian	Williamsburg
Isett, Samuel G.	Pvt. K, 22 Pa. Cav.	1846			
Isett, Samuel K.	Pvt. F, 83 Pa. Inf.	1831	1880	Fairview	Altoona
Isett, Washington	Pvt. E, 3 Pa. Inf.				
	Pvt. A, 110 Pa. Inf.	1841			
Ishler, Emanuel	Pvt. C, 23 Pa. Mil.	1834	1910	Fairview	Altoona
Itinger, Harrison	Pvt. D, 1 Pa. Art.	1847			
Itinger, Samuel H.	Pvt. C, 77 Pa. Inf.	1844	1931	Alexandria	Penna.
Ivory, Jeremiah H.	Sgt. G, 12 Pa. Cav.	1835	1910	Chest Springs	Penna.
Ivory, Thomas	Pvt. G, 12 Pa. Cav.	1841	1865	Salisbury	N. Car.
Jackel, Fred	Pvt. K, 3 N. J. Cav.				
Jackson, George W.	Sgt. G, 41 U.S.C.T.	1825	1903	Eastern Light	Altoona
Jackson, James	Pvt. H, 129 Ohio Inf.	1845	1876	Fairview	Altoona
Jackson, John	Pvt. C, 148 Pa. Inf.	1841	1914	Grandview	Tyrone
Jackson, William	Pvt. F, 28 Pa. Inf.	1844			
Jacobs, George A.	Gnr. U. S. Navy	1825	1889	Presbyterian	Hollidaysburg
Jacobs, Samuel A.	Pvt. Ind. Cav. Pa. Mil.	1844			
Jacoby, Eden B.	Pvt. G, 3 Pa. Art.	1833	1909	Fairview	Altoona
Jacoby, George	Pvt. G, 57 Pa. Inf.	1846			
James, Benjamin	Pvt. C, 193 Pa. Inf.	1845			
James, J. S.	Pvt. Lamberts Cav.		1909	Lewisburg	Penna.
James, Jesse	Pvt. B, 3 Pa. Inf.	1843			
James, Jesse T.	Pvt. A, 84 Pa. Inf.			Horn	Bedford Co.
James, John A.	Pvt. Ind. Cav. Pa. Mil.				
	Pvt. K, 46 Pa. Mil.	1847			
James, Silas	Pvt. K, 22 Pa. Cav.	1843			
Jamison, Benjamin F.	Pvt. I, 110 Pa. Inf.				
	Pvt. B, 125 Pa. Inf.	1843	1920	Reform Church	Loysburg
Jarrett, Joseph	Pvt. F, 49 Pa. Inf.	1844			
Jaris, William	Pvt. B, 136 Pa. Inf.	1843			
Jeffries, William H.	Cpt. H, 63 Pa. Inf.				
Jellison, George	Cpl. I, 40 Pa. Inf.				
	Sgt. I, 190 Pa. Inf.	1832	1912	Fairview	Altoona
Jenkins, Andrew J.	Pvt. F, 205 Pa. Inf.		1920	McVeytown	Penna.
Jenkins, John	Pvt. C, 76 Pa. Inf.	1838			
Jenkins, John	Pvt. K, 78 Pa. Inf.	1848	1904	Oak Ridge	Altoona
Jennings, John	Pvt. C, 84 Pa. Inf.	1823			
Jennings, Michael	Pvt. F, 76 Pa. Inf.	1839			
Jennison, Charles D.	Pvt. A, 5 N. Y. Art.	1840	1903	Fairview	Altoona
Johnson, Benjamin F.	Cpl. A, 49 Pa. Inf.				
Johnston, Collins	Pvt. M, 9 Pa. Cav.	1841			
Johnston, David R. P.	Pvt. G, 125 Pa. Inf.				
	Sgt. F, 77 Pa. Inf.	1839	1917	Fairview	Altoona

THE CIVIL WAR

Name	Rank Organization	Born	Died	Cemetery	Location
Johnston, David S.	Mus. A, 125 Pa. Inf.	1835		Huntingdon	Penna.
Johnston, Franklin R.	Pvt. G, 125 Pa. Inf.				
	Pvt. B, Ind. Bn. Pa. Mil.	1814	1877	Presbyterian	Hollidaysburg
Johnson, Henry	Pvt. A, 15 W. Va. Inf.	1819	1879	St. Patricks	Gallitzin
Johnston, Hugh	Pvt. M, 62 Pa. Inf.	1835			
Johnston, Isaac	Pvt. C, 84 Pa. Inf.	1839			
Johnson, Irvin	Pvt. B, 110 Pa. Inf.				
	Pvt. B, 28 Pa. Inf.				
	Pvt. B, 147 Pa. Inf.	1840	1916	Presbyterian	Birmingham
Johnston, James	Pvt. E, 84 Pa. Inf.		1862	Chancellorsville	Virginia
Johnston, James	Pvt. G, 1 Pa. Art.	1834	1897	St. Patricks	Newry
Johnson, James H.	Pvt. D, 46 Pa. Mil.	1844			
Johnston, James R.	Sgt. A, Ind. Bn. Pa. Mil.	1842			
Johnston, James R.	Pvt. G, 125 Pa. Inf.				
Johnson, James R.	Sgt. B, 13 Pa. Cav.		1864	Petersburg	Virginia
Johnson, John	Pvt. D, 46 Pa. Mil.	1839			
Johnson, John	Pvt. F, 76 Pa. Inf.				
Johnston, John R.	Pvt. I, 105 Pa. Inf.		1864	Wilderness	Virginia
Johnston, John W.	Pvt. C, 133 Pa. Inf.	1843	1912	Lutheran	Claysburg
Johnston, Joseph C.	Pvt. G, 12 Pa. Cav.	1843			
Johnston, Nicodemus	Pvt. D, 14 Pa. Inf.				
	Pvt. K, 5 U. S. Art.	1838	1902	Presbyterian	Sinking Valley
Johnson, Richard T.	Mus. Marine Corps	1844	1918	Fairview	Altoona
Johnson, Robert	2Lt. C, 3 Pa. Inf.				
	Cpt. E, 84 Pa. Inf.				
	Cpt. E, 104 Pa. Inf.	1832		Alexandria	Penna.
Johnston, Robert B.	Pvt. A, 23 Pa. Mil.	1822			
Johnston, Robert M.	Pvt. C, 3 Pa. Inf.				
	Adj. 125 Pa. Inf.	1842	1862	Presbyterian	Williamsburg
Johnson, Samuel	Pvt. B, 3 Pa. Inf.	1842			
Johnson, Samuel	Pvt. C, 84 Pa. Inf.				
	Pvt. K, 57 Pa. Inf.	1842	1884	Fairview	Altoona
Johnston, Samuel	Pvt. C, 110 Pa. Inf.		1864		
Johnston, Samuel A.	Pvt. F, 208 Pa. Inf.	1835	1919	Spring Run	Franklin Co.
Johnson, Seth W.	Pvt. M, 3 Pa. Art.	1838	1913	Frankstown	Hollidaysburg
Johnson, Thomas	Pvt. D, 62 Pa. Inf.			Greenlawn	Roaring Spring
Johnston, Thomas	Pvt. M, 9 Pa. Cav.	1822			
Johnston, Thomas	Pvt. E, 46 Pa. Mil.			Grandview	Tyrone
Johnston, Thomas Eli	Sgt. B, 25 U. S. C. T.	1835	1878	Grandview	Tyrone
Johnston, Thomas G.	Pvt. K, 5 U. S. Art.	1830	1914	Rose Hill	Altoona
Johnson, Thomas M.	Cpl. I, 205 Pa. Inf.	1846			
Johnston, Thomas W.	Pvt. E, 46 Pa. Mil.				
Johnston, William	Pvt. D, 22 Pa. Cav.	1845			
Johnston, William F.	Cpt. I, 137 Pa. Inf.	1834		Milwaukee	Wisconsin
Johnson, William M.	Pvt. U, 84 Pa. Inf.				
	Pvt. I, 57 Pa. Inf.	1845	1923	Rose Hill	Altoona
Jolly, Matthias H.	1Lt. H, 110 Pa. Inf.				
	Cpt. H, 22 Pa. Cav.	1828			
Jones, Arthur M. C.	Cpl. H, 15 Pa. Inf.				
	Pvt. M, 9 Pa. Cav.	1841	1913	Grandview	Tyrone
Jones, Benjamin	Sgt. A, 2 Pa. Cav.				
Jones, Charles H.	Pvt. E, 17 Mich. Inf.	1843	1920	Lutheran	Sinking Valley
Jones, Charles S. W. (S)					
	Cpt. B, 2 Pa. Cav.	1842	1905	Grandview	Tyrone
Jones, Daniel	Pvt. A, 125 Pa. Inf.				
	Cpl. E, 184 Pa. Inf.	1821	1894	Oak Ridge	Altoona
Jones, David M.	Cpl. D, 3 Pa. Inf.				
	Col. 110 Pa. Inf.	1838	1877	Grandview	Tyrone
Jones, Francis	Sgt. E, 184 Pa. Inf.				
Jones, George W.	Pvt. K, 125 Pa. Inf.	1842	1881	Fairview	Altoona
Jones, Harry D.	Pvt. A, 46 Pa. Inf.				
	Pvt. H, Ind. Bn. Pa. Mil.	1842	1911	Calvary	Altoona

SOLDIERS OF BLAIR COUNTY

Name	Rank Organization	Born	Died	Cemetery	Location
Jones, James	Pvt. A, 3 Pa. Inf.				
	Pvt. M, 62 Pa. Inf.	1829	1907	Carson Valley	Duncansville
Jones, John	Pvt. L, 5 Pa. Art.	1826	1906	Oak Ridge	Altoona
Jones, John A.	Pvt. I, 8 U. S. C. T.	1835	1892	Grandview	Tyrone
Jones, John H.	Pvt. D, 4 Pa. Cav.	1847			
Jones, Levi	Pvt. A, 110 Pa. Inf.				
Jones, Nathan S.	Pvt. B, 22 Pa. Cav.	1846	1908	Carlisle	Penna.
Jones, Samuel B.	Pvt. Marine Corps	1845	1917	Rose Hill	Altoona
Jones, Thaddeus	Pvt. G, 125 Pa. Inf.				
Jones, William D.	Pvt. D, 147 N. Y. Inf.	1842	1907	Rose Hill	Altoona
Jones, William L.	Pvt. H, 93 Pa. Inf.				
Jones, William R.	Cpl. A, 205 Pa. Inf.	1839	1892	Oak Ridge	Altoona
Jordan, Charles T.	Pvt. F, 3 N. J. Inf.	1843	1928	Rose Hill	Altoona
Jordan, Daniel	Pvt. A, 84 Pa. Inf.				
	Pvt. G, 57 Pa. Inf.	1840			
Jordan, Daniel	Pvt. F, 37 Pa. Inf.				
	Pvt. C, 5 U. S. Art.				
Jordan, John		1832	1912	Fruitdale	Alabama
Jordan, Sylvester D.	Pvt. M, 62 Pa. Inf.				
	Pvt. K, 91 Pa. Inf.				
Judge, Michael	Pvt. M, 9 Pa. Cav.	1842	1910	Oak Grove	Tyrone
Junkin, David X.	Cpn. U. S. Navy	1808	1880	Bloomburg	New Jersey
Justice, Edward S.	Pvt. C, 110 Pa. Inf.	1864			
Kagarice, Ebenezer	Pvt. C, 76 Pa. Inf.	1840	1863	Fort Wagner	S. Car.
Kahle, John P.	Sgt. E, 127 Pa. Inf.	1832	1908	Fairview	Altoona
Kaisley, William	Pvt. C, 76 Pa. Inf.	1817			
Kane, John M.	Pvt. C, 3 Pa. Inf.				
	Pvt. E, 84 Pa. Inf.	1840	1890	St. Pauls	Williamsburg
Kane, William	Cpl. C, 110 Pa. Inf.				
Kane, William	Pvt. E, 46 Pa. Mil.	1838			
Kantner, David T.	Pvt. G, 12 Pa. Cav.	1846	1924	Greenwood	Altoona
Kantner, Henry F.	Pvt. D, 13 Pa. Cav.	1843		Wilmington	N. Car.
Kantner, John H.	Pvt. A, 205 Pa. Inf.	1844	1926	Fairview	Altoona
Kantner, John H.	Pvt. A, 205 Pa. Inf.	1823	1874	Fairview	Altoona
Kapp, A. H.	Sgn. Pa. Inf.				
Karney, Patrick	Pvt. G, 57 Pa. Inf.	1832	1865	Andersonville	Georgia
Kauffman, David M.	Pvt. D, 49 Pa. Inf.			Union	Bedford Co.
Kauffman, David	Pvt. C, 133 Pa. Inf.	1840	1916	Kauffman	Martinsburg
Kauffman, John	Pvt. C, 205 Pa. Inf.	1841	1922	Greenwood	Altoona
Kauffman, John C.	Pvt. H, 79 Pa. Inf.	1839	1920	Mennonite	Martinsburg
Kauffman, Joseph	Pvt. B, 192 Pa. Inf.	1833	1865	Kauffman	Martinsburg
Kaup, Jacob Stover	Cpl. A, 45 Pa. Inf.	1844	1933	Grandview	Tyrone
Kay, Henry C. H.	1Lt. C, 110 Pa. Inf.				
	Cpt. B, 22 Pa. Cav.				
Kay, Isaac F.	1Lt. K, 110 Pa. Inf.	1828	1873	Logan Valley	Bellwood
Kays, John	Pvt. A, 22 Pa. Cav.	1839			
Kaylor, James	Pvt. C, 46 Pa. Mil.	1820	1914	Calvary	Altoona
Keagy, David F.	2Lt. H, 208 Pa. Inf.	1836	1917	Oak Ridge	Altoona
Keagy, Henry	Pvt. L, 21 Pa. Cav.		1893	Chambersburg	Penna.
Keagy, Jacob S.	Pvt. D, 125 Pa. Inf.		1905	Fairview	Martinsburg
Keagy, John	Pvt. D, 125 Pa. Inf.				
Keagy, Samuel	Pvt. C, 133 Pa. Inf.			Potter	Bedford Co.
Kean, Charles	Pvt. E, 104 Pa. Inf.	1825	1918	Fairview	Altoona
Kean, William C.	Cpl. A, 125 Pa. Inf.			Bedford	Penna.
Kearman, Hugh	Pvt. U, 84 Pa. Inf.				
	Pvt. I, 57 Pa. Inf.	1820			
Kearney, Michael	Pvt. O, 28 Pa. Inf.				
	Pvt. B, 147 Pa. Inf.	1830	1916	St. Johns	Altoona
Kearney, Patrick F.	Pvt. K, 125 Pa. Inf.				
Keasey, William H.	Sgt. L, 12 Pa. Cav.	1843	1884	Frankstown	Hollidaysburg
Keatley, Calvin F.	Pvt. A, 125 Pa. Inf.				
Keatley, James	Cpt. H, 8 Pa. Inf.	1837	1928	Rose Hill	Altoona

THE CIVIL WAR   215

Name	Rank Organization	Born	Died	Cemetery	Location
Keatley, John H.	Pvt. A, 125 Pa. Inf.				
	Q. M. Ind. Bn. Pa. Mil.				
	1Lt. E, 104 Pa. Inf.	1839			
Keckler, Jacob	Pvt. M, 22 Pa. Cav.	1822	1904	Lutheran	Hollidaysburg
Keech, Joseph	Pvt. H, 3 Pa. Inf.	1836			
Keech, Joseph D.	2Lt. C, 76 Pa. Inf.	1836			
Keech, Leo	Pvt. C, 84 Pa. Inf.	1843	1862		
Keeley, Henry	Sgt. A, 3 Pa. Inf.	1828	1888	Presbyterian	Hollidaysburg
Keim, Franklin	Pvt. K, 101 Pa. Inf.	1846			
Keiper, Goswin	Pvt. A, 54 Pa. Inf.	1838	1896	Oak Ridge	Altoona
Keirn, Turbot	Pvt. E, 37 Pa. Inf.				
	Sgt. A, 205 Pa. Inf.	1835	1879	Fairview	Altoona
Keith, Thomas	Pvt. D, 91 Pa. Inf.	1831	1906	Fairview	Martinsburg
Keith, William	Pvt. H, 14 Pa. Inf.	1841			
Keithley, John H.	Pvt. D, 3 Md. Inf.	1838	1898	Fairview	Altoona
Kelch, William F.	Pvt. I, 29 Pa. Inf.	1830		Lutheran	Hollidaysburg
Keller, John C.	Pvt. B, Ind. Bn. Pa. Mil.	1845			
Keller, William B.	Pvt. C, 91 Pa. Inf.	1830	1890	Keller Reform	Williamsburg
Kelley, Alfred H.	Pvt. I, 12 Pa. Cav.				
	Pvt. M, 19 Pa. Cav.	1843	1914	Rose Hill	Altoona
Kelly, Andrew	Pvt. D, 88 Pa. Inf.	1847	1919	Mount Union	Pa.
Kelly, D. R.					
Kelly, David	Pvt. C, 110 Pa. Inf.			Hopewell	Bedford Co.
Kelley, Descartes	Pvt. E, 1 Pa. Cav.	1837	1904	Lewistown	Pa.
Kelly, Edwin	Pvt. 2, Iowa Inf.	1839	1863	Corinth	Mississippi
Kelley, George P.	Cpl. C, 110 Pa. Inf.	1835	1901	Lutheran	Newry
Kelley, George W.	Pvt. E, 84 Pa. Inf.	1834		Methodist	Williamsburg
Kelley, Henry A.	Pvt. M, 9 Pa. Cav.	1843	1908	Greenwood	Altoona
Kelly, Henry F.	Pvt. E, 84 Pa. Inf.				
Kelley, James	Pvt. Ind. Cav. Pa. Mil.	1839			
Kelly, James	Pvt. E, 55 Pa. Inf.	1835	1903	St. Patricks	Gallitzin
Kelly, James D.	Cpl. H, 213 Pa. Inf.	1839	1920	Rose Hill	Altoona
Kelly, James W.	Pvt. E, 84 Pa. Inf.				
Kelly, John	Pvt. F, 3 Pa. Art.			St. Patricks	Gallitzin
Kelly, John	Pvt. E, 84 Pa. Inf.		1862	Winchester	Virginia
Kelly, John	Pvt. D, 22 Pa. Cav.	1843			
Kelly, John	Pvt. C, 3 Pa. Inf.	1828			
Kelly, John	Pvt. I, 205 Pa. Inf.	1836		Fairview	Altoona
Kelley, John A.	Pvt. E, 3 Pa. Inf.	1839			
Kelley, John A.	Cpl. D, 125 Pa. Inf.	1839	1862	Fairview	Altoona
Kelly, John F.	Pvt. F, 22 Pa. Cav.	1843	1937	Reynoldsville	Pa.
Kelly, John W.	Pvt. C, 22 Pa. Cav.	1844			
Kelly, Joseph	Pvt. 183 Pa. Inf.			Beavertown	Pa.
Kelly, Leonard	Pvt. B, 3 Pa. Inf.	1842			
Kelly, Leonard K.	Pvt. M, 9 Pa. Cav.	1839	1912	Rose Hill	Altoona
Kelly, Michael L.	Pvt. U, 22 Pa. Cav.	1843			
Kelly, Michael W.	Lmn. U. S. Navy		1885	St. Patricks	Gallitzin
Kelly, Thomas	Blk. M, 9 Pa. Cav.	1833			
Kelly, William A.	Pvt. H, 110 Pa. Inf.				
Kelly, William D.	Pvt. E, 84 Pa. Inf.				
Kelly, William D.	Pvt. C, 184 Pa. Inf.	1848	1920	Asbury	Altoona
Kelsh, William F.	Pvt. I, 29 Pa. Inf.	1831			
Kemberling, Henry	Pvt. A, Ind. Bn. Pa.Mil.	1823			
Kemmerling, John	Pvt. C, 46 Pa. Mil.	1820			
Kemmerling, John	Pvt. I, 55 Pa. Inf.		1864	Harrisburg	Pa.
Kemmerling, Robert	Pvt. F, 57 Pa. Inf.	1833			
Kemberlin, John G.	Pvt. B, 11 Pa. Inf.		1862	National	Sharpsb'g, Md.
Kemp, Horace	Cpl. G, 125 Pa. Inf.				
	Sgt. A, Ind. Bn. Pa. Mil.	1844	1865	Lutheran	Hollidaysburg
Kemp, Joseph	Pvt. F, 76 Pa. Inf.	1822	1862	Hilton Head	So. Carolina

Name	Rank	Organization	Born	Died	Cemetery	Location
Kendall, O. D.	Pvt.	1 Pa. Art.				
Kendig, Henry B.	Pvt. D,	126 Pa. Inf.				
	Adj. D,	21 Pa. Cav.	1833	1900	Oak Ridge	Altoona
Kennedy, David	Pvt. F,	148 Pa. Inf.	1842	1864	Spring Hope	Martinsburg
Kennedy, James					Milton	Pa.
Kennedy, John	Pvt. H,	22 Pa. Cav.	1846			
Kennedy, John D.	Pvt. B,	110 Pa. Inf.	1837	1907	Greenwood	Altoona
Kennedy, Johnston	Pvt. B,	208 Pa. Inf.				
Kennedy, Johnson	Pvt. F,	14 Pa. Cav.	1836			
Kennedy, Joshua	Pvt. D,	1 Pa. Art.	1827			
Kenney, James R.	Pvt. E,	11 Ohio Inf.	1834	1904	Fairview	Altoona
Kenney, Sanford D.	Pvt. C,	22 Pa. Cav.	1845			
Keogh, Edward J.	Pvt. H,	3 Pa. Inf.				
	Pvt. A,	84 Pa. Inf.				
	Pvt. G,	57 Pa. Inf.	1845			
Kephart, Albert	Pvt. D,	13 Pa. Cav.	1841	1864	Salisbury	N. Car.
Kephart, Caleb M.	Cpl. H,	3 Pa. Inf.	1841			
Kephart, Calvin M.	Pvt. A,	3 Pa. Inf.				
	Pvt. I,	137 Pa. Inf.	1843	1862	Mt. Oliver	Maryland
Kephart, Christian B.	Sgt. D,	13 Pa. Cav.		1865	Andersonville	Georgia
Kephart, Daniel	Pvt. E,	49 Pa. Inf.	1843	1928	Oak Ridge	Altoona
Kephart, David	Pvt. C,	84 Pa. Inf.	1843			
Kephart, David A.	Pvt. D,	13 Pa. Cav.	1844			
Kephart, Jacob	Cpl. K,	46 Pa. Mil.	1838			
Kephart, Jacob	Pvt. E,	125 Pa. Inf.				
Kephart, John	Pvt. B,	Ind. Bn. Pa. Mil.				
	Pvt. D,	13 Pa. Cav.	1843	1898	Hopewell	Pa.
Kephart, Joseph H.	Pvt. D,	184 Pa. Inf.	1820	1900	Maurers	Altoona
Kephart, Perry	Pvt. A,	110 Pa. Inf.				
Kephart, Samuel A.	1Lt. E,	125 Pa. Inf.				
Kephart, Samuel S.	Pvt. A,	110 Pa. Inf.				
Kephart, Simon	Cpl. A,	110 Pa. Inf.				
Kern, James W.	Pvt. F,	154 Pa. Inf.	1846	1899	Oak Ridge	Altoona
Kerns, William	Pvt. L,	12 Pa. Cav.	1829	1904	Greenwood	Altoona
Kerr, David S.	Pvt. F,	55 Pa. Inf.	1844	1929	Carson Valley	Duncansville
Kerr, J. J.	Pvt. F,	162 Ohio Inf.	1836			
Kerr, James G.	Cpl. D,	125 Pa. Inf.				
Kerr, John						
Kerr, Robert	Pvt. A,	125 Pa. Inf.	1844			
Kerr, Robert S.	Pvt. M,	19 Pa. Cav.	1843	1864	Memphis	Tennessee
Kersey, John	Pvt. D,	125 Pa. Inf.	1834	1892	St. Johns	Altoona
Kessler, Cloyd	Pvt. C,	46 Pa. Mil.	1846			
Kessler, John	Pvt. I,	205 Pa. Inf.				
Kessler, Matthias	Pvt. I,	205 Pa. Inf.	1819	1865	Petersburg	Virginia
Ketterman, Albert B.	Pvt. K,	22 Pa. Cav.	1845			
Ketring, Elijah T.	Pvt. I,	194 Pa. Inf.	1845	1903	Holsingers	Bakers Summit
Keys, Elias	Pvt. D,	53 Pa. Inf.				
	Pvt. D,	4 Ohio Inf.	1844	1891	Grandview	Tyrone
Keyes, John M.	Pvt. B,	205 Pa. Inf.	1846	1911	Oak Ridge	Altoona
Keyes, Patrick T.	Cpt. D,	16 U. S. Inf.	1835	1862	St. Johns	Altoona
Kidd, Joseph L. (M)	Sgt. C,	3 Pa. Inf.	1823	1903	Presbyterian	Williamsburg
Kifer, Jacob	Pvt. B,	208 Pa. Inf.	1845	1912	Shellys	Williamsburg
Kifer, Michael B.	Mus. C,	46 Pa. Mil.	1844			
Kilgore, John	Pvt. U,	84 Pa. Inf.				
	Pvt. I,	57 Pa. Inf.	1843			
Killetts, Levi	Pvt. D,	45 Pa. Inf.	1831	1875	Grandview	Tyrone
Killinger, Frank	Pvt. F,	79 Pa. Inf.	1834	1912	Logan Valley	Bellwood
Killinger, John	Pvt. D,	13 Pa. Cav.	1845			
Killinger, John C.	Pvt. B,	Ind. Bn. Pa. Mil.	1846			
Killinger, William	Pvt. A,	Ind. Bn. Pa. Mil.	1846			
Kinch, Israel K.	2Lt. I,	5 Pa. Inf.			Warriors Mark	Pa.
Kinch, John M.	Pvt. I,	136 Pa. Inf.	1815	1891	Grandview	Tyrone

THE CIVIL WAR

Name	Rank	Organization	Born	Died	Cemetery	Location
Kines, Henry	Pvt. E, 126 Pa. Inf.		1844			
King, Daniel	Pvt. I, 57 Pa. Inf.		1845	1865	Salisburg	N. Car.
King, Erastus	Pvt. E, 148 Pa. Inf.		1832	1910	Greenlawn	Roaring Spring
King, Hezekiah	Pvt. E, 3 Pa. Inf.					
	Cpl. G, 16 Pa. Cav.		1837	1916	Rose Hill	Altoona
King, James	Pvt. K, 125 Pa. Inf.					
King, James	Pvt. D, 84 Pa. Inf.					
King, John	Pvt. F, 95 Pa. Inf.		1834	1912	Cascade	Pa.
King, John	Pvt. D, 171 Pa. Inf.				Mt. Zion	Bedford Co.
King, John T.	Pvt. E, 76 Pa. Inf.		1843	1911	Rose Hill	Altoona
King, Thomas	1Lt. 101 Pa. Inf.					
King, William H.	Pvt. A, 3 Pa. Inf.					
	Cpl. M, 102 Pa. Inf.		1841			
Kinkead, David P.	Pvt. K, 22 Pa. Cav.		1833			
Kinley, Samuel	1Lt. C, 110 Pa. Inf.					
Kinney, Jackson	Pvt. M, 9 Pa. Cav.		1823	1904	Grazierville	Tyrone
Kinney, James E.	Pvt. D, 14 Pa. Inf.		1832			
Kinney, John P.	Pvt. D, 3 Pa. Inf.		1839			
Kinney, John T.	Pvt. A, Ind. Bn. Pa. Mil.		1846			
Kinney, Patrick	Pvt. E, 28 Pa. Inf.					
	Pvt. E, 17 U. S. Inf.		1844	1928	Calvary	Altoona
Kinney, Perry	Pvt. D, 3 Pa. Inf.		1838			
Kinney, Thomas	Pvt. A, 110 Pa. Inf.					
Kinsel, Erastus	Pvt. A, 125 Pa. Inf.			1863	Antis	Bellwood
Kinsel, Henry M.	Pvt. H, 110 Pa. Inf.			1863	Gettysburg	Pa.
Kinsel, J. L.						
Kinsel, John M.	Pvt. A, 125 Pa. Inf.		1845	1923	Antis	Bellwood
Kinsel, Jonathon B.	Pvt. F, 76 Pa. Inf.		1841	1863	Fort Wagner	S. Car.
Kinsel, Joseph	Pvt. F, 133 Pa. Inf.		1836	1927	Fairview	Altoona
Kinsel, Miles G.	Cpl. F, 76 Pa. Inf.		1835	1864		
Kinsel, Thomas	Pvt. H, 110 Pa. Inf.				Charlottesville	Bellwood
Kinsel, William H.	Pvt. E, 84 Pa. Inf.					
Kinter, J. Austin	Pvt. F, 206 Pa. Inf.		1848	1915	Pittsburgh	Pa.
Kinzle, William	Pvt. A, 5 Pa. Cav.		1838	1911	Rose Hill	Altoona
Kipple, George H.	Pvt. E, 3 Pa. Inf.		1835	1920	Fairview	Altoona
Kirkpatrick, Chauncey F.	Cpl. A, 125 Pa. Inf.		1836	1885	Logan Valley	Bellwood
Kirkpatrick, James E.	Cpl. K, 22 Pa. Cav.		1841	1864	Antietam	Maryland
Kirkpatrick, William	Pvt. K, 46 Pa. Mil.		1817			
Kirkpatrick, William	Pvt. A, 205 Pa. Inf.					
Kiser, John F.	Pvt. A, 101 Pa. Inf.		1848	1896	Fairview	Altoona
Kissell, John G.	Pvt. D, 125 Pa. Inf.					
	Cpl. C, 46 Pa. Mil.					
	Pvt. G, 5 Pa. Cav.		1845	1930	Oak Ridge	Altoona
Kissinger, John B.	Pvt. B, 202 Pa. Inf.		1848	1897	Oak Ridge	Altoona
Kitchell, Cornelius L.	Pvt. C, 46 Pa. Mil.		1841			
Kite, George W.	1Lt. F, 31 Pa. Inf.					
Kitt, Samuel	Pvt. C, 46 Pa. Mil.		1830	1880	Fairview	Altoona
Klare, Andrew	Pvt. A, 110 Pa. Inf.					
Kleffman, John I.	Pvt. G, 208 Pa. Inf.		1843	1928	Fairview	Altoona
Klepser, Andrew J.	Pvt. O, 28 Pa. Inf.		1841	1862	Fairview	Altoona
Kline, Daniel	Pvt. C, 22 Pa. Cav.		1842			
Kline, Henry Oscar	Pvt. C, 184 Pa. Inf.		1849	1926	Rose Hill	Altoona
Kline, John	Pvt. A, 23 Pa. Mil.		1840			
Kline, John G.	Pvt. D, 192 Pa. Inf.		1840		Greenwood	Altoona
Klinefelter, Aaron	Pvt. A, 148 Pa. Inf.		1842	1918	Rose Hill	Altoona
Klingensmith, William H.	Pvt. C, 46 Pa. Mil.		1847			
Knapp, Harvey W.	Pvt. D, 84 Pa. Inf.					
	Pvt. G, 57 Pa. Inf.		1843			
Knee, David	Cpl. I, 34 Pa. Inf.		1842	1926	Gospel	Gallitzin
Knee, William	Sgt. I, 14 Pa. Inf.		1832	1917	Dayton	Ohio
Knepp, Joseph	Pvt. C, 102 Pa. Inf.			1900	McVeytown	Pa.

SOLDIERS OF BLAIR COUNTY

Name	Rank Organization	Born	Died	Cemetery	Location
Knepper, Henry S.	Pvt. H, 110 Pa. Inf.				
Knepper, Joseph A.	Pvt. E, 23 Pa. Mil.	1837	1884	Fairview	Altoona
Knighton, William C.	Sgt. D, 201 Pa. Inf.		1895	Calvary	Altoona
Knipple, G. W.	Pvt. G, 13 Pa. Cav.			Greenfield	Claysburg
Knipple, John A.	Pvt. A, 84 Pa. Inf.				
	Cpl. L, 3 Pa. Art.	1840	1908	Asbury	Altoona
Knise, Stephen F.	Pvt. 3 Md. Inf.				
Knobb, James	Pvt. B, 22 Pa. Cav.	1827			
Knode, Thomas	Pvt. C, 110 Pa. Inf.				
Knoll, Henry S.	Pvt. E, 125 Pa. Inf.				
Knollen, William	Pvt. C, 205 Pa. Inf.	1845			
Knox, John M.	Mus. F, 76 Pa. Inf.	1842	1864	Cold Harbor	Virginia
Knox, Robert	Pvt. G, 97 Pa. Inf.	1846	1868	Antis	Bellwood
Knox, Thomas	Sgt. 54 Mass. C. T.				
Knox, William	Pvt. F, 76 Pa. Inf.	1844	1862	Hilton Head	S. Car.
Koch, Andrew H.	Pvt. A, 54 N. Y. Inf.	1847	1909	Fairview	Altoona
Koch, David	Pvt. A, 54 N. Y. Inf.	1841	1909	Fairview	Altoona
Koch, John W.	Pvt. Ind. Bn. Pa. Mil.	1845	1915	Fairview	Altoona
Kochendarfer, Jacob C.	Pvt. C, 133 Pa. Inf.	1840	1893	Spring Hope	Martinsburg
Kochenderfer, William W.	Pvt. A, 19 Pa. Cav.	1847	1882	Port Royal	Pa.
Kolb, Henry	Pvt. I, 14 Pa. Inf.	1841			
Koofer, Christian G.	Pvt. H, 12 Pa. Cav.	1842	1864	Frankstown	Hollidaysburg
Kooken, John R.	Cpt. C, 110 Pa. Inf.		1862	Fredericksburg	Virginia
Koons, Charles David	Pvt. K, 131 Pa. Inf.	1827	1910	Grandview	Tyrone
Koon, Henry C.	Pvt. K, 110 Pa. Inf.				
	Pvt. I, 6 U. S. Cav.	1844	1897	Bald Eagle	Tyrone
Koontz, Jacob M.	Pvt. A, 13 Ohio Inf.	1841	1927	Oak Ridge	Altoona
Kopp, Andrew H.	Pvt. D, 78 Pa. Inf.	1837	1918	Fairview	Altoona
Kopp, George W.	Pvt. F, 5 Pa. Art.				
Kough, George	Pvt. H, 6 Md. Inf.				
Kough, John S.	Pvt. F, 76 Pa. Inf.				
	Pvt. E, 125 Pa. Inf.	1827	1903	Fairview	Altoona
Kounsman, David	Pvt. F, 76 Pa. Inf.	1842	1863	Fort Wagner	S. Car.
Kounsman, Samuel	Pvt. F, 76 Pa. Inf.	1844	1863	Fort Wagner	S. Car.
Kraft, J. Penrose	Pvt. K, 200 Pa. Inf.	1839	1909	Oak Ridge	Altoona
Kraft, Phillip	Cpl. F, 31 Pa. Inf.				
	Cpl. A, 191 Pa. Inf.				
Kratzer, John	Pvt. D, 184 Pa. Inf.	1839	1915	Fairview	Altoona
Kreider, E. W. H.	Pvt. G, 49 Pa. Inf.	1833	1901	Fairview	Altoona
Kreider, J. Cloyd	Mus. F, 125 Pa. Inf.				
	Pvt. F, 152 Pa. Inf.	1846	1899	Fairview	Altoona
Krider, Henry H.	Pvt. E, 45 Pa. Inf.	1839	1900	Warriors Mark	Pa.
Kreider, Tobias	Fn. U. S. Navy	1837			
Kreps, James	Pvt. A, 110 Pa. Inf.				
Kress, George G.	Pvt. H, 3 Pa. Inf.				
	Sgt. M, 62 Pa. Inf.	1839	1864	Wilderness	Virginia
Kriner, Henry	Pvt. E, 126 Pa. Inf.	1846	1902	Oak Ridge	Altoona
Kriner, William	Pvt. H, 49 Pa. Inf.	1831			
Krise, John M.	Pvt. H, 110 Pa. Inf.				
Krise, Hugh G.	Sgt. K, 125 Pa. Inf.				
Krise, Stephen J.	Pvt. K, 3 Md. Inf.	1836	1909	St. Johns	Altoona
Krise, Thomas F.	Pvt. M, 102 Pa. Inf.	1848	1920	St. Augustine	Cambria Co.
Krotzen, John	Pvt. F, 76 Pa. Inf.	1841			
Krotzer, Henry	Pvt. F, 76 Pa. Inf.	1844	1864	Salisbury	N. Car.
Krouse, George G.	Pvt. E, 49 Pa. Inf.	1830	1895	Fairview	Altoona
Krouse, John F.	Pvt. M, 12 Pa. Cav.	1830	1879	Fairview	Altoona
Krumick, John	Pvt. Ind. Bn. Cav. Pa. Mil.	1827			
Krupple, John A.	Pvt. A, 84 Pa. Inf.				
Kuchman, J. Adam	Pvt. D, 99 Pa. Inf.	1838	1907	Reform Church	Morrison Cove
Kuhn, George	Pvt. F, 49 Pa. Inf.	1827	1882	Lutheran	Hollidaysburg
Kuhn, George W.	Pvt. D, 3 Pa. Inf.				
	Sgt. M, 9 Pa. Cav.	1839	1925	Greenwood	Altoona

THE CIVIL WAR 219

Name	Rank Organization	Born	Died	Cemetery	Location
Kuhns, John Thomas	Pvt. H, 149 Pa. Inf.	1832	1918	Carson Valley	Duncansville
Kuhn, William C.	Pvt. H, 136 Pa. Inf.	1839	1922	Logan Valley	Bellwood
Kulp, Henry	Pvt. L, 6 Pa. Cav.	1824	1873	Presbyterian	Hollidaysburg
Kurtz, George F.	Pvt. I, 14 Pa. Inf.				
	Pvt. I, 137 Pa. Inf.	1844	1883	Fairview	Altoona
Kurtz, John H.	Pvt. D, 1 Pa. Cav.	1842	1921	Grandview	Tyrone
Kyle, Hugh	Pvt. I, 205 Pa. Inf.	1835			
Kyle, Israel	Pvt. G, 21 Pa. Cav.		1912	Conemaugh	Pa.
Kyle, Silas	Pvt. B, 208 Pa. Inf.				
Kyle, William Franklin	Pvt. B, 208 Pa. Inf.	1847	1921	Presbyterian	Williamsburg
Kylor, Jacob	Pvt. E, 84 Pa. Inf.		1864	Fredericksburg	Virginia
Kyler, Samuel		1844			Iowa
Kyper, George	Pvt. D, 1 Pa. Art.	1841			
Labold, John	Pvt. F, 31 Pa. Inf.				
Lackey, George S.	Sgt. G, 9 Pa. Cav.	1843	1917	Logan Valley	Bellwood
Lafferty, George W.	Pvt. F, 76 Pa. Inf.				
	Sgt. F, 6 U. S. Inf.	1845	1916	Asbury	Altoona
Lafferty, Isaac H.	Pvt. I, 137 Pa. Inf.				
	Smn, U. S. Navy	1843	1893	Oak Ridge	Altoona
Lafferty, John	Cpl. F, 76 Pa. Inf.	1841			
Lafferty, Joseph	Sgt. B, 3 Pa. Inf.	1836			
Lafferty, Joseph W.	Sgt. G, 12 Pa. Cav.	1833			
Lafferty, William H.	Pvt. F, Ind. Bn. Pa. Mil.	1846			
Lafner, Henry	Pvt. A, 181 Ohio Inf.		1926	Arlington	Virginia
Lago, John	Pvt. E, 46 Pa. Mil.	1819			
Lahey, Thomas	Pvt. C, 84 Pa. Inf.	1832			
Laird, John	Pvt. B, 3 Pa. Inf.	1842			
Laird, John B.	Sgn. 4 Ohio Inf.	1825	1898	Logan Valley	Bellwood
Laird, Robert A.	Pvt. Ind. Cav. Pa. Mil.				
	2Lt. I, 22 Pa. Cav.	1843		Grandview	Tyrone
Laise, John H.	Pvt. H, 14 Pa. Inf.				
	Pvt. C, 76 Pa. Inf.	1843	1887	Carson Valley	Duncansville
Lambright, Johnston R.	Pvt. E, 125 Pa. Inf.				
Lambright, Samuel	Mus. E, 46 Pa. Mil.				
	Pvt. H, 110 Pa. Inf.	1845		Grandview	Tyrone
Lambright, William B.	Cpl. A, 84 Pa. Inf.			Mt. Zion	Bedford Co.
Lamburn, Thomas	Pvt. C, 205 Pa. Inf.	1844			
Lamca, John	Pvt. I, 17 Pa. Cav.	1839	1928	Oak Ridge	Altoona
Lammison, George	Pvt. C, 110 Pa. Inf.				
Lammison, Thomas	Pvt. C, 110 Pa. Inf.				
Lander, Jacob Seydell	1Lt. C, 148 Pa. Inf.	1836	1864	Fairview	Altoona
Landon, David	Pvt. B, 133 Ohio Inf.	1845	1924	Logan Valley	Bellwood
Landon, Joel	Pvt. M, 62 Pa. Inf.				
Lane, David C.	Sgt. C, 110 Pa. Inf.				
Lane, David M.	Pvt. A, 84 Pa. Inf.				
	Pvt. G, 57 Pa. Inf.	1843			
Lane, George S.	Pvt. H, 3 Pa. Inf.				
	Pvt. M, 62 Pa. Inf.				
	Pvt. B, 13 Pa. Cav.	1840	1896	Lutheran	Hollidaysburg
Lane, George W.	Pvt. E, 13 Ill. Cav.	1842	1912	Huntingdon	Pa.
Lane, James H.	Pvt. G, 11 Pa. Cav.	1833	1903	Catholic	Lilly
Lane, John S.	Pvt. H, 3 Pa. Inf.				
	Pvt. A, 84 Pa. Inf.				
	Pvt. G, 57 Pa. Inf.	1837	1880	Lutheran	Hollidaysburg
Lane, Milton	Cpl. H, 54 Mass. Inf.	1832	1917	Oak Ridge	Altoona
Lane, William H.	Pvt. H, 84 Pa. Inf.				
	Pvt. H, 57 Pa. Inf.	1813	1868	Lutheran	Hollidaysburg
Lanely, Richard	Pvt. U, 84 Pa. Inf.				
	Pvt. I, 57 Pa. Inf.	1846			
Lang, Benjamin F.	Pvt. B, 208 Pa. Inf.				
Lang, James	Pvt. C, 110 Pa. Inf.		1864	Andersonville	Georgia

Name	Rank Organization	Born	Died	Cemetery	Location
Lang, James	Pvt. C, 76 Pa. Inf.	1831			
Lang, John S.					
Lang, Joseph Hewitt	Pvt. B, 125 Pa. Inf.				
	Sgt. B, 208 Pa. Inf.	1842	1893	Presbyterian	Williamsburg
Lang, Paul M.	Pvt. A, 84 Pa. Inf.		1862	Lutheran	Hollidaysburg
Lang, Robert H.	Pvt. C, 3 Pa. Inf.	1840	1894	St. Pauls	Williamsburg
Lang, Silas					
Lang, William	Pvt. B, 125 Pa. Inf.	1835	1907	Oak Ridge	Altoona
Lang, William L.	Pvt. D, 22 Pa. Cav.				
	Pvt. E, 104 Pa. Inf.	1845	1901	Presbyterian	Hollidaysburg
Langdon, David	Pvt. D, 78 Pa. Inf.	1840	1911	Cherry Tree	Indiana Co.
Langdon, John G.	Pvt. F, 76 Pa. Inf.				
Langer, Lewis	Pvt. H, 117 Pa. Inf.	1843	1911	Rose Hill	Altoona
Langham, James	Pvt. E, 49 Pa. Inf.	1838	1916	Carson Valley	Duncansville
Langham, Samuel	Pvt. A, 55 Pa. Inf.	1844	1868	Carson Valley	Duncansville
Langham, Soloman	Pvt. E, 125 Pa. Inf.				
	Sgt. E, 13 Pa. Cav.			Carson Valley	Duncansville
Landsburgh, Cyrus					
Lantz, Daniel	Pvt. A, 205 Pa. Inf.	1831	1900	Fairview	Altoona
Lantz, Isaac	Pvt. E, 184 Ohio Inf.		1897	Guilford	Altoona
Lantz, Isaac	Pvt. K, 46 Pa. Mil.	1843			
Lantz, Jacob M.	Pvt. L, 12 Pa. Cav.	1844	1896	Rose Hill	Altoona
Lantz, John C.	Pvt. K, 82 Pa. Inf.	1828	1907	Fairview	Altoona
Lantz, Stephen A.	Pvt. F, 28 Pa. Inf.	1840			
Laporte, Adolphus M.	Pvt. A, 125 Pa. Inf.				
	Cpl. L, 2 Pa. Art.	1844	1919	Alexandria	Pa.
Laporte, Anson Parson	Pvt. E, 46 Pa. Mil.				
	Cpl. I, 205 Pa. Inf.	1842	1913	Grandview	Tyrone
Laporte, Lemuel	Pvt. F, 2 Pa. Cav.	1840			
Larman, John S.	Mus. I, 55 Pa. Inf.	1841			
Larrish, Wilbur F.	Pvt. G, 57 Pa. Inf.	1845			
Laskey, Thomas W.	Pvt. U, 22 Pa. Cav.	1844			
Latherow, George W.	Cpl. D, 110 Pa. Inf.				
	Pvt. D, 1 Pa. Art.	1827	1890	Fairview	Altoona
Laub, Charles E.	Sgt. F, 31 Pa. Inf.				
Laub, William A. B.	Pvt. D, 125 Pa. Inf.				
	Pvt. Ind. Cav. Pa. Mil.	1830			
Lauffer, Valentine	Pvt. A, 55 Pa. Inf.		1899	Pine Grove	Puzzletown
Laughlin, John M. C.	Pvt. E, 3 Pa. Inf.	1837			
Laughlin, Patrick	Pvt. A, 46 Pa. Mil.				
	Pvt. C, 91 Pa. Inf.	1841	1934	St. Johns	Altoona
Laughlin, Michael	Pvt. H, 4 Pa. Inf.	1837	1921	St. Johns	Altoona
Laughlin, Samuel			1868		Duncansville
Laughlin, William	Pvt. I, 205 Pa. Inf.	1846			
Lausane, Moses	Pvt. A, 110 Pa. Inf.				
Lauzman, John	Pvt. C, 110 Pa. Inf.				
Law, David	Sgt. D, 1 W. Va. Inf.	1837	1888	Fairview	Altoona
Law, John H.	Pvt. I, 137 Pa. Inf.				
	Pvt. E, 13 Pa. Cav.	1840	1918	Lutheran	Hollidaysburg
Lawly, Thomas	Pvt. E, 14 Wis. Inf.	1838	1878	St. Marys	Hollidaysburg
Lawrence, William H.	Sgt. A, 1 Pa. Art.	1841	1887	Logan Valley	Bellwood
Leake, Adam	Pvt. A, 209 Pa. Inf.	1849	1923	Fairview	Altoona
Leap, Andrew	Cpl. A, 3 Pa. Inf.	1840	1914	Greenlawn	Hollidaysburg
Leaper, William	Pvt. B, Muchler's Bat.	1819	1889	Oak Ridge	Altoona
Leaphart, James C.	Pvt. F, 77 Pa. Inf.	1825			
Lear, Daniel	Pvt. I, 55 Pa. Inf.	1838			
Lear, Franklin	Pvt. F, 77 Pa. Inf.	1846		Hopewell	Pa.
Leer, John	Pvt. E, 125 Pa. Inf.		1862	Antietam	Maryland
Lehr, John	Pvt. Ind. Cav. Pa. Mil.	1818			
Lear, John	Pvt. M, 62 Pa. Inf.	1837			
Lehr, Joseph W.	Cpl. G, 16 Pa. Cav.	1844			
Leer, William	Pvt. C, 110 Pa. Inf.	1847	1912	Greenlawn	Roaring Spring

THE CIVIL WAR

Name	Rank Organization	Born	Died	Cemetery	Location
Lear, William	Pvt. H, 3 Pa. Inf.	1839			
Lebrick, Joseph	Pvt. A, 110 Pa. Inf.		1862	Winchester	Virginia
Lecrone, William K.	Pvt. C, 91 Pa. Inf.	1841	1900	Keagy	Bedford Co.
Ledger, Joseph J.	Pvt. A, 3 Pa. Inf.				
	Cpl. E, 84 Pa. Inf.	1837			
Lee, George F.	Pvt. F, 2 Pa. Cav.	1840	1928		
Lee, James	Pvt. C, 46 Pa. Mil.				
	Pvt. B, 13 Pa. Cav.	1843	1864	Andersonville	Georgia
Lee, John	2Lt. B, 203 Pa. Inf.	1845			
Lee, Martin	Pvt. K, 125 Pa. Inf.				
	Pvt. E, 13 Ohio Cav.				
	Cpl. F, Ind. Bn. Pa. Mil.	1840	1904	Calvary	Altoona
Leedom, Jeremiah	Pvt. G, 1 W. Va. Art.	1839	1893	Houtzdale	Pa.
Leedom, Levi	Pvt. E, 125 Pa. Inf.	1842	1932	Presbyterian	Hollidaysburg
Leepard, Joseph	Pvt. D, 202 Pa. Inf.	1831			
Leeper, Martin V.	Pvt. E, 20 Pa. Cav.	1842	1928	Oak Ridge	Altoona
Leeper, William	Pvt. B, Ind. Bn. Pa. Art.	1829	1889	Oak Ridge	Altoona
Leet, Callohan M.	Pvt. G, 125 Pa. Inf.				
	Pvt. A, Ind. Bn. Pa. Mil.	1841			
Leet, Jonathan T.	Pvt. B, Ind. Bn. Pa. Mil.				
	Pvt. M, 22 Pa. Cav.	1847	1917	Presbyterian	Hollidaysburg
Leffard, Enoch J.	Pvt. D, 1 Pa. Art.	1840			
Leffard, John K.	Pvt. D, 1 Pa. Art.	1843			
Lego, George	Pvt. H, 12 Pa. Cav.	1843	1864	Andersonville	Georgia
Lego, George	Pvt. D, 192 Pa. Inf.				
Lego, John	Cpl. E, 46 Pa. Mil.				
Lego, Martin W.	Pvt. D, 3 Pa. Inf.				
	Sgt. K, 110 Pa. Inf.	1840	1867	Bald Eagle	Tyrone
Lego, William	Pvt. A, 125 Pa. Inf.				
Leidig, Daniel	Pvt. I, 14 Pa. Inf.	1838			
Leightley, James J.	Pvt. C, 34 Pa. Inf.	1844			
Leightner, Henry	Pvt. K, 84 Pa. Inf.	1840	1905	Oak Ridge	Altoona
Leighty, George	Pvt. E, 125 Pa. Inf.				
Leighty, Joseph D.	Pvt. H, 110 Pa. Inf.				
Lighty, William L.	Mus. H, 36 Pa. Inf.				
	Mus. I, 190 Pa. Inf.	1841	1910	Grandview	Tyrone
Leisering, Jacob Shindel	Pvt. G, Ind. Bn. Pa. Mil.	1847	1910	Fairview	Altoona
Leisenring, Peter S.	Pvt. A, 23 Pa. Mil.	1829			
Leisher, Peter	Pvt. I, 137 Pa. Inf.	1838	1919	St. Marys	Altoona
Leman, Robert M.	Pvt. A, 23 Pa. Mil.				
	Pvt. A, Ind. Bn. Pa. Mil.	1822	1863	Presbyterian	Hollidaysburg
Lennihan, Richard P.	Pvt. M, 62 Pa. Inf.				
Leonard, James L.	Pvt. C, 22 Pa. Cav.				
	Pvt. I, 205 Pa. Inf.	1841	1905	Greenwood	Altoona
Leonard, John	Pvt. A, 84 Pa. Inf.				
	Pvt. G, 57 Pa. Inf.				
Leonard, Nathaniel	Pvt. M, 62 Pa. Inf.	1843			
Leonard, William	Pvt. G, Ind. Bn. Pa. Mil.				
	Pvt. I, 194 Pa. Inf.	1843	1915	Salem Reform	Williamsburg
Lessick, Samuel	Pvt. E, 84 Pa. Inf.				
	Pvt. I, 57 Pa. Inf.				
Lever, John	Pvt. C, 84 Pa. Inf.	1824			
Lewis, Benjamin	Pvt. B, Ind. Bn. Pa. Mil.				
	Pvt. M, 13 Pa. Cav.	1847	1929	Rose Hill	Altoona
Lewis, Charles H.	Cpl. E, 20 Pa. Cav.	1844			
Lewis, David J.	Pvt. D, 35 Pa. Inf.	1840	1873	Fairview	Altoona
Lewis, John J.	Pvt. A, 84 Pa. Inf.				
Lewis, Martin	Cpl. D, 46 Pa. Mil.				
	Sgt. E, 49 Pa. Inf.	1813	1898	Fairview	Altoona
Lewis, Reuben M.	Pvt. D, 126 Pa. Inf.				
	Sgt. E, 2 Pa. Art.				
	Sgt. E, 112 Pa. Inf.	1843	1914	Fairview	Altoona

Name	Rank Organization	Born	Died	Cemetery	Location
Lewis, Thomas R.	Pvt. E, 2 Pa. Art.	1845	1891	Fairview	Altoona
Lewis, William A.	Pvt. H, 53 Pa. Inf.	1834	1886	Fairview	Altoona
Levy, William	Pvt. A, 205 Pa. Inf.				
Lias, Frank A.	Sgt. H, 110 Pa. Inf.			Fairview	Altoona
Lias, James M.	Pvt. E, 84 Pa. Inf.				
	Pvt. I, 57 Pa. Inf.	1826			
Lias, John W.	Pvt. I, 205 Pa. Inf.	1831			
Liebhart, James C.	Pvt. F, 77 Pa. Inf.	1829	1923	Coalport	Clearfield Co.
Liebig, Frederick R. (M)	Cpl. D, 192 Pa. Inf.	1826	1914	Oak Ridge	Altoona
Lightner, Charles	Pvt. C, 53 Pa. Inf.	1838	1862	Fair Oaks	Virginia
Lightner, Daniel	Sgt. C, 53 Pa. Inf.	1840	1893	Lutheran	Hollidaysburg
Lightner, George W.	Pvt. A, 54 Pa. Inf.	1838			
Lightner, John	Pvt. C, 110 Pa. Inf.				
Lightner, John	Pvt. D, 3 Pa. Inf.	1833			
Lightner, Samuel		1838			
Lightner, William A.	Pvt. K, 22 Pa. Cav.	1843			
Lilly, Charles S.	Pvt. 14 U. S. Inf.				
Linard, Joseph	Pvt. E, 149 Pa. Inf.		1905	McVeytown	Pa.
Lincoln, Robert E.	Pvt. D, 1 Pa. Art.	1843			
Lindon, Louis	Pvt. H, 39 N. Y. Inf.	1825	1886	Fairview	Altoona
Lindsey, Ambrose	Pvt. M, 9 Pa. Cav.	1838	1924	Frankstown	Hollidaysburg
Lindsey, C. G.					
Lindley, David P.	Pvt. C, 132 Pa. Inf.	1840	1898	Presbyterian	Hollidaysburg
Lindsey Ephriam	Pvt. C, 110 Pa. Inf.		1864	Arlington	Virginia
Lindsey, Jesse M.	Pvt. H, 103 Pa. Inf.	1822	1890	Fairview	Altoona
Lindsay, John T.	Cpl. D, 7 Bn. D. C. Mil.	1837	1916	Rose Hill	Altoona
Lindsey, Miller	Pvt. A, 205 Pa. Inf.	1825	1906	Fairview	Altoona
Linsey, William	Pvt. L, 1 Md. Cav.		1862	Madison Hill	Virginia
Lindsay, William	Pvt. F, 31 Pa. Inf.	1864		Bristoe Station	Virginia
Lindsay, William	Pvt. M, 62 Pa. Inf.				
	Pvt. M, 91 Pa. Inf.	1841			
Ling, John	Pvt. C, 76 Pa. Inf.	1838	1929	Rose Hill	Altoona
Ling, William	Cpl. C, 76 Pa. Inf.	1840	1905	Frankstown	Hollidaysburg
Lingafelt, Aaron	Pvt. A, 55 Pa. Inf.	1845	1912	Calvary	Altoona
Lingafelt, James M.	Pvt. A, 23 Pa. Mil.				
	Pvt. A, Ind. Bn. Pa. Mil.	1844			
Lingafelter, A. J.	Pvt. C, 76 Pa. Inf.				
Lingenfeldt, David	Cpl. H, 14 Pa. Inf.	1823			
Lingenfelter, David	Pvt. I, 55 Pa. Inf.	1822	1890	Greenlawn	Roaring Spring
Lingenfelter, George W.	Pvt. C, 205 Pa. Inf.	1832	1899	Greenlawn	Roaring Spring
Lingenfelter, Josiah	Pvt. D, 125 Pa. Inf.				
Lingenfelter, Josiah	Pvt. A, 55 Pa. Inf.	1829		Union	Gallitzin
Lingenfelter, Martin	Pvt. C, 205 Pa. Inf.	1828	1903	Union	Claysburg
Lingenfelter, Michael	Pvt. L, 19 Pa. Cav.	1845			
Lingenfelter, Thaddeus	Pvt. F, 77 Pa. Inf.	1848	1909	Upper Claar	Bedford Co.
Lingenfelter, Thomas	Pvt. C, 46 Pa.Mil.	1843			
Lindthurst, Isaac M.	Pvt. D, 121 Pa. Inf.				
	Pvt. H, 2 Pa. Cav.	1845	1915	Greenwood	Altoona
Liptrot, Joseph	Pvt. D, 145 Pa. Inf.				
	Pvt. F, 53 Pa. Inf.				
Lisher, Peter	Pvt. I, 137 Pa. Inf.				
List, Leonard	Pvt. F, 84 Pa. Inf.	1829	1907	Oak Ridge	Altoona
Litten, Morris	Mus. E, 14 W. Va. Inf.	1844	1920	Presbyterian	Hollidaysburg
Little, David J.	Pvt. F, 148 Pa. Inf.	1828	1899	Fairview	Altoona
Little, Francis	Pvt. B, 53 Pa. Inf.		1886	St. Patricks	Newry
Little, Harry D.	Pvt. C, 1 Md. Cav.	1848	1914	Gettysburg	Pa.
Little, Irving	Pvt. I, 55 Pa. Inf.	1837	1862	Beauford	S. Car.
Little, Jacob F.	Pvt. I, 142 Pa. Inf.	1837	1890	Eastlawn	Tyrone
Little, James	Pvt. I, 14 Pa. Inf.	1834			
Little, James	Cpl. I, 55 Pa. Inf.	1835			
Litzinger, George O.	Pvt. K, 22 Pa. Cav.	1847			
Litzinger, Joseph	Pvt. A, 110 Pa. Inf.				

Name	Rank Organization	Born	Died	Cemetery	Location
Livingston, Edward	Sgt. B, 149 Pa. Inf.				
Livingston, Ed. J.	Sgt. D, 192 Pa. Inf.				
Livingston, Samuel	Pvt. D, 13 Pa. Cav.	1841			
Livingston, Thomas C.	Sgt. C, 110 Pa. Inf.			Everett	Pa.
Livingston, Thomas M.	Pvt. A, Ind. Bn. Pa. Mil.				
	Pvt. G, Pa. Mil.	1823			
Lloyd, Alexander M.	Cpt. H, 3 Pa. Inf.	1823	1892	Presbyterian	Hollidaysburg
Lloyd, Henry L.	Pvt. A, 23 Pa. Mil.	1842			
Lloyd, John	Cpl. A, 23 Pa. Mil.				
	Pvt. Ind. Cav. Pa. Mil.	1842	1921	Fairview	Altoona
Lloyd, Thomas	Sgt. B, 70 N. Y. Inf.	1838	1907	St. Patricks	Gallitzin
Lloyd, Thomas E.	Mus. H, 14 Pa. Inf.				
	Mus. G, 125 Pa. Inf.				
	Mus. C, 76 Pa. Inf.	1845	1912	Geeseytown	Hollidaysburg
Lockard, George W.	Pvt. I, 205 Pa. Inf.	1829	1895	Oak Ridge	Altoona
Lockard, Joseph	Pvt. A, 205 Pa. Inf.	1839	1911	Rose Hill	Altoona
Lockard, Thomas R.	Pvt. H, 55 Pa. Inf.	1842	1903	Fairview	Altoona
Locke, Enock Eldridge	Pvt. 15 Pa. Cav.	1841	1878	Presbyterian	Hollidaysburg
Loeb, John Henry	Pvt. F, 4 Pa. Cav.	1844	1916	Fairview	Altoona
Loesh, John W.	Pvt. H, 3 Pa. Inf.	1841			
Logan, James	Pvt. K, 22 Pa. Cav.	1844			
Logan, James A.	Pvt. A, 110 Pa. Inf.	1864			
Logan, James A.	Pvt. F, 76 Pa. Inf.				
Logan, Marshall L.	Pvt. F, 22 Pa. Cav.	1834	1885	Grandview	Tyrone
Logan, William J.	Cpl. D, 188 Pa. Inf.	1847	1906	Presbyterian	Arch Spring
Logue, George H.	Pvt. D, 4 U. S. Inf.	1850	1870	St. Johns	Altoona
Logue, John A.	Pvt. A, 36 Pa. Mil.	1846	1910	Fairview	Altoona
Logue, Orin	Cpl. F, Ind. Bn. Pa. Mil.				
	Pvt. E, 3 Pa. Art.	1839	1904	Fairview	Altoona
Logue, Patrick	Pvt. H, 6 Ohio Inf.	1841	1916	St. Johns	Altoona
London, James	Pvt. M, 22 Pa. Cav.	1846			
London, James G.	Pvt. G, 125 Pa. Inf.				
	Pvt. B, Ind. Bn. Pa. Mil.	1846	1916	Greenlawn	Roaring Spring
Loner, George W.	Sgt. E, 45 Pa. Inf.	1836	1923	Gatesburg	Centre Co.
Lonergan, John James	Pvt. B, 54 Pa. Mil.				
	Pvt. H, 111 Pa. Inf.	1845	1907	St. Johns	Altoona
Long, Abram W.	Pvt. A, 9 Pa. Cav.	1846	1902	Fairview	Altoona
Long, Anthony	Pvt. A, 110 Pa. Inf.				
Long, Daniel	Pvt. A, 205 Pa. Inf.				
Long, Daniel	Pvt. E, 125 Pa. Inf.				
Long, Elijah	Pvt. K, 22 Pa. Cav.	1832			
Long, Elijah	Pvt. B, 208 Pa. Inf.	1834	1898	Fairview	Altoona
Long, Jacob	Pvt. D, 205 Pa. Inf.	1831			
Long, James	Pvt. G, 125 Pa. Inf.		1863	Carson Valley	Duncansville
Long, Jeremiah C.	Pvt. K, 21 Pa. Cav.	1843	1922	Oak Ridge	Altoona
Long, John	Pvt. M, 62 Pa. Inf.		1863	Alexandria	Virginia
Long, John D.	Pvt. H, 3 Pa. Inf.	1837			
Long, Joseph	Pvt. D, 46 Pa. Mil.	1825			
Long, Joseph C.	Sgt. H, 208 Pa. Inf.	1838	1916	Rose Hill	Altoona
Long, Joseph R.	Pvt. K, 3 Pa. Art.	1831	1912	Logan Valley	Bellwood
Long, Samuel I.	Pvt. A, 205 Pa. Inf.			Duvoll	Bedford Co.
Long, Samuel L.	Pvt. D, 125 Pa. Inf.				
Long, Thomas	Pvt. C, 84 Pa. Inf.	1826			
Long, William	Pvt. I, 137 Pa. Inf.				
Longabaugh, Cyrus	Pvt. A, 41 Ill. Inf.				
	Cpl. K, 53 Ill. Inf.	1841			
Longabaugh, Thomas		1809	1878	Logan Valley	Bellwood
Longstreth, James	Pvt. B, 10 Pa. Inf.	1846	1926	Grandview	Altoona
Loomis, William A.	Pvt. H, 192 Pa. Inf.	1842	1900	Fairview	Altoona
Loose, Samuel	Pvt. I, 14 Pa. Inf.	1838			
Lorenz, John B.	Pvt. C, 76 Pa. Inf.	1840	1885		

Name	Rank Organization	Born	Died	Cemetery	Location
Lotz, David M.	Cpl. A, Ind. Bn. Pa. Mil.				
	Pvt. A, 205 Pa. Inf.	1844	1930	Carson Valley	Duncansville
Loucks, Samuel	Pvt. H, 135 Pa. Inf.	1841	1931	Logan Valley	Bellwood
Louder, Samuel A.	Cpl. F, 31 Pa. Inf.				
	Cpl. A, 191 Pa. Inf.	1840	1864	Andersonville	Georgia
Louder, William H.	Pvt. I, 137 Pa. Inf.				
	Pvt. G, 12 Pa. Cav.	1839	1913	Logan Valley	Bellwood
Loudon, David M.	Pvt. E, 3 Pa. Inf.				
	Pvt. K, 46 Pa. Mil.	1833	1896	Fairview	Altoona
Loudon, George M.	Pvt. K, 125 Pa. Inf.		1862	Fairview	Altoona
Loudon, James Alfred	Pvt. D, 13 Pa. Cav.	1846	1930	Fairview	Altoona
Loudon, John	Pvt. Ind. Cav. Pa. Mil.	1824			
Louis, Peter	Pvt. C, 3 Pa. Inf.	1826			
Louis, Samuel					
Love, John	Pvt. H, 41 U.S.C.T.	1811	1907	Eastern Light	Altoona
Love, John D.	Pvt. B, 125 Pa. Inf.	1835	1896	Presbyterian	Hollidaysburg
Love, John G.	Sgt. C, 22 Pa. Cav.	1843			
Love, Windield S.	Pvt. D, 201 Pa. Inf.	1846	1905	Grandview	Tyrone
Lovett, John		1847	1922	Topeka	Kansas
Lovett, John	Pvt. D, 13 Pa. Cav.	1845			
Lovett, John	Pvt. B, Ind. Bn. Pa. Mil.	1846			
Lovett, John	Pvt. G, 125 Pa. Inf.				
Lowder, James R.	Pvt. F, 126 Pa. Inf.	1836	1892	Fairview	Altoona
Lowe, Jacob H.	Pvt. E, 15 Pa. Inf.				
	Sgt. A, 9 Pa. Cav.	1841	1918	Duncannon	Pa.
Lowe, John A.	Pvt. B, 125 Pa. Inf.	1837	1911	Royer Mt.	Williamsburg
Lowe, John	Pvt. B, Ind. Bn. Pa. Mil.				
Lowe, John H.	Pvt. A, 9 Pa. Inf.	1845	1916	Fairview	Altoona
Lowe, Joseph	Pvt. M, 9 Pa. Cav.	1839			
Lowe, William H.	Pvt. A, 84 Pa. Inf.				
Lower, George W.	Cpl. G, 84 Pa. Inf.				
Lower, George W.	Cpl. E, 84 Pa. Inf.				
	Sgt. I, 57 Pa. Inf.	1839	1921	St. Johns	Williamsburg
Lower, Henry G.	Pvt. B, 125 Pa. Inf.				
Lower, Henry N.	Pvt. I, 137 Pa. Inf.				
	1Lt. C, 205 Pa. Inf.	1841	1865	Petersburg	Virginia
Lower, Isaiah P.	Pvt. C, 3 Pa. Inf.	1841			
Lower, John C. D.					
Lower, Josiah W.	Pvt. B, 21 Pa. Cav.				
	Pvt. K, 101 Pa. Inf.	1844	1913	Rose Hill	Altoona
Lower, Peoples					
Lower, Samuel	Pvt. C, 45 Pa. Inf.	1827	1898	Oak Ridge	Altoona
Lower, William Harrison	Pvt. I, 206 Pa. Inf.	1846	1934	Snivelys	Williamsburg
Lowry, Garber	Pvt. A, 23 Pa. Mil.	1824			
Lowry, Robert H.	Pvt. B, 1 Pa. Cav.	1841			
Lowther, John	Pvt. D, 46 Pa. Mil.	1837			
Loy, Christian	Pvt. B, 127 Pa. Inf.		1899	Harrisburg	Pa.
Lucas, Abraham	Pvt. C, 3 Pa. Inf.				
	Pvt. B, 125 Pa. Inf.				
	Mus. L, 19 Pa. Cav.	1842			
Lucas, Daniel	Pvt. E, 84 Pa. Inf.		1863	Chancellorsville	Virginia
Lucas, Gabriel	Pvt. B, 125 Pa. Inf.				
Lucas, John	Pvt. D, 1 Pa. Art.	1835			
Lucas, John B.	Pvt. D, 192 Pa. Inf.	1820	1894	Fairview	Altoona
Lucas, John D.	Pvt. F, 148 Pa. Inf.	1821	1905	Fairview	Altoona
Lucas, John H.	Pvt. B, 125 Pa. Inf.				
Luffer, William	Pvt. E, 208 Pa. Inf.		1891	New Bloomfield	Pa.
Lumadue, William	Pvt. H, 110 Pa. Inf.				
Lundegren, Charles A.	Pvt. K, 7 N.Y. Inf.	1830	1910	Fairview	Altoona
Lunden, George W.	Pvt. G, 125 Pa. Inf.		1863	Lutheran	Hollidaysburg
Lundy, George	Cpl. B, Ind. Bn. Pa. Mil.	1844			
Lundy, Joseph F.	Pvt. A, Ind. Bn. Pa. Mil.				
	Pvt. G, 12 Pa. Cav.	1846			

THE CIVIL WAR

Name	Rank Organization	Born	Died	Cemetery	Location
Lusby, Lemuel	Pvt. D, 7 Bn. D. C.	1825			
Luther, Francis	Pvt. C, 76 Pa. Inf.	1830			
Luther, Joseph	Pvt. Ind. Cav. Pa. Mil.	1824			
Lykens, Martin	Pvt. B, 49 Pa. Inf.			Asbury	Altoona
Lynch, Joseph W.	Mus. K, 46 Pa. Mil.	1845			
Lynch, Robert W.	Pvt. D, 84 Pa. Inf.	1815	1872	St. Johns	Altoona
Lyne, John S.	Sgt. C, 9 Pa. Inf.				
	Cpt. G, 130 Pa. Inf.	1836			
Lynn, Levi M.	Pvt. C, 205 Pa. Inf.	1844	1899	Greenlawn	Roaring Spring
Lynn, William M.	Mus. E, 76 Pa. Inf.	1846		Lutheran	Newry
Lyle, Robert V.	Pvt. H, 7 Pa. Inf.				
	Pvt. B, 11 Pa. Art.	1841	1909	Logan Valley	Bellwood
Lyons, George W.	Sgt. F, 41 U.S.C.T.			Union	Hollidaysburg
Lyons, James	Cpl. B, 54 Mass. Inf.	1829			
Lyons, Michael	Pvt. A, 3 Pa. Inf.	1838			
Lysle, James W.	Pvt. E, 3 U.S.C.T.	1840	1906	Oak Ridge	Altoona
Lytle, A. F.	Smn. U. S. Navy			Fairview	Altoona
Lyttle, Albert C.	Pvt. A, 36 Pa. Mil.	1845	1910	Fairview	Altoona
Lytle, Alonzo H.	Pvt. F, 194 Pa. Inf.	1847	1916	Rose Hill	Altoona
Lytle, Benjamin C.	Pvt. D, 149 Pa. Inf.	1838	1864	Spotsylvania C. H.	Virginia
Lytle, Ephriam F.	Pvt. C, 209 Pa. Inf.	1821	1881	Fairview	Altoona
Lytle, George	Pvt. F, 77 Pa. Inf.	1821			
Lytle, Isaac	Pvt. F, 77 Pa. Inf.	1846			
Lytle, John	Pvt. I, 14 Pa. Inf.	1841			
Lytle, Reuben S.	Pvt. K, 22 Pa. Cav.	1844			
Lytle, Robert	Pvt. A, 23 Pa. Inf.	1845			
Lytle, Robert J.	Pvt. K, 14 Pa. Cav.	1840	1895	Fairview	Altoona
Lytle, William	Pvt. D, 14 Pa. Inf.	1836			
Lytle, William	Cpl. A, 110 Pa. Inf.		1864	Arlington	Virginia
Lytle, William M.	Pvt. B, Ind. Bn. Pa. Mil.	1846			
Mabus, Christian	Pvt. D, 46 Pa. Mil.	1832			
Mabus, Leonard	Pvt. K, 125 Pa. Inf.		1862	Maryland Hts.	Maryland
MacDowell, Thomas C.	Col. 84 Pa. Inf.	1814	1883	Harrisburg	Pa.
Mace, John	Mus. F, 31 Pa. Inf.				
Machamer, David	Pvt. B, 22 Pa. Cav.	1844			
Machlan, James L.	2Lt. D, 20 Pa. Cav.	1844	1905	Fairview	Altoona
Machoney, John	Pvt. B, Ind. Bn. Pa. Mil.	1846			
Machtley, John F.	Pvt. C, 82 Pa. Inf.	1844	1916	Alum Bank	Bedford Co.
Mack, John	Pvt. A, 7 Pa. Cav.	1844	1929	St. Patricks	Newry
Mack, Joseph	Pvt. F, 6 Pa. Cav.	1832	1898	German Baptist	Claar
Mackey, John	Cpl. C, 26 Pa. Mil.	1802	1886	Fairview	Altoona
Mackey, Martin H.	Sgt. F, 148 Pa. Inf.	1832	1913	Fairview	Altoona
Mackey, William I.	2Lt. F, 148 Pa. Inf.	1839	1933	Fairview	Altoona
Madara, Daniel	Cpl. D, 46 Pa. Mil.	1836	1865	Logan Valley	Bellwood
Madara, David W.	Cpt. I, 55 Pa. Inf.	1841	1917	Holsingers	Bakers Summit
Madara, George					
Madara, Henry	Pvt. E, 37 Pa. Inf.	1842	1862	South Mountain	Maryland
Madara, Jacob	Pvt. F, 37 Pa. Inf.				
	Pvt. H, 191 Pa. Inf.	1838	1864	Andersonville	Georgia
Madara, Perry	Cpl. E, 37 Pa. Inf.				
	Cpl. G, 191 Pa. Inf.		1865	Salisbury	N. C.
Madara, Samuel	Pvt. A, 110 Pa. Inf.	1840	1917	Newark	Ohio
Madara, Washington					
Madden, Abisha	Pvt. I, 55 Pa. Inf.	1846	1906	Yellow Spring	Williamsburg
Madden, Daniel	Pvt. I, 55 Pa. Inf.	1836			
Madison, John	Pvt. D, 125 Pa. Inf.				
Madison, Joseph W.	Pvt. D, 3 Pa. Inf.	1832			
Maguire, George	Pvt. D, 205 Pa. Inf.	1845			
Maher, Peter M.	Pvt. E, 67 Pa. Inf.	1844	1922	St. Patricks	Newry
Mahoney, Bartholomew	Pvt. B, 12 U. S. Inf.	1831	1871	St. Marys	Hollidaysburg

Name	Rank Organization	Born	Died	Cemetery	Location
Mahoney, John	Pvt. A, 11 Pa. Inf.	1844	1903	Everett	Pa.
Maines, Isaac	Pvt. K, 84 Pa. Inf.				
	Sgt. K, 57 Pa. Inf.	1836	1912	Carson Valley	Duncansville
Maize, Joseph	Pvt. D, 192 Pa. Inf.	1827	1895	Fairview	Altoona
Makin, Abraham	Pvt. H, 110 Pa. Inf.	1821	1864		
Malligan, James	Pvt. G, 36 Pa. Inf.	1827	1905	St. Marys	Hollidaysburg
Mallon, Allen					
Malone, Christian	Pvt. H, 14 Pa. Inf.				
	Pvt. M, 62 Pa. Inf.				
	Pvt. D, 192 Pa. Inf.	1832	1866	Lutheran	Hollidaysburg
Malone, Hezekiah	Pvt. K, 133 Pa. Inf.				
	Pvt. D, 13 Pa. Cav.	1842	1901	Lutheran	Hollidaysburg
Malone, James Y.	Pvt. I, 137 Pa. Inf.				
	Pvt. B, 192 Pa. Inf.	1837	1898	Presbyterian	Hollidaysburg
Malone, John	Pvt. H, 191 Pa. Inf.	1839	1916	Yellow Creek	Bedford Co.
Malone, Robert	Pvt. D, 192 Pa. Inf.	1841	1909	Carson Valley	Duncansville
Maloney, John	2Lt. E, 84 Pa. Inf.	1831			
Maloy, Thomas	Pvt. H, 3 Pa. Inf.				
	Cpl. M, 62 Pa. Inf.				
	Sgt. B, Ind. Bn. Pa. Mil.	1823	1899	St. Marys	Hollidaysburg
Malseed, Charles H.	Pvt. A, Ind. Bn. Pa. Mil.				
	Pvt. D, 1 Pa. Art.	1845			
Mangus, Abraham	Pvt. H, 14 Pa. Inf.	1840			
Mangus, Cyrus A.	Pvt. F, 135 Pa. Inf.				
	Pvt. I, 211 Pa. Inf.	1841	1927	Fairview	Altoona
Manley, David	Pvt. L, 3 Pa. Art.				
	Pvt. D, 188 Pa. Inf.	1828	1918	Asbury	Altoona
Mann, James S.	Pvt. Ind. Cav. Pa. Mil.	1831			
Manning, John W.	Cpl. D, 3 Pa. Inf.				
	1Lt. H, 110 Pa. Inf.	1835	1864	Spotsylvania C. H.	Virginia
Mansberger, Benjamin	Pvt. C, 22 Pa. Cav.	1845			
Mantell, Joseph	Pvt. C, 3 Pa. Inf.	1801			
Marble, Daniel D.	Pvt. D, 83 Pa. Inf.	1845	1917	Oak Ridge	Altoona
Mardia, Jacob	Pvt. G, 206 Pa. Inf.	1820	1888	Fairview	Altoona
Mardis, Richard W.	Pvt. B, 9 Pa. Cav.				
	Pvt. M, 3 Pa. Art.				
	Pvt. 188 Pa. Inf.	1844			
Markey, David C.	Pvt. I, 137 Pa. Inf.	1841	1908	Lutheran	Hollidaysburg
Markey, Joseph	Pvt. G, 184 Pa. Inf.	1833	1917	Reform Church	Loysburg
Markley, Isaac	Smn. U. S. Navy	1826	1865	Fairview	Altoona
Markley, Isaac	Pvt. D, 125 Pa. Inf.	1831	1862	Antietam	Maryland
Markley, John M.	Pvt. H, 22 Pa. Cav.	1838			
Marks, Andrew M.			1912	Alfarata	Pa.
Mark, Anthony S.	Pvt. I, 2 D. C. Inf.	1837	1906	Fairview	Altoona
Marks, Benjamin F.	Cpl. C, 76 Pa. Inf.	1842	1864		
Marks, Jacob	Pvt. C, 76 Pa. Inf.	1827			
Mark, Michael	Pvt. M, 62 Pa. Inf.	1832			
Marlett, Robert L.	Pvt. I, 54 Pa. Inf.	1840	1926	Greenwood	Altoona
Marshall, Alexander W.	Pvt. E, 3 Pa. Inf.				
	Cpt. D, 125 Pa. Inf.	1836	1897	Oak Ridge	Altoona
Marshall, Charles	Pvt. K, 22 Pa. Cav.	1832			
Marshall, George	Pvt. I, 55 Pa. Inf.	1838		National	Lawton
Marshall, James H.	Cpt. I, 208 Pa. Inf.	1833	1897	Oak Ridge	Altoona
Marshall, Winfield S.	Pvt. E, 3 Pa. Inf.				
	Pvt. D, 125 Pa. Inf.				
	Pvt. Ind. Cav. Pa. Mil.	1840			
Marshall, William	Pvt. D, 46 Pa. Mil.				
	Pvt. F, 104 Pa. Inf.	1836	1893	Fairview	Altoona
Marshall, William H.	Pvt. E, 3 Pa. Inf.	1839			
Martin, Andrew	Pvt. F, 76 Pa. Inf.	1838			
Martin, Edmund	Pvt. K, 46 Pa. Mil.	1846			
Martin, Edward	Pvt. F, 76 Pa. Inf.	1844			

THE CIVIL WAR 227

Name	Rank Organization	Born	Died	Cemetery	Location
Martin, Henry	Pvt. G, 125 Pa. Inf.				
	Pvt. D, 192 Pa. Inf.	1833	1922	Lutheran	Hollidaysburg
Martin, James E.	Pvt. K, 34 Pa. Mil.	1846	1916	Fairview	Martinsburg
Martin, James Frederick	Pvt. G, 148 Pa. Inf.	1844	1928	Soldiers Plot	Inglewood, Cal.
Martin, John	Pvt. H, 15 Pa. Inf.			Presbyterian	Williamsburg
Martin, John Calvin		1845	1912	New York	New York
Martin, John	Cpl. F, 76 Pa. Inf.	1840	1864	Chesterfield Hts.	Virginia
Martin, Josiah	Pvt. B, 107 Pa. Inf.	1847	1929	I. O. O. F.	Saxton
Martin, Robert Newton	Pvt. A, 3 Pa. Inf.				
	1Lt. M, 62 Pa. Inf.	1840	1912	Renovo	Pa.
Martin, Samuel	Pvt. F, 101 Ohio Inf.		1863	Nashville	Tennessee
Martin, Thomas Francis	Pvt. B, 101 Pa. Inf.	1843	1909	St. Johns	Altoona
Martin, Wilbur Fiske	1Lt. A, 125 Pa. Inf.	1840	1865	Grandview	Tyrone
Martin, William	Pvt. G, 125 Pa. Inf.				
Martz, William H.	Pvt. D, 42 Pa. Inf.	1840	1881	Fairview	Altoona
Mash, Jacob	Pvt. C, 1 Pa. Art.	1829	1892	Lutheran	Newry
Mason, Charles W.	Pvt. D, 46 Pa. Mil.	1847			
Mason, Robert L.	Pvt. H, 3 Pa. Inf.				
	Sgt. A, 84 Pa. Inf.	1840	1863	Chancellorsville	Virginia
Mason, William H.	Pvt. D, 46 Pa. Mil.				
	Pvt. I, 137 Pa. Cav.	1844	1915	Rose Hill	Altoona
Mateer, Henry H.	Cpl. K, 22 Pa. Cav.	1819	1911	Rose Hill	Altoona
Mattern, Sanford Dewey	Pvt. D, 3 Pa. Inf.	1840	1861	Grandview	Tyrone
Mattern, Tarring S.	Pvt. D, 3 Pa. Inf.	1841	1861	Grandview	Tyrone
Matthew, Edward B.	Pvt. F, 76 Pa. Inf.	1839			
Mathews, James	Pvt. G, 12 Pa. Cav.		1887	Maurers	Altoona
Matthews, James	Pvt. B, 3 Pa. Inf.	1831			
Mathews, James M.	Cpl. E, 125 Pa. Inf.	1844	1911	St. Johns	Altoona
Mathews, John	Pvt. K, 125 Pa. Inf.				
Matthews, Stephen Reed	Pvt. B, 49 Pa. Inf.	1840	1918	Presbyterian	Hollidaysburg
Mattingley, James E.	Pvt. C, 6 Bn. D. C. Mil.	1841	1874	Fairview	Altoona
Mattis, Abraham	Pvt. Ind. Cav. Pa. Mil.	1822			
Maughermer, S. D.	Pvt. A, 84 Pa. Inf.				
Mauk, George W.	Pvt. E, 125 Pa. Inf.		1863	Washington	D. C.
Mauk, Joseph W.	Sgt. H, 14 Pa. Inf.	1836	1861	Union	Claysburg
Mauk, Paul S. (M)	Sgt. I, 55 Pa. Inf.	1829	1896	Union	Claysburg
Maurer, Abraham	Pvt. F, 31 Pa. Inf.				
	Pvt. A, 191 Pa. Inf.	1837			
Mourer, Isaac	2Lt. F, 31 Pa. Inf.				
Maurer, Joseph	Pvt. K, 125 Pa. Inf.				
Maurer, Nathaniel	Pvt. D, 188 Pa. Inf.	1825	1884	Asbury	Altoona
Maus, John	Pvt. A, 55 Pa. Inf.	1845	1916	Calvary	Altoona
Maus, John H.	Pvt. G, 125 Pa. Inf.	1843			
Mausaus, George	Pvt. I, 14 Pa. Inf.	1833			
Maxwell, George W.	Cpl. C, 110 Pa. Inf.	1840	1864	Grandview	Tyrone
Maxwell, James H.	Pvt. A, 72 Pa. Inf.	1839	1866	Fairview	Altoona
Maxwell, Martin M.	Pvt. D, 3 Pa. Inf.				
	2Lt. C, 110 Pa. Inf.	1835			
May, John	Pvt. B, 27 Pa. Inf.	1810	1887	Fairview	Altoona
May, John L.	2Lt. I, 137 Pa. Inf.	1829	1914	Spring Hope	Martinsburg
Mays, William	Pvt. A, 110 Pa. Inf.				
McAdams, William	Pvt. A, 110 Pa. Inf.				
McAlarney, John W.	Cpl. F, 12 Pa. Cav.	1846			
McAninch, William A.	Pvt. F, 76 Pa. Inf.	1844			
McAnnaly, Watson					
McArthur, John	Pvt. F, 19 Pa. Inf.	1840	1920	Oak Ridge	Altoona
McAteer, John J.	Pvt. G, 12 Pa. Cav.	1817			
McAteer, Patrick	Pvt. U, 62 Pa. Inf.	1826			
McAteer, William	Cpl. K, 46 Pa. Mil.	1841			
McAvoy, Michael	Pvt. H, 22 Pa. Cav.	1845			
McAvoy, Michael	Pvt. A, 125 Pa. Inf.				
McBride, Thomas	Cpl. F, Ind. Bn. Pa. Mil.	1837			

SOLDIERS OF BLAIR COUNTY

Name	Rank Organization	Born	Died	Cemetery	Location
McCabe, Edward	Pvt. M, 22 Pa. Cav.	1834			
McCabe, Edward	Pvt. M, 62 Pa. Inf.	1836	1884	St. Marys	Hollidaysburg
McCafferty, James	Pvt. D, 205 Pa. Inf.	1828			
McCahan, David E.	Sgt. G, 125 Pa. Inf.	1841	1897	Presbyterian	Hollidaysburg
McCahan, John	Pvt. C, 3 Pa. Inf.	1831			
McCahan, John A.	Pvt. I, 137 Pa. Inf.				
	Cpt. I, 205 Pa. Inf.	1843	1896	Presbyterian	Hollidaysburg
McCahan, Thomas S.	Pvt. D, 3 Pa. Inf.				
	Cpt. M, 9 Pa. Cav.	1836			
McCahern, James	Pvt. B, 202 Pa. Inf.		1917	Milroy	Pa.
McCall, James	Pvt. M, 62 Pa. Inf.		1863	Bealton Station	Virginia
McCall, Matthew	Pvt. D, 205 Pa. Inf.	1846	1918	Brumbaugh	Hunt'gdon Co.
McCamant, Samuel	Pvt. A, Ind. Bn. Pa. Mil.	1833			
McCamant, Thomas	2Lt. G, 125 Pa. Inf.	1840			
McCandless, David	Pvt. M, 62 Pa. Inf.				
	Pvt. K, 91 Pa. Inf.				
McCarthy, Alvin R.	Pvt. K, 22 Pa. Cav.	1845			
McCartney, Douglass	Pvt. Ind. Cav. Pa. Mil.				
	Cpl. K, 46 Pa. Mil.	1823	1911	Fairview	Altoona
McCartney, George S.	Pvt. A, 125 Pa. Inf.				
McCartney, George S.	Pvt. H, 22 Pa. Cav.	1839	1865		
McCartney, James	Pvt. E, 46 Pa. Mil.	1813			
McCartney, John	Pvt. E, 46 Pa. Mil.	1847			
McCartney, John S.	Pvt. K, 22 Pa. Cav.	1845			
McCartney, James Stephen	Pvt. H, 14 Pa. Inf.				
	Sgt. C, 76 Pa. Inf.	1841	1902	Presbyterian	Williamsburg
McCartney, Thomas C.	Pvt. I, 137 Pa. Inf.				
	Cpt. E, 104 Pa. Inf.	1829	1906	Fairview	Altoona
McCartney, W. Morrison	1Lt. A, 84 Pa. Inf.	1838	1863	Maurers	Altoona
McCarty, Edward Victor	Sgt. G, 12 Pa. Cav.	1844	1905	St. Patricks	Newry
McCarty, Joseph	Pvt. D, 205 Pa. Inf.	1822			
McCaulley, Benjamin F.	Pvt. E, 104 Pa. Inf.	1834	1904	Logan Valley	Bellwood
McCauly, James					
McCauley, James M.					
McCaulley, Martin B.	Pvt. K, 3 Pa. Art.	1830	1898	Logan Valley	Bellwood
McCaulley, William	Pvt. G, 12 Pa. Cav.	1823	1898	Fairview	Altoona
McChesne, John	Pvt. I, 14 Pa. Inf.	1839			
McChesney, John	Cpl. I, 55 Pa. Inf.	1832		Hopewell	Bedford Co.
McClain, Augustus	Pvt. G, 2 Pa. Art.	1825	1899	McMullens	Sinking Valley
McClain, David	Pvt. M, 20 Pa. Cav.	1827	1914	St. Johns	Altoona
McClain, George W.	Pvt. D, 45 Pa. Inf.	1849	1912	Carson Valley	Duncansville
McClain, T. T.					
McClay, William	Pvt. U. S. Marines	1828	1882	Fairview	Altoona
McCleary, George	Pvt. A, Ind. Bn. Pa. Mil.	1845			
McCleary, Samuel	Pvt. K, 125 Pa. Inf.				
McClelland, Adolphus P.	Pvt. G, 125 Pa. Inf.			Charlottesville	Bellwood
McClellan, George A.	Pvt. A, 34 Pa. Inf.				
	Sgt. F, 49 Pa. Inf.	1842	1912	Fairview	Altoona
McClellan, Hugh T.	Pvt. G, 125 Pa. Inf.				
	Pvt. K, 3 Pa. Art.	1841	1892	Fairview	Altoona
McClelland, Jacob	Pvt. A, 205 Pa. Inf.	1836	1905	Hutchisons	Altoona
McClelland, John B.	Sgt. A, 54 Pa. Inf.			Charlottesville	Bellwood
McClellan, John M.	Pvt. U, 1 Pa. Art.	1825	1880	Fairview	Altoona
McClellan, Robert T.	Sgt. I, 205 Pa. Inf.	1834			
McClelland, Thomas	Pvt. G, 125 Pa. Inf.	1835	1894	Charlottesville	Bellwood
McClellan, Thomas R.	Pvt. E, 101 Pa. Inf.	1840			
McClelland, William H.	Pvt. G, 125 Pa. Inf.				
	Pvt. K, 22 Pa. Cav.	1844	1911	Charlottesville	Bellwood
McClintick, David R.	Pvt. K, 205 Pa. Inf.	1848	1929	Grandview	Tyrone
McCloskey, Cornelius	Pvt. K, 46 Pa. Mil.	1846	1863		
McCloskey, Cornelius (m)	Pvt. 55 Pa. Inf.	1817	1889	St. Patricks	Gallitzin

THE CIVIL WAR 229

Name	Rank Organization	Born	Died	Cemetery	Location
McCloskey, David A.	Pvt. D, 125 Pa. Inf.				
McCloskey, Demetrius A.	Pvt. B, 192 Pa. Inf.	1845	1914	St. Patricks	Gallitzin
McCloskey, George A.	Pvt. D, 125 Pa. Inf.	1845	1916	St. Patricks	Gallitzin
McCloskey, Henry	Pvt. E, 84 Pa. Inf.				
McCloskey, John G.	Pvt. A, 55 Pa. Inf.	1850	1906	St. Patricks	Gallitzin
McCloskey, John R. S.	Pvt. H, 139 Pa. Inf.	1844	1931	Grandview	Tyrone
McClossen, Graham					
McCloud, James	Pvt. F, 77 Pa. Inf.	1830			
McClure, Alexander	Pvt. H, 3 Pa. Inf.	1839	1900	Presbyterian	Hollidaysburg
McClure, Andrew A.	Sgt. I, 205 Pa. Inf.	1833			
McClure, Andrew	Sgt. D, 14 Pa. Inf.	1841			
McClure, Andrew	2Lt. H, 12 Pa. Cav.				
McClure, David A.	Pvt. D, 1 Pa. Art.	1844			
McClure, John	Pvt. A, 23 Pa. Mil.				
	Pvt. A, Ind. Bn. Pa. Mil.	1820			
McClure, John H.	Pvt. F, Ind. Bn. Pa. Mil.	1845			
McClure, Joseph	Pvt. A, Ind. Bn. Pa. Mil.	1845			
McClure, William	Cpl. E, 125 Pa. Inf.				
McCluskey, W. J.	Pvt. H, 69 Pa. Inf.				
	2Lt. H, 55 U. S. Inf.				
McCommons, William	Pvt. E, 104 Pa. Inf.				
McConnell, Edmund	Pvt. F, 84 Pa. Inf.				
McConnell, Francis P.	Pvt. D, 46 Pa. Mil.				
	Pvt. A, 205 Pa. Inf.	1844	1900	St. Johns	Altoona
McConnell, Henry	Pvt. E, 57 Pa. Inf.				
McConnell, Jerome	Pvt. A, 205 Pa. Inf.		1886	St. Johns	Altoona
McConnell, John A.	Pvt. C, 76 Pa. Inf.	1839			
McConnell, John H.	Pvt. F, 148 Pa. Inf.				
	Pvt. G, 53 Pa. Inf.		1872	St. Johns	Altoona
McConnell, Joseph D.	Pvt. A, 205 Pa. Inf.				
McConnell, Phil J.	Pvt. I, 55 Pa. Inf.				
McConell, Samuel S.	Pvt. A, 205 Pa. Inf.	1846	1933	Calvary	Altoona
McConnell, William J.	Pvt. H, 14 Pa. Inf.	1837		St. Patricks	Newry
McConnell, William T.	Pvt. H, 110 Pa. Inf.				
McCool, John	Pvt. M, 62 Pa. Inf.				
McCord, Harry C.	Pvt. G, 125 Pa. Inf.	1846	1906	Lutheran	Hollidaysburg
McCormick, Alexander M.	1Lt. Ind. Cav. Pa. Mil.	1831	1872	Fairview	Altoona
McCormick, Charles	Pvt. H, 205 Pa. Inf.	1844			
McCormick, James	Cpl. F, 76 Pa. Inf.	1833			
McCormick, James J.	Pvt. A, 3 Pa. Inf.	1839			
McCormick, John B.	Pvt. A, 205 Pa. Inf.	1843	1925	Grandview	Tyrone
McCormick, John James	1Lt. D, 76 Pa. Inf.	1840	1876	St. Johns	Altoona
McCormick, Robert H.	Pvt. Ind. Cav. Pa. Mil.	1810			
McCormick, Samuel K.	Pvt. A, 205 Pa. Inf.	1829	1898	Fairview	Altoona
McCormick, William		1829	1892	Fairview	Altoona
McCoy, David	Pvt. I, 137 Pa. Inf.	1843	1890	St. Johns	Altoona
McCoy, Dennis	Pvt. E, 125 Pa. Inf.				
McCoy, Francis	Pvt. M, 62 Pa. Inf.	1843			
McCoy, James	Pvt. C, 53 Pa. Inf.	1814	1886	Carson Valley	Duncansville
McCoy, James	Pvt. C, 110 Pa. Inf.				
McCoy, John			1862		
McCoy, John	Pvt. A, 125 Pa. Inf.	1834	1886	Boughmans	Tyrone
McCoy, Patrick	Pvt. C, 84 Pa. Inf.	1831			
McCoy, Robert A.	Col. 40 Pa. Inf.	1835			
McCoy, Ross		1847	1867	Indiana Co.	Pa.
McCoy, William	Pvt. B, 125 Pa. Inf.	1835	1864	Presbyterian	Williamsburg
McCoy, William R.	Pvt. D, 1 Pa. Art.		1864	Baltimore	Maryland
McCoy, William T.	Pvt. B, 110 Pa. Inf.	1835	1895	Fairview	Altoona
McCracken, George M.	Pvt. M, 21 Pa. Cav.	1847	1902	Logan Valley	Bellwood
McCray, James	Pvt. F, 77 Pa. Inf.	1847		Stonerstown	Bedford Co.
McCrea, George R.	Pvt. F, Ind. Bn. Pa. Mil.	1846			
McCrea, William J.	Pvt. G, 125 Pa. Inf.				
	Cpl. C, 46 Pa. Mil.	1844			

SOLDIERS OF BLAIR COUNTY

Name	Rank Organization	Born	Died	Cemetery	Location
McCready, Andrew	Pvt. E, 136 Pa. Inf.		1897	Fairview	Martinsburg
McCue, William	Pvt. F, 77 Pa. Inf.	1831		Focklers	Saxton
McCullough, David G.	Pvt. A, 54 Pa. Inf.	1839	1929	Fairview	Altoona
McCullough, John W.	Cpl. M, 9 Pa. Cav.	1829			
McCullough, Michael	Pvt. A, 84 Pa. Inf.				
McCully, Lisle F.	Sgt. A, 110 Pa. Inf.				
McCummons, William	Pvt. E, 104 Pa. Inf.	1832	1913	Oak Ridge	Altoona
McCune, Joseph M.	Sgt. I, 137 Pa. Inf.				
McCune, Samuel	Pvt. D, 14 Pa. Inf.	1836			
McCune, Samuel	Cpt. A, 110 Pa. Inf.				
McCune, William P.	Pvt. C, 126 Pa. Inf.	1840	1922	Fairview	Altoona
McCurdy, James M.	Pvt. D, 49 Pa. Inf.				
	Sgt. C, 22 Pa. Cav.	1842	1929	Fairview	Altoona
McCurdy, John S.	Cpl. E, 45 Pa. Inf.	1846	1921	Fairview	Altoona
McDermot, Barnabas	Col. 54 Pa. Inf.	1822	1890	St. Johns	Altoona
McDermitt, Charles B.	Pvt. E, 84 Pa. Inf.		1899	St. Josephs	Williamsburg
McDermott, Charles B.	Pvt. E, 84 Pa. Inf.	1840	1880	St. Johns	Altoona
McDermott, Daniel				St. Marys	Hollidaysburg
McDermott, John Daniel	Pvt. A, 25 N. J. Inf.				
	Pvt. E, 3 Del. Inf.	1846	1904	St. Johns	Altoona
McDermitt, Lewis C.	Pvt. K, 125 Pa. Inf.		1862	Boonesville	Maryland
McDermitt, Michael A.	Pvt. K, 125 Pa. Inf.		1862	Philadelphia	Pa.
McDermott, Thomas J. A.	Pvt. E, 49 Pa. Inf.	1838	1864	St. Johns	Altoona
McDermitt, William A.	Cpt. C, 54 Pa. Inf.	1837	1915	Logan Valley	Bellwood
McDeverell, Francis					
McDonald, Cornelius P.	Pvt. K, 187 Pa. Inf.	1848	1930	Calvary	Altoona
McDonald, Daniel	Pvt. A, 84 Pa. Inf.				
McDonald, James	Pvt. C, 3 Pa. Inf.				
	Pvt. I, 205 Pa. Inf.	1835			
McDonald, John	Pvt. D, 13 Pa. Cav.	1839			
McDonald, John	Pvt. H, 49 Pa. Inf.	1844			
McDonald, John	Mus. A, 110 Pa. Inf.				
McDonald, John Thomas	Pvt. A, 84 Pa. Inf.	1834	1881	Fairview	Altoona
McDonald, Owen	Pvt. K, 26 Ind. Inf.				
	Cpl. D, 1 Ind. Cav.	1843	1886	St. Johns	Altoona
McDonald, Samuel	Pvt. A, 97 Pa. Inf.				
	Pvt. D, 110 Pa. Inf.		1865	Potters	Morrisons Cove
McDonald, William	Pvt. H, 110 Pa. Inf.				
McDonough, William P.	Pvt. 73 Ind. Inf.		1863	Nashville	Tennessee
McDowell, William D.	Pvt. D, 4 Pa. Cav.	1843	1928	Rose Hill	Altoona
McElwee, William	Pvt. C, 3 Pa. Inf.				
	Pvt. E, 84 Pa. Inf.	1847		Greenlawn	Roaring Spring
McEnesly, Samuel C.	Pvt. D, 13 Pa. Cav.	1846	1864	City Point	Virginia
McFadden, James S.	Sgt. I, 14 Pa. Inf.	1838	1927	Presbyterian	Hollidaysburg
McFall, Benjamin	Sgt. A, 1 Pa. Art.	°		Presbyterian	Williamsburg
McFalls, Benjamin F.	Pvt. A, 3 Pa. Inf.	1836			
McFalls, Robert	Cpl. B, 125 Pa. Inf.	1830	1901	Fairview	Altoona
McFarland, Crawford E.	Pvt. F, 2 Pa. Cav.	1845	1902	Graziersville	Tyrone
McFarland, John	Pvt. F, 2 Pa. Cav.	1845			
McFarland, John A.	Pvt. A, 125 Pa. Inf.		1863	Strafford C. H.	Virginia
McFarland, Theodore F.	Pvt. F, 2 Pa. Cav.	1844	1874	Grandview	Tyrone
McFarlane, John R.	Cpt. A, 3 Pa. Inf.				
	Cpt. A, 23 Pa. Mil.	1829	1910	Presbyterian	Hollidaysburg
McFarland, Thomas	2Lt. A, 3 Pa. Inf.				
	Cpt. I, 137 Pa. Inf.	1830	1902	Presbyterian	Hollidaysburg
McFeeley, Bernard J.	Cpl. K, 125 Pa. Inf.				
McFeely, Barnabus J.	Pvt. G, 12 Pa. Cav.	1841			
McFeeters, Joseph S.	Pvt. D, 13 Pa. Cav.	1845			
McGahen, Benjamin F.	Mus. D, 205 Pa. Inf.	1847			
McGahen, John	Pvt. D, 205 Pa. Inf.				
McGarvey, Edward					

THE CIVIL WAR   231

Name	Rank Organization	Born	Died	Cemetery	Location
McGarvey, Joseph	Pvt. D, 13 Pa. Cav.				
McGee, James	Pvt. I, 55 Pa. Inf.	1836	1864	Richmond	Virginia
McGee, William	Pvt. I, 55 Pa. Inf.	1838			
McGill, John J.	Pvt. G, Pa. Mil.	1847	1867	Longs	Tyrone
McGill, Thomas T.	Pvt. A, 125 Pa. Inf.				
McGill, William	Pvt. C, 22 Pa. Cav.	1845			
McGinley, James	Pvt. C, 77 Pa. Inf.	1840	1912	Grandview	Tyrone
McGinnis, James	Pvt. G, 125 Pa. Inf.		1904	Greenlawn	Roaring Spring
McGinnis, James	Pvt. D, 192 Pa. Inf.				
McGinnis, John	Pvt. D, 192 Pa. Inf.	1836	1909	Presbyterian	Hollidaysburg
McGinnis, William	Pvt. A, 3 Pa. Inf.	1833			
McGinnis, William	Cpl. E, 125 Pa. Inf.			Carson Valley	Duncansville
McGinley, William	Pvt. K, 12 Pa. Cav.	1832	1901	Fairview	Altoona
McGirr, James	Pvt. C, 84 Pa. Inf.	1818			
McGirr, Philip	Cpl. F, Ind. Bn. Pa. Mil.	1834			
McGlathery, Levi M.	Sgt. B, 3 Pa. Inf.	1842			
McGlathery, Thomas L.	Cpt. F, 76 Pa. Inf.	1841	1865	Ft. Fisher	S. Car.
McGlathery, William C.	Pvt. Ind. Cav. Pa. Mil.	1845			
McGlew, William	Sgt. B, Ind. Bn. Pa. Mil.	1843			
McGlue, William	Pvt. A, 84 Pa. Inf.				
McGonigle, George W.	Pvt. B, 125 Pa. Inf.		1862	Greenlawn	Roaring Spring
McGonigle, Julius C.	Pvt. E, 84 Pa. Inf.				
	Pvt. I, 57 Pa. Inf.	1820		Yellow Spring	Williamsburg
McGough, Charles C.	Pvt. K, 125 Pa. Inf.				
	Pvt. I, 82 Pa. Inf.	1829	1896	St. Johns	Altoona
McGough, John	Pvt. E, 23 Pa. Mil.	1845	1908	St. Johns	Altoona
McGough, Silas A.	Pvt. K, 125 Pa. Inf.	1836	1917	Calvary	Altoona
McGough, William A.	Pvt. D, 5 Pa. Art.	1820	1899	St. Johns	Altoona
McGran, John	Pvt. A, 84 Pa. Inf.				
McGraw, Albert	Pvt. A, 23 Pa. Mil.	1842			
McGraw, Henry A.	Pvt. A, Ind. Bn. Pa. Mil.	1841			
McGraw, John	Pvt. C, 84 Pa. Inf.	1842			
McGraw, John	Pvt. A, 23 Pa. Mil.	1839			
McGraw, John G.	Cpl. A, Ind. Bn. Pa. Mil.	1839			
McGraw, William	1Lt. H, 14 Pa. Inf.				
	Cpt. E, 125 Pa. Inf.	1839	1904	Erie	Pa.
McGregor, James M.					
McGregor, John	Pvt. I, 55 Pa. Inf.	1838	1864	National	Arlington
McGraw, Robert	Pvt. I, 55 Pa. Inf.	1822	1886	Oak Ridge	Altoona
McGregor, William	Pvt. In, 55 Pa. Inf.				
	Pvt. D, 13 Pa. Cav.	1820	1903	Holsingers	Bakers Summit
McGruder, Franklin J.	Pvt. B, 48 Pa. Inf.	1842	1892	Carson Valley	Duncansville
McGuire, Cornelius L.	Pvt. D, 205 Pa. Inf.		1865	National	Arlington
McGuire, Hiram	Pvt. K, 125 Pa. Inf.				
McGuire, Hiram J.	Pvt. E, 104 Pa. Inf.				
McGuire, James N.	Pvt. C, 145 Pa. Inf.	1836	1900	St. Patricks	Gallitzin
McGuire, William A.	Pvt. A, Ind. Bn. Pa. Mil.	1838			
McHale, Austin	Pvt. D, 126 Pa. Inf.	1831	1907	St. Johns	Altoona
McHugh, James E.	Pvt. G, 12 Pa. Cav.	1836	1865	Charleston	W. Va.
McIlnay, James	Pvt. C, 110 Pa. Inf.		1862	Reform Church	Hopewell
McIlnay, John F.	Pvt. H, 14 Pa. Inf.				
	Pvt. I, 137 Pa. Inf.	1837	1921	Albrights	Roaring Spring
McIlvaine, Henry C.	Pvt. A, 125 Pa. Inf.				
McIlvaine, William	Pvt. H, 3 Pa. Inf.	1843			
McIlwain, William W.	Pvt. M, 62 Pa. Inf.	1840	1889	Grandview	Tyrone
McIntosh, Michael P.					
McIntire, Abram	Pvt. U, 13 Pa. Cav.	1844	1864	McIntire	Hollidaysburg
McIntyre, Calvin Clay	Pvt. D, 17 Pa. Cav.	1846	1893	Fairview	Altoona
McIntyre, Eli	Pvt. A, 3 Pa. Inf.	1836			
McIntyre, Eli	Pvt. A, 84 Pa. Inf.	1843	1864	Lutheran	Hollidaysburg
McIntire, Henry M.	Pvt. E, 84 Pa. Inf.	1825	1892	Lutheran	Newry
McIntire, James	Pvt. U, 8 Ind. Inf.	1842	1863	McIntires	Hollidaysburg

SOLDIERS OF BLAIR COUNTY

Name	Rank Organization	Born	Died	Cemetery	Location
McIntyre, John	Sgt. F, Ind. Bn. Pa. Mil.	1840			
McIntire, John	Cpl. G, 12 Pa. Cav.	1842	1924	Presbyterian	Hollidaysburg
McIntire, John A.	Cpl. K, 125 Pa. Inf.				
	Sgt. D, 184 Pa. Inf.				
McIntyre, John A.	Pvt. D, 3 Pa. Inf.	1839			
McIntire, William	Pvt. M, 62 Pa. Inf.				
	Pvt. K, 91 Pa. Inf.				
McKamey, John A.	Mus. C, 3 Pa. Inf.				
	Mus. B, 125 Pa. Inf.				
	Mus. B, 208 Pa. Inf.	1841	1911	Presbyterian	Williamsburg
McKeage, John B. (M)	1Lt. A, 3 Pa. Inf.				
	Cpt. G, 125 Pa. Inf.				
	Col. Ind. Bn. Pa. Mil.				
	Cpt. E, 184 Pa. Inf.	1827	1874	Presbyterian	Hollidaysburg
McKean, James	Pvt. E, 34 Pa. Inf.		1906	Bradford	Clearfield Co.
McKee, Albert	Pvt. G, 12 Pa. Cav.	1846			
McKee, Amos	Pvt. U, 3 Pa. Art.	1835	1907	Greenlawn	Roaring Spring
McKee, David	Pvt. 55 Pa. Inf.			Pote	Morrisons Cove
McKey, David	Pvt. I, 137 Pa. Inf.				
McKee, David	Sgt. I, 14 Pa. Inf.	1838			
McKee, James	Pvt. A, 1 Pa. Cav.	1836	1909	Fairview	Altoona
McKee, James Cooper	Sgn. U. S. Army	1829	1897	Butler	Pa.
McKee, James W.	Pvt. Ind. Cav. Pa. Mil.	1846	1906	Oak Ridge	Altoona
McKee, John Blair	Pvt. G, 84 Pa. Inf.	1845	1915	Fairview	Altoona
McKee, Thomas G.	Pvt. G, 125 Pa. Inf.				
	Sgt. B, Ind. Bn. Pa. Mil.	1844	1926	St. Johns	Altoona
McKee, William H.	Pvt. L, 13 Pa. Cav.	1842	1921	Carson Valley	Duncansville
McKeehan, David	Pvt. A, 205 Pa. Inf.				
McKeehan, James A.	Pvt. A, 3 Pa. Inf.	1837			
McKeehen, Washington L.	Pvt. C, 76 Pa. Inf.	1841			
McKendrick, Joseph	Pvt. B, 105 Pa. Inf.			Grandview	Tyrone
McKeeney, James	Pvt. E, 16 Pa. Inf.				
	Pvt. D, 191 Pa. Inf.	1828	1914		Tyrone
McKenzie, Robert	Pvt. H, 14 Pa. Inf.	1839			
McKibben, Clestine	Pvt. G, 55 Pa. Inf.			St. Patricks	Gallitzin
McKierman, Charles E.	Pvt. E, 104 Pa. Inf.				
McKiernon, Francis M.	Cpl. B, 125 Pa. Inf.	1842	1896	St. Josephs	Williamsburg
McKeirman, Gerald	Sgt. L, 5 Kan. Cav.	1844	1892	Fairview	Altoona
McKiernan, John S.	Cpt. D, 53 Pa. Inf.				
McKiernan, William	Cpl. D, 14 Pa. Inf.	1835			
McKillip, Charles A.	Pvt. C, 101 Pa. Inf.	1827	1917	Spring Hope	Martinsburg
McKinley, George	Pvt. M, 62 Pa. Inf.		1861	Minors Hill	Virginia
McKinney, Henry	Pvt. G, 12 Pa. Cav.	1840			
McKinney, James	Pvt. C, 45 Pa. Inf.				
	Pvt. C, 184 Pa. Inf.	1838	1914	Grandview	Tyrone
McKinney, James	Pvt. G, 12 Pa. Cav.	1848	1901	St. Patricks	Gallitzin
McKinney, James A.	Pvt. G, 12 Pa. Cav.	1828	1916	Antis	Bellwood
McKinney, John G.	Pvt. D, 3 Pa. Inf.	1840	1901	Grandview	Tyrone
McKinney, John W.	Pvt. A, 84 Pa. Inf.	1843			
McKinney, Robert D.	Pvt. A, Ind. Bn. Pa. Mil.				
	Pvt. D, 13 Pa. Cav.	1845			
McKinney, Samuel	Cpl. M, 62 Pa. Inf.				
McKinstry, James A.	Pvt. K, 131 Pa. Inf.				
	Pvt. F, 46 Pa. Mil.				
	Sgt. K, 184 Pa. Inf.	1836	1910	Oak Ridge	Altoona
McKnight, John Andrew	Pvt. E, 15 Pa. Inf.				
	Pvt. B, 36 Pa. Inf.	1840	1917	Presbyterian	Hollidaysburg
McKnight, John P.	Cpl. E, 104 Pa. Inf.	1843	1929	Fairview	Altoona
McLanahan, J. King	Pvt. A, Ind. Bn. Pa. Mil.	1828	1918	Presbyterian	Hollidaysburg
McLanahan, Robert G.	Pvt. D, 49 Pa. Inf.	1840	1916	Grandview	Tyrone
McLanahan, Samuel Calvin	Egr. U. S. Navy	1842	1928	Presbyterian	Hollidaysburg

THE CIVIL WAR 233

Name	Rank Organization	Born	Died	Cemetery	Location
McLane, George	Pvt. K, 125 Pa. Inf.				
McLane, George M.	Cpl. C, 46 Pa. Mil.				
	Cpl. C, 13 Pa. Cav.	1845			
McLaughlin, Cornelius	Pvt. Ind. Cav. Pa. Mil.				
	Pvt. C, 19 Pa. Cav.	1845			
McLaughlin, Henry	Pvt. E, 84 Pa. Inf.				
	Pvt. I, 57 Pa. Inf.	1840	1915	Geeseytown	Hollidaysburg
McLaughlin, Jacob					
McLaughlin, John	Cpl. F, 76 Pa. Inf.	1831	1863	Fairview	Altoona
McLaughlin, Joseph S.	Pvt. D, 125 Pa. Inf.	1843	1862	Fairview	Altoona
McLean, David	Pvt. A, 84 Pa. Inf.				
McLean, Edward	Cpl. Ill. Art.	1843	1914	Fairview	Altoona
McLeary, George	Pvt. D, 13 Pa. Cav.	1846			
McMahan, John	Pvt. I, 137 Pa. Inf.		1884	Gospel	Gallitzin
McMahan, Mordeciah	Pvt. E, 3 Pa. Inf.				
	Cpl. D, 125 Pa. Inf.				
	Pvt. G, 13 Pa. Cav.	1833	1878	Fairview	Altoona
McManamy, John	Pvt. B, 125 Pa. Inf.				
McManamy, Wilson	Pvt. B, 125 Pa. Inf.				
McManus, James	Pvt. E, 84 Pa. Inf.				
McMeans, William T.	Pvt. I, 149 Pa. Inf.	1834	1909	Carson Valley	Duncansville
McMichaels, John	Pvt. B, 125 Pa. Inf.				
McMillan, John A.	Pvt. I, 211 Pa. Inf.		1909	Johnstown	Pa.
McMillen, Francis S.	Pvt. I, 137 Pa. Inf.	1835	1892	Fairview	Altoona
McMonigle, Jacob	Pvt. D, 205 Pa. Inf.	1827	1902	Oak Ridge	Altoona
McMorris, Michael	Pvt. H, 1 Va. Cav.	1841	1889	St. Patricks	Gallitzin
McMullin, Celestine	2Lt. A, 55 Pa. Inf.	1838	1917	Calvary	Altoona
McMullen, Francis P.	Pvt. B, 12 U. S. Inf.	1844	1913	Presbyterian	Birmingham
McMullen, John E.	Pvt. K, 125 Pa. Inf.				
	Pvt. C, 143 Pa. Inf.	1838	1897	St. Johns	Altoona
McMullen, John W.	Pvt. B, 110 Pa. Inf.		1923	Osceola Mills	Pa.
McMullen, Peter B.	Pvt. G, 11 Pa. Cav.			McMullins	Sinking Valley
McMullen, Thomas	Pvt. H, 110 Pa. Inf.				
McMurray, William J.	Pvt. A, 208 Pa. Inf.		1884	Duncannon	Pa.
McMurtrie, Alex. E.	Pvt. F, 1 Pa. Art.	1834			
McMurtrie, George B.	Pvt. A, 102 Pa. Inf.			Grandview	Tyrone
McMurtrie, Robert A.	Pvt. A, 23 Pa. Mil.				
	Pvt. A, Ind. Bn. Pa. Mil.	1811	1880	Presbyterian	Hollidaysburg
McNamara Robert	1Lt. C, 53 Pa. Inf.	1827	1895	Presbyterian	Hollidaysburg
McNamara, Thomas M.	Pvt. A, Ind. Bn. Pa. Mil.	1836			
McNaught, Robert A.	Frn. U. S. Navy	1842	1903	Presbyterian	Hollidaysburg
McNelly, Watson W.	Pvt. H, 103 Pa. Inf.	1838	1912	Royer Mt.	Williamsburg
McNerlin, Orbison	Pvt. H, 22 Pa. Cav.	1841			
McNevin, John	Cpt. C, 76 Pa. Inf.	1845	1910	St. Johns	Altoona
McNew, John W.	Pvt. C, 47 Pa. Inf.	1842	1880	Fairview	Altoona
McNoldy, James F.	Sgt. K, 148 Pa. Inf.	1845	1909	Fairview	Altoona
McNulty, Frank	Pvt. 10 Pa. Inf.	1839	1911	Calvary	Altoona
McPherren, Adams	Pvt. H, 110 Pa. Inf.				
McPherson, Alexander	Pvt. G, 20 Ind. Inf.	1813	1892	Greenlawn	Roaring Spring
McQuillan, Adam W.	Pvt. A, 125 Pa. Inf.				
	Pvt. D, 192 Pa. Inf.				
McQuillen, William	Pvt. A, 125 Pa. Inf.				
McQuillan, William H.	Pvt. A, 110 Pa. Inf.		1864	Petersburg	Virginia
McQuillen, William O.	Sgt. E, 46 Pa. Mil.	1845			
McReady, Andrew	Pvt. E, 136 Pa. Inf.				
	Pvt. C, 6 Pa. Art.	1845			
Meadville, Graham McC.	Pvt. F, 76 Pa. Inf.	1844			
Meadville, John					
Meadville, Joshua B.	Pvt. F, 31 Pa. Inf.				
	Pvt. A, 191 Pa. Inf.	1830	1864	Salisbury	N. Car.

SOLDIERS OF BLAIR COUNTY

Name	Rank Organization	Born	Died	Cemetery	Location
Meadville, Peter H.	Pvt. F, 76 Pa. Inf.				
	Pvt. A, 205 Pa. Inf.	1842	1911	Grandview	Tyrone
Meaher, Thomas	Pvt. A, 110 Pa. Inf.				
Meals, Joseph	Pvt. G, 15 Pa. Cav.				
	Pvt. U. S. Signal Corps	1836	1907	Fairview	Altoona
Mechen, Arthur W.	Pvt. H, 6 Pa. Cav.	1842	1916	Fairview	Altoona
Mechtley, John E.	Pvt. C, 82 Pa. Inf.	1845	1916	Alum Bank	Pa.
Megahen, David	Pvt. H, 4 Pa. Inf.		1913	Petersburg	Hunt'gdon Co.
Megahan, James C.	Pvt. F, 194 Pa. Inf.	1847			
Megahan, John	Pvt. D, 205 Pa. Inf.	1826	1912	Royer Mt.	Williamsburg
Megahan, William B.	Pvt. B, 208 Pa. Inf.	1824	1892	McConnellstown	Pa.
Meinhardt, Lewis	Pvt. D, 125 Pa. Inf.				
Meintel, Henry	Pvt. A, 3 Pa. Inf.				
	Cpl. A, 23 Pa. Mil.				
	Cpl. A, Ind. Bn. Pa. Mil.	1838	1915	Greenlawn	Hollidaysburg
Melcher, Henry	Pvt. A, 201 Pa. Inf.	1844	1928	Mt. Pleasant	Tyrone
Mellin, Felix	Pvt. A, 84 Pa. Inf.				
Meloy, James M.	Pvt. C, 46 Pa. Mil.	1838			
Meloy, John L.	Pvt. C, 133 Pa. Inf.				
	Pvt. D, 99 Pa. Inf.	1830	1919	Greenwood	Altoona
Mench, Isaac	Pvt. G, 171 Pa. Inf.	1804	1887	Sparrs	Williamsburg
Mendenhall, Alfred	Pvt. A, 13 Pa. Inf.	1844			
Mendenhall, Judson	Pvt. D, 13 Pa. Cav.	1845			
Mentzer, Jacob	Pvt. C, 133 Pa. Inf.		1862	Fredericksburg	Virginia
Mentzer, Jeremiah D.	Mus. D, 13 Pa. Cav.	1842	1914	Presbyterian	Sinking Valley
Mentzer, John	Pvt. H, 48 Pa. Inf.	1849	1930	Bald Eagle	Tyrone
Mentzer, William H.	Pvt. E, 104 Pa. Inf.				
Meredith, John Henry	Cpl. A, 38 Pa. Inf.				
	Sgt. I, 7 Pa. Cav.	1847	1920	Rose Hill	Altoona
Meredith, William	Pvt. K, 88 Pa. Inf.	1823	1904	Fairview	Altoona
Meredith, William B.	Pvt. D, 14 Pa. Inf.				
	Sgt. A, 125 Pa. Inf.	1835	1896	Grandview	Tyrone
Merk, Michael	Pvt. M, 62 Pa. Inf.	1834	1896	Fairview	Altoona
Merklin, Thomas	Pvt. D, 11 Pa. Cav.	1839	1868	Fairview	Altoona
Merrell, Charles C.	Cpl. G, 57 Pa. Inf.	1847			
Merritts, Andrew J.	1Lt. C, 53 Pa. Inf.	1841	1903	Frankstown	Hollidaysburg
Merritt, Andrew W.	Pvt. E, 13 Pa. Cav.	1836	1882	Lutheran	Hollidaysburg
Merrits, John	Pvt. F, 77 Pa. Inf.	1835	1865	Galveston	Texas
Merritts, John	Pvt. B, 208 Pa. Inf.	1836	1907	McKeesport	Pa.
Merritts, Joseph	Pvt. M, 9 Pa. Cav.	1847	1918	Huntingdon	Pa.
Merryman, Charles	Sgt. A, 125 Pa. Inf.				
	Cpt. E, 46 Pa. Mil.	1819			
Merryman, George A.	Cpl. H, 22 Pa. Cav.	1836			
Merryman, George W.	Sgt. F, 2 Pa. Cav.	1844			
Merryman, George W.	Cpl. E, 45 Pa. Inf.	1833	1889	Bald Eagle	Tyrone
Merryman, Howell	Pvt. M, 9 Pa. Cav.		1904		
Merryman, John	Pvt. F, 2 Pa. Cav.	1840			
Merryman, John	Pvt. D, 3 Pa. Inf.	1843			
Merryman, Joseph B.	Cpl. E, 45 Pa. Inf.	1835	1909	Bald Eagle	Tyrone
Merryman, William F.	Pvt. A, 125 Pa. Inf.				
	Sgt. E, 46 Pa. Mil.				
	Pvt. F, 2 Pa. Cav.	1845			
Mertz, William H.	Pvt. D, 42 Pa. Inf.	1839	1881	Fairview	Altoona
Messersmith, George	Pvt. H, 22 Pa. Cav.	1846			
Messinger, Robert M.	Sgt. E, 3 Pa. Inf.	1837			
Metz, George M.	Pvt. C, 3 Pa. Inf.				
	Pvt. D, 22 Pa. Cav.				
	Sgt. B, 208 Pa. Inf.	1841	1909	Fairview	Altoona
Metz, Thomas J.	Pvt. B, 125 Pa. Inf.	1843	1901	Presbyterian	Williamsburg
Metz, Thornton B.	Pvt. B, 125 Pa. Inf.				
Metzger, Augustus	Pvt. G, 26 Pa. Inf.	1836	1919	Greenlawn	Hollidaysburg
Metzler, Henry Clay	Pvt. B, 3 Md. Inf.	1845	1935	Bedford	Pa.

THE CIVIL WAR
235

Name	Rank Organization	Born	Died	Cemetery	Location
Metzgar, John	Pvt. I, 14 Pa. Inf.	1842			
Metzker, John L.	Pvt. H, 13 Pa. Cav.	1842	1906	Mennonite	Martinsburg
Metzgar, Joseph	Pvt. E, 61 Pa. Inf.	1835	1900	Fairview	Altoona
Metzlar, Joseph F.	Pvt. G, 125 Pa. Inf.	1841	1902	Lutheran	Newry
Metzker, Levi Y.	Pvt. E, 84 Pa. Inf.				
	Pvt. I, 57 Pa. Inf.	1835	1907	Fairview	Martinsburg
Metzer, Samuel	Pvt. I, 14 Pa. Inf.	1837			
Michaels, Hiram				Washington	D. C.
Michaels, John	Pvt. A, 3 Pa. Inf.	1838			
Middleton, Davis	Pvt. E, 104 Pa. Inf.				
Middleton, James	Pvt. D, 46 Pa. Mil.				
	Pvt. A, 205 Pa. Inf.	1833			
Middleton, Silas	Cpl. G, 12 Pa. Cav.	1840			
Miles, Alfred	Pvt. D, 45 Pa. Inf.	1840	1901	North Bend	Clinton Co.
Miles, George W.	Pvt. A, 125 Pa. Inf.	1842	1930	Logan Valley	Bellwood
Miles, Henry H.	Pvt. H, 110 Pa. Inf.				
Miles, Jacob W.	2Lt. D, 11 Pa. Cav.	1838			
Miles, John M.	Pvt. A, 110 Pa. Inf.	1838	1901	Grandview	Tyrone
Miles, Joseph A.	Pvt. D, 3 Pa. Inf.	1843			
Miles, Samuel A.	Pvt. C, 46 Pa. Mil.	1846			
Miles, Samuel S.	Pvt. F, 200 Pa. Inf.	1845	1920	Port Matilda	Pa.
Miles, William W.	Pvt. I, 190 Pa. Inf.	1840	1930	Grandview	Tyrone
Miller, Abraham	Pvt. B, Ind. Bn. Pa. Mil.	1825			
Miller, Alexander R.	Cpn. 202 Pa. Inf.	1845			
Miller, Andrew A.	Pvt. D, 125 Pa. Inf.	1839	1912	Oak Ridge	Altoona
Miller, Andrew C.	Pvt. C, 110 Pa. Inf.	1824	1891	Carson Valley	Duncansville
Miller, Blanchard	Pvt. F, 27 Pa. Inf.	1842	1919	Neffs Mills	Hunt'gdon Co.
Miller, Charles	Pvt. D, 53 Pa. Inf.	1843	1897	Glasgow	Cambria Co.
Miller, Christopher	Pvt. B, 88 Pa. Inf.	1824	1888	Woomer	Tyrone
Miller, Daniel H.	Pvt. I, 171 Pa. Mil.	1840	1905	Hickory Bottom	Woodbury
Miller, David	Cpl. A, 110 Pa. Inf.				
Miller, David H.	Pvt. G, 34 Pa. Inf.				
	Pvt. C, 191 Pa. Inf.	1841	1905	Oak Ridge	Altoona
Miller, David Ross	Pvt. B, 110 Pa. Inf.				
	Cpt. B, 46 Pa. Mil.				
	Cpt. L, 19 Pa. Cav.	1837	1921	Fairview	Altoona
Miller, Edward B.	Pvt. H, 14 Pa. Inf.	1838			
	2Lt. C, 77 Pa. Inf.				
Miller, Edwin H.	Pvt. I, 13 Pa. Cav.	1833	1905	Spring Hope	Martinsburg
Miller, Elias W.	Pvt. F, 194 Pa. Inf.	1844	1926	Nisky	Bethlehem
Miller, Francis	Pvt. D, 46 Pa. Mil.	1827			
Miller, Gabriel	Pvt. E, 3 Pa. Inf.				
	Mus. G, 12 Pa. Cav.	1842			
Miller, George	Pvt. H, 3 Pa. Inf.	1827			
Miller, George F.	Cpl. I, 205 Pa. Inf.	1843			
Miller, George W.	Pvt. A, 49 Pa. Inf.	1842	1904	Fairview	Altoona
Miller, George W.	Pvt. D, 110 Pa. Inf.				
	Sgt. F, 77 Pa. Inf.	1839	1905	Charlottesville	Bellwood
Miller, George W.	Pvt. F, 76 Pa. Inf.	1843	1884	Carson Valley	Duncansville
Miller, Godfrey W.	Cpl. B, 27 Pa. Inf.		1876	Fairview	Altoona
Miller, Harvey J.	Cpl. H, 78 Pa. Inf.	1833	1908	Grandview	Tyrone
Miller, Henry	Pvt. H, 14 Pa. Inf.	1841			
Miller, Henry	Pvt. C, 76 Pa. Inf.	1841			
Miller, Henry	Pvt. A, 205 Pa. Inf.	1818	1892	Lutheran	Sinking Valley
Miller, Henry	Pvt. E, 84 Pa. Inf.	1819	1892		
Miller, Henry A.	Pvt. B, 3 Pa. Inf.				
	Cpl. F, 76 Pa. Inf.	1843	1921	Fairview	Altoona
Miller, Henry C.	Pvt. E, 45 Pa. Inf.	1843	1920	Fairview	Altoona
Miller, Henry E.	Pvt. E, 39 Pa. Inf.	1841	1890	Fairview	Altoona
Miller, Henry T.	Pvt. B, 208 Pa. Inf.		1865	National	City Point, Va.
Miller, Hezekiah	Pvt. B, 208 Pa. Inf.	1843	1911	Grandview	Tyrone

SOLDIERS OF BLAIR COUNTY

Name	Rank Organization	Born	Died	Cemetery	Location
Miller, Hezekiah H.	Pvt. C, 110 Pa. Inf.		1864	Fairview	Altoona
Miller, Jacob W.	Pvt. E, 84 Pa. Inf.				
	Cpl. I, 57 Pa. Inf.	1828			
Miller, James	Pvt. E, 84 Pa. Inf.				
	Pvt. I, 57 Pa. Inf.	1839	1919	Brumbaughs	Martinsburg
Miller, James	Pvt. I, 50 Pa. Inf.	1820	1878	Nicodemus	Henrietta
Miller, James	Pvt. C, 3 Pa. Inf.	1840			
Miller, James G.	Sgt. G, 34 Pa. Inf.		1875	Grandview	Tyrone
Miller, John	Pvt. D, 205 Pa. Inf.	1836	1916	Frankstown	Hollidaysburg
Miller, John	Mus. H, 3 Pa. Inf.	1838			
Miller, John	Pvt. B, 3 Pa. Inf.	1835			
Miller, John	Cpl. A, 84 Pa. Inf.	1835		Lutheran	Hollidaysburg
Miller, John	2Lt. B, Ind. Bn. Pa. Mil.	1838			
Miller, John	Cpl. A, 205 Pa. Inf.				
Miller, John	Pvt. G, 51 Pa. Inf.				
	Pvt. B, 110 Pa. Inf.	1816	1896	Baughmans	Tyrone
Miller, John	Pvt. H, 1 Pa. Inf.				
	Mus. G, 125 Pa. Inf.				
	Mus. D, 192 Pa. Inf.	1837	1915	Fairview	Altoona
Miller, John	Pvt. K, 20 Iowa Inf.	1833	1915	Fairview	Altoona
Miller, John B.	Pvt. B, Ind. Bn. Pa. Mil.	1842			
Miller, John B.	Pvt. F, 49 Pa. Inf.	1842	1909	Charlottesville	Bellwood
Miller, John E.	Pvt. E, 1 Pa. Mil.				
	Cpl. F, 104 Pa. Cav.	1848	1924	St. Barthelmus	Wilmore
Miller, John G.	Sgt. D, 47 Pa. Inf.	1840			
Miller, John H.	Sgt. D, 51 Pa. Inf.	1827	1893	Bald Eagle	Tyrone
Miller, John I.	Pvt. C, 110 Pa. Inf.			Bedford	Pa.
Miller, John J.	Pvt. M, 9 Pa. Cav.	1842			
Miller, Job	Pvt. A, 84 Pa. Inf.		1862	Lutheran	Hollidaysburg
Miller, Jonathan J.	Pvt. C, 45 Pa. Inf.	1830	1913	Grandview	Tyrone
Miller, Leander	Pvt. I, 34 Pa. Inf.	1843	1890	Fairview	Altoona
Miller, Mark	Pvt. I, 51 Pa. Inf.		1918	Pleasantville	Bedford Co.
Miller, Martin	Pvt. C, 84 Pa. Inf.				
	Pvt. C, 191 Pa. Inf.			Grandview	Tyrone
Miller, Penrose	Pvt. E, 45 Pa. Inf.	1848	1878	Fairview	Altoona
Miller, Peter	Pvt. A, 110 Pa. Inf.				
Miller, Robert G.	Pvt. G, 84 Pa. Inf.	1846	1916	Grandview	Tyrone
Miller, Robert G.	Pvt. M, 9 Pa. Cav.	1834	1861	Charlottesville	Bellwood
Miller, Samuel B.	Pvt. H, 49 Pa. Inf.	1849	1926	Oak Ridge	Altoona
Miller, Samuel H.	Pvt. E, 3 Pa. Inf.	1842	1864	Logan Valley	Bellwood
Miller, Samuel M.	Pvt. A, Ind. Bn. Pa. Mil.	1842			
Miller, Stanley	Pvt. E, 125 Pa. Inf.	1842	1892	Fairview	Altoona
Miller, Thomas	Pvt. G, 125 Pa. Inf.	1844	1922	Rose Hill	Altoona
Miller, Thomas C.	Cpl. F, 77 Pa. Inf.	1830			
Miller, Winfield Scott	Pvt. I, 1 Pa. Art.				
	Pvt. B, 84 Pa. Inf.	1847	1896	Fairview	Altoona
Miller, William	Pvt. D, 192 Pa. Inf.				
Miller, William	Sgt. F, 76 Pa. Inf.	1819	1890	Fairview	Altoona
Miller, William	Sgt. H, 22 Pa. Cav.	1840			
Miller, William	Pvt. D, 3 Pa. Inf.	1839			
Miller, William H.	Pvt. A, 84 Pa. Inf.		1862	Friends	Bedford Co.
Miller, William H.	Sgt. A, 20 Pa. Cav.	1844	1927	Fairview	Altoona
Miller, William H.	Cpl. A, 125 Pa. Inf.	1837	1876	Bald Eagle	Tyrone
Miller, William M.	Pvt. H, 110 Pa. Inf.	1844	1866	Charlottesville	Bellwood
Miller, William T.	Cpl. D, 125 Pa. Inf.	1839	1932	Fairview	Altoona
Miller, Wilson	Cpl. Ind. Cav. Pa. Mil.	1841			
Millhouse, Charles H.	Pvt. L, 13 Pa. Cav.	1846	1911	Juniata Co.	Pa.
Milliger, Robert	Pvt. 203 Pa. Inf.	1849	1930	Warriors Mark	Pa.
Milliken, James	Pvt. A, Ind. Bn. Pa. Mil.	1845			
Milliron, Anthony	Pvt. Ind. Cav. Pa. Mil.	1829			
Millison, Jacob	Pvt. C, 86 Ohio Inf.	1843	1927	Youngwood	Pa.

THE CIVIL WAR

Name	Rank Organization	Born	Died	Cemetery	Location
Mills, Alexander D.	Mus. F, 28 Pa. Inf.	1847	1877	St. Patricks	Gallitzin
Mills, Andrew J.	Pvt. C, 4 Pa. Cav.	1844	1917	Lower Yoder	Johnstown
Mills, David	1Lt. F, 28 Pa. Inf.				
	1Lt. F, Ind. Bn. Pa. Mil.	1818	1892	St. Patricks	Gallitzin
Mills, David	Pvt. K, 51 Pa. Inf.	1821	1898	Greenlawn	Roaring Spring
Mills, Jesse R.	Pvt. I, 137 Pa. Inf.				
Mills, Jesse R.	Pvt. B, 208 Pa. Inf.				
Mills, John	Pvt. G, 188 Pa. Inf.	1839			
Mills, John D.	Pvt. F, Ind. Bn. Pa. Mil.	1847			
Millward, Luke	Pvt. E, 125 Pa. Inf.				
Mimminger, Jacob	Pvt. C, 110 Pa. Inf.				
Minary, Thomas S.	Pvt. Ind. Cav. Pa. Mil.	1826	1906	Grandview	Tyrone
Minehine, Patrick	Pvt. A, 110 Pa. Inf.				
Mingert, Louis					
Minichan, Henry B.	Cpl. A, 29 Pa. Inf.	1839	1922	Harrisburg	Pa.
Minier, Francis P.	Col. 3 Pa. Inf.				
	Cpt. 12 U. S. Inf.				
Minnigh, Henry N.	Cpt. K, 30 Pa. Inf.		1915	National	Gettysburg
Minster, John S.	Pvt. I, 122 Pa. Inf.				
	Pvt. E, 21 Pa. Inf.	1847	1917	Fairview	Altoona
Mitchell, Chalmers M.	Pvt. H, 103 Pa. Inf.	1849	1925	Presbyterian	Hollidaysburg
Mitchell, James S.	1Lt. H, 84 Pa. Inf.				
	1Lt. H, 57 Pa. Inf.	1841			
Mitchell, John	Cpl. A, Ind. Bn. Pa. Mil.	1807			
Mitchell, Moses	Pvt. I, 39 Pa. Inf.				
	Pvt. K, 191 Pa. Inf.	1847			
Mitchell, Thomas C.	Pvt. D, 4 Pa. Cav.	1840	1912	Johnstown	Pa.
Mitchell, Thomas M.	Pvt. C, 105 Pa. Inf.	1839			
Mobley, Denton	Sgt. K, 18 Pa. Cav.	1820	1886	Holsingers	Bakers Summit
Mobley, Ezekial	Pvt. C, 205 Pa. Inf.	1844	1921	Carson Valley	Duncansville
Mock, George	Pvt. D, 19 Ohio Inf.				
Mock, Harry C.	Pvt. C, 133 Pa. Inf.	1843	1919	Barleys	Bedford Co.
Mock, John E.	Pvt. B, 125 Pa. Inf.	1842	1911	Maplewood	Ohio
Mock, Josiah D.	Pvt. A, 84 Pa. Inf.				
Mock, Mathias	Pvt. C, 133 Pa. Inf.				
	Pvt. A, 184 Pa. Inf.		1864		
Mock, Tobias B.	Pvt. K, 55 Pa. Inf.			Mt. Zion	Bedford Co.
Mock, William	Pvt. M, 5 Pa. Art.	1821	1886	Collinsville	Altoona
Mock, William H.	Pvt. E, 84 Pa. Inf.				
Moffit, Albert	Pvt. E, 104 Pa. Inf.				
Molson, William M.	Cpl. B, 43 U.S.C.T.	1840	1918	Eastern Light	Altoona
Monahan, Patrick	Pvt. A, 110 Pa. Inf.				
Monihan, James	Pvt. C, 110 Pa. Inf.				
Montaney, Edmund D.	Cpt. A, 6 Pa. Cav.	1841	1887	Fairview	Altoona
Montgomery, Albert	Pvt. A, 205 Pa. Inf.	1847	1917	Fairview	Altoona
Montgomery, James	Pvt. C, 53 Pa. Inf.	1843			
Montgomery, Levi P.	Pvt. E. 1 Md. Cav.	1843	1917	Fairview	Altoona
Montgomery, Matthew	Pvt. C, 19 Pa. Cav.	1841	1864	Nashville	Tennessee
Montgomery, Robert B.	Pvt. E, 3 Pa. Inf.				
	Sgt. M, 9 Pa. Cav.	1837	1887	Fairview	Altoona
Montgomery, Thomas	Pvt. C, 76 Pa. Inf.	1840			
Montgomery, Thomas	Pvt. H, 110 Pa. Inf.		1865	Sailors Creek	Virginia
Moon, John	Pvt. F, 205 Pa. Inf.	1840	1925	Fairview	Altoona
Moore, Abraham	Cpl. E, 46 Pa. Mil.				
	Pvt. U, 22 Pa. Cav.	1830			
Moore, Albert D.	Cpl. F, 76 Pa. Inf.	1842			
Moore, Charles	Pvt. C, 205 Pa. Inf.	1846		Fayette Co.	Pa.
Moore, Daniel	Pvt. H, 110 Pa. Inf.				
Moore, David A.	Pvt. B, 3 Pa. Inf.				
	Cpl. F, 76 Pa. Inf.	1842			
Moore, David T.	Pvt. I, 136 Pa. Inf.	1837	1912	Logan Valley	Bellwood

SOLDIERS OF BLAIR COUNTY

Name	Rank Organization	Born	Died	Cemetery	Location
Moore, Delano R.	Pvt. Ind. Cav. Pa. Mil	1843	1904	Fairview	Altoona
Moore, Ezra P.	Pvt. G, Ind. Bn. Pa. Mil.	1847	1866	Fairview	Altoona
Moore, George	Pvt. I, 14 Pa. Inf.	1842			
Moore, Henry	Pvt. K, 13 Pa. Cav.	1840	1936	Frankstown	Hollidaysburg
Moore, Ithamar	Pvt. Ind. Cav. Pa. Mil	1835			
Moore, James	Pvt. F, 125 Pa. Inf.	1839	1873	St. Johns	Altoona
Moore, James G.	Pvt. G, 57 Pa. Inf.	1837			
Moore, James S.	Cpl. I, 137 Pa. Inf.				
Moore, James T.	Sgt. F, 31 Pa. Inf.				
	Sgt. A, 191 Pa. Inf.	1829			
Moore, James T.	Pvt. E, 3 Pa. Inf.	1831			
Moore, Jesse S.	Pvt. C, 76 Pa. Inf.				
	Sgt. D, 192 Pa. Inf.	1836	1883	Dayton	Ohio
Moore, John	Pvt. F, 143 Pa. Inf.	1834		Philipsburg	Pa.
Moore, John B.	Sgt. C, 110 Pa. Inf.			Reform Church	Hopewell
Moore, John J.	Pvt. F, 77 Pa. Inf.	1847	1865	Victoria	Texas
Moore, John W.	Pvt. F, 22 Pa. Inf.		1902		Ohio
Moore, John W.	Pvt. C, 76 Pa. Inf.	1841			
Moore, Joseph	Pvt. A, 205 Pa. Inf.	1846	1901	Greenwood	Altoona
Moore, Joseph H.	2Lt. A, 84 Pa. Inf.	1842			
	1Lt. G, 57 Pa. Inf.				
Moore, Joseph L.	Cpl. C, 22 Pa. Cav.				
	Cpl. H, 185 Pa. Inf.				
Moore, Josiah	Pvt. F, 77 Pa. Inf.	1833	1903	Bald Eagle	Tyrone
Moore, Lazarus Lowry	Cpt. Q. M.		1894		
Moore, Miles	Cpl. I, 34 Pa. Inf.				
	Sgt. C, 191 Pa. Inf.	1833	1902	Oak Ridge	Altoona
Moore, Samuel	Pvt. U, 22 Pa. Cav.	1844			
Moore, Thomas	Pvt. I, 105 Pa. Inf.	1840	1898	Oak Ridge	Altoona
Moore, Thomas J.	Sgt. Ind. Bn. Pa. Mil.	1837			
Moore, Warren H.	Pvt. B, 3 Pa. Inf.				
	Sgt. F, 76 Pa. Inf.	1838	1892	Oak Ridge	Altoona
Moore, William	Pvt. F, 31 Pa. Inf.				
	Pvt. A, 191 Pa. Inf.	1840			
Moore, William	Pvt. D, 184 Pa. Inf.		1864	Andersonville	Georgia
Moore, William B.		1836	1911	Birmingham	Alabama
Moore, William Banks	Pvt. B, 202 Pa. Inf.	1836	1921	Grandview	Altoona
Moore, William H.	Pvt. C, 46 Pa. Mil.	1833			
Moorland, John	Pvt. F, 76 Pa. Inf.	1824			
Moran, Miles	Pvt. F, 3 Pa. Inf.				
	Pvt. D, 3 Pa. Art.	1834	1911	St. Johns	Altoona
Moran, W. R.	Pvt. D, 3 Pa. Inf.				
Moran, William	Pvt. I, 137 Pa. Inf.				
Moran, William R.	Pvt. D, 131 Pa. Inf.				
	Pvt. B, Ind. Bn. Pa. Mil.	1843	1904	Fairview	Altoona
Mordos, Samuel	Pvt. I, 14 Pa. Inf.	1839		Bunker Hill	Bedford Co.
Moresy, James	Pvt. A, 110 Pa. Inf.				
Morgan, Dennis	Pvt. C, 110 Pa. Inf.				
Morgan, George W.	Pvt. C, 3 Pa. Inf.	1835			
Morgan, James	Pvt. H, 110 Pa. Inf.	1842	1921		Altoona
Morgan, James	Sgt. H, 110 Pa. Inf.				
Morgan, John	Pvt. D, 202 Pa. Inf.	1825	1894	Grandview	Tyrone
Morgan, John R.	Pvt. F, 76 Pa. Inf.	1843	1863	Ft. Wagner	S. Car.
Morgan, Joshua	Pvt. A, 110 Pa. Inf.				
Morgan, Martin	Pvt. A, 3 Pa. Inf.				
	Cpl. D, 192 Pa. Inf.	1824	1902	St. Marys	Hollidaysburg
Morgan, Michael	Pvt. I, 137 Pa. Inf.	1840	1905	Fairview	Altoona
Morgan, Roger Brady	Pvt. I, 137 Pa. Inf.				
	Smn. U. S. Navy	1844	1920	St. Johns	Altoona
Morgan, Thomas P.	Pvt. C, 187 Pa. Inf.	1845	1930	Grandview	Tyrone

THE CIVIL WAR   239

Name	Rank Organization	Born	Died	Cemetery	Location
Morgan, Thomas W.	Pvt. B, 3 Pa. Inf.				
	Sgt. F, 76 Pa. Inf.	1838	1913	Fairview	Altoona
Morgan, Zachariah T.	Pvt. B, 208 Pa. Inf.				
Morgman, John	Pvt. U, 1 Pa. Art.	1846			
Morningstar, Henry	Cpt. G, 87 Pa. Inf.				
Morningstar, Peter	Pvt. C, 84 Pa. Inf.				
	Pvt. H, 57 Pa. Inf.	1818			
Morris, George W.	Pvt. C, 205 Pa. Inf.		1865	Alexandria	Virginia
Morris, James	Pvt. E, 84 Pa. Inf.			Wilderness	Virginia
Morris, Patrick	2Lt. M, 62 Pa. Inf.	1819	1863	National	Gettysburg
Morrison, George	Cpl. F, 77 Pa. Inf.	1821			
Morrison, John	Pvt. D, 84 Pa. Inf.			Holsingers	Bakers Summit
Morrison, John S.	1Lt. K, 202 Pa. Inf.	1837	1886	Mt. Union	Pa.
Morrissy, Franklin	Pvt. H, 19 Ohio Inf.	1842	1911	Grandview	Tyrone
Morrow, Alexander D.	Cpl. G, 11 Pa. Cav.	1844	1914	Presbyterian	Sinking Valley
Morrow, B. Mortimor	Cpt. C, 84 Pa. Inf.				
	Maj. 22 Pa. Cav.				
	Maj. 205 Pa. Inf.	1835	1867	Presbyterian	Hollidaysburg
Morrow, George T.	Cpl. D, 67 Pa. Inf.	1844	1914	Fairview	Altoona
Morrow, James	Pvt. G, 125 Pa. Inf.				
Morrow, James A.	Pvt. D, Ind. Art. Pa. Mil.				
	Pvt. E, 147 Pa. Inf.	1838	1910	Fairview	Altoona
Morrow, John G.		1834	1864	Fairview	Altoona
Morrow, John H.	Pvt. F, 19 Pa. Cav.	1846			
Morrow, John R.	Pvt. C, 46 Pa. Mil.	1843			
Morrow, William H.					
Morrow, William W.	Pvt. H, 200 Pa. Inf.	1829			
Morrow, Wilson	Pvt. M, 62 Pa. Inf.	1834			
Morse, Charles H.	Pvt. H, 9 Pa. Cav.	1835	1894	Oak Ridge	Altoona
Mort, Adam	Pvt. C, 84 Pa. Inf.	1821			
Mortimer, Absolem F.	Far. D, 13 Pa. Cav.	1834			
Mosel, Frederick M.	Pvt. F, 1 Pa. Art.	1840	1919	Greenlawn	Roaring Spring
Mosel, William	Cpl. I, 55 Pa. Inf.	1836	1864	Spring Hope	Martinsburg
Moss, Edwin	Pvt. I, 14 Pa. Inf.	1832			
Mosser, George W.	Sgt. K, 21 Pa. Cav.	1841	1906	Reform Church	Claysburg
Mothersbaugh, Aaron					
Mottson, William	Pvt. A, 110 Pa. Inf.				
Mountain, Asbury	Pvt. G, 12 Pa. Cav.	1849	1915	Frankstown	Hollidaysburg
Mountain, David	Pvt. G, 12 Pa. Cav.	1847	1919	Geeseytown	Hollidaysburg
Mountain, George R.	Pvt. U, 84 Pa. Inf.				
	Pvt. I, 57 Pa. Inf.	1835	1910	Huntingdon	Pa.
Mountain, John	Pvt. I, 137 Pa. Inf.	1843	1901	Frankstown	Hollidaysburg
Mountain, William	Pvt. G, 12 Pa. Cav.	1827	1897	Greenwood	Altoona
Mountain, William	Pvt. H, 14 Pa. Inf.	1839			
Mountney, Edward D.	Cpl. D, 17 Pa. Inf.				
	Sgt. A, 6 Pa. Cav.	1842	1887	Fairview	Altoona
Mountz, John	Pvt. C, 76 Pa. Inf.				
Mountz, John	Pvt. E, 148 Pa. Inf.	1831	1915	Baughmans	Tyrone
Mouse, John					
Mowrey, Thomas	Pvt. C, 76 Pa. Inf.	1842			
Mowrey, William R.	Pvt. H, 14 Pa. Inf.				
	Sgt. C, 76 Pa. Inf.	1838	1864		
Moyers, Abel	Pvt. C, 205 Pa. Inf.	1833			
Moyer, David	Pvt. A, 205 Pa. Inf.	1827	1907	Gospel	Gallitzin
Moyer, George	Pvt. F, 31 Pa. Inf.	1863			
Moyer, George G.	Pvt. C, 205 Pa. Inf.	1846			
Moyer, George W.	Pvt. G, 12 Pa. Cav.	1838	1919	Grandview	Altoona
Moyer, John Charles	Pvt. E, 194 Pa. Cav.				
	Pvt. F, 4 Pa. Cav.	1820	1874	Fairview	Altoona
Moyer, Martin	Pvt. B, 208 Pa. Inf.				
Moyer, Martin	Pvt. D, 22 Pa. Cav.	1845			

SOLDIERS OF BLAIR COUNTY

Name	Rank Organization	Born	Died	Cemetery	Location
Mufy, James	Pvt. A, Ind. Bn. Pa. Mil.	1845			
Mufty, John	Pvt. A, 3 Pa. Inf.				
	Sgt. M, 62 Pa. Inf.	1836	1902	St. Johns	Altoona
Mulberry, Thomas D.	Pvt. D, 46 Pa. Mil.				
	Pvt. G, Pa. Mil.	1846			
Mulberry, William H.	Pvt. D, 3 Pa. Inf.	1842			
Mullholland, Andrew	Pvt. H, 110 Pa. Inf.				
Mulhollen, Benjamin F.	Pvt. K, 3 Pa. Art.	1835	1919	Fairview	Altoona
Mulholem, David S.	Pvt. D, 188 Pa. Inf.	1819	1892	Logan Valley	Bellwood
Mulhollem, James	Pvt. E, 3 Pa. Art.	1806	1889	Logan Valley	Bellwood
Mulholem, James C.	Pvt. F, 77 Pa. Inf.	1848	1908	Logan Valley	Bellwood
Muhollan, James C.	Pvt. E, 46 Pa. Mil.	1846			
Mulhollern, William	Cpl. E, 104 Pa. Inf.				
Mulhollen, William	Pvt. A, 110 Pa. Inf.				
Mullin, John	Pvt. I, 10 Pa. Inf.				
	Pvt. G, 11 Pa. Cav.	1837			
Mulveny, Patrick	Pvt. D, 14 Pa. Inf.	1832			
Mumper, Jeremiah	Pvt. C, 208 Pa. Inf.		1900	Newton Hamilton	Pa.
Munroe, Thomas	1Lt. C, 28 Pa. Inf.	1842			
Munshower, John N.	Pvt. D, 46 Pa. Mil.	1827			
Munson, D. H.		1847			
Munzert, Lewis	Pvt. A, 205 Pa. Inf.	1832	1896	Fairview	Altoona
Murphy, Edmund	Pvt. I, 205 Pa. Inf.	1826	1904	Fairview	Altoona
Murphy, Henry	Pvt. G, 22 U.S.C.T.				
	Pvt. G, 43 U.S.C.T.			Union	Hollidaysburg
Murphy, James	Pvt. F, 3 Pa. Inf.	1830	1905	St. Marys	Hollidaysburg
Murphy, John	Pvt. C, 34 Ohio Inf.	1810	1863		
Murphey, John	Pvt. C, 84 Pa. Inf.	1827			
Murray, David	Pvt. U, 103 Pa. Inf.	1830	1907	St. Marys	Hollidaysburg
Murray, Ferdinand	Pvt. D, 84 Pa. Inf.				
	Pvt. D, 13 Pa. Cav.	1830	1896	Fairview	Altoona
Murray, Francis B.	Pvt. H, 30 Pa. Inf.				
	Pvt. F, 190 Pa. Inf.	1842	1902	Oak Ridge	Altoona
Murray, Jacob C.	Pvt. A, 84 Pa. Inf.				
Murray, James	Pvt. H, 22 Pa. Cav.	1844	1927	Oak Grove	Tyrone
Murray, John F.	Pvt. H, 3 Pa. Inf.				
	Pvt. G, 11 Pa. Cav.	1825	1882	Dayton	Ohio
Murray, John H.	Pvt. A, 3 Pa. Inf.				
	Cpt. M, 62 Pa. Inf.	1833	1890	St. Marys	Hollidaysburg
Murray, John T.	Pvt. C, 1 Pa. Cav.	1832	1891	Fairview	Altoona
Murray, Joseph	Pvt. D, 130 Ill. Inf.				
	Pvt. E, 77 Ill. Inf.				
	Pvt. E, 130 Ill. Inf.	1835	1907	Oak Grove	Tyrone
Murray, Martin J.	Pvt. M, 62 Pa. Inf.				
	Cpl. K, 91 Pa. Inf.				
Murray, Samuel	Pvt. C, 110 Pa. Inf.				
Murray, William Gray (m)	Col. 84 Pa. Inf.	1825	1862	St. Marys	Hollidaysburg
Murty, James T.	Pvt. F, 31 Pa. Inf.				
	Cpl. A, 191 Pa. Inf.				
Musans, George	Pvt. C, 84 Pa. Inf.	1833			
Mussavous, George	Pvt. A, 84 Pa. Inf.				
Musselman, George	Pvt. C, 205 Pa. Inf.	1846		Reform Church	Hopewell
Musselman, Jacob	Pvt. A, 13 Pa. Cav.	1836	1900	Baptist	Claysburg
Musselman, Jacob	Pvt. H, 147 Pa. Inf.	1828	1897	Selinsgrove	Pa.
Musselman, William	Pvt. C, 148 Pa. Inf.	1842	1887	Fairview	Altoona
Mutzabaugh, George W.	Pvt. G, 3 Pa. Inf.				
	Pvt. A, 133 Pa. Inf.	1840	1926	Rose Hill	Altoona
Myers, Andrew	Pvt. D, 125 Pa. Inf.				
Myers, Benjamin F.	Cpl. D, 13 Pa. Cav.	1841	1912	Carson Valley	Duncansville
Myers, Benjamin F.	Pvt. I, 205 Pa. Inf.	1847	1884	Carson Valley	Duncansville
Myers, Christian B.	Pvt. B, 51 Pa. Inf.	1832	1885	Oak Ridge	Altoona

THE CIVIL WAR 241

Name	Rank Organization	Born	Died	Cemetery	Location
Myers, Charles H.	Pvt. U, 1 Pa. Art.	1843			
Myers, Daniel	Pvt. C, 110 Pa. Inf.		1864	Brattleboro	Vermont
Myers, George	Pvt. D, 13 Pa. Cav.	1844			
Myers, George W.	Pvt. I, 205 Pa. Inf.	1844			
Myers, George W.	Pvt. B, 208 Pa. Inf.				
Myers, Henry W.	Pvt. C, 3 Pa. Inf.	1837			
Myers, Henry W.	Sgt. E, 84 Pa. Inf.	1833	1904	Grandview	Tyrone
Myers, Isaac B.	Pvt. D, 14 Pa. Inf.	1843	1864	Fairview	Martinsburg
Myers, Jacob	Pvt. I, 55 Pa. Inf.	1824	1899	Fairview	Altoona
Myers, James	Pvt. C, 84 Pa. Inf.	1843	1862	Winchester	Virginia
Myers, James H.			1911		
Myers, John	Pvt. A, 125 Pa. Inf.				
	Pvt. E, 104 Pa. Inf.	1841	1917	Logan Valley	Bellwood
Myers, John	Pvt. Ind. Cav. Pa. Mil.				
	Pvt. K, 46 Pa. Mil.	1845			
Myers, John	Pvt. K, 107 Pa. Inf.	1810			
Myers, Joseph	Pvt. E, 3 Pa. Inf.	1816			
Myers, Joseph	Pvt. D, 125 Pa. Inf.				
	Pvt. A, 205 Pa. Inf.	1810	1875	St. Johns	Altoona
Myers, Joseph M.	Pvt. D, 13 Pa. Inf.	1838	1865		
Myers, Joseph R.	Pvt. D, 3 Pa. Inf.	1838			
Miller, Mahlon B.	Pvt. C, 84 Pa. Inf.	1830			
Myers, Peter	Pvt. H, 14 Pa. Inf.	1833			
Myers, Peter S.	Pvt. C, 209 Pa. Inf.	1845	1918	Antis	Bellwood
Myers, Samuel	Pvt. H, 110 Pa. Inf.		1863		
Myers, Seth F.	Sad. D, 22 Pa. Cav.	1842	1923	Shirleysburg	Hunt'gdon Co.
Myers, Sylvester	Pvt. F, 11 Pa. Inf.				
	Pvt. F, 112 Pa. Inf.	1820	1923	Birmingham	Pa.
Myers, Theodore	Pvt. D, 46 Pa. Mil.	1847			
Myers, Thomas B.	Pvt. D, 13 Pa. Cav.	1843	1864	Logan Valley	Bellwood
Myers, Thomas	Cpt. K, 105 Pa. Inf.	1833	1902	Fairview	Altoona
Myers, Thomas	Pvt. A, 125 Pa. Inf.				
Myers, Thomas Y.	Pvt. K, 1 Pa. Inf.	1841	1914	Lancaster	Pa.
Myers, William	Pvt. K, 125 Pa. Inf.		1862	Antietam	Maryland
Myers, William F.	Pvt. D, 13 Pa. Cav.	1841			
Myers, William H.	Pvt. H, 149 Pa. Inf.	1819	1881	Fairview	Altoona
Myers, William H.	Pvt. D, 125 Pa. Inf.				
Myers, William K.	Pvt. F, 210 Pa. Inf.	1846	1909	Greenwood	Altoona
Myers, William T.	Pvt. I, 126 Pa. Inf.	1840	1869	St. Johns	Altoona
Myton, Isaac	Sgt. M, 9 Pa. Cav.	1836			
Naber, Henry	Sgt. C, 205 Pa. Inf.	1839			
Nail, Daniel	Pvt. H, 155 Pa. Inf.			Asbury	Altoona
Nail, Jacob	Pvt. H, 103 Pa. Inf.	1827	1865	Antis	Bellwood
Nash, Adam M.	Pvt. E, 84 Pa. Inf.				
	Pvt. I, 57 Pa. Inf.	1842	1917	Oak Ridge	Altoona
Nash, Benjamin J.	Pvt. B, 208 Pa. Inf.	1845	1907	Frankstown	Hollidaysburg
Nash, Edward M.	Pvt. H, 110 Pa. Inf.				
Nash, Edwin Miles	Pvt. C, 13 Pa. Cav.	1837	1893	Fairview	Altoona
Nash, John	Pvt. I, 34 Pa. Inf.	1839	1910	Grandview	Tyrone
Nash, Samuel	Pvt. E, 84 Pa. Inf.		1863	Chancellorsville	Virginia
Nearhoof, Henry K.	Pvt. I, 91 Pa. Inf.	1830	1897	Bald Eagle	Tyrone
Nearhoof, James B.	Pvt. E, 46 Pa. Mil.				
Nearhoof, John	Pvt. A, 110 Pa. Inf.				
Nearhoof, John A.	Pvt. E, 46 Pa. Mil.	1841			
Nearhoof, Simon	Sgt. A, 19 Pa. Cav.	1833	1908	Grandview	Tyrone
Neely, Robert	Pvt. A, 110 Pa. Inf.		1862	Cumberland	Maryland
Neely, Simon	Pvt. D, 192 Pa. Inf.	1840	1870	Presbyterian	Hollidaysburg
Neely, Thomas D.	Cpl. C, 76 Pa. Inf.	1837	1863	Ft. Wagner	S. Car.
Neff, Albert J.	Pvt. C, 3 Pa. Inf.				
	1Lt. A, 2 U. S. Cav.	1842	1868	Presbyterian	Williamsburg
Neff, George					
Neff, T. Calvin	Cpl. F, 195 Pa. Inf.	1839	1897	Grandview	Tyrone

SOLDIERS OF BLAIR COUNTY

Name	Rank Organization	Born	Died	Cemetery	Location
Neff, William L.	Cpt. C, 3 Pa. Inf.				
	Cpt. D, 22 Pa. Cav.	1832	1910	Presbyterian	Williamsburg
Negley, John C.	Pvt. B, 208 Pa. Inf.				
Neice, Mathias	Cpt. K, 49 Pa. Inf.	1816	1893	McVeytown	Pa.
Neil, William S.	Pvt. K, 88 Pa. Inf.			Grandview	Tyrone
Neiman, William H.	Pvt. D, 49 Pa. Inf.	1832	1891	Dunkard	Lewistown
Nelson, Milton	Mus. F, Ind. Bn. Pa. Mil.	1847			
Nelson, William	Pvt. D, 205 Pa. Inf.	1819	1881	Walters	Duncansville
Nepper, Charles	Pvt. B, 208 Pa. Inf.	1842	1889	Mapleton	Hunt'gdon Co.
Nesbit, James A.	Pvt. F, 49 Pa. Inf.				
Neville, John H.	Pvt. C, 3 Pa. Inf.	1841			
Newberry, James (m)	Pvt. F, 84 Pa. Inf.				
	Pvt. B, 81 Pa. Inf.	1796	1885	Hampton	Virginia
Newhouse, Ludwig	Pvt. E, 104 Pa. Inf.				
Newhouse, Samuel	Pvt. A, 23 Pa. Mil.	1823			
Newhouse, William	Pvt. E, 84 Pa. Inf.				
	Pvt. I, 57 Pa. Inf.	1849	1887	Logan Valley	Bellwood
Newman, John	Pvt. A, 110 Pa. Inf.				
Newman, Richard	Pvt. A, 110 Pa. Inf.				
Newton, James	Pvt. C, 110 Pa. Inf.				
Nicademy, Christopher	Mus. K, 46 Pa. Mil.	1839			
Nicely, Daniel	Pvt. I, 137 Pa. Inf.				
Niswonger, Andrew	Pvt. G, 194 Pa. Inf.	1830	1912	Potters	Woodbury
Nicewonger, Theophilus	Pvt. C, 205 Pa. Inf.	1847	1904	Fairview	Altoona
Nicholas, Jacob	Pvt. A, 46 Pa. Mil.				
	Pvt. D, 194 Pa. Inf.	1811	1881	Fairview	Altoona
Nichols, Samuel I.	Pvt. C, 148 Pa. Inf.	1822	1877	Oak Ridge	Altoona
Nicholson, Thomas C.	1Lt. I, 140 Pa. Inf.	1839	1910	Fairview	Altoona
Nicodemus, Cyrus	Pvt. F, 99 Pa. Inf.	1847	1913	Polo	Illinois
Nicodemus, John H.	Pvt. B, 125 Pa. Inf.	1839	1935	Fairview	Martinsburg
Nicodemus, Josiah					
Nicodemus, Samuel S.	Pvt. M, 62 Pa. Inf.				
	Pvt. K, 91 Pa. Inf.	1840	1919	Spring Hope	Martinsburg
Nicol, John	Pvt. D, 192 Pa. Inf.				
Nicol, Daniel	Sgt. G, 13 U. S. Inf.		1913	Hastings	Pa.
Nightwine, James	Pvt. E, 3 Pa. Inf.	1824			
Nipple, John	Pvt. A, 110 Pa. Inf.				
Nissley, Martin L.	Pvt. E, 36 Pa. Mil.	1843	1931	Coleman	Wilmore
Nixdorf, Henry	Pvt. K, 122 Pa. Inf.	1844	1895	Lancaster	Pa.
Nixdorf, Joseph	Pvt. A, 110 Pa. Inf.	1806	1879	Fairview	Altoona
Nixon, Alban H.	Cpt. K, 84 Pa. Inf.				
Nixon, Albert H.	Pvt. B, 3 Pa. Inf.				
Nixon, Robert	Pvt. I, 2 Pa. Inf.				
	Pvt. A, 9 Pa. Inf.	1826	1919	Donns	Kansas
Noble, James Davis	Sgn. 55 Pa. Inf.				
	Sgn. U. S. Navy	1837	1874	Reform Church	Loysburg
Noel, Charles	Pvt. C, 84 Pa. Inf.	1829			
Noel, Daniel	Pvt. E, 104 Pa. Inf.	1821	1905	Logan Valley	Bellwood
Noel, Daniel F.	Pvt. C, 3 Pa. Inf.	1827	1905	Canoe Creek	Williamsburg
Noel, John C.	Pvt. A, 55 Pa. Inf.	1829			
Noel, Joseph	Cpl. E, 3 Pa. Inf.	1833			
Noel, Michael J.	Pvt. K, 125 Pa. Inf.				
	Sgt. D, 184 Pa. Inf.				
Noffsker, Henry M.	Pvt. I, 55 Pa. Inf.	1828	1870	Lutheran	Newry
Noffsker, Jacob J.	Pvt. A, Ind. Bn. Pa. Mil.				
	Pvt. M, 9 Pa. Cav.	1838	1901	Carson Valley	Duncansville
Nofsker, William	Sgt. E, 125 Pa. Inf.				
Noffsker, William W.	Pvt. H, 14 Pa. Inf.				
	Sgt. H, 4 U. S. Inf.	1843	1922	Union	Hollidaysburg
Noland, David P.	Pvt. E, 104 Pa. Inf.	1845	1912	Royer Mt.	Williamsburg
Nolan, James	Pvt. K, 18 Pa. Cav.	1819	1888	Methodist	Williamsburg

THE CIVIL WAR

Name	Rank Organization	Born	Died	Cemetery	Location
Noland, James H. C.	Pvt. I, 55 Pa. Inf.				
	Pvt. M, 1 U. S. Art.	1832	1915	Greenlawn	Roaring Spring
Noland, John	Pvt. C, 53 Pa. Inf.	1838			
Nolen, John	Pvt. H, 110 Pa. Inf.				
Noland, Joshua	Pvt. I, 22 Pa. Cav.	1844			
Nolen, Sylvester	Pvt. B, Ind. Bn. Pa. Mil.	1845			
Noland, Thomas	Pvt. C, 3 Pa. Inf.				
	Pvt. I, 55 Pa. Inf.				
	Pvt. C, 1 U. S. Art.	1847	1912	Antis	Bellwood
Noland, Thomas	Pvt. F, 77 Pa. Inf.	1836			
Noland, Thomas	Pvt. A, 12 Pa. Inf.		1908	Greenlawn	Roaring Spring
Noland, William	Pvt. C, 53 Pa. Inf.	1840			
Noland, William	Pvt. M, 62 Pa. Inf.	1843		Methodist	Williamsburg
Noonan, Daniel	Pvt. B, 8 Pa. Cav.	1832	1907	Calvary	Altoona
Norman, William	Pvt. E, 104 Pa. Inf.		1893	Bald Eagle	Tyrone
Norris, Robert H.	Pvt. D, 22 Pa. Cav.	1840			
North, Henry	Pvt. H, 110 Pa. Inf.				
North, John L.	Pvt. M, 3 Pa. Art.		1925	Mifflin	Pa.
Norton, James D.	Pvt. F, 46 Pa. Mil.				
	Mus. F, 49 Pa. Inf.	1836	1904	Oak Ridge	Altoona
Norton, William	Pvt. M, 62 Pa. Inf.				
	Pvt. K, 91 Pa. Inf.				
Nugent, Willis J.	1Lt. D, 78 Pa. Inf.	1838	1907	Cherry Tree	Pa.
Numer, David M.	Pvt. D, 130 Pa. Inf.	1842	1914	Newport	Pa.
Numer, William	Pvt. C, 53 Pa. Inf.		1897	Mapleton	Hunt'gdon Co.
Nunemaker, James	Pvt. E, 84 Pa. Inf.				
Nunnemacker, Samuel	Pvt. C, 3 Pa. Inf.				
	Pvt. E, 84 Pa. Inf.				
	Pvt. I, 57 Pa. Inf.	1825	1895	Lutheran	Williamsburg
Nupper, Charles	Pvt. B, 208 Pa. Inf.				
Oakes, Christian R.	Pvt. I, 137 Pa. Inf.			Brumbaughs	Martinsburg
Oakwood, John	Pvt. A, Ind. Bn. Pa. Mil.				
	Pvt. C, 12 Pa. Cav.	1838	1913	Grandview	Tyrone
Oatman, James J.	Cpl. B, 40 Pa. Inf.	1839	1900	Calvary	Altoona
Obenour, Daniel	Pvt. C, 43 Pa. Inf.	1842	1861	Salem Reform	Williamsburg
Obenour, Theobold	Pvt. E, 84 Pa. Inf.	1839	1863	Salem Reform	Williamsburg
O'Brian, Charles T.	Pvt. A, Ind. Bn. Pa. Mil.	1845			
O'Brien, James	Pvt. F, 105 Pa. Inf.			St. Marys	Hollidaysburg
O'Burn, Harrison	Sgt. C, 45 Pa. Inf.	1840	1899	Fairview	Altoona
O'Connor, Bernard J.	Pvt. D, 79 Pa. Inf.	1832	1911	St. Johns	Altoona
O'Connor, William	Pvt. M, 62 Pa. Inf.				
	Pvt. K, 91 Pa. Inf.	1864			
O'Donnell, Hugh O.	Pvt. C, 13 Pa. Cav.	1835	1895	Fairview	Altoona
Oeffinger, Jacob	Pvt. A, 19 U. S. Inf.	1836	1903	Fairview	Altoona
O'Hara, Joshua	Pvt. C, 46 Pa. Mil.	1831	1876	St. Johns	Altoona
Ohlinger, Samuel	Pvt. I, 84 Pa. Inf.	1841	1862	Carson Valley	Duncansville
Oiller, George W.	Pvt. D, 13 Pa. Cav.	1841			
Olewine, John W.	Cpn. Pa. Inf.	1835	1897	Greenwood	Altoona
Olewine, Joseph A.	Pvt. D, 205 Pa. Inf.	1842	1914	Fairview	Altoona
Olinger, George W.	Pvt. C, 110 Pa. Inf.				
Oliver, Robert W.	Cpn. 82 Pa. Inf.				
Olnus, Augustus	Pvt. A, 23 Pa. Mil.	1839			
O'Neil, John	Cpl. I, 137 Pa. Inf.				
	Sgt. B, 192 Pa. Inf.	1838	1925	St. Johns	Altoona
Ormes, Basil	Pvt. I, 127 U. S. C. T.	1823	1902	Oak Ridge	Altoona
Orndorf, William L.	Pvt. I, 98 Pa. Inf.	1847	1910	Reform	Sinking Valley
Orner, George A.	Pvt. H, 14 Pa. Inf.	1836			
Orner, Martin V.	Pvt. G, 208 Pa. Inf.	1841			
O'Rourke, Richard	Pvt. E, 3 Pa. Inf.				
	Pvt. C, 47 Pa. Inf.	1834		St. Johns	Altoona
Orr, Aaron F.	Pvt. K, 125 Pa. Inf.				
	Pvt. G, 12 Pa. Cav.	1842	1892	Fairview	Altoona

SOLDIERS OF BLAIR COUNTY

Name	Rank Organization	Born	Died	Cemetery	Location
Orr, George W.	Pvt. A, 125 Pa. Inf.				
Orr, James A.	Pvt. E, 20 Pa. Cav.		1916	Arcona	Iowa
Orr, James Albert	Pvt. A, 3 Pa. Inf.				
	Pvt. A, 40 Pa. Inf.	1843			
Orr, William	Pvt. M, 62 Pa. Inf.	1839			
Orr, William L.	Pvt. A, 3 Pa. Inf.	1840			
Orth, John	Pvt. E, 84 Pa. Inf.				
Osborne, David P.	Pvt. A, 125 Pa. Inf.				
Osburn, Wesley V.					
Osborne, William	Pvt. C, 84 Pa. Inf.	1843			
Osburn, William R.	Pvt. E, 125 Pa. Inf.				
Osman, Absalom	Pvt. D, 13 Pa. Cav.	1832	1902	Logan Valley	Bellwood
Osman, David C.	Pvt. A, 84 Pa. Inf.				
	Pvt. G, 57 Pa. Inf.	1835			
Osman, Hiram	Pvt. L, 18 Pa. Cav.	1842			
Oster, Henry A.	Pvt. C, 46 Pa. Mil.	1836			
Osterloh, Charles H.	Cpl. A, 23 Pa. Mil.	1840			
Osterloh, John C.	Maj. Militia				
	Maj. 93 Pa. Inf.				
Osterloh, William	Pvt. A, 23 Pa. Mil.	1844			
Oswalt, David W.	Pvt. D, 125 Pa. Inf.		1863	Chancellorsville	Virginia
Oswalt, John	Pvt. G, 5 Pa. Cav.	1823	1862	Williamsburg	Virginia
Oswald, John Calvin	Pvt. K, 5 U. S. Art.	1845	1922	Logan Valley	Bellwood
Ott, Joseph	Pvt. D, 192 Pa. Inf.	1816	1904	St. Patricks	Newry
Otto, Abram	Pvt. I, 55 Pa. Inf.		1864	Petersburg	Virginia
Otto, Henry H.	Pvt. C, 205 Pa. Inf.	1842	1910	Fairview	Altoona
Otto, Jacob William	Pvt. C, 205 Pa. Inf.	1837			
Otto, Samuel	Pvt. E, 104 Pa. Inf.	1838	1924	Carson Valley	Duncansville
Ounkst, Daniel S.	Pvt. G, 125 Pa. Inf.				
	Pvt. C, 76 Pa. Inf.	1836	1910	Presbyterian	Hollidaysburg
Ounkst, James	Pvt. D, 192 Pa. Inf.	1821	1899	Presbyterian	Hollidaysburg
Ounkest, Martin	Pvt. G, 125 Pa. Inf.				
Over, Daniel	Pvt. F, 77 Pa. Inf.	1846			
Over, David H.	Pvt. D, 99 Pa. Inf.	1841	1903	New Enterprise	Woodb'y Twp.
Over, David S.	Pvt. A, 184 Pa. Inf.			New Enterprise	Woodb'y Twp.
Over, James E.	Cpl. E, 138 Pa. Inf.		1905	Osterburg	Pa.
Overcash, James D.	Pvt. D, 2 Pa. Art.	1845	1899	Oak Ridge	Altoona
Owens, James T.	Pvt. D, 3 Pa. Inf.				
	Pvt. H, 15 Pa. Cav.	1840	1908	Grandview	Tyrone
Owens, Matthew	Pvt. D, 125 Pa. Inf.				
Owens, Walter L.	Cpt. D, 151 Pa. Inf.	1840	1912	Lewistown	Pa.
Owens, William J.	Pvt. D, 3 Pa. Inf.	1843			
Oxworth, George	Pvt. F, 76 Pa. Inf.				
	Pvt. Signal Corps	1840			
Page, Edward G.	Pvt. D, 5 Pa. Art.	1842	1921	Oak Ridge	Altoona
Page, Edwin	Pvt. A, 23 Pa. Mil.	1840			
Painter, Harry	Pvt. H, 41 Pa. Inf.		1899	Fairview	Altoona
Painter, Henry	Pvt. E, 190 Pa. Inf.	1845	1929	Fairview	Altoona
Painter, Jacob M.	Pvt. D, 125 Pa. Inf.				
	Sgt. Ind. Cav. Pa. Mil.	1843			
Painter, Leonard	Pvt. B, 208 Pa. Inf.				
Painter, Thomas	Pvt. H, 41 Pa. Inf.				
	Pvt. I, 46 Pa. Inf.	1840	1923	Fairview	Altoona
Painter, William	Pvt. E, 84 Pa. Inf.				
Palmer, Gabriel					
Palmer, George W.	Pvt. H, 36 Pa. Inf.	1846			
Palmer, Jacob W.	Mus. 36 Pa. Inf.	1839	1908	Oak Ridge	Altoona
Palmer, James K.	Pvt. D, 20 Pa. Cav.	1845	1911	Oak Ridge	Altoona
Parisius, William	Pvt. E, 4 Wis. Cav.	1827	1911	Rose Hill	Altoona
Parker, David	Pvt. D, 205 Pa. Inf.	1846			
Parker, John T.	Pvt. C, 126 Pa. Inf.				
	Pvt. D, 21 Pa. Cav.	1840	1908	Rose Hill	Altoona

THE CIVIL WAR

Name	Rank Organization	Born	Died	Cemetery	Location
Parker, William J.	Pvt. H, 125 Pa. Inf.		1863	Jackson Twp.	Hunt'gdon Co.
Parkhurst, George W.	Pvt. E, 13 Md. Inf.	1812	1906	Spring Hope	Martinsburg
Parks, Amos	Pvt. C, 3 Pa. Inf.				
	Pvt. G, 12 Pa. Cav.	1832	1903	Antis	Bellwood
Parks, George W.	Pvt. E, 84 Pa. Inf.				
	Pvt. I, 57 Pa. Inf.	1845			
Parks, James	Pvt. I, 34 Pa. Inf.	1834	1885	Antis	Bellwood
Parks, Miles	Pvt. M, 9 Pa. Cav.	1843			
Parks, William	Pvt. D, 192 Pa. Inf.				
Parks, William	Pvt. A, 22 Pa. Cav.		1906	Newton Hamilton	Pa.
Parrish, Henry	Sgt. B, 133 Pa. Inf.		1886	St. Johns	Altoona
Parsons, Chambers A.	Pvt. D, 125 Pa. Inf.	1832	1879	Oak Ridge	Altoona
Parsons, Charles A.	Pvt. D, 125 Pa. Inf.				
Parsons, George	Pvt. E, 49 Pa. Inf.	1830	1881	Oak Ridge	Altoona
Parsons, John E.	Pvt. H, 22 Pa. Cav.	1839			
Parsons, John F.	Pvt. A, 110 Pa. Inf.	1836	1864	Deep Bottom	Virginia
Parsons, John W.	Cpl. B, 42 Pa. Inf.	1850			
Parsons, Sylvester M.		1845		Grandview	Tyrone
Patch, Isaac P.	Ldm. U. S. Navy	1847	1938	Rose Hill	Altoona
Pates, Thomas	Pvt. C, 205 Pa. Inf.	1820	1897	Carson Valley	Duncansville
Pate, Wesley V.					
Patrick, Dallas	Pvt. B, 190 Pa. Inf.	1845		Fairview	Altoona
Patterson, Andrew J.	Pvt. E, 84 Pa. Inf.				
	Pvt. D, 22 Pa. Cav.	1845	1918	Presbyterian	Williamsburg
Patterson, George M.	Sgt. D, 22 Pa. Cav.	1840	1925	Presbyterian	Williamsburg
Patterson, George McC.	Sgt. C, 3 Pa. Inf.	1837	1873	Presbyterian	Williamsburg
Patterson, John D.	Cpl. B, 125 Pa. Inf.	1842		Harrisburg	Pa.
Patterson, John J.	Sgt. F, 21 Pa. Res. Inf.				
Patterson, John M.	Pvt. B, 77 Pa. Inf.		1897	Alexandria	Pa.
Patterson, John N.	Pvt. B, 49 Pa. Inf.	1843	1917	Franklinville	Hunt'gdon Co.
Patterson, Joseph C.	Pvt. D, 49 Pa. Inf.	1844	1862	Hampton	Virginia
Patterson, Robert G.	Pvt. E, 84 Pa. Inf.	1848	1906	Presbyterian	Williamsburg
Patterson, Samuel	Pvt. D, 205 Pa. Inf.				
Patterson, Samuel N.	Atf. D, 1 Pa. Art.				
	Pvt. D, 49 Pa. Inf.	1829	1899	Grandview	Tyrone
Patterson, Stephen B.	Cpl. M, 9 Pa. Cav.			Burkets	Martinsburg
Patterson, W. C.					
Patterson, William H.	Pvt. C, 1 Pa. Art.	1839	1910	Keller Reform	Williamsburg
Patterson, William J.	Pvt. A, 40 Pa. Inf.		1864	Wilderness	Virginia
Patton, Edward	Pvt. D, 125 Pa. Inf.	1842	1889	St. Patricks	Gallitzin
Patton, Joseph	Pvt. D, 1 Pa. Art.	1840			
Patton, Robert	Pvt. P, 149 Pa. Inf.		1909	Duncannon	Pa.
Patton, Theodore B.	Pvt. C, 46 Pa. Mil.	1847	1922	Fairview	Altoona
Paul, David D.	Pvt. F, 77 Pa. Inf.	1846	1910	Fairview	Martinsburg
Paul, Elias	Pvt. D, 5 Pa. Art.	1834	1917	Grandview	Johnstown
Paul, John C.	Maj. D, 4 Pa. Cav.	1842	1894	Fairview	Altoona
Paulter, John	Pvt. I, 84 Pa. Inf.	1845	1870	St. Marys	Hollidaysburg
Pearson, Thomas K.	Pvt. B, 208 Pa. Inf.				
Pearson, William	Pvt. C, 110 Pa. Inf.				
Peck, Reuben	Pvt. A, 205 Pa. Inf.	1839	1895	Collinsville	Altoona
Peck, William	Pvt. F, 198 Pa. Inf.	1833	1900	Collinsville	Altoona
Peight, Emanuel S.	Pvt. A, 3 Pa. Inf.				
	Cpl. D, 46 Pa. Mil.	1833			
Peight, Jacob	Pvt. D, 46 Pa. Mil.	1835			
Peight, Joseph	Pvt. E, 84 Pa. Inf.				
Pendergast, James T.	Cpl. H, 3 Pa. Inf.	1836			
Penlow, George W.	Pvt. I, 32 U. S. C. T.	1825	1891	Union	Hollidaysburg
Pennock, John L.	Pvt. U, 1 Pa. Art.				
	Pvt. E, 147 Pa. Inf.	1817	1894	Greenwood	Altoona
Penrose, Joseph	Pvt. C, 205 Pa. Inf.				
	Pvt. E, 21 Pa. Cav.	1845		Reform Church	Fishertown
Pensyl, Harry R.	Cpl. H, 21 Pa. Cav.	1846	1923	Fairview	Altoona

SOLDIERS OF BLAIR COUNTY

Name	Rank Organization	Born	Died	Cemetery	Location
Pensyl, J. Frank	Pvt. K, 184 Pa. Inf.	1849	1914	Rose Hill	Altoona
Pensyl, Philip H.	Sgr. 56 Pa. Inf.	1841	1912	Everett	Pa.
Penwell, David	Pvt. C, 46 Pa. Mil.	1817			
Perchey, Henry E.	Pvt. Ind. Cav. Pa. Mil.	1840	1915	Fairview	Altoona
Percival, William H.	Cpl. Ind. Cav. Pa. Mil.	1830			
Perkins, George W.	Pvt. H, 14 Pa. Inf.				
	Sgt. E, 125 Pa. Inf.				
	Pvt. K, 18 Pa. Cav.	1842	1877	Fairview	Altoona
Pervines, Henry	Pvt. B, Ind. Bn. Pa. Mil.	1833			
Peters, Simon	Pvt. B, 19 U. S. C. T.	1824	1892	Union	Hollidaysburg
Peterson, Jacob	Pvt. F, 1 Pa. Art.	1841			
Peterson, William A.	Pvt. A, 84 Pa. Inf.			Pleasantville	Pa.
Pfieffer, Christian F.	Pvt. H, 12 Pa. Cav.	1844	1922	Oak Ridge	Altoona
Pfeifer, John F.	Cpl. C, 12 Pa. Cav.	1842	1921	St. Johns	Altoona
Pfeiffer, John F.	Bks. G, 12 Pa. Cav.	1840	1899	Fairview	Altoona
Pheasant, Joshua R.	Pvt. E, 45 Pa. Inf.	1837	1921	Curtain	Pa.
Phillips, Benjamin F.	Pvt. G, 125 Pa. Inf.	1843	1920	Eastlawn	Tyrone
Phillips, David F.	Pvt. G, 125 Pa. Inf.				
	Pvt. D, 192 Pa. Inf.	1839	1902	Grandview	Tyrone
Phillips, Edward H.	Pvt. H, 50 Ohio Inf.	1845	1914	Fairview	Altoona
Phillips, James	Pvt. F, 77 Pa. Inf.	1836	1870	Charlottesville	Bellwood
Phillips, John H.	Pvt. D, 22 Pa. Cav.	1845			
Phillips, Patrick	Pvt. F, 31 Pa. Inf.				
Phillips, Ralph	Pvt. B, 125 Pa. Inf.				
Phillips, William H.	Pvt. B, 62 Pa. Inf.				
	Pvt. B, 155 Pa. Inf.	1841	1880	Allegheny	Pittsburgh
Pickle, David	Pvt. H, 110 Pa. Inf.				
Pickle, Henry	Pvt. G, 57 Pa. Inf.	1846			
Pickel, Lewis	Pvt. C, 84 Pa. Inf.	1818			
Pickel, Robert	Pvt. C, 84 Pa. Inf.				
Pierce, John E.	Cpl. D, 201 Pa. Inf.		1918	Evergreen	Duncannon
Pierce, William S.	Pvt. E, 84 Pa. Inf.				
	Pvt. G, 57 Pa. Inf.	1816			
Pierson, Francis	Pvt. C, 110 Pa. Inf.			Wagerman	Bedford Co.
Pike, Daniel	Pvt. I, 79 Pa. Inf.				
Piper, Enoch	Cpl. B, 208 Pa. Inf.	1830	1906	Lutheran	Williamsburg
Piper, George	Pvt. A, 3 Pa. Inf.	1835			
Piper, Henry Beam	Cpl. K, 11 Pa. Inf.	1831	1895	Grandview	Tyrone
Piper, Joseph H.	Pvt. G, 125 Pa. Inf.		1862	National	Winchester
Piper, Silas W.	2Lt. A, 84 Pa. Inf.	1841	1921	Carson Valley	Duncansville
Piper, Thompson F.	Pvt. A, 84 Pa. Inf.			Bedford	Pa.
Piper, William M.	Pvt. E, 104 Pa. Inf.	1840	1916	Yellow Springs	Williamsburg
Pitcairn, Hugh	Sgt. C, 46 Pa. Mil.	1845	1911	Fairview	Altoona
Pitzer, William A.	Sgt. G, 138 Pa. Inf.	1841	1917	Oak Ridge	Altoona
Plack, George	Pvt. H, 3 Pa. Inf.	1828			
Plack, George	Pvt. U, 62 Pa. Mil.				
Plaster, William H.	Pvt. C, 110 Pa. Inf.				
Platt, Elias	Pvt. K, 46 Pa. Mil.	1845			
Plowden, Benjamin	Pvt. E, 3 U. S. C.T.	1828	1897	Oak Ridge	Altoona
Plowman, David Calvin	Pvt. F, 21 Pa. Cav.	1847			
Plowman, Wilson L.	Pvt. D, 46 Pa. Mil.	1847			
Plummer, Amos J.	Pvt. A, 110 Pa. Inf.	1841	1864	Grandview	Tyrone
Plummer, Arthur N.	Pvt. 19 Pa. Cav.	1846	1920	Union	Martinsburg
Plummer, Benjamin F.	Pvt. D, 93 Pa. Inf.		1865	Asbury	Altoona
Plummer, Eli B.	Pvt. F, 2 Pa. Cav.	1840	1923	Rose Hill	Altoona
Plummer, Henry E.	Pvt. B, 3 Pa. Inf.				
	Pvt. A, 110 Pa. Inf.	1837	1926	Versailles	McKeesport
Plummer, John R.	Pvt. H, 110 Pa. Inf.				
	Sgt. A, 205 Pa. Inf.	1843	1920	Grandview	Tyrone
Plummer, John W.	Sgt. C, 110 Pa. Inf.	1845	1936	Oak Ridge	Altoona
Plummer, William R.	Sgt. H, 49 Pa. Inf.	1837	1906	Fairview	Altoona
Plumpton, Elijah	Pvt. D, 205 Pa. Inf.	1844			

THE CIVIL WAR 247

Name	Rank Organization	Born	Died	Cemetery	Location
Plunket, William	Pvt. H, 205 Pa. Inf.	1845	1907	St. Augustine	Indiana Co.
Pote, Andrew B.	Pvt. E, 107 Pa. Inf.	1836	1920	Holsingers	Bakers Summit
Poet, Jacob	Pvt. H, 110 Pa. Inf.	1848	1863	Lutheran	Newry
Poet, Michael	Sgt. 76 Pa. Inf.	1845	1929	Fairview	Altoona
Pote, Michael B.	Cpl. C, 76 Pa. Inf.	1821	1901	Holsingers	Bakers Summit
Poffenberger, William H.	Sgt. E, 18 Pa. Cav.	1840	1878	Harrisburg	Pa.
Polk, Henry A.					
Pollard, Alfred J.	Pvt. 18 N. Y. Cav.	1843	1910	Albrights	Roaring Spring
Pollard, Uriah J.	Pvt. K, 88 Pa. Inf.	1846	1925	Oak Ridge	Altoona
Pomeroy, Stephen W.		1836	1912	Harrisburg	Pa.
Port, Jacob	Pvt. B, Ind. Bn. Pa. Mil.	1844			
Port, Levi W.	1Lt. 205 Pa. Inf.	1841	1910	Connellsville	Pa.
Porter, Charles H.	Pvt. A, Ind. Bn. Pa. Mil.	1841			
Postlewait, Samuel C.	Pvt. G, 46 Pa. Mil.				
Potter, John	Far. M, 22 Pa. Cav.	1812	1867	Potter	Morrisons Cove
Potter, Jonas	Pvt. B, 36 Pa. Inf.	1835	1892	Fairview	Altoona
Potter, William M.	Pvt. E, 84 Pa. Inf.	1841	1863	Methodist	Williamsburg
Potts, Andrew J.	Pvt. M, 62 Pa. Inf.	1839			
Potts, John	Pvt. D, 205 Pa. Inf.			Yellow Spring	Williamsburg
Potts, Stephen C.	2Lt. H, 3 Pa. Inf.				
	1Lt. M, 62 Pa. Inf.	1841	1862	Presbyterian	Hollidaysburg
Potts, Thomas P.	Pvt, H, 54 Pa. Inf.				
Poust, Ellis	Pvt. A, 46 Pa. Mil.	1845	1922	Grandview	Tyrone
Powell, Ephriam C.	Pvt. G, 34 Pa. Inf.	1838	1897	Fairview	Altoona
Powell, Handford	Pvt. G, 133 Pa. Inf.	1830	1899	Oak Ridge	Altoona
Powell, Henry H.	Pvt. I, 125 Pa. Inf.	1840	1916	Fairview	Altoona
Powell, John	Pvt. F, 76 Pa. Inf.	1833	1864	Hampton	Virginia
Powell, Joseph	Pvt. D, 22 Pa. Cav.	1839			
Powell, Milton P.	Pvt. C, 3 Pa. Inf.				
	Pvt. B, 125 Pa. Inf.				
	Pvt. I, 22 Pa. Cav.	1842	1881	Presbyterian	Williamsburg
Powell, Samuel D.	Pvt. I, 205 Pa. Inf.	1838	1865		
Powley, Henry L.	Pvt. C, 110 Pa. Inf.		1926	Hutchisons	Altoona
Powley, Richard	Pvt. C, 110 Pa. Inf.				
Powley, Simon	Pvt. D, 46 Pa. Inf.	1838	1905	Fairview	Altoona
Pressel, Jacob	Pvt. H, 12 Pa. Cav.	1837	1914	Pressel	Claysburg
Pressell, Samuel	Cpl. F, 77 Pa. Inf.	1837			
Pressell, Samuel	Pvt. E, 125 Pa. Inf.	1832	1906	Fairview	Altoona
Price, Daniel	Pvt. D, 46 Pa. Mil.	1814			
Price, Daniel M.	Pvt. C, 205 Pa. Inf.	1845			
Price, David	Cpl. C, 110 Pa. Inf.		1912	Bedford	Pa.
Price, Edward G.	Pvt. A, 23 Pa. Mil.	1842			
Price, George	Pvt. D, 99 Pa. Inf.	1849	1916	Fairview	Altoona
Price, Henry H.	Pvt. H, 22 Pa. Cav.	1846			
Price, Jacob W.	Pvt. D, 131 Pa. Inf.				
	Sgt. C, 21 Pa. Inf.	1841	1908	Rose Hill	Altoona
Price, James	Pvt. F, 205 Pa. Inf.			Charlottesville	Bellwood
Price, James	Pvt. E, 20 Pa. Cav.				
Price, John	Pvt. D, 46 Pa. Mil.	1844			
Price, John B.	Pvt. M, 22 Pa. Cav.	1824	1897	Greenlawn	Roaring Spring
Price, John T.	Mus. K, 114 Pa. Inf.	1845			
Price, Joseph B.					
Price, Joseph C.	Pvt. G, 125 Pa. Inf.				
Price, Joseph J.	Pvt. D, 138 Pa. Inf.		1864		
Price, Levi B.	Pvt. E, 20 Pa. Cav.	1826	1899	Fairview	Altoona
Price, Lyman S.	Pvt. G, 31 Pa. Inf.	1847	1903	Carson Valley	Duncansville
Price, Robert	Pvt. A, 205 Pa. Inf.			Charlottesville	Bellwood
Price, William H.	Pvt. E, 3 Pa. Inf.	1841			
Prim, Frank M.	Pvt. M, 19 Pa. Cav.	1846	1880	Fairview	Altoona
Pringle, Daniel S.	Pvt. F, 77 Pa. Inf.	1845	1895	Fairview	Altoona
Printzler, O. P. R.	Pvt. M, 62 Pa. Inf.				
	Pvt. K, 91 Pa. Inf.				

SOLDIERS OF BLAIR COUNTY

Name	Rank Organization	Born	Died	Cemetery	Location
Prizer, Benjamin	Pvt. N, 192 Pa. Inf.		1905	Harrisburg	Pa.
Pross, James H.	Mus. H, 76 Pa. Inf.	1835	1915	Lewisburg	Pa.
Prosser, John	Pvt. I, 137 Pa. Inf.				
	Pvt. D, 192 Pa. Inf.	1845	1892	Summit	Cambria Co.
Prosser, William	Sgt. G, 57 Pa. Inf.	1838			
Protzman, Martin L.	Pvt. D, 1 Pa. Art.	1843			
Prough, Silas	Pvt. D, 192 Pa. Inf.				
	Pvt. D, 107 Pa. Inf.	1841	1927	Eastlawn	Tyrone
Pruner, Daniel J.	Pvt. 11 Pa. Inf.				
	1Lt. A, 21 Pa. Cav.		1864	Bellefonte	
Pruner, Joseph D.	Pvt. D, 3 Pa. Inf.	1838			
Pruner, Robert	Pvt. 45 Pa. Inf.				
	Pvt. 1 Pa. Cav.		1884		
Prunkard, John E.	Pvt. G, 125 Pa. Inf.				
	Cpl. B, Ind. Bn. Pa. Mil.	1842			
Prunkard, Samuel R.	Pvt. Ind. Pa. Cav.	1837	1902	Fairview	Altoona
Pryor, Henry	Pvt. H, 110 Pa. Inf.				
Pryor, William A.	Pvt. C, 205 Pa. Inf.	1845			
Puderbaugh, George	Pvt. D, 56 Pa. Inf.	1832	1882	Fairview	Martinsburg
Pugh, Henry	Pvt. B, 208 Pa. Inf.				
Pugh, Thomas	Pvt. D, 1 Pa. Art.				
Purdue, James M.	Sgt. H, 56 Pa. Inf.	1822	1896	Grandview	Tyrone
Quarry, Alfred	Pvt. F, 31 Pa. Inf.				
	Pvt. A, 191 Pa. Inf.		1865	Salisbury	N. Car.
Quarry, Henry	Pvt. D, 192 Pa. Inf.				
Quarry, Levi	Pvt. F, 31 Pa. Inf.				
	Pvt. A, 191 Pa. Inf.				
Quarry, Michael	Pvt. F, 31 Pa. Inf.				
	Pvt. A, 191 Pa. Inf.				
Quarry, William C.	Pvt. C, 205 Pa. Inf.	1844	1921	Kifers	Woodbury
Quarry, William G.		1845	1929	Dry Hill	Woodbury
Quay, Thomas					
Quinn, James		1835	1872	Grandview	Tyrone
Quinn, John	Pvt. E, 104 Pa. Inf.	1823	1896	St. Johns	Altoona
Rabold, Gotlob	Pvt. I, 34 Pa. Inf.	1836	1904	Burkets	Henrietta
Rabuck, Philip	Pvt. A, 7 Pa. Cav.	1847	1927	Fairview	Altoona
Raffensparger, Daniel B.	Pvt. H, 13 Pa. Cav.	1818	1901	Oak Ridge	Altoona
Ragan, Daniel	Pvt. F, 76 Pa. Inf.	1825	1862	Hilton Head	S. Car.
Ragan, James	Pvt. D, 78 Pa. Inf.		1889	Soldiers Home	Erie
Rager, John L.	Pvt. H, 110 Pa. Inf.	1839	1864	Andersonville	Georgia
Rakestraw, John A.	Pvt. G, 15 Pa. Mil.	1833	1916	Oak Ridge	Altoona
Ralle, Rudolph	Pvt. E, 104 Pa. Inf.	1834	1917	Greenlawn	Roaring Spring
Ralston, David E.	Pvt. C, 110 Pa. Inf.		1863	Chancellorsville	Virginia
Ralston, William	Sgt. C, 110 Pa. Inf.				
Ramage, Thomas R.	Pvt. C, 76 Pa. Inf.	1840			
Ramaley, William R.	Pvt. K, 125 Pa. Inf.				
Rambler, Isaac	Pvt. K, 203 Pa. Inf.	1832	1865	New Berne	N. Car.
Ramey, Frederick	Pvt. A, 23 Pa. Mil.				
	Pvt. A, Ind. Bn. Pa. Mil.	1844	1913	Fairview	Altoona
Ramey, Sanford Dewey	Pvt. A, Ind. Bn. Pa. Mil.				
	Cpl. C, Thompsons Art.	1842	1912	Lutheran	Sinking Valley
Ramsey, Robert	Pvt. D, 46 Pa. Mil.	1833			
Ramsey, Sabret	Mus. E, 28 Iowa Inf.	1844	1908	Rose Hill	Altoona
Ramsey, Samuel S.	Pvt. C, 208 Pa. Inf.				
	Sgt. A, 77 Pa. Inf.	1843	1912	Grandview	Tyrone
Randolph, James	Pvt. D, 205 Pa. Inf.	1837			
Randall, James L.	Pvt. C, 84 Ohio Inf.	1846	1914	Calvary	Altoona
Rankin, John K. M.	Pvt. H, 148 Pa. Inf.	1863			
Raugh, James J.	Pvt. C, 53 Pa. Inf.	1843	1882	Fairview	Altoona
Raugh, John H.	Pvt. C, 53 Pa. Inf.	1837	1891	Fairview	Altoona
Raugh, Sellars	Pvt. C, 125 Pa. Inf.	1840	1910	Logan Valley	Bellwood
Ravenhill, Thomas	Pvt. A, 84 Pa. Inf.	1826	1862	Lutheran	Hollidaysburg

Name	Rank Organization	Born	Died	Cemetery	Location
Rawlins, Isaiah H.	Sgt. 76 Pa. Inf.	1838	1876	Fairview	Martinsburg
Ray, Charles	Pvt. F, 3 Mass. Cav.	1842	1926	Oak Ridge	Altoona
Ray, William	Pvt. H, 205 Pa. Inf.	1827	1911	Fairview	Altoona
Ready, John	Pvt. D, 205 Pa. Inf.	1825			
Reeder, James E.	Pvt. E, 6 U. S. C. T.	1843	1914	Oak Ridge	Altoona
Reeder, Joseph L.	1Lt. C, 131 Pa. Inf.	1821	1904	Grandview	Tyrone
Reeder, Robert B.	Pvt. I, 136 Pa. Inf.	1843	1922	Ross Church	Warriors Mark
Reader, Theodore B.	Sgt. C, 49 Pa. Inf.	1838	1915	Grandview	Tyrone
Reading, William W.	Pvt. F, 66 Ohio Inf.	1838	1907	Rose Hill	Altoona
Ready, William	Pvt. C, 1 Pa. Cav.	1844	1924	Methodist	Lewistown
Ream, David Buchanan	Pvt. B, 195 Pa. Inf.	1846	1918	Rose Hill	Altoona
Ream, W. Charles	Pvt. H, 3 Pa. Inf.				
	2Lt. A, 84 Pa. Inf.	1826	1862	Presbyterian	Hollidaysburg
Rebuck, Henry C.	Cpl. H, 3 Pa. Cav.	1838	1916	Houston	Texas
Reddick, Martin W.	Pvt. B, Ind. Bn. Pa. Mil.	1846			
Redding, John J.	Pvt. A, 3 Pa. Inf.	1834	1902	Calvary	Altoona
Reddy, Henry	Pvt. C, 76 Pa. Inf.	1833			
Reed, Albert Clayton	Pvt. A, Ind. Bn. Pa. Mil.				
	Pvt. D, 2 Pa. Cav.	1845	1886	Presbyterian	Hollidaysburg
Reed, Albert G.					
Reed, Andrew Jackson	Pvt. G, Ind. Bn. Pa. Mil.				
	Pvt. M, 9 Pa. Cav.	1837	1874	Lutheran	Williamsburg
Reed, Clayton	Pvt. A, 23 Pa. Mil.	1844			
Reed, George W.	Pvt. E, 87 Pa. Inf.	1831	1900	Yellow Spring	Williamsburg
Reed, Harrison	Pvt. I, 137 Pa. Inf.				
Reed, James	Pvt. I, 53 Pa. Inf.		1925	Grandview	Tyrone
Reed, John H.	Pvt. G, 12 Pa. Cav.	1826			
Reed, Joseph H.	Pvt. G, 125 Pa. Inf.				
	Pvt. B, Ind. Bn. Pa. Mil.	1841	1920	Lutheran	Hollidaysburg
Reed, Lewis S.	Pvt. C, 84 Pa. Inf.	1839			
Reed, Peter S. (M)	Maj. 2 Neb. Cav.	1824	1882	Golden City	Colorado
Reed, William	Pvt. B, 3 Pa. Inf.	1842			
Reid, William A. D.	Mus. G, 12 Pa. Cav.	1842			
Reed, William J.	Pvt. D, 205 Pa. Inf.	1832			
Reid, William J.	Pvt. F, 31 Pa. Inf.				
	Pvt. A, 191 Pa. Inf.	1828	1865	Salisbury	N. Car.
Reid, William W.	Cpl. B, 3 Pa. Inf.	1811	1889	Frankstown	Hollidaysburg
Reed, William W.	Cpl. B, 202 Pa. Inf.	1837	1911	Oak Ridge	Altoona
Reep, Adam	Pvt. B, Ind. Bn. Pa. Mil.				
	Pvt. H, 110 Pa. Inf.	1844	1911	Carson Valley	Duncansville
Reep, Jacob	Pvt. K, 84 Pa. Inf.				
	Pvt. K, 57 Pa. Inf.	1814	1895	Carson Valley	Duncansville
Reese, Evan C.	Pvt. M, 21 Pa. Cav.	1845	1911	Rose Hill	Altoona
Reese, John F.	Pvt. E, 165 Pa. Inf.	1832	1916	Logan Valley	Bellwood
Reese, Shadrach M.	Pvt. B, 59 Ind.Inf.	1829		Asbury	Altoona
Reese, William B.	Pvt. K, 186 Pa. Inf.	1845	1913	Oak Ridge	Altoona
Reeves, George	Pvt. E, 3 Pa. Inf.	1843			
Reeves, George A.	Pvt. B, 79 Pa. Inf.	1844	1898	Fairview	Altoona
Reffner, Anthony P.	Sgt. F, 63 Pa. Inf.				
	Pvt. K, 105 Pa. Inf.		1889	Lutheran	Hollidaysburg
Reffner, James	Pvt. H, 14 Pa. Inf.				
	Blk. C, 12 Pa. Cav.	1828	1909	Fairview	Altoona
Reffner, Joseph	Pvt. G, 125 Pa. Inf.				
Reffner, Moses	Blk. E, 12 Pa. Cav.			Lutheran	Hollidaysburg
Reich, William	Pvt. D, 46 Pa. Mil.	1842			
Reidy, M. D.	Pvt. H, 7 Pa. Inf.				
Reifsnyder, Alpheus G.	Pvt. E, 194 Pa. Inf.	1845	1918	St. Johns	Altoona
Reiger, August	Pvt. B, 125 Pa. Inf.				
Reigh, Frederick M.	Pvt. G, 12 Pa. Cav.				
	Blk. M, 12 Pa. Cav.		1885	Fairview	Altoona
Reighard, Julius	Pvt. A, 3 Pa. Inf.	1834			
Reighard, Thomas W.	Pvt. C, 11 Pa. Inf.	1842	1902	East Ridge	Clearfield

SOLDIERS OF BLAIR COUNTY

Name	Rank Organization	Born	Died	Cemetery	Location
Reigle, Christian	Pvt. E, 104 Pa. Inf.				
Reigle, Joseph	Sgt. E, 45 Pa. Inf.	1819	1893	Fairview	Altoona
Reinninger, F. M.	Pvt. A, 84 Pa. Inf.		1862	Cumberland	Maryland
Reish, Joseph	Pvt. C, 76 Pa. Inf.				
Reish, Isaac	Pvt. A, 110 Pa. Inf.				
Renner, Matlock	1Lt. A, 1 Pa. Cav.	1835	1903	Fairview	Altoona
Renner, Theodore	Cpl. B, 46 Pa. Mil.				
	Cpl. D, 205 Pa. Inf.	1845		Denver	Colorado
Rentz, John	Pvt. M, 22 Pa. Cav.	1831	1911	St. Marys	Hollidaysburg
Replogle, Simon L.	Pvt. I, 194 Pa. Inf.	1848	1887	Fairview	Altoona
Rentzler, Joseph	Pvt. E, 84 Pa. Inf.				
Rex, Martin Luther	Sgt. I, 22 Pa. Cav.		1920	Mapleton	Pa.
Reynolds, John	Pvt. G, 22 Pa. Cav.	1845	1906	Grandview	Tyrone
Reynolds, Joshua	Pvt. F, 198 Pa. Inf.	1826			
Rhine, George W.	Pvt. I, 76 Pa. Inf.	1849	1913	Fairview	Altoona
Rhodes, A.	Pvt. D, 15 U. S. Inf.				
Rhodes, Abraham	Pvt. K, 125 Pa. Inf.				
Rhodes, Adam W.	Pvt. G, 1 Pa. Cav.	1836	1884	Royer Mt.	Williamsburg
Rhodes, Benjamin F.	Pvt. D, 192 Pa. Inf.	1843	1920	Grandview	Tyrone
Rhodes, Christopher C.	Pvt. I, 14 Pa. Inf.				
	Pvt. D, 14 U. S. Inf.	1839	1894	Greenlawn	Roaring Spring
Rhodes, George H.	Pvt. C, 205 Pa. Inf.	1835	1922	Metzkers	Martinsburg
Rhodes, George H.	Pvt. B, 125 Pa. Inf.				
Rhodes, Isaac	Pvt. K, 125 Pa. Inf.				
Rhodes, Isaac	Pvt. F, 49 Pa. Inf.	1840	1907	Grandview	Tyrone
Rhodes, Isaac	Pvt. C, 46 Pa. Mil.	1840			
Rhodes, Jacob	Pvt. K, 125 Pa. Inf.				
Rhodes, Jacob	Pvt. I, 205 Pa. Inf.	1838			
Rhoads, John A.	Pvt. M, 9 Pa. Cav.	1832	1864	Florence	S. Car.
Rhode, John A.	Cpl. I, 137 Pa. Inf.				
Rhoades, John D.	Pvt. E, 125 Pa. Inf.	1833	1906	Lutheran	Newry
Rhodes, Samuel J.	Pvt. G, 12 Pa. Cav.	1840	1886	Lutheran	Newry
Rhodes, William	Blk. G, 1 Pa. Cav.	1837	1903	Grandview	Tyrone
Rhodes, William D.	Pvt. F, 77 Pa. Inf.	1844	1903	Rhodes	Williamsburg
Rhodes, William H.	Pvt. B, 125 Pa. Inf.				
	Pvt. K, 13 Pa. Cav.	1842	1912	Fairview	Martinsburg
Rhody, Joseph	Pvt. H, 93 Pa. Inf.	1847	1927	Greenlawn	Hollidaysburg
Rhule, James	Pvt. E, 84 Pa. Inf.		1863	Chancellorsville	Virginia
Rhule, Samuel M.	Pvt. M, 9 Pa. Cav.	1844	1925	Dayton	Ohio
Rhule, William G.	Sgt. M, 62 Pa. Inf.	1839	1905		
Rice, Jacob	Pvt. I, 34 Pa. Inf.		1898	Birmingham	Pa.
Rice, Joseph	Pvt. I, 14 Pa. Inf.	1837			
Rice, John G.	Pvt. I, 34 Pa. Inf.	1831	1890	Birmingham	Pa.
Rice, Rhineheart	Pvt. D, 125 Pa. Inf.				
Rice, Samuel H.	Pvt. L, 3 Pa. Art.	1840	1921	Fairview	Altoona
Richards, Alfred	Pvt. D, 40 Pa. Inf.	1846			
Richards, Charles W.	Pvt. E, 84 Pa. Inf.				
	Pvt. I, 57 Pa. Inf.				
Richards, George	Pvt. K, 125 Pa. Inf.				
Richards, George W.	Pvt. A, 110 Pa. Inf.				
Richards, John	Pvt. K, 22 Pa. Cav.	1845			
Richards, John	Pvt. D, 53 Pa. Inf.	1836	1915	Greenwood	Altoona
Richards, John	Pvt. B, 208 Pa. Inf.				
Richards, John	Pvt. B, 125 Pa. Inf.				
Richardson, Isaac	Pvt. G, 11 Pa. Cav.	1836	1912	Rose Hill	Altoona
Richardson, Johnathon	Pvt. A, 205 Pa. Inf.	1846			
Richardson, Michael	Pvt. D, 1 Pa. Art.		1864	Richmond	Virginia
Richardson, Porter	Pvt. E, 46 Pa. Mil.				
	Pvt. K, 13 Pa. Cav.		1923	Birmingham	Pa.
Richmond, Albert E.	Pvt. D, 125 Pa. Inf.				
Richmond, Samuel S.	Pvt. D, 125 Pa. Inf.				
Richter, Adam	Pvt. H, 208 Pa. Inf.	1817	1883	Waterside	Bedford Co.

THE CIVIL WAR

Name	Rank Organization	Born	Died	Cemetery	Location
Rick, Felix	Pvt. C, 84 Pa. Inf.	1843			
Rickabaugh, Jeremiah	Cpl. F, 77 Pa. Inf.	1830			
Ridenour, Jacob D.	Pvt. C, 205 Pa. Inf.	1845		Greenlawn	Roaring Spring
Ridenour, William	Pvt. K, 46 Pa. Mil.	1817			
Ridenour, William B.	Pvt. D, 46 Pa. Mil.	1846			
Riddle, James D.	Pvt. G, 125 Pa. Inf.	1847	1862	Presbyterian	Hollidaysburg
Riddle, James F.	Sgt. E, Ind. Bn. Pa. Mil.				
	Cpl. B, 39 Pa. Inf.	1835	1895	Grandview	Tyrone
Riddle, John B.	Pvt. 129 Pa. Inf.	1787	1863	Presbyterian	Hollidaysburg
Ried, James B.	Sgt. F, 31 Pa. Inf.				
	Sgt. A, 191 Pa. Inf.	1840	1908	Frankstown	Hollidaysburg
Rightenour, Jacob	Pvt. H, 103 Pa. Inf.	1848	1923	Deihl	Martinsburg
Reigal, Joseph	Sgt. E, 45 Pa. Inf.	1820		Fairview	Altoona
Riffle, William	Pvt. E, 138 Pa. Inf.	1844			
Rigby, William	Pvt. 25 U.S.C.T.	1844			
Rigg, James W.	Pvt. H, 110 Pa. Inf.		1863	Chancellorsville	Virginia
Riggle, Joseph	Pvt. E, 45 Pa. Inf.				
Riggle, Martin A.	Pvt. F, 31 Pa. Inf.	1842	1863	Asbury	Altoona
Riggleman, Jonathan	Pvt. F, 31 Pa. Inf.				
Riley, James	Pvt. C, 3 Pa. Inf.	1836	1916	Presbyterian	Williamsburg
Riley, James K.	Pvt. B, 208 Pa. Inf.				
Riley, John	Pvt. E, 184 Pa. Inf.			Everett	Pa.
Riley, John	Pvt. G, 148 Pa. Inf.		1895	Birmingham	Pa.
Riley, Joseph W.					
Riley, Lawrence	Pvt. G, 207 Pa. Inf.		1918	Ogdenburg	Pa.
Riley, Thomas	Pvt. B, 208 Pa. Inf.	1842	1931	Lutheran	Williamsburg
Riley, William A.	Pvt. C, 3 Pa. Inf.	1840	1909	Lutheran	Williamsburg
Reilly, William D.	Pvt. D, 13 Pa. Cav.	1841			
Riley, William H.	Cpl. K, 3 U. S. Cav.				
Riley, William H.	Pvt. B, 125 Pa. Inf.				
Riling, Alexander		1829	1911	Eldorado	Altoona
Riling, John K.	Pvt. L. 102 Pa. Inf.	1850			
Rinard, Jacob	Pvt. C, 84 Pa. Inf.	1843			
Rinehart, Joseph	Pvt. K, 125 Pa. Inf.				
Ring, Charles P.	Pvt. F, 31 Pa. Inf.				
Ritchey, David	Pvt. G, 55 Pa. Inf.	1845	1907	Mt. Hope	Claysburg
Ritchey, George S.	Pvt. F, 77 Pa. Inf.	1833	1910	Mt. Sinai	Blue Knob
Ritchey, Jacob	Pvt. E, 138 Pa. Inf.	1846	1925	Lutheran	Newry
Ritchey, John	Pvt. K, 55 Pa. Inf.	1838	1887	Mt. Hope	Claysburg
Ritchey, John C.	Pvt. E, 138 Pa. Inf.	1844	1925	Mt. Moriah	Blue Knob
Ritchey, Levi	Cpl. G, Ind. Bn. Pa. Mil.	1837	1906	Mt. Hope	Blue Knob
Ritchie, William	1Lt. D, 133 Pa. Inf.	1830	1886	Oak Ridge	Altoona
Ritter, Peter	Pvt. G, 57 Pa. Inf.	1845			
Ritz, John	Pvt. I, 82 Pa. Inf.	1829	1913	Presbyterian	Hollidaysburg
Ritz, William F.	Pvt. F, 7 U. S. Inf.		1902	Carson Valley	Duncansville
Roach, Robert A.	Pvt. D, 3 Pa. Inf.	1838			
Roach, Thomas	Pvt. I, 55 Pa. Inf.				
	Pvt. E, 125 Pa. Inf.	1818		St. Josephs	Williamsburg
Roache, Thomas	Pvt. I, 137 Pa. Inf.				
Robb, James Eaton	Pvt. A, 19 Pa. Cav.	1842			
Robb, Porter A.	Pvt. D, 1 Pa. Art.	1845			
Robb, William Ansen	Mus. 49 Pa. Inf.				
	Pvt. F, 46 Pa. Mil.	1837	1920	Rose Hill	Altoona
Robbins, William	Pvt. G, 99 Pa. Inf.	1838	1902	Oak Ridge	Altoona
Roberts, John H.	Pvt. A, 205 Pa. Inf.	1820	1895	Fairview	Altoona
Roberts, William	Pvt. I, 14 Pa. Inf.				
	2Lt. C, 110 Pa. Inf.				
	Pvt. I, 3 Pa. Art.				
	2Lt. I, 4 U.S.C.T.	1841	1920	Fairview	Martinsburg
Robertson, James H.	Pvt. K, 125 Pa. Inf.				

SOLDIERS OF BLAIR COUNTY

Name	Rank, Organization	Born	Died	Cemetery	Location
Robertson, John H.	Sgt. H, 14 Pa. Inf.				
	2Lt. E, 125 Pa. Inf.				
	2Lt. C, 205 Pa. Inf.	1824	1897	Lutheran	Newry
Robertson, Joseph H.	Pvt. D, 125 Pa. Inf.	1833	1901	Collinsville	Altoona
Robertson, Robert F.	Pvt. F, 2 Pa. Cav.	1828	1908		Tyrone
Robison, Abraham	Pvt. A, 23 Pa. Mil.	1823			
Robinson, Abraham	Pvt. H, 110 Pa. Inf.	1823	1875	Geeseytown	Hollidaysburg
Robeson, Adie	Sgt. D, 13 Pa. Cav.	1839			
Robeson, Adia	Cpl. C, 46 Pa. Mil.	1839			
Robeson, Albert	Pvt. G, 125 Pa. Inf.				
Robison, Charles	Pvt. K, 127 U.S.C.T.	1845		Union	Hollidaysburg
Robison, Henry C.	Pvt. K, 49 Pa. Inf.	1844	1935		Bedford
Robeson, Jacob F.	Pvt. C, 46 Pa. Mil.	1830			
Robison, James	Pvt. A, 125 Pa. Inf.				
Robison, James	Pvt. H, 14 Pa. Inf.	1841			
Robinson, James R.	Cpl. G, 125 Pa. Inf.				
Robinson, John	Pvt. E, 104 Pa. Inf.				
Robeson, Martin L.	Pvt. C, 46 Pa. Mil.	1841			
Robison, Martin L.	Cpl. A, 205 Pa. Inf.				
Robinson, Patrick H.	Pvt. M, 9 Pa. Cav.	1840			
Robison, Samuel	Pvt. A, Ind. Bn. Pa. Mil.	1842			
Robison, William	Sgt. C, 76 Pa. Inf.	1821			
Robinson, William	Pvt. H, 14 Pa. Inf.	1832			
Robinson, William	Pvt. H, 110 Pa. Inf.				
Robison, William A.	Pvt. C, 198 Pa. Inf.	1819	1899	Logan Valley	Bellwood
Robison, William B.	Sgt. 1 Md. Cav.				
Robinson, William M.	Pvt. H, 110 Pa. Inf.	1846	1875	Lutheran	Newry
Robison, Woods W.	Pvt. I, 137 Pa. Inf.				
	Cpl. G, 183 Pa. Inf.	1846	1927	Canoe Creek	Williamsburg
Rock, Williamson J.					
Rockwell, Milton	Pvt. A, 84 Pa. Inf.				
Redamen, John	Pvt. K, 125 Pa. Inf.				
Rodamer, William	2Lt. E, 104 Pa. Inf.				
Rodenizer, William	Pvt. K, 82 Pa. Inf.	1832	1906	Fairview	Altoona
Rodgers, Aaron	Sgt. A, 110 Pa. Inf.				
Rodgers, James	Pvt. A, 3 Pa. Inf.				
	2Lt. A, Ind. Bn. Pa. Mil.				
	Sgt. G, 125 Pa. Inf.				
	1Lt. D, 192 Pa. Inf.	1837	1905	Presbyterian	Hollidaysburg
Rodgers, John	Pvt. K, 78 Pa. Inf.	1833	1896	Ebensburg	Pa.
Rodgers, Samuel	Pvt. A, 110 Pa. Inf.	1844	1906	Birmingham	Pa.
Rodkey, David L.	Pvt. E, 104 Pa. Inf.	1845	1925	Presbyterian	Williamsburg
Rodkey, James	Pvt. E, 84 Pa. Inf.				
Rodkey, James M.	Pvt. D, 13 Pa. Cav.	1840	1892	Fairview	Altoona
Rodkey, William	Pvt. C, 84 Pa. Inf.	1842			
Rodcay, William H.	Pvt. D, 22 Pa. Cav.	1843			
Roe, William I.	Pvt. B, 202 Pa. Inf.			Locust Run	Mifflin
Reoch, George W.	Pvt. D, 13 Pa. Cav.				
Roeloff, John	Pvt. A, 23 Pa. Mil.	1836			
Rorabaugh, George	Pvt. E, 104 Pa. Inf.				
Rohnback, John W.	Pvt. B, 10 Pa. Inf.				
	Sgt. G, 10 Pa. Cav.	1836	1920	Presbyterian	Hollidaysburg
Rohrabaugh, John	Pvt. C, 205 Pa. Inf.	1830		Duvall	Bedford Co.
Rohm, Robert L.	Pvt. F, 19 Pa. Cav.	1847	1939	Riverview	Huntingdon
Rohrer, Jacob A.	Pvt. D, 131 Pa. Inf.	1838	1909	Alexandria	Pa.
Roleson, David	Pvt. A, 23 Pa.Mil.	1806			
Roller, James	Pvt. A, Ind. Bn. Pa. Mil.	1825			
Roller, James C.	Mus. C, 3 Pa. Inf.				
	Pvt. A, 84 Pa. Inf.	1843		Philadelphia	Pa.
Roller, William C.	Sgn. 3 Pa. Inf.				
	Sgn. 23 Pa. Inf.	1838	1897	Presbyterian	Hollidaysburg
Rollins, John	Pvt. D, 125 Pa. Inf.			Lutheran	Hollidaysburg

THE CIVIL WAR

Name	Rank Organization	Born	Died	Cemetery	Location
Rollin, John	Pvt. D, 192 Pa. Inf.				
Rollman, John Henry	Pvt. A, 93 Pa. Inf.	1843	1899	Grandview	Tyrone
Rook, Joseph H.	Pvt. E, 3 Pa. Inf.	1838			
Rook, Joseph H.	Pvt. C, 76 Pa. Inf.	1837	1865	Federal Point	N. Car.
Rooney, John	Pvt. D, 192 Pa. Inf.	1824	1896	Presbyterian	Hollidaysburg
Rooney, Thomas	Pvt. A, 23 Pa. Mil.	1823			
Root, John Matthias	Pvt. B, 6 Pa. Cav.	1827	1904	Antis	Bellwood
Roper, William G.	Pvt. E, 1 Pa. Art.	1845			
Rose, Bernard	Pvt. A, 23 Pa. Mil.	1834			
Rose, Eli E.					
Rose, George W.	Mus. C, 46 Pa. Mil.	1840			
Rose, John	Pvt. D, 125 Pa. Inf.		1862	Antietam	Maryland
Rose, John F.	Pvt. Ind. Cav. Pa. Mil.	1842			
Roseberry, James	Pvt. A, 125 Pa. Inf.	1836	1910	Presbyterian	Sinking Valley
Roseberry, John	Pvt. D, 205 Pa. Inf.				
Roseberry, John T.	Pvt. A, 125 Pa. Inf.				
Roseberry, Thomas J.	Pvt. C, 77 Pa. Inf.	1844	1920	Fairview	Altoona
Rosenberger, Matt's	Pvt. B, 208 Pa. Inf.				
Roseleab, William	Pvt. A, 84 Pa. Inf.				
Ross, Benjamin L.	Pvt. A, 1 Pa. Art.	1838			
Ross, Berney C.	Pvt. F, 148 Pa. Inf.	1838	1915	Greenwood	Altoona
Ross, Christian	Pvt. I, 205 Pa. Inf.	1823			
Ross, George W.	Pvt. A, 102 Pa. Inf.	1845	1866	Grandview	Tyrone
Ross, George W.	Cpl. I, 205 Pa. Inf.	1844			
Ross, Hiram	Pvt. E, 20 Pa. Cav.	1845	1928	Rose Hill	Altoona
Ross, J. Henry				Fairview	Altoona
Ross, James	Pvt. I, 7 Pa. Inf.				
	Pvt. D, 131 Pa. Inf.				
	Pvt. A, 101 Pa. Inf.	1840	1892	Oak Ridge	Altoona
Ross, Jacob	Pvt. I, 14 Pa. Inf.	1829			
Ross, John B.	Pvt. G, 29 Pa. Inf.	1847	1890	Lutheran	Williamsburg
Ross, John R.	Cpt. I, 84 Pa. Inf.				
	Cpt. I, 57 Pa. Inf.			Carson Valley	Duncansville
Ross, Joseph	Pvt. A, 110 Pa. Inf.				
Ross, Laird	Pvt. B, 88 Pa. Inf.	1823	1905	Grandview	Tyrone
Ross, Obadiah J.	Pvt. F, 158 Pa. Inf.	1843	1891	Oak Ridge	Altoona
Ross, Seymour	Pvt. E, 104 Pa. Inf.				
Rote, William H.	Pvt. H, 122 Pa. Inf.		1890	Lancaster	Pa.
Roth, H. C.					
Rothrock, Davis B.	Pvt. H, 14 Pa. Inf.				
	Sgt. C, 53 Pa. Inf.	1839	1916	Oak Ridge	Altoona
Rothrock, Samuel A.	Pvt. K, 131 Pa. Inf.				
	Pvt. C, 19 Pa. Cav.	1846	1913	Rose Hill	Altoona
Roudebush, Michael	Pvt. G, 78 Pa. Inf.	1846			
Rough, Valentine	Pvt. H, 110 Pa. Inf.		1864	Grandview	Tyrone
Rough, Adam	Cpl. E, 125 Pa. Inf.	1835	1876	Greenlawn	Roaring Spring
Rough, Andrew	Pvt. H, 14 Pa. Inf.	1831			
Rough, Andrew	1Lt. I, 55 Pa. Inf.	1826			
Rough, Benjamin	Cpt. I, 55 Pa. Inf.				
Rough, William H.	Cpl. I, 55 Pa. Inf.	1840			
Rounds, William	Pvt. A, 110 Pa. Inf.				
Rounds, Williams	Sgt. E, 125 Pa. Inf.				
Roush, Adolphus	Pvt. D, 46 Pa. Mil.	1834			
Roush, George	Pvt. H, 3 Pa. Inf.	1840			
Roush, George Patrick	Pvt. A, 12 U. S. Inf.			St. Patricks	Newry
Roush, J. Levi	Cpl. D, 35 Pa. Inf.	1838	1906	St. Patricks	Newry
Roush, Justus K.	Pvt. G, 208 Pa. Inf.	1836	1906	Fairview	Altoona
Roush, Simon P.	Pvt. H, 46 Pa. Mil.				
	Pvt. E, 184 Pa. Inf.				
Row, Herman	Mus. 3 Pa. Inf.	1840	1880	Fairview	Altoona
Rowan, George	Sgt. F, 78 Pa. Inf.	1841	1920	Enola	Cumberland
Rowe, Jeremiah W.	Pvt. H, 39 Ohio Inf.	1845	1906	Fairview	Altoona

SOLDIERS OF BLAIR COUNTY

Name	Rank Organization	Born	Died	Cemetery	Location
Rowland, George C.	Pvt. B, 1 U. S. Art.		1910	Windsor	Conn.
Rowles, Isaac B.	Pvt. D, 75 Pa. Inf.	1821	1914	Snyders	Coalport
Rowser, Joseph O.	Pvt. B, 99 Pa. Inf.	1839	1918	Mocks	Bedford Co.
Royer, Henry G.	Pvt. E, 7 Pa. Cav.	1847	1911	Logan Valley	Bellwood
Royer, Martin	Pvt. B, 208 Pa. Inf.	1846	1921	Snivelys	Williamsburg
Royer, Samuel M.	1Lt. C, 53 Pa. Inf.	1838	1921	Fairview	Martinsburg
Ruggles, Albert	Pvt. B, Ind. Bn. Pa. Mil.				
	Cpl. I, 55 Pa. Inf.	1838			
Ruggles, Benjamin F.	Pvt. G, 125 Pa. Inf.				
	Pvt. I, 205 Pa. Inf.	1842			
Ruggles, John	Pvt. I, 14 Pa. Inf.	1830			
Ruggles, John	Pvt. D, 115 Pa. Inf.		1863		
Ruggles, Joseph	Pvt. H, 14 Pa. Inf.				
	Pvt. C, 77 Pa. Inf.	1838	1917	Lutheran	Newry
Ruggles, William	Pvt. D, 205 Pa. Inf.				
Rumbarger, Benjamin	Pvt. E, 84 Pa. Inf.				
	2Lt. D, 46 Pa. Mil.	1843			
Rumberger, Joseph	Pvt. G, 1 Pa. Art.	1842			
Rumberger, Oliver S.	Cpt. H, 49 Pa. Inf.	1840			
Rumbaugh, William	Pvt. M, 62 Pa. Inf.				
	Pvt. K, 91 Pa. Inf.				
Rung, John S.	Pvt. Marine Corps		1894	Huntingdon	Pa.
Runk, John B.	Pvt. H, 22 Pa. Cav.	1845			
Runyen, Amos R. F.	Pvt. C, 46 Pa. Mil.	1845			
Rush, George W.					
Rush, Henry H.	Pvt. E, 3 Pa. Art.	1839	1896	Fairview	Altoona
Rush, Samuel	Pvt. M, 62 Pa. Inf.				
Rush, Stephen P.	Pvt. K, 110 Pa. Inf.				
	Pvt. H, 22 Pa. Cav.	1844	1916	National Home	Indiana
Russ, Edward L.	Sgt. D, 125 Pa. Inf.				
Russ, Joseph Calvin	Pvt. H, 3 Pa. Inf.				
	Pvt. G, 125 Pa. Inf.				
	Pvt. M, 22 Pa. Cav.	1842			
Russell, Carey H.	Pvt. I, 3 Pa. Inf.				
	2Lt. G, 29 Ohio Inf.	1841	1912	Grandview	Tyrone
Russell, Emanuel	Pvt. E, 13 Pa. Cav.	1840	1924	Rose Hill	Altoona
Russel, George	Pvt. E, 46 Pa. Mil.	1846			
Russell, George W.	2Lt. C, 46 Pa. Mil.	1842			
Russell, George W.	Cpl. K, 125 Pa. Inf.				
Russell, George	Pvt. H, 22 Pa. Cav.	1846			
Russell, Jacob K.	Pvt. C, 46 Pa. Mil.	1839			
Russell, John	Pvt. B, 21 Pa. Cav.	1838	1912	Oak Ridge	Altoona
Russell, Pierce	Sgt. G, 57 Pa. Inf.	1835			
Russell, William	Sgt. D, 165 Pa. Inf.	1840	1914	Rose Hill	Altoona
Rustine, Thomas	Pvt. D, 205 Pa. Inf.				
Rutherford, George W.	Pvt. H, 49 Pa. Inf.	1846	1864	Cold Harbor	Virginia
Rutherford, James	Pvt. F, 31 Pa. Inf.				
	Pvt. A, 191 Pa. Inf.	1840			
Rutherford, John	Pvt. I, 205 Pa. Inf.	1825	1879	Oak Ridge	Altoona
Rutherford, Nelson	Pvt. D, 192 Pa. Inf.				
Rutledge, John	Pvt. K, 105 Pa. Inf.		1878	Carson Valley	Duncansville
Rutledge, Thompson	Pvt. K, 105 Pa. Inf.		1882	Fairview	Altoona
Rutter, Elisha B.	Pvt. G, 121 Pa. Inf.	1843	1922	Calvary	Altoona
Rutter, Franklin D.	Cpl. I, 149 Pa. Inf.	1838	1890	Oak Ridge	Altoona
Rutter, John W.	Pvt. F, 19 Pa. Cav.	1849	1925	Oak Ridge	Altoona
Ryan, Michael	Pvt. A, 110 Pa. Inf.				
Ryder, Michael G.	Frn. U. S. Navy	1846	1915	St. Johns	Altoona
Rynn, John	Pvt. A, 77 Pa. Inf.	1843			
Sage, William	Pvt. G, 57 Pa. Inf.	1842			
Sager, Samuel M.	Pvt. K, 205 Pa. Inf.	1842	1903	Oak Ridge	Altoona
Sahler, Isaac	Pvt. B, 34 Pa. Inf.	1832	1921	Phoenixville	Pa.
Salkeld, James W.	Pvt. D, 13 Pa. Cav.	1844			

Name	Rank Organization	Born	Died	Cemetery	Location
Salley, Horace B.	Pvt. H, 30 Pa. Inf.		1904	Pittsburgh	Pa.
Salyards, Joseph	Pvt. D, 192 Pa. Inf.	1833	1899	Lutheran	Hollidaysburg
Salyards, Robert	Pvt. G, 16 Pa. Cav.		1878	Mauers	Altoona
Salyards, William	Pvt. A, 84 Pa. Inf.				
	Pvt. G, 57 Pa. Inf.	1843	1913	Presbyterian	Hollidaysburg
Saltgiver, George	Pvt. M, 62 Pa. Inf.				
Sample, David	Sgt. G, 16 Pa. Cav.	1840	1896	Oak Ridge	Altoona
Sanders, Albert	Pvt. A, 3 Pa. Inf.				
	Sgt. C, 76 Pa. Inf.	1842	1929	Carson Valley	Duncansville
Sanders, Henry	Pvt. B, 164 Pa. Cav.				
Sanders, John	Sgt. B, Ind. Bn. Pa. Mil.	1845			
Sanders, John	Pvt. G, 125 Pa. Inf.				
Sanders, Josiah C.	1Lt. I, 14 Pa. Inf.	1840	1911	Fairview	Martinsburg
Sanderson, William	Pvt. H, 101 Pa. Inf.	1848	1919	Oak Ridge	Altoona
Sandrus, James S.		1842	1916		
Sandrus, John H.	Pvt. D, 84 Pa. Inf.	1816	1877	Oak Ridge	Altoona
Sankey, William	Pvt. D, 205 Pa. Inf.	1819			
Sapp, Jesse	Pvt. F, Ind. Bn. Pa. Mil.	1846			
Sapp, William H.	Pvt. D, 46 Pa. Mil.	1831			
Sarvis, Columbus C.	Sgt. E, 20 Pa. Cav.	1844	1926	East Waterford	Pa.
Saterfield, George B.	Pvt. D, 205 Pa. Inf.				
Satterfield, Harman	Pvt. D, 46 Pa. Mil.	1842			
Satterfield, Herman	Pvt. C, 84 Pa. Inf.	1842		Frankstown	Hollidaysburg
Sauer, George	Pvt. B, 99 Pa. Inf.	1837	1903	Greenlawn	Roaring Spring
Saupp, Frank D.	1Lt. K, 55 Pa. Inf.				
Savets, H.	Pvt. K, 5 U. S. Art.				
Sawyer, John	Pvt. G, 57 Pa. Inf.	1838	1908	Logan Valley	Bellwood
Saxton, Mark A.	Pvt. A, 84 Pa. Inf.				
	Pvt. G, 57 Pa. Inf.	1843			
Schandlemeyer, Jacob	Pvt. E, 3 Pa. Inf.	1839			
Schell, George W.	Pvt. K, 78 Pa. Inf.	1826	1918	Stone Church	Marklesburg
Schettig, John	Pvt. D, 79 N. Y. Inf.	1837	1908	St. Marys	Altoona
Schlag, Adolph	Pvt. D, 125 Pa. Inf.				
	Sgt. D, 46 Pa. Mil.				
	Pvt. G, 12 Pa. Cav.	1833	1872	Fairview	Altoona
Schmidt, Victor	Pvt. C, 2 N. H. Inf.				
Schmittle, George S.	Pvt. C, 110 Pa. Inf.				
	Pvt. C, 13 Pa. Cav.	1846	1922	Rose Hill	Altoona
Schreck, Jacob	Pvt. E, 84 Pa. Inf.				
Schroder, Charles	Mus. C, 110 Pa. Inf.				
Schroeder, Frederick	Pvt. H, 3 Pa. Inf.				
	Pvt. F, 5 U. S. Art.	1829	1906	Lutheran	Hollidaysburg
Schroyer, Andrew G.	Pvt. K, 133 Pa. Inf.				
	Pvt. E, 186 Pa. Inf.	1840	1896	Oak Ridge	Altoona
Schubel, Christian	Pvt. E, 1 Mich. Cav.		1897	Mt. Pleasant	Pa.
Schum, Henry	Pvt. D, 46 Pa. Mil.	1830	1914	Fairview	Altoona
Schwartz, David	Pvt. I, 205 Pa. Inf.	1828			
Swartz, George W.	Pvt. C, 205 Pa. Inf.	1836			
Schwartz, Henry	Cpt. I, 93 Pa. Inf.	1837	1873	Fairview	Altoona
Swartz, Henry J.	Pvt. I, 36 Pa. Mil.	1837	1918	Oak Ridge	Altoona
Swartz, John	Pvt. D, 1 Pa. Art.	1845			
Swartz, John E.	Pvt. H, 206 Pa. Inf.	1848	1931	Salem Reform	Williamsburg
Swartz, John W.	Pvt. I, 194 Pa. Inf.				
	Pvt. Ind. 97 Pa. Inf.	1847	1935	Fairview	Altoona
Swartz, Joseph R.	Cpl. I, 21 Pa. Cav.	1850			
Swartz, Samuel B.	Sgt. C, 110 Pa. Inf.				
Swartz, William B.	Pvt. F, 107 Pa. Inf.	1818	1910	Kifers	Woodbury
Schwedner, Frederick	Pvt. B, 208 Pa. Inf.				
Scoffield, William	Pvt. D, 3 Pa. Inf.	1838			
Scotts, Andrew J.	Pvt. M, 62 Pa. Inf.				
Scott, Charles W.	Pvt. D, 57 Pa. Inf.	1848	1922	Summit	Cresson
Scott, David		1832	1869	Grandview	Tyrone

SOLDIERS OF BLAIR COUNTY

Name	Rank Organization	Born	Died	Cemetery	Location
Scott, David	Pvt. C, 84 Pa. Inf.	1837			
Scott, James H.	Pvt. G, 51 Pa. Inf.				
	Pvt. 2 U. S. Cav.	1835	1904	Oak Ridge	Altoona
Scott, James P.	Pvt. G, 125 Pa. Inf.				
Scott, John	Pvt. C, 76 Pa. Inf.				
Scotten, Elwood P.	Pvt. C, 79 Pa. Inf.	1843	1913	Lancaster	Pa.
Scroffield, William					
Scruder, Leman	Pvt. M, 9 Pa. Cav.	1825			
Scullin, John	Mus. E, 125 Pa. Inf.			St. Patricks	Newry
Seabrooks, George	Pvt. C, 110 Pa. Inf.				
Secrist, David	Pvt. K, 22 Pa. Cav.	1843			
Secrist, Jesse	Pvt. K, 22 Pa. Cav.	1845			
Seeds, Jonathan R.					
Seely, George N.					
Seibert, David	Cpl. B, 148 Pa. Inf.				
Seibert, Oliver	Pvt. G, 205 Pa. Inf.	1830	1910	Mt. Union	Pa.
Seibert, Samuel B.	Pvt. H, 49 Pa. Inf.				
Seigel, Frederick	Pvt. D, 192 Pa. Inf.				
Sellers, David M.	Pvt. G, 125 Pa. Inf.				
	Pvt. D, 192 Pa. Inf.	1832	1891	Lutheran	Hollidaysburg
Sellers, George	Pvt. M, 62 Pa. Inf.	1843			
Sellers, George	Pvt. H, 3 Pa. Inf.				
	Pvt. M, 62 Pa. Inf.	1843			
Sellers, James	Pvt. A, 205 Pa. Inf.	1827	1903	Allegheny Furnace	Altoona
Sellers, John	Pvt. B, 13 Pa. Cav.	1833	1919	Lutheran	Newry
Sellers, Joseph	Pvt. D, 184 Pa. Inf.	1846			
Sellers, Simon	Pvt. E, 104 Pa. Inf.				
Sentman, Samuel	Sgt. I, 198 Pa. Inf.	1830	1904	Oak Ridge	Altoona
Settlemyer, George	Pvt. C, 105 Pa. Inf.		1879	Collinsville	Altoona
Severe, Francis	Pvt. D, 35 Pa. Inf.		1896	Canoe Creek	Williamsburg
Seybert, Samuel W.	Pvt. M, 62 Pa. Inf.				
	Cpl. K, 91 Pa. Inf.				
Seymore, Nicholas	Pvt. A, 55 Pa. Inf.	1842	1912	Calvary	Altoona
Shade, George M.	Pvt. A, 23 Pa. Mil.				
	Sgt. D, 22 Pa. Cav.	1840		Spring Hope	Martinsburg
Shade, James A.	Mus. H, 208 Pa. Inf.	1836	1900	Potters	Morrisons Cove
Shadle, Levi R.	Pvt. B, 167 Pa. Inf.	1840	1908	Spring Hope	Martinsburg
Shaffer, Abraham	Pvt. C, 205 Pa. Inf.	1813	1883	Greenlawn	Roaring Spring
Shafer, Adam	Pvt. I, 55 Pa. Inf.	1807	1879	Lutheran	Hollidaysburg
Shaffer, Christian	Pvt. D, 5 Pa. Art.	1828	1914	Wilmore	Pa.
Shaffer, David	Cpl. H, 125 Pa. Inf.	1829	1883	Oak Ridge	Altoona
Shaffer, David S.	Pvt. E, 104 Pa. Inf.				
Shaeffer, Frank	Pvt. A, 25 Pa. Inf.	1832	1896	Fairview	Altoona
Shafer, Jacob	Pvt. E, 84 Pa. Inf.				
	Pvt. I, 57 Pa. Inf.	1824	1864	City Point	Virginia
Shafer, Jacob	Pvt. K, 125 Pa. Inf.				
Shaffer, Joel	Pvt. F, 191 Pa. Inf.		1879	Freeburg	Snyder Co.
Shafer, John	Pvt. E, 84 Pa. Inf.		1864	Andersonville	Georgia
Shaffer, John	Pvt. G, 12 Pa. Cav.	1820	1889	Fairview	Altoona
Shaffer, John	Pvt. G, 12 Pa. Cav.	1837	1869	Rodman	Roaring Spring
Shaffer, John	Pvt. M, 62 Pa. Inf.				
	Pvt. K, 91 Pa. Inf.	1825			
Shaffer, John	Pvt. H, 49 Pa. Inf.	1845			
Shaffer, Jonathan	Pvt. F, 31 Pa. Inf.				
	Pvt. A, 191 Pa. Inf.				
Shaffer, Joseph	Pvt. D, 125 Pa. Inf.				
Shafer, Levi E.	Pvt. I, 22 Pa. Cav.	1846			
Shafer, Peter	Pvt. U, 76 Pa. Inf.	1840			
Shaffer, Samuel B.	Pvt. C, 3 Pa. Inf.				
	Pvt. B, 125 Pa. Inf.				
	Pvt. B, 208 Pa. Inf.	1842		Parsons	Kansas
Shaffer, Samuel D.	Pvt. D, 18 U. S. Inf.	1842			

THE CIVIL WAR 257

Name	Rank Organizations	Born	Died	Cemetery	Location
Shaffer, Thomas	Sgt. E, 184 Pa. Inf.	1840	1904	Calvary	Altoona
Shaffer, William	Pvt. C, 205 Pa. Inf.	1836	1933	Sharpsburg	Roaring Spring
Shafer, William H.	Pvt. I, 153 Pa. Inf.	1845	1932	Hazelton	Pa.
Shaner, George L.	Pvt. F, 129 Ohio Inf.	1846			
Shaner, John I.	Pvt. L, 6 U. S. Cav.				
	Pvt. E, 34 Pa. Inf.	1840	1901	Logan Valley	Bellwood
Shank, George	Pvt. I, 137 Pa. Inf.			Brumbaughs	Martinsburg
Shank, Joshua	Pvt. H, 14 Pa. Inf.				
	Pvt. I, 55 Pa. Inf.	1830	1900	Carson Valley	Duncansville
Shank, Nicholas	Pvt. F, 31 Pa. Inf.				
Shank Upton E.	Pvt. A, 20 Pa. Cav.	1845			
Shank, William H.	Pvt. E, 184 Pa. Inf.		1864		
Shannon, Charles C.	Cpl. Ind. Cav. Pa. Mil.	1832	1896	Fairview	Altoona
Shannon, James G.	Sgt. A, 84 Pa. Inf.				
	Sgt. D, 192 Pa. Inf.	1830	1898	Greenwood	Altoona
Shannon, John	Pvt. F, 76 Pa. Inf.	1827			
Shannon, William					
Shantz, William H.	Pvt. F, 149 Ill. Inf.	1836	1904	Fairview	Altoona
Sharp, Fleming S.	Pvt. I, 205 Pa. Inf.	1823	1905	Grandview	Tyrone
Sharp, Joseph	Pvt. D, 1 Pa. Art.	1820			
Sharp, Lewis	Pvt. U, 1 Pa. Art.	1838			
Sharp, Richard P.	Sgt. A, 55 Pa. Inf.	1843	1930	St. Johns	Altoona
Sharp, William	Pvt. E, 84 Pa. Inf.				
Sharp, William S.	Pvt. G, Pa. Mil.	1847	1929	Grandview	Tyrone
Sharar, B. M.					
Sharer, Christian	Pvt. B, 208 Pa. Inf.				
Sharrer, Daniel	Pvt. M, 62 Pa. Inf.				
Sharrar, George W.	Pvt. A, 125 Pa. Inf.				
Sharar, Henry Bascom	Pvt. G, 125 Pa. Inf.				
	Sgt. D, 192 Pa. Inf.	1833	1901	Grandview	Tyrone
Sharrer, Jeremiah	Pvt. E, 46 Pa. Mil.	1845			
Shirer, Philip	Pvt. D, 125 Pa. Inf.				
Sharrer, Robert Lytle	Pvt. G, 190 Pa. Inf.	1847	1927	Riverview	Huntingdon
Sharrer, William P.	Pvt. F, 31 Pa. Inf.				
	Pvt. A, 191 Pa. Inf.	1840			
Sharrow, Thomas	Pvt. B, Ind. Bn. Pa. Mil.	1839			
Sharra, Abraham W.	Sgt. F, 28 Pa. Inf.	1826	1874	St. Patricks	Gallitzin
Shaver, H. C.	Pvt. C, 20 Pa. Cav.				
Shaver, John L.	Pvt. U. S. Signal Corps	1843	1922	Rose Hill	Altoona
Shaver, Joseph P.	Pvt. D, 47 Pa. Inf.				
Shaver, Philip	Pvt. D, 125 Pa. Inf.				
Shaver, William	Pvt. I, 149 Pa. Inf.	1839	1909	Mt. Union	Pa.
Shaw, A. Norman	Pvt. I, 205 Pa. Inf.	1836			
Shaw, Alex	Pvt. A, 55 Pa. Inf.	1835	1870	Pine Grove	Puzzletown
Shaw, Daniel	Pvt. A, 125 Pa. Inf.	1842	1862	Logan Valley	Bellwood
Shaw, Edmund	Sgt. K, 110 Pa. Inf.	1836	1919		
Shaw, John	Pvt. F, 76 Pa. Inf.		1865	Wilmington	N. Car.
Shay, Mathias	Pvt. F. 100 Pa. Inf.	1839	1915	Madera	Pa.
Shea, William	Pvt. A, 110 Pa. Inf.				
Shearer, Abraham	Pvt. M, 9 Pa. Cav.	1826			
Sheatern, William	Pvt. F, 77 Pa. Inf.	1837	1882	Asbury	Altoona
Sheeder, Jacob	Pvt. D, 205 Pa. Inf.	1813			
Shollenberger, G.	Pvt. B, 208 Pa. Inf.				
Schollenberger, Garian	2Lt. B, 125 Pa. Inf.				
Shellenberger, Garian	Cpl. C, 3 Pa. Inf.	1838			
Shellenberger, Henry	Pvt. A, 101 Pa. Inf.	1838	1911	Fairview	Altoona
Shellenberger, Henry E.	Pvt. I, 137 Pa. Inf.				
	Pvt. Ind. Cav. Pa. Mil.				
	Pvt. L, 13 Pa. Cav.	1825	1896	Presbyterian	Hollidaysburg
Shellenberger, James	Pvt. C, 46 Pa. Mil.	1832			
Shullenberger, Samuel W.	Pvt. D, 46 Pa. Mil.	1848			
Shelow, John	Cpl. A, 110 Pa. Inf.	1844	1920	Grandview	Tyrone

SOLDIERS OF BLAIR COUNTY

Name	Rank Organizations	Born	Died	Cemetery	Location
Shelow, William Henry	Pvt. B, 3 Pa. Inf.				
	1Lt. A, 110 Pa. Inf.	1843	1916	Grandview	Tyrone
Sheppard, Thomas	Pvt. D, 46 Pa. Mil.	1813			
Sherlock, Stephen	Pvt. A, 77 Pa. Inf.	1824			
Sherman, Robinson T.	Pvt. F, 31 Pa. Inf.		1864		
Shields, William	Pvt. I, 32 Pa. Inf.		1904	Carson Valley	Duncansville
Shiffler, Emanuel	Pvt. I, 14 Pa. Inf.	1843	1861	Sharpsburg	Roaring Spring
Shiffler, Martin J.	Pvt. C, 205 Pa. Inf.	1844	1921	Oak Ridge	Altoona
Shiffler, Nathan B.	Pvt. C, 205 Pa. Inf.	1846			
Shillinger, Frederick	2Lt. E, 3 Pa. Inf.				
	Sgt. Ind. Cav. Pa. Mil.	1824			
Shimer, Alex K.	Cpl. H, 149 Pa. Inf.		1903	Lutheran	Hollidaysburg
Shimer, John W.	Pvt. A, 51 Pa. Inf.	1849	1918	Greenlawn	Roaring Spring
Shimer, Isaac P.	Pvt. G, 194 Pa. Inf.	1846	1924	Fairview	Altoona
Shimer, William H. H.	Sgt. C, 110 Pa. Inf.	1844	1892	Greenlawn	Roaring Spring
Shimmell, John J.	Pvt. A, 110 Pa. Inf.				
Shinefelt, David	Pvt. D, 205 Pa. Inf.	1842			
Shinefelt, Jacob	Col. M, 16 Pa. Cav.		1887	Ardenheim	Pa.
Shinefelt, John Casper	Pvt. B, 125 Pa. Inf.				
	Pvt. U, 84 Pa. Inf.				
	Pvt. I, 57 Pa. Inf.	1830	1898	Lutheran	Williamsburg
Shinefelt, Joseph H.	Pvt. D, 22 Pa. Cav.	1839			
Shirk, Theodore T.	Cpl. D, 205 Pa. Inf.	1846	1933	Eastlawn	Tyrone
Shirley, William J.	Pvt. G, 11 Pa. Cav.	1841	1916	Calvary	Altoona
Shiro, Philip	Pvt. Ind. Cav. Pa. Mil.				
	Cpl. L, 19 Pa. Cav.	1843			
Shive, William C.	Pvt. D, 3 Pa. Inf.	1834			
Shives, Isaac W.	Pvt. B, 208 Pa. Inf.		1865	Petersburg	Virginia
Shock, Daniel	Cpl. G, 194 Pa. Inf.				
	Cpt. F, 77 Pa. Inf.	1824	1911	Reform	Claysburg
Shock, David Wallace	Pvt. C, 87 Pa. Inf.	1833	1912	Fairview	Altoona
Shock, John	Pvt. C, 205 Pa. Inf.	1807	1902	Birmingham	Pa.
Shoemaker, Adam					
Shoemaker, Andrew	Pvt. D, 192 Pa. Inf.	1821	1906	St. Marys	Hollidaysburg
Shoemaker, Austin	Pvt. C, 110 Pa. Inf.	1841	1921	Kifers	Woodbury
Shoemaker, Benjamin F.	Sgt. C, 110 Pa. Inf.	1843	1929	Holsingers	Baker Summit
Shoemaker, George F.	Pvt. D, 101 Pa. Inf.	1840	1937		Bedford Co.
Shoemaker, William H.	Pvt. C, 110 Pa. Inf.				
Shoeman, David	Pvt. I, 14 Pa. Inf.	1839	1913	Fairview	Martinsburg
Shoeman, Peter					
Shoenfelt, Andrew					
Shoenfelt, James	Pvt. B, 76 Pa. Inf.	1842	1865	Rhodes	Roaring Spring
Shoenthal, Moses	Pvt. A, 23 Pa. Mil.	1834			
Shoff, David	Pvt. E, 125 Pa. Inf.				
Shoff, David L.	Pvt. I, Pa. Art.		1864		
Shollar, James Stewart	Pvt. C, 3 Pa. Inf.				
	Sgt. B, 125 Pa. Inf.				
	Cpt. R, 208 Pa. Inf.	1842	1912	Presbyterian	Williamsburg
Shollar, Martin Van B.	Sgt. E, 104 Pa. Inf.	1835	1909	Lutheran	Williamsburg
Shollar, Thaddeus					
Shomo, Allison M.	Mus. B, Ind. Bn. Pa. Mil.	1849			
Shomo, Joseph Henry	Pvt. F, 20 Pa. Inf.	1836	1881		
Shomo, William	Pvt. B, Ind. Bn. Pa. Mil.	1813			
Shoop, William H.	Cpl. F, 1 Pa. Art.	1837	1895	Reform	Loysburg
Shope, David	Cpl. K, 78 Pa. Inf.				
Shope, William E.	Pvt. D, 49 Pa. Inf.	1840	1913	Fairview	Altoona
Shotts, Henry M.	Cpl. B, 3 Pa. Inf.				
	Cpl. K, 125 Pa. Inf.				
	Sgt. F, Ind. Bn. Pa. Mil.	1841			
Shoup, Nathaniel	Pvt. C, 84 Pa. Inf.	1841			
Shreder, John W.	Pvt. C, 84 Pa. Inf.	1843			
Shuck, John N.	Pvt. D, Ind. Bn. Pa. Mil.	1841	1884	Oak Ridge	Altoona

Name	Rank Organization	Born	Died	Cemetery	Location
Shuff, Thomas	Pvt. E, 53 Pa. Inf.	1828	1916	Rose Hill	Altoona
Shultz, Andrew J.	Cpl. D, 126 Pa. Inf.				
Shultz, Levi	Pvt. F, 22 Pa. Cav.	1843			
Shuman, Jeremiah	Pvt. I, 137 Pa. Inf.				
Shutt, Samuel	Pvt. I, 104 Pa. Inf.	1844	1912	Lutheran	Sinking Valley
Sias, David A.	Cpl. C, 53 Pa. Inf.	1833	1897	Snivelys	Williamsburg
Sies, Isaac	Pvt. B, Ind. Bn. Pa. Mil.	1845			
Sias, Joseph	Pvt. C, 3 Pa. Inf.				
	Cpl. B, 125 Pa. Inf.				
	Sgt. E, 104 Pa. Inf.	1833			
Silks, Samuel	Pvt. C, 77 Pa. Inf.	1824	1916	Greenwood	Altoona
Silvey, George W.	Sgt. 37 Pa. Inf.	1847	1923	Presbyterian	Hollidaysburg
Simmers, George	Pvt. A, 55 Pa. Inf.	1864			
Simmers, George	Pvt. E, 125 Pa. Inf.				
Simmers, William	Pvt. E, 125 Pa. Inf.				
Simms, Andrew J.	Pvt. B, 125 Pa. Inf.	1827	1905	Presbyterian	Hollidaysburg
Sims, John T.	Pvt. I, 136 Pa. Inf.				
	Pvt. A, 46 Pa. Mil.				
	Pvt. E, 45 Pa. Inf.	1843	1917	Grandview	Tyrone
Simons, Samuel R.	Pvt. C, 24 Pa. Inf.		1901	Mt. Union	Pa.
Simonton, Thomas	Pvt. B, 3 Pa. Inf.				
	Pvt. C, 205 Pa. Inf.	1839	1865	Petersburg	Virginia
Simpkins, Charles	Pvt. D, 205 Pa. Inf.	1823			
Simpkins, John A.	Pvt. C, 205 Pa. Inf.	1819			
Simpson, James M.	Pvt. A, 3 Pa. Inf.	1843			
Simpson, John W.	Pvt. D, 49 Pa. Inf.	1825	1894	Warriors Mark	Pa.
Simpson, Lloyd	Sgt. F, 5 U. S. Art.				
Simpson, Marion	Cpl. 14 U. S. Inf.		1864	Wilderness	Virginia
Simpson, Thomas M.	Pvt. B, 192 Pa. Inf.	1847	1924	Grandview	Altoona
Singiser, George W.	Pvt. 84 Pa. Inf.				
	Pvt. A, 20 Pa. Cav.	1847	1886	Oak Ridge	Altoona
Singiser, Harry C.	Pvt. G, 84 Pa. Inf.				
	1Lt. A, 20 Pa. Cav.	1842	1916	Mechanicsburg	Pa.
Singiser, Millard F.	Pvt. I, 195 Pa. Inf.	1850	1936	Oak Ridge	Altoona
Singler, Joseph	Pvt. B, 56 Pa. Inf.	1840	1890	Oak Grove	Tyrone
Singleton, George W.	Sgt. F, 2 Pa. Cav.	1848	1914	Presbyterian	Williamsburg
Sipe, Levi	Pvt. F, 76 Pa. Inf.	1841	1864	York	Pa.
Sisler, William	Pvt. E, 3 Pa. Inf.	1834			
Skelly, E. J.	Sgt. K, 101 Pa. Inf.	1847			
Skipper, Augustus R.	Pvt. F, 76 Pa. Inf.	1847			
Skutchall, George W.	Pvt. B, 208 Pa. Inf.	1828			
Slack, John R.	Pvt. K, 22 Pa. Cav.	1845			
Slack, Joseph M.	Pvt. K, 22 Pa. Cav.	1845			
Slater, John	Pvt. B, 208 Pa. Inf.				
Slayman, George W.	Pvt. I, 137 Pa. Inf.	1841	1933	Oak Ridge	Altoona
Sleighter, Levi	Pvt. B, 208 Pa. Inf.				
Sloan, John	Sgt. H, 22 Pa. Cav.	1845	1909	Grandview	Tyrone
Sloan, John	Pvt. A, 125 Pa. Inf.				
Slaugenhoup, Jacob G.	Sgt. G, 11 Pa. Cav.	1830	1907	Charlottesville	Bellwood
Slogenhop, William	Pvt. A, 205 Pa. Inf.	1824	1907	Oak Ridge	Altoona
Slonaker, Joseph	Far. D, 22 Pa. Cav.	1838	1913	Methodist	Williamsburg
Slonaker, Lemuel A.	Pvt. C, 3 Pa. Inf.				
	Pvt. B, 125 Pa. Inf.				
	Pvt. B, 208 Pa. Inf.	1843			
Slossice, Isaac	Pvt. B, Ind. Bn. Pa. Mil.	1841			
Slusser, Isaac	Pvt. B, 13 Pa. Cav.	1841	1899	Gospel	Gallitzin
Smaltz, Charles A.	Pvt. C, 91 Pa. Inf.	1832	1915	Greenlawn	Roaring Spring
Smathers, Alexander	Sgt. F, 32 U.S.C.T.				
Smay, Samuel	Pvt. C, 19 U. S. Inf.	1834	1910	Carson Valley	Duncansville
Smeltzer, Ferdinand	Pvt. G, 12 Pa. Cav.	1848	1932	St. Johns	Altoona
Smeltzer, Franklin S.	Pvt. H, 16 Pa. Inf.		1917	Holsingers	Baker Summit
Smeltzer, Jacob	Pvt. G, 12 Pa. Cav.	1845			

SOLDIERS OF BLAIR COUNTY

Name	Rank Organization	Born	Died	Cemetery	Location
Smeltzer, John B.	Pvt. C, 205 Pa. Inf.	1846		Vicksburg	Roaring Spring
Smiley, Charles J.	Pvt. M, 19 Pa. Cav.	1846	1894	Rose Hill	Altoona
Smiley, John J.	Pvt. K, 22 Pa. Cav.	1846			
Smith, A.	Pvt. A, 13 Md. Inf.				
Smith, Abraham L.	Pvt. F, 31 Pa. Inf.		1864	Spottsylvania	Virginia
Smith, Adam	Sgt. A, 2 Pa. Inf.		1902	Chambersburg	Pa.
Smith, Adolphus H.	Pvt. E, 104 Pa. Inf.	1840	1901	Asbury	Altoona
Smith, Alexander C.	Pvt. L, 19 Pa. Cav.	1837	1907	Lutheran	Claysburg
Smith, Allen D.	Pvt. F, 77 Pa. Inf.				
	Pvt. I, 110 Pa. Inf.	1832	1865	Asbury	Altoona
Smith, Andrew J.	Pvt. D, 22 Pa. Cav.				
	Pvt. B, 208 Pa. Inf.			Smiths	Williamsburg
Smith, Benjamin F.	Pvt. C, 3 Pa. Inf.	1842			
Smith, Benjamin F.	Pvt. D, 22 Pa. Cav.	1831			
Smith, Daniel L.	Cpl. G, 133 Pa. Inf.	1831	1880	Fairview	Altoona
Smith, Daniel W.	Pvt. G, 21 Pa. Cav.	1832	1903	Fairview	Altoona
Smith, David	Pvt. E, 125 Pa. Inf.				
Smith, David	Pvt. H, 14 Pa. Inf.	1838			
Smith, David	Cpl. C, 76 Pa. Inf.	1833	1896	Rodman	Roaring Spring
Smith, David C.	Mus. H, 3 Pa. Art.	1845			
Smith, David C.	Pvt. I, 91 Pa. Inf.	1826	1879	Bald Eagle	Tyrone
Smith, David L.	Cpl. G, 133 Pa. Inf.				
	Pvt. U. S. Signal Corps	1832	1888	Fairview	Altoona
Smith, David S.	Pvt. C, 110 Pa. Inf.				
Smith, Eli	Pvt. C, 205 Pa. Inf.	1843			
Smith, George	Pvt. F, 76 Pa. Inf.	1829			
Smith, George	Pvt. I, 205 Pa. Inf.	1830			
Smith, George	Pvt. D, 192 Pa. Inf.		1866	St. Marys	Hollidaysburg
Smith, George	Pvt. I, 190 Pa. Inf.				
	Pvt. E, 47 Pa. Inf.	1841	1916	Glasgow	Pa.
Smith, George E.	Pvt. C, 205 Pa. Inf.	1829		Reformed	Hopewell
Smith, George C.	Pvt. I, 137 Pa. Inf.				
Smith, George W.	Cpl. C, 110 Pa. Inf.		1864	Petersburg	Virginia
Smith, George W.	Sgn. 54 Pa. Mil.	1835	1907	Presbyterian	Hollidaysburg
Smith, George W.	Pvt. F, 205 Pa. Inf.	1844	1907	Asbury	Altoona
Smith, Hazzard P.	Pvt. E, 104 Pa. Inf.				
Smith, Henry B.	Pvt. D, 192 Pa. Inf.	1824	1904	Lutheran	Hollidaysburg
Smith, Henry	Sgt. C, 76 Pa. Inf.	1840			
Smith, Henry C.	Pvt. F, 77 Pa. Inf.	1827			
Smith, Henry J.	Cpl. C, 53 Pa. Inf.	1837			
Smith, Hugh S.	Sgt. E, 84 Pa. Inf.	1819	1898	St. Marys	Hollidaysburg
Smith, Isaac	Pvt. M, 62 Pa. Inf.				
Smith, Isaac S.	Pvt. G, 1 Pa. Art.	1845			
Smith, Jacob F.	Pvt. E, 127 Pa. Inf.	1842	1917	Fairview	Altoona
Smith, Jacob J.	Sgt. E, 3 Pa. Inf.				
	1Lt. H, 12 Pa. Cav.	1839	1884	Fairview	Altoona
Smith, Jacob M.	Pvt. K, 206 Pa. Inf.	1840	1925	Greenlawn	Roaring Spring
Smith, Jacob N.	Pvt. C, 133 Pa. Inf.	1840			
Smith, Jacob W.	Pvt. C, 53 Pa. Inf.				
	Sgt. H, 39 Pa. Inf.	1838	1911	Lutheran	Newry
Smith, James	Pvt. M, 21 Pa. Cav.	1822	1885	Antis	Bellwood
Smith, James	Pvt. K, 13 Pa. Cav.	1843	1924	Dodsons	Claysburg
Smith, James B.	Pvt. L, 22 Pa. Inf.	1829			
Smith, James M.	Pvt. A, 40 Pa. Inf.				
Smith, James M.	Pvt. D, 22 Pa. Cav.	1845			
Smith, Jesse	Pvt. Ind. Cav. Pa. Mil.	1826	1879	Fairview	Altoona
Smith, John	Pvt. A, 3 Pa. Inf.	1833		St. Johns	Altoona
Smith, John	Cpl. F, 31 Pa. Inf.				
	Sgt. A, 191 Pa. Inf.				
Smith, John	Pvt. H, 14 Pa. Inf.				
	Pvt. C, 76 Pa. Inf.	1834			
Smith, John	Pvt. B, Ind. Bn. Pa. Mil.	1844			

THE CIVIL WAR

Name	Rank Organization	Born	Died	Cemetery	Location
Smith, John	Pvt. C, 76 Pa. Inf.	1832			
Smith, John A.	Pvt. G, 1 Bn. Pa. Mil.				
	Pvt. E, 104 Pa. Inf.	1842	1931	National	Dayton, Ohio
Smith, John B.	Pvt. A, 84 Pa. Inf.			Pleasantville	Bedford Co.
Smith, John C.	Pvt. 3 Pa. Art.				
	Cpl. D, 188 Pa. Inf.	1839	1924	Asbury	Altoona
Smith, John E.				Logan Valley	Bellwood
Smith, John M.	Pvt. C, 76 Pa. Inf.				
	Pvt. E, 104 Pa. Inf.	1833	1882	Asbury	Altoona
Smith, John R.	Pvt. G, 12 Pa. Cav.	1821	1875	St. Johns	Altoona
Smith, John W.	Pvt. C, 47 Pa. Inf.	1845	1911	Grandview	Altoona
Smith, John W.	Pvt. B, 93 Pa. Inf.	1828	1898	Oak Ridge	Altoona
Smith, John W.	Cpl. C, 110 Pa. Inf.			Reformed	Hopewell
Smith, Josiah N.	Sgt. A, 184 Pa. Inf.	1842	1918	St. Johns	Williamsburg
Smith, Josiah Westley	Pvt. B, 82 Pa. Inf.	1842	1929	Charlottesville	Bellwood
Smith, Martin V.	2Lt. E, 5 Pa. Cav.				
Smith, Marion G.	Pvt. F, 76 Pa. Inf.	1842	1891	Logan Valley	Bellwood
Smith, Matthias		1815	1861	Asbury	Altoona
Smith, Michael					
Smith, Oliver G.	Pvt. D, 3 Pa. Inf.				
	Sgt. A, 125 Pa. Inf.	1837	1934	Methodist	Birmingham
Smith, Patrick	Pvt. C, 3 Pa. Inf.	1828			
Smith, Patrick	Smn. U. S. Navy	1831	1882	St. Patricks	Gallitzin
Smith, Peter M.	Cpl. I, 82 Pa. Inf.	1831	1886	Oak Ridge	Altoona
Smith, Philip	Sgt. E, 84 Pa. Inf.		1864	St. Marys	Hollidaysburg
Smith, Philip J.	Sgt. C, 208 Pa. Inf.	1837	1889	St. Marys	Altoona
Smith, Robert	Pvt. K, 125 Pa. Inf.				
Smith, Robert G.	Pvt. D, 78 Pa. Inf.	1840	1918	Rose Hill	Altoona
Smith, Rufus E.	Cpl. C, 205 Pa. Inf.	1844		Reformed	Hopewell
Smith, Sample	Pvt. H, 110 Pa. Inf.				
Smith, Samuel	Pvt. I, 55 Pa. Inf.				
Smith, Samuel H.	Pvt. C, 110 Pa. Inf.				
Smith, Sanford	Pvt. F, 76 Pa. Inf.	1841			
Smith, Stephen D.	Pvt. F, 19 Pa. Cav.	1850	1903	Bald Eagle	Tyrone
Smith, Theodore	Pvt. E, 84 Pa. Inf.				
Smith, Thomas	Pvt. A, 125 Pa. Inf.	1834	1904	Fairview	Altoona
Smith, Victor					
Smith, William	Pvt. H, 14 Pa. Inf.	1842			
Smith, William C.	Pvt. E, 3 Pa. Inf.	1831			
Smith, William Calvin	Pvt. A, 23 Pa. Mil.	1846	1918	Presbyterian	Hollidaysburg
Smith, William H.	Pvt. D, 205 Pa. Inf.	1836			
Smith, William M.	Cpl. H, 9 Pa. Cav.	1838	1907	Fairview	Altoona
Smith, William P.	Cpl. A, Ind. Bn. Pa. Mil.	1841			
Smith, William R.	Sgt. C, 76 Pa. Inf.	1844	1873	Carson Valley	Duncansville
Smith, William R.	Pvt. F, 134 Ill. Inf.				
	Pvt. F, 32 Pa. Inf.	1844	1932	Kifers	Woodbury
Smith, William Wallace	Pvt. C, 3 Pa. Inf.				
	Cpl. C, 46 Pa. Mil.	1832	1920		Harrisburg
Smith, Wilson S.	Pvt. C, 158 Pa. Inf.				
	Pvt. D, 187 Pa. Inf.	1844			
Smyers, Jacob	Pvt. A, 99 Pa. Inf.		1895	Cherry Grove	Hunt'gdon Co.
Smythe, David W.	Sgt. H, 110 Pa. Inf.				
Snadden, John A.	Pvt. A, 84 Pa. Inf.				
	Sgt. G, 57 Pa. Inf.	1838			
Snare, Abraham	Pvt. I, 205 Pa. Inf.	1836			
Snare, Calvin L.	Pvt. C, 194 Pa. Inf.	1847	1898	Presbyterian	Williamsburg
Snare, Henry H.	Pvt. E, 84 Pa. Inf.				
	Sgt. G, 57 Pa. Inf.	1841			
Sneath, John	Pvt. M, 62 Pa. Inf.	1818			
Sneath, John J.	Pvt. D, 190 Pa. Inf.		1877	Shirleysburg	Pa.
Sneath, Robert	Pvt. F, 31 Pa. Inf.				
	Pvt. A, 191 Pa. Inf.				

SOLDIERS OF BLAIR COUNTY

Name	Rank Organization	Born	Died	Cemetery	Location
Sneath, Robert	Pvt. D, 3 Pa. Inf.	1843			
Snitzer, Christian					
Snively, Daniel	Pvt. B, 208 Pa. Inf.	1846	1924	Snivelys	Williamsburg
Snively, Samuel L.	Pvt. B, 208 Pa. Inf.				
Snowberger, Andrew M.	Pvt. C, 205 Pa. Inf.	1847	1869	Rhodes	Roaring Spring
Snowberger, Daniel D.	Pvt. G, 107 Pa. Inf.	1830	1901	Diehls	Martinsburg
Snowberger, Jacob	Pvt. G, 194 Pa. Inf.	1835	1908	Lutheran	Claysburg
Snowberger, John A.		1839	1898	Carson Valley	Duncansville
Snowberger, Joseph B.	Pvt. I, 171 Pa. Inf.	1834	1899	New Enterprise	Bedford Co.
Snowberger, Joseph C.	Pvt. H, 208 Pa. Inf.			S. Woodbury Twp.	Bedford Co.
Snowden, Alexander S.	Pvt. C, 205 Pa. Inf.	1827	1902	Vicksburg	Roaring Spring
Snowden, James	Sgt. M, 62 Pa. Inf.				
	Cpl. K, 127 U.S.C.T.	1829			
Snowden, James R.	Pvt. D, 10 U.S. Inf.	1842	1882	Fairview	Altoona
Snowden, John	Pvt. 54 Mass. C. T.				
Snowden, Joseph	Pvt. B, 53 Pa. Inf.	1830	1915	Kifers	Woodbury
Snyder, Abraham	Pvt. E,,93 Pa. Inf.		1900	Bald Eagle	Tyrone
Snyder, Albert J.	Pvt. K, 111 Pa. Inf.	1849	1913	Calvary	Altoona
Snider, Augustus	Pvt. K, 208 Pa. Inf.	1842	1926	Carson Valley	Duncansville
Snyder, Christian N.	1Lt. H, 3 Pa. Inf.	1838	1911	St. Marys	Hollidaysburg
Snyder, Daniel	Pvt. H, 49 Pa. Inf.	1838	1864	Richmond	Virginia
Snyder, David	Pvt. 1 Pa. Cav.	1840	1898	Lutheran	Hollidaysburg
Snyder, David	Pvt. E, 46 Pa. Mil.	1837	1920	Grandview	Tyrone
Snyder, Frederick	Pvt. H, 201 Pa. Inf.			Bald Eagle	Tyrone
Snyder, George	Pvt. C, 205 Pa. Inf.	1812			
Snyder, George	Pvt. E, 125 Pa. Inf.	1813	1894	Greenlawn	Roaring Spring
Snyder, George	Pvt. E, 125 Pa. Inf.				
	Pvt. I, 55 Pa. Inf.			Greenlawn	Roaring Spring
Snyder, Harrison H.	Cpl. M, 62 Pa. Inf.	1837	1891	Presbyterian	Hollidaysburg
Snyder, Henry	Pvt. I, 57 Pa. Inf.	1844			
Snyder, Henry	Cpl. D, 12 Pa. Inf.	1835	1922	McConnellstown	Pa.
Snyder, Horatio L.	1Lt. F, 2 Pa. Cav.	1845	1920	Clearfield	Pa.
Snyder, Howard E.	Pvt. G, Pa. Mil.	1845	1866	Presbyterian	Hollidaysburg
Snyder, Isaac	Pvt. B, 208 Pa. Inf.	1828	1893	St. Johns	Williamsburg
Snyder, James	Mus. C, 76 Pa. Inf.	1838	1917	Greenlawn	Roaring Spring
Snyder, James D.	Pvt. E, 3 Pa. Inf.	1842	1910	Fairview	Altoona
Snyder, James G.	Pvt. G, 1 Pa. Art.	1840			
Snyder, John	Pvt. D, 205 Pa. Inf.	1844			
Snyder, John	Pvt. H, 110 Pa. Inf.				
Snyder, Theopilus A.	1Lt. K, 91 Pa. Inf.				
	Cpt. H, 213 Pa. Inf.	1816	1889	Fairview	Martinsburg
Snyder, William B.	Cpl. F, 31 Pa. Inf.				
	Cpl. A, 191 Pa. Inf.	1842			
Snyder, William G.	Pvt. H, 110 Pa. Inf.		1864	Wilderness	Virginia
Snyder, William H.	Pvt. G, 125 Pa. Inf.			Duvall	Bedford Co.
Snyder, William L.	Mus. D, 22 Pa. Cav.	1847	1932	Greenlawn	Roaring Spring
Socie, John W.	Pvt. C, 82 Pa. Inf.	1846	1915	St. Marys	Hollidaysburg
Soddens, Emanuel	Pvt. E, 46 Pa. Inf.		1887	Birmingham	Pa.
Soller, Leonard	Pvt. E, 104 Pa. Inf.	1828	1900	St. Marys	Altoona
Souders, Christopher S.	Cpl. F, 31 Pa. Inf.				
	Cpl. A, 191 Pa. Inf.	1840	1865	Salisbury	No. Carolina
Souders, Henry	Pvt. B, 165Pa. Inf.	1826	1896	Logan Valley	Bellwood
Southwood, Thomas	Pvt. M, 20 Pa. Cav.	1846	1912	Carson Valley	Duncansville
Spade, George	Pvt. H, 3 Pa. Inf.				
	Pvt. A, 84 Pa. Inf.	1841			
Spade, George	Cpl. B, Ind. Bn. Pa. Mil.	1842			
Spade, Henry	Sgt. D, 192 Pa. Inf.	1836			
Spade, Henry	Pvt. M, 62 Pa. Inf.	1836			
Spade, William	Pvt. M, 62 Pa. Inf.				
	Pvt. K, 91 Pa. Inf.	1844	1919	Summit	Cambria Co.
Spalding, John F.	Pvt. B, 56 Pa. Inf.	1847	1917	St. Johns	Altoona
Spang, David R. P.	Pvt. L, 19 Pa. Cav.	1841		Stoler	Bedford Co.

Name	Rank Organization	Born	Died	Cemetery	Location
Spang, William E.	Cpl. I, 137 Pa. Inf.				
Spangler, Levi	Pvt. D, 192 Pa. Inf.				
Spanogle, Peter B.	Mus. A, 205 Pa. Inf.				
Spanogle, William L.	1Lt. B, 20 Pa. Cav.	1841	1917	Fairview	Martinsburg
Sparks, William	Pvt. D, 101 Pa. Inf.	1845			
Sparr, Samuel	Pvt. B, 125 Pa. Inf.	1839	1916	Presbyterian	Williamsburg
Spaulding, John F.	Pvt. B, 56 Pa. Inf.	1847			
Speece, Harry	Pvt. F, 77 Pa. Inf.	1841		Fockler	Bedford Co.
Speer, William H.	Pvt. C, 110 Pa. Inf.	1847	1922	Rose Hill	Altoona
Spencer, James	Pvt. I, 14 Pa. Inf.	1829			
Spidel, Jacob	Pvt. C, 84 Pa. Inf.	1843			
Spidel, Joseph	Pvt. E, 84 Pa. Inf.				
Spiece, Louis D.	Sgt. K, 133 Pa. Inf.				
	Cpt. C, 205 Pa. Inf.	1840			
Spielman, William P.	Pvt. K, 125 Pa. Inf.	1843	1933	Fairview	Altoona
Spitler, John L.	Cpl. C, 22 Pa. Cav.	1844			
Spitler, Perry	Pvt. A, 110 Pa. Inf.				
	Pvt. H, 22 Pa. Cav.	1839	1927	Bald Eagle	Tyrone
Spitler, William	Cpl. A, 110 Pa. Inf.	1842			
Spitzer, Edwin					
Sponsler, Augustus	Pvt. D, 13 Pa. Cav.	1844			
Sponsler, John W.	Pvt. I, 22 Pa. Cav.	1847	1916	Everett	Pa.
Sponseller, Oliver	Pvt. C, 202 Pa. Inf.	1846	1920	Grandview	Altoona
Sprankle, David D.	Pvt. F, 77 Pa. Inf.	1844	1894	Grandview	Tyrone
Sprankle, John G.	Pvt. F, 77 Pa. Inf.	1836	1865	Grandview	Tyrone
Sprankle, Moses	Pvt. F, 77 Pa. Inf.	1838	1913	Grandview	Tyrone
Springer, Chambers E.	Pvt. G, 12 Pa. Cav.	1829	1881	Fairview	Altoona
Springer, John M.	Pvt. A, 3 Pa. Inf.	1833			
Springer, William	Cpl. D, 125 Pa. Inf.		1878	Fairview	Altoona
Stackhouse, Charles F.		1817	1872	Fairview	Altoona
Stackhouse, Daniel M.	Pvt. L, 12 Pa. Cav.	1844	1904	Fairview	Altoona
Stackhouse, William H.	Pvt. D, 125 Pa. Inf.				
	Sgt. D, 46 Pa. Mil.				
	Pvt. I, 7 Pa. Cav.	1844	1905	Oak Ridge	Altoona
Stains, Aaron	Pvt. F, 21 Pa. Inf.				
Stains, George H.	Pvt. C, 53 Pa. Inf.	1842			
Stains, Henry T.	Cpl. B, 110 Pa. Inf.	1826	1897	Fairview	Altoona
Stains, Samuel F.	Pvt. C, 53 Pa. Inf.	1838	1863	Philadelphia	Pa.
Stains, William	Pvt. E, 104 Pa. Inf.	1846	1890	Asbury	Altoona
Stall, Rueben	Pvt. A, 149 Pa. Inf.				
Stalman, David	Pvt. C, 84 Pa. Inf.	1841			
Stanley, Joseph B.	Pvt. E, 125 Pa. Inf.			Grandview	Tyrone
Starry, John A.		1835			
States, Henry Lloyd	Pvt. D, 1 Pa. Art.	1847	1921	Huntingdon	Pa.
States, Oliver P.	Pvt. G, 22 Pa. Cav.	1845			
States, William T.	Pvt. D, 1 Pa. Art.	1841			
Stauffer, Samuel S.	Pvt. C, 1 Pa. Art.	1842	1922	Presbyterian	Hollidaysburg
Staum, Jacob	Pvt. H, 110 Pa. Inf.		1864	Wilderness	Virginia
Steckley, John	Pvt. I, 10 Pa. Inf.	1845	1912	Harrisburg	Pa.
Steele, James B.	Pvt. M, 62 Pa. Inf.				
	Pvt. K, 91 Pa. Inf.		1864	Andersonville	Georgia
Steel, John A.	Pvt. D, 13 Pa. Cav.	1830			
Steele, Louden	Pvt. F, 31 Pa. Inf.				
	Pvt. A, 191 Pa. Inf.	1864		Salisbury	N. Car.
Steel, Samuel	Pvt. D, 125 Pa. Inf.	1836			
Steel, Samuel	Pvt. D, 205 Pa. Inf.	1847			
Steiner, Samuel C.	Sgt. F, 49 Pa. Inf.	1835	1903	Antis	Bellwood
Steinman, Matthew C.	Pvt. H, 15 Pa. Inf.				
	Pvt. M, 62 Pa. Inf.	1838	1913	Grandview	Tyrone
Stengal, Jacob	Pvt. K, 55 Pa. Inf.	1833	1910	Mt. Sinai	Blue Knob
Stevens, Adie Allen	Pvt. G, Pa. Mil.				
	Pvt. G, 15 Pa. Cav.	1845	1917	Grandview	Tyrone

SOLDIERS OF BLAIR COUNTY

Name	Rank Organization	Born	Died	Cemetery	Location
Stevens, Alexander	Pvt. H, 13 Pa. Cav.		1897	Lutheran	Williamsburg
Stevens, David M.	Pvt. A, 125 Pa. Inf.				
Stevens, Giles	Pvt. F, 77 Pa. Inf.	1821			
Stevens, Jacob	Pvt. G, 2 Pa. Art.	1821	1883	Grandview	Tyrone
Stephens, John H.	Sgt. C, 205 Pa. Inf.	1843	1915	Greenlawn	Roaring Spring
Stephens, John J.	Pvt. D, 23 Pa. Inf.				
Stephens, John N.	Pvt. B, 23 Pa. Mil.	1845	1929	St. Johns	Altoona
Stevens, Josiah	Pvt. F, 77 Pa. Inf.	1840			
Stephens, Lewis Henry	Pvt. G, 12 Pa. Cav.	1858	1924	Calvary	Altoona
Stephens, Nicholas R.	Sgt. H, 3 Pa. Inf.	1817	1890	Oak Ridge	Altoona
Stephens, Samuel	Pvt. E, 46 Pa. Mil.	1846			
Stevens, Samuel Finley	Pvt. F, 76 Pa. Inf.		1863	Ft. Wagner	S. Car.
Stevens, Thomas	Pvt. 188 Pa. Inf.	1825	1897	Logan Valley	Bellwood
Stevens, Thomas	Pvt. M, 9 Pa. Cav.	1845	1921	Greenlawn	Roaring Spring
Stevens, Valentine	Pvt. F, Ind. Bn. Pa. Mil.	1838			
Stevens, William	Pvt. F, 77 Pa. Inf.	1831	1913	Charlottesville	Bellwood
Stevens, William	Pvt. B, 3 Pa. Inf.	1840			
Stephens, William	Pvt. A, 110 Pa. Inf.				
Stephens, William	Pvt. C, 22 Pa. Cav.	1839			
Stephens, William	Sgt. A, 110 Pa. Inf.				
Stephens, William H.	Pvt. D, 13 Pa. Cav.	1840	1912	Rose Hill	Altoona
Stephens, William H.	Cpt. A, 110 Pa. Inf.				
Stevens, William S.	Pvt. F, 2 Pa. Cav.	1823	1900	Logan Valley	Bellwood
Stevenson, Cyrus	Pvt. B, Ind. Bn. Pa. Mil.				
	Pvt. I, 55 Pa. Inf.	1844			
Stephenson, John	Pvt. E, 46 Pa. Mil.	1846			
Stevenson, Thomas	Cpn. 35 Pa. Inf.				
Stephey, Levi	Pvt. H, 208 Pa. Inf.	1836	1915	Kifers	Woodbury
Stever, George W.	Pvt. D, 192 Pa. Inf.				
Stewart, Alexander H.	Sgt. E, 3 Pa. Inf.	1848	1862	St. Johns	Altoona
Stewart, Andrew	Pvt. D, 125 Pa. Inf.				
Stewart, Benjamin F.	Pvt. A, Ind. Bn. Pa. Mil.				
	Pvt. G, 12 Pa. Cav.	1842			
Stewart, David A.	Pvt. E, 84 Pa. Inf.				
	Cpl. I, 57 Pa. Inf.	1840			
Stewart, David P.	Sgt. D, 110 Pa. Inf.	1838	1910	Rose Hill	Altoona
Stewart, Franklin B.	Mus. D, 3 Pa. Inf.				
	Col. 110 Pa. Inf.		1837	1904 Fairview	Altoona
Stewart, James E.	Pvt. A, Ind. Bn. Pa. Mil.	1830			
Stewart, James G.	Mus. F, 76 Pa. Inf.	1840			
Stewart, James M.	Sgt. D, 13 Pa. Cav.	1835			
Stewart, James P.	Cpl. G, 12 Pa. Cav.	1845	1912	Fairview	Altoona
Stewart, Jesse S.	1Lt. A, 125 Pa. Inf.		1863	Chancellorsville	Virginia
Stewart, John D.	Cpn. 125 Pa. Inf.	1824	1902	Grandview	Tyrone
Stewart, John P.	Pvt. D, 3 Pa. Inf.	1840			
Stewart, John P.	Pvt. K, 22 Pa. Cav.		1908	Grazierville	Tyrone
Stewart, John P.	Pvt. A, 110 Pa. Inf.				
Stewart, Joseph C.	Pvt. A, Ind. Bn. Pa. Mil.	1844			
Steward, Oliver	Pvt. D, 205 Pa. Inf.				
Stewart, Robert	Cpl. A, Ind. Bn. Pa. Mil.	1832			
Stewart, Samuel A.	Pvt. F, 77 Pa. Inf.	1839			
Stewart, Samuel B.	Pvt. F, 31 Pa. Inf.		1863	Gettysburg	Pa.
Stewart, Thomas	Pvt. D, 192 Pa. Inf.				
Stewart, William A.	Pvt. A, 110 Pa. Inf.				
	Pvt. G, Ind. Bn. Pa. Mil.	1835	1883	Grandview	Tyrone
Stewart, William C.	Pvt. E, 84 Pa. Inf.				
	Pvt. I, 57 Pa. Inf.	1843	1864	Salisbury	N. Car.
Stiffler, Harrison T.	Pvt. M, 9 Pa. Cav.	1840	1932	Brethren	Canoe Creek
Stiffler, Henry M.	Pvt. A, 55 Pa. Inf.	1838	1925	Carson Valley	Duncansville
Stiffler, James	Far. C, 13 Pa. Cav.	1816	1904	Lutheran	Newry
Stiffler, John B.	Pvt. B, Ind. Bn. Pa. Mil.				
	Pvt. D, 13 Pa. Cav.	1845			

THE CIVIL WAR

Name	Rank Organization	Born	Died	Cemetery	Location
Stiffler, John H.	Pvt. E, 138 Pa. Inf.			Stiffler	Bedford Co.
Stiffler, Nathaniel	Pvt. E, 138 Pa. Inf.	1841	1923	New Enterprise	Bedford Co.
Stiffler, Peter	Pvt. H, 110 Pa. Inf.	1840	1907	Logan Valley	Bellwood
Stiffler, Sylvanus L.	Pvt. E, 125 Pa. Inf.				
	Pvt. D, 13 Pa. Cav.	1844	1882	Carson Valley	Bellwood
Stiffler, T. M.	Pvt. F, 4 Iowa Inf.	1841	1863	Keokuk	Iowa
Stiffler, Thomas	Pvt. A, 99 Pa. Inf.			Stifflers	Bedford Co.
Stiffler, William J.	Sgt. G, 12 Pa. Cav.	1840	1864	Andersonville	Georgia
Stiffler, William	Pvt. H, 14 Pa. Inf.	1841			
Stiffler, William	Pvt. H, 103 Pa. Inf.	1936	1921	Rose Hill	Altoona
Stiffler, William H.	Pvt. D, 13 Pa. Cav.	1842	1865	Magnolia	N. Car.
Stiffler, William W.	Pvt. A, Ind. Bn. Pa. Mil.	1842			
Stiles, Samuel	Pvt. H, 110 Pa. Inf.				
Stiles, William H.	Pvt. H, 110 Pa. Inf.	1844	1914	Grandview	Tyrone
Stine, Benjamin	Mus. D, 151 Pa. Inf.	1829	1909	Greenwood	Altoona
Stine, David	Pvt. G, 11 Pa. Cav.		1865	Andersonville	Georgia
Stine, Henry	Pvt. D, 2 Pa. Cav.		1881	Asbury	Altoona
Stine, Jacob	Cpl. F, 77 Pa. Inf.	1825	1881	Union	Claysburg
Stine, Irvin	Pvt. D, 2 Pa. Cav.	1844	1926	Oak Ridge	Altoona
Stinemen, Albert A.	Pvt. C, 3 Pa. Inf.				
	Cpt. E, 84 Pa. Inf.	1841			
Stiner, Banjamin F.	Pvt. F, 76 Pa. Inf.	1839	1862	Pocatoligo	S. Car.
Stiner, Samuel	Sgt. I, 55 Pa. Inf.	1829			
Stinger, Samuel H.					
Stiteler, David	Sgt. A, 3 Pa. Inf.				
	1Lt. A, Ind. Bn. Pa. Mil.	1830			
Stitzel, Daniel	Cpl. B, 208 Pa. Inf.				
Stiver, William	Pvt. F, 2 Pa. Cav.		1915	Centre Co.	Pa.
Stocksleger, Peter W.	Pvt. E, 3 Pa. Inf.	1841			
Stoddart, James	Pvt. A, 110 Pa. Inf.		1861	Hagerstown	Maryland
Stoddard, John	Pvt. A, 110 Pa. Inf.		1863	National	Gettysburg
Stoddard, Thomas	Pvt. E, 3 Pa. Inf.	1841			
Stoddart, Thomas	Pvt. A, 110 Pa. Inf.				
Stokes, Joseph	Pvt. K, 76 Pa. Inf.	1845	1917	Oak Ridge	Altoona
Stoke, William	2Lt. D, 14 Pa. Cav.	1828	1904	Oak Ridge	Altoona
Stoltz, Henry O.	Pvt. E, 104 Pa. Inf.	1843	1904	St. Johns	Altoona
Stoltz, Romanus	Cpl. F, 93 Pa. Inf.	1845	1895	Hampton	Virginia
Stom, Jacob H.	Pvt. B, Ind. Bn. Pa. Mil.	1841			
Stambaugh, John	Pvt. K, 55 Pa. Inf.			Mt. Moriah	Blue Knob
Stombaugh, Joseph	Pvt. G, Ind. Bn. Pa. Mil.	1832	1921	Mt. Moriah	Blue Knob
Stone, Andrew T.	Pvt. F, Ind. Bn. Pa. Mil.	1848	1927	Presbyterian	Hollidaysburg
Stone, John H.	Pvt. A, 110 Pa. Inf.				
Stone, Washington, J. (m)	Sgt. C, 5 Ohio Inf.	1826	1862	Lutheran	Hollidaysburg
Stonebraker, Abednego	Pvt. A, 110 Pa. Inf.			Bald Eagle	Tyrone
Stonebraker, David P.	Pvt. K, 110 Pa. Inf.	1841	1904	Baughmans	Tyrone
Stonebraker, Jeremiah	Sgt. H, 148 Pa. Inf.				
	Pvt. G, 53 Pa. Inf.			Bald Eagle	Tyrone
Stonebraker, Sanford	Pvt. D, 3 Pa. Inf.				
	Sgt. F, 19 Pa. Cav.	1840	1921	Bald Eagle	Tyrone
Stonebraker, Valentine	Sgt. K, 56 Pa. Inf.	1842	1882	Grandview	Tyrone
Stonebraker, Winfield F.	Pvt. E, 46 Pa. Mil.	1845			
Stoner, Charles E.	Pvt. D, 125 Pa. Inf.		1862		
Stoner, Daniel F.	Pvt. B, 91 Pa. Inf.	1819	1906	Albrights	Roaring Spring
Stoner, Jacob	Pvt. H, 84 Pa. Inf.				
	Pvt. H, 57 Pa. Inf.	1819			
Stonerook, Aaron B.	Pvt. C, 110 Pa. Inf.				
Stonerook, Jacob B.	Pvt. I, 50 Pa. Inf.	1845	1917	Spring Hope	Martinsburg
Stonerook, Simon B.	Sgt. C, 110 Pa. Inf.				
Stontz, J. B.		1839	1914	Chambersburg	Pa.
Storm, Albert	Pvt. B, Ind. Bn. Pa. Mil.				
	Cpl. E, 13 Pa. Cav.	1844	1865	Raleigh	No. Carolina
Storm, John A.	Pvt. A, 55 Pa. Inf.				

SOLDIERS OF BLAIR COUNTY

Name	Rank Organization	Born	Died	Cemetery	Location
Stotler, Andrew	Pvt. E, 104 Pa. Inf.	1812	1903	St. Pauls	Williamsburg
Stotler, James	Pvt. Ind. Cav. Pa. Mil.	1844			
Stotta, Frederick K.	Pvt. M, 62 Pa. Inf.				
	Pvt. K, 91 Pa. Inf.				
Stouch, Mahlon	Pvt. C, 46 Pa. Mil.	1841	1875	Fairview	Altoona
Stouffler, Jonathon	Pvt. A, 23 Pa. Mil.	1818			
Stouffer, Joseph F.	Pvt. K, 84 Pa. Inf.				
	Pvt. K, 57 Pa. Inf.	1839	1921	Fairview	Altoona
Stouffer, Samuel	Pvt. A, Ind. Bn. Pa. Mil.				
	Pvt. C, 1 Pa. Art.	1842			
Stoughton, Elisha	Pvt. M, 62 Pa. Inf.				
	Pvt. K, 91 Pa. Inf.				
Stouler, Isaac	Pvt. F, 77 Pa. Inf.	1823	1897	Lutheran	Hollidaysburg
Stout, Richard F.	Pvt. C, 110 Pa. Inf.				
Stover, George W.	Pvt. U. S. Marine Corps	1842	1865	Yellow Spring	Williamsburg
Stover, Henry	Pvt. A, 205 Pa. Inf.	1825	1897	Asbury	Altoona
Stover, Theo. Uriah	Pvt. E, 46 Pa. Mil.				
	Pvt. H, 110 Pa. Inf.			Asbury	Altoona
Straddle, John					
Strait, Ely B.	Pvt. B, 8 Pa. Cav.	1842			
Strait, Jacob	Pvt. D, 1 Pa. Art.	1843			
Straley, James	Pvt. C, 110 Pa. Inf.				
	Pvt. B, 22 Pa. Cav.	1839	1875	Eschlemans	Woodbury
Strang, John A.	Mus. A, 23 Pa. Mil.	1833			
Stralford, John F.	Pvt. L, 19 Pa. Cav.				
	Pvt. A, 195 Pa. Inf.	1846	1914	Oak Ridge	Altoona
Stratiff, Ada F.	Cpl. F, 2 Pa. Cav.	1842			
Stratif, Henry H.	Pvt. D, 3 Pa. Inf.	1840	1923	Grandview	Tyrone
Straitiff, Jacob	Pvt. B, 125 Pa. Inf.		1862	Cypress Hill	Long Island
Straitliff, John	Pvt. F, 31 Pa. Inf.				
	Pvt. A, 191 Pa. Inf.				
Straitiff, Johnson	Pvt. B, 125 Pa. Inf.		1863	Mil. Asylum	Wash., D. C.
Streightif, Samuel	Pvt. I, 107 Pa. Inf.	1835	1912	Robinsonville	Bedford Co.
Strayer, George	Cpl. I, 14 Pa. Inf.				
	Blk. H, 22 Pa. Cav.	1821	1892	Oak Ridge	Altoona
Strayer, Henry	Pvt. C, 76 Pa. Inf.	1834			
Strayer, Jacob M. R.	Pvt. E, 148 Pa. Inf.				
	Pvt. E, 53 Pa. Inf.	1837	1917	Albrights	Roaring Spring
Strayer, John	Pvt. E, 125 Pa. Inf.				
Strayer, John D.	Pvt. C, 205 Pa. Inf.	1844	1886	Albrights	Roaring Spring
Strayer, Nicholas	Pvt. C, 205 Pa. Inf.	1834	1865	Arlington	Virginia
Streets, George	Pvt. 54 Mass. C. T.				
Strich, Frederick					
Strickler, Peter	Pvt. M, 22 Pa. Cav.	1831			
Strit, George E.	Pvt. Ind. Cav. Pa. Mil.	1828			
Stroh, John H.	Pvt. C, 79 Pa. Inf.	1837	1911	Calvary	Altoona
Stroh, Philip L.	Mus. D, 93 Pa. Inf.				
	Mus. E, 127 Pa. Inf.	1843	1920	Rose Hill	Altoona
Stroh, Theodore	Pvt. F, 200 Pa. Inf.	1845	1904	Fairview	Altoona
Strong, William	Pvt. K, 125 Pa. Inf.				
	2Lt. Ind. Bn. Pa. Mil.	1840	1932	Fairview	Altoona
Strosser, George M.					
Strought, Henry H.	Pvt. F, 201 Pa. Inf.	1840	1908	Oak Ridge	Altoona
Stroup, Peter	Cpl. E, 125 Pa. Inf.	1838	1909	Lutheran	Newry
Stroup, Samuel S.	Cpl. E, 125 Pa. Inf.	1841	1883	Lutheran	Newry
Struble, George A.	Pvt. I, 198 Pa. Inf.	1836	1889	Broad Top	Bedford Co.
Stuart, Asbury H.	Pvt. B, 125 Pa. Inf.				
Stuard, James Robinson	Pvt. C, 1 Pa. Cav.	1834	1896	Fairview	Martinsburg
Stuart, Madison W.	Pvt. B, 125 Pa. Inf.				
Stuckey, H. Wilson	Pvt. D, 138 Pa. Inf.		1891	New Enterprise	Pa.
Stuff, Valentine	Pvt. G, 125 Pa. Inf.				
Stufft, Michael	Pvt. G, 91 Pa. Inf.			Mt. Zion	Bedford Co.

THE CIVIL WAR

Name	Rank Organization	Born	Died	Cemetery	Location
Stull, Lewis Edward	Pvt. G, 79 Pa. Inf.	1840	1923	Fairview	Altoona
Stull, William	Pvt. C, 17 Pa. Cav.	1841	1916	Holsingers	Baker Summit
Stuller, Ephraim	Pvt. H, 22 Pa. Cav.	1846			
Stumpff, Edward	Pvt. D, 205 Pa. Inf.				
Sturtsman, Henry B.	Pvt. A, 125 Pa. Inf.				
	Pvt. B, 13 Pa. Cav.	1827	1897	Fairview	Altoona
Suckling, John	Pvt. U, 6 Pa. Cav.	1826	1903	Presbyterian	Hollidaysburg
Suder, Charles H.	Mus. E, 125 Pa. Inf.				
	Sgt. D, 13 Pa. Cav.	1839	1890	Walters	Duncansville
Sueger, Hugh	Pvt. K, 125 Pa. Inf.				
Sullivan, James		1842	1863	Oak Grove	Tyrone
Sullivan, John	Smn. U. S. Navy			Logan Valley	Bellwood
Sullivan, Patrick	Pvt. F, 67 Pa. Inf.	1833	1893	St. Johns	Altoona
Sullivan, Patrick O.	Pvt. E, 69 Pa. Inf.	1836	1906	St. Johns	Altoona
Summerland, John	Pvt. I, 55 Pa. Inf.	1837			
Summerland, P. J.	Pvt. I, 55 Pa. Inf.	1837			
Summers, John	Pvt. I, 55 Pa. Inf.				
Sutch, William M.	Pvt. G, 133 Pa. Inf.	1838			
Suter, James P.	Pvt. D, 13 Pa. Cav.	1840	1923	Royer Mountain	Williamsburg
Settlemyer, William	Pvt. F, 49 Pa. Inf.	1838	1893	Fairview	Altoona
Sutton, James C.	Pvt. E, 149 Pa. Inf.	1828	1910	Logan Valley	Bellwood
Sutton, Jonathan A.	Pvt. C, 110 Pa. Inf.	1833	1912	Rose Hill	Altoona
Swaney, David R. P.	Cpl. E, 110 Pa. Inf.	1838	1922	Hickory Bottom	Woodbury
Swaney, Samuel J.	Pvt. C, 110 Pa. Inf.	1844	1923	Oak Ridge	Altoona
Swaney, William S.	Pvt. C, 110 Pa. Inf.				
Swanger, Christopher	Pvt. A, 205 Pa. Inf.	1834	1885	Fairview	Altoona
Swanger, David	Pvt. A, 205 Pa. Inf.	1838	1906	Rose Hill	Altoona
Swanger, Frederick	Pvt. A, 205 Pa. Inf.	1836	1881	Fairview	Altoona
Swanger, Hugh	Pvt. G, 12 Pa. Cav.	1844	1895	Fairview	Altoona
Swatts, Jacob	Pvt. A, 110 Pa. Inf.				
Swicht, Fred	Pvt. G, 199 Pa. Inf.	1826	1897		
Swift, William C.	Pvt. F, 12 U. S. Inf.				
	Pvt. B, 7 U. S. Inf.		1912	Soldiers Home	Wash., D. C.
Swires, Adie	Pvt. B, Ind. Bn. Pa. Mil.	1845			
Swires, John	Sgt. G, 125 Pa. Inf.				
	Cpt. B. Ind. Bn. Pa. Mil.				
	2Lt. D, 192 Pa. Inf.	1836		Lutheran	Hollidaysburg
Sweirs, Joseph C.	Sgt. M, 62 Pa. Inf.	1835			
Swisher, Daniel	Pvt. E, 125 Pa. Inf.			Hopewell	Pa.
Swisher, Henry	Pvt. C, 191 Pa. Inf.	1840	1900	Fairview	Altoona
Swope, Amon W.	Pvt. G, 1 Pa. Art.	1844			
Swope, Henry H.	Pvt. H, 1 Pa. Art.	1840	1920	Mapleton	Hunt'gdon Co.
Swope, James C.	Pvt. D, 1 Pa. Art.	1845			
Sylong, Lewis	Cpl. F, 77 Pa. Inf.	1828	1865	Victoria	Texas
Szink, Henry C.	Pvt. D, 125 Pa. Inf.				
	Pvt. G, Pa. Mil.	1844	1912	Fairview	Altoona
Szink, Jacob S.	Cpt. E, 3 Pa. Inf.				
	Cpt. D, 125 Pa. Inf.				
	Col. 125 Pa. Inf.				
	Maj. Ind. Bn. Pa. Mil.	1824	1872	Fairview	Altoona
Talbott, William A.	1Lt. A, 11 Ind. Inf.	1835	1905	St. Johns	Altoona
Tasker, Eli	Pvt. E, 84 Pa. Inf.				
Tasker, George	Pvt. C, 110 Pa. Inf.				
Tate, Jacob	Pvt. G, 46 Pa. Mil.				
	Pvt. I, 205 Pa. Inf.	1843		Hopewell	Bedford Co.
Tates, Joseph	Pvt. I, 205 Pa. Inf.	1841			
Tate, Wesley V.	Pvt. A, 45 Pa. Inf.	1845	1912	Fairview	Altoona
Tate, William W.	Pvt. C, 76 Pa. Inf.	1835	1861		
Taylor, Alexander H.	Pvt. C, 3 Pa. Inf.				
	1Lt. E, 84 Pa. Inf.	1841		Cannon City	Colorado
Taylor, Alfred H.	Cpn. 137 Pa. Inf.	1811	1866		Hollidaysburg
Taylor, Ambrose K.	Sgt. C, 110 Pa. Inf.		1864	Deep Bottom	Virginia

SOLDIERS OF BLAIR COUNTY

Name	Rank Organization	Born	Died	Cemetery	Location
Taylor, Benjamin K.	Sgt. I, 83 Pa. Inf.	1835	1922	Greenwood	Altoona
Taylor, Charles	Pvt. H, 110 Pa. Inf.				
Taylor, David	Pvt. I, 12 Pa. Cav.			Collinsville	Altoona
Taylor, David	Pvt. F, 32 U.S.C.T.	1844	1926	Oak Ridge	Altoona
Taylor, Elijah L.	Pvt. Ind. Cav. Pa. Mil.	1838			
Taylor, George W.	Blk. I, 21 Pa. Cav.	1839			
Taylor, George W.	Pvt. C, 3 Pa. Inf.	1828	1912		Gallitzin
Taylor, Harrison	Sgt. L, 5 Mass. Cav.	1836	1899	Logan Valley	Bellwood
Taylor, Henry	Pvt. K, 22 Pa. Cav.	1842			
Taylor, Henry C.	Pvt. G, 125 Pa. Inf.				
	Pvt. L, 3 Pa. Art.	1843	1918	Charlottesville	Bellwood
Taylor, Isaiah S.	Cpl. D, 46 Pa. Mil.	1829			
Taylor, James	Pvt. L, 3 Pa. Art.	1827	1918	Charlottesville	Bellwood
Taylor, James C.	Pvt. K, 89 U.S.C.T.				
	Pvt. G, 93 U.S.C.T.				
	Pvt. G, 81 U.S.C.T.	1842	1891	Logan Valley	Bellwood
Taylor, James R.	Pvt. F, 46 Pa. Mil.				
	Sgt. 205 Pa. Inf.	1830	1892	Oak Ridge	Altoona
Taylor, Joseph	Pvt. E, 46 Pa. Inf.	1831			
Taylor, Robert D.	Pvt. C, 84 Pa. Inf.	1840	1914	Fairview	Martinsburg
Taylor, Robert M.	Pvt. K, 46 Pa. Mil.	1845			
Taylor, Samuel	Pvt. G, 125 Pa. Inf.	1832	1896	Charlottesville	Bellwood
Taylor, Thomas T.	Sgt. B, 148 Pa. Inf.	1838	1914	Oak Ridge	Altoona
Taylor, William H.	Pvt. H, 32 U.S.C.T.	1840	1879	Allegheny Fur.	Altoona
Taylor, William M.	Pvt. E, 84 Pa. Inf.		1863	Chancellorsville	Virginia
Tearney, James	Pvt. F, 1 Pa. Inf.				
	Col. 87 Pa. Inf.	1836	1900	Lutheran	Hollidaysburg
Teats, John H.	Pvt. B, 125 Pa. Inf.		1862	Antietam	Maryland
Teeter, John	Pvt. I, 14 Pa. Inf.	1829			
Teeter, John	Pvt. C, 84 Pa. Inf.	1832		Metzkers	Williamsburg
Teeters, John W.	Pvt. B, 147 Pa. Inf.	1830	1887	Lutheran	Hollidaysburg
Teeters, Samuel D.	Pvt. D, 99 Pa. Inf.	1842	1927	Dry Hill	Woodbury
Teeter, Samuel	Pvt. C, 84 Pa. Inf.	1837		Metzkers	Martinsburg
Telfer, John C.	Pvt. B, 202 Pa. Inf.		1921	Pleasant View	Mifflintown
Temple, Franklin	Pvt. F, 77 Pa. Inf.	1847	1865	Victoria	Texas
Temple, James	Pvt. C, 3 Pa. Inf.				
	Pvt. E, 84 Pa. Inf.	1813			
Temple, William M.	Pvt. K, 49 Pa. Inf.	1840	1910	Oak Ridge	Altoona
Templeton, John Kyle	Pvt. A, 125 Pa. Inf.	1844	1897	Grandview	Tyrone
Templeton, John R.	Pvt. A, 125 Pa. Inf.				
	Pvt. C, 205 Pa. Inf.	1845	1908	Carson Valley	Duncansville
Templeton, Roland	Pvt. B, 3 Pa. Inf.				
	Pvt. C, 84 Pa. Inf.	1837			
Templeton, Samuel B.	Pvt. M, 19 Pa. Cav.	1846	1903	Grandview	Tyrone
Terman, Royal	Pvt. M, 9 Pa. Cav.	1831	1874	Fairview	Altoona
Tetwiler, Anthony R.	Pvt. E, 84 Pa. Inf.	1844	1927	Fairview	Martinsburg
Tetwiler, Jacob D.	Pvt. C, 110 Pa. Inf.	1838	1913	Waterside	Bedford Co.
Tetwiler, Peter	Pvt. C, 53 Pa. Inf.	1847		Pote	Morrisons Cove
Tetwiler, William	Pvt. B, 208 Pa. Inf.	1845	1919	St. Johns	Williamsburg
Tetwiler, William	Pvt. C, 110 Pa. Inf.	1831	1897	Kifers	Woodbury
Teufel, William	Pvt. E, 33 Pa. Inf.	1839			
Thomas, Elias	Pvt. D, 45 U.S.C.T.	1844	1933	Grandview	Tyrone
Thomas, George	Pvt. H, 110 Pa. Inf.	1864			
Thomas, George S.	Pvt. B, 21 Pa. Cav.	1827	1887	Fairview	Altoona
Thomas, George W.	Pvt. D, 5 Pa. Art.	1844	1926	Carson Valley	Duncansville
Thomas, George W.	Pvt. A, 125 Pa. Inf.	1841	1902	Fairview	Altoona
Thomas, George Warner	Pvt. K, 208 Pa. Inf.	1840	1912	Greenlawn	Roaring Spring
Thomas, Henry A.	Pvt. H, 45 Pa. Inf.	1835	1910	Greenlawn	Roaring Spring
Thomas, Hezekiah B.	Pvt. G, 16 Pa. Cav.	1834	1916	Logan Valley	Bellwood
Thomas, Isaac	Pvt. H, 110 Pa. Inf.				
Thomas, James D.	Pvt. K, 46 Pa. Mil.	1840			
Thomas, James W.	Pvt. E, 6 U.S.C.T.	1838	1875	Eastern Light	Altoona

THE CIVIL WAR

Name	Rank Organization	Born	Died	Cemetery	Location
Thomas, Jeremiah L.	Pvt. A, 125 Pa. Inf.	1837	1895	Grandview	Tyrone
Thomas, John					
Thomas, Joseph D.	2Lt. K, 9 Pa. Cav.	1841			
Thomas, Meshac	Sgt. E, 104 Pa. Inf.				
Thomas, Orange L.	Pvt. H, 49 Pa. Inf.	1849	1866	Asbury	Altoona
Thomas, Wilkin A.	Pvt. C, 84 Pa. Inf.	1841			
Thomas, William J.	Pvt. M, 22 Pa. Cav.	1846			
Thompson, Austine	Pvt. F, 31 Pa. Inf.				
	Pvt. A, 191 Pa. Inf.				
Thompson, David	Pvt. C, 110 Pa. Inf.		1864	Petersburg	Virginia
Thompson, David	Pvt. G, 12 Pa. Cav.	1839			
Thompson, David	Pvt. B, 3 Pa. Inf.	1838			
Thompson, David	Pvt. A, 8 U.S.C.T.	1833	1902	Riverview	Huntingdon
Thompson, George W.	Pvt. C, 49 Pa. Inf.	1833	1903	Charlottesville	Bellwood
Thompson, James E.	Pvt. D, 3 Pa. Inf.	1833			
Thompson, James E.	Pvt. H, 3 Pa. Inf.				
	Cpl. A, 84 Pa. Inf.				
	Cpl. B, 192 Pa. Inf.				
Thompson, James H.	Pvt. U, 57 Pa. Inf.	1837			
Thompson, James H.	Pvt. A, 128 Pa. Inf.				
	Cpl. H, 88 Pa. Inf.	1839	1920	Calvary	Altoona
Thomson, McLeod W.	Pvt. H, 21 N. J. Inf.	1843			
Thompson, Robert G.	Pvt. H, 10 Pa. Inf.				
	Pvt. G, 11 Pa. Cav.	1822	1899	Wellington	Kansas
Thompson, Roswell D.	Pvt. G, 125 Pa. Inf.				
	Cpl. B, Ind. Bn. Pa. Mil.				
	Pvt. F, 22 Pa. Cav.	1820	1890	Lutheran	Hollidaysburg
Thompson, Samuel S.	Pvt. I, 205 Pa. Inf.	1844	1908	Asbury	Altoona
Thompson, Sanford	Cpl. G, 8 U.S.C.T.		1908	Brethern	Canoe Creek
Thompson, Thomas W.	Pvt. A, 84 Pa. Inf.		1899	Lutheran	Hollidaysburg
Thompson, William	Pvt. B, 3 Pa. Inf.	1840			
Thompson, William	Pvt. M, 9 Pa. Cav.	1842			
Thompson, William	Pvt. G, 12 Pa. Cav.	1838			
Thompson, William F.	Pvt. A, 3 Pa. Inf.	1841	1911	Lutheran	Hollidaysburg
Ticoll, James			1863	Chancellorsville	Virginia
Tierney, Charles W.	Sgt. B, 42 Pa. Inf.	1835	1889	St. Johns	Altoona
Tierney, Francis P.	Pvt. K, 125 Pa. Inf.	1833	1882	Ebensburg	Pa.
Tierney, Thomas	Pvt. A, 3 Pa. Inf.				
	Pvt. F, 76 Pa. Inf.	1843	1915	Greenlawn	Hollidaysburg
Tietze, Emile	Cpl. Ind. Cav. Pa. Mil.	1829			
Tillard, William	Pvt. F, Ind. Bn. Pa. Mil.	1815			
Tippery, Mayberry	Pvt. G, 125 Pa. Inf.				
Tippery, Sanford F.	Pvt. C, 53 Pa. Inf.	1840			
Tipton, B. F.					
Tipton, Caleb	Pvt. H, 3 Pa. Inf.				
	Mus. K, 125 Pa. Inf.	1832	1872	Fairview	Altoona
Tipton, George	Pvt. B, 3 Pa. Inf.	1842			
Tipton, George M.	Pvt. 12 U. S. Inf.				
Tipton, Levi	Pvt. F, 77 Pa. Inf.	1841	1913	Reform	Claysburg
Tipton, Samuel B.	Pvt. A, 3 Pa. Inf.				
	Pvt. M, 62 Pa. Inf.				
	Sgt. K, 91 Pa. Inf.	1842	1920	Fairview	Altoona
Tobias, Calvin N.	Pvt. 22 Pa. Cav.			Hopewell	Pa.
Tobias, John B.	Cpl. F, 84 Pa. Inf.	1840	1919	Everett	Pa.
Tobias, Samuel H. G.	Sgt. C, 110 Pa. Inf.	1842	1863	Hickory Bottom	Woodbury
Tomlinson, Francis	Pvt. G, 12 Pa. Cav.	1841	1894	St. Johns	Altoona
Tomlinson, Harry J.	Cpl. G, 12 Pa. Cav.	1843	1892	St. Johns	Altoona
Tompkins, Joel	2Lt. G, 34 Pa. Inf.				
	Sgt. E, 20 Pa. Cav.	1825	1883	Fairview	Altoona
Tompkins, W. H.			1912	Lima	Ohio
Toner, George	Pvt. K, 26 Pa. Inf.	1834	1913	Milton	Pa.
Tooney, Isaiah W.	Pvt. F, 1 Pa. Cav.	1846			

SOLDIERS OF BLAIR COUNTY

Name	Rank Organization	Born	Died	Cemetery	Location
Toser, Robert	Pvt. A, 110 Pa. Inf.				
Tracy, Thomas J.	Pvt. Md. Inf.		1892	Carson Valley	Duncansville
Trainer, John	Pvt. A, 84 Pa. Inf.	1828			
Traister, George	Pvt. A, 1 Pa. Art.	1828	1892	Grandview	Tyrone
Travis, B. V.	Mus. F, 106 Pa. Inf.	1840			
Travis, Daniel J.	2Lt. K, 125 Pa. Inf.				
	Cpt. F, Ind. Bn. Pa. Mil.	1835			
Travis, John	Pvt. F, Ind. Bn. Pa. Mil.	1839			
Travis, Martin	Pvt. H, 22 Pa. Cav.	1831	1887	St. Johns	Altoona
Traynor, Charles H.	Sgt. H, 1 Md. Cav.	1842	1916	Eastlawn	Tyrone
Trees, Clark	Sgt. Ind. Bn. Pa. Mil.	1844			
Trees, David	Pvt. H, 28 Pa. Inf.	1834			
Treese, David	Pvt. B, 125 Pa. Inf.		1862	Maryland Heights	Maryland
Treese, Francis	Pvt. B, 208 Pa. Inf.	1843	1901	Royer Mountain	Williamsburg
Treese, Harry	Pvt. B, 125 Pa. Inf.				
Treese, Henry	Pvt. C, 76 Pa. Inf.	1832	1862	Hilton Head	South Carolina
Treese, James C.	Sgt. D, 125 Pa. Inf.				
Trees, James C.	Pvt. B, 3 Pa. Inf.	1843			
Trease, James M.	Pvt. H, 110 Pa. Inf.	1845	1910	Greenlawn	Roaring Spring
Treese, Peter	2Lt. D, 125 Pa. Inf.				
Treese, William	Pvt. B, 125 Pa. Inf.	1837	1921	Royer Mountain	Williamsburg
Tremble, Joseph	Pvt. I, 88 Pa. Inf.	1841	1917	St. Marys	Hollidaysburg
Treubner, August	Pvt. G, 2 Pa. Art.		1898	Grandview	Tyrone
Trissler, John A.	Pvt. K, 1 Pa. Inf.				
	Sgt. K, 122 Pa. Inf.	1837	1920	Lancaster	Pa.
Trostle, George W.	Pvt. G, 101 Pa. Inf.	1844	1914	Calvary	Altoona
Trotter, William	Pvt. E, 9 Pa. Cav.	1842	1920	Rose Hill	Altoona
Trout, Alexander	Pvt. B, 125 Pa. Inf.				
Trout, Frederick	Pvt. K, 125 Pa. Inf.				
	Pvt. D, 192 Pa. Inf.				
Trout, James P.	Pvt. B, 3 Pa. Inf.	1841	1894	Fairview	Altoona
Trout, Mayberry G.	Pvt. G, 12 Pa. Cav.	1844	1921	Rose Hill	Altoona
Trout, Robert M.	Pvt. 12 Pa. Cav.				
Trout, William W.	Pvt. 59 U. S. Cav.	1847	1905	Fairview	Altoona
Troxell, Abraham	Pvt. E, 125 Pa. Inf.		1862	Winchester	Virginia
Troxell, George W.	Sgt. A 110 Pa. Inf.				
Troxell, James	Pvt. B, 208 Pa. Inf.	1832	1864	Methodist	Williamsburg
Troxell, John	Pvt. A, 110 Pa. Inf.				
Troxell, John A.	Pvt. A, 55 Pa. Inf.	1849	1920	Rose Hill	Altoona
Troy, Robert J.	Pvt. E, Knapp's Bat.	1839	1914	St. Patricks	Gallitzin
Traux, Elihu	Pvt. F, 31 Pa. Inf.				
	Pvt. A, 191 Pa. Inf.				
Trueman, Jacob	Pvt. F, 77 Pa. Inf.	1840	1865	Victoria	Texas
Tucker, George A.	Pvt. E, 104 Pa. Inf.				
Turman, Harry	Pvt. M, 9 Pa. Cav.	1839			
Turnbaugh, Henry	Pvt. E, 104 Pa. Inf.				
Turnbaugh, Henry C.	Pvt. E, 104 Pa. Inf.				
Turnbaugh, John A.	Pvt. G, 12 Pa. Cav.	1836	1890	Carson Valley	Duncansville
Turnbaugh, Martin	Pvt. G, 12 Pa. Cav.	1836	1909	Antis	Bellwood
Turnbaugh, William	Pvt. G, 12 Pa. Cav.	1835	1917	Antis	Bellwood
Turney, Michael	Pvt. A, 84 Pa. Inf.				
	Pvt. G, 57 Pa. Inf.	1837			
Tussey, Samuel C.	Pvt. M, 9 Pa. Cav.	1844	1925	Presbyterian	Hollidaysburg
Tussey, William M.	Pvt. G, Pa. Mil.	1845	1919	Presbyterian	Sinking Valley
Tweed, John W.	Pvt. I, 83 Pa. Inf.	1847	1917	Logan Valley	Bellwood
Tyler, James D.	Pvt. D, 106 Pa. Inf.				
Typer, John Harrison	2Lt. I, 14 Pa. Inf.	1836	1867	Fairview	Martinsburg
Tyson, Andrew	2Lt. F, 16 Pa. Cav.				
Tyson, Samuel H.	Pvt. C, 110 Pa. Inf.				
Ullery, Daniel	Pvt. H, 3 Pa. Inf.	1817			
Ullery, George	Pvt. D, 13 Pa. Cav.	1847	1911	Oak Ridge	Altoona
Ullery, George	Sgt. I, 137 Pa. Inf.				

Name	Rank Organization	Born	Died	Cemetery	Location
Ullery, James E.	Pvt. G, 12 Pa. Cav.	1833			
Ullery, John E.	Pvt. I, 57 Pa. Inf.	1846			
Ulrich, Frederick	Pvt. L, 21 Pa. Cav.	1844	1908	Fairview	Altoona
Umbower, Samuel	Pvt. B, 76 Pa. Inf.	1842	1920	Spring Hope	Martinsburg
Umholtz, George W.	Pvt. E, 104 Pa. Inf.				
Underhill, John C.	Pvt. A, 23 Pa. Mil.	1834			
Underhill, Jeremiah C.	Sgt. A, Ind. Bn. Pa. Mil.	1834			
Urich, John	Pvt. Ind. Cav. Pa. Mil.				
	Pvt. D, 125 Pa. Inf.	1844			
Urick, Joseph H.	Pvt. Ind. Bn. Pa. Mil.				
	Pvt. D, 22 Pa. Cav.	1846			
Vale, Thomas H.		1840	1868	Oak Grove	Tyrone
Valence, James	Pvt. A, 110 Pa. Inf.				
Vallance, George T.	Pvt. E, 21 Pa. Cav.	1844	1911	Fairview	Martinsburg
Valentine, Cyrus	Cpl. H, 110 Pa. Inf.	1827	1916	Fairview	Altoona
Valentine, H. L.	Pvt. I, 6 U. S. Cav.	1840	1925		California
Valentine, Levi	Pvt. G, 12 Pa. Cav.	1829	1862	Asbury	Altoona
Valentine, Malden	Pvt. G, 12 Pa. Cav.	1846	1915	Fairview	Altoona
Valentine, Samuel	Pvt, H, Ind. Bn. Pa. Mil.	1795	1887	Asbury	Altoona
Valentine, William	Pvt. G, 12 Pa. Cav.	1815			
Van Allman, Joseph	Pvt. B, 192 Pa. Inf.	1836	1920	Lutheran	Hollidaysburg
Vandevander, Robert H.	Cpl. A, 20 Pa. Cav.	1844	1910	Logan Valley	Bellwood
Vandrew, Adam	Pvt. F, 3 Md. Inf.	1824	1892	Fairview	Altoona
Van Ormer, Robert B.	Pvt. E, 101 Pa. Inf.	1834	1907	Rose Hill	Altoona
Vansickle, John W.	Pvt. E, 84 Pa. Inf.		1864	Culpepper C. H.	Virginia
Van Scoyoc, Aaron	Pvt. H, 110 Pa. Inf.	1838	1901	Grandview	Tyrone
Van Scoyoc, Abraham	Pvt. A, 125 Pa. Inf.	1830	1911	Grandview	Tyrone
VanScoyoc, Benjamin F.	Pvt. H, 110 Pa. Inf.			Charlottesville	Bellwood
Van Scoyoc, John	Pvt. D, 192 Pa. Inf.	1849	1916		Cambria Co.
Van Valzah, John F.	Pvt. G, Pa. Mil.				
	Pvt. G, 1 U. S. Engrs.	1844			
Van Zandt, George B.	Pvt. L, 9 Pa. Cav.	1843	1927	Oak Ridge	Altoona
Van Zandt, Jackson A.	Pvt. F, 194 Pa. Inf.	1846	1910	Logan Valley	Bellwood
Van Zandt, James M.	Sgt. K, 22 Pa. Cav.	1843			
Van Zant, William R.	Pvt. F, 31 Pa. Inf.				
	Pvt. A, 191 Pa. Inf.	1840	1865	Salisbury	N. Car.
Varnes, Louis H.	Pvt. A, 3 Pa. Inf.	1840			
Vauclain, Andrew C.		1809	1887	Fairview	Altoona
Vauclain, James L.	A. E. U. S. Navy	1838	1874	Fairview	Altoona
Vaughn, George	Pvt. H, 14 Pa. Inf.	1840			
Vaughn, George	Pvt. A, 125 Pa. Inf.				
Vaughn, George H.	Sgt. G, 125 Pa. Inf.		1922	St. Johns	Altoona
Vaughn, Henry	Pvt. A, 125 Pa. Inf.				
Vaughn, James A.	Mus. Ind. Cav. Pa. Mil.	1838	1921	Oak Ridge	Altoona
Vaughn, Thomas H.	Pvt. C, 76 Pa. Inf.	1830	1898	St. Patricks	Newry
Veach, David C.	Pvt. G, 186 Pa. Inf.	1832	1905	Oak Ridge	Altoona
Vincent, George W.	Pvt. E, 84 Pa. Inf.				
Vogel, Frank	Sgt. H, 3 Pa. Inf.				
	Pvt. D, 192 Pa. Inf.	1826	1904	St. Marys	Hollidaysburg
Vogle, Frederick	Cpl. D, 192 Pa. Inf.				
Vogel, Jacob	Pvt. H, 3 Pa. Inf.	1839	1917	St. Patricks	Gallitzin
Vowinkle, Anthony	2Lt. A, 23 Pa. Mil.	1818			
Wagner, Allison	Pvt. H, 22 Pa. Cav.	1834			
Wagner, Elias	Pvt. H, 149 Pa. Inf.	1845	1912	Oak Ridge	Altoona
Wagner, George	Pvt. C, 53 Pa. Inf.				
Wagner, James H.	Pvt. A, 55 Pa. Inf.	1842	1910	St. Patricks	Gallitzin
Wagoner, John M.	Pvt. E, 125 Pa. Inf.				
	Pvt. C, 205 Pa. Inf.	1833	1910	Lutheran	Williamsburg
Wagner, Joseph	Pvt. G, 79 Pa. Inf.	1837	1903	Grandview	Tyrone
Wagner, Joseph A.	Pvt. B, 208 Pa. Inf.	1846	1911	Royer Mountain	Williamsburg
Wagner, Joseph H.	Pvt. D, 131 Pa. Inf.	1830	1912	Kifers	Woodbury
Wagoner, Monroe	Pvt. U, 22 Pa. Cav.	1845			

SOLDIERS OF BLAIR COUNTY

Name	Rank Organization	Born	Died	Cemetery	Location
Wahl, Christian	Pvt. A, 1 W. Vir. Art.	1838	1883	Fairview	Altoona
Wahl, Joseph F.	Pvt. M, 14 Pa. Cav.	1845	1930	Calvary	Altoona
Wakefield, Thomas H.	Pvt. K, 125 Pa. Inf.				
Waldsmith, John W.	Pvt. H, 125 Pa. Inf.	1843	1903	Donation	Hunt'gdon Co.
Walk, Elias	Pvt. H, 22 Pa. Cav.	1844			
Walk, George W.	Pvt. E, 13 Pa. Cav.	1846	1927	Milroy	Pa.
Walker, Asabel	Pvt. A, 84 Pa. Inf.			Pleasantville	Bedford Co.
Walker, Benjamin H.	Cpl. A, 84 Pa. Inf.				
	Cpl. G, 57 Pa. Inf.	1834			
Walker, Cornelious	Cpl. F, 76 Pa. Inf.	1836	1863	Fort Wagner	S. Car.
Walker, Isaac	Pvt. C, 205 Pa. Inf.	1845		Pleasantville	Bedford Co.
Walker, John	Pvt. C, 110 Pa. Inf.		1863	National	Gettysburg
Walker, John H.	Pvt. A, 84 Pa. Inf.				
Walker, Joseph	Pvt. E, 57 Pa. Inf.	1844	1903	Fairview	Altoona
Walker, Morris	Pvt. A, 84 Pa. Inf.			Pleasantville	Bedford Co.
Walker, Paul	Pvt. E, 20 Pa. Cav.	1845	1885	Walters	Duncansville
Walker, William	Pvt. D, 184 Pa. Inf.		1864	Petersburg	Virginia
Walker, William H.	Pvt. G, 75 Pa. Inf.	1838	1881	Fairview	Altoona
Walker, William M.	Pvt. K, 22 Pa. Cav.	1845			
Wallace, David	Pvt. C, 87 Pa. Inf.	1833	1912		
Wallace, Edward	Cpl. E, 46 Pa. Mil.	1845			
Wallace, Edward	Cpl. D, 192 Pa. Inf.				
Wallace, Edward	Mus. H, 110 Pa. Inf.	1827			
Wallace, Edward A.	Cpl. H, 22 Pa. Cav.	1840			
Wallace, Jesse	Pvt. I, 137 Pa. Inf.	1840	1871	Carson Valley	Duncansville
Wallace, Hays H.	Pvt. I, 22 Pa. Cav.	1842			
Wallace, John	Pvt. H, 110 Pa. Inf.				
Wallace, John G.	Pvt. A, 77 Pa. Inf.	1826	1864	Chambersburg	Pa.
Wallace, Samuel G.	Pvt. 110 Pa. Inf.				
Walls, Ellis	Pvt. U, 22 Pa. Cav.	1844			
Walls, Robert	Pvt. L, 9 Pa. Cav.	1830	1902	Frankstown	Hollidaysburg
Walls, William	Pvt. F, 31 Pa. Inf.				
	Pvt. A, 191 Pa. Inf.				
Walsh, John	Pvt. B, Ind. Bn. Pa. Mil.	1845			
Walsh, Patrick F.	Cpt. E, 84 Pa. Inf.				
Walters, David S.	Pvt. I, 57 Pa. Inf.	1841			
Walters, David	Pvt. K, 48 Pa. Mil.	1834	1909	Rose Hill	Altoona
Walter, George I.	Pvt. A, 13 Pa. Cav.		1888	Reformed	Loysburg
Walters, George W.	Pvt. C, 205 Pa. Inf.	1836	1906	Greenlawn	Roaring Spring
Walters, Jacob A.	Pvt. G, 12 Pa. Cav.	1845	1925	Rose Hill	Altoona
Walter, Jacob D.	Pvt. F, 77 Pa. Inf.	1831	1902	Lutheran	Claysburg
Walter, Jacob W.	Pvt. F, 77 Pa. Inf.	1843	1923	Reformed	Claysburg
Walters, John	Pvt. B, Ind. Bn. Pa. Mil.	1841			
Walters, John	Pvt. I, 205 Pa. Inf.	1840	1917	Fairview	Altoona
Walter, John	Pvt. I, 169 Pa. Inf.			Venango	Pa.
Walters, John E.	Pvt. A, 1 Ky. Inf.				
	Pvt. D, 2 N. J. Cav.	1819	1899	Snyders	Tyrone
Walters, John H.	Pvt. A, 84 Pa. Inf.			Upper Claar	Bedford Co.
Walters, Joseph A.	Pvt. B, 125 Pa. Inf.	1837		Rose Hill	Altoona
Walter, Michael H.	Pvt. L, 1 Md. Inf.	1838	1904		Bedford Co.
Walters, Moses	Pvt. C, 205 Pa. Inf.	1846	1924	Rose Hill	Altoona
Walter, Samuel H.	Pvt. L, 19 Pa. Cav.	1842	1909	Koontz	Morrisons Cove
Walters, William H.	Sgt. A, 16 Pa. Inf.	1834		Presbyterian	Hollidaysburg
Walton, Isaac	Pvt. A, 205 Pa. Inf.	1822	1893	Oak Ridge	Altoona
Walton, Isaac R.	Pvt. D, 205 Pa. Inf.	1824	1877	Lutheran	Sinking Valley
Walton, John	Sgt. A, 205 Pa. Inf.	1837	1880	Collinsville	Altoona
Walton, John	Pvt. D, 125 Pa. Inf.				
Walton, Louis	Pvt. A, 71 Pa. Inf.	1840	1890	Oak Ridge	Altoona
Wambaugh, Sylvester	Cpl. D, 133 Pa. Inf.			Shanksville	Somerset Co.
Wantz, Daniel K.	Pvt. A, 7 Md. Inf.	1843			
Ward, Alexander M.	Pvt. D, 1 Pa. Art.	1843			
Ward, Frederick	Pvt. K, 125 Pa. Inf.	1842	1862	Antietam	Maryland

THE CIVIL WAR

Name	Rank Organization	Born	Died	Cemetery	Location
Ward, John	Pvt. Ind. Cav. Pa. Mil.				
	Cpl. D, 22 Pa. Cav.	1840			
Wareham, Martin	Pvt. B, 3 Pa. Cav.	1839	1912	Albright	Roaring Spring
Warfel, George W.	Sgt. F, 12 Pa. Cav.	1839			
Warfield, John	Pvt. D, 14 Pa. Inf.				
	Pvt. A, 110 Pa. Inf.	1828	1901	Grandview	Tyrone
Warfield, Samuel	Pvt. F, 77 Pa. Inf.	1818			
Waring, Robert W.	Pvt. F, 77 Pa. Inf.	1821	1900	Grandview	Tyrone
Warner, Alfred B.	Pvt. A, 53 Pa. Mil.	1834	1912	Grandview	Tyrone
Warner, John	Pvt. I, 84 Pa. Inf.			St. Marys	Hollidaysburg
Warner, Joseph N.	Pvt. D, 192 Pa. Inf.				
Warner, Joseph P.	Pvt. H, 84 Pa. Inf.	1845	1864	St. Marys	Hollidaysburg
Warren, Edward M.	Cpl. A, 57 Ill. Inf.				
	Cpt. I, 165 Pa. Inf.	1833			
Warrick, John	Pvt. I, 205 Pa. Inf.	1833			
Warrick, William	Pvt. U, 84 Pa. Inf.				
	Pvt. I, 57 Pa. Inf.	1828			
Warsing, James	Pvt. E, 84 Pa. Inf.				
Washburn, Horace V.	Pvt. M, 2 Pa. Inf.		1882	Sunbury	Pa.
Washing, James	Pvt. I, 14 Pa. Inf.	1836			
Watters, Harvey	Pvt. K, 46 Pa. Mil.	1844	1876	Grandview	Tyrone
Waters, Robert		1833	1918	Calvary	Altoona
Waters, William C.	Sgt. H, 9 Pa. Cav.				
Watkins, Jesse	Pvt. I, 55 Pa. Inf.	1827	1863	Beauford	S. Car.
Watkins, John W.	Pvt. D, 205 Pa. Inf.				
Watkins, Samuel	Pvt. 22 U. S. C. T.			Union	Hollidaysburg
Watkins, Thomas	Pvt. M, 62 Pa. Inf.	1822			
Watson, George M.	Pvt. A, 3 Pa. Inf.				
	Pvt. M, 62 Pa. Inf.	1840	1869	Presbyterian	Hollidaysburg
Watson, James	Pvt. A, 187 Ohio Inf.	1836	1898	Fairview	Altoona
Watson, Jeremiah S.	Pvt. D, 3 Pa. Inf.				
	Pvt. A, 125 Pa. Inf.	1836	1888	Grandview	Tyrone
Watt, Albert J.	Sgt. F, 28 Pa. Inf.	1843	1927	Summit	Cambria Co.
Watt, John M.	Pvt. F, 28 Pa. Inf.	1841	1922	Calvary	Altoona
Way, B. S.	Pvt. D, 145 Ohio Inf.	1819			
Wayne, Henry	Cpt. B, 3 Pa. Inf.				
	Cpt. F, 76 Pa. Inf.	1821	1862	Pocotaligo	S. Car.
Wayne, William H.	Mus. F, 76 Pa. Inf.	1846			
Weakland, Augustine	Pvt. C, 53 Pa. Inf.			St. Johns	Altoona
Weakland, Demetrius	Pvt. F, 133 Pa. Inf.	1833	1920	Chest Springs	Cambria Co.
Weaklan, Sylvester J.	Sgt. M, 7 Pa. Cav.	1830	1905	Chest Springs	Cambria Co.
Wear, Emanuel	Pvt. F, 84 Pa. Inf.	1811	1888	Lutheran	Hollidaysburg
Wear, William H.	Pvt. A, Ind. Bn. Pa. Mil.				
	Pvt. K, 67 Pa. Inf.	1845	1902	Lutheran	Hollidaysburg
Weaver, Adam E.	Pvt. I, 195 Pa. Inf.	1843	1874	Fairview	Altoona
Weaver, Albert J.	Pvt. A, 3 Pa. Inf.				
	Pvt. D, 110 Pa. Inf.	1837			
Webber, Daniel B.	Pvt. C, 46 Pa. Mil.	1842			
Weaver, Francis Heyer	Pvt. C, 53 Pa. Inf.	1844		Arlington	Virginia
Weaver, George W.	Pvt. A, 3 Pa. Inf.				
	Pvt. I, 55 Pa. Inf.	1839	1873	Richmond	Virginia
Weaver, James H.	Pvt. C, 2 Pa. Cav.		1911	Valier	Jefferson Co.
Weaver, John J.	Pvt. F, 77 Pa. Inf.	1843	1865	Galveston	Texas
Weaver, John M.	Pvt. A, 84 Pa. Inf.	1843			
Webber, John W.	Cpl. D, 46 Pa. Mil.	1829			
Weaver, Joseph	Pvt. Ind. Cav. Pa. Mil.				
	Cpl. D, 13 Pa. Cav.	1832			
Weaver, Mitchell D.	Pvt. C, 205 Pa. Inf.	1844			
Weber, Morris	Pvt. E, 84 Pa. Inf.				
	Pvt. B, 46 Pa. Mil.	1833	1893	Lutheran	Hollidaysburg
Weaver, Peter M.	Pvt. B, 1 Pa. Art.	1836			
Weaver, Philip					

SOLDIERS OF BLAIR COUNTY

Name	Rank Organization	Born	Died	Cemetery	Location
Weaver, Samuel					
Webb, Henry	Pvt. F, 31 Pa. Inf.		1862		Virginia
Webb, John	Pvt. D, 1 Pa. Art.	1830			
Webb, John B.	Pvt. F, 31 Pa. Inf.				
	Pvt. A, 191 Pa. Inf.	1840	1864	Salisbury	N. Car.
Webster, Robert G.	Pvt. 19 Pa. Cav.	1843	1902	Fairview	Altoona
Weest, Wolfgang	Pvt. D, 46 Pa. Mil.	1828	1900	Oak Ridge	Altoona
Weidensall, Jacob	Pvt. A, 84 Pa. Inf.				
	Pvt. A, 57 Pa. Inf.				
Weidensall, John	Pvt. M, 62 Pa. Inf.	1834	1885	Omaha	Nebraska
Wiedensall, John	Pvt. A, 23 Pa. Inf.	1806			
Widensall, John H.	Pvt. I, 205 Pa. Inf.				
Weidley, Earhart F.	Pvt. K, 187 Pa. Inf.	1817	1880	Oak Ridge	Altoona
Weidner, Jacob	Pvt. M, 9 Pa. Cav.	1842			
Weighaman, George	Mus. H, 3 Pa. Inf.				
	Mus. A, 84 Pa. Inf.				
	Pvt. G, 57 Pa. Inf.	1840	1890	Grandview	Tyrone
Weighaman, John	Mus. A, 3 Pa. Inf.				
	Mus. A, 84 Pa. Inf.	1842	1902	Lutheran	Hollidaysburg
Weighman, William	Mus. A, 3 Pa. Inf.	1842	1873	Lutheran	Hollidaysburg
Weigherman, William H.	Pvt. H, 110 Pa. Inf.		1886	Huntingdon	Pa.
Wighaman, William	Mus. A, 23 Pa. Inf.	1838			
Weight, Aaron	Pvt. C, 84 Pa. Inf.	1838	1862	Frankstown	Hollidaysburg
Weight, Adam	Sgt. A, 110 Pa. Inf.				
Weight, Daniel	Pvt. A, 110 Pa. Inf.	1834	1862	Grandview	Tyrone
Weight, David E.	Pvt. A, 110 Pa. Inf.	1843	1862	Logan Valley	Bellwood
Weight, George	Pvt. D, 205 Pa. Inf.	1824			
Weight, George W.	Pvt. C, 208 Pa. Inf.	1833	1908	Grandview	Tyrone
Weight, George	Cpl. A, 110 Pa. Inf.	1839	1911	Logan Valley	Bellwood
Weight, Henry	Pvt. M, 9 Pa. Cav.	1840			
Waite, James M.	Pvt. E, 104 Pa. Inf.	1833	1912	Logan Valley	Bellwood
Weight, John	Pvt. M, 9 Pa. Cav.	1836			
Weight, John E.	Pvt. 15 Pa. Cav.	1840	1862	Logan Valley	Bellwood
Weight, John	Pvt. D, 192 Pa. Inf.	1824	1904	Grandview	Tyrone
Weight, Samuel G.	Pvt. H, 2 Pa. Art.	1847			
Weight, Thomas	Sgt. 110 Pa. Inf.	1839	1923	Charlottesville	Bellwood
Waight, William	Pvt. C, 87 Pa. Inf.	1845	1932	Oak Ridge	Altoona
Weight, William	Pvt. F, 77 Pa. Inf.	1818	1876	Grandview	Tyrone
Weight, William E.	Pvt. F, 77 Pa. Inf.	1842			
Weimert, Stephen	Pvt. H, 208 Pa. Inf.		1914	Yellow Creek	Morrisons Cove
Weirbaugh, Henry	Pvt. F, 76 Pa. Inf.	1844	1864	Portsmouth	Rhode Island
Weirbaugh, Levi	Pvt. F, 76 Pa. Inf.	1843			
Weisel, John	Pvt. B, 208 Pa. Inf.				
Weisel, John H.	Pvt. A, 84 Pa. Inf.				
	Pvt. G, 57 Pa. Inf.				
Weisgarber, Daniel J.	Pvt. D, 13 Pa. Cav.	1845			
Weisgarver, George W.	Pvt. K, 78 Pa. Inf.	1825	1906	Fairview	Altoona
Weisinger, J. P.	Pvt. C, 54 Pa. Inf.				
Welch, Charles G.	Pvt. C, 46 Pa. Mil.	1845			
Welch, John	Pvt. D, 13 Pa. Cav.	1834			
Welden, James	Pvt. B, 8 Pa. Inf.		1912	Coatesville	Pa.
Weldon, Michael	Pvt. A, 110 Pa. Inf.			Grandview	Tyrone
Weller, John	Pvt. E, 1 Pa. Art.	1843	1934	Oak Ridge	Altoona
Wentling, Jacob B.	Pvt. B, 208 Pa. Inf.				
Wentz, Isaac	Pvt. E, 13 Pa. Inf.			Harrisburg	Pa.
Wentzel, Adam J.	Pvt. C, 76 Pa. Inf.	1818	1881	St. Marys	Altoona
Wensell, Alex C.	Pvt. Ind. Cav. Pa. Mil.	1838	1881	Fairview	Altoona
Wentzell, Frederick	Pvt. M, 62 Pa. Inf.	1834	1864	St. Patricks	Newry
Wensel, John	Pvt. M, 22 Pa. Cav.	1845			
Wentzell, John	Pvt. C, 76 Pa. Inf.				
Wensel, Moses	Pvt. M, 22 Pa. Cav.	1843			
Wertz, Albert M.	Pvt. I, 137 Pa. Inf.	1837	1914	Frankstown	Hollidaysburg

THE CIVIL WAR

Name	Rank Organization	Born	Died	Cemetery	Location
Wertz, Jacob B.	Pvt. A, Ind. Bn. Pa. Mil.				
	Pvt. D, 13 Pa. Cav.	1841	1906	Grandview	Tyrone
Wertz, James E.	Pvt. D, 3 Pa. Inf.				
	Cpl. I, 34 Pa. Inf.	1838			
Wertz, James R.	Cpl. C, 191 Pa. Inf.	1833	1926	Frankstown	Hollidaysburg
Wertz, John C.	Pvt. M, 3 Pa. Art.	1845	1911	Logan Valley	Bellwood
Wertz, Joseph Lee	Pvt. C, 19 Pa. Cav.	1841	1910	Lutheran	Newry
Wertz, Joseph M.	Pvt. A, 46 Pa. Mil.				
	Pvt. E, 131 Pa. Inf.	1845	1909	Grandview	Tyrone
Wertz, Martin	Pvt. A, 110 Pa. Inf.				
	Pvt. F, 209 Pa. Inf.	1836	1913	Grandview	Tyrone
Wertz, Mathias	Pvt. B, Ind. Bn. Pa. Mil.	1826			
Wertz, Philip Martin	Pvt. I, 137 Pa. Inf.	1843	1924	Presbyterian	Hollidaysburg
Wertz, William B.	Cpl. E, 34 Pa. Inf.	1843	1884	Grandview	Tyrone
Wesley, Charles	Pvt. A, 125 Pa. Inf.				
	Sgt. K, 187 Pa. Inf.	1839	1923	Fairview	Altoona
Wesley, Daniel	Pvt. K, 187 Pa. Inf.	1829	1890	Grandview	Tyrone
Wesley, Michael	Pvt. K, 187 Pa. Inf.				Louisiana
West, William	Pvt. D, 125 Pa. Inf.				
Westbrook, Robert S.	Sgt. B, 49 Pa. Inf.	1843	1931	Rose Hill	Altoona
Westbrook, William D.	Pvt. B, 125 Pa. Inf.				
	Pvt. I, 46 Pa. Mil.				
	Pvt. E, 195 Pa. Inf.				
	Pvt. F, 19 Pa. Cav.	1845	1904	Fairview	Altoona
Weston, Alfred	Pvt. D, 14 Pa. Inf.	1839			
Weston, Frederick H.	Cpl. I, 136 Pa. Inf.				
	Cpl. E, 45 Pa. Inf.	1843	1906	Frankstown	Hollidaysburg
Weston, Jeremiah T.	Pvt. I, 34 Pa. Inf.				
	Sgt. A, 2 Pa. Art.	1838	1916	Fairview	Altoona
Weston, William H.	Pvt. A, 205 Pa. Inf.	1847	1932	Oak Ridge	Altoona
Weyant, Alexander	Pvt. A, 188 Pa. Inf.	1829	1918	Diehls	Martinsburg
Wyandt, George Nelson	Pvt. H, 126 Pa. Inf.	1847	1930	Hutchinsons	Altoona
Wyant, Henry C.	Pvt. K, 148 Pa. Inf.	1819	1869	Lutheran	Newry
Wyant, Isaac	Sgt. K, 5 U. S. Art.	1837	1914	Rose Hill	Altoona
Weyandt, Jacob D.	Pvt. L, 3 Pa. Art.	1846	1913	Reform	Claysburg
Weyandt, James	Pvt. H, 99 Pa. Inf.			Upper Claar	Bedford Co.
Wyond, James	Pvt. E, 100 Pa. Inf.	1830	1902	Carson Valley	Duncansville
Weyandt, Joseph	Pvt. A, 13 Pa. Cav.	1830	1901	Upper Claar	Bedford Co.
Weyant, Joseph	Pvt. A, 84 Pa. Inf.				
	Pvt. G, 57 Pa. Inf.	1843		Reformed	Bedford Co.
Weyandt, Samuel S.	Pvt. E, 125 Pa. Inf.				
	Pvt. L, 3 Pa. Art.	1843	1938	Reform	Claysburg
Wharton, William	Pvt. D, 1 Pa. Art.		1865	National	Baltimore
Wheeler, William	Pvt. D, 13 Pa. Cav.	1845			
Wheeler, William S.	Pvt. E, 125 Pa. Inf.				
Wherry, William R.	Pvt. E, 23 Pa. Inf.	1845	1932	Union	Summerhill
Whippo, John	Pvt. C, 49 Pa. Inf.		1909	Warriors Mark	Pa.
Whippo, William H.	Pvt. C, 49 Pa. Inf.	1841	1909	Rose Hill	Altoona
Whiston, Benton	Pvt. G, 123 Pa. Inf.				
	Pvt. H, Ind. Bat. Pa. Art.	1843	1914	Gustavus	Ohio
Whitaker, Henry	Cpl. C, 205 Pa. Inf.	1843			
Whitaker, Joseph E.	Pvt. G, 91 Pa. Inf.	1830	1910	Rose Hill	Altoona
Whitbeck, Joseph	Pvt. G, 205 Pa. Inf.				
White, Andrew	Pvt. D, 205 Pa. Inf.	1819			
White, Andrew J.	Sgt. C, 76 Pa. Inf.	1828	1892	Oak Ridge	Altoona
White, Benjamin	Pvt. H, 3 Pa. Inf.				
	2Lt. C, 76 Pa. Inf.	1836	1898	Frankstown	Hollidaysburg
White, Charles	Pvt. I, 7 Pa. Inf.				
	Pvt. E, 84 Pa. Inf.	1839	1909	Frankstown	Hollidaysburg
White, David	Pvt. D, 1 Pa. Art.	1836			
White, Edward	Sgt. D, 13 Pa. Cav.	1842			

SOLDIERS OF BLAIR COUNTY

Name	Rank Organization	Born	Died	Cemetery	Location
White, Edward	Pvt. H, 3 Pa. Inf.				
	Pvt. C, 84 Pa. Inf.	1841	1915	Frankstown	Hollidaysburg
White, Jacob F.	Pvt. G, 2 Pa. Art.	1842	1907	Logan Valley	Bellwood
White, James	Pvt. C, 84 Pa. Inf.				
	Pvt. D, 13 Pa. Inf.	1846	1933	Oak Ridge	Altoona
White, James H.	Pvt. C, 45 Pa. Inf.	1837	1902	Fairview	Altoona
White, John M.	Pvt. A, 110 Pa. Inf.				
White, John W.	Pvt. C, 46 Pa. Mil.	1824	1909	Oak Ridge	Altoona
White, Lysander M.	Pvt. B, 208 Pa. Inf.				
White, Sanford D.	Pvt. A, 187 Ohio Inf.		1904	Bald Eagle	Tyrone
White, Silas	Pvt. C, 84 Pa. Inf.	1831			
White, Thomas F.	Pvt. D, 1 Pa. Art.	1842			
White, William	Pvt. A, 22 Pa. Cav.	1845			
White, William		1809	1892	Fairview	Altoona
White, William	Pvt. D, 1 Pa. Art.	1845			
White, William	Pvt. D, 1 Pa. Art.	1821			
Whitehead, Charles R.	Pvt. I, 194 Pa. Inf.		1916	Mauch Chunk	Pa.
Whitehead, John M.	Pvt. B, 125 Pa. Inf.				
	Cpl. E, 104 Pa. Inf.	1829	1890	Presbyterian	Williamsburg
Whitehead, Thomas	Pvt. C, 22 Pa. Cav.	1841			
Whitemen, John A.	Pvt. M, 19 Pa. Cav.	1845			
Whitesel, James	Pvt. B, 208 Pa. Inf.				
Whitesides, James	Pvt. E, 46 Pa. Mil.	1844			
Whiteseides, William A.	Pvt. B, 1 Pa. Art.	1842			
Whitney, Walter R.	Cpn. 20 Pa. Cav.	1842			
Whittaker, Thomas S.	Pvt. C, 125 Pa. Inf.				
	1Lt. M, 20 Pa. Cav.			Riverview	Huntingdon
Whittaker, William	Pvt. C, 84 Pa. Inf.	1843			
Wible, Jacob	Pvt. U, 22 Pa. Cav.	1825			
Wible, Peter C.	Pvt. A, 55 Pa. Inf.	1836	1908	St. Johns	Altoona
Wicker, Frederick N.	Pvt. F, 76 Pa. Inf.	1842	1910	Fairview	Altoona
Wicker, John Casper	Cpl. F, 76 Pa. Inf.	1841	1897	Fairview	Altoona
Wickes, David S.	Sgt. F, 3 N. Y. Cav.	1844	1900	Oak Ridge	Altoona
Widmer, Theodore	Pvt. 84 Pa. Inf.	1839	1873	Lutheran	Hollidaysburg
Widner, Jacob	Pvt. I, 137 Pa. Inf.				
Weir, John M.	Pvt. A, 84 Pa. Inf.	1843	1915	Greenlawn	Hollidaysburg
Weir, Richard C.	Pvt. K, 18 Pa. Cav.	1827	1912	Grandview	Tyrone
Wigand, Henry	Pvt. A, 3 Pa. Inf.	1836		Lutheran	Hollidaysburg
Wigton, Theodore H.	Pvt. F, 19 Pa. Cav.	1845	1917		Philadelphia
Wilderson, Peter	Cpl. C, 76 Pa. Inf.	1840			
Wildes, Tillinghast C.	Pvt. H, 3 Pa. Inf.				
	Smn. U. S. Navy	1833	1913	Oak Ridge	Altoona
Wiley, Joseph H.	Pvt. D, 1 Pa. Art.	1837			
Wilgis, William H.	Sgt. F, 31 Pa. Inf.		1862		
Wilkes, William	Sgt. B, 3 Pa. Inf.	1836			
Wilkie, Irvin	Pvt. F, 18 Pa. Mil.		1919	Oak Ridge	Altoona
Williams, Benjamin	Pvt. E, 201 Pa. Inf.	1823			
Williams, David D.	Pvt. D, 192 Pa. Inf.				
Williams, David P.	Pvt. G, 125 Pa. Inf.				
Williams, David S.	Pvt. E, 104 Pa. Inf.			Methodist	Williamsburg
Williams, Edward	Pvt. E, 24 U. S. C. T.		1908	Grandview	Tyrone
Williams, Gains	Smn. U. S. Navy		1865	Fairview	Altoona
Williams, Harrison P.	Sgt. D, Ind. Bn. Pa. Mil.	1837	1899	Everett	Pa.
Williams, James	Pvt. H, 14 Pa. Inf.				
	Pvt. C, 76 Pa. Inf.	1842	1862	Pocotaligo	S. Car.
Williams, James W.	Pvt. H, 3 Pa. Art.	1844	1892	Oak Ridge	Altoona
Williams, James	Sgt. 14 U. S. Inf.				
Williams, John	Pvt. A, 110 Pa. Inf.				
Williams, John	Cpl. I, 14 Pa. Inf.				
	Pvt. A, 84 Pa. Inf.				
	Cpl. H, 57 Pa. Inf.	1832			
Williams, John A. J.	Pvt. C, 67 Pa. Inf.	1833	1909	Greenlawn	Roaring Spring

THE CIVIL WAR

Name	Rank Organization	Born	Died	Cemetery	Location
Williams, John M.	Pvt. M, 1 Vermont Cav.	1833	1884	Fairview	Altoona
Williams, John P.	Pvt. F, 37 Pa. Inf.				
	Pvt. H, 191 Pa. Inf.	1837	1873	Baptist	Salemville
Williams, John R.	Pvt. I, 205 Pa. Inf.	1830			
Williams, Joseph	Pvt. H, 110 Pa. Inf.		1864	Alexandria	Virginia
Williams, Joseph	Pvt. H, 110 Pa. Inf.	1827	1907	Grandview	Tyrone
Williams, Joseph G.	Pvt. B, 149 Pa. Inf.		1913		Tyrone
Williams, Joshua B.	Pvt. G, Pa. Art.	1836	1923	Grandview	Tyrone
Williams, Martin D.	Pvt. C, 46 Pa. Mil.	1846			
Williams, Reese	Cpl. G, 125 Pa. Inf.				
Williams, Samuel	Pvt. E, 104 Pa. Inf.				
Williams, Thomas	Pvt. E, Ind. Bn. Pa. Mil.				
Williams, Thomas R.	Pvt. B, 49 Pa. Inf.				
Williams, William	Pvt. C, 3 Pa. Inf.				
	Mjr. 14 U. S. Inf.	1828	1906	Presbyterian	Hollidaysburg
Williams, William C.	2Lt. I, 55 Pa. Inf.	1821		Rodman	Roaring Spring
Williamson, Charles H.	Pvt. F, 126 Pa. Inf.	1822			
Williamson, Edmund L.	Mus. D, 46 Pa. Mil.	1832			
Williamson, Gideon	Pvt. H, 110 Pa. Inf.				
Williamson, James R.	Sgt. G, 105 Ill. Inf.	1841	1923	Humbolt	Nebraska
Williamson, John H.	Pvt. G, 12 Pa. Cav.	1837			
Williamson, S. H.	Pvt. D, 125 Pa. Inf.				
Wills, James P.	Pvt. A, 205 Pa. Inf.	1846	1880	Mauers	Altoona
Wills, Mark A.					
Wills, Samuel	Pvt. E, 104 Pa. Inf.				
Wills, Samuel A.	Pvt. I, 34 Pa. Inf.	1836	1916	Mauers	Altoona
Wilson, Adam J.	Pvt. B, 46 Pa. Mil.	1808	1885	Fairview	Altoona
Wilson, Alexander C.	Pvt. I, 104 Pa. Inf.	1846	1919	Birmingham	Pa.
Wilson, Andrew	Pvt. D, 192 Pa. Inf.				
Wilson, Calvin B.	Sgt. D, 53 Pa. Inf.	1838	1862	Presbyterian	Williamsburg
Wilson, Charles	Pvt. I, 137 Pa. Inf.				
Wilson, Charles T.	Pvt. K, 15 Pa. Cav.	1832	1906	Fairview	Altoona
Wilson, D. B.		1838	1912		Johnstown
Wilson, Emery E.	Pvt. A, 110 Pa. Inf.	1843	1910	Charlottesville	Bellwood
Wilson, Francis M.	Pvt. D, 46 Pa. Mil.	1832			
Wilson, Henry	Pvt. D, 205 Pa. Inf.	1850	1922	Oak Ridge	Altoona
Wilson, Henry R.	Pvt. C, 84 Pa. Inf.	1840	1869	Presbyterian	Hollidaysburg
Wilson, Hill P.	Sgt. B, 125 Pa. Inf.				
Wilson, James A.	Pvt. C, 110 Pa. Inf.				
Wilson, James M.	Pvt. C, 77 Pa. Inf.	1846	1866	Methodist	Williamsburg
Wilson, James P.	Pvt. H, 3 Pa. Art.	1832	1892	Oak Ridge	Altoona
Wilson, John C.	Sgt. C, 3 Pa. Inf.	1839			
Wilson, John F.	Pvt. E, 84 Pa. Inf.				
Wilson, John J.	Pvt. K, 22 Pa. Cav.	1821			
Wilson, John T.	Pvt. H, 110 Pa. Inf.				
Wilson, Joseph E.	Pvt. F, 90 Pa. Inf.				
	Pvt. H, 11 Pa. Inf.		1897	Logan Valley	Bellwood
Wilson, Joseph L.	Pvt. C, 19 Pa. Cav.		1884	Fairview	Altoona
Wilson, Joseph M.	Pvt. D, 192 Pa. Inf.				
Wilson, Joseph W.	Pvt. A, 125 Pa. Inf.	1834	1911	Logan Valley	Bellwood
Wilson, Matthew C.	Sgt. M, 62 Pa. Inf.				
	Sgt. K, 91 Pa. Inf.	1826	1873	Logan Valley	Bellwood
Wilson, Richard	Pvt. D, 177 N. Y. Inf.				
	Pvt. A, 91 N. Y. Inf.	1825	1902	Fairview	Altoona
Wilson, Samuel H.	Pvt. H, 15 Pa. Inf.				
	Sgt. C, 77 Pa. Inf.	1843			
Wilson, Samuel S.	Sgt. A, 1 Pa. Cav.				
Wilson, Simon M.	Pvt. M, 9 Pa. Cav.	1843			
Wilson, Stewart C.	Pvt. E, 139 Pa. Inf.	1844	1934	Rose Hill	Altoona
Wilson, William	Pvt. A, 110 Pa. Inf.		1862	Harrisburg	Pa.
Wilson, William	Pvt. K, 51 Pa. Inf.		1907	Methodist	Williamsburg
Wilson, William H.	Mjr. Couch's Staff				

SOLDIERS OF BLAIR COUNTY

Name	Rank Organization	Born	Died	Cemetery	Location
Wilson, W. T.	Col. 123 Ohio Inf.				
Wilt, Ephraim	Pvt. G, 18 Pa. Cav.	1825	1911	Lutheran	Newry
Wilt, Frederick S.	Pvt. I, 137 Pa. Inf.	1841	1936	Lutheran	Newry
Wilt, Henry M.	Pvt. E, 125 Pa. Inf.				
	Pvt. B, 107 Pa. Inf.	1837	1908	Lutheran	Newry
Wilt, Isaac W.	Pvt. I, 205 Pa. Inf.	1827	1904	Lutheran	Newry
Wilt, Jacob Y.	Pvt. B, Ind. Bn. Pa. Mil.	1842			
Wilt, Jacob	Pvt. E, 104 Pa. Inf.	1842	1910	Rose Hill	Altoona
Wilt, Joseph	Pvt. H, 14 Pa. Inf.	1836			
Wilt, Joseph	Pvt. H, 110 Pa. Inf.				
Wilt, Silas O.	Pvt. C, 110 Pa. Inf.	1826	1905	Lutheran	Newry
Wilt, William P.	Pvt. B, Ind. Bn. Pa. Mil.	1846			
Wilt, William P.	Pvt. H, 110 Pa. Inf.				
Wimer, John	Pvt. C, 53 Pa. Inf.				
Wimer, Thomas M.	Pvt. D, 192 Pa. Inf.				
Wimer, William R.	Pvt. C, 84 Pa. Inf.	1819			
Wingate, Alex B.	Pvt. H, 125 Pa. Inf.	1843	1885	Grandview	Tyrone
Wingate, J. Brown	1Lt. M, 22 Pa. Cav.	1837	1873	Presbyterian	Hollidaysburg
Wingate, J. Russell	Pvt. H, 3 Pa. Inf.				
	1Lt. G, 84 Pa. Inf.	1832	1864	Presbyterian	Hollidaysburg
Wingate, William B.	Pvt. H, 125 Pa. Inf.	1825	1874	Grandview	Tyrone
Wining, Philip	Pvt. A, 105 Pa. Inf.	1841	1913	Punxsutawney	Pa.
Winkle, William	Sgt. F, 155 Pa. Inf.	1844			
Winnaugle, William F.	Pvt. E, 12 Pa. Cav.	1844	1924	Rose Hill	Altoona
Winter, Ferdinand A.	Mus. 63 Pa. Inf.				
	Pvt. F, 56 Pa. Mil.				
	Mus. 5 Pa. Art.	1844	1926	Greenwood	Altoona
Winters, George	Pvt. B, 125 Pa. Inf.				
Winters, William	Pvt. D, 1 Pa. Art.	1846			
Wise, Cloyd L.	Mus. E, 101 Pa. Inf.	1849	1907	Fairview	Altoona
Wise, Henry A.	Pvt. K, 46 Pa. Mil.	1846			
Wise, Jacob	Pvt. C, 84 Pa. Inf.	1838	1893	Frankstown	Hollidaysburg
Wiseman, Frederick	Pvt. H, 22 Pa. Cav.	1843			
Wisel, George E.	Pvt. H, 55 Pa. Inf.	1845	1912	Fishertown	Bedford Co.
Wiser, Emanuel	Pvt. A, 110 Pa. Inf.				
Witherow, Samuel S.	Pvt. G, 208 Pa. Inf.	1836	1913	Fairview	Altoona
Withers, Henry	Pvt. B, 125 Pa. Inf.				
	Pvt. B, 208 Pa. Inf.				
Witmer, John	Sgt. K, 201 Pa. Inf.	1837	1892	Shippensburg	Pa.
Witmer, John	Pvt. C, 53 Pa. Inf.				
Witters, Levi	Pvt. K, 13 Pa. Cav.	1843			
Wittier, Jacob M.	Pvt. E, 84 Pa. Inf.				
Wogan, James P.	2Lt. H, 22 Pa. Inf.				
Woleslagle, Perry J.	Pvt. A, 195 Pa. Inf.	1847	1917	Oak Ridge	Altoona
Wolf, Daniel J.	Pvt. H, 110 Pa. Inf.				
Wolf, Henry	Pvt. E, 2 Dragoons	1839			Wash., D. C.
Wolf, Isaac P.	Pvt. A, 125 Pa. Inf.	1836	1917	Fairview	Altoona
Wolf, John C.	Pvt. C, 3 Pa. Inf.				
	2Lt. E, 84 Pa. Inf.	1844	1903	St. Josephs	Williamsburg
Wolf, John D.	Pvt. A, 77 Pa. Inf.	1841	1909	Salemville	Pa.
Wolf, John G.	Pvt. A, Ind. Bn. Pa. Mil.				
	Pvt. A, 205 Pa. Inf.	1846	1936	Oak Ridge	Altoona
Wolf, Michael	Pvt. M, 9 Pa. Cav.	1842	1864	Griswoldville	Georgia
Wolf, Michael H.	Pvt. I, 137 Pa. Inf.				
Wolf, Samuel	Pvt. M, 9 Pa. Cav.	1831	1896	Greenwood	Altoona
Wolfe, Theawalt	Pvt. A, 125 Pa. Inf.		1863	Smoketown	Maryland
Wolfe, William M.	Pvt. E, 87 Pa. Inf.	1837	1900	Harrisburg	Pa.
Wolfkill, Benjamin F.	Pvt. B, 125 Pa. Inf.	1829	1911	Fairview	Martinsburg
Wolfkill, Daniel D.	Pvt. I, 125 Pa. Inf.				
	Pvt. C, 78 Pa. Inf.	1844	1895	Oak Ridge	Altoona
Wolford, Edward	Pvt. B, 125 Pa. Inf.				
Wonderly, Forrest	Pvt. G, 12 Pa. Cav.	1847			

THE CIVIL WAR

Name	Rank Organization	Born	Died	Cemetery	Location
Wonderley, Thomas M.	Pvt. Ind. Cav. Pa. Mil.	1845			
Wonderly, William	Pvt. I, 137 Pa. Inf.				
Wonn, Paul	Pvt. K, 22 Pa. Cav.	1844			
Wood, James C.	Pvt. H, 107 N. Y. Inf.	1843	1916	Grandview	Tyrone
Woodall, James T.	Pvt. D, 41 Pa. Inf.				
	Cpl. 191 Pa. Inf.	1837			
Woodcock, Clark	Pvt. C, 110 Pa. Inf.		1865	Sailors Creek	Virginia
Woodcock, George W.	Pvt. C, 53 Pa. Inf.		1864	Spottsylvania	Virginia
Woodcock, William Lee	Pvt. F, 77 Pa. Inf.				
	1Lt. U. S. Signal Corps	1844	1925	Presbyterian	Hollidaysburg
Woodring, Henry S.	Sgt. G, 13 Pa. Cav.			Grandview	Tyrone
Woodring, Jacob	Pvt. C, 22 Pa. Cav.	1844			
Woods, Henry	Pvt. G, 2 Cal. Inf.	1814	1892	St. Johns	Altoona
Woods, John T.	Pvt. C, 46 Pa. Mil.	1846			
Woods, Potter	Pvt. E, 104 Pa. Inf.	1822	1889	Oak Ridge	Altoona
Woods, Richard	Pvt. K, 41 Pa. Inf.	1843			
Woods, Thomas	Pvt. D, 125 Pa. Inf.				
Woodward, James A.	Pvt. C, 110 Pa. Inf.				
Woolet, Sylvester B.	Pvt. C, 110 Pa. Inf.				
Womer, Aaron	Pvt. I, 205 Pa. Inf.	1836			
Woomer, Abednego B.	Pvt. C, 48 Pa. Inf.	1840	1925	Bald Eagle	Tyrone
Woomer, Andrew	Cpl. A, 125 Pa. Inf.	1836	1862	Bald Eagle	Tyrone
Woomer, James Miller	Pvt. E, 4 Pa. Cav.	1848	1912	Fairview	Altoona
Woomer, Jonathan	Pvt. H, 103 Pa. Inf.	1835	1911	Grandview	Tyrone
Woomer, Joseph	Pvt. H, 103 Pa. Inf.	1836	1926	Bald Eagle	Tyrone
Woomer, William	Pvt. H, 103 Pa. Inf.	1831	1865	Bald Eagle	Tyrone
Work, Lawrence T.	Pvt. Ind. Cav. Pa. Mil.	1826			
Worley, Aaron C.	Pvt. F, 6 U.S.C.T.	1840	1895	Oak Ridge	Altoona
Worley, William	Pvt. D, 205 Pa. Inf.	1827			
Wright, Charles C.	Pvt. A, 184 Pa. Inf.	1841	1916	Alum Bank	Bedford Co.
Wright, Jacob	Pvt. K, 55 Pa. Inf.			Upper Claar	Bedford Co.
Wright, John M.	Pvt. F, 31 Pa. Inf.				
	Pvt. A, 191 Pa. Inf.	1840			
Wright, Levi	Pvt. F, 31 Pa. Inf.				
Wright, Thomas	Pvt. E, 125 Pa. Inf.				
	Pvt. E, 13 Pa. Cav.	1841	1918	Greenfield	Bedford Co.
Wright, William D.	Pvt. E, 101 Pa. Inf.	1844	1903	Fairview	Altoona
Wunderlick, Charles A.	Pvt. A, 36 Pa. Inf.	1842	1904	Carlisle	Pa.
Wyland, John Jacob	Pvt. D, 163 Ohio Inf.	1823	1888	Oak Ridge	Altoona
Wynekoop, William H.	Pvt. E, 5 Mich. Inf.	1847	1922	Greenwood	Altoona
Yarnell, Reuben	Pvt. A, 45 Pa. Inf.	1862			
Yarrick, Joseph	Pvt. E, 104 Pa. Inf.				
Yeager, Henry C.	Pvt. H, 2 Pa. Inf.	1840			
Yeager, John	Cpl. D, 46 Pa. Inf.	1845	1918	Calvary	Altoona
Yerger, George W.	Pvt. C, 3 Pa. Inf.				
	Pvt. B, 125 Pa. Inf.				
	Sgt. H, 22 Pa. Cav.	1843			
Yerger, Henry	Pvt. K, 125 Pa. Inf.				
Yingling, Benjamin F.	Pvt. D, 22 Pa. Cav.	1845			
Yingling, Calvin	Pvt. D, 13 Pa. Cav.	1840			
Yingling, David C.	Cpl. C, 3 Pa. Inf.	1829			
Yingling, Henry M.	Pvt. H, 143 Pa. Inf.	1832	1916	Bald Eagle	Tyrone
Yingling, Jacob C.	1Lt. C, 3 Pa. Inf.	1833	1888	Yellow Springs	Williamsburg
Yingling, James A.	Pvt. E, 84 Pa. Inf.				
	Pvt. I, 57 Pa. Inf.	1836	1918	Fairview	Martinsburg
Yingling, James M.	Blk. D, 22 Pa. Cav.	1842			
Yingling, Lazarus	Pvt. C, 46 Pa. Mil.	1832			
Yingling, Martin	Pvt. L, 34 Pa. Inf.			Lutheran	Claysburg
Yingling, Moses	Pvt. C, 46 Pa. Mil.				
	Blk. D, 12 Pa. Cav.	1843	1912	Grandview	Altoona

SOLDIERS OF BLAIR COUNTY

Name	Rank Organization	Born	Died	Cemetery	Location
Yingling, Thomas C.	Cpl. B, 3 Pa. Inf.				
	Pvt. G, 12 Pa. Cav.				
	Cpl. A, 205 Pa. Inf.	1838		Mauers	Altoona
Yingling, Washington	Pvt. I, 29 Pa. Inf.	1821			
Yingling, William L.	Blk. C, 22 Pa. Cav.				
Yocum, Andrew D.	1Lt. C, 166 Pa. Inf.	1837	1889	Fairview	Altoona
Yocum, Elmer W.	Pvt. D, 205 Pa. Inf.	1841			
Yon, David A.	Pvt. D, 188 Ohio Inf.	1840	1923	Carson Valley	Duncansville
Yon, Henry	Pvt. B, 208 Pa. Inf.	1826	1906	Fairview	Altoona
Yon, Henry	Pvt. I, 102 Pa. Inf.	1842	1927	Logan Valley	Bellwood
Yon, Henry M.	Pvt. G, 88 Pa. Inf.	1846	1926	Carson Valley	Duncansville
Yon, Henry S.	Pvt. D, 46 Pa. Mil.	1828			
Yon, William	Pvt. I, 102 Pa. Inf.	1846	1927	Charlottesville	Bellwood
Yon, William W.	Pvt. K, 78 Pa. Inf.	1849	1908	Fairview	Altoona
Yost, William B.	Cpl. K, 149 Pa. Inf.	1831	1887	Doylestown	Pa.
Young, Abraham C.	Pvt. E, 3 Pa. Art.	1835	1902	Logan Valley	Bellwood
Young, Benjamin F.	Pvt. E, 104 Pa. Inf.				
Young, Charles	Cpl. B, Ind. Bn. Pa. Mil.	1825			
Young, Charles F.	Pvt. I, 205 Pa. Inf.	1825			
Young, Charles H.	Pvt. F, 84 Pa. Inf.	1842	1904	Calvary	Altoona
Young, Edwin	Pvt. C, 110 Pa. Inf.			Hopewell	Bedford Co.
Young, George B.	Sgt. I, 137 Pa. Inf.	1829	1906	Lutheran	Newry
Young, George N.	Pvt. C, 110 Pa. Inf.				
Young, Henry	Pvt. A, 100 Pa. Inf.	1844	1912	Yellow Springs	Williamsburg
Young, Jesse B.	Cpt. B, 84 Pa. Inf.	1845			
Young, John	Pvt. E, 46 Pa. Mil.	1817			
Young, John	Pvt. H, 22 Pa. Cav.	1846	1892	Oak Ridge	Altoona
Young, John W.	Mus. C, 205 Pa. Inf.	1837	1902	Greenlawn	Roaring Spring
Young, John Y.	Pvt. G, 148 Pa. Inf.				
	Pvt. B, 53 Pa. Inf.	1845	1901	Calvary	Altoona
Young, Joseph M.	Pvt. A, Ind. Bn. Pa. Mil.				
	Pvt. D, 28 Pa. Inf.	1844	1889	St. Marys	Hollidaysburg
Young, Martin L.	Pvt. C, 84 Pa. Inf.	1840	1906	Rose Hill	Altoona
Young, Peter	Pvt. A, 23 Pa. Mil.	1838			
Young, Peter H.	Pvt. A, 3 Pa. Inf.	1840	1919	St. Marys	Altoona
Young, Philip	Pvt. I, 137 Pa. Inf.	1842			
Young, Samuel	Pvt. I, 45 Pa. Inf.	1828	1912	Oak Ridge	Altoona
Young, William	Pvt. F, 49 Pa. Inf.				
Yount, James	1Lt. E, 171 Pa. Inf.	1840	1938	Huff	Altoona
Yundt, Oliver W.	Pvt. K, 158 Pa. Inf.	1841	1893	Oak Ridge	Altoona
Zeek, Emanuel	Pvt. C, 77 Pa. Inf.		1906	Birmingham	Pa.
Zeeke, Lewis R.	Pvt. C, 76 Pa. Inf.	1840	1863	Fort Wagner	South Carolina
Zeigler, John B.	Pvt. B, 149 Pa. Inf.	1843	1916	Grandview	Tyrone
Zeigler, Josiah	Pvt. C, 77 Pa. Inf.		1927	Newport	Pa.
Zemsch, Erhard	Pvt. K, 89 N. Y. Inf.	1836	1905	St. Johns	Altoona
Zentzer, Frederick	Pvt. G, 57 Pa. Inf.	1830			
Zeth, George W.	Pvt. C, 19 Pa. Cav.	1842	1916	Reform	Claysburg
Zimmerman, Henry	Pvt. A, 188 Pa. Inf.	1845	1920	Salem Reform	Williamsburg
Zimmerman, Jacob M.	Pvt. K, 3 Pa. Inf.				
	Pvt. F, 77 Pa. Inf.	1844	1907	Presbyterian	Hollidaysburg
Zimmerman, James	Pvt. D, 192 Pa. Inf.				
Zimmerman, John	Pvt. A, 84 Pa. Inf.	1794	1888	Lutheran	Hollidaysburg
Zimmerman, John K.	Pvt. D, 192 Pa. Inf.	1844	1883	Frankstown	Hollidaysburg
Zimmerman, Samuel	Pvt. F, 77 Pa. Inf.	1840	1908	Reform	Claysburg
Zimmerman, William	Pvt. F, 77 Pa. Inf.	1847	1916	Reform	Claysburg
Zimmerman, William	Pvt. A, 84 Pa. Inf.				
Zimmerman, William M.	Pvt. A, 101 Pa. Inf.	1824	1889	Grandview	Tyrone
Zitch, John W.	Cpl. B, 2 Pa. Inf.		1909	Maryville	Pa.
Zonker, Joseph	Cpl. A, 3 Pa. Inf.				
	Sgt. A, 23 Pa. Mil.	1824	1876	St. Marys	Hollidaysburg
Zook, Charles W.	Pvt. E, 37 Pa. Inf.	1844	1929	Greenlawn	Roaring Spring

THE CIVIL WAR
ADDITIONAL RECORDS

Name	Rank	Organization	Born	Died	Cemetery	Location

SOLDIERS OF BLAIR COUNTY

Name	Rank	Organization	Born	Died	Cemetery	Location

PART V
THE SPANISH-AMERICAN WAR

A brief history of the War with Spain, the Philippine Insurrection, the China Campaign (Boxer Rebellion), giving the causes, important events, battles and the ending.

A history of the military organizations of Blair County prior to the Spanish-American War, and the military organizations during the War.

A history of the camps and posts of all organizations of Spanish-American Veterans of Blair County.

A register of all Spanish-American War veterans, giving the rank, organization, year of birth and death and place of burial of deceased veterans.

SPECIAL ABBREVIATIONS USED IN THIS SECTION

B. M.......*Boiler maker*

Cps.......*Coppersmith*

Elc.......*Electrician*

G. M.......*Gunner Mate*

H. S.......*Hospital Stewart*

P. I.......*Philippine Islands*

(c)......*also served in the Civil War*

(w)......*also served in the World War*

INDEX TO PART V

THE SPANISH-AMERICAN WAR

Brief History of the Spanish-American War	285
Brief History of the Philippine Insurrection	286
Brief History of the China Campaign	286
The Pennsylvania National Guard	287
Logan Zouaves of Altoona	287
Keystone Guards of Altoona	288
Latta Guards of Altoona	288
Company F, of Altoona	288
Company D, of Altoona	288
Sheridan Troop of Tyrone	288
Company C, of Hollidaysburg	289
Company D, of Altoona	289
The Pennsylvania Volunteers	291
Company C, 5th Infantry	291
Sheridan Troop, Pennsylvania Volunteer Cavalry	291
The Home Guards	292
Veterans Organizations	293
Tyrone Camp No. 85, United Spanish War Veterans	294
Admiral Geo. Dewey Camp No. 86, United Spanish War Veterans	295
Joseph C. Robinson Camp No. 131, United Spanish War Veterans	296
Register of Spanish-American War Veterans	297

A BRIEF HISTORY OF THE SPANISH-AMERICAN WAR

The war with Spain was brought on by Spanish misrule and cruelty in the nearby island of Cuba, and involved in addition the islands of Porto Rico, the Philippines and other smaller island possessions of Spain.

The struggle of the Cubans for independence from Spanish rule first broke out in the island in 1868. Other attempts were made without success and resulted in the Spanish Government taking strong coercive action to end the insurrection. The final movement began early in 1895, and a large army was sent over, which under General Weyler proceeded ruthlessly to destroy houses and growing crops, and to prohibit, as far as possible, all productive industry. Non-combatants as well as insurgents were penned up in filthy camps, and poorly fed, where thousands died of starvation or disease.

The people of the United States aided the distressed natives with money and food, and the government tendered its good offices to bring about a termination of the conflict, but without effect. Conditions grew worse and on the evening of the 15th of February, 1898, the United States Battleship *Maine* was blown up in the harbor of Havana by a tremendous explosion, and 266 of the vessel's crew lost their lives. News of the disaster created great excitement throughout the United States, but judgment was withheld until an investigation could be made. Responsibility for the destruction of the vessel was never determined, but it was generally thought to be Spanish treachery.

President McKinley's message to Congress on the 11th of April, 1898, stated that the existing condition of affairs in Cuba was a constant menace to our peace and that the war must stop. Congress, on the 25th of April, passed a formal declaration reciting that war existed between the United States and Spain, and had existed since the 21st.

On the 25th of April, the President called for 125,000 two-year volunteers, and the regular army was reorganized and its strength increased from 27,000 to 61,000 men.

Not only the national government, but State as well, took part in the preparation for war. The various National Guards were prepared for mobilization at a moment's notice, and scores of provisional regiments were raised and offered to the governors of the various States, so they could be called out as soon as the expected call for volunteers occurred. Of these provisional regiments, the most famous was one commanded by Colonel Theodore Roosevelt, known as Roosevelt's Rough Riders, which as the First Volunteer Cavalry saw active duty in Cuba.

The principal engagements and events of the Spanish-American War were:

Las Mantanzas	West Indies	Apr. 27, 1898
Manila Bay	Philippine Islands	May 1, 1898
Manila	Philippine Islands	Aug. 13, 1898
Las Quasimas	Cuba	June 24, 1898
San Juan	Cuba	July 1, 1898
El Caney	Cuba	July 1, 1898
Santiago Bay	Cuba	July 3, 1898
Santiago	Cuba	July 17, 1898
Ponce	Porto Rico	Aug. 9, 1898

By the terms of peace as negotiated at Paris on the 10th of November, 1898, Spain relinquished Cuba, the United States assuming international responsibility for the protection of life and property in the Island; Porto Rico, Guam in the Ladrones, and the Philippine Archepelago were ceded to the United States. For the cession of the Philippines the United States agreed to pay Spain $20,000,000.

THE PHILIPPINE INSURRECTION

The Philippine Archipelago ceded by the Spanish Government for the sum of $20,000,000, comprised over fifteen hundred islands with a population of about 8,000,000. The two largest islands, Mindanao and Luzon, about the size of an average American State, were inhabited by warlike natives who resisted the authority of the United States.

Shortly after Dewey's victory in Manila Bay, and before the capture of Manila, the Filipinos under the leadership of Aguinaldo revolted against American rule, declaring that they desired independence and not a mere change of masters. A Philippine republic was proclaimed, and an insurgent government was organized with Aguinaldo at the head.

An army of Filipinos was raised and attacks were launched against the American lines about Manila, and the outbreak extended throughout the entire islands and continued for three years, during which time additional troops were shipped to the Islands and guerrilla warfare was engaged in, until all the principal towns were captured by the American forces and the hostile natives were driven into the mountains.

Many pitched battles and engagements were fought during the Philippine Insurrection, but none of them resembled a battle of major importance. Detachments of the American forces were stationed at many points and were constantly harassed by the insurgents.

The President of the United States, on the 4th of July, 1902, issued a proclamation officially declaring the insurrection in the Philippines at an end everywhere, except among the Moros.

CHINA CAMPAIGN

An anti-foreign society existing in China, known as the "Boxers," demanded the expulsion of all foreigners from the empire, and an uprising resulted in the murder of foreigners and the destruction of their property.

The foreign residents took refuge in the legations and defended their lives with arms. Telegraphic connections with the outside world were cut off and the safety of the besieged was unknown, while troops of the various nations fought their way to the aid of the besieged.

American troops participated in the relief expedition which extended from the 20th of June, 1900, until the 12th of May, 1901.

The principal events in which American troops participated were:

Yangstun	China	Aug. 6, 1900
Tientsin	China	Aug. 19, 1900
Hoshiwu	China	Aug. 24, 1900
Chang Ping Chow	China	Sept. 4, 1900

The members of the society were defeated and punished where ever found and the government of China was required to pay an indemnity to cover damages to the property of the foreigners.

PENNSYLVANIA NATIONAL GUARD

Following the close of the Civil War, interest in the activities and organization of the Pennsylvania Militia received the attention of those persons connected with the military affairs of the State, and a re-organization of the militia was inaugurated. The Act of the 7th of April, 1870, increased the number of divisions from twenty to twenty-one and changed the title from the Pennsylvania Militia to the National Guard of Pennsylvania.

The military system of the United States had changed from the compulsory responding to militia muster that had been in effect during the early days, and was of more recent years on an entirely volunteer system, except for the necessary drafts during the war periods when insufficient numbers of volunteers responded.

The organization of military companies was almost entirely a local affair. Members were enrolled and continued in good standing so long as they attended drill or displayed some interest in the activities of the company. They could be discharged or resign at any time, and many were discharged or dropped from the rolls for failing to attend drills.

The officers were elected by the members of the organization, and they continued to hold their rank and title until voted out at the next annual election, or their services terminated by resignation, death or other causes.

Very little equipment or support was furnished the units by the State during these days. The State furnished arms and such equipment, but the uniforms and other items were supplied by the individual.

A re-organization of the National Guard of Pennsylvania was enacted by law on the 12th of June, 1878, at which time the twenty-one divisions were abolished in favor of a single division as in existence at the present time.

This law provided that each soldier of the National Guard be provided with a uniform similar to that worn by the troops of the United States, and other equipment consisting of an overcoat, blanket bag, haversack, canteen, ration can, knife, fork, spoon, tin cup and rubber blanket. The law also authorized the State to appropriate the sum of six hundred dollars to each company of infantry, and one thousand dollars to each troop of cavalry or battery of artillery.

A history of the Blair County units of the Pennsylvania Militia and National Guard is found herewith. Infantry companies located in this section of the State were part of the 5th Regiment and at the time of an inspection held at Hollidaysburg, on the 3rd of May, 1876, the regiment was commanded by Colonel James F. Milliken, and the Adjutant was J. Irvin Brotherline.

LOGAN ZOUAVES

A military company known as the Logan Zouaves was organized at Altoona on the 1st of December, 1866. Forty-three of the full strength of one hundred and three members were secured at the original meeting. Requirements for membership included that the men had seen service during the Civil War. This was the first military unit to be formed in Blair County following the Civil War.

Official recognition was accorded this company as a unit of the Pennsylvania Militia on the 9th of February, 1867, and the following members were mustered into the service as the officers: Captain Frank B. Stewart, First Lieutenant William H. Mulberry, Second Lieutenant Henry A. Folk, all from Altoona.

This company was armed with short Enfield rifles and sabre bayonets, furnished by the State, and continued as an active unit of the State Militia until the 7th of December, 1869, when it disbanded.

KEYSTONE GUARDS

Another effort to form a military organization was attempted in 1871, at which time a company of infantry, known as the Keystone Guards, was formed.

This company was mustered into the service as a unit of the Pennsylvania National Guard on the 3rd of June, 1871, with the following officers: Captain Harry A. Miller, First Lieutenant Theodore Burchfield, and Second Lieutenant Charles L. Gettinger.

LATTA GUARDS

The Keystone Guards were designated the Latta Guards on the 11th of February, 1874, without any changes in the names of the officers.

The Latta Guards were named in honor of Colonel James W. Latta, who commanded the First Regiment of Infantry, Pennsylvania National Guards. He was named the Adjutant General of Pennsylvania on the 2nd of June, 1873, and through his untiring efforts, the National Guard of Pennsylvania became an efficient organization. He commanded the National Guard under the one division organization and retired, after years of service, as a Major General.

COMPANY F

The Latta Guards were re-designated Company F, 5th Regiment of Infantry, Pennsylvania National Guard, on the 30th of June, 1874, without any change in the commanding personnel.

COMPANY D

Company F, was re-designated Company D, 5th Regiment of Infantry, Pennsylvania National Guard, on the 1st of August, 1874, with the following named officers: Captain Theodore Burchfield, First Lieutenant Malden Valentine, and Second Lieutenant G. H. Manson.

This unit continued active until the 5th of September, 1877, when it disbanded.

SHERIDAN TROOP

The Sheridan Troop of Cavalry, Pennsylvania National Guard, was organized at Tyrone on the 15th of July, 1871. Forty-two members were present at this meeting and steps were taken to secure recognition by the State and to secure the sabres and belts which was the only equipment furnished by the State at that time.

The following named officers were elected at the time of organizing: Captain Charles S. W. Jones, First Lieutenant Johnson C. Akers, Second Lieutenant Rudolph Ginerick.

The first order issued by this troop read as follows: "Headquarters, Sheridan Troop, Tyrone, Pa., June 9, 1871. Company Order No. 1; Sheridan Troop will assemble at Headquarters June 16, 8:30 P. M. Uniforms, Equipment and other business of importance requires your presence. Be prompt and plenty. C. S. W. Jones, Captain. S. B. Templeton, 1st Sergeant."

This Troop was named in honor of Major General Philip H. Sheridan of Civil War fame, who commanded the cavalry forces under General Ulysses S. Grant during the operations in Virginia in the latter years of the war.

The Sheridan Troop has been in continuous existence since 1871, except for short periods for re-organization, but the interest in cavalry activities dates prior to the Civil War, when a Troop of Cavalry was organized at Tyrone with James Crowthers as Captain.

Captain Charles S. W. Jones served in command of this Troop until his death in 1905, during which time the Troop served on riot and emergency duty on different occasions, and attended the annual encampments, one of which was held at Lakemont, Blair County, in 1893.

During the early days of the history of the Troop, armories were maintained at Tyrone, Warriors Mark, Bellwood and in Sinking Valley, for each platoon. A large three story building was later erected at Tyrone for troop headquarters and dedicated on the 16th of June, 1893.

The Sheridan Troop saw active service during the Spanish-American War, as the Sheridan Troop, Pennsylvania Volunteer Cavalry.

COMPANY C

A unit of the Pennsylvania National Guard was organized at Hollidaysburg, during the early part of 1879. The application was dated the 27th of February, 1879, and forwarded to Harrisburg where it was approved on the 19th of March, 1879.

The inspection and muster was held at Hollidaysburg on the 5th of April, 1879, at which time the following officers were commissioned: Captain Trevanion Dallas Wilkins, First Lieutenant James P. Stewart, and Second Lieutenant Joseph Dysart Hemphill.

The old Methodist Church building on Walnut Street, now the Gildea Garage, was used as the armory for many years. The dedication of this building as recorded in the *Altoona Tribune* of the 12th of April, 1883, read as follows: "The old Methodist Church building on Walnut Street, Hollidaysburg, having been purchased by Company C, 5th Regiment, National Guard of Pennsylvania, and having been remodeled and re-arranged, to suit the convenience and the taste of the military was formally dedicated Thursday evening, April 7, 1883.

"The Social Cornet band was present and began the proceedings by treating the audience to several artistically rendered pieces of music. Then Company C, under command of Captain E. Gerst, its new commander, gave a drill which made it perfectly manifest to the military critics in attendance that the company is about as near perfection as they make them and that the new Captain is the right man in the right place.

"The first speaker of the evening was Martin Bell, Esq., who in an admirable address gave a graphic picture of the military history of the denizens of the Juniata Valley from the earliest times down to the revolutionary struggle, the War of 1812, the Mexican War and the great War of the rebellion.

"The next and last speaker of the evening was W. I. Woodcock, Esq., who confined his remarks to a history of Company C, the changes in its officers, its financial standing, etc."

The names of those who served this company as Captain are as follows: James P. Stewart, Ephraim Gerst, Martin Bell and John H. West. Company C, attended the regimental encampment held at Camp William G. Murray, at Roaring Spring, in July, 1886 and one held at Camp Lieutenant S. C. Potts, near Altoona, in August, 1893.

Company C, 5th Regiment of Infantry, Pennsylvania National Guard, took part in the inauguration of President Garfield on the 4th of March, 1881, and that of President Harrison on the 4th of March, 1889. It was one of the twelve companies to attend the centennial anniversary of the surrender of Cornwallis at Yorktown on the 19th of October, 1881, and also attended the centennial anniversary of the inauguration of President Washington at New York in 1889.

This company had active service during the Spanish-American War as Company C, 5th Regiment of Infantry, Pennsylvania Volunteers.

COMPANY D

A company of the Pennsylvania National Guard was organized at Elway's Hall, Altoona, on the 7th of August, 1879, at which time the following named officers were elected and mustered: Captain R. W. Guthrie, First Lieutenant Thomas W. Jackson, and Second Lieutenant John Miller.

The muster roll contained the names of fifty members; however, only thirty-three members were present when the company was mustered by Captain McLean.

Colonel Theodore Burchfield, Commander of the 5th Regiment, spoke at the occasion of the mustering of Company D into the service as a unit of the Pennsylvania Guard.

This company did not continue active long, but passed out of existence within a few years.

COMPANY D

In 1882, another attempt was made to organize a company in Altoona, as evidenced by the following item which appeared in the *Altoona Tribune* of the 13th of April, 1882: "Special Order No. 10; An election for officers of the military company, lately recruited at Altoona, Pa., by W. C. Westfall and others, will be held at Altoona on Tuesday, April 18, 1882, and will be conducted by Colonel Theodore Burchfield, 5th Regiment, who is hereby authorized to fix the hour at which the same will open. The Company will be known as Company 'D', 5th Regiment, National Guard.

"By order of Brigadier General James A. Beaver, D. S. Keller, Assistant Adjutant General."

Company D, 5th Regiment of Infantry, Pennsylvania National Guard, was mustered on the 22nd of April, 1882, and the results of the election were as follows: Captain Robert B. Guthrie, First Lieutenant Vincent D. Hudson, and Second Lieutenant William L. Nagele.

This company continued in existence until the 13th of April, 1887, when it disbanded.

No other attempt is known to have been made to revive or to organize a military unit of the Pennsylvania National Guard in Altoona during the period from 1887 until the Spanish-American War, and no unit of the Guard represented Altoona in that war. However, a number of Altoona citizens enrolled in Company C, of Hollidaysburg, and in other units, and a number of them saw active duty during the period of the war.

THE PENNSYLVANIA VOLUNTEERS

Upon the declaration of war with Spain on the 21st of April, 1898, the entire National Guard of Pennsylvania was called for duty, and responded on the 27th of April. The troops were mobilized at Mount Gretna where they were mustered into Federal Service.

Some units of the Pennsylvania National Guard saw service in the Philippine Islands, while other units were stationed in southern camps and did not see active field duty.

Company C of the 5th Regiment of Infantry of Hollidaysburg, and the Sheridan Troop of Tyrone were the only units composed entirely of residents of Blair County and vicinity. A number of men were recruited at Altoona for service with the 28th and 43rd regiments of Infantry, United States Volunteers, and saw service in the Philippine Islands.

COMPANY C, 5TH REGIMENT INFANTRY, PENNSYLVANIA VOLUNTEERS

Company C, 5th Regiment of Infantry, Pennsylvania Volunteers under the command of Captain John H. West, left Hollidaysburg on the 27th of April, 1898, and arrived at Mount Gretna on the morning of the 28th, being one of the first units to report.

On May 11, 1898, the regiment was mustered into the service of the United States by Major W. A. Thompson, United States Army, and was comprised of thirty-seven officers and six hundred and four enlisted men. The regiment broke camp at Mount Gretna on the 17th of May, 1898, and entrained for Chickamauga, Georgia, where it arrived on the 19th. It bivouacked for the night on Snodgrass Hill, and on the following day went into camp along the Alexander Bridge road, where it remained until the 12th of August, when it moved to a better camp site along the Brotherton road.

While encamped at Chickamauga Park, Georgia, the regiment was recruited to full strength and trained for active warfare. The sanitary conditions being unsatisfactory, resulting in much sickness, the regiment was moved by rail on the 22nd of August, to Camp Hamilton, near Lexington, Kentucky.

The objective of the war having been accomplished by the sinking of the Spanish Fleet, and the surrender by the Spanish of the Philippine and West Indies Islands, the services of the army being no longer required, the 5th Regiment was accordingly granted, on the 17th of September, 1898, a thirty-day furlough and Company C arrived at Hollidaysburg on the 18th.

Headquarters for the 5th Regiment were established at Altoona and after the expiration of the furlough, ten days were given for muster out, which time was increased twenty additional days to permit the regiment to participate in the Peace Jubilee at Philadelphia, on the 27th of October, 1898.

The members of the 5th Regiment of Infantry, Pennsylvania Volunteers, were finally discharged on the 7th of November, 1898. Company C, served under the following officers: John H. West, Captain; David S. Barr, First Lieutenant; William A. Van-Allman, Second Lieutenant.

SHERIDAN TROOP, PENNSYLVANIA VOLUNTEER CAVALRY

The Sheridan Troop entrained at Tyrone on the 27th of April, 1898, for Mount Gretna where it arrived on the following day. Here it was mustered into the service of the United States on the 11th of May, as the Sheridan Troop, Pennsylvania Volunteer Cavalry. Upon being equipped and drilled for field service, the Troop entrained on the

7th of July, for Camp Alger, Virginia, as a part of a temporary squadron, and was there attached to the Second Army Corps.

The squadron proceeded on the 24th of July, 1898, to Newport News, Virginia, where it embarked on the 5th of August, aboard the transport *"Manitoba"* for Porto Rico. On the 10th of August, the transport ran aground two miles off Port de Ponce, requiring the transfer of the men and horses to other boats, and by the time the squadron was ready to proceed to the front, information of the signing of the Peace Protocol was received and the Troops were ordered to land at Port de Ponce, where a camp was established on the Cathedral grounds. The squadron was later moved to a camp several miles northwest of the City of Ponce.

The Sheridan Troop with other units returned to the United States aboard the transport *"Mississippi,"* sailing on the 3rd of September and arriving at Jersey City, New Jersey, on the 10th of September. The troop proceeded at once to Tyrone, where it arrived on the 11th, and after a sixty-day furlough was finally mustered out of the United States service on the 16th of November, 1898.

The Sheridan Troop was commanded by Captain Charles S. W. Jones until the 27th of July, 1898, when he was promoted to Major, and First Lieutenant Luther F. Crawford was promoted to Captain. The other officers were: Harry S. Fleck, First Lieutenant, and Adam L. Dickson, Second Lieutenant.

THE HOME GUARDS

During the absence of Company C, 5th Regiment of Infantry, a unit known as Company F, 21st Regiment of Provisional Guards, was organized at Hollidaysburg on July 2, 1898, as a home defense unit, under the following officers: Harry A. Miller, Captain; Samuel Royer Dibert, First Lieutenant, and Charles A. Beswick, 2nd Lieutenant.

VETERANS ORGANIZATIONS

Organizations composed of the returned veterans of the Spanish-American War, the Philippine Insurrection and the China Campaign were formed soon after the return of the soldiers. The first units took into membership only those who had seen foreign service, but as time advanced an organization of these veterans came into existence which included all who had honorable military service during the war.

The origin and early history of the first organizations is as follows:

An organization known as the American Veterans of Foreign Service was chartered in the State of Ohio on the 11th of October, 1899, and this name continued in use, upon the consolidation of several units, until the year 1913.

The Colorado Society, Army of the Philippines, was organized in Denver, Colorado, on the 12th of December, 1899, and upon its consolidation with other units, was given number one, and continues to the present time as Post No. 1, Veterans of Foreign Wars of the United States.

On the 6th of June, 1901, members of the Forty-third United States Volunteers were welcomed home from the Philippine Islands by the citizens of Altoona, and a few days later several of the returned soldiers took steps to form an organization. A meeting was held in the Eagle House on the 10th of July, and an organization perfected to be known as the Society of Philippine War Veterans. This unit was first assigned the number 2, when it consolidated with other units as the American Veterans of Foreign Service. The number was later changed to 3, and it is now known as the James L. Noble Post No. 3, Veterans of Foreign Wars of the United States.

In June, 1902, an organization was formed at Philadelphia and called the Society of American Veterans of the Philippine and China Wars, and when merged with other units into the American Veterans of Foreign Service it was assigned number 1. Its number was changed when Denver joined and is known at present as Post No. 2.

Efforts were made elsewhere along the same line to organize the returned war veterans. Several units were organized, then consolidated, and out of these efforts we have today two prominent organizations—the Veterans of Foreign Wars of the United States and the United Spanish War Veterans.

Three camps of the United Spanish War veterans exists in Blair County at present. Eligibility to membership includes all persons who served during the period of the Spanish-American War, the Philippine Insurrection and the China Campaign.

The David Cassidy Camp of the United Spanish War Veterans was organized at Hollidaysburg early in 1920, but became inactive after a few years.

The first officers of the David Cassidy Camp were: Commander, William A. Van Allman; Senior Vice Commander, Samuel C. Kagarise; Junior Vice Commander, Nelson Lynn; Officer of the Day, Joseph W. Shufflebotham; Officer of the Guard, William J. Long; Adjutant, Samuel Calvin; Quartermaster, George C. Irwin; Chaplain, Herman Treese; Historian, Charles R. Simpson.

This camp was named in honor of the memory of David Cassidy, who was born on the 25th of November, 1864. He enlisted as a Private in Company C, 5th Regiment of Infantry, Pennsylvania Volunteers, on the 10th of May, 1898, and was discharged on the 7th of November, 1898. He died on the 8th of August, 1899, and is buried in the St. Johns Cemetery at Altoona.

The members of the Sheridan Troop of Tyrone who participated in the service performed by the Troop in Porto Rico during the Spanish-American War, have formed an organization known as the Sheridan Troop Veterans Association, and meetings are held annually at which time officers are elected and plans are made to continue their organization so long as any of their members survive.

SOLDIERS OF BLAIR COUNTY
TYRONE CAMP NO. 85

A camp of the United Spanish War Veterans was organized at Tyrone on the 11th of August, 1920, by the veterans of the Spanish-American War, Philippine Insurrection and the China Campaign; assigned the number 85, and named after the town of Tyrone.

The names of the charter members are as follows: G. Conrad Albright, Charles F. Bateman, Roger T. Bayard, Walter C. Biddle, C. P. Blain, Paul L. Bonner, Philip Carper, Warren F. Conrad, Luther F. Crawford, Adam L. Dickson, George M. Eckroth, Harry S. Fleck, John K. Fleck, John S. Fleck, Verne C. Fortney, Harry H. Gensimore, William H. Gingery, John H. Grazier, William J. Hain, John B. Hastings, Edward W. Herlt, Lannie C. Keefer, Adam J. List, J. Howard Lotz, J. Milliken McWilliams, James F. Moore, James O. Noll, George W. Owens, William P. Owens, Rudolph H. D. Raabe, Jacob D. Rutherford, Edward K. Steets, Jesse G. Smith, Ralph L. Stryker, Alexander C. Trimble, James Trimble and W. E. Williams.

The names of the past commanders are as follows:

1920	Adam L. Dickson
1921	Alexander C. Trimble
1922	G. Conrad Albright
1923	Verne C. Fortney
1924	John B. Smith
1925	Luther F. Crawford
1926	Roger T. Bayard
1927	Harry S. Fleck
1928-1929	Charles F. Bateman
1930-1931	Herbert E. Akers
1932	John B. Hastings
1933-1934-1935	J. Howard Lotz
1936	Walter C. Biddle
1937-1938	Ralph L. Stryker
1939	George O. Derrick

The members of the Tyrone Camp of the United Spanish War Veterans took over the duties of the Colonel D. M. Jones Post No. 172, Grand Army of the Republic, when the Civil War veterans were no longer able to care for the graves of their comrades or to arrange for the observance of patriotic occasions. All cemeteries are visited annually prior to Memorial Day by the members of Camp No. 85 at which time they decorate the graves of all deceased veterans and hold appropriate services.

The officers of Tyrone Camp No. 85, for the year 1939 were:

Commander	George O. Derrick
Senior Vice Commander	G. Conrad Albright
Junior Vice Commander	John G. Smith
Adjutant	George W. Owens
Quartermaster	Adam L. Dickson
Chaplain	John B. Hastings
Officer of the Day	Rudolph H. D. Raabe
Officer of the Guard	Alexander C. Trimble

Trustees—Adam L. Dickson, George W. Owens and Harry S. Fleck

The Tyrone Camp meets on the last Friday of each month in the Municipal Building, in rooms used for many years by the veterans of the Civil War, which were set aside by ordinance for the use of organizations of the veterans of the various wars.

The newly elected officers for the year 1940 are: Commander, Alexander C. Trimble; Senior Vice Commander, Lannie C. Keefer; Junior Vice Commander, Harry E. Kauffman; Adjutant, George W. Owens; Quartermaster, Adam L. Dickson; Historian, John S. Fleck; Chaplain, John D. Hastings; Officer of the Day, G. Conrad Albright; Officer of the Guard, John E. Ghaner; Trustees—Harry S. Fleck, Adam L. Dickson and George W. Owens.

ADMIRAL GEORGE DEWEY CAMP NO. 86

The veterans of the Spanish-American War, Philippine Insurrection and China Campaign of Altoona and vicinity are organized as the Admiral George Dewey Camp No. 86, United Spanish War Veterans.

A charter dated the 17th of September, 1920, but which took effect the 30th of August, 1920, contains the following names as the charter members: George A. Breckbeil, Frank Y. Brehman, David S. Barr, J. Hewitt Christy, Harry L. Clarke, Benjamin H. DeTurk, Daniel J. Finn, Joseph Fonner, Wesley L. Goodman, Michael L. Geisinger, Harry H. Hess, Joseph H. Hamilton, Stephen E. Isaac, Harry L. Johnston, Joseph F. Kelly, Edward M. Lotz, William C. Leamer, William J. Long, Harry E. Myers, Perle S. Nevitt, Elmer J. Noland, George L. Olewine, Harry S. Parker, William J. Samuels, Robert F. Sassaman, Walter B. Seward, H. Joseph Schwartz, J. Harry Shearer, Samuel E. Shoup, Raphael R. Sites, Ellis M. Stewart, Ernest D. Thompson, Gilbert H. Weiss, H. B. Weiser and Samuel F. Yocum.

Many of the veterans of the Spanish-American War, Philippine Insurrection and China Campaign had previously affiliated with other organizations, some of which passed out of existence while others consolidated. Upon the re-organization of the James L. Noble Post No. 3, Veterans of Foreign Wars of the United States, in 1919, when many returned veterans of the World War who had foreign service became eligible for membership, a group of the veterans of the Spanish-American War found it advisable to form an organization whose membership would be distinctly of the Spanish-American War service.

Camp No. 86, United Spanish War Veterans, was named in honor of the memory of George Dewey, an American naval officer, who as Commader of the Asiatic Squaddron, when war was declared with Spain, was ordered to "capture or destroy the Spanish Squadron." Admiral Dewey's Squadron entered the channel of Manila and there, on Sunday morning, the 1st of May, 1898, sank, burned or captured all the ships of the Spanish Squadron in the bay, silenced and destroyed three land batteries, obtained complete control of the bay, without losing a single man.

The names of those who served as commander of Camp No. 86, are as follows: George A. Brechbeil, David S. Barr, J. Harry Shearer, Frank Y. Brehman, Samuel F. Yocum, Robert F. Sassaman, Charles C. Harris, John B. Roland, John P. Huller, Norman R. Palmer, Charles E. Knighton, Ormond H. Kyle, John P. Huller, Samuel E. Shoup, Herbert F. Fleck, Harry H. Hess, George P. Hoover, Wesley L. Goodman, Henry J. Waltz, Henry Mitchell and Joseph F. Kelly.

A ladies auxiliary organization known as Camp Dewey No. 46, was instituted in May, 1923, with a charter dated the 6th of August, 1923. Mrs. Robert G. Prosser is serving as President for the year 1940.

A marching unit numbering thirty-eight members, dressed in uniforms of blue and gray colors, represents the Camp on all public and patriotic occasions as well at all conventions.

Camp No. 86 was instrumental in having a shell erected in front of the new Post Office, Eleventh Avenue and Twelfth Street, Altoona, on which a bronze plaque was placed containing this inscription, "Memorial Projectile, Erected in honor of the Soldiers and Sailors of the Spanish-American War. This projectile was fired from one of the guns of the Fleet of the United States Navy at Santiago, Cuba, June 23, 1898. Erected by U. S. W. V. and V. F. W. of Altoona, Pa."

The Altoona Camp meets on the first and third Tuesdays of each month in the V. F. W. Memorial Home, 1301 17th Street. The officers for the year 1939 are as follows: Commander, Henry Mitchell; Senior Vice Commander, Joseph F. Kelly; Junior Vice Commander, Robert C. Prosser; Adjutant, David S. Barr; Officer of the Day, Chester F. Hutchison; Officer of the Guard, Norman R. Palmer; Chaplain, Ormond H. Kyle; Quartermaster, Herbert F. Fleck; Trustees, David S. Barr, Ormond H. Kyle and Samuel E. Shoup. The commander for the year 1940 is Joseph F. Kelly.

SOLDIERS OF BLAIR COUNTY
JOSEPH C. ROBINSON CAMP NO. 131

A Camp of the United Spanish War Veterans was organized at Hollidaysburg on the first of June, 1929, with twenty-six charter members, fifteen of whom transferred from the Admiral George Dewey Camp of Altoona, and named the Joseph C. Robinson Camp No. 131.

The names of the charter members are as follows: Samuel A. Andrews, Howard W. Burket, Samuel Calvin, Paul Clodgu, Edward T. Eboch, Edgar W. Hill, George C. Irwin, Samuel C. Kagarise, Asberry Kantner, Nelson Lynn, Charles A. Malone, James D. Malone, Harry Martin, Harry D. McKee, Edward B. Metzer, John I. Mock, Harry E. Myers, William Onkst, Joseph W. Shufflebotham, William Smith, Charles S. Stiffler, George A. Sullivan, William A. Van Allman, John F. Walsh, Charles H. Womer and Blaine Yingling.

This camp was named in honor of the memory of Joseph C. Robinson, who was born in 1877, and who enlisted as a Private in Company C, 5th Regiment of Infantry, Pennsylvania Volunteers, for duty during the Spanish-American War, on the 21st day of June, 1898, and served with his regiment at Chickamauga, Georgia, where he died on the 15th day of August, 1898. His body was returned to his home and buried in the Presbyterian Cemetery at Hollidaysburg.

The members of the Joseph C. Robinson Camp who have served in the capacity of Commander are as follows:

1929	Georges C. Irwin
1930	Samuel Calvin
1931	Paul Clodgu
1932	Harry Martin
1933	Samuel C. Kagarise
1934	James D. Malone
1935	William J. Samuels
1936	Joseph W. Shufflebotham
1937	Simon R. Wert
1938	Asberry Kantner
1939	Martin B. Christy

The members of this Camp take an active part in the observance of public and patriotic occasions, and hold their meetings on the second and fourth Fridays of each month in the rooms of the Fort Fetter Post, American Legion, in the Wolf Building, corner of Allegheny and Front Streets. The membership for the year 1939 was twenty-six.

Joseph W. Shufflebotham, a member of this Camp, served as President of the Mid-Western council of the State of Pennsylvania, and received for the year of 1940, the appointment of Aide to the National Commander, George Eberly.

The officers for the year 1939 are as follows:

Commander	Martin B. Christy
Senior Vice Commander	Edward T. Eboch
Junior Vice Commander	J. Patrick Cummings
Adjutant	Joseph W. Shufflebotham
Quartermaster	John F. Walsh
Chaplain	Harry Martin
Officer of the Day	Joseph Ditzer

Trustees—John F. Walsh, Martin B. Christy and Harry Martin

The Joseph C. Robinson Camp No. 131, succeeded the David Cassidy Camp in conducting the affairs of the Spanish-American War Veterans of Hollidaysburg when the David Cassidy Camp became inactive.

The officers elected to serve the Camp during the year 1940 are as follows: Commander, Edward T. Eboch; Senior Vice Commander, J. Patrick Cummings; Junior Vice Commander, Charles A. Malone; Adjutant, Joseph W. Shufflebothom; Quartermaster, John F. Walsh; Chaplain, Harry Martin; Officer of the Day, Joseph Ditzer; Trustees, John F. Walsh, Martin B. Christy and Harry Martin.

THE SPANISH-AMERICAN WAR 297

Name	Rank Organization	Born	Died	Cemetery	Location
Ackerman, Lee H.	Art. A, 20 Inf.	1873	1929	Grandview	Altoona
Addleman, Ernest L.	Sgt. Sheridan Troop		1901	Burkets	Warriors Mark
Addleman, Verner C.	Pvt. Sheridan Troop	1874	1933		Oregon
Aiken, Richard					
Aikey, L. D.	Cpt. A, 41 US. Vol. Inf.				
Akers, Herbert E.	Pvt. C, 43 US. Vol. Inf.	1875	1935	Logan Valley	Bellwood
Albright, G. Conrad	Pvt. Sheridan Troop				
Allen, David A.	Pvt. M, 28 US. Vol. Inf.		1899	Grandview	Tyrone
Anderson, Blake W.	Pvt. C, 5 Pa. Inf.	1879	1932	Fairview	Martinsburg
Andrews, Samuel A.	Cpl. C, 5 Pa. Inf.				
Arble, Adam B.	Cpl. Sheridan Troop				
Archey, James M.	Pvt. Marine Corps	1880	1932	Conemaugh	Pa.
Ayres, Charles W.					
Baker, Jesse D.	Cpl. I, 8 Pa. Inf.				
Barnes, Carl L.	Cpl. E, 14 Pa. Inf.	1873	1932	Rose Hill	Altoona
Barr, David S.	1Lt. C, 5 Pa. Inf.				
Barrett, Harry M.	Pvt. F, 5 Pa. Inf.				
Bartley, James P.	Pvt. C, 5 Pa. Inf.	1870	1936	Calvary	Altoona
Bashart, J. J.					
Bateman, Charles F.	Pvt. Sheridan Troop	1874	1938	Boalsburg	Pa.
Bateman, Thomas P.	Pvt. Sheridan Troop				
Baumgardner, Thomas R.	Pvt. K, 8 Inf.	1877	1933	Oakridge	Altoona
Bayard, Roger Thomas	Sgt. B, 5 Pa. Inf.				
Beard, Charles C.	Pvt. C, 5 Pa. Inf.				
Bender, Francis A. (w)	Pvt. A, 43 US. Vol. Inf.				
	Mus. M, 22 Inf.	1878	1918	Oise-Argonne	France
Biddle, Walter C.	Pvt. Sheridan Troop				
Beihl, Charles W.	Smn. U. S. Navy				
Bingman, Edgar L.	Pvt. A, 43 US. Vol. Inf.	1879	1913	Fairview	Altoona
Black, Harry A.	Pvt. Sheridan Troop				
Black, James E.	Sgt. C, 43 US. Vol. Inf.				
Black, Victor H.	Sgt. A, 5 Pa. Inf.	1880	1930	Grandview	Altoona
Blackburn, Lloyd E.	Pvt. Sheridan Troop				
Blackstone, Wesley S.	Pvt. B, 17 Inf.				
Blake, Roland G. (w)	Pvt. C, 5 Pa. Inf.				
Blanchard, Alcyone D.	Smn. U. S. Navy				
Blover, Thos. H.					
Bookhamer, David G.	Pvt. C, 5 Pa. Inf.				
Bookhamer, Isaac L.	Cpl. A, 5 Pa. Inf.	1870	1918	Green Lawn	Roaring Spring
Bowers, James E.	Pvt. E, 3 Cav.				
Bradley, William S.	Pvt. B, 5 Pa. Inf.				
	Pvt. B, 7 Inf.				
	Pvt. L, 37 US. Vol. Inf.	1871	1911	Rose Hill	Altoona
Brawley, William J.					
Brechbiel, George A.	Mus. D, 5 Pa. Inf.				
Brehman, Frank Yenser	Sgt. C, 5 Pa. Inf.	1870	1933	Fairview	Altoona
Brickner, Wilbert J.	Pvt. C, 43 US. Vol. Inf.	1879	1911	St. Patricks	Gallitzin
Briggs, Lloyd M.	Sgt. L, 8 Cav.	1877	1901	Grandview	Tyrone
Brown, Charles B.	Pvt. Sheridan Troop	1870	1901	Grandview	Tyrone
Brown, Henry E.	Pvt. C, 5 Pa. Inf.				
Brown, Walter A.	Cpl. Field Art.	1877	1922	Fairview	Altoona
Brubaker, John Lambert	Sgt. Sheridan Troop				
Buchanan, Samuel W.	Pvt. I, 8 Inf.				
Bumgardner, Roy	Pvt. C, 8 Inf.				
Burchfield, Herbert E.	2Lt. K, 5 Pa. Inf.				
Burchfield, James N.	Sgt. F, 2 Va. Inf.	1864	1933	Logan Valley	Bellwood
Burchfield, Theodore (c)	Col. 5 Pa. Inf.	1842	1923	Fairview	Altoona
Burket, Howard W.	Sgt. I, 28 US. Vol. Inf.				
Butler, Edwin J.	Pvt. Sheridan Troop				
Butler, Joseph H.	Sgt. 5 Pa. Inf.	1861	1916	St. Johns	Altoona
Butt, Gilbert S.	Pvt. M, 2 Cav.	1879	1939	Mifflintown	Pa.

SOLDIERS OF BLAIR COUNTY

Name	Rank Organization	Born	Died	Cemetery	Location
Caldwell, David	Pvt. C, 5 Pa. Inf.	1868	1937	Gollipolis	Ohio
Calvin, Samuel (w)	Pvt. C, 5 Pa. Inf.				
Campbell, Edward S.	Pvt. C, 5 Pa. Inf.				
Carlin, Thomas B.	Pvt. Signal Corps	1865	1900	St. Johns	Altoona
Carper, Philip	Pvt. Sheridan Troop				
Cartwright, Orville B.	Mus. E, 5 Pa. Inf.	1879	1920	Oak Ridge	Altoona
Cassidy, David	Pvt. C, 5 Pa. Inf.	1864	1899	St. Johns	Altoona
Chamberlain, John S.	Pvt. Sheridan Troop	1869	1911	Warriors Mark	Pa.
Cherry, Benjamin H.	Cpl. C, 43 US. Vol. Inf.	1877	1902	Logan Valley	Bellwood
Chidwick, John P.	Cpn. U. S. Navy	1863	1935	New York	New York
Christy, James Hewitt	Pvt. C, 5 Pa. Inf.				
Christy, Martin B.	Cpl. A, 12 Pa. Inf.				
Clark, Frank S.	Pvt. M, 1 Ky. Inf.	1869	1929	Calvary	Altoona
Clark, Harry L.	Pvt. G, 5 Pa. Inf.				
Clodgu, Paul	Pvt. 1 Vt. Inf.				
Cole, Newton E.	Pvt. Sheridan Troop				
Cole, Thomas H.	Pvt. L, 5 Pa. Inf.				
Coleman, James E.	Sgt. Sheridan Troop	1873	1939	Fairview	Altoona
Collary, James D.	Pvt. H, 3 Inf.				
Confer, Harry T.	Pvt. Sheridan Troop				
Confer, Lloyd E.	Pvt. Sheridan Troop		1937	Burkets	Warriors Mark
Conrad, Warren F.	Cpl. Sheridan Troop				
Cover, William T.	Pvt. C, 5 Pa. Inf.	1872	1909	Fairview	Altoona
Cox, Robert Edward (w)	G. M. U. S. Navy	1875	1937	Rose Hill	Altoona
Crawford, James C.	Pvt. Sheridan Troop				
Crawford, Luther F.	Cpt. Sheridan Troop	1859	1930	Grandview	Tyrone
Crum, Ira A.	Pvt. C, 5 Pa. Inf.	1878	1916	Fairview	Altoona
Cummings, J. Patrick	Pvt. D, 17 Inf.				
Cunningham, Harry C.	Pvt. C, 5 Pa. Inf.				
Curry, Robert C.	Pvt. C, 43 US. Vol. Inf.				
Curtin, James L.	Pvt. B, 5 Pa. Inf.				
Curtis, Burch E.	Pvt. F, 8 Inf.	1883	1925	Fairview	Altoona
Darby, Arthur	Mus. D, 5 Pa. Inf.				
Davison, John C.	Pvt. Sheridan Troop	1876	1908	Eastlawn	Tyrone
Delozier, Frederick	Pvt. C, 5 Pa. Inf.				
Delozier, Joseph L.	Pvt. C, 5 Pa. Inf.	1880	1933	Presbyterian	Hollidaysburg
Deneen, George P.	Pvt. H, 4 Inf.	1878	1915	Greenwood	Altoona
Derrick, George O. (w)	Sgt. I, 8 Inf.				
Desch, Charles					
Detrick, Logan	Pvt. U. S. Marines				
DeTurk, Benjamin H.	Mus. A, 5 Pa. Inf.				
Detwiler, Calvin	Pvt. C, 5 Pa. Inf.				
Detwiler, Clarence					
Dickson, Adam L.	2Lt. Sheridan Troop				
Dickson, Andrew A.	Pvt. Sheridan Troop				
Dickson, George L.	Pvt. Sheridan Troop	1875	1933	Rose Hill	Altoona
Dickson, Harry W.	Pvt. Sheridan Troop				
Dickson, J. L.	Sgt. A, Light Art.				
Diehl, James F.	Pvt. M, 5 Pa. Inf.	1873	1929	Gettysburg	Pa.
Dillon, Benjamin F.	Pvt. E, 10 Inf.	1869	1929	Oak Ridge	Altoona
Ditzer, Joseph	Pvt. C, 5 Pa. Inf.				
Dively, Charles T.	Pvt. I, 28 US. Vol. Inf.	1877	1929	Alto Reste	Hollidaysburg
Doloway, Charles E.	Pvt. Sheridan Troop	1872	1938	Philadelphia	Pa.
Dougal, F.	Pvt. D, 2 Inf.				
Douglas, Harrie A. (w)		1869	1935	Stoverdale	Pa.
Downing, Sankey L.	Pvt. 17 Ohio Inf.	1875	1914	Geeseytown	Hollidaysburg
Drexler, Carl W.	Pvt. C, 43 US. Vol. Inf.				
Dunlap, Robert E.	Pvt. Sheridan Troop	1875	1927	Rose Hill	Altoona
Dupman, Harmon					
Dwyer, Edward	Smn. U. S. Navy				
Eaken, William J.	Pvt. I, 2 Art.	1879		Grazierville	Tyrone

THE SPANISH-AMERICAN WAR

Name	Rank	Organization	Born	Died	Cemetery	Location
Eardley, Deroy M.	Pvt. E, 7 Cav.		1878	1938	Greenwood	Altoona
Earl, Edward A.	Pvt. A, 43 U. S. Vol. Inf.		1877	1939	Fairview	Altoona
Ebersole, George W.	Sgt. H, 14 Inf.		1869	1932	Holsingers	Bakers Summit
Ebersole, Preston	Pvt. C, 3 U. S. Art.		1874			
Eboch, Edward T.	Pvt. B, 5 Pa. Inf.					
Ebright, Josiah M.	Mus. H, 5 Pa. Inf.		1877	1929	Oak Ridge	Altoona
Eckert, William	Pvt. U. S. Marines					
Ecklay, Don P.	Pvt. L, 5 Pa. Inf.					
	Pvt. K, 12 Inf.					
Eddie, Angus J.						
Edmiston, John Collins	Smn. U. S. Navy					
Eichenburg, Edward	Pvt. I, 35 U. S. Vol. Inf.		1876	1934	Rose Hill	Altoona
Ellis, Harry Edward	Pvt. E, 2 Pa. Inf.					
Ellis, William A.	Pvt. G, 5 Pa. Inf.		1877	1936	South Bend	Indiana
Ensbrenner, John	Pvt. K, 27 U. S. Vol. Inf.		1870	1936	Blain	Pa.
Ensminger, C. E.	Pvt. E, 38 U. S. Vol. Inf.					
Evans, Gomer	Pvt. 84 C. A. C.		1878	1939	Calvary	Altoona
Eversole, John R.	Pvt. M, 47 U. S. Vol. Inf.					
Fagley, Daniel D.	Cpl. C, 43 U. S. Vol. Inf.		1880	1939	Los Angeles	California
Fair, John Sherman (w)	1Lt. 5 Pa. Inf.					
	Cpt. 43 U. S. Vol. Inf.					
	1Lt. 9 Cav.					
Fair, Philip W.	Pvt. C, 5 Pa. Inf.					
Finn, Daniel J.	Pvt. C, 5 Pa. Inf.					
Fisher, John Barkley	1Lt. I, 4 Pa. Inf.		1866	1939	Oak Ridge	Altoona
Fissel, Frank Bacon	Pvt. C, 5 Pa. Inf.		1874	1933	Lutheran	Newry
Fleck, Charles H.	Sgt. Sheridan Troop					
Fleck, Frank E.	Sgt. Sheridan Troop		1867	1939	Rose Hill	Altoona
Fleck, Harry S.	1Lt. Sheridan Troop					
Fleck, Herbert F.	Pvt. Sheridan Troop					
Fleck, John Kistler	Cpl. Sheridan Troop					
Fleck, John Stoner	Sgt. Sheridan Troop					
Fleck, Marsh Frank	Pvt. M, 47 U. S. Vol. Inf.		1872	1928	Fairview	Altoona
Fleck, Wesley Wayne	Pvt. Sheridan Troop					
	Cpl. M, 47 U. S. Vol. Inf.					
Fonner, Joseph	Pvt. C, 5 Pa. Inf.					
Fortney, Verne C.	Pvt. Sheridan Troop					
Foster, Zackary T.	Cpl. D, 8 Pa. Inf.					
	Cpl. D, 46 U. S. Vol. Inf.					
Frazier, Harry D.	Pvt. C, 5 Pa. Inf.					
Frederick, Samuel F.	Pvt. G, 21 Inf.					
Funk, Charles	Pvt. E, 8 Inf.					
Funk, Levi H.	Pvt. Sheridan Troop					
Galbraith, Robert C.	Pvt. Sheridan Troop		1859	1918	Arlington	Virginia
Gardner, Harry A.	Pvt. B, 5 Pa. Inf.					
Gardner, Robert C.	Pvt. Sheridan Troop		1858	1907	Grandview	Tyrone
Garland, George W.	Pvt. C, 5 Pa. Inf.					
Gearhart, Roy F.	Pvt. C, 43 U. S. Vol. Inf.			1900	Arlington	Virginia
Geesey, Charles H.	Pvt. D, 5 Pa. Inf.		1870	1925	Presbyterian	Hollidaysburg
Geisinger, Michael L.	Pvt. A, 5 Pa. Inf.			1924	Mill Creek	Pa.
Gensimore, Charles W.	Pvt. Sheridan Troop		1875	1918	Bedford	Pa.
Gensimire, Daniel W.	Pvt. Sheridan Troop					
Gensimore, Edward C.	Pvt. Sheridan Troop					
Gensimire, Harry H.	Pvt. Sheridan Troop					
Gensimore, Jesse F.	Pvt. Sheridan Troop					
Gettys, Edward B.	Pvt. A, 18 Pa. Inf.		1879	1931	Greenwood	Altoona
Ghaner, John E.	Pvt. E, 5 Pa. Inf.					
Gheer, John R.	Pvt. K, 2 Cav.					
Gibbons, Walker G.	Pvt. C, 5 Pa. Inf.					
Gilbert, Fred John	Pvt. A, 5 Pa. Inf.					
Gillam, Roy D.	Pvt. Sheridan Troop					

SOLDIERS OF BLAIR COUNTY

Name	Rank Organization	Born	Died	Cemetery	Location
Gillaspie, John A.	Pvt. C, 5 Pa. Inf.	1876	1924	Grandview	Altoona
Gingery, Andrew C.	Pvt. Sheridan Troop	1863	1926	Union	Centre Co.
Gingery, William H.	Sgt. H, 12 Inf.	1866	1927	Highland	Lock Haven
Ginter, John William	Pvt. E, 10 Pa. Inf.				
Girts, Bertram I.	Pvt. L, 3 Inf.				
Glover, Samuel P.	Sgn. 5, Pa. Inf.	1860	1936	Hartleton	Pa.
Goetz, Fred Z.					
Goodman, George B.					
Goodman, Samuel W.	B. M. U. S. Navy				
Goodman, Wesley L.	Pvt. C, 5 Pa. Inf.				
Graf, Christian					
Grafius, David E.	Pvt. C, 1 Ariz. Inf.				
	Pvt. C, 42 U. S. Vol. Inf.	1878	1904	Fairview	Martinsburg
Gray, Winfield S.	Pvt. C, 12 Inf.				
	Pvt. C. A. C.		1905	Frankstown	Hollidaysburg
Graybill, Frank E.	Cpl. A, 43 U. S. Vol. Inf.				
Grazier, John H.	Pvt. Sheridan Troop	1863	1932	Grandview	Tyrone
Greene, William A.	Pvt. C, 5 Pa. Inf.				
	Pvt. C, 43 U. S. Vol. Inf.	1875	1931	Logan Valley	Bellwood
Grove, Albert	Pvt. A, 5 Pa. Inf.				
Gunderman, Edward C.	Pvt. I, 40 U. S. Vol. Inf.				
Guthridge, John E.	Pvt. H, 8 Inf.				
Hain, William J.	Pvt. Sheridan Troop	1875	1924	Grandview	Tyrone
Hainley, William E.	Pvt. C, 5 Pa. Inf.				
Hainsey, Fred	Cpl. G, 17 Pa. Inf.				
Hainsey, Harry (w)	Pvt. B, 5 Cav.	1873	1934	Frankstown	Hollidaysburg
Haley, George D.	Cpl. K, 4 Inf.	1875	1925	Calvary	Altoona
Hamilton, Joseph H.	Pvt. C, 5 Pa. Inf.				
Hammaker, Samuel H.	Pvt. C, 5 Pa. Inf.				
Hammel, Blair	Pvt. C, 5 Pa. Inf.				
Harber, Josiah F. (w)	Pvt. F, 8 Inf.	1880	1938	Grandview	Altoona
Harner, John V.	Bks. Sheridan Troop	1869	1933	Dayton	Ohio
Harpster, Edward L.					
Harpster, Harry W.					
Harrier, Orin	Pvt. E, 5 Pa. Inf.				
Harris, Charles C.	Sgt. E, 4 Pa. Inf.				
Hartman, Joseph F.	Cpn. 5 Pa. Inf.				
Hastings, John B.	Pvt. Sheridan Troop				
Hauser, Harry	Pvt. C, 5 Pa. Inf.				
Heath, Arthur L.	Pvt. Hospital Corps				
Hengst, Allison	Pvt. C, 5 Pa. Inf.				
Herlt, Edward W.	Pvt. Sheridan Troop				
Herring, George A.	Pvt. D, 5 Pa. Inf.	1874	1899	Oak Ridge	Altoona
Hess, Harry H.	Cpl. L, 5 Pa. Inf.				
Hileman, Philip A.	Pvt. Sheridan Troop	1874	1918	Presbyterian	Hollidaysburg
Hill, Edgar Walter	Cpl. C, 5 Pa. Inf.	1870	1932	Greenlawn	Hollidaysburg
Hoff, Robert C.	Pvt. C, 5 Pa. Inf.				
Hollen, Ira A.	Pvt. C, 5 Pa. Inf.	1874	1937		California
Holt, Edward	Pvt. E, 43 U. S. Vol. Inf.				
Homan, George W.	Pvt. H, 5 Pa. Inf.	1878	1898	Presbyterian	Hollidaysburg
Hoopes, C. E.	2 Cav.				
Hoopes, Harry S.	Pvt. L, 2 Cav.				
Hoover, George P.	Pvt. B, 5 Pa. Inf.				
Hopkins, Miles S.	Pvt. C, 5 Pa. Inf.	1877	1910	Oak Ridge	Altoona
Hornauer, Max A.	Cpl. Marine Corps				
Houser, Martin	Pvt. G, 43 U. S. Vol. Inf.	1881	1903	Oak Ridge	Altoona
Huller, John P.	Sgt. Marine Corps				
Hunsinger, William H.	Pvt. F, 4 N. J. Inf.	1873	1935	Meyers	Bellefonte
Hutchison, Chester F.	Pvt. E, 5 Pa. Inf.				
Hvnick, George	Pvt. L, 8 Inf.				
Irwin, George Caleb	Cpl. C, 5 Pa. Inf.	1871	1934	Presbyterian	Hollidaysburg

Name	Rank Organization	Born	Died	Cemetery	Location
Isaac, Stephen Edward	Pvt. D, 3 Pa. Inf.	1879	1937	National	Philadelphia
Isett, Samuel E.	Pvt. C, 5 Pa. Inf.				
Ivison, John J.	Pvt. C, 5 Pa. Inf.				
Jacobs, E. W.	Pvt. E, 5 Pa. Inf.				
Jamison, Andrew	Pvt. H, 23 Kan. Inf.	1870	1935	Grandview	Altoona
Jewett, Mark I.	Pvt. 3, Wis. Inf.				
Johnson, Albert S.	Mus. F, 5 Pa. Inf.				
Johnson, Joseph M.	Mus. G, 5 Pa. Inf.	1870	1931	Fairview	Altoona
Johnston, Harry Long	Sgt. 5 Pa. Inf.				
Johnston, Thomas (w)	Pvt. A, 47 U. S. Vol. Inf.	1876	1939	Birmingham	Pa.
Jones, Charles S. W.	Cpt. Sheridan Troop				
	Maj. 1 Pa. Cav.	1842	1905	Grandview	Tyrone
Kabella, Frank J.	Cpl. A, Col. Art.				
Kagarise, Samuel C.	Pvt. L, 47 U. S. Vol. Inf.				
Kamerly, James C.	Pvt. C, 5 Pa. Inf.				
Kantner, Asberry	Pvt. C, 5 Pa. Inf.				
	Sgt. H, 12 U. S. Inf.				
Kaufman, Harry E.	Pvt. Sheridan Troop				
Keefer, Lannie C.	Pvt. Sheridan Troop				
Keime, Urban G.					
Keiper, Henry	Pvt. E, 19 Inf.		1913	Philadelphia	Pa.
Keller, John S.	Pvt. C, 43 U. S. Vol. Inf.				
Kelly, Herbert O.	Mus. K, 14 Pa. Inf.				
	Pvt. I, 28 U. S. Vol. Inf.	1872	1929	Greenwood	Altoona
Kelly James R.	Pvt. F, 1 Cav.				
Kelly, Joseph Francis	Pvt. K, 21 Inf.				
Kendig, Wilford M.	Mch. U. S. Navy	1871	1918	Rose Hill	Altoona
Kennedy, Jesse F.	Pvt. A, 5 Pa. Inf.	1876	1937	Rose Hill	Altoona
Killinger, Claude C.	Pvt. C, 5 Pa. Inf.				
Kinney, James M.	Cpl. C, 43 U. S. Vol. Inf.				
Kline, Frank L.	Pvt. Marine Corps				
Knighton, Charles E.	Pvt. B, 12 Inf.	1872	1936	Calvary	Altoona
Knipple, Dillinger C.	Pvt. I, 5 Pa. Inf.	1871	1929	Greenfield	Bedford Co.
Kniseley, Calvin	Pvt. I, 5 Pa. Inf.			Shellsburg	Pa.
Kocher, Harry A.	Pvt. Sheridan Troop				
Kurtz, Harvey Daniel	Pvt. G, 28 U. S. Vol. Inf.	1881	1919	Fairview	Martinsburg
Kutz, William Henry	Frn. U. S. Navy				
Kyle, Ormond H.	Cpl. M, 3 Ohio Inf.				
Lackey, Charles H.	Cpl. F, 6 Pa. Inf.	1876	1932	Mapleton	Pa.
Lasher, Edward	Pvt. C, 5 Pa. Inf.	1879	1932	Oak Ridge	Altoona
Lathero, Thomas J. (w)	Pvt. C, 5 Pa. Inf.				
Leamer, Samuel G.	Pvt. D, 4 Va. Inf.	1855	1937	San Diego	California
Leamer, William Canan	Pvt. C, 5 Pa. Inf.	1873	1935	Rose Hill	Altoona
Leman, Charles W.	U. S. Navy				
Lewis, John					
Lewis, Thomas	Cpl. K, 1 Pa. Inf.				
Liebig, Frederick T.	Pvt. A, Col. Art.	1871	1919	Greenwood	Altoona
Lightfoot, Charles C.	Mus. G, 5 Pa. Inf.				
Lightner, Blake (w)	Pvt. E, 5 Pa. Inf.				
	Pvt. L, 28 U. S. Vol. Inf.	1871	1938	Coalport	Pa.
List, Adam J.	Cpl. G, 43 U. S. Vol. Inf.				
Locker, Vernon					
Long, William J.	Pvt. C, 5 Pa. Inf.				
Longenecker, Ira	Pvt. K, 14 Pa. Inf.	1879	1937	Greenlawn	Roaring Spring
Lotz, Edward M.	Pvt. C, 5 Pa. Inf.				
Lotz, John Howard	Cpl. Sheridan Troop	1854	1938	Lutheran	Sinking Valley
Loucks, Charles F.	Pvt. C, 43 U. S. Vol. Inf.	1878	1933	Logan Valley	Bellwood
Lusk, Joseph M.					
Luther, Urban A.	Pvt. F, 14 Cav.				
Lynn, Nelson	Sgt. C, 5 Pa. Inf.				
Lytle, William B.					
Mackin, William A.					

SOLDIERS OF BLAIR COUNTY

Name	Rank Organization	Born	Died	Cemetery	Location
Maclay, William P.	Pvt. A, 43 U. S. Vol. Inf.		1938	Philadelphia	Pa.
Macready, William E.	Pvt. Sheridan Troop	1878	1938	Grandview	Tyrone
Malone, Charles A.	Sgt. H, 17 Inf.				
	Pvt. G, 23 Inf.				
Malone, James Daniel	Pvt. C, 5 Pa. Inf.				
Mann, William A. (w)	Cpt. 17 Inf.				
	Maj. 14 Inf.	1854	1934	Arlington	Virginia
Manspeaker, Oliver	Pvt. D, 8 Inf.				
Markley, Milton C.	Pvt. C, 5 Pa. Inf.				
Martin, Harry	Pvt. C, 5 Pa. Inf.				
Martin, Lemon	Pvt. C, 5 Pa. Inf.	1877	1905	Lutheran	Hollidaysburg
Mateer, Nelson	Pvt. C, 5 Pa. Inf.				
Matthews, Charles L.	Pvt. C, 5 Pa. Inf.				
Matthews, William R.	Pvt. Sheridan Troop				
Mauk, Charles					
Mauk, Robert	Pvt. I, 8 Inf.				
Mauk, William David	Pvt. M, 47 U. S. Vol. Inf.				
Mavity, W. H.					
Meadville, Walker S.	Sgt. Sheridan Troop				
Mench, Homer F.	Pvt. C, 5 Pa. Inf.				
Mendenhall, Edward					
Mentzer, Edmund H.	Pvt. Sheridan Troop				
Mentzer, Edward B.	Pvt. C, 5 Pa. Inf.				
Mentzer, Howard D.	Pvt. Sheridan Troop	1878	1935	Eastlawn	Tyrone
Middlekauff, Wallace W.	Pvt. H, 4 Inf.				
Miller, Bruce D.	Pvt. A, 5 Pa. Inf.				
Miller, David P.	Pvt. Sheridan Troop	1878	1924	Elizabeth City	Virginia
Miller, Harry B.	Pvt. C, 5 Pa. Inf.				
Miller, Harry Leonard	Cpl. C, 5 Pa. Inf.	1877	1918	Fairview	Altoona
Miller, J. R.					
Miller, James Sumner	Pvt. L, 5 Cav.				
Miller, Lloyd S.	Pvt. A, 5 Pa. Inf.				
Minary, Joseph O.	Pvt. G, 1 Md. Inf.	1866	1913	Grandview	Tyrone
Minnigh, John Harry	Mus. E, 5 Pa. Inf.	1860	1920	Oak Ridge	Altoona
Mitchell, Henry	Pvt. F, 12 Pa. Inf.				
	Pvt. K, 28 U. S. Vol. Inf.				
Mock, John Irvin	Pvt. L, 47 U. S. Vol. Inf.				
Mong, Jerry W.	Pvt. Sheridan Troop	1867	1936	Burkets	Warriors Mark
Moore, James E.	Cpl. Sheridan Troop				
Moore, William E.	Sgt. Sheridan Troop				
Morgan, Bertram G. (w)	Cpl. C, 43 U. S. Vol. Inf.	1879	1931	Fairview	Altoona
Morgan, Fenton C.	Pvt. G, 21 Inf.				
Morrow, Charles E.	Pvt. Sheridan Troop				
Mosser, William Frank	Pvt. 20 C. A. C.				
	Pvt. K, 2 Art.				
Mountain, Joseph C.	Pvt. A, 5 Pa. Inf.				
Mulhollen, William C.	Pvt. C, 43 U. S. Vol. Inf.	1878	1901	Logan Valley	Bellwood
Murphy, James E.	Pvt. Sheridan Troop	1874	1925	Uniondale	Pittsburgh
Murphy, William B.	Pvt. Sheridan Troop				
Murray, Clinton G.	Pvt. B, 5 Pa. Inf.				
Murray, John H.	Pvt. G, 28 U. S. Vol. Inf.				
Mutzabaugh, Robert M.	Pvt. 64 C. A. C.	1877	1920	Union	Duncannon
Myers, Charles E.	Mus. H, 5 Pa. Inf.				
Myers, Harry E.	Cpl. C, 5 Pa. Inf.				
Myers, Horace C.	Cpl. Sheridan Troop	1869	1937	Logan Valley	Bellwood
Myers, James W.	Pvt. Sheridan Troop				
Myers, William Clyde	Pvt. Sheridan Troop	1878	1921	Grandview	Tyrone
McCloskey, George A.	Mus. F, 5 Pa. Inf.				
McCoy, John F.	Pvt. G, 1 Inf.	1878	1931	Pleasant Hill	Glasgow
McCracken, George H.	Pvt. Marine Corps	1876	1917	Logan Valley	Bellwood
McCullough, Charles H.	Pvt. C, 5 Pa. Inf.				
McCully, Dorsey P.	Atr. I, 12 Inf.	1877	1933	Logan Valley	Bellwood

THE SPANISH-AMERICAN WAR

Name	Rank Organization	Born	Died	Cemetery	Location
McElwee, Wilson H.	Pvt. A, 5 Pa. Inf.	1872	1920	Fairview	Altoona
McFadden, John	Pvt. C, 5 Pa. Inf.	1878	1902	St. Marys	Hollidaysburg
McGonigal, Samuel A.	Pvt. H, 5 Pa. Inf.				
McGuire, James	23 Inf.			Pittsburgh	Pa.
McIntyre, Robert W.	Pvt. G, 7 Cav.	1878	1932	Presbyterian	Hollidaysburg
McKee, Harry Dwellinger	Pvt. C, 5 Pa. Inf.	1864	1937	Greenlawn	Roaring Spring
McKinney, Edgar	Pvt. Sheridan Troop				
McLaughlin, Charles	Pvt. 43 US. Vol. Inf.		1899	St. Johns	Altoona
McLaughlin, John A.	Cpl. F, 5 Pa. Inf.				
McLain, David Roswell	Sgt. 2 Art.	1876	1939	Ft. Lewis	Washington
McMonigal, James B.	Smn. U. S. Navy	1875	1930	Oak Ridge	Altoona
McNamara, Robert C.	Maj. 5 Pa. Inf.		1912	Bedford	Pa.
McNelis, Edward F.	Cpl. F, 1 W. Va. Inf.				
McWilliams, J. Milliken	Pvt. Marine Corps	1875	1923	Eastlawn	Tyrone
Neil, Luther	U. S. Navy				
Neugebauer, Henry	Pvt. M, 8 Cav.		1901	Grandview	Tyrone
Nevitt, Perle Sylvin	Cpl. I, 2 Ohio Inf.	1878	1938	Greenwood	Altoona
Nicodemus, Edward G.	Pvt. E, 8 Inf.	1878	1938	Grandview	Altoona
Noble, James L.	Pvt. A, 18 Pa. Inf.				
	Cpl. C, 43 US. Vol. Inf.	1878	1900	Greenwood	Altoona
Nolan, Elmer J.	Mus. A, 5 Pa. Inf.				
Noll, James Orin	Pvt. B, 5 Pa. Inf.	1875	1927	Eastlawn	Tyrone
Noll, John S.	Pvt. C, 5 Pa. Inf.	1876	1923	Lutheran	Newry
Nothnagle, George	Pvt. I, 17 Inf.	1876	1922	Rose Hill	Altoona
Nute, George W.	Pvt. C, 8 Pa. Inf.	1873	1926	Chambersburg	Pa.
O'Dell, Benton	Pvt. E, 5 Pa. Inf.				
Olewine, George L.	Sgt. C, 5 Pa. Inf.				
Olmes, Edw. A.	Mus. C, 5 Pa. Inf.				
Onkst, William	Pvt. C, 5 Pa. Inf.				
Oschea, Albert L.					
Otto, George H.					
Over, Harvey	Cpl. C, 43 US. Vol. Inf.				
Oves, Henry B.	Pvt. C, 5 Pa. Inf.				
Owens, George Wilkins	Pvt. Sheridan Troop				
Owens, William P.	Pvt. Sheridan Troop				
Palmer, Norman R.	Pvt. B, 15 Pa. Inf.				
Parker, Harry Strickler	Pvt. C, 5 Pa. Inf.				
Patterson, Robert M.	Pvt. Sheridan Troop				
Patterson, Samuel A.	Pvt. Sheridan Troop				
Pennebaker, James M.	Pvt. I, 2 Cav.				
Port, Vance J.	Pvt. A, 5 Pa. Inf.				
Potter, Henry C.	Mus. 5 Pa. Inf.				
Potter, Irwin R. (w)	Pvt. C, 8 Inf.				
Pross, James H. (c)		1835	1919	Lewisburg	Pa.
Prosser, Robert Gale	Pvt. D, 16 Pa. Inf.				
Puckle, Archie F.	Cpl. D. 5 Inf.				
Raabe, Rudolph H. D.	Pvt. Sheridan Troop				
Ragen, E. S.					
Ralston, George	Pvt. I, 28 US. Vol. Inf.				
Randolph, Scott E.	Pvt. A, 5 Pa. Inf.				
Raney, David L.	Pvt. Sheridan Troop	1871	1926		
Reamey, Lazarus Lowrey	Com. U. S. Navy	1849	1914	Woodlawn	New York
Reed, G. Wallace	Cpl. K, 17 Inf.	1880	1926	Calvary	Altoona
Reigh, James David	Pvt. D, 19 Inf.	1859	1932	Los Angeles	California
Richabaugh, Claire					
Ritter, William H.	Pvt. E, 15 Pa. Inf.	1871	1905	Fairview	Altoona
Robinson, Joseph C.	Pvt. C, 5 Pa. Inf.	1877	1898	Presbyterian	Hollidaysburg
Rodgers, Elmer B.	Pvt. E, 38 US. Vol. Inf.				
Rohrer, Ralph A.	Pvt. A, 5 Pa. Inf.				
Roland, John B.	Sgt. E, 38 US. Vol. Inf.				
Roller, William C. (w)	Pvt. C, 5 Pa. Inf.	1879	1929	Brownsville	Pa.

SOLDIERS OF BLAIR COUNTY

Name	Rank	Organization	Born	Died	Cemetery	Location
Rooney, Wm. R. A. (w)	Com.	U.S.Navy	1854	1932	Arlington	Virginia
Roseberry, David G.	Pvt.	Sheridan Troop	1876	1931	Eastlawn	Tyrone
Ross, J. Harry	Pvt.	Sheridan Troop				
Ross, Samuel H.	Pvt.	Sheridan Troop	1879	1936	Grandview	Tyrone
Rote, Frederick S.	Pvt.	C, 10 Inf.	1877	1925	Baughman	Tyrone
Rothrock, Percival B.	Pvt.	C, 5 Pa. Inf.	1876	1902	Oak Ridge	Altoona
Roush, Harry J.	Pvt.	C, 5 Pa. Inf.	1868	1918	Greenlawn	Roaring Spring
Ruggles, David	Pvt.	F, 8 Inf.				
Rupert, Henry						
Russell, Hubert H.	2Lt.	12 Pa. Inf.				
Russell, James S.	Pvt.	L, 5 Pa. Inf.				
Rutherford, Jacob D.	Pvt.	Sheridan Troop				
Samuels, William Joel	Cpl.	C, 5 Pa. Inf.	1865	1937	Carson Valley	Duncansville
Sassaman, Robert F.	Pvt.	C, 5 Pa. Inf.				
Schultz, George H.	Pvt.	C, 5 Pa. Inf.				
Schwartz, H. Joseph	Pvt.	K, 9 Inf.	1882	1939	Oak Park	New Castle
Seads, Herbert John	Pvt.	G, 12 Pa. Inf.				
Seward, Walter B.	Mus.	4 Ohio				
	Mus.	10 Ohio				
Shaffer, William B.	Pvt.	F, 5 Pa. Inf.	1877	1926	Fairview	Altoona
Shaner, George R.	Mus.	C, 43 US Vol. Inf.				
Shearer, Jacob Harry	Elc.	U. S. Navy				
Sheets, Edward K.	Pvt.	Sheridan Troop	1872	1924	Eastlawn	Tyrone
Shelow, John L.	Pvt.	K, 4 Art.				
	Cpl.	D, 1 Inf.	1877	1938	National	San Francisco
Sherlock, Thomas M.	Pvt.	B, 5 Pa. Inf.				
Shirley, William						
Shoemaker, John S.	Pvt.	C, 5 Pa. Inf.				
Shoenfelt, Franklin A.	Pvt.	63 C.A.C.				
	Pvt.	G, 12 Inf.	1876	1902	Grandview	Roaring Spring
Shontz, Edgar	Pvt.	L, 5 Pa. Inf.				
Shoup, Samuel E.	Mus.	B, 5 Pa. Inf.				
Showalter, Howard W.	Pvt.	I, 8 Inf.	1879	1928	Presbyterian	Hollidaysburg
Shufflebothom, Joseph W.	Pvt.	C, 5 Pa. Inf.				
Simpson, Charles R.	H.S.	5 Pa. Inf.				
Sites, Raphael R.	Pvt.	G, 8 Pa. Inf.	1875	1930	Churchtown	Pa.
Slater, John R.	Pvt.	C, 5 Pa. Inf.				
Smawley, Robert M.	Pvt.	C, 5 Pa. Inf.	1872	1903	Massillon	Ohio
Smeltzer, Frank S.	Pvt.	H, 16 Pa. Inf.			Holsingers	Bakers Summit
Smeltzer, Frederick	Pvt.	M, 8 Inf.				
Smith, Charles A.	Sgt.	A, 14 Inf.	1866	1934	South Side	Pittsburgh
Smith, Frank H.	Pvt.	C, 5 Pa. Inf.	1877	1914	Huntingdon	Pa.
Smith, James E.	Pvt.	C, 5 Pa. Inf.				
Smith, Jesse G.	Pvt.	Sheridan Troop				
Smith, John B.	Pvt.	Sheridan Troop				
Smith, Joseph L.	Pvt.	A, 8 Cav.				
Smith, Samuel W.	Pvt.	C, 20 Inf.	1879	1905	Fairview	Altoona
Smith, William	Sgt.	12 Inf.				
Smith, William J.	Pvt.	G, 19 Inf.	1869	1902	Calvary	Altoona
Snider, Lyman E.	Pvt.	Hospital Corps	1881	1925	Grandview	Tyrone
Snyder, Carl E.	Pvt.	C, 5 Pa. Inf.				
Snyder, Charles D.	Pvt.	C, 5 Pa. Inf.				
Snyder, Charles W.	Cpl.	C, 5 Pa. Inf.				
Snyder, Norman R.	Pvt.	M, 8 Ohio Inf.				
Snider, Simon J.	H. S.	4 Pa. Inf.				
Solt, Samuel A.	Pvt.	K, 47 US. Vol. Inf.				
Stange, Louis A.	Pvt.	B, 2 Pa. Inf.				
Stayer, Andrew S.	Maj.	5 Pa. Inf.				
Stayer, Edgar Simon (w)	1Lt.	5 Pa. Inf.				
	1Lt.	28 US. Vol. Inf.				
	1Lt.	23 Inf.				

THE SPANISH-AMERICAN WAR 305

Name	Rank Organization	Born	Died	Cemetery	Location
Stayer, Morrison Clay	Pvt. H, 5 Pa. Inf.				
Stewart, Ellis M.	Pvt. A, 5 Pa. Inf.				
Steward, General W.	Pvt. Sheridan Troop		1937	Huntingdon	Pa.
Stewart, Jesse A.	Pvt. Sheridan Troop				
Stewart, John E.					
Stewart, Samuel C.	Pvt. Sheridan Troop				
Stiffler, Charles S.	Sgt. C, 5 Pa. Inf.				
Strayer, Charles E.	8 Inf.	1878	1901	Greenwood	Altoona
Stryker, Harry C.	Pvt. Sheridan Troop		1934	Cleveland	Ohio
Stryker, Ralph L.	Pvt. Sheridan Troop				
Sullivan, George A. (w)	Pvt. C, 5 Pa. Inf.				
Sunday, George W.	Pvt. B, 5 Pa. Inf.				
Swenk, David I.	Cpl. G, 12 Inf.				
Swigert, Charles T.	Far. Sheridan Troop	1866	1918	Grandview	Tyrone
Swisher, Benjamin E.	Cpl. C, 43 US. Vol. Inf.	1878	1908	Oak Ridge	Altoona
Tate, Thomas W.	Pvt. Sheridan Troop	1876	1902	Spruce Creek	Pa.
Tate, William E.	Pvt. Sheridan Troop	1862	1911	Seven Stars	Hunt'gdon Co.
Taylor, Grant	Pvt. Sheridan Troop				
Taylor, John G.	Pvt. Sheridan Troop				
Taylor, Robert Frank		1869	1936	Roanoke	Virginia
Teufel, Christ F.	Pvt. C, 43 US. Vol. Inf.				
Thomas, Jacob L.	Pvt. Sheridan Troop				
Thompson, Carl	Smn. U. S. Navy	1878	1934	Grandview	Altoona
Thompson, Ernest D.	Cpl. A, 5 Pa. Inf.				
Thompson, George B.	Pvt. Sheridan Troop				
Treese, Elhannan J.	Pvt. C, 5 Pa. Inf.				
Trimble, Alexander C.	Cpl. Sheridan Troop				
Trimble, James	Pvt. Sheridan Troop	1872	1936	East Lawn	Tyrone
Tweed, Bruce W.	Pvt. L, 16 Pa. Inf.	1877	1898	Logan Valley	Bellwood
Ullery, James E.	Pvt. K, 8 Inf.				
Utter, Paul	102 C.A.C.		1910	Rose Hill	Altoona
VanAllman, William A.	2Lt. C, 5 Pa. Inf.				
Vogt, Charles F.	Pvt. E, 1 Engrs.				
Wahl, Frederick W.	Pvt. C, 5 Pa. Inf.		1929	Harrisburg	Pa.
Waite, Charles B.	Pvt. Sheridan Troop	1877	1936	Burkets	Warriors Mark
Walker, Robert J.					
Walsh, John F.	Sgt. C, 5 Pa. Inf.				
Walter, William M.	Cpl. A, 1 S. Dak. Inf.				
Walters, Edw. M.					
Walters, Lloyd A.	Pvt. C, 5 Pa. Inf.	1877	1918	Vicksburg	Roaring Spring
Waltz, Henry Jackson	Pvt. K, 2 Cav.				
Warfel, George	Pvt. G, 5 Pa. Inf.				
Waughtel, Ora	Bks. G, 2 Cav.				
Way, George W.	Pvt. Sheridan Troop				
Weaver, George D.	Pvt. M, 5 Pa. Inf.				
Weaver, Lewis S.	Pvt. M, 5 Pa. Inf.				
Weibley, Frank	Pvt. A, 43 US. Vol. Inf.				
Weight, David W.	Pvt. C, 5 Pa. Inf.				
Weiser, H. B.	Pvt. G, 5 Md. Inf.				
Weiss, Gilbert Haven (w)	Cps. U. S. Navy	1874	1925	Fairview	Altoona
Wert, Simon R.	Pvt. F, 47 US. Vol. Inf.				
West, John H.	Cpt. C, 5 Pa. Inf.	1860	1937	Presbyterian	Hollidaysburg
Wester, Albert V.	Pvt. K, 2 Cav.				
Whelan, Frank					
Whittaker, Ralph R. (w)	Pvt. A, 5 Pa. Inf.				
Wickes, Walter E.	Pvt. F, 1 Inf.	1882	1927	Oak Ridge	Altoona
Wildes, Clayton B.	Pvt. C, 5 Pa. Inf.				
Williams, Harrison G.	Pvt. B, 5 Pa. Inf.				
Williams, Harvey C.	Cpl. D, 28 US. Vol. Inf.				
Williams, James Blaine	Sgt. G, 5 Cav.				
Williams, Robert S.	Pvt. C, 5 Pa. Inf.				

SOLDIERS OF BLAIR COUNTY

Name	Rank Organization	Born	Died	Cemetery	Location
Williams, William G.	Cpl. C, 43 US. Vol. Inf.				
Williams, William H.					
Winter, Walter F.	Cpl. A, 43 US. Vol. Inf.	1876	1901	Greenwood	Altoona
Woleslagle, John Alvin	Pvt. C, 5 Pa. Inf.				
Wolfe, LeRoy L.	Pvt. Sheridan Troop				
Womer, Charles H.	Pvt. D, 2 Cav.				
	Sgt. F, 7 Cav.	1874	1933	Presbyterian	Hollidaysburg
Woods, Emory A.	Pvt. G, 7 Inf.				
Woods, Richard B.	Cpl. F, 1 W. Va. Inf.				
Yingling, Blaine	Pvt. I, 47 US. Vol. Inf.				
Yingling, David A.	Pvt. A, 1 Ala. Inf.				
	Pvt. G, 23 Inf.	1871	1934	National	Washington,
Yocum, Samuel F.	Cpl. C, 5 Pa. Inf.	1874	1938	Fairview	Altoona
Young, Ellis S.	Pvt. Sheridan Troop				
Young, John A.	Sgt. A, 43 US. Vol. Inf.				
Youngman, Charles E.	Pvt. 21 Inf.		1907	Huntingdon	Pa.
Zimmerman, William H.	Pvt. E, 5 Cav.	1874	1939	Logan Valley	Bellwood

ADDITIONAL RECORDS

PART VI

THE WORLD WAR

A brief history of the World War, giving the causes, important events, the American Expeditionary Forces, battles, and the ending.

A history of the military organizations of Blair County prior to and during the World War.

A history of all veterans organizations of Blair County.

A register of World War Veterans who died prior to January 1, 1940, giving their rank, organization, year of birth, year of death, and the place of burial.

SPECIAL ABBREVIATIONS USED IN THIS SECTION

Amb. ......*Ambulance*
Amn. ......*Ammunition*
Ck. ....*Cook*
Clk. ....*Clerk*
Con. ....*Construction*
Conv. ......*Convalescent*
C. P. O. ....*Chief Petty Officer*
Cps. ....*Coppersmith*
Ct. ....*Centre*
D. B. ....*Depot Brigade*
Dept. ......*Department*
Det. ....*Detachment*
Dev. ....*Development*
Div. ....*Division*
Engr. ......*Engineer*
Ens. ....*Ensign*
F. A. ....*Field Artillery*
H. A. ......*Hospital Apprentice*
Hosp. ......*Hospital*
Hqs. ....*Headquarters*
Mch. ......*Mechanic*
M. D. ......*Medical Department*
M. E. ......*Master Engineer*
Med. ......*Medical*
M. G. ......*Machine Gun*

M. M. ......*Machinists Mate*
Mt. ....*Motor*
Mtr. ....*Mortar*
Ord. ....*Ordnance*
Pion. ......*Pioneer*
Rep. ....*Replacement*
Rpr. ....*Repairman*
R. R. ......*Railroad*
R. T. C. ....*Recruit Training Centre*
San. ....*Sanitary*
S. A. T. C. .*Students Army Training Corps*
Ser. ....*Service*
Sfr. ....*Shipfitter*
Sig. ....*Signal*
Skr. ....*Storekeeper*
Sqn. ....*Squadron*
Sup. ....*Supply*
Tel. ....*Telegraph*
Tr. ....*Trench*
Trn. ....*Train, Training*
Trans. .....*Transportation*
U. ....*Unassigned*
Ymn. ......*Yeoman*

(s) ......*also served in the Spanish-American War*

INDEX TO PART VI

THE WORLD WAR

Brief History of the World War	309
The Pennsylvania National Guard	311
Sheridan Troop, of Tyrone	311
Company C, of Hollidaysburg	313
Company E, of Altoona	315
Company M, of Altoona	315
Provisional Headquarters Company	315
Home Defense Police	316
The United States Army	317
Sheridan Troop of Tyrone	317
Company G, of Altoona	319
Pennsylvania Reserve Militia	320
Chronicles of the Hollidaysburg Draft Board	321
Veterans Organizations of Blair County	335
James L. Noble Post No. 3, Veterans of Foreign Wars	337
Benjamin H. Hewit Post No. 185, Veterans of Foreign Wars	339
D. Merl Tipton Post No. 43, Veterans of Foreign Wars	340
Chas. R. Rowan Post No. 228, The American Legion	341
Howard Gardner Post No. 228, The American Legion	344
Bonner-Sollenberger Post No. 456, The American Legion	346
Murray-Appleman Post No. 147, The American Legion	347
Fort Fetter Post No. 516, The American Legion	348
John M. Anderson Post No. 424, The American Legion	350
Claysburg Post No. 522, The American Legion	351
Robinson-Herring Post No. 529, The American Legion	353
Altoona Chapter No. 34, Disabled American Veterans	354
Blair County Voiture No. 350 La Societe 40 Hommes et 8 Chevaux	356
Twenty-first District Council	358
Register of deceased World War Veterans	359

A BRIEF HISTORY OF THE WORLD WAR

The principal cause of America's participation in the World War was Germany's actions in sinking vessels without warning, by her submarines.

Other causes such as the natural alliance between English speaking nations. the invasions of neutral nations, and the ruthless acts of the German Army and secret service system in disregarding the rights of non-belligerents, the placing of bombs in neutral vessels and committing sabotage in industrial plants.

Germany's policy of sinking merchantmen without warning and without providing for the safety of the passengers and crew was contrary to international warfare; however, the use of submarines required quick destruction of the vessels, lest the vessels be armed and the submarines destroyed; and as a result of the sinking of several vessels, including the Lusitania on the 7th of May, 1915, a number of notes were exchanged between the United States and Germany.

Some concessions in the use of submarines were secured from the German Government, but on the 30th of January, 1917, the United States was advised that all vessels would be sunk in certain prescribed zones without warning by German submarines.

On the 3rd of February, 1917, the German Ambassador, Count Von Bernstorff, was dismissed from Washington, the American Ambassador Gerard was recalled from Berlin, and diplomatic relations with Germany were severed.

By Executive Order, formal notice was given on the 12th of March, 1917, "that the Government of the United States has determined to place upon all American merchant vessels sailing through the barred areas an armed guard for the protection of the vessels and the lives of the persons on board."

Congress was called into special session on the 2nd of April, 1917, and in the President's message, he stated that "The world must be made safe for democracy." By an act of Congress and the approval of President Woodrow Wilson, war was declared between the United States and the German Imperial Government, on the 6th of April 1917.

On the 18th of May, 1917, Congress authorized the Regular Army to recruit to 287,000 men, the National Guard to 625,000, and the building of a National Army of one million members.

The National Army to be organized by means of a system of selective draft of men between 21 and 31, through Local Boards. All men were required to register in their election districts, each to receive a serial number, and their turn of entering the service was determined by the drawing in a lottery at Washington. The order in which the numbers were drawn was the order in which the men were called for service.

General John J. Pershing was appointed as commander of the American Expeditionary Force and arrived in Paris on the 8th of June, 1917. As early as the 16th of May, 1917, a squadron of American torpedo boats under the command of Rear Admiral Sims, was aiding the British fleet in patrolling the seas, and American troops first occupied French front-line trenches in a quiet part of the battle zone on the 27th of October, 1917.

One year, one month and twenty-five days after the declaration of War, American troops were first engaged in action on a large scale when 28,000 stopped the German Offensive at Chateau-Thierry, in the Marne Valley.

Of a total of about 4,800,000 men, who served in the armed forces of the United States during the war period, 2,000,000 were transported to Europe over a period of nineteen months, without the loss of an American troop transport on its eastward voyage.

At the time of the Armistice, the American Expeditionary Force consisted of the following divisions: Number 1 to 8 inclusive of the Regular Army, numbers 26 to 42, inclusive of the National Guard, and numbers 76 to 93, inclusive of the National Army. The strength of a division was 28,105 men, divided into two brigades of infantry, one brigade of artillery, division troops and trains. Each brigade of Infantry consisted of two regiments of infantry and one machine gun battalion. The brigade of Artillery consisted of three regiments of Field Artillery and one Trench Mortar Battery. The division troops included Headquarters, one machine gun Battalion, one regiment of Engineers, one Field Signal Battalion. The Trains were: Train Headquarters and Military Police, Ammunition Train, Supply Trains, Engineer Train and Sanitary Train which included ambulance companies and Field Hospitals.

The battles and engagemnts in France according to government statistics, participated in by American soldiers during 1918 were as follows:

German Offensive

Somme	March 21 to April 6
Lys	April 9 to 27
Aisne	May 27 to June 5
Moyon-Mondidier	June 9 to 15
Champagne-Marne	July 15 to 18

Allied Offensive

Aisne-Marne	July 18 to Aug. 6
Somme	August 8 to November 11
Oise-Aisne	August 18 to November 11
Ypres-Lys	August 19 to November 11
St. Mihiel	September 12 to 15
Meuse-Argonne	September 26 to November 11

With the signing of the Armistice on the 11th of November, 1918, the homeward march of the men of the American Expeditionary Force began and the millions of men who enlisted or were called into the service of their country were rapidly discharged and their peace time occupations resumed.

THE PENNSYLVANIA NATIONAL GUARD

Upon the return home of the local units of the Pennsylvania National Guard, from their service in the Spanish-American War, they were immediately reorganized for future duty and anticipated service in the Philippine Islands.

However, service in the Islands was limited to the National Guard troops already there, and the use of the regular army, supplemented by the enrollment of volunteers, such as the 28th and 43rd, which contained a number of volunteers from Blair County.

The Pennsylvania National Guard was re-organized by the Dick Act which went into effect on the 1st of January, 1910. This law changed the designation of many companies, consolidated companies and regiments, increasing the number of members of the various units.

A new National Defense Act was prepared during the winter and spring of 1916, and was approved by the President on the 3rd of June, 1916.

This law provided that the National Guard of the various states could be called into Federal Service within the limits of the United States, that it could be drafted as an organization for service outside the continental limits of the United States, that the members of the Guard would receive Federal pay for attendance at drills, and that it would be under Federal supervision at all times.

Mexican internal troubles brought about strained relations with that country and a crisis developed when on the 9th of March, 1916, Francisco Villa with a bandit force crossed into New Mexico and attacked the town of Columbus, New Mexico, setting fire to the houses and killing eighteen persons, some of them soldiers of the United States Cavalry, guarding the border there.

A punitive expeditionary force under Brigadier General John J. Pershing crossed the Mexican line on the 16th of March in a fruitless effort to capture Villa and his band. The pursuing column comprised almost the entire regular force and in order to protect the exposed border from further raids, the National Guard of Texas, New Mexico and Arizona were called out on the 9th of May

Nine days later, by the call of the President, the entire National Guard of the United States were ordered to assemble for duty on the Mexican Border. Within a month an army of more than one hundred thousand guardsmen formed a line along the border.

SHERIDAN TROOP

The Sheridan Troop of Tyrone, a unit of Cavalry of the Pennsylvania National Guard was re-organized upon its return home from the Spanish-American War service in Porto Rico, and officially recognized on the 20th of December, 1898.

Captain Charles S. W. Jones resumed command of the Troop, and upon his death in 1905, Luther F. Crawford became Captain, followed by Captain James F. Moore.

The 2nd Brigade of the National Guard of which the Sheridan Troop was a part, encamped at Tipton, Blair County, from the 20th to 27th of July, 1907, at "Camp Homer J. Lindsay."

On the 15th of May, 1910, the Sheridan Troop was assigned to Squadron B, and this Squadron was redesignated as 2nd Squadron Cavalry, on the 21st of June, 1911. On the 6th of June, 1914, this Troop was assigned to the 2nd Squadron of the 1st Regiment of Cavalry, and upon being mustered into the Federal service for duty on the Mexican Border the Sheridan Troop was designated as Troop B, 1st Regiment of Cavalry.

The administrator's building of the present armory, located at 926 South Logan

Avenue, was dedicated in 1912, and the riding hall and stables were added in 1917 and 1918.

The officers of the Sheridan Troop responded to the President's call of June 18, 1916, for troops to guard the Mexican Border, and the following order was issued: "Order No. 7-A. Armory, Sheridan Troop, 1st Cavalry, Pennsylvania National Guard, Tyrone, Pennsylvania, June 21, 1916. In compliance with General Order No. 21, dated Harrisburg, Pennsylvania, June 19, 1916, the Division Order No. 3, dated Sunbury, Pennsylvania, June 19, 1916, the Division Pennsylvania National Guard, will mobilize at Mt. Gretna, Pennsylvania, Saturday, June 24, 1916, in response to the call of the President for the mobilization of the militia of the United States for Federal Service.

"Therefore, Sheridan Troop will assemble at the armory Thursday morning, June 22, 1916, dismounted and will at once arrange for movement to Mt. Gretna, Pennsylvania. Previous instructions as to personal kits and schedule of equipment must be complied with. Each man will be allowed a suitcase, also must provide himself with a large gunny sack and pack his entire horse equipment therein. Details for this packing will be announced on bulletin board. Each man must see to it, that each article of equipment is properly numbered and that he has every piece of his number as he will be strictly accountable to the Quartermaster Department of the army. Any shortage of equipment occurring while in the Federal Service will be deducted from the soldiers pay each month.

"The 1st Sergeant will arrange his detail work and will take up the routine work of the Troop at 8.:30, Thursday morning, June 22nd. The Quartermaster Sergeant and squad leaders will report to the Troop Commander on Thursday morning for instructions.

"The Troop will assemble in service uniforms at the above named date and hour and will be on duty and remain at the Armory thereafter. Subsistence will be provided. James F. Moore, Captain."

The Sheridan Troop with other units of the Pennsylvania National Guard arrived at Mt. Gretna, on the 25th of June, 1916, and was mustered in the Federal Service on the 6th of July. It performed duty at El Paso, on the Mexican Border as Troop B, 1st Regiment of Cavalry, National Guard of the United States, and was mustered out of the Federal Service on the 23rd of January, 1917.

The names of the members of the Sheridan Troop who served on the Mexican Border, with the highest rank acquired during that period are as follows:

ROSTER SHERIDAN TROOP

Captain	James F. Moore
First Lieutenant	Edgar M. McKinney
First Lieutenant	Reuben H. Harris
Second Lieutenant	Joseph A. Dickson

	Sergeants	*Corporals*	*Saddler*
First	Alva J. Addleman	Eugene H. Ammerman	William N. Beam
Quartermaster	Godfrey J. Maurer	Gilbert E. Kanour	*Cooks*
Mess	John F. Johnson	Elmer E. Mong	Norris E. Hildebrand
Stable	Millard F. Brownlee	William H. Sweet	Albert F. Dahlstrom
	Richard H. Gilbert	George G. Naylor	*Horseshoer*
	Charles T. Snyder	Walter B. Woodbridge	Edward T. Long
	John Elliot Trego	Frank L. Dickson	*Wagoners*
	James C. Trimble	Cecil B. Meadville	James H. Mauk
	John Boyd Goheen		Benjamin F. Dickson
			Musicians
			Chester L. Stewart
			Samuel C. Leeper
			Amon L. DeArment

Privates

Anderson, John M.	Harkness, Orville M.	Patterson, Francis G.
Armstrong, James H.	Herzog, Clarence W.	Peary, Harry D.
Askey, Max McKinley	Hockenberry, William E.	Preston, Charles A.
Barr, Andrew R.	Horning, James B.	Reed, James Chalmer
Beam, John Leroy	Huber, John G.	Robinson, John F.
Bell, Edward M.	Irvin, Plummer J.	Root, James Dean
Beyer, Francis David	Johnson, Fred G.	Sankey, John L.
Branstetter, Raymond B.	Kester, Carl W.	Schopp, Walter L.
Bressler, Arthur D.	Krape, Joseph R.	Scullin, Robert P.
Brossman, Harry B.	Kolessy, John F.	Shires, Joseph A.
Daniels, Theodore L.	Lewis, Clair	Shoemaker, Edward C.
Davis, Edward R.	Love, Frederick F.	Sprague, William H.
Dean, Fay	McClain, Edward R.	Steel, Harry E.
Dennis, Benjamin F.	McDonnell, Owen F.	Steel, Charles Morgan
Dunlap, John E.	Martz, George D.	Stewart, Alexander M.
Gensimore, Milton F.	Metzger, Charles D.	Shultzaberger, Robert L.
Gilmore, Cloyd P.	Milligan, Elmer H.	Thompson, Harold M.
Glenn, Randolph F.	Moore, Chester D.	Wallace, Bernard B.
Grazier, Jesse C.	Moore, Orlando B.	Woodring, Alton Cherry
Grove, Clair Nelson	Newlin, J. F.	Yergy, John Levan
Hampton, Milroy H.	Parks, Preston O.	Yingling, Chester M.

COMPANY C

Soon after the return of the members of the Hollidaysburg Company from service in the Spanish-American War at Chickamauga, Georgia, and Lexington, Kentucky, steps were taken to reorganize Company C, of the Pennsylvania National Guard, for future service. The organization was effected on the 7th of January, 1899, and the company was mustered into the service as a unit of the Pennsylvania National Guard on the 27th of January, 1899.

Captain John H. West was promoted to the rank of Major on the 3rd of August, 1899, and interest in the activities of the company lagged, so that Company C, was disbanded on the 15th of November, 1899.

Company F, 21st Regiment of the Pennsylvania National Guard, an organization which was formed at Hollidaysburg during the absence of Company C, as a Home Guard unit, was re-designated Company C, 5th Regiment of the Pennsylvania Guard, and under the command of Captain Harry A. Miller, it was mustered into the service of the State on the 15th day of November, 1899.

Harry A. Miller continued in command of this company until the 20th of July, 1904, when John A. Woleslagle became Captain.

Company C, 5th Regiment of Infantry, as part of the 2nd Brigade of the Pennsylvania National Guard, attended an encampment held at Camp Homer J. Lindsay, at Tipton, Blair County, from the 20th to the 27th of July, 1907.

On the 1st of January, 1910, when the Dick Act reorganizing the National Guard of Pennsylvania, went into effect the Hollidaysburg Company was re-designated Company G, 10th Regiment of Infantry, and the officers at that time were: Captain John A. Woleslagle, First Lientenant William C. Weaver, Second Lieutenant Frank Brehman.

John A. Woleslagle continued in command of Company G, until the 7th of February, 1913, when William C. Leamer became Captain, and on the 8th of December, 1914, John R. Dunkel became Captain.

The reorganization of the National Guard of Pennsylvania under the Dick Act required each Regiment to have twelve companies. In order to accomplish this, the 5th Regiment, along with other organizations, was demobilized and Company C, received its new designation of Company G, 10th Regiment of Infantry.

SOLDIERS OF BLAIR COUNTY

On the 18th of June, 1916, fifteen days after the passage of the National Defense Act which gave the National Guard a federal status, the President of the United States called the Pennsylvania Guard into the Federal Service for duty on the Mexican border.

Company G, 10th Regiment of Infantry, responded to the call and arrived at Mt. Gretna on the 24th of June, and was mustered into the Federal Service on the 2nd of July, 1916.

The long journey to El Paso, Texas began at 10 o'clock, Sunday evening, July 2nd, over route 9 of the American Railway Association which was by way of Corry, Chicago, St. Louis and Dallas, and arrived at its destination on the 8th of July. The 10th Regiment was stationed at Camp Stewart, near El Paso, where it received extensive training in the art of warfare.

The names of the members of Company G, 10th Regiment of Pennsylvania Infantry, United States National Guard, at Camp Stewart, El Paso, Texas, in October of 1916, were as follows:

Captain   John R. Dunkel
First Lieutenant   Albert O. King
Second Lieutenant   Charles R. Rowan

Sergeant	*Corporals*	*Buglers*
Bruce I. Ebersole	Foster K. Burket	James E. Simpson
Francis A. Bender	John F. Devine	John F. Wicker
Gomer Evans	William McK. Hay	*Cooks*
Blake Lightner	Robert S. Krause	Harry L. Cuthbert
John G. Kimmell	Clarence B. Mock	John H. Minnigh
Ira D. Keirn	David Nelson	*Mechanic*
	Earl J. Plunket	Joseph B. Hill
	John R. Russell	

Privates

Aikens, Joseph V.	Fowkes, William McK.	Morse, Harry E.
Ake, Samuel M.	Good, Edward F.	Myers, Charles A.
Albright, Edward L.	Greene, Amos B.	Page, Charles W.
Anderson, William W.	Green, Thomas C.	Rhoades, Charles
Armstrong, Irving E.	Gutshall, Jesse C.	Robinson, Arthur L.
Bathurst, Clarence I.	Hartzell, Leon E.	Rourke, James F.
Benthamer, Fred D.	Hess, Harry G.	Rutherford, Richard K.
Bilger, Joseph	Hetrick, John S.	Shade, Charles M.
Bradley, Paul D.	Hill, Fred	Simpson, Ira E.
Breslin, Patrick A.	Hunt, Hearvey E.	Smith, Harry A.
Brown, Clifford	Hunter, Frederic D.	Spielman, John E.
Brown, Joseph C.	Koontz, Guy C.	Stewart, John D.
Brunner, Lawrence E.	Lightner, Willis C.	Stiffler, Logan E.
Cadle, Josiah D.	Loucks, Howard M.	Stouch, Ralph W.
Caldwell, Walter	Lowe, Lester L.	Stumpt, Bruce C.
Clarke, Harry E.	MacDonald, John A.	Taylor, Eli S.
Corbo, Thomas	McClellan, Harry A.	Wert, Edwin A.
Curry, Edward O.	McGee, Fred W.	Williams, Edwin W.
Dodson, Walter C.	Mathews, Morris J.	Wilt, Charley W.
Edwards, Watson N.	Mason, Frank L. B.	Wilt, Homer R.
Ehredt, Charles F.	Meloy, Herman L.	Wolf, John P.
Ferguson, Edward P.	Minnigh, Chester	Young, James H.
Fickes, Calvin R.	Murray, William W.	Zumsteg, Walter H.

The 10th Regiment returned from the Mexican Border on the 5th of October, 1916, and on the 11th it arrived in Pittsburgh where it was given a great ovation. Thousands of people lined the streets and the buildings were profusely decorated for the occasion.

THE WORLD WAR 315

A parade was formed and marched along Smithfield Street, and Fifth Avenue to the Soldiers Memorial Hall where speeches of welcome were made by Governor Brumbaugh.

The regiment then disbanded and Company G. returned on the 12th of October, 1916, and was mustered out of the service on the 15th of January, 1917.

COMPANY E

Company E, 5th Regiment of Infantry, Pennsylvania National Guard, was organized at Altoona during the spring of 1903, and mustered into the service on the 29th of June, 1903.

An account of the mustering of this company as printed in the *Altoona Mirror* of the 30th of June, reads as follows: "After many years of waiting, Altoona, at last has a military organization. Last evening Major John H. West, of Hollidaysburg, mustered into the service of Pennsylvania and the United States a company of about fifty-five men, the mustering being done in the Murray building. It will be known as Company E, Fifth Regiment, and will take the place of the company disbanded at Clearfield, June 22nd, by Major West. These officers were chosen for a term of five years: Captain Elmer K. Rupp, First Lieutenant William C. Leamer, and Second Lieutenant William P. Maclay. The Company will receive its equipment shortly and will start the drill at once, to be ready for camp on July 25th.

"All the officers are experienced military men. Captain Rupp and Lieutenant Leamer having served in the 5th Regiment in the Spanish War. Lieutenant Maclay spent two years in the Philippines.

"The new Company will drill tonight at 8 o'clock in the Uniform Rank, K of P. Hall, in the Morrow Block, Eleventh Avenue and Twelfth Street. A full attendance is desired, as important announcements will be made."

On the 1st of January, 1910, when the Dick Act went into effect reorganizing the National Guard and increasing the numerical strength of the various units, the Altoona Company was redesignated as Company M, and assigned to the 10th Regiment of Infantry, Pennsylvania National Guard.

COMPANY M

At the time of the mustering of the Altoona Company as Company M, 10th Regiment of Infantry, the 24th of January, 1910, the officers were as follows: Captain Urban G. Keime, First Lieutenant Harry B. Wise, and Second Lieutenant Frank G. Webber.

Captain Urban G. Keime was discharged on the 11th of June, 1910, and First Lieutenant Harry B. Wise was promoted to Captain on the 1st of July, 1910. The officers in command of Company M, on the 28th of February, 1912, at which time the Company was disbanded and transferred to Latrobe, were: Captain Harry B. Wise, First Lieutenant Frank G. Webber, and Second Lieutenant Edward R. Hunter. These officers were discharged on the 6th of April, 1912, and the Altoona Company passed out of existence.

PROVISIONAL HEADQUARTERS COMPANY

A unit designated as the Provisional Headquarters Company, 10th Regiment of Infantry, Pennsylvania National Guard, was organized at Altoona, on the 31st of December, 1914. This, Company was re-organized on the 14th of October, 1916, and recognized as Headquarters Company, 10th Regiment of Infantry.

SOLDIERS OF BLAIR COUNTY

HOME DEFENSE POLICE

A semi-military organization known as the Blair County Home Defense Police of Pennsylvania was organized during 1917, soon after the departure of the National Guard for camp. The members of the Home Defense Police in this county numbered close to one thousand and were commissioned police officers by the Governor of the Commonwealth of Pennsylvania.

They were drilled and received instruction in their duties which were to investigate reports of un-American activities and to make arrests and prosecutions when necessary. Each member was issued a badge, a whistle, an armband and a blackjack, and were given rank similar to a soldier in the army.

The officers of the Regimental Staff were as follows:

Colonel	J. L. Minick
Lieutenant Colonel	W. B. C. Allen
Lieutenant Colonel	B. J. Clark
Major	W. S. Greevy
Major	James W. Hayes
Major	J. R. Sloan
Major	Edgar McKinney
Captain and Adjutant	B. F. Barr
Captain and Quartermaster	J. N. Drass
Captain and Commissary	J. C. Sell
Captain and Chaplain	Rev. M. J. Canole
Captain and Chaplain	Rev. E. L. Eslinger

The locations of the various companies of the Regiment and their officers were as follows:

Co.	Location	Captain	First Lieutenant	Second Lieutenant
A	Altoona	B. I. Ebersole	Edmond H. Turner	C. R. Kunes
B	Altoona	W. C. Weaver	Francis M. Anderson	Wilbur L. Kunes
C	Altoona	Harry Wise		
D	Altoona	David S. Barr	Lloyd B. Ickes	Edgar C. Rice
E	Altoona	W. A. Silliman	J. H. Shearer	Elmer C. Ake
F	Bellwood	D. E. Wentzel	H. F. Cox	
G	Hollidaysburg	S. R. Dibert	William H. Haller	Benjamin F. Warfel
H	Roaring Spring	Samuel C. Kagarise	Harry Roush	Frank H. Logan
I	Duncansville	Asberry Kantner	C. G. Shaffer	Merritt L. Kunney
K	Llyswen	R. M. Steward	S. H. Owens	R. A. White
L	Williamsburg			
M	Juniata	A. V. Wester	L. W. Ferguson	H. C. Trout

THE UNITED STATES ARMY

With the entry of the United States into the World War on the 6th of April, 1917, the work of recruiting and training the National Guard was hastened. Members who had dependents and those who were unable to pass the rigid examinations were discharged and others recruited to take their places.

Several units of the Pennsylvania National Guard were called to the colors as soon as it was seen that war was inevitable for the purpose of guarding tunnels, bridges and other important points throughout the State.

The 3rd Regiment of Pennsylvania Infantry, from Philadelphia, was assigned to this section and regimental headquarters were established at Altoona. This regiment left Philadelphia on the 2nd of April, and arrived at Altoona the next morning. It was relieved on the 14th of August, 1917, and returned to Philadelphia.

During the period that the 3rd Regiment was stationed in this section, a number of Blair County men enrolled in its ranks. This regiment became part of the 110th Infantry when called to the Federal Service, which placed the Blair County members of this regiment with the members of Company G, from Blair County.

SHERIDAN TROOP

The Sheridan Troop, of Tyrone, continued as a unit of the Pennsylvania National Guard following its return from the Mexican Border, and was designated as Troop B, 1st Pennsylvania Cavalry, Pennsylvania National Guard.

Upon the call of the President for service during the World War, the members of the Sheridan Troop mobilized at their armory at Tyrone on the 15th of July, 1917. Here it was mustered into the Federal Service on the 20th of July, 1917, and on the 5th of August, it was drafted into the United States army for service outside the continental limits of the United States.

The 1st Cavalry, National Guard of the United States, entrained for Camp Hancock, Augusta, Georgia, where it arrived on the 11th of September, 1917, and trained as part of the 28th Division.

Under the new table of organization the 1st Cavalry was designated the 101st Cavalry. However, as cavalry units were not desired for the type of warfare being fought in Europe, the personnel of the 101st Cavalry were transferred to other units, and the 101st Cavalry was disbanded on the 12th of November, 1917.

The entire enlisted personnel of the Sheridan Troop was transferred to the 103rd Trench Mortar Battery, and about one month later many of the Tyrone members were transferred to other units, including the 103rd Engineers, the Military Police, the 103rd Veterinary Corps, and Headquarters Troop, 28th Division.

Practically all of the members of the Sheridan Troop saw service in France with the American Expeditionary Forces.

The roster of the Sheridan Troop, as Troop B, 1st Cavalry, during its training period at Camp Hancock, Augusta, Georgia, was as follows:

Major   James F. Moore
Captain   Reuben H. Harris
First Lieutenant   Joseph A. Dickson
Second Lieutenant   John Boyd Goheen

SOLDIERS OF BLAIR COUNTY

Sergeants	*Corporals*	*Cooks*
First — Frank L. Dickson	John L. Beam	Plumer J. Irvin
Supply — Bernard B. Wallace	Charles M. Steel	James H. Armstrong
Stable — Milton F. Gensimer	Alton C. Woodring	Albert F. Dahlstrom
Mess — Norris E. Hildebrand	Max M. Askey	*Horseshoers*
Elmer E. Mong	James C. Reed	Walter E. Conrad
Milroy H. Hampton	Clair N. Grove	Orlando B. Moore
William H. Sprague	Chester D. Moore	*Saddler*
Edward M. Bell	Walter L. Schopp	Frederick F. Love
Harry D. Peary		*Musicians*
		Amon L. DeArment
		Paul C. Conrad

Privates

Barrett, Whitford R.
Burrows, Paul W.
Brant, Fred L.
Bressler, Arthur D.
Calbert, George O.
Cassady, Charles H.
Castranio, James A.
Cryder, Harry E.
Davis, Christian K.
Davis, Edward R.
Dennis, Benjamin F.
Deshong, Oscar Earl
Diggins, Hugh E.
Dunlap, John E.
Ehrhart, Lisle C.
Eyer, Donald J.
Fagley, John D.
Felty, John A.
Fields, Guyer R.
Fink, James G.
Fleck, Verne W.
Frazier, William A.
Fry, Jesse L.
Gardner, Paul F.
Gibson, Newton E.
Gill, William L.
Gillam, Sewell P.
Gilmore, Cloyd P.
Griffin, Paul F.
Herzog, Clarence W.
Hildebrand, John W.
Holden, Ralph A.
Horning, James B.
Huber, John G.
Hughes, John T.
Jones, Burton K.
Kaiser, George B.
Kanour, Gilbert E.
Kester, Carl W.
Klepser, John M.

Kloss, David S.
Kolessy, John F.
Krape, Joseph R.
Lucas, James H.
Lytle, Fred M.
McCann, James W.
McCullough, Chester B.
McDonnell, Owen F.
McFadden, Charles E.
McFarland, Ralph G.
McNeal, Orris L.
Martz, George D.
Maugle, Edward H.
Meehan, Robert F.
Meredith, David H.
Morrison, Albert O.
Nicodemus, Albert H.
Patterson, Robert D.
Parks, Preston O.
Rhodes, Gilbert D.
Root, James D.
Runk, William A.
Schell, Richard J.
Sears, William O.
Sellers, Harry N.
Shires, Joseph A.
Shollenberger, Edward M.
Sickler, John J.
Seibert, Jerome T.
Snyder, Adam T.
Stewart, Alexander M.
Stratiff, Paul F.
Tate, Joseph L.
Thompson, Harold M.
Tyson, Edwin L.
VanScoyoc, John H.
Waring, Monroe C.
Wiley, Harry E.
Yergy, John L.
Yingling, Chester M.

COMPANY G

Upon the return of Company G, 10th Regiment of Infantry, Pennsylvania National Guard, from duty on the Mexican Border, it was decided not to reestablish headquarters in its armory at Hollidaysburg, as the great majority of the personnel of the company were from Altoona, but rather to secure rooms somewhere in Altoona. Quarters were therefore secured in the Stehley Building, where activities were resumed and the members trained and prepared for future emergencies.

The members of Company G, responded to the call of the President of the United States on the 15th of July, 1917, for duty against the Imperial German nation and mobilized at the armory at Altoona. The company was mustered into Federal Service at Altoona on the 20th of July, 1917, and drafted into the United States Army on the 5th of August, 1917.

Company G entrained at Altoona on the 7th of September, 1917, and arrived at Camp Hancock, Augusta, Georgia, on the 10th. Here the 10th Regiment of Infantry was consolidated with the 3rd Infantry to form the 110th Regiment of Infantry, 28th Division.

As part of the 2nd Battalion, 110th Infantry, the Blair County company entrained at Camp Hancock during the latter part of April, 1918, for Camp Merritt at Hoboken, New Jersey, from where it departed on the 2nd of May, and boarded the British ship "Corsican." It debarked on the 17th of May, at Liverpool, England, and traveled by train by way of London to Dover. On the afternoon of the 19th of May, 1918, the organization left Dover and arrived at Calais, France, during the evening and was taken to Rest Camp No. 6.

As a unit of the 28th Division, American Expeditionary Forces, Company G, saw extensive service, participating in the following battles and engagements: Lorraine, Champagne, Champagne-Marne, Aisne-Marne, Oise-Aisne, and Meuse-Argonne.

The roster of Company G, as of the 20th of July, 1917, was as follows:

Captain John R. Dunkel
First Lieutenant Charles R. Rowan
Second Lieutenant Robert S. Krause

	Sergeants	Corporals	Bugler
First	Ira D. Keirn	John R. Russell	Alfred W. Milleisen
Mess	Foster K. Burket	John D. Stewart	*Cooks*
Supply	William McK. Hay	William W. Murray	Ralph W. Stouch
	Blake Lightner	John F. Wicker	Charles W. Page
	Francis A. Bender	Samuel M. Ake	William L. Smith
	Clarence B. Mock	Josiah D. Cadle	*Mechanics*
	Earl J. Plunket	John F. Foley	Charles F. Ehredt
	Harry A. Smith	Thomas C. Green	Richard K. Rutherford
	Harry E. Morse	Arthur A. Glunt	
	Harry E. Clarke	Jesse C. Gutshall	
	Bruce Stump	Charles A. Myers	
		John P. Wolf	
		Ira E. Simpson	
		James H. Young	
		John M. Black	
		Edwin W. Williams	
		Harold M. Haworth	

Privates

Amrhein, Jacob	Hildebrand, Cloyd A.	Rhine, Thomas A.
Anderson, John M.	Hoffman, Herbert H.	Robinson, Arthur L.
Ashburn, Paul M.	Hoover, John L.	Robison, Bernard D.
Black, William A.	Hunter, Frederick D.	Rothrock, Roy R.
Bollinger, George E.	Huston, Harvey H. S.	Rourke, James F.
Bower, William L.	Imler, William F.	Russell, Robert N.
Bradley, Paul D.	Johnston, Harry N.	Rutherford, Raymond A.
Brandt, Henry U.	Kelly, Raymond X.	Saylor, Mac R.
Brown, Clifford	Kelley, William L.	Schaaf, Gilbert E.
Brown, Joseph T.	Keller, William E.	Shelly, William
Bruner, Lawrence E.	Kitchen, Martin O.	Showalter, Daniel C.
Buck, Walter S.	Koontz, Guy C.	Showers, Lewis McC.
Carson, David F.	Kottman, Martin E.	Smith, Alfred E.
Chase, Robert W.	Kreuz, John	Smith, Dennie M.
Chilcoat, Harry D.	Lewis, Leon	Smith, Herbert A.
Cichon, Walter	Lightner, Willis C.	Smith, Roy A.
Corl, Robert A.	Loucks, Howard M.	Stewart, Charles F.
Coxey, Charles R.	Lowe, Lester L.	Stiver, Warren
Curry, Edward	Lucas, Samuel C.	Tarr, Isadore
Decker, Jacob A.	Lynn, William E.	Taylor, Eli S.
Decker, James D.	Maraldo, Domenick	Temple, William H.
Decker, Raymond F.	Marshall, Samuel A.	Vance, George H.
Dodson, Walter C.	Mathews, Morris J.	Wagner, Harry A.
Ferguson, Edward P.	McDonald, John A.	Walker, Riley A.
Fickes, Calvin R.	McIntire, Duncan R.	Walsh, John B.
Flanagan, John P.	Meloy, Herman L.	Wicker, Harry A.
Forrester, Harry W.	Metzger, Eugene A.	Wileman, Charles E.
Fowkes, William M.	Metzgar, George J.	Williams, Maurice B.
Frederick, John S.	Miller, Joseph F.	Wilt, Charley W.
Gearhart, Donald L.	Mobley, Russell E.	Wilt, Homer R.
Giarth, William C.	Nale, Clair P.	Wolfe, Clyde E.
Gill, Boyd R.	Nale, Gilbert E.	Wolf, George C.
Grassmyer, Nelson G.	Nelson, Ray E.	Wood, John R.
Green, Edward E.	Noel, Herbert W.	Woomer, Nathan C.
Gunsallus, Harry W.	Olewine, Robert E.	Young, Hiram L.
Gunsallus, Ira D.	Oswalt, Raymond H.	Zobel, Samuel C.
Hauser, Edward F.	Paul, Earl	Zumsteg, Ralph R.
Heinbaugh, Herman E.	Policastro, Joseph	Zumsteg, Walter H.
Heller, Josiah L.	Rhine, Harry E.	

Among other units to receive soldiers from Blair County were the 19th Engineers, the Spruce Division, and the 305th Engineers. Many of the young men who came in the Draft were enrolled in the college vocational course as members of the Student Army Training Camp, while others from this County were assigned to the 79th and 80th Divisions of the National Army, and trained at Camp Lee, Virginia.

PENNSYLVANIA RESERVE MILITIA

Troop C, of the Squadron Cavalry, of Tyrone, Pennsylvania Reserve Militia, was organized during the early part of 1918, and mustered out of the service of the Commonwealth of Pennsylvania on the 17th of May, 1920.

The officers of Troop C, were: Captain Edgar McKinney, First Lieutenant John C. Trego, and Second Lieutenant Charles T. Snyder.

CHRONICLES

OF

LOCAL DRAFT BOARD FOR DIVISION NO. 1
BLAIR COUNTY

located at

324½ Allegheny Street

HOLLIDAYSBURG, PA.

CHRONICLERS:—

W. LOVELL BALDRIGE, *Chairman*
ROBERT W. SMITH, *Secretary*
MISS ELIZABETH W. SMITH, *Chief Clerk*

ROSTER OF

LOCAL DRAFT BOARD FOR DIVISION NO. 1
BLAIR COUNTY

W. Lovell Baldrige .... *Chairman*
Robert W. Smith .... *Secretary*
Wayland R. Palmer, M. D. .... *Chief Medical Examiner*
Roy Deck .... *Member*
    (resigned to enter United States Army)
Harry S. Holland .... *Member*
    (resigned to enter United States Army)
J. Lee Plummer, Esq. .... *Government Appeal Attorney*
Robert C. Irwin, M. D. .... *Medical Examiner*
Frank R. Shoemaker, M. D. .... *Medical Examiner*
Elizabeth W. Smith .... *Chief Clerk*
Laura S. Baldrige .... *Clerk*
Elizabeth C. Stanley .... *Clerk*
Private Victor Paul Gearhart .... *Sergeant at Arms*
James L. Lusardi .... *Official Interpreter*
E. E. Fuller .... *Clerk to Medical Examiner*
J. Henry Albright .... *Page*
Corporal John Brenneman .... *Messenger*
Rev. William H. Orr .... ⎧ Emergency Workers
Rev. Julius F. Seebach .... ⎨   during
Rev. E. E. Harter .... ⎩ Influenza Epidemic

INTRODUCTION

The history of the selective draft would not be complete without tribute being paid to the patriotic eagerness of the boys to serve, when called, and the equally patriotic eagerness of the mothers of these boys to bear their burden of sorrow, over the departure of their sons.

The element of sorrow was, of course, prevalent throughout the draft; partings, with probable permanency, made it impossible to conduct such a heart-breaking governmental service with anything like elation or buoyancy, but the profound patriotism of the mothers was impressive.

Cases of absolute disloyalty were isolated; indeed, there were but several cases coming within the knowledge of this Local Board, and, considering that over 6000 registrants were handled by it, the percentage of disloyalty was nil.

Cases of slackerism were isloated; there were, of course, many who did not understand their duty and who naturally thought the evasion of it was not a crime, nor even despicable, but they were not nearly so numerous as reports from time to time tried to make it appear.

On the other hand, sons of German emigrants were enthusiastic in almost all cases; some of them went forth in officers' uniforms, displaying loyalty which was remarkable considering their previous home training and surroundings.

The sincere desire of our boys to "stand up front," and to prove the stuff of which real men are made, was the rule; the Local Board was helpful in showing some of them their duty and, by argument and logic, was able to strengthen those who displayed any weakness of patriotic desire.

The stoicism of the parents was magnificent; they accepted the inevitable and lent their acquiescence to the governmental demands with universal resignation and satisfaction.

The development of their sons into soldiers, accompanied with the usual advancements and recognition for special qualifications, were noted by parents and friends alike with that satisfaction which was natural and this process of interest had its effect upon their intensity of service in war activities at home.

Voluntary enlistments in this section of Blair County compared more than favorably with those of other sections of the Union and those who volunteered reflected credit upon themselves and friends without exception.

The selective service board was ably assisted by an enthusiastic public opinion, which proved its value in giving information through which the Local Board was able to conduct its work with smoothness, and without arousing more than the ordinary amount of antagonism and which latter was confined to those opposed to conscription or disloyal at heart.

The members of the Local Board never felt that they had borne any burdens of consequence; their labors were, of course, distasteful since they dealt with a peculiarly close relationship of each home affected, but even with the long hours often necessary to accomplish the work assigned them, they remembered that "over there" hours of duty were not counted nor even decent living conditions considered, so with full knowledge that their lot was incomparable with that of the boys who were making supreme sacrifices, they are prepared to say that their duties were not more than inconvenient.

GENERAL ACTIVITIES OF THE BOARD

There were one hundred partriotic demonstrations and parades, under the direction of this Board. Two Clergymen, Rev. Harry F. Strong, Methodist, and Rev. George R. Ehrgood, Reformed, were inducted as Chaplains in the Army. Harry S. Holland, the Board Chairman, resigned to accept a commission as Captain in the Remount Service. Miss Orphea Wilt was inducted into the Army as a Red Cross Nurse. Stirring receptions were accorded these military recruits. The Red Cross Society provided one thousand Comfy Kits for the departing soldiers.

A Soldiers' Farewell in Hollidaysburg meant the suspension of business in the town, the assembling of the Liberty Band, Home Defense Guards, Girls Escort Battalion, Boy Scouts, Public School pupils, all public officials, Catholic and Protestant clergymen at the Court House, for a rousing and fervent "Good Bye and God Bless You."

When the limited service soldiers went away to Syracuse to enter the service as fire fighters, the local fire company turned out and the recruits rode in triumph to the station aboard the fire motor truck.

There were fifteen hundred physical examinations held at the Y. M. C. A. Home. The draftees were given access to the Gymnasium, Swimming Pool, and Bowling Alleys.

CONTRIBUTIONS TO THE MILITARY SERVICE

This Board had the military destinies of SIX THOUSAND AND FIFTY (6,050) under its control, apportioned as follows:—

Registration of June, 1917 2359
Registration of June and August, 1918 258
Registration of September, 1918 3433

Total 6,050

Seven Hundred and Six (706) Registrants of the Local Board were inducted into the military service:—

To Camp Lee, Virginia, the General Supply Camp for this Local Board, were sent .... 403 Registrants

The Draftees and Volunteers of this Local Board were distributed among forty-nine (49) Cantonments, camps, barracks, colleges, and training stations.

Twenty (20) Volunteers went to Vancouver Barracks, Washington, as Soldiers in the Spruce Division.

Six (6) went to Kelly Field, Texas to engage in military aeronautics work, and eight (8) Registrants were forwarded to Camp Sevier, South Carolina, to engage in similar service.

One Registrant was inducted in the Gas Defense Section in Washington, D. C.

One Hundred and Thirty-seven (137) young men entered the College Vocational Courses. This Local Board claims the honor of sending the largest number of registrants into special college vocational courses of any local board in Pennsylvania.

THE FIRST SELECTIVE SERVICE BOARD ON EARTH

Addressing an assemblage of five hundred Draftees at the Court House, Hollidaysburgh, Pennsylvania, Robert W. Smith, the Secretary of the Board, outlined this story of the first Selective Service Board on earth:—

"Let us recall the olden story of the first drafted man on earth. Gideon was the commander of the Israelites. He had an army of 32,000 men at his back. He sought to draft out of that army only the strongest and best warriors to fight the enemy. He thereupon constituted himself the first Selective Service Board in the history of the world. His first draft order was that all his soldiers, who had dependents, or were slackers, or who were afraid and wanted to go home, may go. Thereupon 22,000 Israelites deserted the colors and went home, leaving 10,000 comrades behind to fight the battle. The commander then proceeded to separate the physically disqualified from the army. So, this novel test of efficiency was applied. The 10,000 soldiers were marched down to a stream and commanded to drink. Ninety-seven hundred got down on all fours to drink, thereby proving that they were physically unfit, lacking both the agility and virility to wage successful combat against the foe. But the three hundred remaining soldiers were so eager for the coming fray, so alert against any possible surprise attack of the enemy, that they disdained to stoop and kneel. They stood erect. Each one scooped up the water in the palms of his hands, and drank.

"These brisk, energetic men, swift of limb and steady of purpose, were the soldiers chosen in the selective service of the long, long ago. Better three hundred picked men, than 32,000 doubtful fighters for Gideon's Army. Holy Writ tells us, that these drafted men were entrusted with the sword of the Lord and of Gideon, and achieved a glorious victory. The American Nation enters the world war, for the sake of justice, righteousness and humanity. She is calling her sons to rally around her banner, as modern Gideons, that freedom, and equality and liberty may not perish from the earth.

"The conscript ages of 21 to 30 were the ages of the great and mighty captains in the army of the Lord. David, the shepherd boy, was a warrior, who prayed in his Psalm, 'Thou hast taught my hands to war, and my fingers to fight.' A boy of the plains became Joseph, the first food conservator and food controller of Egypt. Our Saviour began his sacred ministry, at the age of 30. He, too, was within the conscript age. We rejoice, that America's Selective Service Army of ten million, in the pink and flower of their early manhood, will fight in a righteous cause, and will fight all the harder for so knowing.

"From the jury wheel in this Court House are drawn the names of jurors, who are to render justice between man and man. From the conscription wheel are drawn the names of Gideon soldiers, who are to render justice between nation and nation.

"Rich man, poor man, beggarman, saint and sinner, all have an equal chance to enter Gideon's Army.

CAMP RECLAMATION, IN THE STATE OF CORRECTION

"In this District, three physicians have certified, that 564 young men are physically deficient, and unfit for service in the National Army. I commend these figures to your sober and intelligent consideration. One hundred and forty-three men were rejected, because their hearts were not right. The alcoholic heart, the tobacco heart, the youthful folly heart, the heart that pounds like a motor car of ancient make, are where the good, right beating heart ought to be. O, you mother who did not raise your boy to be a soldier, have a care for the heart of that boy. One hundred and eighty-two were rejected because their bodies have been overtaxed. Thoughtless and inconsiderate fathers make pack horses, burden bearers of their sons. We are taught, that the human body was made, in the Divine image. Why shatter the physical vase, in which God put the precious jewel of eternity? The physicians rejected forty-nine men for underweight, nineteen for defective hearing, thirty-seven for defective vision. These ills and imperfections may in the main be corrected.

This Nation is conserving its food power. It is conserving its fuel power. Why should not Uncle Sam also conserve his man power develop all the boys called to the army to their fullest, physical perfection? This District will send five hundred accepted soldiers to Camp Lee, in the State of Virginia. Why should not the District also send 564 rejected soldiers to CAMP RECLAMATION, IN THE COUNTRY OF GOOD WILL AND STATE OF CORRECTION? There are 564 stars lost to our Service Flag. In your jubilation for the laddies, who won, remember in kindness and sympathy, the laddies who tried and lost, the stars lost to the Flag."

THE FINDING OF GEORGE WASHINGTON HICKS, DELINQUENT

His name was George Washington Hicks. His Order Number was in the two hundreds of the First Draft. We smiled when we mailed him a questionnaire. We were so sure that a namesake of Truthful George would rush to the first call to the colors. But the Questionnaire came back "Unclaimed." We waited a few weeks and sent him another—a perfectly fresh one. Back it came to us with the Village Postmaster's pencil notation thereon—"Party Unknown Here." Weeks went by and then we sent him a summons for physical examination. Like the cat and the dandelion on our lawn—it came back. We then mailed a peck of "BE ALERT" cards to him and then a second summons for physical examination. And they all came back to our office unclaimed. Evidently George Washington Hicks had vanished off of the face of the earth after Registration Day. Now, the Hicks family was celebrated throughout the whole Northern end of the District for patriotism. No contigent departing for Camp was complete without a Hicks.

It seemed to us that we had drawn so heavily from this particular family that there were none left but Four A's and Five G's. And they all went willingly and gladly—eager for the Big Fight. It was unbelievable that there was a slacker in the Hicks family.

We made up our Delinquent List in May. And we placed thereon the name of Charley Ross of the Hicks Family. In a few weeks the Adjutant General had located a missing registrant of our Board, a certain gentleman of color who used to step around town in a polka dot shirt and play a banjo all day long. He was hustled off to Camp with his banjo under his arm. And they found four of our Italians up in Yonkers, New York, and a tubercular boy in a Detroit sanitarium. The Adjutant General was working hard on that list. One by one the great dragnet of the Selective Service System was pulling the slackers in. But George Washington Hicks was not of these.

It was in June when he came to us. We were hard at work one sunny afternoon when the screen door flapped with a very vigorous flap. We looked up and beheld one of the most grotesque figures that had visited our office during the draft. The newcomer was tall—so tall he was obliged to stoop to enter the door. He was built on the macaroni style of architecture—long and lean like Uncle Sam. He looked more like a cartoon clipped from the pages of *Life* or *Judge* than a real man. On his head was an immense straw hat with a big piece of the brim torn out—probably chewed out by a hungry calf. He wore a patched seersucker shirt, and his dirty suspenders clutched at two lone buttons on his shabby overalls. Those buttons could have given William G. McAdoo pointers on responsibility. His feet were gigantic and he had incased them in mud-bespattered shoes, which he told us later had been made from the hide of a calf he had butchered. Topping off this tall, thin body was the full, round face of a boy, with big brown eyes, and a wide, toothy smile. At his heels was a little fat woman in a faded calico wrapper and an old-fashioned slat sunbonnet. We could not see her face, but we caught the gleam of sharp, dark eyes.

At first the Secretary thought he was the victim of a practical joke. A few moments' conversation with the new arrivals allayed his suspicion. This was the real, righty, honest-to-goodness George Washington Hicks. The village postmaster had at last gotten busy. He did a little detective work, and sent a messenger up into the Alleghenies, and ordered George to hustle back to civilization and lift his mail. After a conversation with the postmaster and an explanation of the Adjutant General's admonitions, our delinquent registrant and his wife walked fifteen miles to Hollidaysburg.

The Secretary explained to Hicks the seriousness of his delinquency, and informed him that he must immediately submit to physical examination, and if he was found fit for service he would be sent to Camp at once.

Hicks crossed one long leg over the other. We trembled lest he would smash the glass in the bookcase on the opposite side of the room.

"Well, Gents," said he, "You see, I thought this war was over long ago. My old pap said it didn't take no more than a few months to beat up Spain, and he reckoned old Germany would git the stuffins lammed out of her in about two weeks. The feller what registered me said he reckoned I was safe. They'd never need me till they started to put lightnin' rods in the trenches. So I just went off and got married, moved away up on the mountain and didn't bother no more about war. I never wrote and I never got a letter in my life.

"And Gents, if you are goin' to send me to war now, one thing's certain and that is —you've got to take my missus too. You don't leave her behind, no siree! We ain't been separated since we was hitched up. She sticks closer to me than a burr to a cow's tail. If you takes me, you takes her too. She could wash dishes and patch pants for the boys in camp."

The Secretary explained that it was impossible to grant this request, and that the Government would provide for Mrs. Hicks financially while her husband was at war. And he added cheerfully that the war would soon be over and the separation would be of very short duration.

The little fat figure straightened up. Fire flashed from under the sunbonnet. The Secretary winced for he had heard somewhere that "The female of the species was more deadly than the male." She burst out—"My George ain't for sale or rent to no one. If he goes, I got to go too. I don't want your money—I jest wants George." She was like a vicious little terrier on guard before her master. And it looked as though the draft members were in danger of contracting Hydrophobia if they insisted upon sending George to camp.

Arguments were useless. Finally, George experienced a sudden change of heart. He announced his willingness to submit to physical examination. "Bring on your Doc," said he, "I'll let him look me over. And you'd better take my missus with me 'cause she kin give the Doc pointers on my ailments. Git a wiggle on, because we got to git home 'for milkin' time."

So George Washington Hicks was folded up in our Medical Examiner's Ford, his knees almost puncturing the top, and conveyed to the Y.M.C.A. Gymnasium for examination. Down the street they sped, and following close behind was the fat and faithful one in the calico wrapper. Down on the steps of the "Gym" she sank, and waited outside for the doctor's verdict in a perfect passion of rage and rebellion.

Hicks was duly examined. He refused to remove his clothing and only under threat of arrest did he disrobe. He said he hadn't changed his clothes for three months—he was too busy and it was too much bother. He had an Ingersoll watch. He lived in mortal fear that the watch would be stolen from him. Throughout the examination his eyes never once left the spot where he had laid it. He even distrusted the doctor, for he could not understand how any human being could fail to be attracted to such a magnificent time piece. In his eyes it was a test of any man's honesty.

Well, we lost George Washington Hicks. That doctor found everything wrong with him—underweight, overheight, hypertrophy and flat feet. The doctor stated that he had superintended the examination of two thousand pairs of feet, but never had he beheld a pair of feet built just like George's. We sent Hicks away with a Five-G card in his pocket. As they passed out of the office, Mrs. Hicks flashed from under her sunbonnet a triumphant black eye, and then stuck her tongue out at the Secretary.

We never forgave the medical examiner for refusing to let us have George Washington Hicks. We had gleefully picture how fine he would look marching down to the depot with our next contingent of future Guy Empeys and Sergeant Peats on their way to Camp.

OUR LIBERTY BAND

To keep the people of the District on the tiptoes of enthusiasm, the Board organized the Liberty Band. Patriotic devotion ran the marching force of this unique musical society up to fifty, and the Flu Epidemic kept the numbers down to four.

As each young bandman was drafted into the service, the Board drafted a superannuated musician under the *Blow or Fight Regulations*, as his successor.

The bandmen ranged in ages from thirteen to seventy, and in avoirdupois from eighty-five to two hundred and sixty pounds. The two hundred and sixty pound basso marched side by side with the eighty-five pound trombonist.

There was a chocolate brown who would never take his place in the ranks until the first tune, "Keep the Home Fires Burning," was played. The lump in his throat during the rendition of that tune shut off the wind from his tenor horn.

The Hollidaysburg Burgess, the G. A. R., Colonel, and a red-headed color bearer, who had fought under Grant, could always be depended upon to lead the Band. The Hollidaysburg Postmaster, druggist, Court House Clerks, tinshop man and mechanics, kept their horns upon their desks and work-benches, ready for immediate use and service. Whenever the War Board called them, these Musical Minute-men assembled in front of the Board Headquarters, prepared to escort to the railroad station either a contingent of seventy-five Camp Lee recruits, or one lone volunteer for the Spruce Division on the Pacific Slope.

When the news of the big American victories came in piping hot over the Associated Press wires at the witching hour of midnight, our own Liberty Band paraded to the homes of the Blair County Judge and the Board Officials, separated them from their downy couches, and summoned them to participate in a glorious all-night parade in honor of the achievement of Yankee arms.

When the New York newspapers captured the Crown Prince, the Liberty Band, with four musicians in line, started the parade of two Draft Board Officials, one Burgess, one hot dog restaurant man, and one undertaker, by playing "The Star Spangled Banner." Four hours later, the dawn of day saw that Band, fifty strong, and two thousand paraders, tramping wearily down the street, and the musicians had kept continuously and unceasingly playing that tune.

The Liberty Band may justly claim the long time record for the rendition of our National Anthem. When Fame distributes her chaplets of glory, the Liberty Band will not be forgotten.

HOW HEINE PIPPERT SAVED THE FLAGS

One of our Board's biggest problems was how to get rid of the waste paper. We bought an immense clothes hamper. It was in a chronic state of engorgement. There was a perpetual Niagara of paper overflowing the sides and flooding the floor. So we awarded to Heine Pippert the exclusive contract for keeping that basket empty. Thereafter, every time we flashed an S.O.S. Our Basket Runneth Over, Pippert would pull up in front of our office with a fat and lazy old horse hitched to a ramshackle cart, and take away our paper.

Now, Pippert was a German—born in Germany. At the outbreak of the War he was a staunch admirer of the Man with the Mailed Fist, and a loyal son of the Fatherland that had starved and frozen him into exile. So outspoken was he in his denunciations of England, so rabid in his hatred of France, that he grew to be about as popular as a smallpox patient at a health resort. Little by little, as America was drawn into the great whirlpool of war, Pippert was constantly under suspicion and surveillance. He became involved in frequent quarrels and on several occasions narrowly escaped arrest.

One day a certain long, lean gentleman, who always has his pictures taken in striped trousers, a long tailed blue coat and a high hat with a starry band, reached down into a humble little home on the outskirts of Hollidaysburg, and took away a boy in the pride and prime of his young manhood, clothed him in khaki, gave him a gun and sent him on a sea voyage.

Pippert was stricken dumb. Physical suffering showed in every line of his face. He aged ten years. He grew as silent and morose as he had formerly been loud and boastful. Days went by and then a wonderful thing happened. A little flag with a blue star peeped shyly out of the front window in Pippert's home. Then a big red cross slipped up by its side, and over them all went the sign that Pippert owned a Liberty Bond. And one Spring morning a pole went up in the neat little front yard and from it waved a starry banner that was the pride and envy of the whole neighborhood. Then Pippert invariably occupied the Amen corner at all the patriotic demonstrations in Hollidaysburg; he read all the newspapers and could locate the exact spot of the legions of Uncle Sam in Flanders. And after Chateau Thierry, he broke a twenty year record for sobriety by getting shamefully drunk.

One bright Spring morning, Pippert drove up to our office. He had a perfect poultice of Red Cross and Liberty Bond buttons on his chest and his horse was gay with penny flags. He was whistling "Over There" in a downright hilarious manner.

Our Board had scheduled seven hearings for that morning. Witnesses had been subpoenaed from the country round about. So full was the office that they overflowed out into the street. Our office had no rear exit, and Pippert was obliged to peddle the hamper out through the front door. He was busy packing into the basket when a fat and fiery patriot, a Captain in the Home Defense Guards, who had no confidence in Heine's conversion to the principles of Democracy, flung open the door and yelled to Heine to come out at once—his crazy old horse was eating the flags of the Allies on an automobile.

Heine made a mad dive for the front door with the hamper in his arms, deluging the waiting witnesses and Board Members with waste paper and leaving a long white trail out into the street.

A motorist had left his car standing in front of our office and the horse had started to devour the flags on the machine. When Heine arrived on the scene, the animal had completely eaten up poor little Belgium, had only a shred of Great Britain dangling from his teeth, and was already casting an anticipatory eye on the banner of France. Pippert struck the animal a stinging blow, and pulled him away from his Banquet of Flags. The overfed and over-petted beast was so startled and frightened by his master's cruelty that he started down the street like a winner of the blue ribbon at a Blair County Fair. The crowd had grown in the twinkling of an eye. The Home Defense Captain took the matter in a very serious light, but when the crowd beheld the enraged Pippert beating the unpatriotic and disloyal horse, everybody broke into a hearty laugh.

ABSURDITIES REVEALED BY THE WORK OR FIGHT ORDERS

The enforcement of the Work or Fight regulations revealed many oddities and absurdities of domestic life.

One tearful wife, anxious to defend her husband from the charge of being a chronic loafer, explained to the Chairman of the Board:

"Indeed, he isn't idle all the time. He beats me part of the time. But then he never beats me hard."

Excusing her husband for filling a non-essential job of driving a milk wagon, a woman wrote:

"He is too fat to fill any but a settin' job." To which the Government Appeal Attorney replied: "Give him the hen's job."

Another idler's wife offered the Board this compromise settlement:

"I am willing that he go to the Army, but the Government must give him back to me at the end of three months. That will teach him to git up and hustle."

Three veracious farmers made affidavits that a young man was usefully engaged as a skilled laborer on a farm. A little later, the village Vigilantes produced indubitable evidence that the extent of the boy's agricultural labors consisted in stirring plum butter in the back kitchen of his mother's home.

THE DOUGHNUT SYMBOL

Twenty-two conscientious objectors to war were sent by the Board to War. One objector, who aired his views in a manner displeasing to the commanding officer, spent the greater portion of the year in a guard house at Camp Lee.

A brawny blacksmith was appointed leader of a contingent that included two objectors. The leader, while aboard train en route to Camp, broke the seal of the Board envelope that contained the military records of his men. He noticed there the non-combatant symbol (O) opposite the names of the two objectors.

Summoning the men before him, the leader inquired, "What is the meaning of this doughnut?" The objectors told him that they were men of peace. The doughnut symbol so incensed the blacksmith that he beat and mauled the objectors so severely that they were placed in a Hospital Ward, upon their arrival at Camp.

The majority of the Board's list of objectors were of the Mennonite faith. A leader of the clan gave this viewpoint:

"The blood and iron Kings of Germany expelled Menno, the Father of our faith, from the realm. We are now going back to Germany to do what we can as non-combatant soldiers, to break the despotic powers that drove Father Menno and our ancestors into exile four centuries ago."

NO PEACE FOR THE BEE MAN

The District Board exempted the proprietor of an apiary from military service on the grounds that "he is engaged in a necessary agricultural enterprise."

This judgment provoked a torrent of condemnation. A father who had a three star service flag in the front window of his home, led a cohort of complaints. A mother, whose boy was in the bullet swept trenches of Flanders, headed a solid phalanx of poisoned pen pushers.

This Board vainly explained that five wise old owls, sitting on the District Board at Greensburg, one hundred miles away, had decided that the maker of honey was helping to win the war.

The complainants retorted that Mr. Hoover's bread was sticky enough without a top layer of a slacker's honey. The hornets swarmed to the sacred precincts of the office of the Provost Marshal General. There was a rehearing of the bee man's case, and his name went on the military service rolls.

A SHARP TURN ON A SHARP SHOOTER

A deserted wife whose husband was compelled by Court authority to support her, indited these lines:—
"Dear Draft Board:—

You may send my husband to War. He pays me only $16.00 a month for the support of myself and child. He does this because the Court ordered him so to do. I am told that the Government will pay me $32.50 a month, if he goes to War.

My man is a great hunter. He is the best marksman in this neighborhood. He has spent more money on guns, powder, and hunting dogs than he ever spent on me. He can help both me and his Country by going to France as a sharpshooter.

Yours Patriotically, H--R--."

A BULLY WITH A WEAK HEART

This Board was waited upon by delegations of citizens who wanted men kept out of the war, and by other delegations who wanted men sent to war.

Prominent citizens of a town of the District besieged the Board one day with the request, that the town bully be inducted into the service.

Their tale of woe was that the bully had battered and mauled the adult males, big and little, robust and weaklings, until none was left to dispute the supremacy of his big fist.

The town constable held the bully, in awe. The District Attorney had exhausted his powers, and jail incarcerations bore no terrors to the strong man.

The protesting citizens thought that a pugilist who could hold an entire community in subjection, would be a fit match for the Hun.

The Board rejected the bully's claim of exemption, and ordered him to appear for physical examination. He swaggered into the Examination Room. The Medicos held a solemn pow wow, and then decided that the bully could not go to war because he had a weak heart—a heart that could not endure the din and stress of battle. The bully was afterwards known in his native town as the "Kaiser", on the theory that the royal craven and coward also had a weak heart.

IT WAS WORTH A TRY

In the early days of the draft, many draftees received with fear and trembling their notices to appear for physical examination. A twenty-one year old boy, after receiving his official notice, confided his trouble to his landlady, a thirty-nine year old widow, and mother of two bouncing big boys.

The woman thus explained a scheme to defeat the Service Law:—"Marry me. Then make exemption affidavit that you have a wife and two children to support."

The scheme worked. There was an immediate marriage, and this trusting Board duly honored the exemption claim.

The patriotic countryside, however, soon exposed the deception. The bridegroom was called to the colors. When the weeping widow was asked by the Board why she exhibited undue haste in her second marriage, she dried her tears and smiled, exclaiming, "Well, it was worth a try."

THE MOTHERS AND THE BIBLES

The Registration Day of September 12th, 1918, requiring all eighteen year old boys to go on the military rolls, developed an odd situation in this District.

A surprisingly large number of eighteen year old boys, employed in the Pennsylvania Railroad shops and offices, failed to register. Pennsylvania Law forbids the employment of boys under eighteen years of age. Both the Draft Board and the Corporation were mystified by the action of the delinquents.

A list of the youthful railroad employees was prepared and subpoenas were issued in the name of the President, commanding them to explain why they had failed to obey their Country's call. The boys soon came to the chalk line in the Board Office. So did their mothers and the Family Bibles. And the mothers' stories, coupled with the Bible record of date of birth, furnished indisputable proof that the boys were all under eighteen years of age.

They explained that they had misstated their ages to the Railroad Officials for the purpose of obtaining employment. Other boys confessed that they had practiced similar deceptions on the Court House Clerks for the purpose of obtaining licenses to marry.

The people of Hollidaysburg became accustomed to the sight of a boy, headed for the Board Office, toting a big Bible under his arm, and accompanied by a determined looking matron. The awestruck multitude knew that the youthful George Washington was going to prove his alibi-old enough to marry and get a job, but too young to go to war.

THE KAISER MARK AND DOUBLE EAGLES

There strolled into the examination room of the Board one day a man of dark and forbidding visage. In obedience to the command of the Medical Examiner, the strange draftee stripped. The physician gasped when he beheld on the bare breast of this candidate for the National Army a faithful picture of the German War Lord. Tattooed on the flesh were the helmet and plume, and resplendent uniform and medals, the great white cloak, the Mephistophelean countenance, sneering lips and withered arm of the Imperial Master of the Hun, and below were the double eagles of the countries ruled by his mailed fist.

The man was willing that the examination proceed and he be inducted into the Army. But the Examiner was firm that the khaki was the one uniform in which the Kaiser should not be decked.

Inquiry made by the Home Defence Police developed the fact that the man was a sailor from an interned Hamburg liner, who had wandered up into the mountains of Central Pennsylvania and obtained employment in a limestone Quarry.

HONORABLES AND ESQUIRES TO STAND ASIDE FOR ARMY TITLES

When the Selective Service Machine got in full operation, political wiseacres began to predict that new titles of distinction would follow the war.

It was pointed out at patriotic demonstrations that the title "Honorable" is a king-made title. The title, "Esquire" is also king-made. But no king can make an American soldier, the greatest fighting man on earth. After the war is over, the king-made titles, "Honorable" and "Esquire" are going to the junk heap, as out of place in a war to make the world safe for Democracy.

At the Court House Assemblage, attended by all the honor men of the District, it

was predicted that when County Chairman J. Lee Plummer comes two years hence to frame a winning ticket, it will read something like this in the newspapers:—
For Congress—Colonel Webster Calvin.
For State Senator—Captain Frank H. Fay.
For Sheriff—Top Sergeant Myrl Gildea.
For County Treasurer—Corporal John Elliott.

And that the platform will be, "THERE IS NOTHING TOO GOOD FOR THE BOYS WHO WENT TO WAR."

Predictions were made by the wiseacres that there will be a brand new crop of fine Army titles when the boys come back, and the Honorables and Esquires must clear the track when they are coming.

JULES VERNE'S STORIES IN REAL LIFE

If a prophet in the Year 1913, looking forward five years, had predicted these things to happen in this District, he would have been straightway consigned to a padded cell in the incurables ward of Bedlam:—

A Hollidaysburg boy Commanding a Company of two hundred and fifty Chinese Coolies on the Battlefields of France.

A Hollidaysburg boy sewing wings on air ships at Kelly Field, Texas.

A Hollidaysburg boy running a sawmill near Bordeaux, France, and his chum operating an artificial ice plant at Paris.

A bunch of Hollidaysburg boys fashioning out of the virgin forests at Vancouver, Washington, the ships that float the air and the ships that float the sea.

A Hollidaysburg boy tumbling out of a seaplane three thousand feet in midair into the gulf of Mexico, and being rescued by a tramp steamer, en route to Cuba.

And yet this sober-minded War Board set the wheels in motion for these Jules Verne's stories in real life.

THE GOOD SHIP HOLLIDAYSBURG

An activity of this Board was the agitating of the project for naming one of the new fleet of American Ships "Hollidaysburg."

These limestone foothills of the Alleghenies once sheltered the youthful Carnegie, Schwab, Replogle, Blackburn, and Vauclain, the men whose gold and talents are building the ships that will win the war for America.

"May the day come and that right soon, when the President of the Young Women's Christian Association of Hollidaysburg shall crack a bottle,—of grapejuice,—across the prow and christen a good ship—'Hollidaysburg'."

A SPANKING FOR DISLOYALTY

There were one hundred and fifty-three enemy aliens in this District. Let it be said, however, to the credit of boys of German parentage, that when they were summoned for military duty, they filed no claim for exemption, or deferred classification, and responded to the Call without murmur, or complaint.

Only one case of open disloyalty was reported to the Board. The young farmer guilty of this offence appeared before the Board and, in the presence of his mother, took the oath of allegiance. And that mother gave her pledge that the next time her son so offended, she would administer to him a sound spanking.

THE ARMY WAITS ON NO MAN

All the boys going to Camp were cautioned by the Board that punctuality and discipline were cardinal virtues in a soldier. This caution was diregarded by a departing soldier.

At the station, he kept both eyes on his sweetheart and nary a peeper on his train.

Locked in each other's embrace, the lovers were oblivious to the tooting of whistle and sounding of bell. The result was that the train pulled out for Camp, and the soldier and his sweetheart were left behind.

The Board gave the delinquent lover a fresh start in his military career, and he arrived at Camp seven hours late. For this first breach of discipline the young soldier was assigned to a different Company from that of the boys of his home town, and he thereby lost their fellowship and society.

The Board, holding this incident in remembrance, warned the honor men on their induction day, that when they arrive at Camp they will be there greeted by a gruff and surly, baldheaded, mustering-in-officer, who will accept no apologies nor explanations for delinquency.

WHAT IS A HIGHLY SPECIALIZED MECHANICAL EXPERT?

One hundred and fifty nineteen year old boys, who were railroad laborers, made claims in their questionnaires, for deferred classifications in Class Three-J, on the grounds that they were "highly specialized mechanical experts."

As these boys had only been in the railroad employ for periods of time ranging from three weeks to a year, the Board was at a loss to understand how the railroad corporation was raising a crop of youthful Schwabs, Edisons and Fords in short order.

A subpoena was accordingly issued, commanding prominent Railroad superintendents to appear before the Board and substantiate their claims.

The Superintendents and the railroad counsel, Thomas H. Greevy, Esq., appeared before the Board. It was contended that owing to the unprecedented scarcity of railroad workmen and the fear that railroads might be compelled to suspend business owing to labor market conditions, the field for mechanical experts had become greatly enlarged.

GENERAL CROWDER AND MR. McADOO

The debate became quite caustic. The six foot frame of Mr. Greevy towered above the four foot, four body of Chairman W. L. Baldridge.

Mr. Greevy:—"We make this claim on the orders of Mr. McAdoo."
Chairman Baldridge:—"And we refuse this claim on the orders of General Crowder."
Mr. Greevy:—"Remember, you are not a Czar."
Chairman Baldrige:—"Yes, and I also remember Webster's definition of an expert."

The War conditions along the Juniata would have surely extended to the District Board at Greensburg, and one hundred appeals would have gone up to Washington, had not the Armistice ended the controversy.

A WAR LOTTERY

In September, 1918, eighty-eight young men of the District filed written applications with the Board to enter the War Vocational Courses, at the Colleges.

The morning's mail brought an official document from State Headquarters, allowing the Board only a quota of five men in the War Colleges.

The officials were in a quandary how best to avoid the ire and displeasure of the would-be students, their parents, sisters, cousins and aunts.

It was finally decided to dump slips of paper with the names of the eighty-eight volunteers thereon, into the Chairman's Stetson and have Judge Thomas J. Baldrige, of the County Court, draw therefrom the names of the five winners.

This War lottery pleased both the winners and the losers and the Board was thus rescued from an unpleasant dilemma.

HUN BOOKS KEPT HOME FIRE BURNING

Yielding to the popular sentiment that the Hun Armies, books and literature should be destroyed at the same time, the Board, at the close of the Public School Term in

THE WORLD WAR 333

June, 1918, called upon the School Officials to supply the German text books for an immense bonfire in honor of the Selectives leaving for Camp Forrest, Georgia.

The books were arranged in the form of a pyramid in the public square of Hollidaysburg, crowned with a German dictionary and a painting of the Kaiser, and treated to a coal oil bath.

The Burgess of the town applied the match as the Camp Forrest men marched in front of the bonfire, the Liberty Band playing, "Keep the Home Fires Burning."

The bonfire made German a dead language in Hollidaysburg.

ITALY A GRANDMOTHER TO AMERICAN SOLDIERS

This District sent one contingent to Camp that was made up almost entirely of Italians.

Vito Criscione was its Captain. They were dismissed by the Board with this word:—

"All the world is ringing today with plaudits and huzzas for the gallant Italian Chasseurs, who are fast driving the invader from their soil. You recognize America as your mother and Italy as your grandmother, and we believe that you will do glorious honor to both your native and adopted countries, in the conflict."

THE 139,687TH SMITH

George Leo Smith, of Hollidaysburg, was the Captain of a large contingent of the District, going to Camp Lee. The parting word of the Board was this:

"You are the last of three brothers to enter the service."

"You are also the 139,687th member of the Smith Family to enter the service."

The latest word received from Captain Smith was that he was at close quarters with his cousin, Hans Schmidt, along the River Rhine.

PARIS GREEN FOR THE KAISER

Charles Murphy, of Tunnel Hill, was assigned the Captaincy of an Irish contingent of the District. The Board charged him:—

"Charley, no matter what the Irish in Ireland are going to do, the Irish in America are going over there to make Paris Green for the Kaiser."

BLOW THE DINNERHORN FOR THE HUN

Harry Salyards, of Hollidaysburg, was inducted into the service as a bugler. The Board gave him this parting salute:—

"You may blow the bugle for the Sammy Boys at Amiens and Verdun. But when you reach the River Rhine, you may blow the dinnerhorn for the Hun. The foe is now awaiting an invitation to surrender and sit down at a Yankee Feast of white bread and plenty."

COAL FOR THE HOME FIRES

John B. Elliott, of Hollidaysburg, a prominent coal merchant of the district, was inducted by the Board into the Motor Mechanics. The Liberty Band and two hundred fellow citizens turned out as an escort of honor.

Mr. Elliott thus addressed them:—

"I am sacrificing my business to go to war. If you want to honor me, then help my business. By my coal and keep your 'Home Fires Burning'."

THE KAISER TO BE SENTENCED

Eleven colored men were sent by this Board to Camp. The first National Army man of this District to set foot on the soil of France was a son of Africa. The parting word of a colored Draftee to the Board was:—

"I'se goin' to capture that Kaiser and bring him before Judge Baldrige for sentence at the next Term of Court."

HOW MAJOR MURDOCK SPOILED A WEDDING

A robust young farmer walked into the Board Headquarters one day and startled the Members with the request, "I want the Board to marry me the day I leave for camp."

The Board Secretary suggested that this was not a matrimonial agency, and that the P. M. G. O. bore no application to nuptial contracts. Nevertheless, the farmer insisted that because he and the girl of his choice were of different religious faiths, the Board should induct him into war and marriage at one and the same time.

The prospective soldier was under orders to go to Camp Greenleaf, on November 11th. The Board accordingly arranged that the marriage ceremony should immediately follow the induction ceremony, before the assembled Selective Service men, at the Court House; that the Judge of the County Court perform the ceremony, that the Board Chairman give away the bride and that the Liberty Band play, "Good Bye Girls, I'm Through," as the bridegroom marched away with his comrades.

November 11th, and Armistice news came together. A telegram from Major Murdock at the State Headquarters stayed the departure of the Camp Greenleaf men.

When the Secretary told the young farmer that he could still enter the married state, even if he could not enter the Army, the latter retorted, "If I can't fight, I won't marry."

And leaving the Board, the disappointed draftee went back to his farm.

SOLDIERS' VICTORY ARCH

The crowning achievement of the Board was the building of a Soldiers' Victory Arch and Court of Honor in the Public Square of Hollidaysburg. The names of the soldier dead and of the French battle fields are inscribed on the arch. The work of building the Arch was begun December 20, 1918, and it will be completed at an approximate outlay, derived from public contributions, of $2000.

VETERANS ORGANIZATIONS

Approximately 5,500 men and women of Blair County performed military service during the World War. These veterans upon their return made possible the organizing of a number of units of the various veterans organizations. The Veterans of Foreign Wars of the United States being already formed, received into membership many of the overseas veterans, and within a few years, there was organized the two other major veterans organizations, namely; The American Legion, and the Disabled American Veterans of the World War, which now maintain active units within the county. No units of the Jewish War Veterans, or the Order of the Purple Heart exists in Blair County at present. However, a number of residents of the county are eligible for membership in these organizations.

The Veterans of Foreign Wars of the United States was known prior to 1913, as the American Veterans of Foreign Service,—the latter name having been adopted at the First National Convention, which was held at Altoona, on the 10th to 12th of September, 1903. At this convention a number of organizations composed of veterans of the Spanish-American War, the Philippine Insurrection and the China Campaign, who had foreign-service, consolidated their units into one. The origin and early history of these organizations is found in the history of the Spanish-American War section of this book.

The Veterans of Foreign Wars of the United States was incorporated by an Act of Congress in 1936. Its national headquarters is located at Kansas City, Missouri, and the State headquarters is located at Harrisburg.

The American Legion was incorporated by an Act of Congress on the 16th of September, 1919, though it had been informally organized in Paris during the spring of 1919, by a group of representative members of the American Expeditionary Forces. Its First National Convention was held at Minneapolis, Minnesota, on the 10th and 11th of November, 1919. National Headquarters is located at Indianapolis, Indiana, and the membership has exceeded one million members, divided among 12,000 posts.

The Preamble to its constitution sets forth its objects and reads as follows; "For God and Country, We associate ourselves together for the following purposes; To uphold and defend the Constitution of the United States of America; to maintain law and order; to foster and perpetuate a one hundred per cent Americanism; to preserve the memories and incidents of our association in the great war; to inculcate a sense of individual obligation to the community, state and nation; to combat the autocracy of both the classes and the masses; to make right the master of might; to promote peace and good will on earth; to safeguard and transmit to posterity the principles of justice, freedom and democracy; to consecrate and sanctify our comradeship by our devotion to mutual helpfulness."

The Disabled American Veterans of the World War was founded at Cincinnati, Ohio, in March, 1920. A National Caucus was held in the same city on the 25th of September, 1920, and the First National Convention was held at Detroit, Michigan, on the 27th to 30th of June, 1921, at which time a permanent organization was formed, a national constitution, ritual and program adopted, and permanent headquarters established at Cincinnati, Ohio.

This organization is congressionally chartered and was the first of the three major organizations to receive that distinction.

The membership of the Disabled American Veterans numbers about 40,000, divided among some 800 chapters scattered throughout the United States.

La Societe des Quarente Hommes et Huit Chevaux was founded at Philadelphia, Pennsylvania, during the spring of 1920. This organization is the fun-making unit of the

American Legion and is commonly known as the 40 and 8. National headquarters is maintained at Indianapolis, Indiana, and its membership has exceeded 40,000, divided among some seven hundred voitures located throughout the United States, and a few in foreign countries.

Eligibility to membership in the La Societe des Quarante Hommes et Huit Chevaux is restricted to those members of the American Legion who have performed some outstanding service for the Legion.

The Twenty-first District Council was organized during 1932, for the purpose of co-ordinating the activities of the various American Legion Posts of Bedford and Blair Counties. Its membership is composed of representatives from its member organizations.

The eligibility requirements for membership in the three major World War veterans organizations of the United States are given herewith:

Eligibility for membership in the Veterans of Foreign Wars of the United States, as defined by a resolution passed at their first national convention, reads as follows; "That all Soldiers, Sailors and Marines who served on foreign soil or on hostile waters in the service of the United States in the War zone in the time of war, shall become eligible for membership". These requirements have changed but little in the past thirty-odd years, as the regulations of to-day, briefly stated, is that membership is available to those men who served in the armed forces of the United States in any foreign war, isurrection or expedition, which service shall be recognized by the authorization of the issuance of a campaign badge.

The American Legion requirements for membership read as follows; "Any person shall be eligible for membership in The American Legion who was regularly enlisted, drafted, inducted or commissioned, and who was accepted for and assigned to active duty in the Army, Navy or Marine Corps of the United States at some time during the period between April 6, 1917, and November 11, 1918, both dates inclusive, or who, being a citizen of the United States, at the time of his entry therein, served on active duty in the Naval, Military or Air forces of any Government associated with the United States during the Great War."

Eligibility to membership in a Chapter of the Disabled American Veterans of the World War is defined as, "Any man or women who was wounded, gassed, injured or disabled in line of duty while in the service of either the military or naval forces of the United States of America between the dates of April 6, 1917, and July 2, 1921, and who was in the service between the dates of April 6, 1917, and November 11, 1918, and who received an honorable discharge. Others who were disabled while serving with any of the armed forces of the nations associated with the United States during the World War and who are now American citizens and who were honorably discharged."

The only World War veterans organization formed in Blair County which became inactive and has not renewed its charter was the John W. Colabine Post No. 343, Veterans of Foreign Wars of the United States, of Bellwood. This Post was formed shortly after the close of the World War and was named in honor of the memory of John W. Colabine, who was born at Bellwood, on the 31st of March, 1895. He enlisted on the 18th of July, 1917, and served as a Corporal in Company L, 110th Infantry, 28th Division, and died in France on the 28th of July, 1918, of wounds received in action. His body was returned to his home and buried in the Logan Valley Cemetery at Bellwood.

A group of World War veterans residing in Juniata Borough, now the 13th Ward of the City of Altoona, formed a local organization which was chartered in the Blair County Courts on the 20th day of September, 1921, under the title of "Juniata's Soldier, Sailor and Marine Club," with the following officers; Commander, Bernard F. O'Connor; Vice Commander, Harry N. Oakwood; Adjutant, Thomas G. Peoples; and Finance Officer, Max C. Dunmire.

Employees of the Pennsylvania Railroad, residents of Altoona, who served in the 19th Railway Engineers during the World War, are eligible to membership in a local organization which holds regular meetings, elects officers and endeavor to keep alive the memory of their association during the war.

JAMES L. NOBLE POST NO. 3

The James L. Noble Post No. 3, Veterans of Foreign Wars of the United States traces its origin to an organization founded in Altoona on the 10th of July, 1901, when returned members of the 43rd Infantry, United States Volunteers, took action to perpetuate their services in the Philippine Islands and to honor the memory of their departed comrades. This organization adopted the name of The Society of Philippine War Veterans, and elected Herbert O. Kelly as its first commander.

This organization was named in honor of the memory of James L. Noble, who was born on the 26th of October, 1876, a son of Mr. and Mrs. John Noble. He served an enlistment in Company A, 18th Infantry, Pennsylvania Volunteers, from the 8th of May, 1898, until the 10th of October, 1898. He then re-enlisted, and served as a Corporal in Company C, 43rd Infantry, United States Volunteers, from the 9th of September, 1899, until the 30th of September, 1900, at which time he was killed near Palo Leyte, Philippine Islands, during an engagement.

The name of this organization was changed at the time of the consolidation of several similar organizations during the first convention which was held at Altoona, on the 10th of September, 1903, and a charter was issued to the James L. Noble Post No. 2, American Veterans of Foreign Service, on the 8th of August, 1904, with the following named veterans as the charter members; Herbert E. Akers, Richard Aiken, Chas. W. Ayers, E. L. Bingman, Wilber Birchner, Samuel Buchanan, Roy Bumgardner, James E. Black, Thos. H. Blover, William J. Brawley, J. E. Coleman, H. A. Douglass, Carl W. Drexler, Chas. E. Dolaway, Harmon Dupman, Edward A. Earl, Angus J. Eddie, Marsh F. Fleck, Wesley W. Fleck, Charles Funk, Frank E. Graybill, Christian Graf, Fred Z. Goetz, George B. Goodman, Edward L. Harpster, Harry W. Harpster, Martin Hauser, Edward Holt, George Hynick, Thomas Johnson, Herbert O. Kelly, J. S. Keller, Urban G. Kimes, Charles E. Knighton, John Lewis, Chas. W. Lemon, Joseph M. Lusk, Henry Rupert, Vernon Locker, Bertram G. Morgan, Henry Mitchell, Edward Mendenhall, Oliver Manspeaker, William A. Macklin, W. H. Mavity, Edward Nicodemus, George H. Otto, Albert L. Oschea, R. H. Raabe, Claire Richabaugh, William F. Ritter, E. S. Ragen, David Ruggles, David G. Roseberry, George R. Shaner, William Smith, Joseph L. Smith, George W. Sunday, Samuel A. Solt, Joseph Swartz, E. M. Stewart, James E. Ullery, Christ Tuefel, Edw. M. Walters, H. C. Williams, William H. Williams, Frank Whelen, Robert J. Walker, D. C. Yingling and William H. Zimmerman.

The Second National Convention of the American Veterans of Foreign Service was held at Pittsburgh, Pennsylvania, at which time Herbert O. Kelly of the James L. Noble Post No. 2, of Altoona, was elected National Commander. The Third National Convention returned to Altoona for its deliberations.

During the 1913 convention the name of American Veterans of Foreign Service was changed to the name as used at present, the Veterans of Foreign War of the United States.

During the years 1917 and 1918, this Post became inactive due to War conditions and the enlistment of some of its members into the service of their Country. Upon the return home of the World War soldiers and their eligibility to membership by reason of having performed foreign service, interest in the organization was renewed and as a result a charter, dated the 12th of September, 1919, was granted to the James L. Noble Post No. 3, with the following named veterans as the charter members; Hyman Abelson, George E. Alleman, Myer Abelson, Emmet J. Athey, Samuel W. Buchanan, J. L. Bosserman, Raymond J. Brenner, C. G. Boffenmyer, Samuel Brudensky, Frederick H. Bloomhardt, Everett O. Bidwell, Christopher W. Burns, Robert T. Billon, C. C. Burns, Harold B. Baird, Foster K. Burket, Alton B. Briggs, Harry T. Byrne, F. R. Baumgardner, Walter Ball, Stewart B. Brown, E. G. Bowers, James D. Collary, Francis C. Carl, Frederick F. Crosson, William L. Cramer, Ralph E. Devore, Edward A. Earl, Lucian W. Ferguson, Russell L. Forsyth, C. A. Formwalt, Frank C. Fonner, H. Fisher, Edward P. Ferguson,

SOLDIERS OF BLAIR COUNTY

John L. Frederick, Albert R. Fonner, William L. Fluke, Robert E. Fleck, C. L. Fletcher, George N. Green, Calvin B. Goodman, Homer H. Glass, Carl F. Gamber, William B. Gonter, David L. Grossman, George M. Greene, Alvin V. Greene, Frank J. A. Gamber, Frank H. Good, Edward Holt, Edward F. Houser, Harold Holmes, Amos P. Huber, C. C. Hiner, Walter P. Horton, Lawrence F. Harpster, Joseph B. Hill, William A. Hall, Clyde J. Hartman, John W. Hileman, Philip Klevan, Arthur J. Kiser, William E. Keller, Guy C. Koontz, Charles L. Ketrow, Harry E. Loomis, Ross U. Lockard, Oliver Manspeaker, William Montage, George E. Musselman, Charles A. Myers, Henry Mitchell, Frederick O. Maeder, Orville B. Mann, Edgar B. McGuire, Charles M. McKee, George O. Nothnagle, Frederick U. Noble, George W. Nale, Myruen H. Naeffer, Jr., Ernest R. Otto, George H. Otto, George E. Olewine, Jr., Earl J. Plunkett, Jacob Parish, Edgar C. Rice, Raymond A. Rutherford, Ralph W. Richards, L. K. Riling, Joseph E. Robinson, Bernard D. Robinson, Foster C. Ross, F. J. Reiser, George W. Ralston, H. J. Schwartz, Edward M. Stewart, Joseph L. Smith, Harry A. Schnavely, Harry A. Smith, Charles E. Stout, Jacob H. Shearer, W. J. Strohmyer, William M. Smith, James M. Shollar, Harry Singerman, Walter J. Smithoover, Samuel R. Stephens, Charles F. Stewart, C. E. Teufel, Edwin A. Taylor, Edward Ullery, John F. Vaughn, Joseph Wise, Gilbert H. Weiss, Paul W. Wilbur, William M. Walter, Albert V. Wester, Charles E. Wolford, Lloyd R. Wilson, Harvey C. Williams, Harry A. Wicker, Morris Wayne, John F. Wolf, Lemon L. West, James D. Webster and Donald M. Yarnall.

Post meetings were first held in the City Hall, then in the Stehle building, and the Post conducted the following activities; Organization of the V. F. W. band with Bruce Crumm as Business Manager and Director E. C. Stewart, Thomas McFarlane and Wilfred Beck; Maintenance of a Service Bureau under, George H. Lersch, Fred F. Crosson, Philip A. Burket and Edward Holt;—Annual sale of Buddy Poppies;—Publication of The Noble Spirit magazine;—Formation of a Rifle Club;—Organization of a unit of the Military Order of the Cooties;—Operation of a Veterans of Foreign Wars Club;—and the maintenance of a French Renault tank.

A Post home, at 917 Lexington Avenue, was purchased during 1923, and remains today as property of the Post. The "James L. Noble Post No. 3, Veterans of Foreign Wars Home Association of Altoona" was chartered on the 5th of May, 1924. The present home at 1301-05 17th Street was purchased during 1929, and was dedicated as a Memorial Home on the 9th of November, 1929, by the National Commander, Admiral R. E. Coontz. A ladies auxiliary was chartered on the 29th of June, 1920, and the President for 1939 is Mrs. Ruth Wyland.

Philip A. Burket was elected Department Historian for 1939, Junior Vice Commander for 1934, Senior Vice Commander for 1935, and Department Commander for 1936. James E. Van Zandt was elected Department Junior Vice Commander for 1927, and Department Commander for 1928 and 1929. He was elected National Junior Vice Commander in 1931, Senior Vice Commander in 1932, and National Commander in 1933, 1934 and 1935.

Those known to have served as commanders are; Herbert O. Kelly, Charles E. Knighton, Edward M. Walters, Edward Holt, Oliver Manspeaker, Marsh F. Fleck, Edward L. Harpster, Henry Mitchell, Albert V. Wester, Joseph L. Smith, Norman B. Snyder, Harry Singerman, H. Joseph Schwartz, Robert J. Puderbaugh, Frank A. Duncan, Raymond K. Snyder, Bruce Crumm, Martin Baird, Arthur J. Kiser, Philip A. Burket, J. Harry Shearer, Bruce Crumm, J. Lester Laughlin, Glenn Kaufman, John J. Jonsonbaugh, Edgar Soyke, Clair P. Nale and Harry R. Hallett.

The 1934 Department Convention was held in the City of Altoona on the 8th, 9th and 10 of June, with the James L. Noble Post acting as host.

The officers for the year 1939-40 are; Commander, Harry R. Hallett; Senior Vice Commander, Raymond F. Decker; Junior Vice Commander, Harry Smith; Adjutant, Gilbert Wyland; Chaplain, Naseeb Masood; Quartermaster, John C. Emme; Trustees, Ernest Hopkins, Glenn Kaufman and Samuel Bradinsky.

BENJAMIN H. HEWIT POST NO. 185

A Post of the Veterans of Foreign Wars of the United States was organized at Hollidaysburg a few years after the World War and designated the Benjamin H. Hewit Post No. 509.

The name of Benjamin H. Hewit had previously been adopted as the name for Post No. 516, the American Legion, but as the Legion Post had become inactive, Post 509 of the Veterans of Foreign Wars took care of veterans affairs in the community and endeavored to perpetuate the name of Captain Hewit by naming their Post in his honor.

Captain Benjamin Hartley Hewit was born at Jamestown, North Dakota, on the 26th of July, 1884, a son of Oliver H. and Elizabeth Myers Hewit. He was called into active service from civil life on the 15th of August, 1917, and commissioned a Captain of Infantry. He was killed in action in France on the 29th of September, 1918, while serving as Captain of Company F, 316th regiment of Infantry, 79th Division, and is buried in the Meuse-Argonne cemetery in France.

Post No. 509 of the Veterans of Foreign Wars became inactive a few years after its organization and remained so until the 2nd of March, 1937, at which time officers were elected and the Post was assigned the number 185.

The first officers elected under the reorganization were; Commander, King T. Rhodes; Senior Vice Commander, Richard J. Louther; Junior Vice Commander, Samuel R. Manning; Adjutant, Samuel E. Shelley; Quartermaster, Joseph F. Reiser; Chaplain, Edgar M. Geesey; Trustees; J. Frank Kauffman, Edgar R. Vipond, and Fred J. Wolf.

A home association was chartered in the Courts of Blair County on the 8th of April, 1937, as the "Veterans of Foreign Wars Post No. 185 Home Association of Hollidaysburg", for the purpose of holding and controlling property. A club was operated by the home association for some time on Broad Street, Hollidaysburg. Post meetings are held on the second and fourth Sundays of each month at 509 South Juniata Street.

Post No. 509, when active during the years following the World War, secured twelve rifles from the United States Government for use on ceremonial occasions and to fire volleys over the graves of deceased veterans. These rifles were secured by giving bond, and in later years when the Fort Fetter Post was organized, these rifles were used by the Legionnaires and were eventually purchased by the Legion Post.

Richard J. Louther of the Hollidaysburg Post of the Veterans of Foreign Wars has been named as the District Commander of the organization for this vicinity.

The names of those who have served as Post Commanders during past years, so far as known are:

 1922 Charles W. Douglass
 1937 King T. Rhodes
 1938 Richard J. Louther
 1939 Samuel R. Manning.

The officers chosen to serve the Post during the year 1939-1940 were:

Commander — Samuel R. Manning
Senior Vice Commander — Samuel E. Shelley
Junior Vice Commander — John A. Heininger
Adjutant — David E. Carl
Quartermaster — Joseph J. Austin
Chaplain — George A. Stock
Trustees; Richard J. Louther, Harry J. Boland and King T. Rhodes.

D. MERL TIPTON POST NO. 43

A Post of the Veterans of Foreign Wars of the United States was formed at Martinsburg during the early part of 1935, by veterans who had performed service in a foreign country or waters during the period of hostilities.

The Martinsburg Post was named in honor of the memory of D. Merl Tipton and was assigned the number 43. The charter was dated the 1st of August, 1935, and the members whose names appear on the charter are as follows: Albert H. Tipton, Arch R. Lykens, Joseph D. Bechtel, Samuel C. Kagerise, Walter A. Bassler, Irvin L. Gouchnour, George Ross, George W. Swartz, Chalmer J. Shoeman, J. Elvin Kurtz, Russell E. Scrafford, L. Earl Daughenbaugh, Herman E. Rhodes, John Mellott, Earl N. Dilling, Emory W. Myers, Charles A. McGraw, Earl Paul, Oscar Samuels, D. Emmert Brumbaugh, Julius V. Pote, Charles O. Long and Charles W. McPerson.

D. Merl Tipton was born at Martinsburg, Blair County, on the 15th day of July, 1893, a son of Jacob S. and Ellen Barbara Tipton. He entered the service on the 10th of March, 1918, and served as a Private in Company G, 319 Infantry, 79th Division. He was killed in action in France on the 5th of October, 1918, while engaged with his unit in the battle of the Argonne Forest. His body was returned to his home and buried with military honors in the Fairview Cemetery at Martinsburg.

The officers chosen to serve this Post during the first year of its existence were as follows:

Commander	Albert H. Tipton
Senior Vice Commander	Arch R. Lykens
Junior Vice Commander	L. Earl Daughenbaugh
Adjutant	Samuel C. Kagerise
Quartermaster	Walter A. Bassler
Chaplain	Chalmer J. Shoeman
Officer of the Day	Russell E. Scrafford
Officer of the Guard	John Mellott

The installation of the D. Merl Tipton Post took place on the 1st of August, 1935, with a ceremony and a street parade, at Martinsburg. The parade was headed by Chief Burgess C. Guy Barley of Martinsburg and the James L. Noble Post No. 3, Color bearers and guard, of Altoona,—followed by the James L. Noble Post No. 3, Band, members of the various Veterans of Foreign Wars Posts, the charter members of the D. Merl Tipton Post, and notables of the vicinity.

The parade came to a halt at the pavilion in Memorial park and the meeting was called to order by J. Lester Laughlin, of Altoona, District Commander of the Veterans of Foreign Wars. Burgess Barley made a short address of welcome and expressed the hope that the new Post would prosper, assuring the veterans of the heartly cooperation of the citizens of Martinsburg.

The meeting was then turned over to Philip A. Burket, Senior Vice Commander of the Department of Pennsylvania, who instituted the new Post and obligated the officers, and the charter was turned over to the officers. Commander Tipton then assumed charge of the meeting and following the voicing of congratulations and best wishes, refreshments were served at the kitchen in the park.

Since the formation of the Martinsburg Post, the members have taken an active part in the social and community affairs. The Post meetings are held in the Municipal building, and the officers for the year 1939-1940 are; Commander, Arch R. Lykens; Senior Vice Commander, George Ross; Junior Vice Commander, Fred L. Gunnett; Adjutant, Samuel C. Kagerise; Quartermaster, Albert H. Tipton; Chaplain, Oscar Samuels; Sergeant of the Day, Joseph Rape.

CHAS. R. ROWAN POST NO. 228

A few months after the national body of the American Legion came into existence, and while the founders were still perfecting details of organization, two groups of World War veterans of Altoona were directing their efforts towards organizing local units. The first group to make application for a charter was composed chiefly of business and professional men of the city. This application was dated the 14th of August, 1919, and a temporary charter was granted on the 21st of August. The names appearing on the application were; Fred H. Bloomhardt, John E. Surrick, Edward Cassel, Harry D. McNamara, Leonard M. Wissinger, John H. Carson, C. S. Downs, C. H. Jacobs, S. W. Hilemen, John O. Ullrich, Martin B. Bechtel, Chester B. Tindle, ... Brought, Paul B. Cooley, Robt. T. Billin, Paul R. Bennett, Otis K. Daugherty, Theodore M. Tousdale, Allen E. Kay, A. J. Handwork and H. Frank Culp. This application was given the number 228, and a permanent charter was granted on the 29th of November, 1920.

The second group, composed of employees of the Pennsylvania Railroad Company, made application for a charter on the 22nd of August, 1919, with the following names; H. H. Mansfield, J. R. Stewart, Frank Riddell, Stewart H. Barwis, A. O. King, William C. Cole, J. S. Koesel, George D. Sprankle, William F. Crowl, Jr., Harry D. Else, A. A. Thompson, Karl W. Collins, Leo P. Trevis, C. W. Gilliford, J. H. Mattern and W. R. O'Hara. This application was given the number 235.

The two Posts merged at a meeting held in the City Hall on the 6th of April, 1920, and adopted the title of the Chas. R. Rowan Post No. 228.

Lieutenant Charles R. Rowan was born at Altoona on the 4th of July, 1869, a son of Richard M. and Ida McConnell Rowan. As a member of Company G, 10th Infantry, Pennsylvania National Guard, he saw service on the Mexican Border in 1916, and as a member of Company G, 110th Infantry, 28th Division, he served in France, where he was promoted to First Lieutenant of his company, and was wounded on the 29th of September, 1918. He died two days later and was posthumously awarded the Distinguished Service Cross.

The Post meetings were first held in the council chamber of the old City Hall. As the membership increased and its program of activities required more adequate facilities, quarters were obtained in various buildings about the business section of the town. A home association was chartered in the Blair County Courts on the 9th of May, 1922, as "The American Legion Home Association of Altoona," and a permanent home was acquired in 1923, when the Post purchased the site of the present home from Miss Elizabeth L. Snyder. An old frame dwelling on the site served as quarters for some time after some necessary alterations had been made. The present home was erected in 1928, and formally dedicated during the Armistice Day celebration, November 12th, 1928.

Membership was the chief interest of the Post during the first few years of its existence and considerable time had to elapse before the aims of the organization could be impressed upon the minds of the veterans and the public at large. However, with a sufficiently large and formidable membership, and permanent quarters, and an outlined program of activities, the Post gradually applied the principles of Legionism locally. The first sub-unit of the local Post was a Ladies Auxiliary to the Chas. R. Rowan Post, which was formally organized at the Penn Alto Hotel on the 14th of March, 1923. Like the Legion Posts with which it is affiliated, this Post carried out a vast program of service, including rehabilitation, child welfare, national defense, Fidac, radio, care of orphans and widows, school awards, and many other interests. The following ladies have served as President of the Auxiliary: Mrs. Richard M. Rowan, Mrs. J. Robert Morrow, Mrs. Samuel Washabaugh, Mrs. Elmer C. Ake, Mrs. Ruth Pincin, Mrs. Miriam Diggins, Mrs. C. J. Rodgers, Mrs. Fern Norton, Mrs. Harry Piper, Mrs. Fay Hetrick, Mrs. J. H. Galbraith, Mrs. Edna White, Mrs. C. W. Burns, Mrs. Harry E. Slep and President-elect Mrs. H. Baker Reed.

The Senior Drum Corps was organized during the spring of 1926, and made its initial appearance on Memorial Day. Walter Gipprich served as Director, R. E. Van Ormer as Drum Major, and Robert S. Krause as Drill Master. During the next eight years the Corps served the post as its only musical unit, turning out for all events. Not only did it serve the Post locally, but it also represented the local unit in many events elsewhere. The Senior Drum Corps continues to function under the present leadership of James H. Armstrong.

Youth activities have been one of the chief interests of the Chas. R. Rowan Post since the early years of its existence. The first unit to be sponsored by this Post was the Legion Boy Scout Troop No. 22, which was organized during 1924, and formally installed on the 6th of June. This Troop has had four Scoutmasters during its existence, namely: William C. Cole, Wallace J. White, H. Baker Reed and the present Scoutmaster R. Harold Counsman. In the fifteen years of its existence, the troop has grown from a group of eight boys to its present enrollment of thirty-two. Two Senior Scout units, the Explorer Scouts and the Rover Scouts are affiliated with this troop. At one time the troop had an enrollment of more than fifty boys. It is one of the most successful troops of the Blair-Bedford Council, having to its credit twenty-two Eagle Scouts.

In December, 1927, another youth organization was added to the Legion family, when the Ladies Auxiliary sponsored a unit of the Junior League. A program adapted to the age of children was arranged, regular meetings were held on Saturday afternoons, but the unit passed out of existence after a year.

The Sons of the Legion Squadron was organized during the summer months of 1934, and formally installed on the 26th of October. The charter was presented in December. The following year the Junior Drum Corps, which is a sub-unit of the squadron, was organized and has served the Post in local parades, convention parades, and out-door exhibitions, and has traveled over the entire state of Pennsylvania, and to many places outside of the state. The Corps has been from the start under the direction of John E. Stewart, and under his direction it has progressed and merited for the Legion high honors and much favorable comment. The present enrollment of the Legion Squadron is about 250 members. Five Squadron members have held the office of Captain (President) since its formation, namely: James Haight, 1934-1935; William Shugarts, 1935-1936; John Stewart, 1936-1937; Joseph Willoughby, 1937-1938; and the present Captain Robert Cole.

The Junior Auxiliary, the latest unit to be added to the Legion group, was organized on the 30th of April, 1936. Its membership is composed of daughters of Auxiliary members under the age of 18 years. Regular meetings are held at which time a suitable program is carried out. The Junior Auxiliary recently organized a drill team, which will represent the unit in parades and outdoor exhibitions. The following members have held the office of President since its organization, namely: Madelyn White, 1936; Jane Burns, 1937; Dorothy Koush, 1938; and the present incumbent, Dorothy Reighter.

During the twenty years of its existence the Chas. R. Rowan Post No. 228, has carried out a program of service, which has centered chiefly on veteran service, community service, charities, education, school medal awards, safety programs, and flood relief. The Flag Day program which is observed annually on June 14th or a day conveniently close to that day has become one of the Post's elaborate events. The street parade and drum corps exhibition attracts thousands and has merited much favorable comment from the citizens and visitors.

One of the early events in the history of the Post was a visit on Sunday, the 30th of October, 1921, of Marshal Ferdinand Foch, Commander-in-chief of the Allied forces during the World War; and General John J. Pershing, Commander-in-chief of the American Expeditionary Forces, who stopped for a brief period in Altoona while on their way to Kansas City, Missouri, where the third national convention of the American Legion was in session. A crowd of approximately 14,000 gathered at the local station to greet the visitors.

The body of Charles R. Rowan was returned to his home and the burial took place on the 26th of December, 1921. An elaborate military funeral was accorded the hero, in which, the local Legion Post accompanied by other military and veterans organizations marched in rain and sleet to do honor to the deceased. The Post erected an attractive memorial at his grave in St. Johns Cemetery, the unveiling of which took place on the 27th of May, 1929, with a program of exercises which included a parade.

One of the outstanding accomplishments was the raising of a fund of over $17,000, during July, 1925, as the Post's quota towards the $5,000,000 Legion Endowment Fund, the income of which is expended in the rehabilitation of the disabled veterans and in child welfare work among the World War orphans.

The Post has joined in the planting of trees along the road leading from Altoona to the Horse-shoe Curve, which will be known as "Highway of Memory" and the trees are in memory of those who suffered and died for their country.

The local Post rendered great service during the flood of the 17th of March, 1936, when central Pennsylvania was flooded and many persons were desperately in need of assistance. Hardly had the call for aid been voiced over the radio until the Post had recruited a number of members who collected large supplies of food and clothing for the relief of the sufferers in the stricken areas. In a very short time the Legion home became a veritable store-house, where, under the direction of John E. Stewart with the aid of Legion and Auxiliary members, the food and clothing was packed and shipped by truck to points where needed. Several truck loads of provisions and clothing were sent to Johnstown, the first consignment to reach that city. The same service was rendered in February, 1937, when two car loads of food and clothing were sent to the suffers in the Mississippi.

The local Post has also been interested in the Boys State Camp, which is held annually at Indiantown Gap. This Camp is sponsored by the Pennsylvania Department of the American Legion, and is conducted for a period of ten days. Boys from over the entire state are sent by various organizations, and are schooled in the principles of government and citizenship.

The names of the members who served the Post as commander are: Fred H. Bloomhardt, 1919; John D. Logue, 1920; Donald J. Howard, 1921; Albert O. King, 1922; John J. Haberstroh, 1923; J. Murray Shollar, 1924; Homer I. Smith, 1925; William Bradford, 1926; Paul R. Kuhn, 1927; Harry E. Clarke, 1928; David Kaufman, 1930; George E. Alleman, 1930; Frank E. Hennaman, 1931; Harry E. Slep, 1932; John H. Galbraith, 1933; William Diamond, 1934; William W. Shugarts, 1935; Wilfred A. Morgan, 1936; Clyde B. Saylor, 1937; Daniel Bohn, 1938; John J. R. Williams, 1939; and the commander-elect John E. Stewart.

The Post's membership for the year 1939 was 655, and the names of the officers were as follows:

Commander	John J. R. Williams
Senior Vice Commander	Harry W. Piper
Junior Vice Commander	Wallace J. White
Adjutant	Daniel D. Carey
Finance Officer	Joseph Tate
Historian	Raphael L. Seidel
Chaplain	C. Myrle McKee
Sergeant at arms	Adam Muri

The history of this Post as presented herewith was prepared by the Post Historian, Raphael L. Seidel.

HOWARD GARDNER POST NO. 281

The Tyrone Post of the American Legion was organized during the summer of 1919, its application for a charter being dated the 27th of August, 1919, and the temporary charter being dated the 4th of September, 1919. The names of those who signed the application for the charter were: Joseph A. Dickson, David S. Kloss, Jr., Whitford R. Barrett, Paul F. Stratiff, George E. Kienzle, Jr., E. Lloyd Tyson, Benjamin C. Jones, Albert O. Morrison, Walter L. Schopp, John J. Clark, James W. McCann, George E. Gillam, Charles G. Waple, Richard J. Schell and G. O. Calbert.

The officers elected to serve during the first year were: Commander, John B. Nason; Vice Commander, Joseph A. Dickson; Adjutant, E. Lloyd Tyson; and Finance Officer, Carey C. Bradin.

The permanent charter was granted on the 15th of September, 1920, and the Post was named in honor of the memory of John Howard Gardner who was born at Tyrone on the 26th of June, 1895, a son of Amos and Cordelia Gardner. He enlisted on the 5th of August, 1917, as a Private in Company G, 110th Infantry, 28th Division, and was killed in action at Courmont, France, on the 28th of July, 1918, being the first Tyrone soldier to be killed on the battlefields of France. The body of John Howard Gardner was returned to his home and buried in the Bald Eagle Cemetery, near Tyrone.

The first community activity of this Post was the erection of a memorial to perpetuate the names of the soldiers from Tyrone who gave their lives to their country during the World War. This monument, located at Washington Avenue and 10th Street, Tyrone, consists of a bronze tablet placed on a large native boulder. The dedication took place on Armistice Day, the 11th of November, 1920, and the following inscription is found on the tablet: "Dedicated to the boys of Tyrone and vicinity who gave full measure of devotion to their country that civilization might live, Edward M. Beightol, Paul W. Borrows, George Briggs, Francis Diehl, Harry G. Dossler, Richard G. Fisher, John H. Gardner, John C. Gates, Simeon H. Glassco, Achileppe Karansta, Oscar Kennedy, Frank Lodick, Orris W. McNeal, D. Blair Mingle, Charles C. Norman, Donald Richards, John G. Robinson, John J. Sickler, Warren Stiver, Nathan C. Woomer."

Another memorial was erected at Tyrone by the Pennsylvania Railroad Company to the memory of the soldiers of the Tyrone Division. This monument is located near the Passenger Station and was dedicated on the 31st of May, 1921.

The following auxiliary units were organized by the Post to aid and assist in its many community activities:

The Ladies Auxiliary of Post No. 281 was chartered on the 7th of April, 1925. The President for 1939 was Mrs. Esther Lebkicker, and the President-elect for 1940 is Mrs. Myrtle Adams, wife of the Post Commander.

The American Legion Drum and Bugle Corps of Tyrone was organized during the year 1924, and has won distinction under the leadership of Drum Majors: Joseph A. Dickson, Robert W. Owens, Benjamin C. Jones and James C. Warrender, the corps placing second in the competitive drills at the Erie Convention.

A Squadron of the Sons of the Legion was organized during the year 1938, and the Captain for the year 1940 is Lee E. Adams, Jr., the only son of the Post Commander.

An organization of daughters of members of the Ladies Auxiliary, known as the Junior Auxiliary, was organized during the year 1932.

A Rifle Club, having as its object the creation of interest in the use of the rifle and the development of marksmanship, was organized during the year 1933.

Other activities include the awarding of School Medals to pupils of the eighth grade, the maintenance of a burial plot in the Grandview Cemetery where any soldier may be buried without expense, the care and distribution of National flags used on the curbs for street decorations, and an annual sale of Legion poppies.

THE WORLD WAR

The Tyrone Post of the American Legion became one of the most active Posts in the central part of Pennsylvania, and has continued to this day as one of those Posts whose membership and support of Legion policies can be depended upon by the Department and National headquarters. The patriotism and comradeship of the soldiers of Tyrone and vicinity are well exemplified by the interest shown in the promotion and advancement of military and veterans organizations in their community.

A Post home, located at the corner of Logan Avenue and 10th Street, was purchased in 1923, for the sum of $40,000. This followed the chartering of a home association in the Blair County Courts on the 9th of April, 1923, as the "Howard Gardner Post of the American Legion No. 281." A second charter was secured on the 1st of March, 1937, as the "Legion Home Association of Tyrone." A residence was first used as the Post home, but as the activities increased, a garage located on the rear of the lot on Logan Avenue, was utilized. On the 17th of March, 1936, both buildings were damaged and practically all equipment belonging to the Drum Corps, the Post, and other units, was destroyed by flood waters. This Post was the recipient of a gift of money amounting to $25,000 from John G. Anderson, a public spirited citizen of the town, and this sum was used in acquiring the J. K. Johnston property at Lincoln Avenue and 15th Street, where extensive alterations and repairs have converted this property into a most attractive home for the Legionnaires and their guests, and where a Legion Club is being operated along with the Posts many other activities.

At the present time the Post is engaged in carrying to completion one of its largest projects,—the construction of a public playground on the lot adjacent to the Post home on West Fifteenth Street. This project is sponsored jointly by the Post and the Tyrone Borough Council. When completed playground equipment will be installed and a portion of the project devoted to Post activities, including a drill field for the Drum Corps and a small park for picnic purposes.

The past commanders and the year during which they served are as follows: John B. Nason, 1920; Joseph A. Dickson, 1921; Emmett K. McClintock, 1922; Walter E. Lotz, 1923; George D. Wands, 1924; Herman Work, 1925; James C. McConahy, 1926; Benjamin C. Jones, 1927; Rudolph R. Reinschmidt, 1928; John J. Clark, 1929; Robert W. Owens, 1930; Howard M. Stone, 1931; George O. Calbert, 1932; Wilbur C. Van Scoyoc, 1933; Albert O. Morrison, 1934; James C. Warrender, 1935; Richard W. Wingate, 1936; John W. Hildebrand, 1937; Edwin A. Lebkicker, 1938; Charles H. Cassady, 1939.

The elected officers for the year 1939 are as follows:

Commander	Charles H. Cassady
Senior Vice Commander	Lee E. Adams
Junior Vice Commander	Samuel T. Lewis
Adjutant	John J. Clark
Treasurer	John A. Hiller
Historian	A. Ray Flenner
Chaplain	James C. Warrender
Sergeant at Arms	Admiral D. Mencer
Sergeant at Arms	Domenic Castagnola
Executive Committee	Richard W. Wingate John W. Hildebrand Albert J. Friday Horace L. Frantz Clark C. Ginter

For the year 1940, Lee E. Adams was elected Post Commander. The membership for the year 1939 was 155, and the regular meetings are held in the Post home on the second Monday of each month.

BONNER-SOLLENBERGER POST NO. 456

A temporary charter was granted the Williamsburg Post of the American Legion under date of the 18th of December, 1919, and the permanent charter was issued on the 27th of April, 1921, with the following names: Joseph D. Bechtel, Floyd W. Coble, Lloyd E. Wilt, J. E. Devereaux, John Figurelli, Paul C. Lytle, Clarence G. Price, Herbert H. Smith, Thomas A. Lindsay, Joseph T. Pitcher, Anthony Filorimo, Robert S. Brehmen, George Obenour, Ralph R. Whittaker, and Paul E. Henderson.

Post No. 456 was named in honor of the memory of Guy Leslie Bonner and Robert Franklin Sollenberger, the first two soldiers of Williamsburg or vicinity to be killed in action during the World War.

Guy Leslie Bonner was born on the 31st of August, 1893, at Martinsburg, a son of Martin Bonner. He enlisted as a Private and served in the Headquarters Troop, 5th Marines. He was wounded during the battle of the Argonne on the 2nd of October, 1918, and died the same day. His body was returned to his home and buried in the Fairview Cemetery at Martinsburg.

Robert Franklin Sollenberger was born at Isett, Blair County, on the 28th of November, 1895, a son of Joseph and Clara Sollenberger. He served as a Private in Company G, 319 Infantry, 79th Division, and was killed in action on the 4th of August, 1918, near Ayette, France. His body was returned home and buried in the Sparr Cemetery, near Williamsburg.

The first meetings of Post 456 were held in the Wilt Hotel, then more permanent quarters were established over the Justice Printing Shop, afterwards when larger quarters were needed the Post moved to rooms above the Eastep and Flaig Store. About 1925, interest in the Post and Legion work diminished when a number of members moved elsewhere, and the Post remained in an inactive state until the year 1930 when through the efforts of the District Commander, Floyd G. Hoenstine of Hollidaysburg, interest was revived and the Post resumed its activities and quarters were secured above the Norris garage. In 1935 the Post moved its headquarters to the "Dugout" on East 2nd Street, where regular meetings are held on the 1st and 3rd Mondays of each month, and a membership of 56 was secured for the year 1939.

This Post has organized the following auxiliary units: Legion Drum and Bugle Corps in 1932, Ladies Auxiliary in 1935, Sons of the Legion in 1936, Junior Drum and Bugle Corps in 1936, Junior Baseball team in 1938, and also conducts an annual sale of poppies and sponsors an annual Legion picnic.

Mrs. Linnie Wilt, mother of Past Commander Lloyd E. Wilt, who died on the 4th of January, 1939, was a guiding influence in the activities of the Post and was known as the "Mother of the American Legion of Williamsburg."

The names of the Past Commanders of Post 456 are: Lloyd E. Wilt, Joseph D. Bechtel, Paul E. Henderson, Frank P. Ross, Ralph T. White, Everett Miller, Joseph Shawley and Clarence G. Price.

The elected officers who served this Post during the year 1939 were:

Commander	Frank H. Good
Senior Vice Commander	Lloyd E. Wilt
Junior Vice Commander	W. Earl Bell
Adjutant	Frank B. Mann
Finance Officer	George S. Havens
Historian	Paul E. Henderson
Chaplain	Charles Suter
Sergeant at arms	Anthony Wance

The officers elected to serve for the year 1940 are: Commander, Frank B. Mann; Senior Vice Commander, Charles Hoover; Junior Vice Commander, Ralph T. White; Adjutant, Warren Detwiler; Finance Officer, George S. Havens; Historian, Charles Suter; Chaplain, Glenn Zeilinger, and Sergeant at arms, William Shade.

MURRAY-APPLEMAN POST NO. 147

The Roaring Spring Post of the American Legion was granted a temporary charter on the 26th of December, 1922, and the permanent charter as issued on the 1st of April, 1924, contained the following names: J. R. Wike, Chas S. Stephens, R. B. Kaufman, Geo. L. Horner, F. J. Wood, C. S. Albright, J. V. Pote, E. W. Myers, L. O. Burket, W. L. Hair, Harry Albright, Jack Echman, Blair Hartman, John Curry, S. M. Morgart, J. F. Stonerook, and Robert Riley.

The first officers elected were: Commander, J. R. Wike, First Vice Commander, L. O. Burket; Second Vice Commander, J. V. Pote; Adjutant, Chas S. Stephens; Finance Officer, Ralph B. Kaufman; Historian, F. J. Wood; Chaplain, Harold Morgart; Sergeant at arms, Dewey S. Hayes; Executive Committee, Geo. L. Horner, W. L. Hair, Oren S. Cowen, J. F. Stonerook, W. L. Grounds, E. W. Myers, Tom Hamilton, Park Ferry, John Curry.

Post No. 147 was named in honor of the memory of Jesse L. Murray and Clyde E. Appleman. Jesse L. Murray was born nead Roaring Spring on the 16th of September, 1899. He enlisted on the 26th of April, 1917, and served as a Private in the Machine Gun Company, 28th Infantry, 1st Division, and died on the 22nd of July, 1918, of wounds received the previous day near Berzy-le-Sec, France. His body was returned to his home and buried in the Greenlawn Cemetery at Roaring Spring.

Clyde E. Appleman was born at Bakers Summit on the 10th of June, 1893. He enlisted on the 12th of February, 1918, and served as a Private in Company B, 305th Engineers, 80th Division, and died of wounds and complications on the 17th of October, 1918. His body was returned to his home and buried in the Holsinger Cemetery at Bakers Summit.

A mass meeting of the World War veterans of Roaring Spring was held in the office of Lorenz and Wike, on the 12th of December, 1922, at which time an organization was perfected. Post meetings were held in various rooms in the borough until May, 1933, when an American Legion Home was erected at the corner of Cemetery and Poplar Streets. The home association was chartered in the Blair County Courts on the 4th of October, 1926, as "The American Legion Home Association of Roaring Spring." A portion of the ground purchased on the 26th of April, 1926, was donated to the School District for the purpose of providing a site for a gymnasium.

The Murray-Appleman Drum and Bugle Corps which was in existence from 1931 to 1938, won many distinctions, including the Class "B," Department of Pennsylvania Championship, under the leadership of Drum Major, George L. Horner; Director, Robert F. Moore, and Assistant Director, Miss Marian Holsinger.

The Ladies Auxiliary to Post No. 147 was organized November 15th, 1923.

A Squadron of the Sons of the Legion was organized on the 26th of February, 1934, with sixty-five members.

The Glee Club was organized during the spring of 1939 with 35 members.

The latest community activity of this Post was the purchase of an oxygen tent and its presentation on the 14th of December, 1939, to the Nason Hospital.

The names of the Past Commanders are: Jesse R. Wike, George L. Horner, Fred J. Wolf, James W. McMillan, George B. Replogle, Roy G. McGinnis, John E. Parry, William H. Heuston, Abram Barley and John A. Whitman.

The officers who served during 1939 were: Commander, John A. Whitman; First Vice Commander, W. A. Bassler; Second Vice Commander, C. S. Albright; Adjutant, Chas. S. Stephens; Finance Officer, Lyman Reffner; Historian, Chas. Hiney, Jr.; Chaplain, Samuel P. Snyder; Sergeant at arms, John Curry.

The Post meets on the second Friday of each month and has 103 members.

The officers for the year 1940 are: Commander, Jacob Yingling; First Vice Commander, Clarence E. Lauer; Second Vice Commander, Park Ferry; Adjutant, Chas. S. Stephens; Finance Officer, V. E. Lane; Historian, E. L. Burket; Chaplain, George B. Replogle; Sergeant at arms, John Curry.

FORT FETTER POST NO. 516

Post No. 516, The American Legion of Hollidaysburg, as organized in 1920, was named in honor of the memory of Benjamin H. Hewit, who was killed in action while serving as Captain of Company F, 316th Infantry.

The charter was dated the 26th of March, 1920, and contained the following names: Webster Calvin, John A. Matthews, Edwin R. Baldrige, F. J. Wolf, Joseph G. Stultz, Joseph F. Reiser, Edgar R. Vipond, W. E. Bice, Charles W. Moore, J. R. Creamer, A. H. Christy, F. C. Brenner, J. A. Smith, R. C. Nowell and J. Stewart Shatzer.

This post became inactive and upon the organization of Post No. 509, of the Veterans of Foreign Wars, the name of Benjamin H. Hewit was selected.

A temporary charter was issued on the 28th of January, 1925, for a revived Post of the American Legion, to be known as the Fort Fetter Post No. 516. The permanent charter was issued on the 2nd of March, 1927, and contained the following names: John B. Elliott, C. R. Skinner, Adam C. Leonard, Amos C. Mellott, J. Calvin Lang, Jr., Chester Elliott, Donald G. McIntyre, F. J. Wolf, Joseph F. Reiser, William M. Corbin, M. H. Gildea, W. E. Bice, J. B. Mauk, Paul H. Smith, E. W. Hewitt, and Frank J. Reiser.

The officers elected for the year 1925 were: Commander, Frank J. Reiser; Vice Commander, W. Earl Bice; Adjutant, Fred J. Wolf; Finance Officer, Amos C. Mellott; Historian, Samuel Calvin; Chaplain, Joseph G. Stultz; Sergeant at arms, Harry L. Ireland; and chairman of the Executive Committee, J. Blaine Mauk.

Fort Fetter Post was so named to commemorate a Revolutionary War fort which stood near the New Portage Junction, one mile west of Hollidaysburg.

Some of the many activities of this Post are as follows:

The Post has decorated annually the graves of all deceased veterans buried in this vicinity, and has sponsored parades and conducted patriotic observances on Memorial and Armistice Days.

An Auxiliary unit to Post 516 was chartered on the 28th of December, 1926, consisting of the mothers, wives, widows and daughters of Legionnaires.

The Fort Fetter Post Service Unit was formed during the year 1927, for the purpose of administering the last rites to departed comrades, and to represent the Post on public and patriotic occasions.

Post rooms were secured in the Wolf building, corner of Allegheny and Front Streets, during 1929, and have continued to the present time as the meeting place for the Post, its auxiliaries and other groups.

A plot of ground in the Alto Reste Cemetery was presented to the Post by the cemetery association, and dedicated on Memorial Day, 1929, as a burial ground for any veteran. The remains of three Civil War veterans were moved from the County Almshouse cemetery and re-interred in the Legion Plot.

The Fort Fetter Post Drum and Bugle Corps was organized during 1929, and has represented the Post and town at many public events, including State Conventions, and has won many distinctions in competitive drills. The Corps made its first public appearance at Hollidaysburg, on Armistice Day, 1929, and its first appearance away from home at Bellwood the following May, under the leadership of Drum Major Floyd G. Hoenstine. The Drum Major during recent years has been Matthew Calvin.

The Americanism committee has presented school medal awards to a boy and girl of each of the graduating classes of the grammar schools, since 1930.

A Boys Band was organized in 1931, and under the leadership of Andrew Schroeder served as the official band for the Hollidaysburg Centennial.

A sum of money amounting to over four thousand dollars was presented to the Post on the 4th of November, 1932, by the officers of the United War Work Fund, John N. Drass, General Chairman, and Jonathan G. Shope, Treasurer. This money had been raised during the closing days of the World War and was intended for welfare work among the soldiers.

THE WORLD WAR

"The American Legion Home Association of Hollidaysburg" was chartered by the Blair County Courts on the 21st of August, 1933, for the purpose of legally holding and controlling all property belonging to the Post.

During the fall of 1933, the Post expended the sum of seven hundred dollars towards the installation of flood lights on Dysart Park. The Post's half interest in the flood lights was later transferred to the Hollidaysburg High School Athletic Association, as a donation from the Post.

The first Squadron of the Sons of the Legion to be formed in Blair County was organized on the 18th of December, 1933, as the Fort Fetter Squadron No. 516, and chartered on the 12th of January, 1934.

A plot of ground at the intersection of the Juniata, Mulberry and Blair Streets, was purchased from the Pennsylvania Railroad on the 28th of August, 1934, as the site of a possible future home, for the sum of six hundred dollars.

The Dell Delight Park, containing fifty-two acres, was purchased on the 9th of July, 1935, from the First National Bank of Altoona, for the sum of four thousand dollars. The money received from the officers of the United War Work Fund was used for this purpose. The name of Dell Delight Park was changed to American Legion Memorial Park.

A Legion Club was opened on the first floor of the Wolf Building, underneath the Legion rooms, on the first of August, 1935.

In December, 1935, work was started on the improvements to the Memorial Park, under a public works project sponsored by the Blair County Commissioners.

During the St. Patrick's Day flood of the 17th of March, 1936, the Legion rooms and facilities, as well as the service of the officers and members, were freely given towards alleviating distress among the flood sufferers. Immediate relief was furnished by the Legion, and the Post rooms were used as headquarters for the collection and distribution of food, clothing, medicine and other supplies.

The services of the officers and members of the Post, and its auxiliaries, contributed in a large measure to the success of the observance of the Hollidaysburg Centennial, which was held from the 9th to 16th of August, 1936.

The Junior Auxiliary, composed of daughters of the members of the Ladies Auxiliary, was chartered on the 18th of January, 1939.

The names of the Past Commanders and their membership, are as follows:

1925	Frank J. Reiser and W. Earl Bice	56
1926	Joseph G. Stultz	43
1927	Amos C. Mellott	101
1928	John B. Elliott	102
1929	Floyd G. Hoenstine	110
1930	J. Calvin Lang, Jr.	112
1931	Samuel Calvin and John W. Allen	143
1932	John W. Allen	110
1933	Edwin S. Warner	113
1934	John Hughes	123
1935	John W. Allen and Kay A. Hansen	101
1936	Kenneth D. Forsht	153
1937	John G. Kelly	135
1938	Chas. C. Shoemaker	111
1939	Robert N. Mutzabaugh	142

The officers for the year 1939 were: Commander, Robert N. Mutzabaugh; Senior Vice Commander, Samuel B. Hainley; Junior Vice Commander, Stanton C. Funk; Adjutant, Kay A. Hansen; Finance Officer, J. Calvin Lang, Jr.; Historian, Floyd G. Hoenstine; Chaplain, Mark Sloan; Sergeant at Arms, Frank H. Claar; Executive Committee members, John G. Kelly, A. W. Martin, Hobson C. Wagner and John Hughes.

Fort Fetter Post meets on the first and third Mondays of each month, and the Commander for the year 1940 is Samuel B. Hainley.

JOHN M. ANDERSON POST NO. 424

A Post of the American Legion was organized at Bellwood during the summer of 1926 by the World War veterans residing in Bellwood and vicinity, and an application was signed and forwarded to the Department Headquarters of the American Legion at Philadelphia, requesting that a charter be granted. A temporary charter was issued on the 9th of August, 1926, and the members proceeded with the election of officers and the organization of the Post. The charter remained open while additional members were solicited and the permanent charter was granted on the 16th of April, 1927.

The names appearing on the charter were: H. C. Emerick, William Sitman, Jr., R. A. Pickens, Cloyd P. Gilmore, H. F. Singleton, H. D. Sitman, E. J. Garland, J. Wiggans Thorn, Robert B. Greenland, Blair W. Dunn, S. G. Orris, H. R. Gwin, John F. Davis, B. F. Hughes and J. M. Douglass.

The Bellwood Post was given the number 424, and named in honor of the memory of John M. Anderson who was killed in action near Chateau Thierry, France, on the 31st of July, 1918. He was born at York, Pennsylvania, on the 17th day of January, 1899, a son of Reverend Joseph F. and Drucilla Anderson, who resided at Bellwood. John M. Anderson enlisted as a Private in Company G, 110th Infantry, 28th Division, at Altoona on the 21st of May, 1917. His body was returned to his home and buried in the Rose Hill Cemetery at Altoona.

This Post first held its meetings in the community room in the First National Bank Building, and later in the home purchased from the Pennsylvania Railroad on the 1st of March, 1927. A home association was chartered in the Blair County Courts on the 10th of January, 1927, under the title of the "John M. Anderson Post of the American Legion No. 424."

Several auxiliary units have been organized during the life of the Post to assist in carrying on the Legion work, among which the Ladies Auxiliary was chartered on the 16th of March, 1928. The president for the year 1939 was Mrs. C. L. Bush, and the recently elected President for 1940 is Mrs. Ethel Hirsch.

A firing squad equipped with rifles, uniforms and flags has served the Post and community on all public and patriotic occasions and has administered the last rites to all deceased veterans of that vicinity.

The names of those who have served as commander during the history of the Post are as follows: H. Clark Emerick, W. Murray Ermine, William Sitman, Jr., Raymond M. Strunk, Harry R. Gwin, Lincoln F. Henry, Justus M. Douglass, Charles F. Wertz, William P. Bush, Jay M. Stevens, John E. Harvey, Earl M. Goshorn, and Frank L. Wogan.

During the year 1939, thirty-one members were secured through the efforts of the following elected officers:

Commander	Frank L. Wogan
Senior Vice Commander	B. Franklin Hughes
Junior Vice Commander	Lewis M. Hample
Adjutant	William P. Bush
Finance Officer	Lincoln F. Henry
Historian	Edward R. Weight
Chaplain	Harry R. Gwin
Sergeant at arms	George E. Vandevender
Executive Committee	Charles F. Wertz, John E. Harvey, Blair W. Dunn, Earl M. Goshorn

The officers elected for the year 1940 are as follows: Commander, B. Franklin Hughes; Senior Vice Commander, J. Howard Stone; Junior Vice Commander, Jacob K. Cramer; Adjutant, John E. Harvey; Finance Officer, Lincoln F. Henry; Historian, Edward R. Weight; Chaplain, Harry R. Gwin; Sergeant at arms, George E. Vandevender; Executive Committee members: Fred Irwin, Merrill M. Doran, Jay M. Stevens.

Post No. 424 meets on the first Thursday of each month.

CLAYSBURG POST NO. 522

The World War veterans residing at Claysburg and vicinity held a meeting in the Kindergarten building on the evening of the 14th of October, 1932, for the purpose of determining as to whether an American Legion should be organized at Claysburg. About forty former soldiers were present and it was decided to form a Post. Accordingly, a temporary organization was formed with D. Emmert Brumbaugh as chairman, who in turn appointed a committee, consisting of Warren C. McCarty and Charles L. Reighard, to arrange for the securing of a charter. Of the eligible members who were present on this occasion, a number belonged to American Legion Posts in other towns, principally Roaring Spring, while others had never held membership in the Legion due to there being no Post in the vicinity of their place of residence.

A temporary charter was granted by the Department of Pennsylvania under date of the 9th of December, 1932, and the permanent charter was dated the 11th of March, 1933, with the following named veterans as the charter members: D. Emmert Brumbaugh, Warren C. McCarty, Harry E. Diehl, Boyd L. Murray, Peter M. Stufft, Maurice T. McCullough, Chauncey F. Lingenfelter, Charles L. Reighard, Wilmer H. Bennett, Leslie L. Weyandt, Jacob S. Barnhart, David R. Reighard, Harry S. Lingenfelter, Stanley Helsel, Albert E. Langley, Henry L. Isenber, John T. Spence, Charles O. Garver, Egbert B. Dodson, J. Elvin Kurtz, Fred E. Shaffer, William Diehl, Charles B. Weyant, Shannon C. Weyant, Murray H. Ake, Thaddeus Feathers, Edward Lingenfelter, Taylor L. Dively, Carl A. Senn, Andrew Patterson, Isaac Patterson, Paul E. Coller, Charles R. Ross, Warren S. Mock, Emory H. Cowher, John E. Leslie, Earl D. Replogle, Wesley Weyant, H. Ross Brumbaugh, Charles H. Close, Raymond Nale, Luther Nycum, William M. Bush, Lester D. Burket, William B. Dively, Howard Harpster, John Hengst, Winfield Ickes, Chester Shaffer, Howard Roudabush, Hervey Berkey, John Kauffman, Harry Plummer, Warren Hengst, Shannon Helsel, Herman Colabaugh, Albert Walter, Herbert Emeigh, Clarence Burket, James Eyler, Calvin Williams, Chester Lingenfelter, Shannon Kauffman, Edward Wombacher, Russell Burger, Ellsworth Croyle, James Hammel and Tony Saya.

The Post was assigned the number 522 by the Department Headquarters and by action of the members of the Post, it was named in commemoration of the town of Claysburg, which had been so named in memory of Henry Clay, an American statesman and member of the United States Senate.

The following named members were elected to fill the various offices of the Post during its initial year: Commander, D. Emmert Brumbaugh; Senior Vice Commander, Harry E. Diehl; Junior Vice Commander, Boyd L. Murray; Adjutant, Warren McCarty; Finance Officer, Peter M. Stufft; Historian, Chauncey F. Lingenfelter; Chaplain, Maurice T. McCullough; Sergeant at arms, Charles T. Reighard; Executive Committee members: John T. Spence, J. Elvin Kurtz, Stanley T. Helsel, Raymond Nale and Earl D. Replogle.

This Post, with the exception of the Robinson-Herring Post of Altoona, was the last to be organized in Blair County and since its formation it has been a very active unit of the American Legion. Among its many community activities is the annual Legion Day celebration held at Claysburg on the 4th of July. This event consists of a street parade, competitive drills by visiting bands and drum corps, and a display of fireworks, interspersed with athletic contests, band concerts and other entertainment.

Action was taken at the March, 1933, meeting to secure the use of an old brick school house, property of the General Refractories Company, as a meeting place. This building served the Post, its auxiliaries and other groups as a meeting place for its various activities until the 1st of April, 1939, when a home, located at the northern edge of the town, was purchased, where meetings of the Post are now held on the first and fourth Thursdays of each month.

SOLDIERS OF BLAIR COUNTY

The new home, formerly a residence, after some alterations will provide comfortable and adequate quarters for the activities of the Claysburg veterans, their auxiliary organizations, and the entertainment of their friends.

The Ladies Auxiliary of the Claysburg Post was organized during the year 1934, with Mrs. Hazel McCullough as President. This unit has performed valuable service to the Post and continues its activities with Miss Goldie Weyandt as the President for the year 1940.

During the year 1934 this Post organized and sponsored a band, known far and near as the Claysburg Legion Band, which under the leadership of E. Mauguman Ickes, Carl A. Senn and J. Elvin Miller, has participated in many parades at home as well as in distant towns where it won distinction in competitive drills and brought credit to the town it represents.

During the year 1935, a Squadron of the Sons of the Legion was organized, consisting of the sons of Legionnaires, with Paul Dodson as the first Captain.

Other activities of the Claysburg Post of the American Legion are:

The annual observance of Memorial and Armistice Days with the decoration of all soldiers' graves in the vicinity by placing a small American flag on the grave prior to Memorial Day.

The sponsoring of a joint banquet annually with the ladies of the Auxiliary, at which time the Post and community have been honored by the presence of several Department Commanders of the American Legion as well as many other distinguished Legionnaires, county officials, and others of prominence.

The names of the Past Commanders, their membership is as follows:

Year	Name	Membership
1933	D. Emmert Brumbaugh	74
1934	D. Emmert Brumbaugh	127
1935	Charles L. Reighard	131
1936	Warren C. McCarty	124
1937	Wilmer A. Bennett	114
1938	Carl A. Senn	76
1939	Maurice T. McCullough	74

The membership for this Post is drawn from Claysburg, which is the only town not incorporated as a borough in Blair County that supports a Legion Post, East Freedom and Sproul in Greenfield Township, and a number from Bedford County.

The names of the elected officers for the year 1939 were as follows:

Commander	Maurice T. McCullough
Senior Vice Commander	D. Ray Hengst
Junior Vice Commander	William Diehl
Adjutant	Warren C. McCarty
Finance Officer	D. Emmert Brumbaugh
Historian	C. Blair Burket
Chaplain	Taylor L. Dively
Sergeant at arms	Moses Claar
Sergeant at arms	George Homan
Executive Committee members	J. Elvin Kurtz, Jacob S. Barnhart, Warren A. Hengst, J. Irvin Eyler, Henry Lingenfelter

The names of the officers elected to serve this Post during the year 1940 are: Commander, George A. Knighton; Senior Vice Commander, Egbert B. Dodson; Junior Vice Commander, Henry L. Isenberg; Adjutant, Warren C. McCarty; Finance Officer, D. Emmert Brumbaugh; Chaplain, Maurice T. McCullough; Historian, C. Blair Burket; Sergeant at arms, Harry J. Dibert and Moses Claar; Executive Committee members: William Fowkes, J. Elvin Kurtz, Hugh Ernest, D. Ray Hengst, and Boyd L. Murray.

ROBINSON-HERRING POST NO. 529

An American Legion Post, whose membership consists entirely of the colored World War veterans who reside in Blair and adjacent counties, was organized at Altoona during the spring of 1939, through the efforts of District Commander Wilbur C. Van Scoyoc of Tyrone. The application for a charter, which was forwarded to the Department Headquarters at Philadelphia and which resulted in the issuance of a temporary charter, contained the following names of eligible members: Hugh Barnes, Pat Burns, Irvin Brown, Paul Cochran, John Cooksey, Wilbur A. Cuff, Arthur J. Fitzgerald, James C. Francis, Robert Hart, Arthur J. Johnson, W. Thomas Johnson, Arnold Knox, John A. Pattillo, Marshall Pattillo, Robert A. Pattillo, William Pendleton, William J. Russell, Albert M. Slaughter, William D. Shields, John C. Smith, Arthur Stephenson, Opal Surratt, Riley N. Tucker, John H. Walker, Eugene Warren, William W. White, John Willis, Frederick D. Wims, Jesse Woodland and Roland E. Woolridge. Other names will be added to the permanent charter as additional members are secured up until the time set for closing the charter.

Post 529 of the American Legion was named in honor of the memory of Joseph F. Robinson and Lovey J. Herring, two colored soldiers of this vicinity who gave their last full measure of devotion to their country's cause while serving in the armed forces of the United States.

Joseph F. Robinson, a resident of Huntingdon, Pennsylvania, was born at Pittsburgh, Pennsylvania, in 1882. He enlisted in the service at Newport News, Virginia, on the 3rd of September, 1917, and served as a Private in Company K, 301st Stevedore Regiment, Quartermaster Corps. He died on the 5th of January, 1918, of a fractured skull received in an accident and is buried in the Riverview Cemetery at Huntingdon.

Lovey J. Herring, a resident of 1616½ 17th Street, Altoona, was born at Wallace, North Carolina, in 1888. He entered the service at Altoona on the 27th of October, 1917, and served as a Private in Company A, 505th Engineers. He died at Camp Lee, Virginia, on the 18th of November, 1917, of pneumonia and is buried at Berwyn, Pennsylvania.

The names of the officers elected to serve this Post during its initial year were as follows:

Commander	Albert Slaughters
Senior Vice Commander	Robert A. Pattillo
Junior Vice Commander	Wilbur A. Cuff
Adjutant	Arthur J. Johnson
Finance Officer	Robert Hart
Historian	W. Thomas Johnson
Chaplain	John Cooksey
Sergeant-at-Arms	Pat Burns
Sergeant-at-Arms	John C. Smith
Executive Committee Members	Sam Pattillo, Opal Surrat, John Willis

The Robinson-Herring Post No. 529, The American Legion, meets on the first and third Wednesdays of each month in the Community Center Building, Thirteenth Avenue and Eighteenth Street, Altoona. However, several of its meetings have been held in the American Legion homes at the various towns where the Post's members reside. The members of this Post enrolled thirty-five members during the year 1939, and through the efforts of its members, individually and jointly, this Post promises to be one of the most active in the district. Various social events have been conducted in an effort to arouse interest in the Post's membership drive and to provide funds with which to conduct its program.

The election of officers for the year 1940 resulted in the retention of all of the 1939 officers.

ALTOONA CHAPTER NO. 34

An organization known as the Disabled American Veterans of the World War was founded at Cincinnati, Ohio, during March, 1920. Delegations from local organizations of disabled veterans gathered at the same place on the 25th of September, 1920, in a caucus and decided to federate into a national body, composed of a National Department, State Department and local chapters.

The First National Convention was held at Detroit, Michigan, on the 27th to 30th of June, 1921, at which time a permanent organization was perfected. The Disabled American Veterans of the World War was incorporated by an Act of Congress on the 17th of June, 1932.

All persons who served honorably during the World War and suffered disabilities from wounds, gas, accident or disease are eligible for membership.

National headquarters are maintained at 2840 Melrose Avenue, Cincinnati, Ohio, and national conventions are held annually at which time a national commander and other officers are elected by the assembled delegates.

The National Commander elected at the 1939 convention is Lewis J. Murphy, and the National Adjutant, also editor of the semi-monthly newspaper, is Vivian D. Corbly, who has served for several years by appointment.

Headquarters for the Department of Pennsylvania are maintained at Harrisburg, Pa., and a Department Convention is held annually at which time officers are elected by the assembled delegates.

The State officers serving for the year 1939-1940 are:

Commander	Henry Rivlin
Senior Vice Commander	William C. McKelvie
Junior Vice Commander	James J. Dunphy
Junior Vice Commander	Harry E. Loomis
Judge Advocate	George S. Fay
Chaplain	William R. Cummings

Chapters, existing in every state in the union, are founded upon a spirit of fellowship, comradeship, mutual aid and co-operation, and many own and operate their own club rooms where social rehabilitation has been a chief accomplishment.

Plans for the formation of a Chapter in Altoona were considered at a meeting held in the Young Mens Christian Association building at Altoona, during the spring of 1931, when a number of disabled veterans of Blair County met at the invitation of a national organizer.

Officers were elected, members enrolled and a charter was granted by the National Organization on the 1st of May, 1931. The names of the members appearing on the charter are as follows: Paul L. Hall, Floyd G. Hoenstine, M. A. Wolfberg, Joe Gionfriddo, J. W. Burkholder, James E. Moore, Harry E. Clarke, Frank J. Reiser, Alfred K. Hall, H. E. Beck, W. E. Bice, John F. Royer, W. R. Charles, Wm. C. Giarth, Jasse C. Gutshall and C. L. Savage.

The Altoona Chapter of the Disabled American Veterans maintain a service office here and assistance is given any disabled veteran or his dependents. The Chapter also conducts a weekly radio broadcast over WFBG, joins in the plans for the observance of Memorial Day and Armistice Days in Altoona, jointly sponsors with the Brotherhood Class of the Greenwood Brethren Church the memorial services in the Greenwood Cemetery, the evening of each Memorial Day, distributes Christmas baskets to needy veterans each year, and supports all public and patriotic endeavors.

The Chapter is dependent on an annual sale of forget-me-nots for funds with which to conduct its various activities, and a sum in excess of four hundred dollars was secured during the sale of September, 1939, through the support of an Advisory Committee consisting of J. Harry Shearer, Chairman; Mayor J. Harry Moser, Hon. Thomas J. Baldrige, Hon. Marion D. Patterson, William H. Wade, Levi Gilbert, Rev. John E.

O'Connor, Rev. Burleigh A. Peters, S. Arthur Coffey, Robert C. Haberstroh, Roy F. Thompson, N. A. Stevens, Robert P. MacDonald and J. Virgil Taylor.

A number of distinctive honors have been conferred on members of the Altoona Chapter during the past years, in the election and appointment of its members to National and State offices. George S. Fay was elected National Executive Committeeman at the Cincinnati Convention in 1933, and re-elected at the Colorado Springs Convention in 1934. He was elected National Junior Vice Commander at the New Haven Convention in 1935, and appointed a member of the National Finance Committee following the Grand Rapids Convention in 1938. He also was elected to the office of Department Judge Advocate for the years 1936, 1937, 1938, 1939 and 1940.

Harry E. Loomis of this Chapter was elected to the office of State Junior Vice Commander at the Punxsutawney Convention in 1938, and re-elected at the Philadelphia Convention in 1939.

The Fifth Department Convention of the Disabled American Veterans of Pennsylvania was held at the Penn Alto Hotel, Altoona, on the 24th to 27th of January, 1935, with the Altoona Chapter acting in the capacity of host.

During the year 1931, the Altoona Chapter was honored by a visit from the National Commander, E. Claude Babcock, and in 1935 the National Adjutant Vivian D. Corbly, visited Altoona at the time of the Fifth Department Convention.

The names of the Past Commanders of the Altoona Chapter are:

1931   Paul L. Hall and Harold E. Beck
1932   Alva R. Dunaway and George S. Fay
1933   George S. Fay
1934   John M. Yingling
1935   J. Lester Laughlin
1936   Ray E. Nelson and Harry E. Loomis
1937   Harry E. Loomis
1938   Floyd G. Hoenstine
1939   Randolph M. Clark

For the past several years the Chapter has met on the first and third Tuesdays of each month in the G. A. R. building, 911 Chestnut Ave., its membership now is 96.

An auxiliary organization known as the Altoona Chapter Memorial Unit, consisting of all members in good standing, was formed in 1938 for the purpose of representing the Chapter on all public and patriotic occasions as a uniformed group, and to have charge of Memorial and Armistice Day observances.

The Altoona Chapter has presented Certificates of Merit to four citizens of Altoona who have rendered faithful, efficient and outstanding service to the cause of the disabled veterans. These certificates are provided for by the National Constitution and By-laws and are awarded on the approval of the Department and National Officers. The names of the recipients of these awards are:

J. Harry Shearer, President, Pennsylvania Edison Company
S. Arthur Coffey, Manager Credits, *Altoona Mirror*
J. Virgil Taylor, Editor, Veterans Activities, *Altoona Mirror*
Roy F. Thompson, Managing Director, WFBG Radio Station

The elected officers who served the Chapter during the year 1939 were:

Commander	Randolph M. Clark
Senior Vice Commander	Michael F. Cole
Junior Vice Commander	William E. Roles
Treasurer	Floyd G. Hoenstine
Chaplain	Wade R. McDowell
Officer of the Day	George E. Bollinger
Sergeant-at-Arms	Oliver G. Langer
Trustees	Jesse T. Harmon, J. Lester Laughlin, and M. A. Wolfberg
State Executive Committeeman	Floyd G. Hoenstine

The Commander elected to serve for the year 1940 is Michael F. Cole.

BLAIR COUNTY VOITURE NO. 350

La Societe des Quarante Hommes et Huit Chevaux is an organization of World War veterans affiliated with the American Legion. Eligibility for membership requires the applicant to have been a member of the American Legion for a period of at least twelve months, and to have rendered service in some capacity to the Legion. It is organized primarily as a fun-making unit, but it also has a program of service relative to that of the parent organization. The name "Forty and Eight" is derived from the French boxcar used during the period of the World War to convey men and horses to the battlefront. On the side of the car was painted a rectangle, in the enclosure of which was printed the numerals and words "40 Hommes et 8 Chevaux," meaning "Forty men or Eight horses."

La Societe is composed of three component bodies similar to that of the parent organization, the American Legion, namely Voiture Nationale, corresponding to the National body of the Legion; the Grand Voiture, corresponding to the State department of the Legion; and the Voiture Locale, which is the County unit whose membership is recruited from the outstanding members of the Legion Posts within the County. The French word "Voiture" corresponds more nearly to our English word "Chapter."

Blair County Voiture 350 was organized at Tyrone during the month of August, 1922, when a group of active Legionnaires in that town perfected plans for the formation of a Voiture. The charter is dated the 16th of August, 1922, and on its roster of charter members are included the following names: Joseph P. Arnold, Charles M. Aultz, J. L. Bosserman, Carey C. Bradin, Charles E. Cole, Joseph A. Dickson, Roger W. Franciscus, Paul F. Griffin, John J. Haberstroh, Louis F. Haberstroh, John A. Hiller, John D. Logue, Donald J. Howard, Raymond V. Kearns, Paul M. Kienzle, A. O. King, Philip Klevan, Paul R. Kuhn, Roy J. Landis, B. B. Levengood, Walter E. Lotz, Wilfred A. Morgan, Edward R. Musser, Jr., E. K. McClintock, John B. Nason, Robert W. Owens, David R. Perry, Richard J. Schell, Harry N. Sellers, Morgan J. Sheedy, Raymond J. Sheedy, J. Murray Shollar, Gerald H. Stevens, Norman E. Stryker, William S. Swope, Chester H. Wagner, Richard W. Wingate, Paul T. Winter and Herman Work.

The early meetings of the Voiture were held at Tyrone, where it originated, but as the unit was without permanent quarters, meetings were held at several places in that town. The City of Altoona eventually became the center because of its convenience and central location within the county. During the intervening years between 1922 and 1933 various places in Altoona served as meeting places, no attempt being made to acquire a permanent home. From records available it is apparent that no outstanding activities interested the membership other than the periodical "wrecks" and a few informal social affairs. During the years intervening between 1929 and 1933 it is evident that the Voiture was on the decline as little is recorded showing any activity and the membership was reduced to a small figure and the Voiture became inactive.

However, a revival of interest was effected in 1933 when a number of interested members undertook the task of re-organizing the unit. A campaign of membership renewal was inaugurated for the purpose of reviving interest and activity. A home association was chartered in the Blair County Courts, effective on the 31st day of May, 1933, as "The 40 and 8 Club, Voiture 350," permanent quarters were secured in a small but cosy and comfortable bungalow back of Lakemont Park along the Frankstown Road. The building was adequately equipped to serve as a home until more spacious accommodations could be secured. So rapidly was Voiture interest revived that after a year of occupying the bungalow it became necessary to obtain new and larger quarters to accommodate the increasing members. Accordingly, in the summer of 1934 the Voiture acquired the Hatch property in Pleasant Valley on the outskirts of Altoona, along the Pleasant Valley Boulevard, which was originally a part of the Hileman Estate. The property included an old but comfortable frame house, spacious and well constructed, which after alterations and improvements has served as a home for the Voiture. A con-

THE WORLD WAR

siderable sum was spent to recondition the house and premises, and when finished was one of the most attractive and comfortable veterans clubs in Central Pennsylvania. The formal opening was held with a three-day observance on the 13th, 14th and 15th of December, 1934.

Since occupation of the present quarters, the Voiture home has been the scene of many elaborate social events, which have attracted and entertained its members on many occasions. Not only has the Voiture had its socials and rounds of frivolity, but it has also adhered to its purpose of organization namely,—service to the Legion and community. Lengthy accounts could be written of all that has transpired within its circles, and occasions when services were rendered, but limited space will not permit it in this account. However, a few of the outstanding are here recorded.

Voiture 350 has been interested in the activities of the Legion Posts of Blair County, especially Legion membership and Americanism. It has been interested in child welfare work. It is interested in the "Highway of Memory." It has given its support to the work of the Red Cross and Blair County Tuberculosis Society. It has presented flags to the Blair-Bedford Council Boy Scouts of America and the Mercy Hospital. During the flood periods of 1936 and 1937 it co-operated with and extended donations of money and food to the Legion Posts of Blair County which were active at that time in extending relief to the stricken areas. Every year a Christmas party is given for the children of the community. It has supported the Keystone Boys State Camp of the American Legion by sending a number of boys from Altoona and Blair County to the camp at the expense of the Voiture.

During the seventeen years of its existence fifteen of its members have held the office of Chef de Gare, which is the President of the unit. This number includes the following: Paul F. Griffin, Wilfred A. Morgan, John R. Hurd, Hyman Goldberg, William Diamond, R. E. Van Ormer, Samuel J. Constance, John E. Weidley, T. Don Willoughby, J. Murray Shollor, John C. Haller, Morgan J. Sheedy, L. Paul Shafer, Henry H. Pennock and the present incumbent, David Kaufman. Of the above mentioned, one has answered the final call, namely, Hyman Goldberg, who died on the 10th of February, 1935.

The membership of the Voiture has always been relatively small as compared with the Legion membership in Blair County, but this difference is more than repaid by the active interest of its membership in Legion and Voiture activities. The average age of the World War veteran is now approaching the half-century mark and the future of the Voiture cannot be a promise of many years, but while the members are still agile and alert, it can safely be assured that an indefinite number of years are still ahead for the unit, if unexpected adversities do not suddenly disrupt its march of progress.

The officers who served for the year 1939 were as follows:

Chef de Gare	Henry H. Pennock
Chef de Train	C. Wesley Burns
Comissaire Intendent	Zane A. W. Green
Correspondant	Charles A. McManamy
Conducture	Carl G. Frank
Garde de la Porte	Clyde G. Levan
Comis Voyageur	Adam Muri
Lampiste	Louis Ehringer
Aumonier	Naseeb Masood
Cheminots	Morgan J. Sheedy
	John J. R. Williams
	John B. Elliott
	John H. Galbraith and
	William C. Cole

The above history written by Raphael L. Seidel, Correspondent Passee.

THE TWENTY-FIRST DISTRICT COUNCIL

An organization known as The Twenty-first District Council of the Department of Pennsylvania, The American Legion, was formed during the year 1932 for the purpose of promoting closer co-operation between the various American Legion Posts located in Blair and Bedford Counties.

Membership in the Council consists of the District Commander and Deputy District Commanders as ex-officio members without vote; delegates representing the various Posts of the District, including the Commander, Adjutant, one elected delegate-at-large, and one elected delegate for each one hundred members or fraction thereof. The Council meets on the first Sunday of January, April, July and October.

Since the organization of the Council the following members served as Chairman:

1933	John W. Allen	Hollidaysburg
1934	George C. Heit	Bedford
1935	John H. Galbraith	Altoona
1936	J. William Richey	Everett
1937	George L. Horner	Roaring Spring
1938	Ivan R. White	Saxton
1939	Harry E. Diehl	Claysburg

The functions of the District Council are similar in many respects to the duties of the District Commander and his deputies, both having as their object the advancement of the Legion program through increased membership, dissemination of information and unified action in carrying out the policies of the parent organization. Prior to the formation of the Council the District Commanders endeavored to carry out the Legion program by holding district conferences, and the present District Council is the outcome of such efforts.

A District Commander is elected by the delegates who attend the Department Convention in the odd numbered year and serves for a period of two years. The District Commander also appoints representatives from the various Posts in his District as members of the various Department Committees.

The names of those who served as District Commanders of the District in which Blair County has been a part, are as follows:

1922-1923	George D. Wands	Tyrone
1924-1925	Paul R. Kuhn	Altoona
1926-1927	George L. Horner	Roaring Spring
1928-1929	Jay M. Walters	Everett
1930-1931	Floyd G. Hoenstine	Hollidaysburg
1932-1933	Floyd G. Hoenstine	Hollidaysburg
	Robert C. Amos	Bedford
1934-1935	Edwin S. Warner	Hollidaysburg
1936-1937	Ivan R. White	Saxton
	John H. Galbraith	Altoona
1938-1939	C. Wilbur Van Scoyoc	Tyrone
1940-1941	George C. Heit	Bedford

The office of the Chairman of the Council rotates among the Posts of the District, providing the Post has a candidate at the time that its turn comes around. The officers elected to serve the Twenty-first District Council for the year 1939 were as follows: Chairman, Harry E. Diehl; Vice Chairman (Blair County), William C. Cole, Vice Chairman (Bedford County), William Gearinger; Adjutant-Finance Officer, Daniel D. Carey; Historian, George L. Horner; Chaplain, Daniel R. Wilt; Sergeant at arms, John E. Parry.

The Chairman elected at the meeting in January to head the organization during the year 1940 is William Gearinger of Six Mile Run.

THE WORLD WAR

Name	Rank Organization	Born	Died	Cemetery	Location
Ackers, Levi Ernest	Pvt. B, 314 F. A.	1895	1919	Salem Reform	Williamsburg
Alexander, John Ralph	Smn. U. S. Navy	1897	1918	Homewood	Pa.
Allingham, Jesse P.	Pvt. C, 26 Inf.	1890	1918	Presbyterian	Williamsburg
Allison, Steward L.	Pvt. 1 Prov. Con. Co.	1895	1937	Spring Hope	Martinsburg
Anderson, John M.	Pvt. C, 110 Inf.	1899	1918	Rose Hill	Altoona
Anderson, Lester McK.	Pvt. E, 4 Cav.	1896	1931	Fairview	Altoona
Appleman, Clyde E.	Pvt. B, 305 Engrs.	1893	1918	Holsingers	Bakers Summit
Arble, Charles L.	Ck. D, 305 Engrs.	1896	1936	Carrolltown	Pa.
Armstrong, Edward L.	Pvt. 72, Trans. Corps	1882	1932	Greenwood	Altoona
Auker, Carl S.	Sgt. 100 Trans. Corps	1896	1939	Rose Hill	Altoona
Auman, Charles	Ck. Sup. 109 F. A.	1891	1918	Oak Ridge	Altoona
Aurandt, George Howard	Pvt. G, 387 Inf.	1887	1918	Fairview	Altoona
Baker, John Jennings	Pvt. Bal. Group	1897	1937	Carson Valley	Duncansville
Baker, Thomas	Pvt. K, 166 Inf.	1890	1918	Meuse-Argonne	France
Barnes, Charles	Cpl. Marine Corps	1891	1937	Alto Reste	Hollidaysburg
Barr, Clifford Allen	Pvt. Sup. 347 Inf.	1896	1922	East Lawn	Tyrone
Bason, Garwood	Pvt. I, 165 Inf.		1924	Rays Cove	Everett
Bathurst, Clarence I.	Pvt. G, 110 Inf.	1894	1930	Greenwood	Altoona
Bathurst, Thomas E.	U. S. Navy	1891	1939		Tyrone
Battista, Guiseppe	Pvt. D, 18 Inf.	1898	1934	Calvary	Altoona
Bauman, Frank Joseph	Pvt. M. P. 6 Corps	1893	1938	St. Marys	Altoona
Baumgardner, Thomas S.	Pvt. 3, 154 D. B.	1894	1936	St. Marys	Altoona
Beach, Freeman B.	Pvt. D, 158 D. B.	1894	1918	Carson Valley	Duncansville
Becher, Joseph C.	Pvt. 5 Ord. Guard	1889	1920	St. Patricks	Gallitzin
Behe, William C.	Pvt. Med. Dept.	1896	1936	Oak Ridge	Altoona
Behm, Carl F.	Pvt. 106, Trans. Corps	1888	1939	Fairview	Altoona
Beightol, Edward M.	Pvt. G, 110 Inf.	1898	1918	Mt. Pleasant	Centre Co.
Bell, Charles Chester	Cpl. Med. 341, Ser. Bn.	1887	1932	Oak Ridge	Altoona
Bender, Francis A. (s)	Sgt. G, 110 Inf.	1878	1918	Oise-Argonne	France
Bendheim, Roy G.	Pvt. B, 13 Inf.	1891	1920	Mt. Siani	Altoona
Bennett, Francis S.	Sgt. 309 Q. M. C.	1893	1937	Greenlawn	Roaring Spring
Bennett, John Henry	Pvt. D, 28 Inf.	1893	1918	Muese-Argonne	France
Beringer, Harold Elton	Pvt. S. A. T. C.	1898	1938	Grandview	Tyrone
Berkey, Benjamin H.	Pvt. I, 320 Inf.	1888	1918		France
Berkey, John H.	Pvt. Gas Med. Rep. Unit	1897	1918	Greenfield	Claysburg
Berney, Samuel E.	Pvt. 27, 155 D. B.	1895	1917	Adudath Achim	Altoona
Bickhart, Harry J.	Sgt. A, 16 Inf.	1892	1918		France
Biehl, Charles Wolfgang	Pvt. B, 332 Inf.	1888	1938	St. Marys	Altoona
Bilger, George Francis	Pvt. Spruce Div.	1888	1918	Grandview	Tyrone
Black, John Michael	Sgt. G, 110 Inf.	1880	1918	Carson Valley	Duncansville
Blackburn, George Leroy	Pvt. Spruce Div.	1901	1922	Calvary	Altoona
Blair, Charles Field	Cpl. D, 425 Tel. Bn.	1896	1937	Grandview	Tyrone
Blair, George Wm.	Pvt. Ord. Dept.	1896	1928	Alto Reste	Hollidaysburg
Blair, Ralph G.	Pvt. 258 Aero Sqn.	1892	1919	Oak Ridge	Altoona
Bleicher, Frank Xavier	2Lt. Marine Corps	1884	1926	St. Patricks	Newry
Bloomhardt, Fred H.	Lt. Col. Med. 321 Inf.	1872	1929	Fairview	Altoona
Bolyar, Charles R.	Sgt. L, 803 Pioneer Inf.	1889	1922	Rose Hill	Altoona
Bonner, Guy Leslie	Pvt. Hqs. 5 Marines	1893	1918	Fairview	Martinsburg
Boone, George William	Sgt. Cavalry	1890	1937	Rose Hill	Altoona
Boring, Elmer H.	Pvt. Hqs. 166 Inf.	1890	1929	Rose Hill	Altoona
Borrows, Paul W.	Pvt. 103 Tr. Mtr. Bn.	1894	1918	Highland	Lock Haven
Boyles, Burt H.	Pvt. Base Hosp. 41	1895	1937	Lutheran	Newry
Bradley, Albert Miller	Pvt. 62, 153 D. B.	1893	1919	Fairview	Altoona
Bradley, Frank J.	Cpl. C, 14 M. G. Bn.	1889	1925	St. Patricks	Gallitzin
Brandt, Henry U.	Cpl. G, 110 Inf.	1896	1918	York	Pa.
Brandt, Willoughby B.	Pvt. 1, 153 D. B.	1893	1934	Alto Reste	Hollidaysburg
Brannen, Eugene J.	Pvt. K, 10 Inf.	1886	1935	St. Patricks	Gallitzin
Bratton, George M.	Cpl. Q. M. C.	1888	1931	Glasgow	Pa.
Brede, Charles F.	Cpl. 30 Trans Corps	1889	1924	Oak Ridge	Altoona
Briggs, George H.	Pvt. G, 110 Inf.	1893	1918	Lutheran	Sinking Valley
Brightbill, William	Pvt. Q. M.C.	1883	1937	Carson Valley	Duncansville

SOLDIERS OF BLAIR COUNTY

Name	Rank Organization	Born	Died	Cemetery	Location
Brogan, Jonathan Robert	Pvt. M, 35 Engrs.	1894	1934	Rose Hill	Altoona
Brophy, Thomas Edward	Cpl. 243 Aero Sqn.	1896	1934	St. Patricks	Gallitzin
Brown, Clarence W.	Pvt. 235 Aero Sqn.	1899	1922	Rose Hill	Altoona
Brubaker, Gilbert Earl	Pvt. D, 156 D. B.	1892	1918	Carson Valley	Duncansville
Brubaker, Samuel James	Pvt. A, 1 F. A.	1889	1938	Decatur	Illinois
Brumbaugh, Henry Ross	Pvt. Q. M. C.	1893	1934	Fairview	Martinsburg
Brumbaugh, Harry Victor	Pvt. Mt. Trans. Corps.	1897	1921	Brumbaugh	Martinsburg
Brumbaugh, Rolland Edw.	2Lt. Marine Corps	1895	1922	Greenlawn	Roaring Spring
Brumbaugh, Walter P.	Sgt. A, 5 F. A.	1887	1920	New Enterprise	Bedford Co.
Buck, Henry Franklin	Pvt. 22 Spruce Sqn.	1888	1930	Grazierville	Tyrone
Buchanan, Clarence E.	Pvt. Mt. Sup. Train	1888	1935	Grandview	Altoona
Buchanan, James Wm.	Sgt. Medical Dept.	1892	1930	Grandview	Altoona
Buck, Elmer W.	Pvt. Amb. Corps	1891	1938	Woodward	Clearfield Co.
Buhler, William M.	Pvt. 79 F. A.	1891	1930	Rose Hill	Altoona
Burger, Russell Conwell	Pvt. 17 M.G. Bn.	1894	1936	Vicksburg	Roaring Spring
Burke, Joseph B.	Sgt. D, 116 Sup. Train	1892	1929	Greenlawn	Roaring Spring
Burket, Charlie	Pvt. B, 3 Dev. Bn.	1888	1931	St. Patricks	Newry
Burley, Paul C.	Pvt. 21 Amb.	1889	1927	St. Johns	Altoona
Burns, Thomas M.	Cpl. I, 35 Engrs.	1889	1919	Fairview	Altoona
Burnshire, Charles H.	Pvt. G, 110 Inf.	1895	1925	Grandview	Tyrone
Butler, Henry	Cpl. D, 72 F. A.	1900	1935	Greenlawn	Roaring Spring
Butler, John A.	Wgr. E, 55 F.A.	1899	1919	Spring Hope	Martinsburg
Byers, Frank B.	Cpt. R. R. Engrs.	1876	1921	Rose Hill	Altoona
Caldwell, Artie Blair	Pvt. 3 Engrs.	1894	1919	Rose Hill	Altoona
Calvin, Webster	Lt. Col. 303 San Train	1882	1929	Presbyterian	Hollidaysburg
Campbell, Lester Lyman	Pvt. A, 321 F. A.	1892	1937	Eastlawn	Tyrone
Capri, Guido	Pvt. Hos. 162 Inf.	1890	1936	St. Patricks	Gallitzin
Carl, Bernard E.	Pvt. Spruce Sqn.	1892	1932	St. Johns	Altoona
Carl, Francis Clare	Pvt. B, 49 Engrs.	1896	1926	St. Marys	Hollidaysburg
Carles, William H.	Cpl. M, 328 Inf.	1893	1930	Grandview	Altoona
Carlson, Ralph A.	Sgt. B, 9 Inf.	1899	1929	Eastlawn	Tyrone
Carson, David F.	Pvt. G, 110 Inf.	1896	1918	Rose Hill	Altoona
Carson, John Houser	Smn. U. S. Navy	1895	1921	Fairview	Altoona
Cashman, William McK.	Pvt. B, 49 Engrs.	1895	1918	Arlington	Virginia
Cassatta, Engelbert M.	Pvt. 118 Trans. Corps	1896	1938	Calvary	Altoona
Castel, Julius	Mus. 16 Inf.	1889	1933	Mt. Moriah	Blue Knob
Cathers, William S. P.	Pvt. L, 112 Inf.	1894	1918	Pavia	Bedford Co.
Cerullo, Lewis	Pvt. M. G. 110 Inf.	1898	1918	Calvary	Altoona
Chase, Milton H.	Pvt. 406 Mt. Trans.	1899	1939	Blandsburg	Cambria Co.
Cheslock, Michael J.	Pvt. B, 109 Inf.	1894	1935	St. Patricks	Gallitzin
Chilcoat, Harry D.	Pvt. G, 110 Inf.	1898	1918	Arlington	Virginia
Chirdon, Clyde Peter	Pvt. Marine Corps	1897	1935	Calvary	Altoona
Claar, Franklin Clyde	Pvt. G, 26 Inf.	1899	1918	Lutheran	Claysburg
Clark, Charles Alex	Wgr. Sup. 309 F. A.	1892	1937	Grandview	Tyrone
Clark, James Francis	Cpl. C, 13 Inf.	1896	1922	Calvary	Altoona
Clarke, John M.	Cpt. F, 111 Inf.	1888-1918		Oise-Aisne	France
Clossin, John Joseph	Pvt. K, 124 Inf.	1894	1918	St. Patricks	Gallitzin
Coble, Floyd W.	M. E. Hqs. 216 Engrs.	1885	1929	Sparrs	Williamsburg
Cochran, Joseph Milton	Pvt. 34, 153 D. B.	1890	1928	Carson Valley	Duncansville
Colabine, John Wesley	Cpl. L, 110 Inf.	1895	1918	Logan Valley	Bellwood
Cole, Alton C.	Pvt. D, 28 Inf.	1899	1918	Suresnes	France
Colledge, John W.	Pvt. C, 147 Engrs.	1897	1931	Carson Valley	Duncansville
Condon, Gordon John	Pvt. 152 Aero Sqn.	1899	1932	Fairview	Altoona
Condon, Miles Marion	Pvt. M, 12Bn.Trn. Center	1895	1939	Grandview	Altoona
Confer, John W.	Maj. 10 Cav.	1893	1928	West Roxbury	Mass.
Conlon, Stephen S.	Pvt. 83 Trans Corps	1896	1922	Calvary	Altoona
Corl, Robert A.	Pvt. G, 110 Inf.	1894	1918	Vicksburg	Roaring Spring
Cotter, John James	Pvt. 9 Recruit Camp	1889	1930	Rose Hill	Altoona
Cowan, Robert B.	Pvt. 808 Aero Sqn.	1895	1935	Snow Shoe	Centre Co.
Cox, Jesse R.	Pvt. 155 D. B.	1894	1935	Claar	Claysburg
Cox, Robert Edward (S)	Gnr. U. S. Navy	1875	1937	Rose Hill	Altoona

THE WORLD WAR

Name	Rank Organization	Born	Died	Cemetery	Location
Coxey, Charles Robert	Pvt. G, 110 Inf.	1899	1938	Greenwood	Altoona
Craiger, Thomas C.	Pvt. F, 43 C. A. C.	1899	1924	Rose Hill	Altoona
Crawford, Wm. Morrow	Smn. U. S. Navy	1890	1918	At Sea	
Crider, Harry E.	Pvt. F, 103 Engrs.	1891	1920	Antis	Bellwood
Crissman, Luther H.	Wgr. Sup. 108 F. A.	1894	1931	Rose Hill	Altoona
Croft, Cloyd Stanley	Pvt. A, 54 Engrs.	1894	1918	Holsingers	Bakers Summit
Croft, Elmer Ellsworth	Pvt. C, 111 Inf.	1887	1935	Holsingers	Bakers Summit
Crook, Charles E.	Pvt. Marine Corps	1890	1929	Calvary	Altoona
Crowl, John Thomas	Frn. U. S. Navy	1883	1938	St. Marys	Altoona
Crum, Edwin	Smn. U. S. Navy	1890	1921	Fairview	Altoona
Crum, John Oliver	Sgt. Marine Corps	1881	1929	Greenlawn	Hollidaysburg
Crumbaker, Charles Grant	Clk. U. S. Navy	1894	1931	Fairview	Altoona
Curfman, John Edwin	Pvt. S. A. T. C.	1898	1918	Fairview	Martinsburg
Curtis, Charles R.	Pvt. B, 359 Inf.	1891	1937	Pomona	California
Dahlberg, Arthur	Sgt. D, 308 M. G. Bn.	1891	1933	Elmwood	Wisconsin
Davidson, William A.	Cpl. D, 131 Inf.	1888	1930	Eastlawn	Tyrone
Davis, Lloyd Franklin	Pvt. 8, 153 D. B.	1890	1930	Carson Valley	Duncansville
DeArment, William McK.	Pvt. C, 602 Engrs.	1893	1937	Fairview	Altoona
Decker, Willis D.	Pvt. A, 2 Engrs.	1894	1936	Rose Hill	Altoona
Dell, Clarence Edgar	Pvt. I, 146 Inf.	1896	1932	Carson Valley	Duncansville
de Lozier-Morris, Mary M.	Nrs. U. S. Army		1939	Arlington	Virginia
Dempsie, James	Cpl. L, 51 Inf.	1894	1933	Presbyterian	Williamsburg
Denny, Charles E.	Sgt. Med. Dept.	1887	1923	Grandview	Tyrone
Denny, Reuben	Pvt. C, 5 Prov. Engrs.	1886	1918	Grandview	Tyrone
Denocenzo, Angelo	Pvt. C, 3 Bn. 105 D. B.	1893	1918	St. Josephs	Williamsburg
Desch, Charles F.	Sgt. Q. M. C.	1894	1920	Rose Hill	Altoona
Detwiler, Frank S.	Mch. 109 Trans. Corps	1895	1923	Rose Hill	Altoona
Devereaux, John Earle	Pvt. Field Art.	1897	1924	Johnstown	Pa.
Devine, James R. M.	Pvt. Marine Corps	1899	1939	Calvary	Altoona
Devore, George F.	Pvt. 10 Mt. Mch.	1878	1919	Rose Hill	Altoona
Diehl, Francis Richard	Pvt. G, 110 Inf.	1899	1918	Oak Grove	Tyrone
Dillalogi, Alphonzo	Pvt. C, 601 Engrs.	1893	1924	St. Patricks	Gallitzin
Dillon, Thomas R.	Pvt. D, 53 C. A. C.	1900	1924	Calvary	Altoona
Dively, James Ellsworth	Sgt. E, 305 Engrs.	1894	1932	Lutheran	Claysburg
Dixon, Matthew	Pvt. 117 Trans. Corps	1892	1937	Calvary	Pittsburgh
Dodson, Harvey Francis	Pvt. A, 109 M. G. Bn.	1896	1918	Patton	Pa.
Dollinger, Benjamin H.	Pvt. B, 60 Inf.	1889	1938	Greenwood	Altoona
Donahoe, Hugh B.	Pvt. 476 Aero Sqn.	1891	1921	Calvary	Altoona
Donnelly, Edward J.	Pvt. 60 Spruce Sqn.	1891	1934	Calvary	Altoona
Donnelly, Patrick J.	Pvt. C, 30 Inf.	1892	1938	Calvary	Altoona
Dooley, Chalmer	Pvt. I, 147 Engrs.	1896	1925	Warriors Mark	Pa.
Dossler, Harry G.	Pvt. D, 15 F. A.	1892	1918	Eastlawn	Tyrone
Dougherty, Glenn Edgar	Pvt. Marine Corps	1891	1920	Rose Hill	Altoona
Dougherty, Thomas E.	Pvt. C, 27 Engrs.	1879	1923	Fairview	Altoona
Douglas, Harrie A. (s)	Cpt. Q. M. C.	1869	1935	Stoverdale	Pa.
Douglass, Charles W.	Cpl. A, 19 Engrs.	1888	1933	Riverview	Huntingdon
Douglass, Paul E.	Pvt. D, 309 Inf.	1892	1934	St. Patricks	Gallitzin
Downs, James Roy	Pvt. L, 38 Inf.	1891	1932	Greenwood	Altoona
Doyle, Morgan James	Pvt. Med. Dept.	1897	1928	Calvary	Altoona
Doyle, Michael David	Pvt. 61 Spruce Sqn.	1887	1939	Greenlawn	Hollidaysburg
Doyle, Vincent James	Pvt. E, 305 Mt. Sup.Trn.	1892	1939	Greenlawn	Hollidaysburg
Drass, Lawrence Patrick	Sgt. Spruce Sqn.	1892	1921	St. Marys	Hollidaysburg
Dubbs, Clarence Ray	Pvt. E, 319 Inf.	1891	1919	Oise-Aisne	France
Dubbs, Lawrence T.	Pvt. 158 Aero Sqn.	1877	1925	Las Vegas	Nevada
Duffield, Foster Wm.	Pvt. B, 305 Engrs.	1891	1939	Fairview	Altoona
Duffy, Burton Owen	Pvt. G, 110 Inf.	1893	1931	Woodland	Clearfield
Duffy, John F.	Pvt. Q. M. C.	1878	1929	Calvary	Altoona
Duffy, Joseph C.	Cpl. I, 4 Inf.	1894	1939	Calvary	Altoona
Dunaway, Alva R.	Sgt. C, 314 Engrs.	1894	1933	Grandview	Altoona
Duncan, William Lewis	Pvt. 2, Del. C. A. C.	1897	1939	Carson Valley	Duncansville
Dunn, Matthew G.	Gnr. U. S. Navy	1895	1920	St. Johns	Altoona

SOLDIERS OF BLAIR COUNTY

Name	Rank Organization	Born	Died	Cemetery	Location
Earl, Homer W.	Pvt. A, 11 Inf.	1893	1918		France
Earnest, Roy Elmer	Pvt. 6, Signal Corps	1896	1934	Rose Hill	Altoona
Ebersole, Harry Clinton	Pvt. C, 14 Engrs.	1872	1928	Oak Ridge	Altoona
Ebersole, Herbert N.	Cpl. M, 320 Inf.	1894	1928	Salemville	Bedford Co.
Eckenrode, Paul S.	Pvt. Med. Corps	1896	1937	St. Patricks	Gallitzin
Eckhard, Julius Roy	Pvt. E, 5 F. A. R. D.	1893	1935	Dayton	Ohio
Eisel, William Jacob	Cpl. B, 163 Inf.	1890	1937	St. Marys	Altoona
Emeigh, George Ellis	Pvt. Hqs. 60 C. A. C.	1897	1931	Greenlawn	Roaring Spring
Emerick, Harry Clark	Pvt. C, 110 Inf.	1888	1936	Logan Valley	Bellwood
England, Samuel Arthur	Pvt. Signal Corps	1896	1918	Keller Reform	Williamsburg
Epple, Frank Joseph	Cpl. Marine Corps	1893	1935	St. Marys	Altoona
Erb, Levi C.	Pvt. 696 Mt. Truck	1897	1935	Vicksburg	Roaring Spring
Ermin, Edward Vance	Pvt. 46, 153 D. B.	1893	1932	Greenwood	Altoona
Ernest, John Bernard	Pvt. K, 18 Inf.	1893	1918	Arlington	Virginia
Evans, John A.	Pvt. Med. Dept.	1890	1939	Grandview	Tyrone
Ewing, Leroy Baker	Pvt. B, 316 Engrs.	1892	1918	Rose Hill	Altoona
Fagan, Germain R. M.	M. M. U. S. Navy	1891	1922	St. Johns	Altoona
Fagan, William Lawrence	1Lt. Engrs.	1889	1918	Clifton Heights	Philadelphia
Fagley, Ray H.	Pvt. K, 319 Inf.	1894	1918	Grandview	Altoona
Fanning, Winthrop C.	Lt. Air Service	1893	1919	Thiacourt	France
Fay, Frank H.	Pvt. Q. M. C.	1869	1936	Presbyterian	Hollidaysburg
Feathers, Owen Daniel	Pvt. L, 118 Inf.	1891	1932	Reform	Claysburg
Felker, Mark Roush	Mus. 305 Engrs.	1895	1936	Beaver Springs	Pa.
Feltwell, Frank H.	1Lt. Tank Corps	1894	1925	Rose Hill	Altoona
Fetters, Charles I.	Pvt. L, 112 Inf.	1896	1938	Imler	Bedford Co.
Fickes, David Elmer	Pvt. C, 103 F. Sig. Bn.	1887	1918	Union	Bedford Co.
Field, Harry James W.	Pvt. Marine Corps	1900	1918	Belleau	France
Fields, Guyer R.	Pvt. Hqs. 28 Inf.	1896	1933	Grandview	Tyrone
Fink, Aden Fay	Pvt. E, 158 Inf.	1896	1919	Presbyterian	Williamsburg
Fiore, Harry	Pvt. Med. Dept.	1892	1933	Calvary	Altoona
Fisher, Frank Gilbert	Sgt. Q. M. C.	1893	1931	Rose Hill	Altoona
Fisher, Richard Gilbert	Pvt. Med. Dept.	1893	1918	Grandview	Tyrone
Flannagan, John P.	Pvt. G, 110 Inf.	1886	1925	Rose Hill	Altoona
Fleck, Aaron J.	Sgt. A. S. M.	1886	1932	Oak Ridge	Altoona
Fleck, Thomas J.	Sgt. Construction Div.	1886	1934	Presbyterian	Hollidaysburg
Fleisher, Cloyd S.	Pvt. 16 Balloon	1897	1935	Mt. Union	Pa.
Fleming, Malcolm D.	Lt. Marine Corps	1889	1933	Logan Valley	Bellwood
Flick, Paul A.	Sgt. 333 F. R. S.	1890	1931	Calvary	Altoona
Fluke, Edgar P.	Pvt. 2 Conv. Center	1897	1924	Rose Hill	Altoona
Fluke, Harry Earl	Sgt. 39 Trans. Corps	1893	1920	Rose Hill	Altoona
Foley, John Francis	Cpl. G, 110 Inf.	1889	1918	Calvary	Altoona
Follette, Oliver W.	Cpl. M, 117 Inf.	1888	1925	Greenlawn	Roaring Spring
Fonner, Charles W.	Pvt. Veterinary Corps	1891	1927	Greenwood	Altoona
Forcarille, Mark	Pvt. 12 Balloon	1896	1920	Calvary	Altoona
Franzoni, Lodovico	Pvt. B, 45 Engrs.	1888	1937	St. Patricks	Gallitzin
Friel, John R.	Pvt. D, 134 F. A.	1890	1939	Akron	Ohio
Fry, Daniel Kime	Pvt. B, 2 R. T. C.	1888	1934	Rose Hill	Altoona
Frye, Edmond M.	Pvt. E, 33 F. A.	1899	1934	Greenwood	Altoona
Frye, William Roy	Pvt. 7, 2 Trn. Bn.	1895	1924	Reform	Claysburg
Fulton, Frank	Sgt. E, 320 Inf.	1892	1918	Belleau	France
Furlong, John F.	Sgt. A, 20 F. A.	1881	1935	Calvary	Altoona
Furrer, Jacob Charles	Smn. U. S. Navy	1895	1918	At Sea	
Fusco, Biago	Smn. U. S. Navy	1889	1933	Calvary	Altoona
Galbraith, Benjamin B.	Pvt. G, 7 Inf.	1886	1935	Alto Reste	Hollidaysburg
Gallagher, William A.	Pvt. 63 Trans. Corps	1883	1932	Calvary	Altoona
Gardner, John Howard	Pvt. G, 110 Inf.	1895	1918	Bald Eagle	Tyrone
Garland, Harry	Oiler, U. S. Navy	1887	1923	Carson Valley	Duncansville
Garland, Martin H.	Pvt. Q. M. C.	1889	1923	Grandview	Tyrone
Garrity, James J.	Cpl. H, 50 Inf.	1886	1934	St. Johns	Altoona
Gates, John C.	Pvt. A, 21 Engrs.	1892	1918	At Sea	
Gearhart, Donald L.	Pvt. G, 110 Inf.	1899	1918	Rose Hill	Altoona

Name	Rank Organization	Born	Died	Cemetery	Location
Gearhart, Earl Russell	Pvt. B, 313 M. G. Bn.	1887	1935	Rose Hill	Altoona
Geesey, Norman Elwood	Pvt. F. A.	1901	1937	Fairview	Altoona
Gibbons, John	Pvt. 67, C. A. C.	1889	1927	Calvary	Altoona
Gibbons, Michael Thos.	Sgt. 37, 55 D. B.	1886	1924	St. Johns	Altoona
Giboney, Oscar Fred	Pvt. Med. Dept.	1898	1933	Alto Reste	Hollidaysburg
Gibson, Wilbur J.	Pvt. 103 San. Engrs.	1885	1919	Danville	Pa.
Gildea, Myrel H.	Pvt. B, 7 Trn. Bn.	1896	1931	Greenlawn	Hollidaysburg
Gill, Wilfred Paul	Sgt. Med. Corps	1890	1937	Calvary	Altoona
Gillette, Charles C.	Cpt. I, 3 Inf.	1895	1938	Presbyterian	Hollidaysburg
Glasgow, Jesse L.	Mch. I, 60 Inf.	1886	1923	Oak Ridge	Altoona
Glass, Calvin Luther	Pvt. E, 305 Engrs.	1889	1932	Nicodemus	Martinsburg
Glassco, Simeon H.	Pvt. E, 131 Inf.	1888	1918	Grandview	Tyrone
Gleason, Charles H.	Pvt. 18, 158 D. B.	1891	1918	Logan Valley	Bellwood
Goetz, George Baringer	Col. Q. M. C.	1863	1937	Greencastle	Pa.
Goldberg, Hyman	Sgt. Sup. 11 F. A.	1891	1935	Sons of Jacob	Altoona
Gonder, William M.	Pvt. 262 Aero Sqn.	1887	1936	Rose Hill	Altoona
Goodman, Clyde W.	Pvt. C, 1 Tr. Mtr.	1891	1930	Huntingdon	Pa.
Gorsuch, Frederick L.	Pvt. General Service	1884	1920	Geeseytown	Hollidaysburg
Goshorn, Ethel May	Nrs. Army Nurse Corps	1895	1918	Logan Valley	Bellwood
Graffius, William E.	Sgt. Sup. 316 Inf.	1896	1929	Grandview	Tyrone
Grant, Charles R.	Pvt. Med. Dept.	1896	1926	Greenlawn	Hollidaysburg
Grathwohl, Charles M.	Pvt. A, 307 Mt. Repairs	1891	1918	St. Marys	Altoona
Gray, Caleb A.	Pvt. A, 305 F. Signal Bn.	1890	1918	Romagne	France
Green, Amos B.	Sgt. I, 7 Inf.	1895	1930	Logan Valley	Bellwood
Green, Clair E.	Sgt. Sup. 326 Inf.	1895	1923	Rose Hill	Altoona
Greiner, Frank Joseph	Pvt. 2, Prov. E. M. P.	1888	1935	St. Marys	Altoona
Griffin, Perry T.	Pvt. Q. M. C.	1890	1938	Grays	Centre Co.
Grimes, Samuel Louis	Pvt. Med. Corps	1897	1934	Alto Reste	Hollidaysburg
Gugluzo, Joseph	Pvt. D, 4 Inf.	1891	1918	Belleau	France
Guido, Saverio	Pvt. 305 M. G. Bn.	1892	1926	Calvary	Altoona
Gullarmod, Norman A.			1918		France
Gunsallus, Harry W.	Pvt. Hqs. 50 Inf.	1900	1927	Rose Hill	Altoona
Gutwald, Clyde Frank	Pvt. A, 318 Inf.	1891	1935	Calvary	Altoona
Gutwald, Francis J.	Pvt. 315 Aero Sqn.	1898	1920	Calvary	Altoona
Gutzwiller, Louis P.	Pvt. H, 15 Cav.	1901	1921	Calvary	Altoona
Guyer, Fred Raymond	Pvt. B, 155 D. B.	1895	1923	Fairview	Altoona
Gwin, Joseph R.	Pvt. 29 Amb.	1892	1923	Grandview	Altoona
Haberstroh, John J.	2Lt. Ord. Dept.	1894	1939	Calvary	Altoona
Hainsey, Harry (s)	Sgt. I, 2 Inf.	1873	1934	Frankstown	Hollidaysburg
Hall, Alfred K.	Cpl. 82 Trans. Corps	1889	1939	Greenwood	Altoona
Hall, Samuel Conrad	Pvt. 77 Spruce Sqn.	1887	1939	Oak Ridge	Altoona
Hamilton, Albert R.	Pvt. 501 Aero Sqn.	1889	1932	Oak Ridge	Altoona
Hammer, Charles A.	Pvt. Q. M. C.	1888	1939	Philadelphia	Pa.
Hammond, Charles Henry	Pvt. 77 Spruce Sqn.	1895	1932	Calvary	Altoona
Hempsher, Joseph	Sgt. M. G. 13 Inf.	1888	1922	Rose Hill	Altoona
Hancock, Benjamin	Mch. I, 61 Inf.	1875	1936	Philipsburg	Pa.
Hancuff, Karl Wm.	Pvt. Q. M. C.	1890	1921	Presbyterian	Williamsburg
Hand, Joseph W.	Wgr. G, 307 Amb. Trn.	1893	1931	Eastlawn	Tyrone
Hanley, Michael C.	Pvt. D, 320 Inf.	1886	1918	Meuse-Argonne	France
Harber, Josiah F.	Cpl. Sup. 13 Inf.	1880	1938	Grandview	Altoona
Harman, Fred W.	Pvt. A, 28 Inf.	1895	1925	Alto Reste	Hollidaysburg
Harney, William J.	Pvt. Spruce Sqn.	1886	1926	St. Johns	Altoona
Harper, Clyde Miller	Cpl. E, 305 Mt. Sup. Trn.	1890	1932	Rose Hill	Altoona
Harper, Henry G.	2Lt. B, 18 F. A.		1927	Bloomfield	Pa.
Harpster, Charles M.	Pvt. I, 2 Inf.	1897	1923	Steffeys	Hunt'gdon Co.
Harrington, Thomas	Pvt. M. G. 23 Inf.	1889	1933	Calvary	Altoona
Harris, David James	2Lt. Ord. Dept.	1893	1935	Rose Hill	Altoona
Harrison, Chester Benj.	Cpl. A, 120 Engrs.	1887	1930	Fairview	Altoona
Harvey, Fred	Pvt. B, 16 Cav.	1900	1918	St. Patricks	Gallitzin
Hawkins, James Bruce	Pvt. B, 880 Pioneer Inf.	1893	1933	Oak Ridge	Altoona
Hayes, Adolphus W.	Pvt. B, 75 R. R. Art.	1889	1920	Eastlawn	Tyrone

SOLDIERS OF BLAIR COUNTY

Name	Rank Organization	Born	Died	Cemetery	Location
Hayes, Ivan Edison	Pvt. Hqs. 114 F. A.	1892	1939	Greenlawn	Roaring Spring
Hazard, Harold George	Smn. U. S. Navy	1899	1936	Arlington	Virginia
Heath, James T.	Pvt. 141 Inf.	1898	1923	Broad Top City	Hunt'gdon Co.
Herberling, Norman D.	Pvt. 27 Amb.	1896	1932	Eastlawn	Tyrone
Heberling, Omer S.	Pvt. Spruce Sqn.	1888	1919	Eastlawn	Tyrone
Heinbaugh, Herman E.	Cpl. G, 110 Inf.	1896	1936	Presbyterian	Hollidaysburg
Heinike, Herbert R.	Cpl. 102 Tr. Mtr. Bn.	1897	1934	Buffalo	New York
Heller, Josiah Lawrence	Pvt. G, 110 Inf.	1890	1936	Logan Valley	Bellwood
Hendricks, Hiram G.	Mus. Hqs. 111 Inf.	1887	1936	Grandview	Altoona
Henry, Ernest E.	Pvt. I, 10 Inf.	1898	1934	Mt. Lebanon	Lebanon
Herr, Ralph	Sgt. B, 305 Engrs.	1891	1929	Grandview	Altoona
Herr, Raymond Davis	Pvt. 11, 154 D. B.	1890	1930	Greenwood	Altoona
Herring, Lovey J.	Pvt. A, 505 Engrs.	1888	1917	Berwyn	Pa.
Herring, Rae F.	2Lt. H, 35 Engrs.	1887	1919	Rose Hill	Altoona
Hess, Harry Edison	Pvt. Marine Corps	1898	1918	Oak Ridge	Altoona
Hetherington, Seth Cald.	1Lt. D, 315 Inf.	1883	1918		France
Hewit, Benjamin Hartley	Cpt. F, 316 Inf.	1884	1918	Meuse-Argonne	France
Hewitt, Ernest W.	1Lt. Air Service			Fairview	Martinsburg
Hewitt, Raymond M.	Cpl. Hqs. 319 M. G. Bn.	1892	1939	Dayton	Ohio
Hilbert, Paul E.	Pvt. Chemical Service	1897	1932	Greenwood	Allentown
Hildebrand, Harold W.	Pvt. Medical Corps	1896	1933	Eastlawn	Tyrone
Hileman, Samuel Walter	Sgt. Ord. Dept.	1893	1928	Fairview	Altoona
Hillard, Stephen H.	Sgt. Q. M. C.	1897	1926	Logan Valley	Bellwood
Hiner, Chester C.	Pvt. 305 Signal Corps	1894	1935	Oak Ridge	Altoona
Hoffman, Harry T.	Sgt. H, 59 Inf.	1889	1924	Rose Hill	Altoona
Hoffman, Howard Adam	Frm. U. S. Navy	1894	1934	Rose Hill	Altoona
Hoffman, Sylvester E.	Sft. U. S. Navy	1893	1932	Calvary	Tyrone
Hoffman, William Edw.	Pvt. 153 D. B.	1895	1921	Eastlawn	Tyrone
Hofmann, Joseph Pious	Pvt. 66 Engrs.	1898	1930	St. Marys	Hollidaysburg
Hollabaugh, Thomas L.	Pvt. Med. Dept.	1892	1918	Lutheran	Sinking Valley
Holland, Harry Stanford	Cpt. Q. M. C.	1861	1931	Riverside	Roaring Spring
Holland, Leland E.	Pvt. S. A. T. C.	1899	1935	Alto Reste	Hollidaysburg
Holland, Leo M.	Cps. U. S. Navy	1892	1936	Calvary	Altoona
Holliday, William F.	2Lt. Air Service	1892	1926	Logan Valley	Bellwood
Holsinger, Paul S.	Pvt. 155 D. B.	1893	1932	Holsingers	Bakers Summit
Holtzapple, Richard C.	Cpl. C, 5 Bn. Tr. Art.	1902	1926	Logan Valley	Bellwood
Hommon, Frank Palmer	Pvt. F, 112 Inf.	1898	1918	Aisne-Marne	France
Hopkins, Ray Clinton	Pvt. D, 145 Inf.	1888	1918	Meuse-Argonne	France
Hostler, Merrill R.	Sgt. H, 33 Inf.	1898	1925	Rose Hill	Altoona
Houck, Ernest O.	Pvt. 80 Trans. Corps	1898	1929	Calvary	Altoona
Houck, Kenneth Jones	Sgt. Ord. Corps	1897	1939	Alto Reste	Altoona
Houston, Thomas Edw.	Pvt. 67 Spruce Sqn.	1892	1924	Logan Valley	Bellwood
Huebner, Leonard Wm.	Pvt. L, 167 Inf.	1887	1918		France
Huey, Walter Joseph	Sgt. C, 305 Engrs.	1893	1929	St. Patricks	Gallitzin
Huling, Meryl R.	Sgt. 662 Aero Sup. Sqn.	1898	1934	Lutheran	Newry
Humphries, Dwight L.	Ck. 4, 158 D. B.	1900	1931	Sinking Spring	Ohio
Hunter, Roy M.	Ck. A, 305 Engrs.	1896	1918		France
Hurd, William Edmond		1891	1939	Absecon	New Jersey
Hutchison, Robert Guyer	Cpl. I, 64 Inf.	1886	1936	Los Angeles	California
Iachini, Giovanni	Pvt. M, 30 Inf.	1891	1937	St. Patricks	Gallitzin
Irvin, Wilbur Landis	Pvt. Inf.	1888	1935	Grandview	Tyrone
Isenberg, Alvin Roy	Pvt. D, 109 Inf.	1889	1918		France
Isenberg, Orville Juette	Pvt. B, 111 Inf.	1892	1937	Presbyterian	Williamsburg
Izzo, Frank X.	Pvt. D, 109 Inf.	1896	1918	Calvary	Altoona
Jackson, George F.	Sgt. F, 811 Pioneer Inf.	1890	1924	Rose Hill	Altoona
James, John William	Sgt. Med. Dept.	1895	1932	Rose Hill	Altoona
Johns-Dalton, Gertrude	Nrs. Army Nurse Corps	1875	1923	Logan Valley	Bellwood
Johnston, James E.	Pvt. F, 16 F. A.	1894	1938	Carson Valley	Duncansville
Johnson, Paul R.	Pvt. E, 304 Engrs.		1938	Port Royal	Pa.
Johnston, Thomas (s)	Cpl. 352 Mt. Trans.	1876	1939	Birmingham	Pa.
Jones, Claude L.	Pvt. 113 Engrs.	1890	1932	Rose Hill	Altoona

THE WORLD WAR 365

Name	Rank Organization	Born	Died	Cemetery	Location
Jones, Frank Stanley	Pvt. 262 Aero Sqn.	1893	1918	Arlington	Virginia
Jones, Glenn Harrison	Rpn. U. S. Navy	1890	1921	Rose Hill	Altoona
Jones, Russell Wm.	Pvt. Marine Corps	1898	1918	Grandview	Altoona
Kaiser, George B.	Pvt. 103 Engrs.	1893	1926	Calvary	Altoona
Kaliway, George John	Pvt. C, 314 Inf.	1894	1918		France
Kane, John E.	Pvt. 42 C. A. C.	1890	1933	Presbyterian	Williamsburg
Kane, Joseph X.	Sgt. F, 344 Inf.	1890	1939	Oak Grove	Tyrone
Karansta, Achileppa	Pvt. D, 159 M. G. Bn.	1894	1918		France
Karl, Peter Paul	Sgt. Hqs. 111 Inf.	1891	1931	Calvary	Altoona
Kay, Allen Edw.	Pvt. Hqs. 119 Inf.	1893	1933	Oak Ridge	Altoona
Keefe, John W.	Pvt. 525 Mt.Trans.	1892	1927	Riddlesburg	Pa.
Keil, Gordon J.	Pvt. A, 109 F.A.	1901	1921	Watsontown	Pa.
Keller, Franklin P.	Sgt. 220 F. Signal Corps	1891	1931	Keller Reform	Williamsburg
Kelley, Cecil A.	Pvt. F, 19 Inf.	1897	1917	Oak Ridge	Altoona
Kelley, Harry Edward	Sgt. 502 Aero Sqn.	1892	1919	Calvary	Altoona
Kelly, Andrew F.	Pvt. Ord. Dept.	1887	1924	Calvary	Altoona
Kelly, Raymond X.	Pvt. K, 110 Inf.	1900	1936	Arlington	Virginia
Kennedy, James Oscar	Pvt. 155 D. B.	1890	1918	Eastlawn	Tyrone
Kephart, James Watson	Pvt. B, 109 Inf.	1893	1918		France
Kepner, Frank P.	Cpl. C, 21 Engrs.	1890	1932	Carson Valley	Duncansville
Kerber, George E.	Pvt. Marine Corps	1891	1939	Cleveland	Ohio
Kilgalon, Edward	Pvt. B, 7 M.G. Bn.	1882	1933	Calvary	Altoona
Killian, Harry Clair	Pvt. Spruce Sqn.	1896	1923	Calvary	Altoona
Killinger, Bert H.	Pvt. C, 305 Engrs.	1892	1918	St. Patricks	Gallitzin
Kimmel, Harry Frank	Pvt. 741 Mt. Mch.	1891	1918	Oak Ridge	Altoona
Kirby, Guy J.	Pvt. M, 308 Inf.	1889	1924	Summit	Cambria Co.
Kirk, Elizabeth Krebs	Nrs. U. S. Navy	1884	1920	Presbyterian	Hollidaysburg
Kitto, William	Pvt. K, 319 Inf.	1893	1918		France
Klein, Paul Peter	Cpl. G, 56 Engrs.	1895	1925	Presbyterian	Hollidaysburg
Klepser, Frank W.	Pvt. Med. Dept.	1893	1917	Oak Ridge	Altoona
Kline, Benjamin F.	Mch. E, 132 Inf.	1893	1924	Greenwood	Altoona
Klink, Charles William	Sgt. 156 Trans Corps	1888	1934	Rose Hill	Altoona
Koenig, Joseph William	Pvt. Med. Dept.	1895	1934	St. Marys	Altoona
Kreuz, John J.	Cpl. G, 110 Inf.	1897	1918	Meuse-Argonne	France
Krumrine, Byron F.	1Lt. 387 Inf.	1895	1921	Rose Hill	Altoona
Kuhn, Paul Hudson	Pvt. G, 167 Inf.	1894	1918	Glasgow	Pa.
Kunsman, William H.	Pvt. D. B.	1892	1921	Carson Valley	Duncansville
Kyper, Don Cameron	Cpl. Med. Corps	1888	1928	Logan Valley	Bellwood
Lafferty, Harry J.	Pvt. 135 D. B.	1889	1929	Rose Hill	Altoona
Laird, Elmer L.	Pvt. Q. M. C.	1896	1922	Eastlawn	Tyrone
Lake, Leon Eben	Sgt. 121 Trans. Corps	1889	1934	Alto Reste	Hollidaysburg
Landeck, William A.	Pvt. 23 Amb. Co.	1897	1937	Greenwood	Altoona
Langham, Grace Helen	Nrs. Nurse Army Corps	1888	1922	Rose Hill	Altoona
Langham, Roy		1884	1938	San Diego	California
Lasher, William A.	Sgt. E, 9 Inf.	1896	1920	St. Marys	Altoona
Lay, Bryan Kenneth	Ck. U. S. Navy	1899	1931	Rose Hill	Altoona
Lear, Howard E.	Pvt. K, 59 Inf.	1889	1920	Oak Ridge	Altoona
Leasure, Clarence J.	Cpl. 2, 154 D. B.	1896	1926	Rose Hill	Altoona
Lee, Francis Joel	Smn. U. S. Navy	1898	1936	Oak Ridge	Altoona
Lees, Allen Eugene	Cpl. 525 Amb. Corps	1892	1919	Grandview	Altoona
Lehle, Fred John	Bug. C, 45 Trans. Corps	1895	1918	Oak Ridge	Altoona
Lehman, Peter H.	Med. Corps	1882	1938	Montoursville	Pa.
Lehr, George Milroy	Pvt. I, 165 Inf.	1897	1936	Pittsburgh	Pa.
Leonard, James Beaver	Pvt. L, 363 Inf.	1886	1929	Oak Ridge	Altoona
Lewis, Arthur L.	Pvt.		1925	Brisbin	Clearfield Co.
Lewis, Lawrence L.	Pvt. 305 Son. Tr.	1895	1929	Grandview	Tyrone
Lewis, Leon	Pvt. A, 103 Amn. Trn.	1898	1936	Rose Hill	Altoona
Liebegott, Elvin Harold	Pvt. S. A. C. T.	1899	1922	Greenlawn	Roaring Spring
Light, Frank F.	Pvt. F, 305 Inf.	1893	1924	Baughman	Tyrone
Lightner, Blake (s)	2Lt. G, 110 Inf.	1871	1938	Coalport	Pa.
Lipsey, Joseph Gillmore	Pvt. B, Labon. Bn.	1896	1932	Grandview	Altoona

SOLDIERS OF BLAIR COUNTY

Name	Rank Organization	Born	Died	Cemetery	Location
Little, Oscar J.	Sgt. Marine Corps	1890	1929	Fairview	Altoona
Litzinger, Charles Edw.	Pvt. D, 305 Engrs.	1896	1931	St. Patricks	Gallitzin
Litzinger, Norman J.	Cpl. K, 26 Inf.	1890	1918		France
Lloyd, William C.	Cpt. Railway Service	1884	1935	Calvary	Altoona
Locke, John C.	Pvt. 6, 153 D. B.	1897	1935	Calvary	Altoona
Lodick, Frank	Pvt. A, 60 Inf.	1890	1918	Oak Grove	Tyrone
Lohmer, Michael Albert	Pvt. Marine Corps	1893	1918	St. Marys	Altoona
Long, Dwight Elmer	Cpt. Med. Corps	1886	1932	Alto Reste	Hollidaysburg
Lonsdale, Leroy P.	Pvt. 352 Aero Sqn.	1897	1932	Rose Hill	Altoona
Loucks, Howard M.	Pvt. G, 110 Inf.	1898	1918	Rose Hill	Altoona
Lordeman, Maxwell W.	Maj. Ord. Dept.	1887	1939	Denver	Colorado
Lucas, James Harold	Cpl. B, 103 F. Sig. Bn.	1895	1934	Osceola Mills	Clearfield Co.
Lucas, Lee M.	Ck. 5 B. R. T. C.	1888	1932	Charlottsville	Bellwood
Lynch, Edward Augustus	Sgt. A, 29 M. G. Bn.	1894	1922	Presbyterian	Hollidaysburg
Lynam, Thomas M.	Smn. U. S. Navy	1892	1939	Calvary	Altoona
Lynn, William E.	Pvt. G, 110 Inf.	1899	1918	Fairview	Altoona
Lytle, William Andrew	M. E. 19 Engrs.	1890	1934	Grandview	Tyrone
MacArthur, Edwin D.	Cpl. D. B.	1886	1918	Oak Ridge	Altoona
Maeder, Frederick O.	Pvt. Hqs. 25 Engrs.	1890	1938	Calvary	Altoona
Malhoit, Alfred W.	Pvt. B, 102 F. A.	1894	1920	Calvary	Altoona
Mallam, Thaddeus L.	Cpt. C, 19 Engrs.	1869	1930	Oak Ridge	Altoona
Mann, William Abram (s)	Maj. General Inf.	1854	1934	Arlington	Virginia
Manning, John C.	Pvt. B, 58 Amn. Trn.	1885	1918	Yellow Spring	Williamsburg
Mapes, Joseph F.	Sgt. Marine Corps	1881	1938	Greenlawn	Roaring Spring
Marshall, Calvin			1918		
Marshall, Michael J.	Pvt. Mt. Truck	1899	1922	Grandview	Altoona
Martin, J. W.	Pvt. 97 Aero Sqn.	1874	1922	Fairview	Altoona
Martin, Warren Lee	2Lt. Inf.	1893	1938	Miami	Florida
Mascia, Leonardo G.	Pvt. H, 319 Inf.	1889	1918	Calvary	Altoona
Mastantuono, Pasquale	Pvt. G, 48 Inf.	1899	1936	Calvary	Altoona
Masterson, Arthur J.	Sgt. Med. Dept.	1893	1937	Calvary	Altoona
Masterson, John J.	Cpl. Hqs. 317 Inf.	1888	1925	Calvary	Altoona
Mattioli, Luigi	Pvt. C, 315 M. G. Bn.	1891	1930	Calvary	Altoona
Mauk, Paul C.	Cpl. H, 110 Inf.	1899	1918	Antis	Bellwood
Means, Fred J.	Cpl. 697 Mt. Trans.	1900	1928	Calvary	Altoona
Meck, Chester F.	Pvt. 34 Trans. Corps	1889	1938	Oak Ridge	Altoona
Meintel, Howard Charles	Pvt. B, 111 Inf.	1891	1937	St. Patricks	Gallitzin
Mertle, Charles Vincent	Pvt. 2, Prov. E. M. P.	1890	1936	St. Patricks	Gallitzin
Miller, Byron C.	Sgt. Med. Dept.	1896	1936	Alto Reste	Hollidaysburg
Miller, Earl	Pvt. A, 303 Engrs.	1889	1928	Greenwood	Altoona
Miller, Elwood C.	Pvt. E, 75 C. A. C.	1896	1934	Logan Valley	Bellwood
Miller, John A.	Sgt. Air Service	1888	1927	Calvary	Altoona
Miller, Ralph	Pvt. 7, 155 D. B.	1895	1929	St. Marys	Hollidaysburg
Miller, Samuel Warren	1Lt. Med. Corps	1888	1938	Fairview	Altoona
Miller, William A.	Lt.	1894	1939		Bellwood
Mills, Paul A.	Pvt. 48, 153 D. B.	1894	1933	Fairview	Altoona
Mingle, David Blair	Ens. U. S. Navy	1897	1919	Grandview	Tyrone
Mitchell, Harry Edgar	Pvt. G, 319 Inf.	1892-1918		Meuse-Argonne	France
Mock, Arthur C.	Cpl. H, 28 Inf.	1899	1918		France
Mogle, James Woomer	Pvt. 33, 153 D. B.	1896	1923	Alexandria	Pa.
Moist, Norman E.	Pvt. 81 Aero Sqn.	1897	1932	Rose Hill	Altoona
Mong, Elmer Ellsworth	Sgt. Q. M. C.	1893	1919	Oak Ridge	Altoona
Montgomery, John	Pvt. M, 27 Inf.	1902	1920	St. Patricks	Newry
Moore, Harry Allen	Pvt. E, 50 C. A. C.	1894	1937	Rose Hill	Altoona
Morgan, Bertram G. (s)	Cpl. D, 21 Engrs.	1878	1931	Fairview	Altoona
Morgan, William James	M. M. U. S. Navy	1896	1922	Rose Hill	Altoona
Morgan, William Russell	Pvt. E, 5 Inf.	1894	1920	Greenlawn	Roaring Spring
Morrelli, Arcangelo	Pvt. 170 Aero Sqn.	1891	1932	Presbyterian	Williamsburg
Morse, Clarence W.	Pvt. M. G. 372 Inf.	1899	1934	Oak Ridge	Altoona
Morse, Harry Elwood	Sgt. G, 110 Inf.	1898	1918	Oak Ridge	Altoona
Mosel, Roy P.	Cpl. B, 330 Inf.	1891	1939	Eastlawn	Tyrone

Name	Rank Organization	Born	Died	Cemetery	Location
Mowry, Frederick L.	Cpl. D, 20 F. A.	1889	1937	Grandview	Tyrone
Moyer, Joseph P.	Pvt. 305 F. Sig. Bn.	1895	1934	Kylertown	Pa.
Mulhaern, William Lee	Cpl. E, 21 Engrs.	1892	1919	St. Johns	Altoona
Mullen, Ralph A.	Pvt. 2, 154 D. B.	1889	1928	Rose Hill	Altoona
Murphy, Charles R.	Pvt. K, 49 Inf.	1889	1918	St. Patricks	Gallitzin
Murphy, Daniel Patrick	Pvt. 152 Trans. Corps	1891	1937	St. Marys	Hollidaysburg
Murphy, Joseph Ryan	Cpl. B, 30 Inf.	1895	1934	St. Patricks	Gallitzin
Murray, Jerome J.	Pvt. 155 D. B.	1890	1921	St. Patricks	Gallitzin
Murray, Jesse L.	Pvt. M. G. 28 Inf.	1899	1918	Greenlawn	Roaring Spring
Musselman, Harvey R.	Pvt. A, 56 Inf.	1894	1926	Fairview	Altoona
Musselman, Stewart S.	Pvt. M, 348 Inf.	1898	1936	East Sharpsburg	Roaring Spring
Myers, Allen S.	Pvt. Hqs. 319 Inf.	1892	1929	Rose Hill	Altoona
Myers, Harry Earle	Pvt. E, 305 Engrs.	1887	1930	Greenlawn	Roaring Spring
Myers, John Edward	Pvt. M, 61 Inf.	1893	1937	St. Patricks	Gallitzin
Myers, William	Sgt. Hqs. 30 Inf.	1891	1939	St. Patricks	Gallitzin
McCann, Archie P.	Pvt. Hqs. 4 F. A.	1883	1934	Calvary	Pittsburgh
McCann, Edward	Fr. U. S. Navy	1889	1928	Osceola Mills	Clearfield Co.
McCartney, Charles M.	Pvt. Med. Dept.	1896	1925	Grandview	Altoona
McConnell, Charles O.	Pvt. C, 167 Inf.	1895	1918		France
McConnell, Robert A.	Smn. U. S. Navy	1898	1931	St. Thomas	Ashville
McCormick, William Dean	Cpl. B, 54 Engrs.	1893	1925	Lutheran	Sinking Valley
McCoy, Raymond B.	Pvt. E, 160 Inf.	1895	1918		France
McCreight, William L.	Sgt. M. P.	1893	1939	Phoenix	Arizona
McDonough, John M.	Sgt. 119 Trans. Corps	1896	1933	Calvary	Altoona
McDowell, Edward B.			1918		
McDowell, Ralph Walker	Cpt. U. S. Navy	1883	1935	Arlington	Virginia
McFarland, Lloyd B.	Pvt. C, 93 Engrs.	1893	1931	Cedar Grove	Petersburg
McGarry, Gerald	Pvt. D. B.	1890	1938	St. Johns	Altoona
McGough, Cyril A.	Sgt. 60 Trans. Corps	1887	1938	Calvary	Altoona
McGraw, David D.	Pvt. E, 36 Inf.	1897	1937	Catholic	Penn
McGraw, Earl S.	2Lt. 373 Inf.	1890	1925	Fairview	Martinsburg
McGraw, John William	Pvt. D, 59 Amn. Trn.	1886	1937	St. Patricks	Gallitzin
McGraw, Paul Joseph	Pvt. 869 Trans. Corps	1890	1935	Calvary	Altoona
McGregor, Earl J.	Pvt. 75 C. A. C.	1893	1938	Oak Ridge	Altoona
McIntire, Homer Austin	Pvt. A, 70 Engrs.	1898	1937	McIntires	Hollidaysburg
McIntosh, Charles Edgar	Pvt. I, 146 Inf.	1893	1918	Meuse-Argonne	France
McKamey, Robert E.	Pvt. E, 28 Inf.	1897	1918	Oak Ridge	Altoona
McKelvey, Blain J.	Pvt. 20 M. P.	1892	1938	Mecks	Pa. Furnace
McLain, David Roswell	2Lt. Signal Corps	1876	1939	Ft. Lewis	Washington
McMullen, LeRoy F.	Pvt. M. D. 327 Inf.	1895	1927	Calvary	Altoona
McMullen, Thomas P.	Pvt. Inf.	1888	1935	St. Josephs	Coupon
McMurray, James C.	Cpl. D, 323 F. A.	1889	1930	Presbyterian	Hollidaysburg
McNeal, Orris L.	Pvt. 103 Tr. Mtr. Bat.	1897	1918		France
Nau, James Andrew	Pvt. Q. M. C.	1890	1928	Baughmans	Tyrone
Nearhoof, William D.	Pvt. Hqs. 109 F. A.	1900	1920	Grandview	Tyrone
Neeley, Calvin G.	Wgr. 1 Anti-Air Craft	1895	1918		France
Neff, Wayne A.	Pvt. C, 33 Engrs.	1900	1921	Rose Hill	Altoona
Nicodemus, Clyde Mahlon	M. M. U. S. Navy	1894	1934	Rose Hill	Altoona
Noel, Herbert W.	Cpl. G, 110 Inf.	1894	1918		France
Norman, Charles C.	Pvt. G, 110 Inf.	1885	1918		France
O'Brien, William J.	Sgt. 320 F. Hosp.	1890	1936	St. Patricks	Gallitzin
O'Hair, Edward	Pvt. D, 162 D. B.	1895	1927	Baptist	Claysburg
Olver, Fern Archibald	C. P. O. U. S. Navy	1897	1935	Dunmore	Pa.
Onkst, Martin R.	Ck. A, 21 M. G. Bn.	1888	1927	Grandview	Johnstown
Orner, Chester W.	Pvt. G, 25 Cav.	1891	1927	Rose Hill	Altoona
Otto, Ernest R.	Pvt. M, 328 Inf.	1894	1929	Oak Ridge	Altoona
Pacey, Benjamin	Cpl. Hqs. 58 Inf.	1889	1928	Rose Hill	Altoona
Park, Jesse David	Cpl. Hqs. 158 D. B.	1893	1918	Rose Hill	Altoona
Parson, Chester A.	Cpl. A, 23 Inf.	1896	1918	Rose Hill	Altoona
Patterson, Andrew	Pvt. Med. Dept.	1898	1938	Lutheran	Claysburg
Patterson, Francis S.	1Lt. F, 313 Inf.	1894	1918		France

SOLDIERS OF BLAIR COUNTY

Name	Rank Organization	Born	Died	Cemetery	Location
Patterson, Robert D.	Ck. F, 103 Engrs.	1896	1934	Alto Reste	Hollidaysburg
Pfoutz, Samuel R.	Pvt. E, 7 Mt. Sup. Trn.	1896	1939	Osceola Mills	Clearfield Co.
Piper, William Fluke	Sgt. Med. Dept.	1893	1918	Fairview	Altoona
Plank, John Joseph	Cpl. E, 310 Mt. Tank Tr.	1889	1939	Calvary	Altoona
Plempel-McLemore, Mae K.	Nrs. U. S. Army	1894	1925	Lutheran	Newry
Porta, Albert J.	Pvt. 29, 153 D. B.	1886	1933	Calvary	Altoona
Price, Earl S.	Cpl. C. A. C.	1889	1932	Alto Reste	Hollidaysburg
Price, Reamer E.	Pvt. B, 12 M. G. Bn.	1894	1934	Calvary	Altoona
Quinn, Paul Charles	Pvt. Prov. Recruit	1896	1926	St. Patricks	Gallitzin
Rahm, John W.	Cpl. D, 145 Inf.	1892	1933	Carson Valley	Duncansville
Raible, Joseph Paul	Pvt. Service Corps	1886	1926	St. Marys	Altoona
Rauton, George Mason	Sgt. D, 306 Amn. Trn	1895	1936	Rose Hill	Altoona
Ray, Charles Conrad	Pvt. G, 56 Pioneer Inf.	1888	1938	Oak Ridge	Altoona
Reamey, Brewster	2Lt. Marine Corps	1888	1937	Woodlawn	New York
Reed, Paul Wilson	Pvt. Ord. Dept.	1891	1918	Carson Valley	Duncansville
Reiser, Edward W.	Cpl. D, 10 Bn. R. T. C.	1896	1923	Greenlawn	Hollidaysburg
Reiser, Frank Joseph	2Lt. 2 M. C.	1893	1939	Arlington	Virginia
Rhodes, Frank M.	Pvt. B, 111 Inf.	1894	1937	Chambersburg	Pa.
Rhodes, George A.			1939		
Rhodes, Levi A.	Pvt. 1, C. A. C.	1894	1921	Grandview	Altoona
Rhodes, Scott A.	Sgt. B, 305 Engrs.	1895	1933	Grandview	Altoona
Rhodes, Walter Scott	Pvt. E, 51 Inf.	1891	1919	Royer Mt.	Williamsburg
Rhodes, William Martin	Ymn. U. S. Navy	1895	1937	Grandview	Tyrone
Rice, Harry Melvin	Pvt. Hqs. 17 Cav.	1896	1918	Logan Valley	Bellwood
Rich, George B.	Pvt. Air Service	1889	1935	Fairview	Altoona
Rickard, Russell L.	Pvt. M, 362 Inf.	1892	1936	Cedar Spring	Clinton Co.
Rigaldello, Donato	Pvt. G, 110 Inf.	1892	1918	Calvary	Altoona
Riling, Chester C.	Pvt. E, 361 Inf.	1893	1923	Carson Valley	Duncansville
Ritchey, Francis B.	Pvt. C. A. C.	1898	1918	Mt. Hope	Claysburg
Ritts, Ellis V.	Sgt. C, 21 Engrs.	1894	1925	Rose Hill	Altoona
Robertozzi, Gregorio	Pvt. 7 Dev. Bn.	1891	1926	Calvary	Altoona
Robertson, Clyde C.	Pvt. B, 60 Inf.	1893	1932	Fairview	Altoona
Robidaro, Joe	Pvt.	1887	1927	Calvary	Altoona
Robinson, Arthur L.	Pvt. G, 110 Inf.	1897	1918	Suresnes	France
Robinson, John Glenn	Pvt. A, 151 F. A.	1895	1919		France
Robinson, Joseph F.	Pvt. K, 301 Stevedore	1882	1918	Riverview	Huntingdon
Rockwell, Raymond M.	Pvt. G, 60 Inf.		1918		
Rocus, Michael John	Pvt. F, 305 Engrs.	1894	1931	St. Marys	Gallitzin
Rodgers, Guard I.	Pvt. 117 Amn. Trn.	1893	1928	Grandview	Tyrone
Roller, William Calvin	Maj. Med. Corps	1879	1929	Brownsville	Pa.
Rooney, Wm. Reed Alex (s)	Lt. Com. U. S. Navy	1854	1932	Arlington	Virginia
Ross, Earl E.	Pvt. D, 49 Inf.	1894	1919	Keller Reform	Williamsburg
Roudabush, Howard E.	Pvt. D, 318 Inf.	1894	1937	New Enterprise	Bedford Co.
Rourke, Mitchell James	Pvt. Marine Corps	1896	1925	Oak Ridge	Altoona
Rouzer, Paul Ellsworth	Cpl. E, 41 Art.	1889	1938	Asbury	Altoona
Rowan, Charles R.	1Lt. G, 110 Inf.	1889	1918	St. Johns	Altoona
Rupe, Paul Clinton	Pvt. 29 Sqn. M. P. C.	1895	1930	Rose Hill	Altoona
Ryan, Francis E.	Cpl. M, 7 Inf.	1893	1926	Calvary	Altoona
Ryder, Anthony H.	Cpl. 7, 4 Mt. Mch. Aero	1885	1918		France
Sadler, Paul L.	Pvt. Inf.	1899	1924	Rose Hill	Altoona
Sager, David P.	Hsr. Sup. 110 Inf.	1895	1931	Grandview	Altoona
Sanderson, William R.	Pvt. Med. Corps	1896	1919	Oak Ridge	Altoona
Sandrus, William H.	Pvt. A, Dev. Bn.	1890	1936	Presbyterian	Hollidaysburg
Sangiorgi, Natale	Pvt. 4, 153 D. B.	1893	1928	Calvary	Altoona
Saylor, Leroy C. D.	Cpl. 411 Sup. Trn.	1899	1935	Rose Hill	Altoona
Schafhirt, Richard W.	Pvt. S. A, T, C.	1898	1933	Greenwood	Altoona
Schoellkopt, Christian	Ck. Med. Dept.	1887	1925	Grandview	Tyrone
Schulz, George A.	Sgt. Med. Dept.	1883	1931	Rose Hill	Altoona
Shade, Ralph M.	Cpl. L, 29 Inf.	1892	1918		France
Shaffer, Guy William	Pvt. 28 Balloon	1897	1926	McVeytown	Huntingdon
Shaffer, Harold C.	Sgt. 40 Aero Sqn.	1900	1926	Rose Hill	Altoona
Shaffer, Joseph Evan	Pvt. Med. Dept.	1894	1928	Fairview	Altoona

Name	Rank Organization	Born	Died	Cemetery	Location
Shamp, Cloyd Samuel	Pvt. S. A. T. C.	1897	1937	Rose Hill	Altoona
Shaver, Harry D.	Pvt. 2, 1 Dev. Bn.	1881	1937	Fairview	Altoona
Shaver, McKinley	Sft. U. S. Navy	1896	1939	Calvary	Altoona
Sheedy, Raymond J.	Pvt. Q. M. C.	1898	1933	St. Johns	Altoona
Shelow, John L. (s)	Sgt. Hqs. 32 Inf.	1877	1938	San Francisco	California
Shingler, Charles H.	Pvt. Med. Dept.	1896	1918	Rose Hill	Altoona
Shirley, Harry A.	Sgt. 875 Aero Sqn.	1880	1919	Calvary	Altoona
Shoemaker, John H.	Pvt. L, 38 Inf.	1891	1930	Everett	Pa.
Shriner, Charles Darvin	Pvt. C, Mt. Mch.	1897	1919	Spring Hope	Martinsburg
Sickler, John J.	Pvt. Hqs. 110 Inf.	1898	1918	Arlington	Virginia
Sicuranzo, Francis N.	Pvt. G, 116 Engrs.	1898	1937	Rose Hill	Altoona
Sideras, James A.	Pvt. 64, 153 D. B.	1896	1930	Rose Hill	Altoona
Sietenspinner, Charles	Pvt. 1, 1 Trn. Bn.	1897	1922	Rose Hill	Altoona
Slack, John Franklin	Smn. U. S. Navy	1884	1934	Rose Hill	Altoona
Slagle, David H.	Pvt. F, 111 Inf.	1891	1918	Oisne-Aisne	France
Slep, Harry Edward	Sgt. Med. Corps	1887	1935	Rose Hill	Altoona
Slep, Jack Levan	Cpl. Marine Corps	1901	1932	Rose Hill	Altoona
Smeltzer, John Irvin	Pvt. 167 Amb. Corps		1939	Albrights	Roaring Spring
Smith, George Wash.	Lt. U. S. Navy	1866	1937	Arlington	Virginia
Smith, Herbert A.	Pvt. G, 110 Inf.	1895	1934	Presbyterian	Williamsburg
Smith, Hugh B.	Sgt. Q. M. C.	1895	1929	St. Marys	Hollidaysburg
Smith, John Alexander	Mus. C. A. C.	1889	1929	Frankstown	Hollidaysburg
Smith, John P.	Pvt. H, 6 Inf.	1888	1930	Calvary	Altoona
Smith, Joseph E.	Wgr. Sup. 52 Inf.	1888	1935	Grandview	Altoona
Smith, Paul	Pvt. F. A.	1900	1931	Presbyterian	Williamsburg
Smith, Samuel Calvin	Maj. Med. Dept.	1881	1939	Presbyterian	Hollidaysburg
Smith, Simon J.	Pvt. 32, 155 D. B.	1888	1934	Calvary	Altoona
Smith, Walter C.	Pvt. C, 51 Engrs.	1895	1919	Logan Valley	Bellwood
Smith, William Donald	Pvt. S. A. T. C.	1899	1918	Calvary	Altoona
Smith, William E.	Cpl. E, 19 F. A.	1890	1936	Lilly	Pa.
Smithoover, Walter Jacob	Pvt. 378 Aero Sqn.	1894	1921	Antis	Bellwood
Smoll, Samuel W.	Smn. U. S. Navy	1903	1928	Adudath Achim	Altoona
Smouse, Earl R.	Pvt. B, 319 M. G. Bn.	1891	1918	Rose Hill	Altoona
Sollenberger, Isaac H.	Sgt. B, C. A. C.	1891	1936	Lutheran	Claysburg
Sollenberger, Robert F.	Pvt. G, 319 Inf.	1895	1918	Sparrs	Williamsburg
Spact, Clayton C.	Pvt. Hqs. 103 Engrs.	1899	1932	Grandview	Tyrone
Sprankle, Arthur S.	Pvt. Med. Dept.	1895	1933	Calvary	Altoona
Stabinski, Leon	Pvt. Med. Dept.	1889	1936	Alto Reste	Hollidaysburg
Stambaugh, Chester J.	Pvt. A, 320 Inf.	1892	1918		France
Stambaugh, Ralph James	Pvt. 10 Engrs.	1893	1935	Presbyterian	Mifflintown
Steel, Lewis Clay	Pvt. E, 305 Engrs.	1893	1931	Greenlawn	Hollidaysburg
Stehel, Bernard D.	Pvt. 38, 155 D. B.	1889	1934	St. Marys	Altoona
Steindel, Harry A.	Pvt. A, 506 Engrs.	1896	1939	Grandview	Altoona
Stevens, William Hatton	Maj. Engrs.		1937	Arlington	Virginia
Stevenson, Benjamin A.	Cpl. B, 511 Engrs.	1887	1926	Rose Hill	Altoona
Stewart, Charles F.	Pvt. Hqs. 110 Inf.	1897	1920	Rose Hill	Altoona
Stewart, George W.	Pvt. C, 1 Tr. Mtr. Bn.	1900	1921	Logan Valley	Bellwood
Stewart, Kenneth	Pvt. A, 160 D. B.	1896	1926	Oak Ridge	Altoona
Stiver, John Warren	Pvt. G, 110 Inf.	1895	1918	Grandview	Tyrone
Stotler, Havice	Cpl. B, 5 F. A.	1877	1928	Lutheran	Williamsburg
Stouch, Edward Emmett	Pvt. 63 Spruce Sqn.	1890	1934	Fairview	Altoona
Stoudnour, David B.	Pvt. G, 339 Inf.	1888	1918	Mt. Pleasant	Henrietta
Stout, Charles E.	Pvt. C. A. C.	1886	1939	Alto Reste	Hollidaysburg
Strayer, George L.	Ck. Med. Dept.	1881	1920	Greenwood	Altoona
Strobel, Ralph Eliott	Pvt. C. A. C.	1897	1919	Fairview	Altoona
Stultz, Wilmer L.	Sgt. 634 Aero Sqn.	1900	1929	Presbyterian	Williamsburg
Sturm, Russell Alfred	H. A. U. S. Navy	1897	1934	Rochester	Pa.
Sukowski, Joseph Edward	Cpl. E, 305 Engrs.	1894	1920	St. Patricks	Gallitzin
Summers, Joseph Foster	Pvt. 155 D. B.		1935	Bald Eagle	Tyrone
Sunderland, Grover E.	Sgt. M. G. 38 Inf.	1895	1918		France
Sunderland, John A.	Ck. A, 47 Engrs.	1896	1921	Rose Hill	Altoona
Sutton, Walter J.	Pvt. B, 17 M. G. Bn.	1895	1924	Calvary	Altoona

SOLDIERS OF BLAIR COUNTY

Name	Rank Organization	Born	Died	Cemetery	Location
Swab, Arthur McK.	Pvt. Sup. 112 Inf.	1900	1935	Thompsontown	Pa.
Swails, Earl F.	Pvt. I, 314 Inf.	1890	1934	Carson Valley	Duncansville
Swayne, Harry B.	Pvt. 148 Sqn. Sig. Corps	1888	1927	Rose Hill	Altoona
Swisher, Amani	Pvt. E, L. Prov.	1885	1932	Calvary	Altoona
Swisher, Edward	Pvt. Hqs. 313 F. A.	1893	1935	Calvary	Altoona
Tanneyhill, James	Pvt. 2, 153 D. B.	1887	1919	Asbury	Altoona
Taylor, George S.	Pvt. E, 319 Inf.	1895	1926	Fishertown	Bedford Co.
Taylor, Samuel Paul	Pvt. S. A. T. C.	1894	1932	Alto Reste	Hollidaysburg
Temple, Homer A.	Pvt. Med. Dept.	1884	1929	Oak Ridge	Altoona
Temple, William H.	Cpl. G, 110 Inf.	1899	1922	Oak Ridge	Altoona
Temple, William S.	Sgt. A, 38 Inf.	1896	1918	Oise-Aisne	France
Teramano, Domenico	Pvt. H, 319 Inf.	1892	1919	Calvary	Altoona
Tharp, George Edgar	Pvt. B, 305 Engrs.	1890	1938	Liverpool	Pa.
Thompson, Franklin	Pvt. 333 Sup. Q. M. C.	1887	1927	East Lawn	Tyrone
Tindle, Chester B.	Pvt. San. Sqn.	1891	1937	Rose Hill	Altoona
Tipton, D. Merl	Pvt. G, 319 Inf.	1893	1918	Fairview	Martinsburg
Titler, John J.	Pvt. C, 19 F. A.	1894	1918	St. Patricks	Gallitzin
Tracy, John Earl	Pvt. 22, C. O. T. S.	1892	1937	Rose Hill	Altoona
Treese, Earl Stanton	Ck. 25 Trans. Corps	1894	1938	Lutheran	Clappertown
Troutwine, Frank King	Pvt. General Service	1892	1928	East Lawn	Tyrone
Tussey, Moore C.		1879	1927	Presbyterian	Sinking Valley
Updyke, Charles E.	Pvt. D, Dev. Bn.	1893	1938	Franklinville	Hunt'gdon Co.
Vadacchino, Gennaro	Pvt. I, 319 Inf.	1895	1918	Camp Lee	Virginia
Vance, George Richard	Pvt. Air Service	1895	1935	Rose Hill	Altoona
Vanneman, William	Pvt. B, 19 Engrs.	1893	1922	Grandview	Altoona
Veach, Earl James	Pvt. 150 Trans. Corps	1895	1920	Rose Hill	Altoona
Villini, Joseph	Pvt. B, 601 Engrs.	1895	1920	Calvary	Altoona
Vogel, Charles L. G.	Cpl. L, 110 Inf.	1900	1937	Grandview	Johnstown
Vogel, George Karl	Pvt. B, 305 Engrs.	1890	1921	Calvary	Altoona
Wagner, Harry A.	Pvt. G, 110 Inf.	1896	1935	Calvary	Altoona
Walker, Joseph F.	Wgr. Sup. 808 Pion. Inf.	1890	1922	Grandview	Altoona
Walker, Ralph G.	Pvt. Sn. Sqn. 20	1888	1918	Grandview	Tyrone
Walker, Riley Alden	Pvt. G, 110 Inf.	1898	1918	Aisne-Marne	France
Walter, Roy M.	Pvt. E, 8 Trn. Bn.	1895	1918	New Enterprise	Bedford Co.
Walter, David	Pvt. H, 319 Inf.	1894	1921	Rose Hill	Altoona
Walter, Dewey M.	Pvt. General Service	1897	1922	Reform	Claysburg
Waring, Monroe	Pvt. 103 Tr. Mtr.	1898	1929	Eastlawn	Tyrone
Weaver, Charles Elwood	Bug. D, 1Bn. U. S. Guards	1894	1935	Pine Grove Mills	Centre Co.
Weaver, Raymond Russell	Pvt. Hqs. 319 Inf.	1896	1936	Alto Reste	Hollidaysburg
Weible, William E.	Pvt. B, 30 Inf.	1895	1918	Arlington	Virginia
Weiss, Gilbert Haven (s)	Cps. U. S. Navy	1874	1925	Fairview	Altoona
Weller, Chester W.	Cpl. Hqs. 12 F. A.	1895	1939	Bellefonte	Pa.
Werkheiser, Clarence M.	Pvt. L, 56 Inf.	1896	1938	Athens	Pa.
Werner, George Carl	Pvt. B, 305 Engrs.	1890	1926	Oak Ridge	Altoona
Wesner, Daniel Wertz	Pvt. I, 61 Inf.	1895	1937	Grandview	Tyrone
Weston, Warner S.	Pvt. C, 110 Inf.	1891	1930	Rose Hill	Altoona
Weyandt, Charles A.	Pvt. 641 Aero Sqn.	1895	1935	Lewistown	Pa.
Weyandt, Leslie L.	Pvt. G, 319 Inf.	1891	1936	Lutheran	Claysburg
White, Jesse Lou	2Lt. F. A.	1892	1923	Grandview	Tyrone
White, Martin Morgan	Pvt. F, 606 Engrs.	1896	1935	Rose Hill	Altoona
Whitehead, John Smith	Pvt. M. G. School	1893	1930	Fairview	Altoona
Wilcox, Jacob J.	Cpl. C, 37 Inf.	1891	1936	Burkets	Warriors Mark
Williams, Arthur P.	Pvt. 71 Spruce Sqn.	1886	1926	Alto Reste	Hollidaysburg
Williams, Charles H.	Sgt. 351 San. Det.	1897	1920	Eastlawn	Tyrone
Williams, David Morris	Cpl. C, 602 Engrs.	1892	1933	Fairview	Altoona
Williams, Edgar T.	Pvt. A, 33 M. G. Bn.	1895	1937	Fairview	Altoona
Williams, George W.	Pvt. Med. Dept.	1897	1931	Fairview	Altoona
Williams, Gilbert E.	Pvt. M, 3 Inf. Rep. Tr. Ct.	1893	1929	Oak Ridge	Altoona
Williams, Howell W.	Pvt. Air Service	1890	1918	Pittston	Pa.
Williams, Maurice B.	Pvt. G, 110 Inf.	1897	1918	Meuse-Argonne	France
Williams, Percy L.	Pvt. K, 6 Inf.	1890	1939	Bald Eagle	Tyrone
Winn, Robert Oliver	Sgt. 7 Aero Sqn.	1885	1939	Oak Ridge	Altoona

THE WORLD WAR

Name	Rank	Organization	Born	Died	Cemetery	Location
Winter, Stanley A.	Skr.	U. S. Navy	1896	1922	Rose Hill	Altoona
Wiseman, John Henry	Pvt.	D, 81 Engrs.	1890	1918	McIntires	Hollidaysburg
Wisorek, John Paul	Pvt.	C, 15 F. A.	1896	1927	St. Marys	Altoona
Wolfe, Ernest S.	Sgt.	Air Service	1892	1919	Frankstown	Hollidaysburg
Witts, Herbert Lewis	Pvt.	M. G. 319 Inf.	1895	1923	Carson Valley	Duncansville
Wolf, John J.	Smn.	U. S. Navy	1895	1926	St. Johns	Altoona
Wood, Arthur Paul	Pvt.	A, 51 Inf.	1890	1937	Calvary	Altoona
Wood, Fred Johnston	Pvt.	Unassigned	1888	1939	Greenlawn	Roaring Spring
Woomer, Earl Herbert	Sgt.	A, 8 F. A. R. D.	1891	1939	Bald Eagle	Tyrone
Woomer, Lester Elgin	1Lt.	Med. Corps	1892	1931	Grandview	Tyrone
Woomer, Nathan Clark	Pvt.	G, 110 Inf.	1891	1918	Bald Eagle	Tyrone
Wright, Leroy Reed	Frn.	U. S. Navy	1893	1933	Baptist	Colfax
Wyandt, Victor Dewy	Pvt.	12 Recruit	1898	1918	Hutchison	Altoona
Wyerman, Albert R.	Pvt.	B, 115 F. A.	1892	1918	Carson Valley	Duncansville
Yeager, Ralph George	Pvt.	153 D. B.	1895	1932	Calvary	Altoona
Yingling, Edgar Dean	Pvt.	B, S. A. T. C.	1897	1918	Greenlawn	Roaring Spring
Yingling, Joseph	Ck.	E, 52 Inf.	1893	1935	St. Patricks	Gallitzin
Yingling, Landis T.	Smn.	U. S. Navy	1895	1939	Greenlawn	Roaring Spring
Yohn, Charles J.	Pvt.	E, 147 Engrs.	1897	1922	Grandview	Altoona
Yohn, John Russell	Sgt.	Sp. Tr. O. T. C.	1893	1934	Newport	Pa.
Yon, Charles B.	Pvt.	G, 51 Inf.	1893	1934	Alto Reste	Hollidaysburg
Yon, Raymond Grant	Pvt.	Med. Dept.	1892	1936	Greenwood	Altoona
Yost, Charles J.	Cpl.	Hqs. 5 F. A.	1896	1918	Rose Hill	Altoona
Young, James H.	Cpl.	G, 110 Inf.	1888	1928	Oak Ridge	Altoona
Zimberlin, John Earl	Pvt.	C, 25 Trans. Corp	1894	1919	St. Patricks	Gallitzin
Zimmerman, Robert L.	Smn.	U. S. Navy	1899	1918	Logan Valley	Bellwood
Zorger, George F.	Smn.	U. S. Navy	1895	1938	Chicago	Ill.

ADDITIONAL RECORDS

SOLDIERS OF BLAIR COUNTY

Name	Rank	Organization	Born	Died	Cemetery	Location
....	....		....			....

THE WORLD WAR

Name	Rank	Organization	Born	Died	Cemetery	Location

SOLDIERS OF BLAIR COUNTY

Name	Rank	Organization	Born	Died	Cemetery	Location

Name	Rank	Organization	Born	Died	Cemetery	Location

SOLDIERS OF BLAIR COUNTY

Name	Rank	Organization	Born	Died	Cemetery	Location
....	....		....		....
....	....		....		....
....	....		....		....
....	....		....		....
....	....		....		....
....	....		....		....
....	....		....		....
....	....		....		....
....	....		....		....
....	....		....		....
....	....		....		....
....	....		....		....
....	....		....		....
....	....		....		....
....	....		....		....
....	....		....		....
....	....		....		....
....	....		....		....
....	....		....		....
....	....		....		....
....	....		....		....
....	....		....		....
....	....		....		....
....	....		....		....
....	....		....		....
....	....		....		....
....	....		....		....

PART VII

INDIVIDUAL RECORDS

A complete military and genealogical record of the soldier, identifying the soldier for all time to come by recording together the military services and the names of the members of his family, giving the rank, organization, date of enlistment and discharge, place and date of birth, place of residence or burial, where discharge is recorded, names of parents, names of brothers and sisters, and children, name of wife, and wife's parents, and date of marriage.

INDEX TO PART VII

Abelson, Myers 391
Auker, Charles Arlon 414
Bailey, Joseph 410
Baird, Harris 411
Baldrige, Howard Malcolm 385
Bice, Frank Lee 384
Bice, William Earl 380
Bigley, Edward James 417
Black, John Michael 407
Bohn, Daniel 392
Bolger, Herbert Sanders 379
Bollinger, George Earl 399
Bossert, Henry M. 423
Brehman, John Andrew 396
Brumbaugh, David Emmert 380
Burket, Philip Arnold 394
Calvin, Webster 383
Carberry, Ambrose Lear 405
Clark, Randolph Mitchell 392
Clones, Nicholas Hristo 397
Coffey, Seneca Williamson 421
Cole, Michael Fenlon 384
Cole, William Clifford 381
Curran, Paul Reedy 426
Davis, Fred McDowell 387
Deal, Augustus R. 393
DeHaas, James Floyd 423
de Haas, John Philip 423
Dickson, Joseph Adam 388
Diehl, Harry Edmund 398
Drass, Lawrence Patrick 416
Dughi, Lazarus Arthur 409
Eastep, William Raymond 405
Elliott, John Brua 385

Fair, John Sherman 386
Farrell, Timothy Garrihan 383
Fay, Frank Hugus 425
Fay, George Simon 412
Fleck, Wesley Wayne 408
Funk, Stanton Chislett 406
Galbraith, John Hugus 409
Garber, John Joseph 426
Garver, Ivan Edison 403
Gast, Christian 417
Gibbons, Patrick Joseph 382
Gilbert, Richard Henry 387
Glass, Harry Nelson 402
Good, Frank Heyer 407
Green, Leslie Wilbur 424
Greenland, Robert Brooks 403
Grounds, Wilbert Lee 410
Gwin, Harry Richard 394
Haberstroh, John Joseph 414
Hainley, Samuel Blair 396
Hall, Edward Samuel 382
Haller, John Christian 391
Hanson, Oscar Aage 413
Hare, Robert Forster 395
Hare, Samuel Lesley 420
Harvey, John Edwin 420
Hays, David Sterrett 412
Hemphill, Joseph Dysart 387
Hennaman, Frank Field 385
Hewit, Benjamin Hartley 418
Hewit, Benjamin Lightner 418
Hewit, Herndon 418
Hoenstine, Floyd Guanar 419
Hughes, Benjamin Franklin 422
Johnston, Harry Lang 416
Johnston, John Wilson 409
Jones, Benjamin Charles 381
Kagarise, Samuel Calithan 404
Kantner, Asberry 412
Keatley, James 422
Kienzle, Paul Michael 395
Klepser, John Mark 381
Kurtz, John Elvin 396
Lang, John Calvin, Jr. 392
Laughlin, James Lester 389
Lawley, Thomas 397
Leamer, Samuel William 379
Leedom, Levi 390
Leet, Jonathan T. 402
Liebegott, Harvey Milton 421
Lingenfelter, Henry Stanley 403
Loomis, Harry Ellsworth 415
Louther, Richard James 411
Lynn, Nelson 380
McAlarney, John Wesley 395
McCarty, Warren Charlton 384
McCullough, Maurice Thomas 404
McFarlane, John Robert 394
McIntosh, Charles Edgar 379
McKeage, John Burns 424
McMicken, James 425
Mallery, Charles Richard 407
Malone, Charles Augustus 426
Mastos, Charles Richard 390
Mauk, James Blaine 386
Mauk, William David 414
Megahan, James Campbell 413
Mohler, Homer Foster 424
Morgart, Samuel M. F. 419
Morris, Lloyd McKinley 389
Murray, Boyd Lindley 389
Myers, Daniel 388
Nale, Clair Perry 400
Nason, John Blaisdell 400
Patterson, George Marion 404
Pearce, Guy Zane 402
Peoples, Thomas Gettemy 421
Peters, Burliegh Alvin 383
Reighard, Charles Lloyd 400
Reiley, William Benjamin 416
Ritchey, Clyde Roy 397
Royer, John Fleck 399
Saylor, Clyde Bartley 417
Schroeder, Andrew Henry 406
Shearer, Jacob Harry 410
Sheedy, Morgan John 420
Shilling-Yates, Edith Agnes 388
Shoenfelt, Charles Edgar 401
Slep, James Gallatin 405
Smith, Gordon Patrick 406
Smith, Homer Irwin 398
Smith, Hugh 393
Smith, William Calvin 391
Snyder, Harrison Herbert 425
Stevens, Joseph 398
Strunk, Raymond McAlvey 390
Swartz, George William 401
Trease, James Melville 408
Van Zandt, James Edward 382
Van Allman, Joseph 411
Warfield, John 386
Watts, Gilbert Searle 413
West, John Heiss 401
Whittaker, Ralph Rohrer 419
Williams, John Jacob Russell 422
Williams, William 415
Wilson, Benner Marshall 415
Yingling, Blaine 399

INDIVIDUAL RECORDS 379

HERBERT SANDERS BOLGER

BE IT HERE RECORDED, that Herbert Sanders Bolger served in the UNITED STATES Army during the World War as a Private in the 75th Company, Transportation Corps; enlisting on the 3rd day of May, 1918, and honorably discharged on the 15th day of July, 1919.

Said Herbert Sanders Bolger was born at Martinsburg, Penna., on the 17th day of April, 1895; and resides at 510 Bellview Street, Altoona, Penna.

The discharge is recorded in Volume 5, Page 142, Soldier's Discharge Record, Register and Recorder's office, Blair County Court House, Hollidaysburg, Penna.

The genealogical data relating to this soldier is as follows:

Parents	Brothers and Sisters	Children
	William Harold Bolger	Mary Lenore Bolger
	Herbert Sanders Bolger	
William M. Bolger	Levi Cortney Bolger	Patricia Ann Bolger
	Joseph Tranter Bolger	
Gelia Sanders	Carl Richard Bolger	Herbert Sanders Bolger
	Donald LeRoy Bolger	
	Theodore Roosevelt Bolger	
	Grace Hoover	

Married Mary Ruth, daughter of Fred S. and Gertrude J. Martin, on Sept. 1, 1921.

CHARLES EDGAR McINTOSH

BE IT HERE RECORDED, that Charles Edgar McIntosh served in the UNITED STATES Army during the World War as a Private in Company I, 146th Regiment of Infantry; enlisting on the 30th day of April, 1918, and killed in action on the 28th day of September, 1918.

Said Charles Edgar McIntosh was born at Newry, Penna., on the 30th day of June, 1893, and is buried in the Meuse-Argonne Cemetery, France.

The genealogical data relating to this soldier is as follows:

Parents	Brothers and Sisters	Children
	Charles Edgar McIntosh	
	James Joseph McIntosh	
Harry A. McIntosh	Mary Jessie McIntosh	
	Francis Joseph McIntosh	
Myrtle J. Diehl	Leanna Edna McIntosh	
	Eleanor Drass	
	Harry Eugene McIntosh	

This record placed by Harry A. McIntosh, of Hollidaysburg.

SAMUEL WILLIAM LEAMER

BE IT HERE RECORDED, that Samuel William Leamer served in the UNITED STATES Army during the Spanish-American War as a Private in Company D, 4th Infantry, Virginia Volunteers; enlisting on the 11th day of July, 1898, and honorably discharged on the 27th day of April, 1899.

Said Samuel William Leamer was born at Leamersville, Penna., on the 29th of January, 1855; died on the first of October, 1937, and is buried in the Fort Rosecrans National Cemetery at San Diego, California.

The genealogical data relating to this soldier is as follows:

Parents	Brothers and Sisters	Children
	Emily Gemella Leamer	
Samuel G. Leamer	Laura Adella Lorenz	
Sarah Ann Shriner	Annie Leamer	
	Samuel William Leamer	
(Second Marriage)		
Bernard Lorenz	Fannie Hair	

This record placed by R. D. Lorenz, of Roaring Spring.

SOLDIERS OF BLAIR COUNTY

WILLIAM EARL BICE

BE IT HERE RECORDED, that William Earl Bice served in the UNITED STATES Army during the World War as a Master Engineer, Headquarters Detachment, 305th Engineers, 80th Division; enlisting on the 19th day of September, 1917, and honorably discharged on the 11th day of June, 1919.

Said William Earl Bice was born at Frankstown, Penna., on the 16th day of March, 1887; and resides at 538 Hickory Street, Hollidaysburg, Penna.

The discharge is recorded in Volume 2, Page 60, Soldier's Discharge Record, Register and Recorder's Office, Blair County Court House, Hollidaysburg, Penna.

The genealogical data relating to this soldier is as follows:

Parents	Brothers and Sisters	Children
	William Earl Bice	
John Fay Bice	Blair Rodkey Bice	
	Frank Lee Bice	Dorothy Kathryn Bice
Annie E. Rodkey	Isabell Boggs Smith	
	Ralph Waldo Bice	
	Nanna Marie Baird	
(Second Marriage)		
Eva Kate Turner	Robert Andrew Bice	

Married Mary Pearl, daughter of William and Eva Kate Turner, on April 3, 1920.

NELSON LYNN

BE IT HERE RECORDED, that Nelson Lynn, served in the UNITED STATES Army during the Spanish-American War as a Sergeant in Company C, 5th Regiment of Infantry, Pennsylvania Volunteers; enlisting on the 27th day of April, 1898, and honorably discharged on the 7th day of November, 1898.

Said Nelson Lynn was born at East Sharpsburg, Blair County, on the 4th day of July, 1871; and resides at 511 Clark Street, Hollidaysburg, Penna.

The discharge is recorded in Volume 4, Page 207, Soldier's Discharge Record, Register and Recorder's Office, Blair County Court House, Hollidaysburg, Pa.

The genealogical data relating to this soldier is as follows:

Parents	Brothers and Sisters	Children
	Mary E. Lynn	
William M. Lynn	Anna F. Brown	
	Caroline Malone	
Susan D. Snyder	Nelson Lynn	
	Grace L. Lee	

DAVID EMMERT BRUMBAUGH

BE IT HERE RECORDED, that David Emmert Brumbaugh served in the UNITED STATES Army during the World War as a Private in Headquarters Company, 58th Field Artillery Brigade, 33rd Division; enlisting on the 15th day of June, 1918, and honorably discharged on the 9th day of June, 1919.

Said David Emmert Brumbaugh was born at Martinsburg, Penna., on the 8th day of October, 1894; and resides at Claysburg, Penna.

The genealogical data relating to this soldier is as follows:

Parents	Brothers and Sisters	Children
	Charles Albert Brumbaugh	
	Henry Ross Brumbaugh	
Moses Robert Brumbaugh	David Emmert Brumbaugh	David Robert Brumbaugh
	William Elvin Brumbaugh	Summer Emmert Brumbaugh
Sara Florence Stuard	Minnie Marie Keiser	Carol Brumbaugh
	Sara Irene Brumbaugh	Carolyn Brumbaugh
	Susanna Agnes Brumbaugh	
	Carrie Ethel Banks	

Married Carolyn, daughter of Henry D. and Sara Acker, on October 29, 1919.

INDIVIDUAL RECORDS 381

WILLIAM CLIFFORD COLE

BE IT HERE RECORDED, that William Clifford Cole served in the UNITED STATES Army during the World War as a Captain in Company I, 35th Regiment of Engineers, Railway Transportation Division; enlisting on the 17th day of November, 1917, and honorably discharged on the 30th day of July, 1919.

Said William Clifford Cole was born at Altoona, Pennsylvania, on the 20th day of April, 1885; and resides at 2210 Fourth Street, Altoona, Penna.

The genealogical data relating to this soldier is as follows:

Parents	Brothers and Sisters	Children
	Molley Galbraith	
	James Foster Cole	
	Lara Ann Cole	
	Rosa Cole	
James Benjamin Cole	Adda Caswell	Robert Thomas Cole
	Arthur B. Cole	
	Sarah B. Long	
Isabella Ann Bartley	William Clifford Cole	Doris Jean Cole
	Albert Lewis Cole	
	Charles Chester Cole	
	Viola Bell Taylor	
	George Hiram Cole	

Married Charlotte Marie, dau. of George T. and Effie Hyatt, on June 30, 1915.

BENJAMIN CHARLES JONES

BE IT HERE RECORDED, that Benjamin Charles Jones served in the UNITED STATES Army during the World War as a First Lieutenant in the 311th Machine Gun Battalion, 79th Division; enlisting on the 15th day of May, 1917, and honorably discharged on the 5th day of August, 1919.

Said Benjamin Charles Jones was born at Tyrone, Pennsylvania, on the 9th day of June, 1896; and resides at 303 West 11th Street, Tyrone, Penna.

The discharge is recorded in volume 2, page 532, Soldier's Discharge Record, Register and Recorder's office, Blair County Court House, Hollidaysburg, Pa.

The genealogical data relating to this soldier is as follows:

Parents	Brothers and Sisters	Children
Claude Jones	Benjamin Charles Jones	Benjamin Charles Jones
Stella Alice Armor	Elizabeth Lintgen	David Mattern Jones
		Kathleen Elizabeth Jones

Married Kathleen Adeline, dau. of James G. and Drucie Stover, on Aug. 28, 1929.

JOHN MARK KLEPSER

BE IT HERE RECORDED, that John Mark Klepser served in the UNITED STATES Army during the World War as a Second Lieutenant of Battery A, 20th Regiment of Field Artillery; enlisting on the 1st day of June, 1917, and honorably discharged on the 18th day of January, 1919.

Said John Mark Klepser was born at Martinsburg, Pennsylvania, on the 20th day of May, 1896; and resides at Sylvan Hills, Hollidaysburg, Penna.

The genealogical data relating to this soldier is as follows:

Parents	Brothers and Sisters	Children
	Frank W. Klepser	
	M. Ruth Findley	John M. Klepser
Harry M. Klepser	John M. Klepser	Frederick L. Klepser
	June Stewart	Eric A. Klepser
Minnie Bateman	J. Ralph Klepser	Allen W. Klepser
	George M. Klepser	
	Helen G. Patterson	

Married Mary Adele, daughter of John H. and Ellanora Snyder, on June 20, 1924.

EDWARD SAMUEL HALL

BE IT HERE RECORDED, that Edward Samuel Hall served in the UNITED STATES Army during the Civil War as a Private in Company K, 125th Regiment of Pennsylvania Infantry; enlisting on the 14th day of August, 1862, and honorably discharged on the 18th day of May, 1863; also, served as a Sergeant in Company G, Pennsylvania Militia; enlisting on the 16th day of July, 1864, and honorably discharged on the 14th day of November, 1864.

Said Edward Samuel Hall was born in Dauphin County, Pennsylvania, on the 30th day of December, 1843; died on the 30th day of January, 1900, and is buried in lot 59, section P, Fairview Cemetery at Altoona, Pa.

The genealogical data relating to this soldier is as follows:

Parents	Brothers and Sisters	Children
		Maria Catherine Mitchell
		George W. Hall
	Elizabeth Zuber	Annie Caswell
George Hall		Carrie Rhue
	Charlotte B. Boyer	Rebecca Metzler
		Edward Hall
Maria Drye	Edward Samuel Hall	Margaret Hall
		William Hall
		Robert Hall
		Clifford Hall

Married Margaret Beatty on February 28, 1867.

This record placed by Mrs. Charles W. Morrow, of 2807 Walnut Av., Altoona, Pa.

JAMES EDWARD VANZANDT

BE IT HERE RECORDED, that James Edward VanZandt served in the UNITED STATES Navy during the World War as a Chief Quartermaster; enlisting on the 29th day of April, 1917, and honorably discharged on the 19th day of September, 1919.

Said James Edward VanZandt was born at Altoona, Pennsylvania, on the 18th day of December, 1898; and resides at 1017 Eighteenth Avenue, Altoona, Penna.

The genealogical data relating to this soldier is as follows:

Parents	Brothers and Sisters	Children
	George H. VanZandt	
James T. VanZandt	Eleanor Spang	
	Katherine Wayland	
Katherine Smith	James Edward VanZandt	
	Alice Roscher	

Married Frances S., dau. of Frederick and Teressa Schoen, on January 10, 1921.

PATRICK JOSEPH GIBBONS

BE IT HERE RECORDED, that Patrick Joseph Gibbons served in the UNITED STATES Navy during the World War as a Ship Fitter, 2 Class; enlisting on the 10th day of June, 1918, and honorably discharged on the 9th day of June, 1920.

Said Patrick Joseph Gibbons was born at Altoona, Pennsylvania, on the 14th day of May, 1893; and resides at 1610 Nineteenth Avenue, Altoona, Penna.

The genealogical data relating to this soldier is as follows:

Parents	Brothers and Sisters	Children
	John A. Gibbons	Kathleen Mary Gibbons
	Patrick Joseph Gibbons	Elaine Gibbons
Michael M. Gibbons	Ella Brede	Maurice Holland Gibbons
	Margaret Hoyer	Robert Gibbons
Ella Healy	Thomas B. Gibbons	Mary Gene Gibbons
	Catharine Unverdorben	
	Mary Irwin	

Married Marguerite, dau. of Maurice J. and Mary E. Holland, on July 2, 1917.

INDIVIDUAL RECORDS

TIMOTHY GARRIHAN FARRELL

BE IT HERE RECORDED, that Timothy Garrihan Farrell served in the UNITED STATES Army during the Indian Campaign as a Private in Company A, 22nd Regiment of United States Infantry; enlisting on the 25th day of April, 1866, and honorably discharged on the 25th day of April, 1869.

Said Timothy Garrihan Farrell was born in County Roscommon, Ireland, on the 4th day of April, 1849; died on the 21st day of September, 1920, and is buried in Lot 50, section G, Calvary Cemetery at Altoona, Penna.

The discharge is recorded in volume 1, page 151, Soldier's Discharge Record, Register and Recorder's Office, Blair County Court House, Hollidaysburg, Pa.

The genealogical data relating to this soldier is as follows:

Parents	Brothers and Sisters	Children
		Timothy George Farrell
		Patrick Farrell
Patrick Farrell	Ellen Harper	Katherine Farrell
		Margaret Nell Godfrey
Margaret Garrihan	Timothy Garrihan Farrell	Ann Mary Gallagher
		Mary Ann Farrell
		Matildo Jo Madden

Married Catharine, daughter of John and Catherine Mulligan, about 1880.
This record placed by Mrs. David S. Madden of Hollidaysburg, Penna.

BURLEIGH ALVIN PETERS

BE IT HERE RECORDED, that Burleigh Alvin Peters served in the UNITED STATES Army during the World War as a First Lieutenant and Chaplain, 107th Regiment of Field Artillery, 28th Division; enlisting on the 17th day of July, 1917, and honorably discharged on the 2nd day of July, 1919.

Said Burleigh Alvin Peters was born at McVeytown, Pennsylvania, on the 15th day of February, 1892; and resides at 102 Logan Avenue, Altoona, Penna.

The discharge is recorded in volume 1, page 509, Soldier's Discharge Record, Register and Recorder's Office, Somerset County Court House, Somerset, Penna.

The genealogical data relating to this soldier is as follows:

Parents	Brothers and Sisters	Children
	John Banks Peters	
Levi Peters	Edward James Peters	James Burleigh Peters
Anna M. Patton	Burleigh Alvin Peters	Janet Louise Peters
	Albert Peters	

Mar. Ruth Gertrude, dau. of Edward H. and Rosa Gertrude Leffler, on Oct. 21, 1919.

WEBSTER CALVIN

BE IT HERE RECORDED, that Webster Calvin served in the UNITED STATES Army during the World War as a Lieutenant Colonel, Medical Corps; enlisting on the 23rd day of April, 1917, and honorably discharged on the 6th day of January, 1919.

Said Webster Calvin was born at Hollidaysburg, Pennsylvania, on the 31st day of May, 1882; died on the 15th day of January, 1929, and is buried in lot 149, section D, Presbyterian Cemetery at Hollidaysburg, Penna.

The discharge is recorded in volume 4, page 416, Soldier's Discharge Record, Register and Recorder's Office, Blair County Court House, Hollidaysburg, Pa.

The genealogical data relating to this soldier is as follows:

Parents	Brothers and Sisters	Children
	Samuel Calvin	
Matthew Calvin	Webster Calvin	
	Hayes Calvin	Webster Calvin
Mary Henry	King Calvin	
	Matthew Calvin	

Married Elizabeth May, dau. of Andrew T. and Mary H. Stone, on September 29, 1909.
The record placed by Mrs. Elizabeth M. Calvin of 411 Allegheny St., Hollidaysburg.

MICHAEL FENLON COLE

BE IT HERE RECORDED, that Michael Fenlon Cole served in the UNITED STATES Army during the World War as a Private in Battery D, 151st Regiment of Artillery, 42nd Division; enlisting on the 1st day of September, 1917, and honorably discharged on the 7th day of February, 1919. He enlisted under the name of Michael P. Fenlon in memory of Peter Fenlon, an uncle who served in the Confederate Army during the Civil War as a Lieutenant of the 19th Georgia Infantry and who died of wounds received at the battle of Fredericksburg.

Said Michael Fenlon Cole was born at Atlanta, Georgia, on the 9th day of December, 1901; and resides at 538 Wharton Avenue, South Lakemont, Penna.

The discharge is recorded in volume 4, page 413, Soldier's Discharge Record, Register and Recorder's Office, Blair County Court House, Hollidaysburg, Penna.

The genealogical data relating to this soldier is as follolws:

Parents	Brothers and Sisters	Children
	Thomas Joseph Cole	
	Michael Fenlon Cole	
Michael Jeremiah Cole	Anna May Cole	Robert Francis Cole
	Catherine Anatasia Brown	
Mary Boylan	Louis Boylan Cole	Catherine Claire Cole
	Irene Claire Cole	
	Robert Maurice Cole	

Married Thelma, daughter of Frank and Pearl Rothrauff, on March 17, 1930.

WARREN CHARLTON McCARTY

BE IT HERE RECORDED, that Warren Charlton McCarty served in the UNITED STATES Army during the World War as a Private in the X-ray Repair Shop; enlisting on the 16th day of Feb., 1918, and honorably discharged on the 5th of Aug. 1919.

Said Warren Charlton McCarty was born at Barree, Pennsylvania, on the 4th day of May, 1896; and resides at Claysburg, Penna.

The discharge is recorded in volume 5, page 244, Soldier's Discharge Record, Register and Recorder's Office, Blair County Court House, Hollidaysburg, Pa.

The genealogical data relating to this soldier is as follows:

Parents	Brothers and Sisters	Children
George B. McCarty	Cloyd A. McCarty	
Emma Sharp	Roy I. McCarty	
	Warren C. McCarty	

Married Virgie D., daughter of Benjamin F. and Generva Dively, on Dec. 14, 1923.

FRANK LEE BICE

BE IT HERE RECORDED, that Frank Lee Bice served in the UNITED STATES Army during the World War as a Wagoner in Company C, 103rd Ammunition Train, 28th Division; enlisting on the 9th day of June, 1917, and honorably discharged on the 20th day of May, 1919.

Said Frank Lee Bice was born at Frankstown, Pennsylvania, on the 16th day of April, 1892; and resides at 1304 Spruce Street, Hollidaysburg, Penna.

The discharge is recorded in volume 2, page 257, Soldier's Discharge Record, Register and Recorder's Office, Blair County Court House, Hollidaysburg, Pa.

The genealogical data relating to this soldier is as follows:

Parents	Brothers and Sisters	Children
	William Earl Bice	
John Fay Bice	Blair Rodkey Bice	Virginia Alice Bice
	Frank Lee Bice	Anna Isabell Bice
Annie E. Rodkey	Isabell Boggs Smith	Frank Lee Bice
	Ralph Waldo Bice	William Harrison Bice
(second marriage)	Nanna Marie Baird	
Eva Kate Turner	Robert Andrew Bice	

Married Ethel Dell, dau. of Samuel C. and Isabell Kemberling, on Dec. 26, 1917.

INDIVIDUAL RECORDS 385

HOWARD MALCOLM BALDRIGE

BE IT HERE RECORDED, that Howard Malcolm Baldrige served in the UNITED STATES Army during the Civil War, as a Private in Company A, 23rd Regiment of Pennsylvania Militia, enlisting on the 21st day of September, 1862, and honorably discharged on the 30th day of September, 1862, also, as a Private in Company A, Independent Battalion, Pennsylvania Militia; enlisting on the 3rd day of July, 1863, and honorably discharged on the 8th day of August, 1863.

Said Howard Malcolm Baldrige was born at Hollidaysburg, Penna., on the 15th day of January, 1842; died on the 18th day of March, 1895, and is buried in Lot 98, Section A, Presbyterian Cemetery, Hollidaysburg, Penna.

The genealogical data relating to this soldier is as follows:

Parents	Brothers and Sisters	Children
	Howard Malcolm Baldrige	Howard H. Baldrige
Joseph Baldrige		Katharine McLanahan
	Edwin Rockfellow Baldrige	Joseph M. Baldrige
Sophia Frampton		Sophie Baldrige
	Joseph Harry Baldrige	Thomas J. Baldrige

Married Laura, daughter of Jacob and Catharine Mattern, on December 8, 1863.
This record placed by Hon. Thomas J. Baldrige, of Hollidaysburg.

JOHN BRUA ELLIOTT

BE IT HERE RECORDED, that John Brua Elliott served in the UNITED STATES Army during the World War as a Private in Company 2, Motor Transportation Corps; enlisting on the 24th of October, 1918, and honorably discharged on the 3rd of December, 1918.

Said John Brua Elliott was born at Hollidaysburg, Penna., on the 6th day of October, 1884; and resides at 515 Montgomery Street, Hollidaysburg, Pa.

The discharge is recorded in volume 2, page 394, Soldier's Discharge Record, Register and Recorder's Office, Blair County Court House, Hollidaysburg, Penna.

The genealogical data relating to this soldier is as follows:

Parents	Brothers and Sisters	Children
	John Brua Elliott	
	Mabel Elliott Ovelman	
Robert A. Elliott	Merrill Robert Elliott	
	Blanche Elliott Young	Margaret Gallagher Elliott
Clara Brua	Chester Holliday Elliott	
	Ruth Amanda VanAllman	
	Fay Crawford Elliott	

Married Mary Elizabeth, dau. of Jeffrey and Margaret Taylor, on March 23, 1929.

FRANK FIELD HENNAMAN

BE IT HERE RECORDED, that Frank Field Hennaman served in the UNITED STATES Army during the World War, as a Major, General Staff, Camp Meade, Maryland; enlisting on the 9th day of May, 1917, and honorably discharged on the 9th day of January, 1919.

Said Frank Field Hennaman was born at Altoona, Penna., on the 12th day of September, 1895; and resides at Sylvan Hills, Hollidaysburg, Penna.

The genealogical data relating to this soldier is as follows:

Parents	Brothers and Sisters	Children
	Margaret E. Foshay	
John Mitchell Hennaman	Edward Hennaman	
	Howard Hennaman	
Kate Irene Hooper	John J. Hennaman	
	Helen H. Miller	
	Frank F. Hennaman	

Married Martha B., dau. of William J. and Nancy Jane Heinsling, on May 25, 1918.

JOHN WARFIELD

BE IT HERE RECORDED, that John Warfield served in the UNITED STATES Army during the Civil War, as a Private in Company D, 14th Pennsylvania Infantry; enlisting on the 23rd of April, 1861, and honorably discharged on the 6th day of August, 1861, also, as a Private in Company A, 110th Pennsylvania Infantry; enlisting on the 29th day of August, 1861, and honorably discharged on the 28th day of June, 1865.

Said John Warfield was born near Petersburg, Penna., on the 4th day of March, 1828; died on the 25th day of November, 1901, and is buried in lot 2240, Section 122, Grandview Cemetery at Tyrone, Penna.

The discharge is recorded in volume 1, page 1, Soldier's Discharge Record, Register and Recorder's Office, Court House, Huntingdon, Penna.

The genealogical data relating to this soldier is as follows:

Parents	Brothers and Sisters	Children
	Catharine McMahan	Ella Maude Fleck
Adam Warfield	Adam Warfield	Catharine Warfel
	George Warfield	Alice M. Glasgow
Maria Rudy	John Warfield	Benjamin F. Warfel
	Hannah Warfield	U. Grant Warfel
		Margaret Bell Bailey
		Emma Blanche Warfel

Married Margaret, daughter of Daniel and Mary Conrad, on the 31st of Jan., 1866. This record placed by Benjamin F. Warfel, of Hollidaysburg.

JOHN SHERMAN FAIR

BE IT HERE RECORDED, that John Sherman Fair served in the UNITED STATES Army during the Spanish-American War, Mexican Border Campaign and the World War; enlisting on the 11th day of April, 1898, and retired as a Colonel, United States Army, on the 30th day of April, 1938.

Said John Sherman Fair was born at Dakota City, Nebraska, on the 13th day of April, 1873; and resides at Sylvan Hills, Hollidaysburg, Penna.

The genealogical data relating to this soldier is as follows:

Parents	Brothers and Sisters	Children
	John Sherman Fair	
Lemuel Fair	Mary Wilson	John Sherman Fair
	Elda M. Fair	David Ramey Fair
Mary Bridenbaugh	Philip W. Fair	Nancy Montgomery
	Helen Glass	

Married Lorene, dau. of David K. and Ann Rebecca Ramey, on June 25, 1903.

JAMES BLAINE MAUK

BE IT HERE RECORDED, that James Blaine Mauk served in the UNITED STATES Army during the World War, as a Private in Company F, Student Army Training Corps, Carnegie Institute of Technology; enlisting on the 15th day of October, 1918, and honorably discharged on the 20th day of December, 1918.

Said James Blaine Mauk was born at Bennington, Penna., on the 23rd of October, 1881; and resides at 805 Penn Street, Hollidaysburg, Penna.

The discharge is recorded in volume 2, page 415, Soldier's Discharge Record Register and Recorder's Office, Blair County Court House, Hollidaysburg, Pa.

The genealogical data relating to this soldier is as follows:

Parents	Brothers and Sisters	Children
	Annie Mauk	
H. Blair Mauk	Sanford Mauk	
	Robert Mauk	
Sarah Treese	J. Blaine Mauk	
	Mabel Leedom	

INDIVIDUAL RECORDS 387
JOSEPH DYSART HEMPHILL

BE IT HERE RECORDED, that Joseph Dysart Hemphill served in the UNITED STATES Army during the Civil War as a Private in Company A, 23rd Regiment of Pennsylvania Militia; enlisting on the 21st day of September, 1862, and honorably discharged on the 30th day of September, 1862; also, as a Private in Company B, Independent Battalion, Pennsylvania Militia; enlisting on the 3rd day of July, 1863, and honorably discharged on the 8th day of August, 1863; also, as a Private in Company H, 110th Regiment of Pennsylvania Infantry; enlisting on the 9th day of February, 1864, and honorably discharged on the 7th day of June, 1865.

Said Joseph Dysart Hemphill was born at Hollidaysburg, Pennsylvania, on the 4th day of May, 1846; died on the 26th day of December, 1939, and is buried in lot 233 section B, Presbyterian Cemetery at Hollidaysburg.

The genealogical data relating to this soldier is as follows:

Parents	Brothers and Sisters	Children
John Laird Hemphill	Joseph Dysart Hemphill	Elizabeth Patton Hemphill
Rebecca Parks McKee	John Laird Hemphill	
(second Marriage)	Thomas Johnston Hemphill	
Margaret Johnston	Mabel Hemphill Gardner	

Married Sarah Isabelle, dau. of Joseph and Elizabeth Milliken, on Oct. 22, 1873.

RICHARD HENRY GILBERT

BE IT HERE RECORDED, that Richard Henry Gilbert served in the UNITED STATES Army during the Mexican Border Campaign as a Sergeant in the Sheridan Troop, (B) 1st Pennsylvania Cavalry; being mustered into the Federal Service on the 1st day of June, 1916, and mustered out on the 15th day of March, 1917.

Said Richard Henry Gilbert was born at Emporium, Pennsylvania, on the 26th day of March, 1885; and resides at 907 Jefferson Avenue, Tyrone, Penna.

The discharge is recorded in volume 2, page 509, Soldier's Discharge Record, Register and Recorder's Office, Blair County Court House, Hollidaysburg, Pa.

The genealogical data relating to this soldier is as follows:

Parents	Brothers and Sisters	Children
Richard Henry Gilbert	Fred John Gilbert	Jane Louise Gilbert
	Cleo Clark Kloss	
Julia Lau	Richard Henry Gilbert	Julia Ann Gilbert

Married Missoura, dau. of Elias and Elmira Wolfgang, on September 25, 1912.

FRED McDOWELL DAVIS

BE IT HERE RECORDED, that Fred McDowell Davis served in the UNITED STATES Army during the World War as a Second Lieutenant of Headquarters Company, 320 Regiment of Infantry, 80th Division; enlisting on the 12th day of February, 1918, and honorably discharged on the 8th day of July, 1919.

Said Fred McDowell Davis was born at Altoona, Pennsylvania, on the 16th day of November, 1893; and resides at Johnstown, Penna.

The discharge is recorded in volume 2, page 367, Soldier's Discharge Record, Register and Recorder's Office, Blair County Court House, Hollidaysburg, Pa.

The genealogical data relating to this soldier is as follows:

Parents	Brothers and Sisters	Children
	E. Grace Gearhart	
	E. Margaret Davis	
Tarring S. Davis	Fred McDowell Davis	Sarah Ann Davis
	Edna B. Davis	
	Mary A. Davis	
Sarah E. McDowell	Joseph E. Davis	Helen Margaret Davis
	John T. Davis	
	Sarah C. Davis	

Married Mary Margaret, dau. of Frank P. and Elizabeth Koontz, on Feb. 14, 1924.
This record placed by Prof. Tarring S. Davis of 632 Rose Hill Dr., Altoona, Pa.

SOLDIERS OF BLAIR COUNTY
DANIEL MYERS
BE IT HERE RECORDED, that Daniel Myers served in the UNITED STATES Army during the Civil War as a Private in Company C, 110th Regiment of Pennsylvania Infantry; enlisting on the 22nd day of February, 1864, and died of wounds received in the Battle of the Wilderness.

Said Daniel Myers was born at Duncansville, Pennsylvania, in 1825; died on the 19th day of April, 1864, and is buried at Brattleboro, Vermont.

The genealogical data relating to this soldier is as follows:

Parents	Brothers and Sisters	Children
	John Myers	
	Maria Myers	David Miles Myers
Abram Myers	Jesse Myers	Alfred Blair Myers
	Daniel Myers	Martha Jane Richards
	David Myers	Abram Lloyd Myers
	Samuel Myers	Estella Beamer
Catherine	William Henry Myers	Anna Mary Hess
	Levi Myers	Daniel Grant Myers
	Josiah Myers	
	Anne Elizabeth Haun	

Married Mary, daughter of Jacob Haun, at Bellwood, Penna., in 1850.
This record placed by Mrs. Isaac Hess of Duncansville, Penna.

JOSEPH ADAM DICKSON
BE IT HERE RECORDED, that Joseph Adam Dickson served in the UNITED STATES Army during the World War as a Captain and Adjutant of the 111th Regiment of Infantry, 28th Division; enlisting on the 5th day of August, 1917, and honorably discharged on the 9th day of May, 1919.

Said Joseph Adam Dickson was born in Sinking Valley, Blair County, Penna., on the 29th day of December, 1891; and resides at 1058 Lincoln Ave., Tyrone, Pa.

The genealogical data relating to this soldier is as follows:

Parents	Brothers and Sisters	Children
	Mary Martha Kauffman	
Adam Leffard Dickson	Annie Louise Gill	George Gibbs Dickson
	Susan Rebecca Schirm	Joseph Adam Dickson
Ellen Morrow	David Charles Dickson	John Hancock Dickson
	Joseph Adam Dickson	

Married Edith Hancock, dau. of George J. and Nettie Gibbs, on May 22, 1917.

EDITH SHILLING-YATES
BE IT HERE RECORDED, that Edith Shilling-Yates served in the UNITED STATES Navy during the World War as a Red Cross Nurse in the United States Navy Reserve; enlisting on the 15th day of March, 1918, and honorably discharged on the 1st day of October, 1920.

Said Edith Agnes Shilling-Yates was born in Ringgold, Jefferson County, Pa., on the 8th day of December, 1887; and resides at 717 4th Ave., Juniata, Altoona.

The genealogical data relating to this soldier is as follows:

Parents	Brothers and Sisters	Children
	William H. Shilling	
	Jacob Shilling	
	Martha Shick	
Samuel Shilling	Jennie Gahagan	
	Effie Hall	
	Elizabeth Bauer	
Mary Jane Comiskey	Bertha Seanor	
	Alonza S. Shilling	
	Blaine M. Shilling	
	Edith Agnes Yates	

Married Walter James, son of James and Joann S. Yates, on April 4, 1925.

INDIVIDUAL RECORDS

BOYD LINDLEY MURRAY

BE IT HERE RECORDED, that Boyd Lindley Murray served in the UNITED STATES Army during the World War, as a Private in the 69th Squadron, Aviation Section, Signal Corps; enlisting on the 9th day of December, 1917, and honorably discharged on the 24th day of January, 1919.

Said Boyd Lindley Murray was born at LeContes Mills, Penna., on the 20th day of January, 1893; and resides at Claysburg, Penna.

The discharge is recorded in the Register and Recorder's Office, Clearfield County Court House, Clearfield, Penna.

The genealogical data relating to this soldier is as follows:

Parents	Brothers and Sisters	Children
	Minnie Bell	
	Bessie Baumgardner	
	Samuel A. Murray	Boyd Ross Murray
Jacob Kyler Murray	Blanche Murray	
	Maida Woodling	Meriam May Murray
	Lena Sumburg	
Ada Wells Stewart	Boyd Lindley Murray	Wayne Allen Murray
	Olive Brinton	
	Marian Haney	
	Walter Murray	
	Donald Murray	

Married Isabell, daughter of William and Arvilla Ross, on September 17, 1919.

LLOYD McKINLEY MORRIS

BE IT HERE RECORDED, that Lloyd McKinley Morris served in the UNITED STATES Army during the World War as a Second Lieutenant, Students Army Training Camp, Lafayette College; enlisting on the 5th day of July, 1918, and honorably discharged on the 6th day of January, 1919.

Said Lloyd McKinley Morris was born at Holbrook, Greene County, Penna., on the 4th day of December, 1895; and resides at 1515 22nd Ave., Altoona, Penna.

The discharge is recorded in volume 4 page 414, Soldier's Discharge Record, Register and Recorder's Office, Blair County Court House, Hollidaysburg, Penna.

The genealogical data relating to this soldier is as follows:

Parents	Brothers and Sisters	Children
Samuel R. Morris	Lloyd McKinley Morris	
Violet M. Scott	Laura DeCelcia Gilbert	

Married Helen Margaret, dau. of Edward and Agnes Wood, on September 7, 1921.

JAMES LESTER LAUGHLIN

BE IT HERE RECORDED, that James Lester Laughlin served in the UNITED STATES Marine Corps during the World War as a Private 1st Class in Company 45, 5th regiment of Marines; enlisting on the 7th day of April, 1918, and honorably discharged on the 12th day of September, 1919.

Said James Lester Laughlin was born at Huntingdon, Penna., on the 10th day of September, 1896; and resides at 2036 Broad Avenue, Altoona, Penna.

The discharge is recorded in volume 4, page 412, Soldier's Discharge Record, Register and Recorder's Office, Blair County Court House, Hollidaysburg, Penna.

The genealogical data relating to this soldier is as follows:

Parents	Brothers and Sisters	Children
	Merle Louder	
Harry P. Laughlin	James Lester Laughlin	Lester Harry Laughlin
	Carey N. Laughlin	
Ella M. Smith	Fred S. Laughlin	Sara Luella Laughlin
	Donald V. Laughlin	

Married Sara Crystal, dau. of Harry E. and Lulu K. Lingenfelter, on Aug. 25, 1920.

LEVI LEEDOM

BE IT HERE RECORDED, that Levi Leedom served in the UNITED STATES Army during the Civil War as a Private in Company E, 125th Regiment of Pennsylvania Infantry; enlisting on the 6th day of August, 1862, and honorably discharged on the 18th day of May, 1863.

Said Levi Leedom was born in Berks County, Pennsylvania, on the first day of February, 1842; died on the 4th day of January, 1932, and is buried in lot 11, section D, Presbyterian Cemetery, Hollidaysburg, Penna.

The discharge is recorded in volume 1, page 46, Soldier's Discharge Record, Register and Recorder's Office, Blair County Court House, Hollidaysburg, Penna.

The genealogical data relating to this soldier is as follows:

Parents	Brothers and Sisters	Children
		Lucy A. Leedom
		Paul Leedom
Thomas Leedom	Jeremiah Leedom	Ella K. Hart
	Levi Leedom	Jerry W. Leedom
Leah Witman	Elizabeth Leedom	George C. Leedom
		Walter H. Leedom
		Leah E. Leedom
		Ruth J. Leedom

Married Emma L., daughter of Paul and Ellen McCahan, on March 25, 1873. This record placed by Paul Leedom, of Hollidaysburg, Penna.

GUST THOMAS MASTOS

BE IT HERE RECORDED, that Gust Thomas Mastos served in the UNITED STATES Army during the World War as a Cook, Headquarters Company, School Troops, C.O.T.S.; enlisting on the 24th day of July, 1918, and honorably discharged on the 31st day of January, 1919.

Said Gust Thomas Mastos was born at Spartan, Greece, on the 21st day of June, 1891; and resides at 2010 15th Avenue, Altoona, Penna.

The discharge is recorded in volume 6, page 142, Soldier's Discharge Record, Register and Recorder's Office, Blair County Court House, Hollidaysburg, Penna.

The genealogical data relating to this soldier is as follows:

Parents	Brothers and Sisters	Children
	Louis Mastos	Helen Mastos
Thomas Mastos	Gust Thomas Mastos	Stabroula Mastos
Olga Poledares	Willis Mastos	Thomas Mastos
	Peter Mastos	

Married Mary G., dau. of George and Mary Stathake, on February 20, 1921.

RAYMOND McALEVY STRUNK

BE IT HERE RECORDED that Raymond McAlevy Strunk served in the UNITED STATES Army during the World War as a Sergeant in Company K, 320th Regiment of Infantry, 80 Division; enlisting on the 6th day of October, 1917, and honorably discharged on the 13th day of June, 1919.

Said Raymond McAlevy Strunk was born at McAlevy's Fort, Huntingdon County, Penna., on the 13th day of November, 1889, and resides at Bellwood, Penna.

The discharge is recorded in volume 6, page 230, Soldier's Discharge Record, Register and Recorder's Office, Blair County Court House, Hollidaysburg, Penna.

The genealogical data relating to this soldier is as follows:

Parents	Brothers and Sisters	Children
	Ethel D. Hirsch	
Thomas Lunger Strunk	Raymond M. Strunk	Raymond M. Strunk
Susan Martha McAlevy	Maude Strunk	Suzanne M. Strunk
	Thomas F. Strunk	

Married Florence H., dau. of Harry and Anna Manley, on September 6, 1926.

INDIVIDUAL RECORDS

MYER ABELSON

BE IT HERE RECORDED, that Myer Abelson served in the UNITED STATES Army during the World War as a Sergeant in Company A, 30th Regiment of Infantry, 3rd Division; enlisting on the 19th day of September, 1917, and honorably discharged on the 31st day of January, 1919.

Said Myer Abelson was born at Altoona, Penna., on the 23rd day of October, 1893; and resides at Sylvan Hills, Hollidaysburg, Penna.

The discharge is recorded in volume 3, page 265, Soldier's Discharge Record Register and Recorder's Office, Blair County Court House, Hollidaysburg, Pa.

The genealogical data relating to this soldier is as follows:

Parents	Brothers and Sisters	Children
	Myer Abelson	
	Hyman Abelson	
	Harry Abelson	Shirley Eleanor Abelson
Abraham Abelson	Bessie Goodfriend	
	Martha Macks	
	Hilda Moses	Roselyn Abelson
Ida Izenstein	Isadore Abelson	
	Lena Kroll	
	Anna O'Blonsky	Arlene Abelson
	Mary Stein	

Married Fannie, dau., of Jacob and Rebecca Silberstein, on January 4, 1920.

WILLIAM CALVIN SMITH

BE IT HERE RECORDED, that William Calvin Smith served in the UNITED STATES Army during the Civil War as a Private in Company A, 23rd Regiment of Pennsylvania Militia; enlisting on the 21st day of September, 1862, and honorably discharged on the 30th day of September, 1862.

Said William Calvin Smith was born in Turkey Valley, Blair County, Pa., on the 3rd day of September, 1846; died on the 28th day of November, 1918, and is buried in Lot 222, Section D, Presbyterian Cemetery, Hollidaysburg, Pa.

The genealogical data relating to this soldier is as follows:

Parents	Brothers and Sisters	Children
	Gretta B. Smith	
Samuel Smith	William Calvin Smith	Guy Hamilton Smith
	Elizabeth Tussey	
Elizabeth Brotherlin	Clara King	Samuel Chester Smith
	Thomas Smith	

Married Angeline, daughter of Hamilton and Angeline McKenzie, about Nov. 1869. This record placed by Guy H. Smith, Hollidaysburg, Pa.

JOHN CHRISTIAN HALLER

BE IT HERE RECORDED, that John Christian Haller served in the UNITED STATES Army during the World War as a Cook in Company C, 52nd Regiment of Infantry, 6th Division; enlisting on the 3rd day of May, 1918, and honorably discharged on the 17th day of June, 1919.

Said John Christian Haller was born at Altoona, Pa., on the 8th day of November, 1894; and resides at 3000 Fourth Avenue, Altoona, Pa.

The discharge is recorded in volume 2, page 101, Soldier's Discharge Record, Register and Recorder's Office, Blair County Court House, Hollidaysburg, Pa.

The genealogical data relating to this soldier is as follows:

Parents	Brothers and Sisters	Children
John Haller	John Christian Haller	
	William Herman Haller	Sally Haller
Anna Weiss	Fred Martin Haller	

Married Alma Elizabeth, daughter of William and Laura Piper, on June 23, 1924.

RANDOLPH MITCHELL CLARK

BE IT HERE RECORDED, that Randolph Mitchell Clark served in the UNITED STATES Army during the World War as a Private in Battery B, 1st Battalion F.A.R.D., 26th Division; enlisting on the 26th day of June, 1918, and honorably discharged on the 14th day of May, 1919.

Said Randolph Mitchell Clark was born at Grampian, Pa., on the 25th day of May, 1901; and resides at 421 3rd Avenue, Altoona, Pa.

The discharge is recorded in volume 2, page 457, Soldier's Discharge Record, Register and Recorder's Office, Blair County Court House, Hollidaysburg, Pa.

The genealogical data relating to this soldier is as follow:

Parents	Brothers and Sisters	Children
	John A. Clark	
	Helen Linn	
	Wilfred Clark	
Thomas H. Clark	George A. Clark	
	Violet Withers	
	Maude Ebersole	Donald Orville Clark
	Nellie Thompson	
Martha Allen	May Glenn	
	Paul Clark	
	Randolph M. Clark	
	Kenneth B. Clark	

Married Sarah May, daughter of Robert M. and Ella Morgan, on April 6, 1921.

JOHN CALVIN LANG

BE IT HERE RECORDED, that John Calvin Lang served in the UNITED STATES Army during the World War as a Sergeant, Depot Detachment, 446th Engineers; enlisting on the 30th day of November, 1917, and honorably discharged on the 8th day of May, 1919.

Said John Calvin Lang was born at Hollidaysburg, Pa., on the 18th day of January, 1891; and resides at 921 Penn Street, Hollidaysburg, Pa.

The discharge is recorded in volume 2, page 112, Soldier's Discharge Record, Register and Recorder's Office, Blair County Court House, Hollidaysburg, Pa.

The genealogical data relating to this soldier is as follows:

Parents	Brothers and Sisters	Children
	Effie Thompson	
John Calvin Lang	E. Rea Lang	John Calvin Lang
	Estella Young	
Martha Ann Kephart	Nell J. Lang	Virginia Anne Lang
	John Calvin Lang	

Married Ethel May, daughter of Gilbert L. and Dollie M. Nokes, on June 25, 1924.

DANIEL BOHN

BE IT HERE RECORDED, that Daniel Bohn served in the UNITED STATES Army during the World War as a Captain, Medical Department; enlisting on the 26th day of August, 1917, and honorably discharged on the 22nd day of July, 1919.

Said Daniel Bohn was born at Lickdale, Pa., on the 9th day of May, 1873; and resides at 1208 Seventh Avenue, Altoona, Pa.

The genealogical data relating to this soldier is as follows:

Parents	Brothers and Sisters	Children
	Samuel Bohn	Violet Lenore Geary
John G. Bohn	Daniel Bohn	Charles Earl Bohn
	Charles Bohn	Ralph Warren Bohn
Amanda Bucher	Amy Bohn	

Married Bertha C., daughter of John C. and Anna Wentz, on June 13, 1895.

INDIVIDUAL RECORDS 393
AUGUSTUS ROUMFORT DEAL
BE IT HERE RECORDED, that Augustus Roumfort Deal served in the UNITED STATES Army during the Civil War as a Private in Company I, 137 Regiment of Pennsylvania Infantry; enlisting on the 8th day of August, 1862, and honorably discharged on the 1st day of June, 1863, also, as a Sergeant in Company B, 192nd Regiment of Pennsylvania Infantry; enlisting on the 10th day of February, 1865, and honorably discharged on the 24th day of August, 1865.

Said Augustus Roumfort Deal was born at Frankford, Pennsylvania, on the 21st day of November, 1839; died on the 30th day of January, 1929, and is buried lot 335, section B, Presbyterian Cemetery at Hollidaysburg, Pa.

The discharge is recorded in volume 1, page 115, Soldier's Discharge Record, Register and Recorder's Office, Blair County Court House, Hollidaysburg, Pa.

The genealogical data relating to this soldier is as follows:

Parents	Brothers and Sisters	Children
		Edith Houck
	Jacob Francis Deal	May Houck
	Edith Alvira Deal	Bess Deal
Joseph Deal	Robert Whitaker Deal	Joseph Deal
	Emma R. Deal	Charles Reese Deal
	Margaret Ann S. Deal	Elmer Howard Deal
Margaret Whitaker	Augustus Roumfort Deal	Margaret Hileman
	Joseph Clancy Deal	Robert Ernest Deal
	Myers Deal	Mary Caroline Goodfellow
	Clara Mary Deal	Jacob Frank Deal
		Helen Frances Deal

Married Mary Caroline, daughter of Jacob and Anna Mary Ebaugh on Feb. 8, 1864.
This record placed by Miss Helen F. Deal of Hollidaysburg, Pa.

HUGH SMITH
BE IT HERE RECORDED that Hugh Smith served in the UNITED STATES Army during the Civil War as a Color Sergeant in Company E, 84th Regiment of Pennsylvania Infantry; enlisting on the 3rd day of October, 1861, and honorably discharged on the 9th day of December, 1862.

Said Hugh Smith was born at Kilkern, County Galway, Ireland, on the 22nd day of June, 1819; died on the 21st day of February, 1898, and is buried in lot 96, St Marys Cemetery at Hollidaysburg, Pa.

The discharge is recorded in volume I, page 6, Soldier's Discharge Record, Register and Recorder's Office, Blair County Court House, Hollidaysburg, Pa.

The genealogical data relating to this soldier is as follows:

Parents	Brothers and Sisters	Children
		Mary Brady Davis
		B. Berdelia Clay
	Hugh Smith	Annie J. Prendergast
		Michael Smith
	Thomas Smith	Julia Smith
Michael Smith		Rose Etta Carlin
	Patrick Smith	Thomas Barbour Smith
Mary		John Brady Smith
	Michael Smith	H. Steele Smith
		Katherine Smith
	Bridget Ganan	Katherine J. Van Zandt
		Retta Clark Bice
		William B. Smith
		Edward Smith

Married Catherine, daughter of Terrence and Mary Brady, on April 11, 1849.
This record placed by H. Steele Smith of Hollidaysburg, Pa.

JOHN ROBERT McFARLANE

BE IT HERE RECORDED, that John Robert McFarlane served in the UNITED STATES Army during the Civil War as a Captain in Company A, 3rd Regiment of Pennsylvania Infantry; enlisting on the 20th day of April, 1861, and honorably discharged on the 30th day of July, 1861, also, served as a Captain in Company A, 23rd Regiment of Pennsylvania Militia; enlisting on the 21st day of September, 1862, and honorably discharged on the 30th day of September, 1862.

Said John Robert McFarlane was born at Philadelphia, Pennsylvania, on the 5th day of March, 1829; died on the 11th day of July, 1910, and is buried in lot 80, section A, Presbyterian Cemetery at Hollidaysburg, Pa.

The genealogical data relating to this soldier is as follows:

Parents	Brothers and Sisters	Children
		Mary Walker McFarlane
	John Robert McFarlane	Maria Riter McFarlane
George Rowan McFarlane		John Fluke McFarlane
	Thomas McFarlane	Carrie Griffin Burley
		Catharine Roberta Bollinger
Maria Riter McCrea	Catharine Roberta West	Bessie Kaziah Tyree
		George Rowan McFarlane
		Howard King MacFarlane
		Park Richardson McFarlane

Married Mary Virginia, daughter of John and Kaziah Fluke, on March 7, 1859.

This record placed by H. King MacFarlane, of 2425 W. Chestnut Ave., Altoona, Pa.

PHILIP ARNOLD BURKET

BE IT HERE RECORDED that Philip Arnold Burket served in the UNITED STATES Army during the World War as a Wagoner, Hoboken Casual Company 17; enlisting on the 12th day of July, 1917, and honorably discharged on the 23rd day of July, 1919.

Said Philip Arnold Burket was born at East Freedom, Pa., on the 13th day of August, 1898; and resides at 2827 Fifth Avenue, Altoona, Pa.

The discharge is recorded in volume 5, page 336, Soldier's Discharge Record, Register and Recorder's Office, Blair County Court House, Hollidaysburg, Pa.

The genealogical data relating to this soldier is as follows:

Parents	Brothers and Sisters	Children
	Chester H. Burket	
George W. Burket	Edna M. Burket	
Elizabeth G. Hileman	Philip A. Burket	

HARRY RICHARD GWIN

BE IT HERE RECORDED, that Harry Richard Gwin served in the UNITED STATES Army during the World War as a Mechanic in Company D, 145th Regiment of Pennsylvania Infantry, 37th Division; enlisting on the 6th day of October, 1917, and honorably discharged on the 10th day of April, 1919.

Said Harry Richard Gwin was born in Antis Township, Blair County, Pa., on the 25th day of January, 1894; and resides in Antis Township, Blair County, Pa.

The discharge is recorded in volume 3, page 105, Soldier's Discharge Record, Register and Recorder's Office, Blair County Court House, Hollidaysburg, Pa.

The genealogical data relating to this soldier is as follows:

Parents	Brothers and Sisters	Children
	Harry Richard Gwin	Anna Elizabeth Gwin
George Richard Gwin	Nellie Rose Cherry	Sara Elinor Gwin
	Dean Russell Gwin	Ruth Evagene Gwin
Anna Rose Turnbaugh	James Martin Gwin	Harry Snyder Gwin
	Pearl Ruth Horrobin	Bruce Ray Gwin

Married Tressa Elizabeth, daughter of Ira J. and Sara Alice Snyder on Nov. 27, 1919.

INDIVIDUAL RECORDS

JOHN WESLEY McALARNEY

BE IT HERE RECORDED, that John Wesley McAlarney served in the UNITED STATES Army during the Civil War as a Corporal in Troop F, 12th Regiment of Pennsylvania Cavalry; enlisting on the 13th day of February, 1862, and honorably discharged on the 20th day of July, 1865.

Said John Wesley McAlarney was born in West Township, Centre County, Pa., on the 17th day of March, 1846; and resides in Loop Station, Pa.

The discharge is recorded in volume 1, page 119, Soldier's Discharge Record, Register and Recorder's Office, Blair County Court House, Hollidaysburg, Pa.

The genealogical data relating to this soldier is as follows:

Parents	Brothers and Sisters	Children
		Henry C. McAlarney
	Catherine Foust	Terrence McAlarney
	Mary Robinson	Edmund R. McAlarney
Terrence McAlarney	John Wesley McAlarney	Clara Bell McAlarney
	Malinda Reynolds	Emma Hart
	James McAlarney	Ida McAlarney
Elizabeth Gregg	Sarah Gray	John W. McAlarney
	William McAlarney	Davis H. McAlarney
	Terrence McAlarney	William McAlarney
		Chester A. McAlarney

Married Lidia, daughter of Henry and Feba Cronister, on January 12, 1868.
Married Ida V., daughter of John and Mehala Culver, about 1910.

ROBERT FORSTER HARE

BE IT HERE RECORDED, that Robert Forster Hare served in the UNITED STATES Army during the World War as a Sergeant, Escort Detachment, Medical Corps; enlisting on the 5th day of September, 1918, and honorably discharged on the 26th day of July, 1919.

Said Robert Forster Hare was born at Altoona, Pa., on the 21st day of February, 1897; and resides at 2905 3rd Avenue, Altoona, Pa.

The discharge is recorded in volume 3, page 318, Soldier's Discharge Record, Register and Recorder's Office, Blair County Court House, Hollidaysburg, Pa.

The genealogical data relating to this soldier is as follows:

Parents	Brothers and Sisters	Children
Thomas C. Hare	Eleanor Gertrude Hare	Robert Forster Hare
Louise Kurtz	Robert Forster Hare	Thomas Franklin Hare

Married Blanda Irene, daughter of Franklin and Sarah Crooks, on June 27, 1923.

PAUL MICHAEL KIENZLE

BE IT HERE RECORDED, that Paul Michael Kienzle served in the UNITED STATES Army during the World War as a Master Electrician, 460th Aero Squadron, A. S. A. P.; enlisting on the 22nd day of February, 1918, and honorably discharged on the 8th day of February, 1919.

Said Paul Michael Kienzle was born at Tyrone, Pa., on the 29th day of June, 1894; and resides at 533 5th Street, Tyrone, Pa.

The discharge is recorded in volume 3, page 214, Soldier's Discharge Record, Register and Recorder's Office, Blair County Court House, Hollidaysburg, Pa.

The genealogical data relating to this soldier is as follows:

Parents	Brothers and Sisters	Children
	Frank Kienzle	
John Michael Kienzle	Carl Kienzle	Constance M. Kienzle
	Paul M. Kienzle	Janice R. Kienzle
Catherine Hewel	Agnes M. Kienzle	Paul M. Kienzle
	Kathryn C. Vaugh	

Married Ruth M., daughter of J. Harry and Myrtle E. Hayward, on Oct. 16, 1924.

JOHN ANDREW BREHMAN

BE IT HERE RECORDED, that John Andrew Brehman served in the UNITED STATES Army during the Civil War as a musician in Company C, 4th Regiment of Pennsylvania Militia; enlisting on the 15th day of September, 1862, and honorably discharged on the 23rd day of September, 1862.

Said John Andrew Brehman was born at McVeytown, Pa., on the 5th day of September, 1840, died on the 19th day of July, 1911, and is buried in lot 41, section B, Fairview Cemetery, Altoona, Pa.

The genealogical data relating to this soldier is as follows:

Parents	Brothers and Sisters	Children
		Mary Gertrude Coy
		Frank Yenser Brehman
	Mary Catherine Brehman	George Edmund Brehman
George W. Brehman	John Andrew Brehman	Herbert Sylvester Brehman
	Elizabeth Durr Brehman	Grace Irene Brehman
Mary Troxell	George Edmund Brehman	Cora May Tobias
	Charles Schaffer Brehman	Jessie Marian Brehman
		Emma Margaret Barry
		Helen Elizabeth Brehman

Married Elizabeth, daughter of Thomas and Margaret Ann Keesey, on June 4, 1867. This record placed by Herbert S. Brehman, of Williamsburg, Pa.

SAMUEL BLAIR HAINLEY

BE IT HERE RECORDED, that Samuel Blair Hainley served in the UNITED STATES Army during the World War as a Private in Headquarters Detachment, 30th Artillery Brigade, C. A. C.; enlisting on the 3rd day of May, 1917, and honorably discharged on the 11th day of January, 1919.

Said Samuel Blair Hainley was born at McKee, Pa., on the 7th day of July, 1897; and resides at 508 Allegheny Street, Hollidaysburg, Pa.

The discharge is recorded in volume 3, page 139, Soldier's Discharge Record, Register and Recorder's Office, Blair County Court House, Hollidaysburg, Pa.

The genealogical data relating to this soldier is as follows:

Parents	Brothers and Sisters	Children
Jeremiah S. Hainley	Samuel Blair Hainley	
Sarah Lucy Raffensberger	Nellie Margaret Hainley	

Married Chloe Myrtle, daughter of Decker and Madie Sellars, on August 16, 1924.

JOHN ELVIN KURTZ

BE IT HERE RECORDED, that John Elvin Kurtz served in the UNITED STATES Navy during the World War as a Shipfitter; enlisting on the 5th day of March, 1918, and honorably discharged on the 4th day of March, 1922.

Said John Elvin Kurtz was born at Martinsburg, Pa., on the 5th day of February, 1893; and resides at Claysburg, Pa.

The discharge is recorded in volume 4, page 33, Soldier's Discharge Record, Register and Recorder's Office, Blair County Court House, Hollidaysburg, Pa.

The genealogical data relating to this soldier is as follows:

Parents	Brothers and Sisters	Children
	Cora May Stearn	
	Harvey Daniel Kurtz	
Robert Kurtz	Henry Clyde Kurtz	John Robert Kurtz
	William George Kurtz	
Sarah Paul	Elizabeth Baker	Walter Paul Kurtz
	John Elvin Kurtz	
	Mary Matilda Shoemaker	

Married Jennie F., daughter of Calvin and Mollie Helsel, on November 25, 1924.

INDIVIDUAL RECORDS 397

THOMAS LAWLY

BE IT HERE RECORDED, that Thomas Lawly (Laulaa) served in the UNITED STATES Army during the Civil War as a private in Company E, 14th Regiment of Wisconsin Infantry; enlisting on the 1st day of November, 1861, and honorably discharged on the 7th day of December, 1864.

Said Thomas Lawly was born in County Limerick, Ireland, during 1838; died on the 30th day of April, 1878, and is buried in lot 204, St. Marys Cemetery, Hollidaysburg, Pa.

The discharge is recorded in volume 1, page 138, Soldier's Discharge Record, Register and Recorder's Office, Blair County Court House, Hollidaysburg, Pa.

The genealogical data relating to this soldier is as follows:

Parents	Brothers and Sisters	Children
		Thomas Lawly
		Sarah Lawly
Jeremiah Lawly		John Lawly
		Ann Lawly
....	Thomas Lawly	Jeremiah Lawly
		Mary Plummer
		Joseph Lawly

Married Ellen, daughter of James and Sarah S. Simcox, about 1859.
This record placed by Thomas Lawly, of Hollidaysburg, Pa.

CLYDE ROY RITCHEY

BE IT HERE RECORDED, that Clyde Roy Ritchey served in the UNITED STATES Army during the World War as a chauffeur in the 25th Aero Squadron, A. S. A.; enlisting on the 17th day of October, 1917, and honorably discharged on the 14th day of June, 1919.

Said Clyde Roy Ritchey was born at Everett, Penna., on the 24th day of June, 1894; and resides at 515 Allegheny Street, Hollidaysburg, Penna.

The discharge is recorded in volume 5, page 312, Soldier's Discharge Record, Register and Recorder's Office, Blair County Court House, Hollidaysburg, Penna.

The genealogical data relating to this soldier is as follows:

Parents	Brothers and Sisters	Children
	Cora B. Parker	
William A. Ritchey	Olive M. Spriggs	
	Alice M. Mumma	Dorothy Rose Ritchey
Susan Shaffer	William C. Ritchey	
	Clyde Roy Ritchey	

Married Sara, daughter of Benjamin and Rose Foor, on December 16, 1919.

NICHOLAS HRISTO CLONES

BE IT HERE RECORDED, that Nicholas Hristo Clones served in the UNITED STATES Army during the World War as a Corporal in Company L, 9th Regiment of Infantry, 2nd Division; enlisting on the 29th day of September, 1917, and honorably discharged on the 25th day of July, 1919.

Said Nicholas Hristo Clones was born at Sparta, Greece, on the 20th day of December, 1894; and resides at 1113 13th Avenue, Altoona, Penna.

The discharge is recorded in volume 6, page 242, Soldier's Discharge Record, Register and Recorder's office, Blair County Court House, Hollidaysburg, Penna.

The genealogical data relating to this soldier is as follows:

Parents	Brothers and Sisters	Children
	James Clones	
Hristo Clones	Rose Sangus	
	Gust Clones	
Catherine Papatheodovacos	George Clones	
	Peter Clones	

JOSEPH STEVENS

BE IT HERE RECORDED, that Joseph Stevens served in the CONSTRUCTION Corps of the United States Government during the Civil War, for a period of three years.

Said Joseph Stevens was born at Frankstown, Penna., on the 22nd day of April, 1844; died on the 1st day of March, 1910, and is buried in lot 48, section G, Calvary Cemetery, Altoona, Penna.

The genealogical data relating to this soldier is as follows:

Parents	Brothers and Sisters	Children
		Nicholas A. Stevens
	Henry H. Stephens	Agnes M. Luther
	Thomas Stephens	Gertrude N. Stevens
Nicholas R. Stephens	Mary Conroy	J. Edward Stevens
	Joseph Stevens	Charles C. Stevens
	Samuel Stephens	Theresa A. Stevens
Ruth Curry	John Stephens	Frank Stevens
	James M. Stephens	Clara E. Lambour
		Vincent L. Stevens
		Gerald H. Stevens

Married Matilda, daughter of Augustine and Theresa Flaugh, on February 20, 1870. This record placed by Nicholas A. Stevens, of 1421 8th Avenue, Altoona, Penna.

HARRY EDMUND DIEHL

BE IT HERE RECORDED, that Harry Edmund Diehl served in the UNITED STATES Navy during the World War as a Seaman; enlisting on the 9th day of September, 1918, and honorably discharged on the 30th day of January, 1919.

Said Harry Edmund Diehl was born at Blue Knob, Blair County, Penna., on the 6th day of February, 1896; and resides at Claysburg, Penna.

The discharge is recorded in volume 4, page 266, Soldier's Discharge Record, Register and Recorder's Office, Blair County Court House, Hollidaysburg, Penna.

The genealogical data relating to this soldier is as follows:

Parents	Brothers and Sisters	Children
	Allen J. Diehl	
George Calvin Diehl	William Diehl	Helen Jaqueline Diehl
	Emory Aaron Diehl	
Emma Jane Berkhimer	Harry Edmund Diehl	Robert Andrew Diehl
	Austin Blair Diehl	
	Homer Diehl	

Married Ida Elizabeth, daughter of Howard and Rebecca Gochnour, on June 20, 1926.

HOMER IRWIN SMITH

BE IT HERE RECORDED, that Homer Irwin Smith served in the UNITED STATES Army during the World War as a Quartermaster Sergeant in the Quartermaster Corps; enlisting on the 2nd day of February, 1918, and honorably discharged on the 2nd day of May, 1919.

Said Homer Irwin Smith was born at Frankstown Township, Blair County, Penna., on the 3rd day of September, 1891; and resides at 809 Penn St., Hollidaysburg, Penna.

The discharge is recorded in volume 3, page 259, Soldier's Discharge Record, Register and Recorder's Office, Blair County Court House, Hollidaysburg, Penna.

The genealogical data relating to this soldier is as follows:

Parents	Brothers and Sisters	Children
	Homer Irwin Smith	
Thomas Irwin Smith	Mary Jane Smith	Eloise Elizabeth Smith
Blanche Elizabeth Brua	Janet Elizabeth Smith	
	Helen Matilda Smith	

Married Vera Elizabeth, daughter of Abraham L. and Ella Garver, on Sept. 15, 1926.

INDIVIDUAL RECORDS

BLAINE YINGLING

BE IT HERE RECORDED, that Blaine Yingling served in the UNITED STATES Army during the Spanish-American War as a Private in Company I, 47th Regiment of Infantry, United States Volunteers; enlisting on the 25th day of September, 1899, and honorably discharged on the 2nd day of July, 1901.

Said Blaine Yingling was born at Elliott's Mills, Fayette County, Penna., on the 19th day of November, 1877; and resides in Greenfield Twp., Blair Co., Pa.

The discharge is recorded in volume 4, page 214, Soldier's Discharge Record, Register and Recorder's Office, Blair County Court House, Hollidaysburg, Penna.

The genealogical data relating to this soldier is as follows:

Parents	Brothers and Sisters	Children
	Alonza M. Yingling	
	William W. Yingling	
	Iva Myrtle Feathers	
Martin M. Yingling	Angus C. Yingling	
	Jennie M. Shaeffer	James Allen Yingling
	Herbert R. Yingling	
Susan R. Moore	Oscar L. Yingling	
	Herman E. Yingling	
	Blaine Yingling	

Married Mary Jane, daughter of William and Christina Feathers, on April 17, 1910.

GEORGE EARL BOLLINGER

BE IT HERE RECORDED, that George Earl Bollinger served in the UNITED STATES Army during the World War as a Wagoner in the Supply Company, 110th Regiment of Infantry, 28th Division; enlisting on the 3rd day of July, 1917, and honorably discharged on the 23rd day of May, 1919.

Said George Earl Bollinger was born at Barnesboro, Penna., on the 15th day of March, 1896; and resides at Greenwood, Blair County, Penna.

The discharge is recorded in volume 4, page 409, Soldier's Discharge Record, Register and Recorder's Office, Blair County Court House, Hollidaysburg, Penna.

The genealogical data relating to this soldier is as follows:

Parents	Brothers and Sisters	Children
	Virginia Bollinger	
George V. Bollinger	George Earl Bollinger	
Rose Elmira Kelley	Howard Bollinger	
	Donald A. Bollinger	

JOHN FLECK ROYER

BE IT HERE RECORDED, that John Fleck Royer served in the UNITED STATES Army during the World War as a Private in Company B, 109th Regiment of Infantry, 28th Division; enlisting on the 26th day of February, 1918, and honorably discharged on the 31st day of July, 1919.

Said John Fleck Royer was born at Arch Spring, Blair County, Penna., on the 16th day of August, 1895; and resides at 2203 Chestnut Street, Harrisburg, Pa.

The discharge is recorded in volume 2, page 102, Soldier's Discharge Record, Register and Recorder's Office, Blair County Court House, Hollidaysburg, Penna.

The genealogical data relating to this soldier is as follows:

Parents	Brothers and Sisters	Children
	Fannie Elizabeth Miller	John Gregg Royer
Jacob Royer	Samuel Keagy Royer	Alan Fleck Royer
	William Moore Royer	James Glenn Royer
Margaret Mae Sprankle	Clarence Sprankle Royer	Anna Lois Royer
	John Fleck Royer	Margaret Louise Royer
	Carl Frederick Royer	

Married Grace Pauline, dau. of Theodore G. and Anna M. Lucas, on Dec. 30, 1921.

CLAIR PERRY NALE

BE IT HERE RECORDED, that Clair Perry Nale served in the UNITED STATES Army during the World War as a Corporal in Company G, 110th Regiment of Infantry, 28th Division; enlisting on the 8th day of June, 1917, and honorably discharged on the 23rd day of May, 1919.

Said Clair Perry Nale was born at Milroy, Penna., on the 10th day of March, 1899; and resides at 832 18th Avenue, Altoona, Penna.

The discharge is recorded in volume 2, page 193, Soldier's Discharge Record, Register and Recorder's Office, Blair County Court House, Hollidaysburg, Penna.

The genealogical data relating to this soldier is as follows:

Parents	Brothers and Sisters	Children
	Clair Perry Nale	
	Jessie N. Shirley	Margaret E. Merkle
Perry R. Nale	Charles E. Nale	
	Gertrude Figart	Donald C. Nale
Florence M. Naginey	Ethel Lowther	
	Esther Nale	Richard D. Nale
	Ray Nale	
	Dean Nale	

Married Bertha E., daughter of Samuel and Lula Arnold, on April 27, 1920.

CHARLES LLOYD REIGHARD

BE IT HERE RECORDED, that Charles Lloyd Reighard served in the UNITED STATES Army during the World War as a Cook, 305th Engineers Train, 80th Division; enlisting on the 19th day of September, 1917, and honorably discharged on the 11th day of June, 1919.

Said Charles Lloyd Reighard was born at Claysburg, Penna., on the 28th day of January, 1896; and resides at Claysburg, Penna.

The discharge is recorded in volume 3, page 50, Soldier's Discharge Record, Register and Recorder's Office, Blair County Court House, Hollidaysburg, Penna.

The genealogical data relating to this soldier is as follows:

Parents	Brothers and Sisters	Children
	David Ross Reighard	
Harry M. Reighard	Elizabeth Reighard	Donald Lloyd Reighard
Elizabeth Winkler	Charles Lloyd Reighard	William McClelland Reighard
	Thomas Reighard	

Married Margaret Bertha, daughter of John and Anna Elizabeth Moore, on May 10, 1923.

JOHN BLAISDELL NASON

BE IT HERE RECORDED, that John Blaisdell Nason served in the UNITED STATES Army during the World War as a Captain in the Medical Department; enlisting on the 28th day of December, 1917, and honorably discharged on the 4th day of August, 1919.

Said John Blaisdell Nason was born at Townville, Penna., on the 14th day of February, 1871; and resides at 1207 Logan Avenue, Tyrone, Penna.

The discharge is recorded in volume 4, page 50, Soldier's Discharge Record, Register and Recorder's Office, Blair County Court House, Hollidaysburg, Penna.

The genealogical data relating to this soldier is as follows:

Parents	Brothers and Sisters	Children
	Lillian A. Lehenthaler	
	Charles A. W. Nason	William Nason
William Nason	William R. Nason	Ardis Williams
Catharine Breed	Sherman E. Nason	John B. Nason
	Frank T. Nason	Lyman Breed Nason
	John B. Nason	

Married Stella R., daughter of Charles and Louise Lyman, on June 12, 1895.

INDIVIDUAL RECORDS

CHARLES EDGAR SHOENFELT
BE IT HERE RECORDED, that Charles Edgar Shoenfelt served in the UNITED STATES Army during the World War as a Corporal in Company I, 4th Regiment of Infantry, 3rd Division; enlisting on the 20th day of July, 1917, and honorably discharged on the 26th day of October, 1919.

Said Charles Edgar Shoenfelt was born at Duncansville, Penna., on the 14th day of March, 1892; and resides at Duncansville, Penna.

The genealogical data relating to this soldier is as follows:

Parents	Brothers and Sisters	Children
	Nancy C. Lowry	
	Carrie Shoenfelt	
John K. Shoenfelt	Ray A. Shoenfelt	Helen Marie Shoenfelt
	J. Lloyd Shoenfelt	Edith May Shoenfelt
Jennie Hicks	Edith M. Webb	John Thomas Shoenfelt
	Emely M. Kyle	
	Nellie C. Hughes	
	Charles Edgar Shoenfelt	

Married Mildred M., daughter of Thomas and Mary Duggan, on November 24, 1920.

JOHN HEISS WEST
BE IT HERE RECORDED, that John Heiss West served in the UNITED STATES Army during the Spanish-American War as a Captain in Company C, 5th Regiment of Infantry, Pennsylvania Volunteers; enlisting on the 27th day of April, 1898, and honorably discharged on the 7th day of November, 1898.

Said John Heiss West was born at Hollidaysburg, Penna., on the 29th day of July, 1860; died on the 30th day of October, 1937, and is buried in lot 71, section B, Presbyterian Cemetery, Hollidaysburg, Penna.

The genealogical data relating to this soldier is as follows:

Parents	Brothers and Sisters	Children
	George Rowan West	
John Charles West	Julia West	
	William Henry West	
Catherine Roberta	John Heiss West	
McFarlane	Maria Louisa West	

This record placed by Miss Maria L. West, of 2013 4th Avenue, Altoona, Pa.

GEORGE WILLIAM SWARTZ
BE IT HERE RECORDED, that George William Swartz served in the UNITED STATES Army during the World War as a Corporal in Company C, 313th Machine Gun Battalion, 80th Division; enlisting on the 3rd day of October, 1917, and honorably discharged on the 12th day of June, 1919.

Said George William Swartz was born in Huston Township, Blair County, Penna., on the 20th day of June, 1890; and resides in Huston Twp., Blair County, Penna.

The discharge is recorded in volume 3, page 110, Soldier's Discharge Record, Register and Recorder's Office, Blair County Court House, Hollidaysburg, Penna.

The genealogical data relating to this soldier is as follows:

Parents	Brothers and Sisters	Children
	Mary Swartz	
	Margaret Ketner-Ford	
	John E. Swartz	
John E. Swartz	Arch Swartz	
Angeline Fetterman	Matilda Swartz	Audrey Jean Swartz
	Jane Booth	
	Sam Swartz	
	George W. Swartz	

Married Verna C., daughter of Jacob and Jane Detwiler, on December 25, 1921.

SOLDIERS OF BLAIR COUNTY

JONATHAN T. LEET

BE IT HERE RECORDED, that Jonathan T. Leet served in the UNITED STATES Army during the Civil War as a Private in Company B, Independent Battalion Pennsylvania Militia; enlisting on the 3rd day of July, 1863, and honorably discharged on the 8th day of August, 1863; also, served as a Private in Company M, 22nd Regiment of Pennsylvania Cavalry; enlisting on the 11th day of February, 1864, and honorably discharged on the 14th day of August, 1865.

Said Jonathan T. Leet was born at Washington, Penna., on the 15th day of February, 1847; died on the 12th day of February, 1917, and buried in lot 80, section B, Presbyterian Cemetery, Hollidaysburg, Penna.

The discharge is recorded in volume 1, page 152, Soldier's Discharge Record, Register and Recorder's Office, Blair County Court House, Hollidaysburg, Penna.

The genealogical data relating to this soldier is as follows:

Parents	Brothers and Sisters	Children
	Calahan M. Leet	
Jonathan Duke Leet	Mary L. Martin	Joseph Irwin Leet
Mary Ann Calahan	Jonathan T. Leet	Mary Martin Pitcairn
		William Buxton Leet
(Second Marriage)	Katherine May Collin	
Mary Jane Saunders	William Charles Leet	

Married Ruth Elliott, daughter of Joseph and Mary Irwin, on December 18, 1879. This record placed by William B. Leet, 826 Walnut Street, Hollidaysburg, Pa.

GUY ZANE PEARCE

BE IT HERE RECORDED, that Guy Zane Pearce served in the UNITED STATES Navy during the World War as a Machinist Mate, 1cl.; enlisting the 18th day of August, 1917, and honorably discharged on the 14th day of July, 1919.

Said Guy Zane Pearce was born at Huntingdon, Pennsylvania, on the 22nd day of November, 1895; and resides at 2715 Seventh Avenue, Altoona, Penna.

The discharge is recorded in volume 4, page 35, Soldier's Discharge Record, Register and Recorder's Office, Blair County Court House, Hollidaysburg, Penna.

The genealogical data relating to this soldier is as follows:

Parents	Brothers and Sisters	Children
John Pearce	Guy Zane Pearce	Richard Dutt Pearce
Annie Musser		Doris Jean Pearce

Married Kathryn Marie, dau. of Charles L. and Matilda D. Zimmerman, on Oct. 7, 1925.

HARRY NELSON GLASS

BE IT HERE RECORDED, that Harry Nelson Glass served in the UNITED STATES Army during the World War as a Private in the 153rd Depot Brigade; enlisting on the 6th day of September, 1918, and honorably discharged on the 12th day of December, 1918.

Said Harry Nelson Glass was born at Millerstown, Blair County, Penna., on the 26th day of July, 1893; and resides at 861 Washington Avenue, Tyrone, Pa.

The genealogical data relating to this soldier is as follows:

Parents	Brothers and Sisters	Children
	Elizabeth A. Glass	
	John Elvin Glass	
Elias G. Glass	Anna M. Burget	
	Margaret N. Ritchey	Frances Susan Glass
	Katherine G. Hoover	
Mary Margaret Wolfe	Charles F. Glass	
	Harry Nelson Glass	
	George E. Glass	
	I. Melvin Glass	

Married Mabel Elizabeth, daughter of John A. and Maude H. Boyd, on May 18, 1922.

HENRY STANLEY LINGENFELTER

BE IT HERE RECORDED, that Henry S. Lingenfelter served in the UNITED STATES Army during the World War as a Private in Company B, 7th Trench Mortar Battalion; enlisting on the 15th day of August, 1918, and honorably discharged on the 15th day of January, 1919.

Said Henry Stanley Lingenfelter was born at Claysburg on the 28th day of October, 1896; and resides at Claysburg, Pennsylvania.

The genealogical data relating to this soldier is as follows:

Parents	Brothers and Sisters	Children
	Thomas J. Lingenfelter	
	Ray S. Lingenfelter	
	Jennie Lingenfelter	
Martin Adam Lingenfelter	John S. Lingenfelter	Donald Ray Lingenfelter
	Charles A. Lingenfelter	
	Anne E. Stufft	
Laura Belle Snowberger	Henry S. Lingenfelter	John Roger Lingenfelter
	Frank Lingenfelter	
	Rebecca Marie Berg	
	Ida Elliott	
	Clair M. Lingenfelter	

Married Grace Mildred, daughter of Archie and Jennie Moore, on February 2, 1921.

ROBERT BROOKS GREENLAND

BE IT HERE RECORDED, that Robert Brooks Greenland served in the UNITED STATES Army during the World War as a Sergeant in the 50th Aero Squadron; enlisting on the 1st day of August, 1917, and honorably discharged on the 19th day of May, 1919.

Said Robert Brooks Greenland was born at Bellwood, Pennsylvania, on the 17th day of August, 1898; and resides at 300 S. 2nd Street, Bellwood, Penna.

The discharge is recorded in volume 2, page 246, Soldier's Discharge Record, Register and Recorder's Office, Blair County Court House, Hollidaysburg, Penna.

The genealogical data relating to this soldier is as follows:

Parents	Brothers and Sisters	Children
	Kathleen Irvin	
	Robert Brooks Greenland	
Bruce Everett Greenland	Lena Hayward	Robert Brooks Greenland
	Bruce Everett Greenland	
Carrie May Thompson	Laura Day	William Wilson Greenland
	Edna Emeigh	
	Milton Greenland	

Married Irene Rebecca, daughter of William A. and Hilda Love, on September 22, 1923.

IVAN EDISON GARVER

BE IT HERE RECORDED, that Ivan Edison Garver served in the UNITED STATES Army during the World War as a Private in Company H, 1st Provisional Regiment, O. T. C.; enlisting on the 29th day of July, 1918, and honorably discharged on the 11th day of January, 1919.

Said Ivan Edison Garver was born at Roaring Spring, Penna., on the 18th day of October, 1887; and resides at 715 Spang Street, Roaring Spring, Penna.

The discharge is recorded in volume 3, page 173, Soldier's Discharge Record, Register and Recorder's Office, Blair County Court House, Hollidaysburg, Penna.

The genealogical data relating to this soldier is as follows:

Parents	Brothers and Sisters	Children
Abraham Lincoln Garver	Ivan Edison Garver	
	Russell Bare Garver	
Ella Bare	Vera Elizabeth Smith	

MAURICE THOMAS McCULLOUGH

BE IT HERE RECORDED, that Maurice T. McCullough served in the UNITED STATES Army during the World War as a Corporal in the 14th Balloon Company Air Service; enlisting on the 8th day of February, 1918, and honorably discharged on the 12th day of August, 1919.

Said Maurice Thomas McCullough was born at Sinclairville, New York, on the 16th day of April, 1898; and resides at Claysburg, Pennsylvania.

The discharge is recorded in volume 6, page 228, Soldier's Discharge Record, Register and Recorder's Office, Blair County Court House, Hollidaysburg, Penna.

The genealogical data relating to this soldier is as follows:

Parents	Brothers and Sisters	Children
	Earl E. McCullough	
Martin T. McCullough	Evah Mulkin	Maurice Thomas McCullough
	Glenn L. McCullough	Whitford Barratt McCullough
Hattie Sylvester	Hazel E. Lowan	
	Allen M. McCullough	
	Maurice Thomas McCullough	

Married Hazel Eline, daughter of James and Sarah Barratt on October 30, 1922.

GEORGE MARION PATTERSON

BE IT HERE RECORDED, that George Marion Patterson served in the UNITED STATES Army during the Civil War as a Quartermaster Sergeant in the 22nd Regiment of Pennsylvania Cavalry; enlisting on the 17th day of July, 1863, and honorably discharged on the 5th day of February, 1864.

Said George Marion Patterson was born at Williamsburg, Penna., on the 14th day of February, 1840; and died on the 22nd day of February, 1925, and is buried in the Presbyterian Cemetery at Williamsburg, Pennsylvania.

The genealogical data relating to this soldier is as follows:

Parents	Brothers and Sisters	Children
	Mary A. Patterson	Mabel M. Patterson
Thomas S. Patterson	Jane Patterson	James T. Patterson
	George Marion Patterson	Marion Dean Patterson
Margaret Dean	John Dean Patterson	John Carl Patterson
	Robert G. Patterson	George G. Patterson
		Mary Mildred Ross

Married Mary Rebecca, daughter of James and Margrette Roller, on January 13, 1870. This record placed by Hon. George G. Patterson, of Hollidaysburg, Penna.

SAMUEL CALITHAN KAGARISE

BE IT HERE RECORDED, that Samuel C. Kagarise served in the UNITED STATES Army during the Spanish-American War as a Private in Company L, 47th Regiment of Infantry, United States Volunteers; enlisting on the 27th day of September, 1899, and honorably discharged on the 2nd day of July, 1901.

Said Samuel Calithan Kagarise was born at New Enterprise, Penna., on the 27th day of August, 1876; and resides at Roaring Spring, Penna.

The discharge is recorded in volume 4, page 267, Soldier's Discharge Record, Register and Recorder's Office, Blair County Court House, Hollidaysburg, Penna.

The genealogical data relating to this soldier is as follows:

Parents	Brothers and Sisters	Children
	Daniel S. Kagarise	
	Minnie Gates	
Jacob R. Kagarise	Andrew C. Kagarise	
Elizabeth Calithan	Samuel Calithan Kagarise	Janet Louise Kagarise
	Susan Hartman	
	Jacob C. Kagarise	

Married Rosella B., daughter of John and Henrietta Fisher on December 25, 1910.

INDIVIDUAL RECORDS 405

WILLIAM RAYMOND EASTEP

BE IT HERE RECORDED, that William Raymond Eastep served in the UNITED STATES Army during the World War as a Private in the Students Army Training Corps; The Pennsylvania State College, enlisting on the 15th day of October, 1918, and honorably discharged on the 12th day of December, 1918.

Said William Raymond Eastep was born at Williamsburg, Pennsylvania, on the 6th day of July, 1898; and resides at 531 Pine Street, Hollidaysburg, Penna.

The discharge is recorded in volume 6, page 240, Soldier's Discharge Record, Register and Recorder's Office, Blair County Court House, Hollidaysburg, Penna.

The genealogical data relating to this soldier is as follows:

Parents	Brothers and Sisters	Children
	Mazzie Beryl Eastep	
	William Raymond Eastep	
George William Eastep	James Calvin Eastep	William Raymond Eastep
	Alverta Blanche Eastep	
Laura Elizabeth Sorrick	Wayland Palmer Eastep	Helen Louise Eastep
	George Eugene Eastep	

Married Grace Amanda, daughter of William E. and Clara M. Rodkey, on Nov. 30, 1922.

JAMES GALLATIN SLEP

BE IT HERE RECORDED, that James Gallatin Slep served in the UNITED STATES Navy during the World War as a Storekeeper; enlisting on the 23rd day of July, 1917, and honorably discharged on the 8th day of January, 1919.

Said James Gallatin Slep was born at Altoona, Pennsylvania, on the 7th day of July, 1898; and resides at 2410 Twelfth Street, Altoona, Penna.

The discharge is recorded in volume 4, page 416, Soldier's Discharge Record, Register and Recorder's Office, Blair County Court House, Hollidaysburg, Penna.

The genealogical data relating to this soldier is as follows:

Parents	Brothers and Sisters	Children
	James Gallatin Slep	
Daniel Neff Slep	Daniel Potter Slep	Dorothy Helen Slep
Elda Pearl Potter	Eugene Gilland Slep	James Daniel Slep
	Philip Potter Slep	

Married Helen Cora, daughter of Ellwood P. and Susanna K. Jester, on Sept. 6, 1919.

AMBROSE LEAR CARBERRY

BE IT HERE RECORDED, that Ambrose Lear Carberry served in the UNITED STATES Army during the World War as a Private in the Student Army Training Corps; enlisting on the 15th day of October, 1918, and honorably discharged on the 9th day of December, 1918.

Said Ambrose Lear Carberry was born at Saxton, Pennsylvania, on the 5th day of December, 1898; and resides at 1414 Allegheny St., Hollidaysburg, Penna.

The discharge is recorded in volume 3, page 7, Soldier's Discharge Record, Register and Recorder's Office, Blair County Court House, Hollidaysburg, Pa.

The genealogical data relating to this soldier is as follows:

Parents	Brothers and Sisters	Children
	John L. Carberry	
	Andrew L. Carberry	Lyla Rose Hainey
	Jesse L. Carberry	
	Calvin L. Carberry	Doris Lorine Carberry
Wilson H. Carberry	Ambrose L. Carberry	
	Elnora L. Sleek	Nancy Fay Carberry
	Anna Thomas	
Lydia A. Lear	Clara Thomas	Joe Lear Carberry
	Isadore O. Haire	
	Sadie B. Carberry	
	Jeannette Moore	

Married Arda Rosalie, daughter of William E. and Della MacGregar, on March 13, 1919.

SOLDIERS OF BLAIR COUNTY

GORDON PATRICK SMITH

BE IT HERE RECORDED, that Gordon Patrick Smith served in the UNITED STATES Army during the World War as a Corporal in Company 481, Motor Transport Corps; enlisting on March 27, 1918, and honorably discharged on August 23, 1919.

Said Gordon Patrick Smith was born at Altoona, Pennsylvania, on the 26th day of January, 1901; and resides at Hollidaysburg, Penna.

The discharge is recorded in volume 6, page 248, Soldier's Discharge Record, Register and Recorder's Office, Blair County Court House, Hollidaysburg, Penna.

The genealogical data relating to this soldier is as follows:

Parents	Brothers and Sisters	Children
	William Donald Smith	
	Gordon Patrick Smith	
J. Frank Smith	Eugene Smith	
	Herbert Paul Smith	Mary Suzanne Smith
Catherine Rose Sullivan	J. Frank Smith	
	Catherine Julia Conley	
	Robert Zuern Smith	

Married Mary Elizabeth, daughter of Harry H. and Helen Blackburn, on July 2, 1938.

STANTON CHISLETT FUNK

BE IT HERE RECORDED, that Stanton Chislett Funk served in the UNITED STATES Army during the World War as a Private in Company E, 15th Regiment of Engineers; enlisting on the 23rd day of April, 1917, and honorably discharged on the 15th day of May, 1919.

Said Stanton Chislett Funk was born at Altoona, Pennsylvania, on the 5th day of February, 1894; and resides at 503 Walnut Street, Hollidaysburg, Pa.

The discharge is recorded in volume 10, page 193, Soldier's Discharge Record, Register and Recorder's Office, Allegheny County Court House, Pittsburgh, Penna.

The genealogical data relating to this soldier is as follows:

Parents	Brothers and Sisters	Children
	Edith Coates	George Ehrenfeld Funk
Nicholas G. Funk	Mary Sue Weber	Sue Morgan Funk
Sue Cornelia Goudy	Stanton Chislett Funk	Stanton Curtiss Funk
	Nicholas Ward Funk	

Married Ina G., daughter of George and Eliza Jane Ehrenfeld, on April 22, 1920.

ANDREW HENRY SCHROEDER

BE IT HERE RECORDED, that Andrew Henry Schroeder served in the UNITED STATES Army during the World War as a Private in the 1st Provisional Company, 98th Division; enlisting on the 29th day of August, 1918, and honorably discharged on the 7th day of December, 1918.

Said Andrew Henry Schroeder was born at Hollidaysburg, Pennsylvania, on the 9th day of February, 1896; and resides at 804 Jones St., Hollidaysburg, Pa.

The discharge is recorded in volume 5, page 101, Soldier's Discharge Record, Register and Recorder's Office, Blair County Court House, Hollidaysburg, Pa.

The genealogical data relating to this soldier is as follows:

Parents	Brothers and Sisters	Children
	Charles L. Schroeder	
	Katherine Runyeon	Harold Lloyd Schroeder
Henry Schroeder	Martin Schroeder	
	Henry Schroeder	
	Andrew Henry Schroeder	Lucille Frances Schroeder
Alice Mary Lesley	Genevieve Stubler	
	Helen Yon	
	Isabelle Schmerbeck	Melvin Richard Schroeder
	Mary Schmerbeck	
	Jule M. Schroeder	

Married Alice Emma, daughter of Charles H. and Rebecca Jane Bush, on June 28, 1917.

INDIVIDUAL RECORDS 407

JOHN MICHAEL BLACK

BE IT HERE RECORDED, that John Michael Black served in the UNITED STATES Army during the World War as a Sergeant in Company G, 110th Infantry, 28th Division; enlisting on the 10th day of May, 1917, and killed in action.

Said John Michael Black was born at Royer, Blair County, Pennsylvania, on the 2nd day of December, 1880; died on the 7th day of September, 1918, and is buried in lot 20, section 1, row C, Carson Valley Cemetery, near Duncansville, Pa.

The genealogical data relating to this soldier is as follows:

Parents	Brothers and Sisters	Children
	Olive Louise Gibboney	
	Elmira Amanda Colbert	
Adam Black	Araminta Manerva Stewart	
	Mary Ann Andrews	
Mary Ellen Trexler	John Michael Black	
	Ettie Catherine Shipe	
	Charles Glenn Black	

This record placed by Mrs. Mary Ann Andrews, of Hollidaysburg, Pa.

CHARLES RICHARD MALLERY

BE IT HERE RECORDED, that Charles Richard Mallery served in the UNITED STATES Army during the World War as a First Lieutenant, Field Artillery, Central Officers Training School; enlisting on the 27th day of August, 1917, and honorably discharged on the 20th day of December, 1918.

Said Charles Richard Mallery was born at Altoona, Pennsylvania, on the 18th day of June, 1888; and resides at 605 Allegheny Street, Hollidaysburg, Pa.

The discharge is recorded in volume 4, page 17, Soldier's Discharge Record, Register and Recorder's Office, Blair County Court House, Hollidaysburg, Pa.

The genealogical data relating to this soldier is as follows:

Parents	Brothers and Sisters	Children
	Margaret May Hutchison	
James Richard Mallery	John W. Mallery	
Laura Medora Hatton	Leonard S. Mallery	
	Charles Richard Mallery	

Married Ethel, daughter of J. Lee and Mary Ann Plummer, on October 14, 1939.

FRANK HEYER GOOD

BE IT HERE RECORDED, that Frank Heyer Good served in the UNITED STATES Army during the World War as a Corporal in Headquarters Company, 335th Battalion, Tank Corps; enlisting on the 30th day of June, 1918, and honorably discharged on the 17th day of July, 1919.

Said Frank Heyer Good was born at Eldorado, Blair County, Pennsylvania, on the 31st day of July, 1886; and resides at 714 W. 2nd St., Williamsburg, Pa.

The discharge is recorded in volume 6, page 74, Soldier's Discharge Record, Register and Recorder's Office, Blair County Court House, Hollidaysburg, Pa.

The genealogical data relating to this soldier is as follows:

Parents	Brothers and Sisters	Children
	William Good	
	S. Peter Good	
William Howard Good	James M. Good	
	Frank Heyer Good	
	Oline Gains	
Lavinia Weaver	Florence Williams	
	Fred A. Good	
	Rebecca Brumbaugh	
	Pearl Hargraves	
	Adalaide Brantlinger	
	Russel A. Good	

Married Nora, daughter of Miles and Lydia Benton, on August 16, 1921.

WESLEY WAYNE FLECK

BE IT HERE RECORDED, that Wesley Wayne Fleck served in the UNITED STATES Army during the Spanish-American War as a Private in the Sheridan Troop, 1st Regiment of Pennsylvania Cavalry; enlisting on the 27th day of April, 1898, and honorably discharged on the 21st day of November, 1898; also, served as a Corporal in Company M, 47th Regiment of United States Infantry; enlisting on the 5th day of October, 1899, and honorably discharged on the 6th day of July, 1901.

Said Wesley Wayne Fleck was born in Sinking Valley, Blair County, Pennsylvania, on the 26th day of November, 1877; and resides at 204 First Avenue, Altoona, Pa.

The genealogical data relating to this soldier is as follows:

Parents	Brothers and Sisters	Children
	J. Emerson Fleck	
	C. Hayden Fleck	
	Minnie Myrtle Fleck	
	Ella Maude Fleck	
John Francis Fleck	H. Clyde Fleck	Oscar Ellsworth Fleck
	Frank Marsh Fleck	
	John Kistler Fleck	
	Abraham Lloyd Fleck	
Barbara Ellen Ramey	Wesley Wayne Fleck	Ruth Naomi Fleck
	Elsor Dean Fleck	
	James Ramey Fleck	
	Nannie Neff Beck	
	George W. B. Fleck	

Married Maude, daughter of William E. and Flora Banks, on December 5, 1901.

JAMES MELVILLE TREASE

BE IT HERE RECORDED, that James Melville Trease served in the UNITED STATES Army during the Civil War as a Private in Company H, 110th Regiment of Pennsylvania Infantry; enlisting on the 18th day of September, 1862, and honorably discharged on the 3rd day of May, 1863.

Said James Melville Trease was born at Maria Forge, Blair County, Pennsylvania, on the 13th day of May, 1845; died on the 9th day of February, 1910, and is buried in the Greenlawn Cemetery at Roaring Spring, Pa.

The genealogical data relating to this soldier is as follows:

Parents	Brothers and Sisters	Children
	James Melville Trease	David K. Trease
John Treese	Samuel Treese	Harry Melville Trease
Elizabeth Gates	Aden D. Treese	May Hoover
	Calvin Treese	
	Caroline Treese	
(second marriage)	Wesley Treese	
	Allen Treese	
Barbara Snyder	Fannie McGinnis	
	Matilda Treese	
	Janealice Treese	
	Henry Treese	
	Louis Treese	
	Edmund Treese	
	Albert Treese	
	Collins Treese	

Married Caroline, daughter of Amos and Nancy McKee, on November 29, 1865.
This record placed by James G. Trease of 2811 W. Chestnut Ave., Altoona, Pa.

INDIVIDUAL RECORDS 409

JOHN WILSON JOHNSTON

BE IT HERE RECORDED, that John Wilson Johnston served in the UNITED STATES Army during the Civil War as a Private in Company C, 133rd Regiment of Pennsylvania Infantry; enlisting on the 13th day of August, 1862, and honorably discharged on the 26th day of May, 1863.

Said John Wilson Johnston was born at Woodbury, Pennsylvania, on the 17th day of January, 1841; died on the 8th day of May, 1912, and buried in lot 7, section A, Lutheran Cemetery at Claysburg.

The genealogical data relating to this soldier is as follows:

Parents	Brothers and Sisters	Children
	Samuel Johnston	
	James Johnston	Charles O. Johnston
Thomas Johnston	William F. Johnston	
	David Sheaffer Johnston	Jennie D. Walter
	Sallie Decker	
Margaret Cantner	Eliza Jane Durborrow	William C. Johnston
	John Wilson Johnston	
	Mary E. Berkstresser	Annie B. Johnston
	Charles Wesley Johnston	
	Nannie A. Johnston	Maggie E. Johnston
	Daniel I. Johnston	

Married Ella Barbara, daughter of Paul and Anna Mauk, on November 3, 1870. This record placed by Doctor C. O. Johnston of Claysburg.

JOHN HUGHES GALBRAITH

BE IT HERE RECORDED, that John Hughes Galbraith served in the UNITED STATES Army during the World War as a Captain, Divisional Orthopedist, 90th Division; enlisting on the 31st day of August, 1917, and honorably discharged on the 8th day of August, 1919.

Said John Hughes Galbraith was born at Altoona, Pennsylvania, on the 11th day of June, 1886; and resides at Oak Knoll, Hollidaysburg, Pa.

The discharge is recorded in volume 4, page 418, Soldier's Discharge Record, Register and Recorder's Office, Blair County Court House, Hollidaysburg, Pa.

The genealogical data relating to this soldier is as follows:

Parents	Brothers and Sisters	Children
James S. Galbraith	Cleona Shaver	John Hughes Galbraith
Katherine R. Hughes	John Hughes Galbraith	Mary Katherine Galbraith
		Jean Elizabeth Galbraith

Married Julia Elizabeth, daughter of Robert R. and Mary E. Le Van, on July 28, 1915.

LAZARUS ARTHUR DUGHI

BE IT HERE RECORDED, that Lazarus Arthur Dughi served in the UNITED STATES Army during the World War as a Private in the Medical Department; enlisting on the 24th day of December, 1917, and honorably discharged on the 20th day of December, 1918.

Said Lazarus Arthur Dughi was born at Altoona, Pennsylvania, on the 18th day of May, 1895; and resides at 1224 5th Avenue, Altoona, Pa.

The genealogical data relating to this soldier is as follows:

Parents	Brothers and Sisters	Children
	Mossimo V. Dughi	
	Adam J. Dughi	
Dominic Dughi	Lazarus Arthur Dughi	
Mary Lusardi	A. Catherine Crawford	
	Mary A. Ruble	
	Stella M. Cruse	

Married Edna Jean Bryan, daughter of John Vowinkle, on November 11, 1929.

JOSEPH BAILEY

BE IT HERE RECORDED, that Joseph Bailey served in the UNITED STATES Army during the Civil War as a Private in Company G, 77th Regiment of Pennsylvania Infantry; enlisting on the 22nd day of February, 1864, and honorably discharged on the 6th day of December, 1865.

Said Joseph Bailey was born at Huntingdon, Pennsylvania, on the 4th day of April, 1845; died on the 30th day of September, 1921, and is buried in the Geeseytown Cemetery, near Hollidaysburg.

The discharge is recorded in volume 4, page 106, Soldier's Discharge Record, Register and Recorder's Office, Blair County Court House, Hollidaysburg, Pa.

The genealogical data relating to this soldier is as follows:

Parents	Brothers and Sisters	Children
	John Bailey	George C. Bailey
	Joseph Bailey	Cora Bell Grove
John Bailey	Catherine Roach	Mary M. McMasters
	Harriett Emerick	William F. Bailey
	Stuard Bailey	John Edgar Bailey
	William Bailey	James Henry Bailey
Catherine	Samuel Bailey	Stella May Weaver
	Isabelle Jackson	
	George Bailey	
	Benjamin Bailey	

Married Nancy M., daughter of Joseph and Anna Rager, on October 5, 1870.
This record placed by Mrs. Cora Bell Grove, of Loop Station, Blair County, Pa.

WILBERT LEE GROUNDS

BE IT HERE RECORDED, that Wilbert Lee Grounds served in the UNITED STATES Army during the World War as a First Lieutenant, Medical Corps; enlisting on the 7th day of August, 1918, and honorably discharged on the 3rd day of February, 1919.

Said Wilbert Lee Grounds was born at Washington, Pennsylvania, on the 2nd day of October, 1883; and resides at 532 Park Avenue, Roaring Spring, Pa.

The discharge is recorded in volume 3, page 505, Soldier's Discharge Record, Register and Recorder's Office, Blair County Court House, Hollidaysburg, Pa.

The genealogical data relating to this soldier is as follows:

Parents	Brothers and Sisters	Children
William Henry Grounds	Anna Della Sprowls	Mary Elizabeth Good
Mary Martha Henderson	Wilbert Lee Grounds	Dorothy Lee Grounds

Married Eleanor, daughter of A. Mack and Nellie Smith, on September 6, 1911.

JACOB HARRY SHEARER

BE IT HERE RECORDED, that Jacob Harry Shearer served in the UNITED STATES Navy during the Spanish-American War as Gunners Mate and Electrician; enlisting on the 23rd day of April, 1898, and honorably discharged on the 23rd day of December, 1898.

Said Jacob Harry Shearer was born at Philadelphia, Pennsylvania, on the 2nd day of November, 1868; and resides at Rose Hill Lodge, near Altoona, Pa.

The genealogical data relating to this soldier is as follows:

Parents	Brothers and Sisters	Children
	Jacob Harry Shearer	
	Walter Shearer	
Jacob J. Shearer	William B. Shearer	
Alice N. Pine	Richard L. Shearer	
	Mary Rodman Howard	
	Alice N. Shearer	

Married Lurline Lisbet, daughter of Wm. and Exa Priere du Branch, on Feb. 10, 1902.

INDIVIDUAL RECORDS 411

JOSEPH VAN ALLMAN

BE IT HERE RECORDED, that Joseph Van Allman served in the UNITED STATES Army during the Civil War as a Private in Company B, 192nd Regiment of Pennsylvania Infantry; enlisting on the 13th day of February, 1865, and honorably discharged on the 24th day of August, 1865.

Said Joseph Van Allman was born at Frankstown, Pennsylvania, on the 30th day of June, 1836; died on the 4th day of October, 1920, and is buried in the Lutheran Cemetery at Hollidaysburg, Pa.

The genealogical data relating to this soldier is as follows:

Parents	Brothers and Sisters	Children
	Joseph Van Allman	Minnie Stevens
	Samuel Van Allman	Ida Blanche Hamilton
Adam Van Allman	William Van Allman	Catherine Robinson
	Henry Van Allman	William A. Van Allman
	Elizabeth Baird	Charles A. Van Allman
Catherine Mogul	Sarah Boyer	Rose Anna Van Allman
	Christina Wertz	Daisy Van Allman
	John Van Allman	Lillian Eberst
		S. Ross Van Allman
		Joseph Van Allman

Married Sarah Elizabeth, daughter of John and Rosanna C. Sisler on May 4, 1862.
This record placed by S. Ross Van Allman, of Hollidaysburg, Pa.

RICHARD JAMES LOUTHER

BE IT HERE RECORDED, that Richard James Louther served in the UNITED STATES Army during the World War as a Private in Headquarters Company, 320th Regiment of Infantry, 80th Division; enlisting on the 2nd day of April, 1918, and honorably discharged on the 7th day of June, 1919.

Said Richard James Louther was born at Stoystown, Pennsylvania, on the 11th day of February, 1895; and resides at 503 Spruce Street, Hollidaysburg, Pa.

The discharge is recorded in volume 1, page 452, Soldier's Discharge Record, Somerset County Court House, Somerset, Pa.

The genealogical data relating to this soldier is as follows:

Parents	Brothers and Sisters	Children
Snyder J. H. Louther	Richard J. Louther	Lois Louther
Amanda Hostetler		Louise Louther

Married Elizabeth Ogle, daughter of Earl O. and Ida Belle Houpt on January 21, 1921.

HARRIS BAIRD

BE IT HERE RECORDED, that Harris Baird served in the UNITED STATES Navy during the World War as a Machinist Mate, 2nd Cl.; enlisting on the 22nd day of June, 1918, and honorably discharged on the 21st day of June, 1922.

Said Harris Baird was born at Altoona, Pennsylvania, on the 28th day of June, 1892; and resides at 515 Front Street, Hollidaysburg, Pa.

The discharge is recorded in volume 4, page 75, Soldier's Discharge Record, Register and Recorder's Office, Blair County Court House, Hollidaysburg, Pa.

The genealogical data relating to this soldier is as follows:

Parents	Brothers and Sisters	Children
	Mary Teresa Baird	
	Harris Baird	
Ira Fay Baird	Helen Gertrude Ertl	Robert Bruce Baird
Katherine Stich	Harriet Charlotte Hoenstine	Richard Fay Baird
	Evelyn Violet Trease	
	Ira Russell Baird	

Married Nanna Marie, daughter of John F. and Annie E. Bice, on June 4, 1917.

SOLDIERS OF BLAIR COUNTY

DAVID STERRETT HAYS

BE IT HERE RECORDED, that David Sterrett Hays served in the UNITED STATES Army during the Civil War as a Surgeon, 110th Regiment of Pennsylvania Infantry; enlisting on the 1st day of November, 1861, and honorably discharged on the 3rd day of June, 1865.

Said David Sterrett Hays was born in Jackson Township, Huntingdon County, on the 10th day of December, 1833; died on the 10th day of July, 1898, and is buried in lot 105, section A, Presbyterian Cemetery at Hollidaysburg.

The genealogical data relating to this soldier is as follows:

Parents	Brothers and Sisters	Children
		Harry Price Hays
	David Sterrett Hays	David Arthur Hays
John Hays	Samuel Dale Hays	Elizabeth Griest Hays
	William Hays	Mary Edith Hays
Elizabeth Ferron	Mary Hays	Charles Ferron Hays
	Elizabeth Morrison	Bernice Woodrow Kelly
		Emma Adelaide Jackson

Married Mary Emma, daughter of Charles C. and Eliza Greist Price on June 10, 1869. This record placed by Charles F. Hays of Hollidaysburg.

ASBERRY KANTNER

BE IT HERE RECORDED, that Asberry Kantner served in the UNITED STATES Army during the Spanish-American War as a Private in Company C, 5th Regiment of Infantry, Pennsylvania Volunteers; enlisting on the 27th day of April, 1898, and honorably discharged on the 7th day of November, 1898, also, served as a Sergeant in Company H, 12th Regiment of United States Infantry; enlisting on the 6th day of December, 1898, and honorably discharged on the 5th day of December, 1901.

Said Asberry Kantner was born at Altoona, Pennsylvania, on the 10th day of October, 1875; and resides at Duncansville, Pa.

The genealogical data relating to this soldier is as follows:

Parents	Brothers and Sisters	Children
	Mary Lowe	
John Henry Kantner	Margaret Reed	Agnes Sylvina Miller
	Hannah Baker	William Marshall Kantner
Sarah Marshall	William A. Kantner	
	Asberry Kantner	

Married Annie Myrtle, daughter of George and Agnes Sylvina Walters on July 17, 1902.

GEORGE SIMON FAY

BE IT HERE RECORDED, that George Simon Fay served in the UNITED STATES Navy during the World War as a Machinists Mate, 1st Class; enlisting on the 27th day of February, 1918, and honorably discharged on the 8th day of October, 1919.

Said George Simon Fay was born at Altoona, Pennsylvania, on the 22nd day of April, 1897; and resides at 2721 Walnut Avenue, Altoona, Pa.

The discharge is recorded in volume 4, page 418, Soldier's Discharge Record, Register and Recorder's Office, Blair County Court House, Hollidaysburg, Pa.

The genealogical data relating to this soldier is as follows:

Parents	Brothers and Sisters	Children
	Matilda Fay	
George Fay	Charles Fay	Harold George Fay
	Archie W. Fay	Audrey Lorraine Fay
Catherine E. Keister	George Simon Fay	Phyllis Jean Fay
	Frank G. Fay	

Married Grace Bertha, daughter of William H. and Isa Stiver on February 21, 1921.

JAMES CAMPBELL MEGAHAN

BE IT HERE RECORDED, that James Campbell Megahan served in the UNITED STATES Army during the Civil War as a Private in Company F, 194th Regiment of Pennsylvania Infantry; enlisting on the 6th day of May, 1864, and honorably discharged on the 6th day of November, 1864.

Said James Campbell Megahan was born at McConnellstown, Pa., on the 5th day of October, 1847; and resides at 510 West 14th Street, Duncansville, Pa.

The genealogical data relating to this soldier is as follows:

Parents	Brothers and Sisters	Children
	George Washington Megahan	
	Abraham Jackson Megahan	
Jacob Megahan	Mary Jane Megahan	Martha Stephens Megahan
	J. B. Luden Megahan	
(first marriage)	Susana Margaretta Lohr	
Martha L. Stephens	James Campbell Megahan	James Jackson Megahan
	Abraham Lemon Megahan	
	Isaac Megahan	
(second marriage)		
Margaret Leonard	Acenith J. Kyler	
	John Megahan	
	Daniel Bollinger Megahan	
	Ida Gill	

Married Felice, daughter of John and Maria Jane Jackson on May 7, 1890.

GILBERT SEARLE WATTS

BE IT HERE RECORDED, that Gilbert Searle Watts served in the UNITED STATES Navy during the World War as a Chief Quartermaster, Student Aviator, Naval Reserve Force; enlisting on the 19th day of July, 1918, and honorably discharged on the 22nd day of November, 1918.

Said Gilbert Searle Watts was born at Knoxville, Tennessee, on the 14th day of December, 1896; and resides in Antis Township, Blair County, Pa.

The genealogical data relating to this soldier is as follows:

Parents	Brothers and Sisters	Children
Ralph L. Watts	Gilbert Searle Watts	Marjorie Jane Watts
	Curtis McClure Watts	
Hattie Searle	Grace Elizabeth Bell	Elizabeth Ross Watts

Married Mary Agnes, daughter of James Irvin and Laura Ross Lytle on June 29, 1918.

OSCAR AAGE HANSON

BE IT HERE RECORDED, that Oscar Aage Hanson served in the UNITED STATES Army during the World War as a Cook in Company E, 305th Regiment of Engineers, 80th Division; enlisting on the 19th day of September, 1917, and honorably discharged on the 11th day of June, 1919.

Said Oscar Aage Hanson was born at Korsor, Denmark, on the 5th day of January, 1889; and resides at Dell Delight, Hollidaysburg, Pa.

The discharge is recorded in volume 2, page 399, Soldier's Discharge Record, Register and Recorder's Office, Blair County Court House, Hollidaysburg, Pa.

The genealogical data relating to this soldier is as follows:

Parents	Brothers and Sisters	Children
	Julius August Hansen	
	Elna Dagmas Hansen	
George August Hansen	Rigmor Hansen	
Camilla Hansen	Oscar Aage Hanson	
	Helge Camilla Hansen	
	Marie Elizabeth Jacobsen	

Married Hellen Mary, daughter of Alexander L. and Martha E. Figart on Jan. 31, 1925.

JOHN JOSEPH HABERSTROH

BE IT HERE RECORDED, that John Joseph Haberstroh served in the UNITED STATES Army during the World War as a Second Lieutenant, Ordnance Department; enlisting on the 30th day of January, 1918, and honorably discharged on the 15th day of April, 1919.

Said John Joseph Haberstroh was born at McKeesport, Pennsylvania, on the 6th day of August, 1894; died on the 10th day of May, 1939, and is buried in lot 49, section C, Calvary Cemetery at Altoona, Pa.

The genealogical data relating to this soldier is as follows:

Parents	Brothers and Sisters	Children
	Louis W. F. Haberstroh	
	John Joseph Haberstroh	
Louis F. Haberstroh	Helen C. Schmid	Lillian Esther Haberstroh
Mary A. Fitzpatrick	A. Rea Haberstroh	John Joseph Haberstroh
	Ruth C. Walton	
	James H. Haberstroh	
	Robert C. Haberstroh	

Married Mary Esther, daughter of John E. and Anna A. Nowland, on August 22, 1922. This record placed by Robert C. Haberstroh, of Altoona, Pa.

WILLIAM DAVID MAUK

BE IT HERE RECORDED, that William David Mauk served in the UNITED STATES Army during the Spanish-American War as a Private in Company M, 47th Regiment of Infantry, United States Volunteers; enlisting on the 25th day of September, 1899, and honorably discharged on the 22nd day of March, 1901.

Said William David Mauk was born at Claysburg, Pennsylvania, on the 14th day of July, 1877; and resides at Pitcairn, Pa.

The genealogical data relating to this soldier is as follows:

Parents	Brothers and Sisters	Children
	Hattie Sophie Kurfman	
George W. Mauk	Samuel P. Mauk	
	William D. Mauk	
Henrietta Shafer	G. Edmund Mauk	
	John S. Mauk	

Married Minnie Gorman.
This record placed by Samuel P. Mauk, of Claysburg, Pa.

CHARLES ARLON AUKER

BE IT HERE RECORDED, that Charles Arlon Auker served in the UNITED STATES Army during the World War as a Private in the Students Army Training Corps, Dickinson College; enlisting on the 1st day of October, 1918, and honorably discharged on the 14th day of December, 1918.

Said Charles Arlon Auker was born at Mifflintown, Pennsylvania, on the 10th day of January, 1899; and resides at 1106 26th Avenue, Altoona, Pa.

The discharge is recorded in volume 6, page 243, Soldier's Discharge Record, Register and Recorder's Office, Blair County Court House, Hollidaysburg, Pa.

The genealogical data relating to this soldier is as follows:

Parents	Brothers and Sisters	Children
	Hazel May Auker	
	Theorus R. Auker	
Reuben L. Auker	Jay Stoner Auker	Charles Arlon Auker
	Charles Arlon Auker	
Minnie N. Stoner	Rebecca Smith	Howard Reuben Auker
	Samuel Irvin Auker	
	Katherine Kreps	

Married Grace Beatrice, daughter of Howard K. and Gertrude Jacoby, on Sept. 1, 1928.

INDIVIDUAL RECORDS 415

WILLIAM WILLIAMS

BE IT HERE RECORDED, that William Williams served in the UNITED STATES Army during the Mexican War as a First Lieutenant in Company B, 2nd Regiment of Infantry, Pennsylvania Volunteers; enlisting on the 21st day of December, 1846, and honorably discharged on the 14th day of July, 1848; also, served during the Civil War as a Major, 14th Regiment of United States Infantry; enlisting on the 14th day of May, 1861, and honorably discharged on the 8th day of June, 1863.

Said William Williams was born at Greensburg, Pennsylvania, on the 7th day of June, 1827; died on the 30th day of January, 1906, and is buried in lot 88, section A, Presbyterian Cemetery at Hollidaysburg, Pa.

The genealogical data relating to this soldier is as follows:

Parents	Brothers and Sisters	Children
		Rebecca Calvin Fleniken
		Marian Catharine Fleniken
Joseph Williams		Thomas B. M. Williams
	William Williams	Jane E. M. Williams
....		Sarah Ruth Frazier
		Thomas B. M. Williams
		William C. Williams
		George Riddle Williams
		Harry Williams

Married Sarah Jane, daughter of Thomas B. and Jane E. Moore, on November 4, 1849.
Married Mary Jane, daughter of Louis H. and Lydia E. Williams, on April 2, 1868.
This record placed by John C. McKone of 424 Allegheny Street, Hollidaysburg, Pa.

BENNER MARSHALL WILSON

BE IT HERE RECORDED, that Benner Marshall Wilson served in the UNITED STATES Army during the World War as a First Lieutenant, Air Service; enlisting on the 4th day of June, 1917, and honorably discharged on the 15th day of Mar., 1920.

Said Benner Marshall Wilson was born at Altoona, Pennsylvania, on the 15th day of December, 1893, and resides at 114 Ruskin Drive, Altoona, Pa.

The discharge is recorded in volume 6, page 222, Soldier's Discharge Record, Register and Recorder's Office, Blair County Court House, Hollidaysburg, Pa.

The genealogical data relating to this soldier is as follows:

Parents	Brothers and Sisters	Children
Harry L. Wilson	Benner Marshall Wilson	
Sarah Elsie Pringle	Kenneth E. Wilson	Sarah Virginia Wilson
	Esther Jane Glass	

Married Helen R. C., daughter of John G. and Virginia Sellers, on September 26, 1924.

HARRY ELLSWORTH LOOMIS

BE IT HERE RECORDED, that Harry Ellsworth Loomis served in the UNITED STATES Army during the World War as a Private in the 15th Ambulance Company, attached to the 5th Marines; enlisting on the 7th day of June, 1917, and honorably discharged on the 14th day of August, 1919.

Said Harry Ellsworth Loomis was born at Altoona, Pennsylvania, on the 18th day of June, 1894; and resides at 1113 Seventeenth Avenue, Altoona, Pa.

The genealogical data relating to this soldier is as follows:

Parents	Brothers and Sisters	Children
	Edgar Loomis	
	Harry Ellsworth Loomis	
Mayberry Milton Loomis	Sarah May Loomis	
	Anna May Loomis	Charlotte Jean Loomis
Sadie Cashling	Madeline June Loomis	
	Clarence Loomis	
	Raymond M. Loomis	

Married Leona Lucy, daughter of John and Alice Bogle, in 1923.

SOLDIERS OF BLAIR COUNTY

LAWRENCE PATRICK DRASS

BE IT HERE RECORDED, that Lawrence Patrick Drass served in the UNITED STATES Army during the World War as a Sergeant in the 113th Squadron, 2nd Regiment A.S.A.P.; enlisting on the 1st day of March, 1918, and honorably discharged on the 27th day of January, 1919.

Said Lawrence Patrick Drass was born at Hollidaysburg, Pennsylvania, on the 16th day of March, 1892; died on the 27th day of May, 1921, and is buried in lot 452, St. Marys Cemetery at Hollidaysburg, Pa.

The discharge is recorded in volume 2, page 30, Soldier's Discharge Record, Register and Recorder's Office, Blair County Court House, Hollidaysburg, Pa.

The genealogical data relating to this soldier is as follows:

Parents	Brothers and Sisters
	John N. Drass
	Alexander L. Drass
John Baptist Drass	Joseph F. Drass
	Mary M. Drass
	Benjamin T. Drass
Elizabeth Gill	Lawrence P. Drass
	Isabelle G. Drass
	Bernard M. Drass

This record placed by John N. Drass, of 412 Allegheny St., Hollidaysburg, Pa.

WILLIAM BENJAMIN REILEY

BE IT HERE RECORDED, that William Benjamin Reiley served in the UNITED STATES Army during the World War as a Private in the Machine Gun Company, 315th Regiment of Infantry, 79 Division; enlisting on the 29th day of April, 1918, and honorably discharged on the 6th day of June, 1919.

Said William Benjamin Reiley was born at Seidersville, Pennsylvania, on the 16th day of April, 1896; and resides at Loop, Pa.

The discharge is recorded in volume 3, page 46, Soldier's Discharge Record, Register and Recorder's Office, Blair County Court House, Hollidaysburg, Pa.

The genealogical data relating to this soldier is as follows:

Parents	Brothers and Sisters	Children
	Lovean Freeman Reiley	Betty Marie Reiley
George Henry Reiley	Emma Grace Pfeiffer	Irene Priscilla Reiley
Angelico Sheetz	William Benjamin Reiley	Jean Georgetta Reiley
	Mary Grossett	Jane Grace Reiley

Married Hattie May, daughter of George and Priscilla Lyons, on February 12, 1918.

HARRY LANG JOHNSTON

BE IT HERE RECORDED, that Harry Lang Johnston served in the UNITED STATES Army during the Spanish-American War as Sergeant Major of the 5th Regiment of Infantry, Pennsylvania Volunteers; enlisting on the 27th day of April, 1898, and honorably discharged on the 7th day of November, 1898.

Said Harry Lang Johnston was born at Hollidaysburg, Pennsylvania, on the 1st day of April, 1873; and resides at 3508 Oneida Avenue, Altoona, Pa.

The discharge is recorded in volume 4, page 81, Soldier's Discharge Record, Register and Recorder's Office, Blair County Court House, Hollidaysburg, Pa.

The genealogical data relating to this soldier is as follows:

Parents	Brothers and Sisters	Children
	Harry Lang Johnston	
William Noble Johnston	Nellie Bricker	Helen Louise Hammitt
	Charles Vowinkle Johnston	
Laura Lang	Marie Lawson Johnston	Anna Margaret Sheldon
	Mary Keyes Johnston	

(First marriage)
Catherine Snively   Annie Maria Leader

Married Annie Cherry, daughter of Benjamin M. and Louisa Bunker, on May 4, 1899.

INDIVIDUAL RECORDS

CHRISTIAN GAST

BE IT HERE RECORDED, that Christian Gast served in the UNITED STATES Army during the Revolutionary War as Private in Captain John Schneider's Company of Northumberland County Militia during May and June, 1780.

Said Christian Gast was born in Pennsylvania, on the 11th day of August, 1762; died on the 25th day of September, 1843, and is buried in the Frankstown Cemetery, near Hollidaysburg, Pa.

The genealogical data relating to this soldier is as follows:

Parents	Brothers and Sisters	Children
		Christian Gast
	Catherine Maurer	John Gast
John Christian Gast		George Gast
		Jacob Gast
	John Nicholas Gast	William Gast
Catherine Brandt		Samuel Gast
		Catherine Leamer
	Christian Gast	Mary Myers
		Margaret Geesey
		Sallie Koofer

Married Margaretta, daughter of Peter Boras about 1787.
This record placed by R. D. Lorenz, of Roaring Spring, Pa.

EDWARD JAMES BIGLEY

BE IT HERE RECORDED, that Edward James Bigley served in the UNITED STATES Army during the Mexican Border Campaign as a First Lieutenant and Adjutant of the 3rd Battalion, 10th Regiment of Infantry, Pennsylvania National Guard; being mustered into the Federal Service on the 4th day of July, 1916, and mustered out on the 25th day of October, 1916.

Said Edward James Bigley was born at Brisbin, Clearfield County, Pa., on the 12th day of March, 1876; and resides at 1211 Fifteenth St., Altoona, Pa.

The genealogical data relating to this soldier is as follows:

Parents	Brothers and Sisters	Children
William Bigley	Edward James Bigley	John Allen Bigley
Evelyn Weakland	Marcellus J. Bigley	Martha Elizabeth Hauber

Married Leona, daughter of Wesley and Carrie Brumbaugh, on October 29, 1901.

CLYDE BARTLEY SAYLOR

BE IT HERE RECORDED, that Clyde Bartley Saylor served in the UNITED STATES Army during the World War as a Sergeant in the 16th Company, C.M.G.O.-T.S.; enlisting on the 16th day of May, 1917, and honorably discharged on the 26th day of November, 1918.

Said Clyde Bartley Saylor was born at Altoona, Pennsylvania, on the 13th day of May, 1895; and resides at 2515 Eighth Avenue, Altoona, Pa.

The discharge is recorded in volume 4, page 420, Soldier's Discharge Record, Register and Recorder's Office, Blair County Court House, Hollidaysburg, Pa.

The genealogical data relating to this soldier is as follows:

Parents	Brothers and Sisters	Children
	William Saylor	
	James L. Saylor	
	Laura Orner	
John Calvin Saylor	Howard D. Saylor	
	Sarah Plitt	
	Ira Saylor	
	Mary Crawford	
Annie Maria Bartley	Clyde Bartley Saylor	
	Herbert S. Saylor	
	Leroy Saylor	

Married Blanche Edna, daughter of William H. and Rosanna Kemberlin, on Nov. 27, 1919

SOLDIERS OF BLAIR COUNTY

BENJAMIN LIGHTNER HEWIT

BE IT HERE RECORDED, that Benjamin Lightner Hewit served in the UNITED STATES Army during the Civil War as a Private in Company A, 23rd Pennsylvania Militia; enlisting on the 21st day of September, 1862, and honorably discharged on the 30th day of September, 1862; also, served as a Private in Company A, Independent Battalion Pennsylvania Militia; enlisting on the 3rd day of July, 1863, and honorably discharged on the 8th day of August, 1863; also, served as a Major, Paymaster of Cavalry; enlisting on the 18th day of March, 1864, and honorably discharged on the 1st of November, 1865.

Said Benjamin Lightner Hewit was born at Petersburg, Pennsylvania, on the 4th day of June, 1833; died on the 10th day of March, 1894, and is buried in lot 52, section A, Presbyterian Cemetery at Hollidaysburg, Pa.

The genealogical data relating to this soldier is as follows:

Parents	Brothers and Sisters	Children
Nicholas Hewit	Benjamin Lightner Hewit	Oliver Hartley Hewit
Mary Murphy		Harry Davis Hewit

Married Lillian, daughter of Samuel and Margarette Davis, on June 18, 1857.
Married Mary W., daughter of Joseph and Mary Smith, on December 4, 1874.
This record placed by Herndon Hewit of 719 Allegheny St., Hollidaysburg, Pa.

BENJAMIN HARTLEY HEWIT

BE IT HERE RECORDED, that Benjamin Hartley Hewit served in the UNITED STATES Army during the World War as a Captain of Company F, 316th Regiment of Infantry, 79th Division; enlisting on the 12th day of May, 1917, and killed in action near Montfaucon, France, on the 29th day of September, 1918.

Said Benjamin Hartley Hewit was born at Jamestown, North Dakota, on the 26th day of July, 1894; and is buried in grave 1, plot B, Meuse-Argonne Cemetery, Nantillois, France.

The genealogical data relating to this soldier is as follows:

Parents	Brothers and Sisters	Children
	Mary Lillian Brotherlin	
Oliver Hartley Hewit	Benjamin Hartley Hewit	
	Elizabeth Myers Hewit	
Elizabeth Patton Myers	Herndon Hewit	
	Oliver Hartley Hewit	

This record placed by Herndon Hewit of 719 Allegheny St., Hollidaysburg, Pa.

HERNDON HEWIT

BE IT HERE RECORDED, that Herndon Hewit served in the UNITED STATES Army during the World War as a First Lieutenant and Instructor, Officers Training School; enlisting on the 27th day of August, 1917, and honorably discharged on the 13th day of December, 1918.

Said Herndon Hewit was born at Duluth, Minnesota, on the 31st day of October, 1892; and resides at 719 Allegheny Street, Hollidaysburg, Pa.

The genealogical data relating to this soldier is as follows:

Parents	Brothers and Sisters	Children
	Mary Lillian Brotherlin	Benjamin Hartley Hewit
Oliver Hartley Hewit	Benjamin Hartley Hewit	Alice Bubb Hewit
	Elizabeth Myers Hewit	Elizabeth Myers Hewit
Elizabeth Patton Myers	Herndon Hewit	George Good Hewit
	Oliver Hartley Hewit	

Married Sarah Burrows, daughter of George M. H. and Alice Bubb Good, on Dec. 7, 1920.

INDIVIDUAL RECORDS 419
RALPH ROHRER WHITTAKER
BE IT HERE RECORDED, that Ralph Rohrer Whittaker served in the UNITED STATES Army during the Spanish-American War as a Private in Company A, 5th Regiment of Infantry, Pennsylvania Volunteers; enlisting on the 7th day of May, 1898, and honorably discharged on the 7th day of November, 1898; also, served during the World War as a Captain in the Medical Corps; enlisting on the 15th day of June, 1918, and honorably discharged on the 3rd day of July, 1919.

Said Ralph Rohrer Whittaker was born in Porter Township, Huntingdon County, Pa., on the 25th day of November, 1878; and resides at Williamsburg, Pa.

The discharges are recorded in volume 4, pages 414 and 415, Soldier's Discharge Record, Register and Recorder's Office, Court House, Hollidaysburg, Pa.

The genealogical data relating to this soldier is as follows:

Parents	Brothers and Sisters	Children
	Fred A. Whittaker	
William A. Whittaker	Wilbur H. Whittaker	Helen Louise Pryor
Caroline A. Huyette	Mabel C. Whittaker	Ralph Rohrer Whittaker
	Ralph Rohrer Whittaker	

Married Helen W., daughter of George and Elizabeth Ullery, on November 24, 1909.
Married Marie A., daughter of David and Chana Gates, on December 19, 1936.

SAMUEL M. F. MORGART
BE IT HERE RECORDED, that Samuel M. F. Morgart served in the UNITED STATES Army during the World War as a Private in the Medical Corps; enlisting on the 12th of December, 1917, and honorably discharged on the 17th of April, 1919.

Said Samuel M. F. Morgart was born at Everett, Pennsylvania, on the 9th day of June, 1894; and resides at 311 Main Street, Roaring Spring, Pa.

The discharge is recorded in volume 5, page 28, Soldier's Discharge Record, Register and Recorder's Office, Blair County Court House, Hollidaysburg, Pa.

The genealogical data relating to this soldier is as follows:

Parents	Brothers and Sisters	Children
	Jessie Ritchey	
	Lena Morgart	
Andrew J. Morgart	Samuel M. F. Morgart	Dorothy Marie Morgart
	Fannie Morgart	
Amanda E. Heckman	G. Harold Morgart	Donald Theodore Morgart
	Theodore O. Morgart	
	Marie Bechtel	

Married Mary M., daughter of Solomon S. Horton, on December 27, 1922.

FLOYD GUANAR HOENSTINE
BE IT HERE RECORDED, that Floyd Guanar Hoenstine served in the UNITED STATES Army during the World War as a Second Lieutenant in Company C, 55th Regiment of Infantry, 7th Division; enlisting on the 27th day of August, 1917, and honorably discharged on the 11th day of September, 1919.

Said Floyd Guanar Hoenstine was born at St. Clairsville, Bedford County, Pa., on the 31st day of July, 1895; and resides at 418 Wayne St., Hollidaysburg, Pa.

The discharge is recorded in volume 4, page 68, Soldier's Discharge Record, Register and Recorder's Office, Blair County Court House, Hollidaysburg, Pa.

The genealogical data relating to this soldier is as follows:

Parents	Brothers and Sisters	Children
	Bertha Olive Saupp	
	Floyd Guanar Hoenstine	
Wilson Elmer Hoenstine	Homer Harold Hoenstine	Floyd Baird Hoenstine
	Carl Ross Hoenstine	
Mary Elizabeth Claycomb	Charles Arthur Hoenstine	Barbara Ann Hoenstine
	Harry Calvin Hoenstine	
	Alvin Daniel Hoenstine	

Married Harriett Charlotte, daughter of Ira Fay and Katherine Baird, on Aug. 27, 1928.

SAMUEL LESLEY HARE

BE IT HERE RECORDED, that Samuel Lesley Hare served in the UNITED STATES Army during the Civil War as a Private in Company E, 84th Regiment of Pennsylvania Infantry and transferred to Company I, 57th Regiment of Pennsylvania Infantry; enlisting on the 2nd day of October, 1861, and honorably discharged on the 29th day of June, 1865.

Said Samuel Lesley Hare was born at Allenville, Mifflin County, Pa., on the 6th day of November, 1841; died on the 16th day of March, 1916, and is buried in lot 87, section CC, Rose Hill Cemetery at Altoona, Pa.

The genealogical data relating to this soldier is as follows:

Parents	Brothers and Sisters	Children
	Sara Aurandt	Martha M. Lafferty
	John T. Hare	Maude H. Smith
William M. Hare	Mary Hyle	Harry I. Hare
	William M. Hare	Thomas C. Hare
Matilda Goodman	Samuel Lesley Hare	Elizabeth S. Hare
	Adam L. Hare	Fern H. Hahn
	Caroline Hare	

Married Mary D., daughter of John and Mary Donelly.
This record placed by Hon. Thomas C. Hare, of 2012 Broad Avenue, Altoona, Pa.

JOHN EDWIN HARVEY

BE IT HERE RECORDED, that John Edwin Harvey served in the UNITED STATES Army during the World War as a Sergeant in Headquarters Company, 35th Engineers; enlisting on the 12th day of September, 1917, and honorably discharged on the 12th day of June, 1919.

Said John Edwin Harvey was born at Milroy, Pennsylvania, on the 1st day of May, 1898; and resides at Bellwood, Pennsylvania.

The discharge is recorded in volume 6, page 246, Soldier's Discharge Record, Register and Recorder's Office, Blair County Court House, Hollidaysburg, Pa.

The genealogical data relating to this soldier is as follows:

Parents	Brothers and Sisters	Children
	Mary A. Barron	John William Harvey
William B. Harvey	John Edwin Harvey	Ann Elizabeth Harvey
Annie E. Russler	Charlotte Haupt	Samuel Edwin Harvey
	Helen G. Harvey	

Married Sara Ann, daughter of Orla C. and Martha E. Brenneman, on June 22, 1922.

MORGAN JOHN SHEEDY

BE IT HERE RECORDED, that Morgan John Sheedy served in the UNITED STATES Navy during the World War as a Seaman, 1 Class; enlisting on the 30th day of July, 1918, and honorably discharged on the 30th day of September, 1921.

Said Morgan John Sheedy was born at Altoona, Pennsylvania, on the 25th day of September, 1896; and resides at 310 Wopsononock Ave., Altoona, Pa.

The discharge is recorded in volume 3, page 517, Soldier's Discharge Record, Register and Recorder's Office, Blair County Court House, Hollidaysburg, Pa.

The genealogical data relating to this soldier is as follows:

Parents	Brothers and Sisters	Children
	Michael Morgan Sheedy	
	Elizabeth Josephine Coghlan	Mary Madelyn Sheedy
John Madden Sheedy	Morgan John Sheedy	Marie Eileen Sheedy
	John Austin Sheedy	Morgan Madden Sheedy
	Thomas Madden Sheedy	Virginia Ann Sheedy
Marcella Young	Paul Sheedy	Morgan Madden Sheedy
	Morgan John Sheedy	John Patrick Sheedy
	Raymond Joseph Sheedy	
	Gerald Patrick Sheedy	

Married Madelyn Kathryn, daughter of Elmer G. and Pauline Rhodes, on Oct. 17, 1928.

INDIVIDUAL RECORDS 421

SENECA WILLIAMSON COFFEY

BE IT HERE RECORDED, that Seneca Williamson Coffey served in the UNITED STATES Army during the Civil War as a Private in Company B, 38th Regiment of New Jersey Infantry; enlisting on the 5th day of September, 1864, and honorably discharged on the 30th day of June, 1865.

Said Seneca Williamson Coffey was born at Ringoes, New Jersey, on the 22nd day of July, 1846; died on the 2nd day of November, 1933, and is buried in lot 58, section S, Greenwood Cemetery at Wheeling, West Virginia.

The genealogical data relating to this soldier is as follows:

Parents	Brothers and Sisters	Children
		Seneca Arthur Coffey
	Seneca Williamson Coffey	Jennie May Gerard Coffey
Nathaniel Coffey		Florence Margaret Elig
	Lottie Gathercole	Anna Rachel Coffey
Elizabeth MacManus		William Augustus Coffey
	William Coffey	Gerald Joseph Coffey
		Nathaniel Seldon Coffey

Married Sarah Frances, daughter of Gideon O. and Mary Jane Gerard, on Feb. 16, 1876. This record placed by S. Arthur Coffey, of Sylvan Hills, Hollidaysburg, Pa.

THOMAS GETTEMY PEOPLES

BE IT HERE RECORDED, that Thomas Gettemy Peoples served in the UNITED STATES Army during the World War as a Sergeant in Company A, 622nd Field Signal Battalion; enlisting on the 10th day of May, 1918, and honorably discharged on the 18th day of December, 1918.

Said Thomas Gettemy Peoples was born at New Florence, Pa., on the 12th day of July, 1888, and resides at 528 Fourth Avenue, Juniata, Altoona, Pa.

The genealogical data relating to this soldier is as follows:

Parents	Brothers and Sisters	Children
James Newton Peoples	Thomas Gettemy Peoples	Thomas Gettemy Peoples
Levina Gettemy	Grace Bailey	Mary Virginia Peoples
	May Cochran Grimminger	

Married Alma M., daughter of John H. and Annie Shoemaker, on November 24, 1932

HARVEY MILTON LIEBEGOTT

BE IT HERE RECORDED, that Harvey Milton Liebegott served in the UNITED STATES Army during the World War as a Private in the Aviation Section; enlisting on the 16th day of January, 1918, and honorably discharged on the 17th day of July, 1918; also, served as a Private in the Medical Department; enlisting on the 29th day of August, 1918, and honorably discharged on the 6th day of May, 1919.

Said Harvey Milton Liebegott was born at New Enterprise, Pennsylvania, on the 22nd day of February, 1890; and resides at Duncansville, Pa.

The discharge is recorded in volume 3, page 295, Soldier's Discharge Record, Register and Recorder's Office, Blair County Court House, Hollidaysburg, Pa.

The genealogical data relating to this soldier is as follows:

Parents	Brothers and Sisters	Children
	George H. Liebegott	
	Minnie K. Liebegott	
	Alleta M. Liebegott	
Christian Liebegott	M. Luther Liebegott	
	Charles E. Liebegott	
	E. Grace Lykens	
Annetta Furry	H. Emory Liebegott	
	Thella V. Liebegott	
	Annetta Liebegott	
	John C. Liebegott	
	Alice R. Liebegott	

JAMES KEATLEY

BE IT HERE RECORDED, that James Keatley served in the UNITED STATES Army during the Civil War as a Captain of Company H, 37th Regiment of Pennsylvania Infantry; enlisting on the 30th day of April, 1861, and honorably discharged on the 24th day of May, 1864.

Said James Keatley was born at Strattonville, Pennsylvania, in 1837; died on the 19th day of November, 1928, and is buried in lot 411, section OO, Rose Hill Cemetery at Altoona, Pa.

The genealogical data relating to this soldier is as follows:

Parents	Brothers and Sisters	Children
	James Keatley	
	Hattie Keatley	Annetta Belle Stolz
John Keatley	Frank Keatley	John Crawford Keatley
	Clara Keatley	Claire Keatley
	Homer Keatley	Charles Keatley
Katherine Jack	John Keatley	Evelyn Smead
	Emma Keatley	Verna Davidson
	William Keatley	
	Katherine Keatley	

Married Emma Bell, daughter of James C. and Mary Liebhart, in 1875.
This record placed by Doctor Paul K. Stolz, of Hollidaysburg, Pa.

BENJAMIN FRANKLIN HUGHES

BE IT HERE RECORDED, that Benjamin Franklin Hughes served in the UNITED STATES Army during the World War under the name of Frank Hughes as a Corporal in the 507th Aero Squadron; enlisting on the 5th day of February, 1918, and honorably discharged on the 24th day of March, 1919.

Said Benjamin Franklin Hughes was born at Altoona, Pennsylvania, on the 25th day of December, 1899, and resides at Bellwood, Pa.

The discharge is recorded in volume 5, page 263, Soldier's Discharge Record, Register and Recorder's Office, Blair County Court House, Hollidaysburg, Pa.

The genealogical data relating to this soldier is as follows:

Parents	Brothers and Sisters	Children
Scott Edward Hughes	Benjamin Franklin Hughes	Martha Louise Hughes
Rosie Marie Green		

Married Sarah Leffard, daughter of Edward and Jennie Keyes, on Nov. 29, 1920.

JOHN JACOB RUSSELL WILLIAMS

BE IT HERE RECORDED, that John Jacob R. Williams served in the UNITED STATES Army during the World War as a Private, Military Guard Section, Ordnance Department; enlisting on the 21st day of July, 1918, and honorably discharged on the 13th day of March, 1919.

Said John Jacob Russell Williams was born at Blanchard, Pennsylvania, on the 21st day of June, 1895; and resides at 1310 21st Avenue, Altoona, Pa.

The discharge is recorded in volume 1, page 158, Soldier's Discharge Record, Register and Recorder's Office, Centre County Court House, Bellefonte, Pa.

The genealogical data relating to this soldier is as follows:

Parents	Brothers and Sisters
	Harrison Glenn Williams
	Shuman Sylvester Williams
Isaac Richard Williams	Eliza Catherine Lucas
	Henry Scott Williams
Catherine Matilda Holter	Nancy Idella Williams
	George Frank Williams
	Laura Claudia Stolz
	John Jacob Russell Williams

Married Mary Celestia, daughter of Jacob and Elizabeth Reish, on March 30, 1927.

INDIVIDUAL RECORDS 423

JOHN PHILIP DE HAAS

BE IT HERE RECORDED, that John Philip de Haas served in the UNITED STATES Army during the Revolutionary War as a Brigadier General, Continental Line; enlisting on the 22nd day of January, 1776, and honorably discharged on the 3rd day of November, 1783.

Said John Philip de Haas was born in Holland, about 1735; died on the 3rd day of June, 1786, and is buried at Philadelphia, Pa.

The genealogical data relating to this soldier is as follows:

Parents	Brothers and Sisters	Children
John Nicholas de Haas	John Philip de Haas	John Philip de Haas
Eleanor Bingham		Henrietta Craig

This record placed by James F. De Haas of 1008 21st Avenue, Altoona, Pa.

HENRY M. BOSSERT

BE IT HERE RECORDED, that Henry M. Bossert served in the UNITED STATES Army during the Civil War as a Captain in Company C, 11th Regiment of Pennsylvania Infantry; enlisting on the 25th day of April, 1861, and honorably discharged on the 25th day of July, 1861; also, served as a Colonel of the 137th Regiment of Pennsylvania Infantry; enlisting on the 25th day of August, 1862, and honorably discharged on the 3rd day of March, 1863.

Said Henry M. Bossert was born in Northampton County, Pennsylvania, on the 13th day of January, 1825, died on the 25th day of January, 1892, and is buried in the Noyes Cemetery at Westport, Pa.

The genealogical data relating to this soldier is as follows:

Parents	Brothers and Sisters	Children
	Henry M. Bossert	George Bossert
	John Y. Bossert	Elizabeth E. Bossert
Jacob Bossert	Frances Bossert	John S. Bossert
....		Anna C. Heilman
		William Bossert
		Caroline Bossert
		M. Frances de Haas

Married Mary Catherine, daughter of George and Elizabeth Brown, on Nov. 11, 1846.

This record placed by James F. De Haas, of 1008 21st Avenue, Altoona, Pa.

JAMES FLOYD DE HAAS

BE IT HERE RECORDED, that James Floyd DeHaas served in the UNITED STATES Army during the World War as a Private in the 379th Aero Squadron; enlisting on the 11th day of February, 1918, and honorably discharged on the 3rd day of February, 1919.

Said James Floyd DeHaas was born at Westport, Pennsylvania, on the 12th day of September, 1898; and resides at 1008 21st Avenue, Altoona, Pa.

The discharge is recorded in volume 1, page 291, Soldier's Discharge Record, Register and Recorder's Office, Clinton County Court House, Lock Haven, Pa.

The genealogical data relating to this soldier is as follows:

Parents	Brothers and Sisters	Children
	John Henry DeHaas	
Joseph R. DeHaas	Mable Berry	(first marriage)
	William LeRoy DeHaas	Inez Margaret DeHaas
M. Frances Bossert	Florence Sterner	
	John Yost Bossert DeHaas	
	Ruth DeHaas	(second marriage)
	James Floyd DeHaas	Joseph Francis DeHaas
	Clair Hiram DeHaas	

Married Blanche, daughter of Anson O. and Sarah Thomas, on March 11, 1922.
Married Esther E. Elder, daughter of James C. and Esther Hatch, on September 27, 1933.

SOLDIERS OF BLAIR COUNTY

JOHN BURNS McKEAGE

BE IT HERE RECORDED, that John Burns McKeage served in the UNITED STATES Army during the Mexican War. (Services not available.) Also, served during Civil War as a First Lieutenant in Company A, 3rd Regiment of Pennsylvania Infantry; enlisting on the 20th day of April, 1861, and honorably discharged on the 29th day of July, 1861, also served as Captain in Company G, 125th Regiment of Pennsylvania Infantry; enlisting on the 13th day of August, 1862, and honorably discharged on the 18th day of May, 1863, also served as a Lieutenant Colonel, Independent Battalion Pennsylvania Militia, enlisting on the 3rd day of July, 1863, and honorably discharged on the 18th day of May, 1863, also served as a Captain in Company E, 184th Regiment of Pennsylvania Infantry; enlisting on the 13th day of May, 1864, and honorably discharged on the 14th day of July, 1865.

Said John Burns McKeage was born at Baltimore, Maryland, on the 15th day of April, 1827; died on the 12th day of February, 1874, and is buried in lot 14, section A, Presbyterian Cemetery at Hollidaysburg, Pa.

The genealogical data relating to this soldier is as follows:

Parents	Brothers and Sisters	Children
		Fannie E. Myers
Robert McKeage	Jane Elizabeth Bracken	Jane Bracken Barr
Elizabeth Lewis	John Burns McKeage	Ann Fletcher McKeage
(second marriage)		Robert Burns McKeage
Ann Catherine Fletcher		Elizabeth B. Fisher

Married Sarah, daughter of William and Elizabeth Butler, in June, 1863.
This record placed by Robert M. Barr, of 511 Union St., Hollidaysburg, Pa.

HOMER FOSTER MOHLER

BE IT HERE RECORDED, that Homer Foster Mohler served in the UNITED STATES Army during the World War as a Private in Evacuation Unit No. 49; enlisting on the 19th day of October, 1917, and honorably discharged September 3, 1919.

Said Homer Foster Mohler was born at Maitland, Pennsylvania, on the 9th day of March, 1898; and resides at 214 Second Avenue, Altoona, Pa.

The discharge is recorded in the Soldier's Discharge Record, Register and Recorder's Office, Mifflin County Court House, Lewistown, Pa.

The genealogical data relating to this soldier is as follows:

Parents	Brothers and Sisters	Children
John Stroup Mohler	Homer Foster Mohler	
(second marriage)	Herman Walter Mohler	
Ada Brenneman	Samuel Boyd Mohler	
	Sarah Romayne Catherman	

Married Susan, daughter of Lewis and Laura Fleck, on October 14, 1920.

LESLIE WILBUR GREEN

BE IT HERE RECORDED, that Leslie Wilbur Green served in the UNITED STATES Army during the World War as a Private in Battery E, 51st Coast Artillery Corps; enlisting on the 1st day of May, 1917, and honorably discharged on the 28th day of March, 1919.

Said Leslie Wilbur Green was born at Roaring Spring, Pennsylvania, on the 29th day of July, 1886; and resides at 750 Church St., Roaring Spring, Pa.

The discharge is recorded in volume 5, page 126, Soldier's Discharge Record, Register and Recorder's Office, Blair County Court House, Hollidaysburg, Pa.

The genealogical data relating to this soldier is as follows:

Parents	Brothers and Sisters	Children
	Pearl G. Burket	
Collins D. Green	Leslie Wilbur Green	Max Leslie Green
Florence M. McKee	Chester R. Green	
	Loretta Wood	

Married Laura M., daughter of John A. and Anna W. Shultz, on November 21, 1920.

INDIVIDUAL RECORDS 425

JAMES McMICKEN

BE IT HERE RECORDED, that James McMicken served in the UNITED STATES Army during the Revolutionary War as a Lieutenant in the Bucks County Militia, from the 1st of May, 1783.

Said James McMicken was born in Bucks County, Pennsylvania, on the 29th day of December, 1756; died on the 18th day of September, 1815, and is buried in the Pine Creek Cemetery, at Jersey Shore, Pa.

The genealogical data relating to this soldier is as follows:

Parents	Brothers and Sisters	Children
	James McMicken	David McMicken
		James McMicken
		Charles McMicken

Married Elizabeth, daughter of Charles and Mary Walker on July 4, 1778.
This record placed by John Lafferty, of 1023 58th Street, Altoona, Pa.

HARRISON HERBERT SNYDER

BE IT HERE RECORDED, that Harrison Herbert Snyder served in the UNITED STATES Army during the Civil War as a Private in Company M, 62nd Regiment of Pennsylvania Infantry; enlisting on the 9th day of August, 1861, and honorably discharged on the 15th day of August, 1864.

Said Harrison Herbert Snyder was born at Hollidaysburg, Pa., on the 15th day of January, 1837; died on the 25th day of February, 1891, and is buried in lot 15, section A, Presbyterian Cemetery, Hollidaysburg, Pa.

The genealogical data relating to this soldier is as follows:

Parents	Brothers and Sisters	Children
	Harrison Herbert Snyder	
	John Milton Snyder	
Jacob Snyder	Anna Marie Snyder	
	Henry Baxter Snyder	John Milton Snyder
	William Lamertine Snyder	
Sarah Cecelia Bowers	Plymouth Warren Snyder	
	George Bowers Snyder	
	Howard Edward Snyder	

Married Ella McClain, daughter of John and Catherine Dipner, on May 18, 1868.
This record placed by John M. Snyder, of 417 Allegheny St., Hollidaysburg, Pa.

FRANK HUGUS FAY

BE IT HERE RECORDED, that Frank Hugus Fay served in the UNITED STATES Army during the World War as a Private, Remount Service Training Camp, Q.M.C.; enlisting on the 2nd day of September, 1918, and honorably discharged on the 30th day of November, 1918.

Said Frank Hugus Fay was born at Williamsburg, Pennsylvania, on the 10th day of November, 1869; died on the 23rd day of March, 1936, and buried in lot 710, section C, Presbyterian Cemetery at Hollidaysburg, Pa.

The discharge is recorded in volume 2, page 12, Soldier's Discharge Record, Register and Recorder's Office, Blair County Court House, Hollidaysburg, Pa.

The genealogical data relating to this soldier is as follows:

Parents	Brothers and Sisters	Children
	Joseph B. Fay	
George Fay	William M. Fay	
Martha Fluke	Orville J. Fay	
	Alice Beattie	
(second marriage)	Frank Hugus Fay	
Catherine S. McCoy	Charles R. Fay	

Married Anna Perry, daughter of Samuel and Mary Milliken, on October 4, 1913.
Married Bessie Janet, daughter of Willis J. and Mary A. Nugent, November 9, 1929.
This record placed by Mrs. Bessie Janet Fay, of 418 Allegheny St., Hollidaysburg.

SOLDIERS OF BLAIR COUNTY

JOHN JOSEPH GARBER

BE IT HERE RECORDED, that John Joseph Garber served in the UNITED STATES Army during the Civil War as a Corporal in Company C, 205th Regiment of Pennsylvania Infantry; enlisting on the 9th day of August, 1864, and honorably discharged on the 2nd day of June, 1865.

Said John Joseph Garber was born in Adams County, Pennsylvania, on the 12th day of June, 1838; died on the 8th day of November, 1927, and is buried in the St. Patricks Cemetery at Newry, Pa.

The genealogical data relating to this soldier is as follows:

Parents	Brothers and Sisters	Children
	Catherine Heron	Ella N. Hartman
	Mary Walden	Silas H. Garber
Daniel Garber	Ellen Snyder	Lewis F. Garber
	Susan Morgan	James E. Garber
	Daniel Garber	Leo A. Garber
Catherine Schrader	Frank Garber	William J. Garber
	Henry Garber	Erastus B. Garber
	Eli Garber	Maggie Garber

Married Adaline, daughter of Alexander and Mary Bonner, on March 4, 1869.

This record placed by Lewis F. Garber, of Roaring Spring, Pa.

CHARLES AUGUSTUS MALONE

BE IT HERE RECORDED, that Charles Augustus Malone served in the UNITED STATES Army during the Spanish-American War as a Corporal in Company H, 17th Regiment of Infantry; enlisting on the 9th day of December, 1898, and honorably discharged from Company G, 23rd Infantry on the 8th day of December, 1901.

Said Charles Augustus Malone was born at Hollidaysburg, Pa., on the 2nd day of September, 1877; and resides at 219 Franklin St., Hollidaysburg, Pa.

The discharge is recorded in volume 4, page 203, Soldier's Discharge Record, Register and Recorder's Office, Blair County Court House, Hollidaysburg, Pa.

The genealogical data relating to this soldier is as follows:

Parents	Brothers and Sisters	Children
	Minnie Malone	
Robert Malone	Elizabeth Housman	Kenneth Augustus Malone
	Robert D. Malone	
Margaret S. Malone	Samuel S. Malone	John Francis Malone
	Charles A. Malone	

Married Catharine, daughter of John P. and Bridget Reilly, on September 15, 1903.

PAUL REEDY CURRAN

BE IT HERE RECORDED, that Paul Reedy Curran served in the UNITED STATES Army during the World War as a Sergeant in Company F, 2nd Corps A.P.; enlisted on the 1st day of June, 1918, and honorably discharged on June 26, 1919.

Said Paul Reedy Curran was born at Hollidaysburg, Pennsylvania, on the 13th day of April, 1889; and resides at 305 Clark Street, Hollidaysburg, Pa.

The genealogical data relating to this soldier is as follows:

Parents	Brothers and Sisters	Children
	Frank Curran	
	John A. Curran	
Charles Curran	Rebecca M. Curran	Clara Margaret Curran
	Charles Curran	
	William Curran	
Margaret Doran	Thomas W. Curran	Paul Anthony Curran
	Porter Curran	
	Howard J. Curran	
	Paul Reedy Curran	
	Lowry Curran	

Married Catherine A., daughter of Anthony J. and Clara Stormer, on May 26, 1920.

www.ingramcontent.com/pod-product-compliance
Lightning Source LLC
Chambersburg PA
CBHW030224100526
44585CB00012BA/212